What's New in This Edition

Given the explosion of tools for building Java applications and the wide variety of things that people are doing with Java, for the Web and for general-purpose applications, there is no shortage of new things to talk about when it comes to Java.

This edition, therefore, is a fully revised edition of the original *Teach Yourself Java in 21 Days*. It has been updated to cover Java 1.1, and it has been significantly enhanced, with all the original content updated, the weak parts fixed, and more examples added.

- ☐ Updated to include the new and expanded Java 1.1 packages
- ☐ Coverage of new Java topics such as Inner Classes and Reflection
- ☐ Examples that put to use the new capabilities found in Java 1.1
- ☐ An additional chapter dedicated to the newly expanded AWT
- ☐ Entirely revised Class Hierarchy Diagrams and Class Library Reference updated for Java 1.1
- ☐ Discussion of JavaBeans—Java's new component technology
- ☐ New coverage of events and how they have changed
- ☐ Overviews of JDBC and RMI
- ☐ Expanded discussion on networking
- ☐ New Java security features including how to create signed applets
- ☐ In-depth discussions about moving from Java 1.0.2 to Java 1.1

Praise for *Teach Yourself Java 1.1 in 21 Days*

"If you get only one Java book, it should be *Teach Yourself Java in 21 Days*. Authors Laura Lemay and Charles L. Perkins cover all aspects of Java programming in an easy-to-read guide organized around daily lesson plans."

—Jay Munro, *PC Magazine*

" . . .this is where to begin. Java in all its details: classes to applets, methods to multithreading."

—Thom Gillespie, *Library Journal*

"If you are a hands-on learner, this book is perfect for you."

—*Books & Bytes*

"*Teach Yourself Java* gives a thoughtful treatment to under-the-hood issues of Java's implementation."

—Peter Coffee, *PC Week*

"If you buy one book on Java, this is the one to buy. *Teach Yourself Java* is one of the best introductions to hands-on Java programming. The setup of the book is extremely well-thought-out."

—Scott Sidel, *Independent Web Review*

"This book does not assume that you know C or C++, but it offers tips for those who do. Laura Lemay is my favorite tech author. . . .If you can afford only *one* Java book, then this is the one to get."

—David Geary

Contents

Acknowledgments

From Laura Lemay:

To Sun's Java team, for all their hard work on Java, the language, and on the browser, and particularly to Jim Graham, who demonstrated Java and HotJava to me on very short notice in May 1995 and planted the idea for this book.

To everyone who bought my previous books and liked them: Buy this one, too.

From Charles L. Perkins:

To Patrick Naughton, who first showed me the power and the promise of Oak (Java) in early 1993.

To Mark Taber, who shepherded this lost sheep through his first book.

About the Authors

Lead Authors

Laura Lemay is a technical writer and a nerd. After spending six years writing software documentation for various computer companies in Silicon Valley, she decided that writing books would be much more fun (but has still not yet made up her mind). In her spare time she collects computers, e-mail addresses, interesting hair colors, and nonrunning motorcycles. She is also the perpetrator of *Teach Yourself Web Publishing with HTML in 14 Days* and *The Official Marimba Guide to Castanet*.

You can visit her home page at `http://www.lne.com/lemay/`.

Charles L. Perkins is the founder of Virtual Rendezvous, a company building a Java-based, real-time meta-service for shared activities that will foster socially-focused and computer-mediated interactions between people's personas in the virtual environments of the near future. In previous lives, he has evangelized NeXTSTEP, Smalltalk, and UNIX, and has degrees in both Physics and Computer Science. Before attempting this book, he was an amateur columnist and author. He's done research in speech recognition, neural nets, gestural user interfaces, computer graphics, and language theory, but had the most fun working at Thinking Machines and Xerox PARC's Smalltalk group. In his spare time, he reads textbooks for fun.

You can reach him via e-mail at `virtual@rendezvous.com`, or visit his Java page at `http://rendezvous.com/java`.

Contributors

Rogers Cadenhead (`rogers@prefect.com`) is a writer, computer programmer, and Web developer whose inner child is a knuckleball pitcher with the worst walk-to-strikeout ratio in the American League. He is the author of *Teach Yourself Java 1.1 Programming in 24 Hours*, and is a co-author of *Teach Yourself SunSoft Java WorkShop in 21 Days* from Sams.net. He also writes a question-and-answer trivia column for the Fort Worth Star-Telegram and New York Times News Syndicate. He lives in North Texas and occasionally harbors members of the Dallas Cowboys when they need to dodge a subpoena. Visit his home page at `http://www.prefect.com/rogers`.

Michael Morrison is the author of *Teach Yourself Internet Game Programming with Java in 21 Days*, and a contributing author to *Tricks of the Java Programming Gurus*, *Java Unleashed*, and *Game Developer* magazine. Michael lives in Scottsdale, Arizona, with his (now legally recognized) female cohort, Mahsheed. In his spare time, Michael enjoys testing his threshold of pain on skateboard ramps. You can reach Michael via e-mail at mmorrison@thetribe.com, or check out his Web site at www.thetribe.com.

Tell Us What You Think!

As a reader, you are the most important critic and commentator of our books. We value your opinion and want to know what we're doing right, what we could do better, what areas you'd like to see us publish in, and any other words of wisdom you're willing to pass our way. You can help us make strong books that meet your needs and give you the computer guidance you require.

Do you have access to CompuServe or the World Wide Web? Then check out our CompuServe forum by typing GO SAMS at any prompt. If you prefer the World Wide Web, check out our site at http://www.samspublishing.com.

 NOTE

> If you have a technical question about this book, call the technical support line at 317-581-3833 or send e-mail to support@mcp.com.

As the publishing manager of the group that created this book, I welcome your comments. You can fax, e-mail, or write me directly to let me know what you did or didn't like about this book—as well as what we can do to make our books stronger. Here's the information:

FAX: 317-581-4669

E-mail: newtech_mgr@sams.mcp.com

Mail: Mark Taber
          Sams.net Publishing
          201 W. 103rd Street
          Indianapolis, IN 46290

Introduction

The World Wide Web, for much of its existence, has been a method for distributing passive information to a widely distributed number of people. The Web has, indeed, been exceptionally good for that purpose. With the addition of forms and image maps, Web pages began to become interactive—but the interaction was often simply a new way to get at the same information. The limitations of Web distribution were all too apparent once designers began to try to stretch the boundaries of what the Web can do. Even other innovations, such as Netscape's server push to create dynamic animations, were merely clever tricks layered on top of a framework that wasn't built to support much other than static documents with images and text.

Enter Java, and the capability for Web pages to contain Java applets. Applets are small programs that create animations, multimedia presentations, real-time (video) games, multiuser networked games, and real interactivity—in fact, most anything a small program can do, Java applets can. Downloaded over the Net and executed inside a Web page by a browser that supports Java, applets are an enormous step beyond standard Web design.

The disadvantage of Java is that to create Java applets right now, you need to write them in the Java language. Java is a programming language, and, therefore, creating Java applets is more difficult than creating a Web page or a form using HTML.

There are a variety of tools and programs available that make creating Java applets easier, but the only way to truly delve into Java is to learn the language and start playing with the raw Java code. Even if you have one of these tools to help you out, you may want to do more with Java than the tool can provide, and you're back to learning the language.

That's where *Teach Yourself Java 1.1 in 21 Days, Second Edition,* comes in. This book teaches you all about the Java language and how to use it to create not only applets, but also applications, which are more general Java programs that don't need to run inside a Web browser. By the time you get through with this book, you'll know enough about Java to do just about anything, inside an applet or out.

How This Book Is Organized

Teach Yourself Java 1.1 in 21 Days, Second Edition, covers the Java language and its class libraries in 21 days, organized as three separate weeks. Each week covers a different broad area of developing Java applets and applications.

In the first week, you'll learn about the Java language itself:

- ☐ Day 1 is the basic introduction: what Java is, why it's cool, and how to get the software. You'll also create your first Java applications and applets.

- ☐ On Day 2 you'll explore basic object-oriented programming concepts as they apply to Java.

- ☐ On Day 3 you'll start getting down to details with the basic Java building blocks: data types, variables, and expressions—such as arithmetic and comparisons.

- ☐ Day 4 goes into detail about how to deal with objects in Java: how to create them, how to access their variables and call their methods, and how to compare and copy them. You'll also get your first glance at the Java class libraries.

- ☐ On Day 5 you'll learn more about Java with arrays, conditional statements, and loops.

- ☐ Day 6 is the best one yet. You'll learn how to create classes, the basic building blocks of any Java program, and how to put together a Java application (a Java program that can run on its own without a Web browser).

- ☐ Day 7 builds on what you learned on Day 6. On Day 7, you'll learn more about how to create and use methods, including overriding and overloading methods and creating constructors.

Week 2 is dedicated to applets and the Java class libraries:

- ☐ Day 8 provides the basics of applets—how they're different from applications, how to create them, and about the most important parts of an applet's life cycle. You'll also learn how to create HTML pages that contain Java applets.

- ☐ On Day 9 you'll learn about the Java classes for drawing shapes and characters on the screen—in black, white, or any other color.

- ☐ On Day 10 you'll start animating shapes and other images using threads. You'll also learn to add sound using Java.

- ☐ Day 11 delves into interactivity—handling mouse and keyboard clicks from the user in your Java applets.

- ☐ Day 12 is ambitious; on that day you'll learn about using Java's Abstract Windowing Toolkit to create a user interface in your applet including menus, buttons, check boxes, and other elements.

- ☐ Day 13 will continue teaching you about the AWT, picking up where Day 12 left off.

- ☐ On Day 14 you'll explore the last of the main Java class libraries for creating applets: windows and dialogs, networking, and a few other tidbits.

Week 3 includes advanced topics, useful when you start doing larger and more complex Java programs, or when you want to learn more:

- ☐ On Day 15 you'll learn more about the Java language's modifiers—for abstract and final methods and classes as well as for protecting a class's private information from the prying eyes of other classes.
- ☐ Day 16 covers interfaces and packages, useful for abstracting protocols of methods to aid reuse, and for the grouping and categorization of classes.
- ☐ Day 17 covers exceptions: errors and warnings and other abnormal conditions, generated either by the system or by you in your programs.
- ☐ Day 18 builds on the thread basics you learned on Day 10 to give a broad overview of multithreading and how to use it to allow different parts of your Java programs to run in parallel.
- ☐ On Day 19 you'll learn all about the input and output streams in Java's I/O library.
- ☐ Day 20 teaches you about native code—how to link C code into your Java programs to provide missing functionality or to gain performance.
- ☐ On Day 21 you'll get an overview of some of the behind-the-scenes technical details of how Java works: the bytecode compiler and interpreter, the techniques Java uses to ensure the integrity and security of your programs, and the Java garbage collector.

Conventions Used in This Book

Text that you type and text that should appear on your screen is presented in monospace type:

```
It will look like this
```

to mimic the way text looks on your screen. Placeholders for variables and expressions appear in monospace italic.

The end of each chapter offers common questions asked about that day's subject matter with answers from the authors.

Sources for Further Information

Before, while, and after you read this book, there are several Web sites that may be of interest to you as a Java developer.

The official Java Web site is at `http://java.sun.com/`. At this site, you'll find the Java development software and online documentation for all aspects of the Java language, including the previously mentioned Java 1.1 preview page. It has several mirror sites that it lists online, and you should probably use the site "closest" to you on the Internet for your downloading and Java Web browsing.

There is also an excellent site for developer resources, called Gamelan, at `http://www.gamelan.com/`, which contains an enormous number of applets and applications with sample code, help, and plenty of information about Java and Java development.

For discussion about the Java language and the tools to develop in it, check out the Usenet Newsgroups for `comp.lang.java`. This set of newsgroups—which includes `comp.lang.java.programming`, `comp.lang.java.api`, `comp.lang.java.misc`, `comp.lang.java.security`, and `comp.lang.java.tech`—is a terrific source for getting questions answered and for keeping up on new Java developments.

The Java Language

Day **1**

An Introduction to Java Programming

by Laura Lemay

Hello and welcome to *Teach Yourself Java 1.1 in 21 Days*! Starting today and for the next few weeks you'll learn all about the Java language and how to use it to create programs that run inside Web pages (called *applets*) and programs that can run on their own (called *applications*).

That's the overall goal for the next couple of weeks. Today the goals are somewhat more modest, and you'll learn about the following:

☐ What exactly Java is, and its current status

☐ Why you should learn Java—its various features and advantages over other programming languages

☐ Getting started programming in Java—what you'll need in terms of software and background, as well as some basic terminology

☐ How to create your first Java programs—to close this day, you'll create both a simple Java application and a simple Java applet!

What Is Java?

Based on the enormous amount of press Java is getting and the amount of excitement it has generated, you may get the impression that Java will save the world—or at least solve all the problems of the Internet. Not so. Java's hype has run far ahead of its capabilities, and although Java is indeed new and interesting, it really is another programming language with which you write programs that run on the Internet. In this respect, Java is closer to popular programming languages such as C, C++, Visual Basic, or Pascal than it is to a page description language such as HTML or a simple scripting language such as JavaScript.

More specifically, Java is an object-oriented programming language developed by Sun Microsystems, a company best known for its high-end UNIX workstations. Modeled after C++, the Java language was designed to be small, simple, and portable across platforms and operating systems, both at the source and at the binary level, which means that Java programs (applets and applications) can run on any machine that has the Java virtual machine installed (you'll learn more about this later).

Java is usually mentioned in the context of the World Wide Web, where browsers such as Netscape Navigator and Microsoft's Internet Explorer claim to be "Java enabled." Java enabled means that the browser in question can download and play Java programs, called applets, on the reader's system. Applets appear in a Web page much the same way as images do, but unlike images, applets are dynamic and interactive. Applets can be used to create animation, figures, forms that immediately respond to input from the reader, games, or other interactive effects on the same Web pages among the text and graphics. Figure 1.1 shows an applet running in Netscape 3.0. (This applet, at `http://prominence.com/java/poetry/`, is an electronic version of the refrigerator magnets that you can move around to create poetry or messages.)

 Applets are programs that are downloaded from the World Wide Web by a Web browser and run inside an HTML Web page. You'll need a Java-enabled browser such as Netscape Navigator or Microsoft's Internet Explorer to run applets.

To create an applet, you write it in the Java language, compile it using a Java compiler, and refer to that applet in your HTML Web pages. You put the resulting HTML and Java files on a Web site in the same way that you make ordinary HTML and image files available. Then, when someone using a Java-enabled browser views your page with the embedded applet, that browser downloads the applet to the local system and executes it, allowing your reader to view and interact with your applet in all its glory. (Readers using other browsers may see text, a static graphic, or nothing.) You'll learn more about how applets, browsers, and the World Wide Web work together later in this book.

Although applets are probably the most popular use of Java, the important thing to understand about Java is that you can do so much more with it than create and use applets.

Java was written as a full-fledged general-purpose programming language in which you can accomplish the same sorts of tasks and solve the same sorts of problems that you can in other programming languages, such as C or C++.

Figure 1.1.

Netscape running a Java applet.

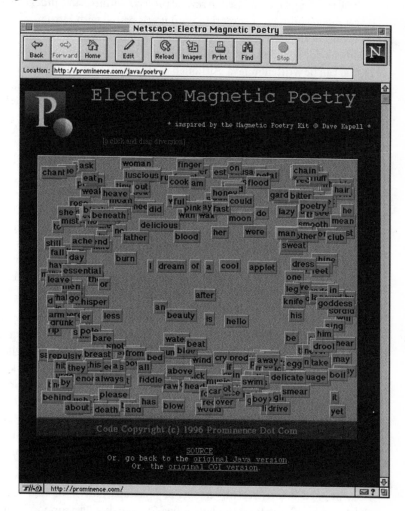

Java's Past, Present, and Future

The Java language was developed at Sun Microsystems in 1991 as part of a research project to develop software for consumer electronics devices—television sets, VCRs, toasters, and the other sorts of machines you can buy at any department store. Java's goals at that time were to be small, fast, efficient, and easily portable to a wide range of hardware devices. Those same goals made Java an ideal language for distributing executable programs via the World Wide

Web and also a general-purpose programming language for developing programs that are easily usable and portable across different platforms.

The Java language was used in several projects within Sun (under the name Oak) but did not get much commercial attention until it was paired with HotJava. HotJava, an experimental World Wide Web browser, was written in 1994 in a matter of months, both as a vehicle for downloading and running applets and also as an example of the sort of complex application that can be written in Java. Although HotJava got a lot of attention in the Web community, it wasn't until Netscape incorporated HotJava's ability to play applets into its own browser that Java really took off and started to generate the excitement that it has both on and off the World Wide Web. Java has generated so much excitement, in fact, that inside Sun, the Java group spun off into its own subsidiary called JavaSoft.

Versions of Java itself, or, as it's most commonly called, the Java API, correspond to versions of Sun's Java Developer's Kit, or JDK. As I write this book, there are actually two versions of the JDK that are competing for attention: the older 1.02 JDK, which is in wide use and supported by the most common browsers (Netscape 3.0 and MSIE 3.0) and development tools such as Symantec's Cafe and Microsoft's Visual J++. The recently released Java 1.1 has lots of extra new features, but because it is still very new, it's not as widely supported as the 1.02 version. This book describes both Java 1.02 and Java 1.1, noting the differences where they exist. Note that 1.02 Java programs will work just fine in Java 1.1, but the reverse is not true; version1.1 programs will not run in a 1.02 environment.

To program in Java, you'll need a Java development environment of some sort for your platform. Sun's JDK works just fine for this purpose and includes tools for compiling and testing Java applets and applications. In addition, several excellent Java development environments have been developed, including Sun's own Java Workshop, Symantec's Café, Microsoft's Visual J++ (which is indeed a Java tool, despite its name), and Natural Intelligence's Roaster, with more development tools appearing all the time. If you're writing code for Java 1.1, make sure that your development environment supports the 1.1 JDK; as I write this, the only development environment for Java 1.1 is Sun's JDK. If you're less interested in 1.1 features, you can use either a 1.02 or 1.1 environment.

To run and view Java applets, you'll need a Java-enabled browser or other tool. As I mentioned before, recent versions of Netscape Navigator (2.0 and higher) and Internet Explorer (3.0) can both run Java applets. (Note that Java support in different browsers varies widely, so check with the documentation that comes with your browser to make sure it supports Java.) Even if you don't have a Java-enabled browser, many development tools provide simple viewers with which you can run your applets. The JDK comes with one; it's called the appletviewer. As with the development environments, watch out for differences between Java 1.02 and 1.1; as I write this there are no browsers that support Java 1.1, and the only way to test applets written using the 1.1 JDK is through Sun's appletviewer. Netscape 3.0 and Internet Explorer do NOT support 1.1-based applets.

NOTE

> As I write this, Netscape Communicator is in beta, and although it supports some features of the 1.1 JDK, it does not appear to support all of them. This may have changed by the time the final version of Netscape Communicator is released.

What's in store for Java in the future? Java 1.1 provides a number of significant revisions to help Java move from an interesting and fun language for writing applets into one that is more powerful and flexible for creating large-scale applications. As this book progresses, you'll learn about many of those changes and why they're useful for Java development. Further revisions of Java will include more powerful features for different types of Java applications—for example, sets of Java classes and APIs for multimedia, for sophisticated graphics and layout, for advanced security features, and for more flexibility in the development of graphical user interfaces in Java.

In addition, Java is broadening from a simple programming language into many other different realms. Sun is developing Java microprocessors, to provide fast environments for Java applications. Sun's Network Computer uses a Java operating system, which is designed to run on very small and limited systems. Sun's vision of the future is of a computer that runs Java from top to bottom, inside and out.

Why Learn Java?

At the moment, probably the most compelling reason to learn Java—and probably the reason you bought this book—is that applets are written in Java. Even if that were not the case, Java as a programming language has significant advantages over other languages and other environments that make it suitable for just about any programming task. This section describes some of those advantages.

Java Is Platform Independent

Platform independence—that is, the ability of a program to move easily from one computer system to another—is one of the most significant advantages that Java has over other programming languages, particularly if your software needs to run on many different platforms. If you're writing software for the World Wide Web, being able to run the same program on many different systems is crucial to that program's success. Java is platform independent at both the source and the binary level.

New Term *Platform independence* means that a program can run on any computer system. Java programs can run on any system for which a Java virtual machine has been installed.

At the source level, Java's primitive data types have consistent sizes across all development platforms. Java's foundation class libraries make it easy to write code that can be moved from platform to platform without the need to rewrite it to work with that platform. When you write a program in Java, you don't need to rely on features of that particular operating system to accomplish basic tasks. Platform independence at the source level means that you can move Java source files from system to system and have them compile and run cleanly on any system.

Platform independence in Java doesn't stop at the source level, however. Java-compiled binary files are also platform independent and can run on multiple platforms (if they have a Java virtual machine available) without the need to recompile the source.

Normally, when you compile a program written in C or in most other languages, the compiler translates your program into machine code or processor instructions. Those instructions are specific to the processor your computer is running—so, for example, if you compile your code on an Intel-based system, the resulting program will run only on other Intel-based systems. If you want to use the same program on another system, you have to go back to your original source code, get a compiler for that system, and recompile your code so that you have a program specific to that system. Figure 1.2 shows the result of this system: multiple executable programs for multiple systems.

Figure 1.2.

Traditional compiled programs.

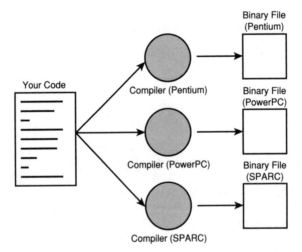

Things are different when you write code in Java. The Java development environment actually has two parts: a Java compiler and a Java interpreter. The Java compiler takes your Java program and, instead of generating machine codes from your source files, it generates *bytecodes*. Bytecodes are instructions that look a lot like machine code but are not specific to any one processor.

To execute a Java program, you run a program called a bytecode interpreter, which in turn reads the bytecodes and executes your Java program (see Figure 1.3). The Java bytecode interpreter is often also called the Java virtual machine or the Java runtime.

Figure 1.3.

Java programs.

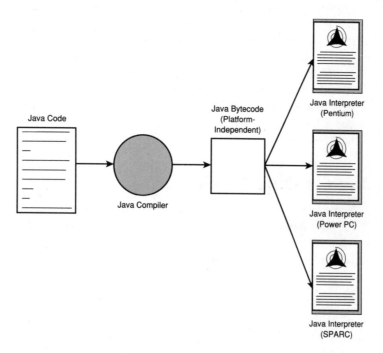

Java Code

Java Compiler

Java Bytecode (Platform-Independent)

Java Interpreter (Pentium)

Java Interpreter (Power PC)

Java Interpreter (SPARC)

NEW TERM　　Java *bytecodes* are a special set of machine instructions that are not specific to any one processor or computer system. A platform-specific bytecode interpreter executes the Java bytecodes. The bytecode interpreter is also called the Java virtual machine or the Java runtime interpreter.

Where do you get the bytecode interpreter? For applets, the bytecode interpreter is built into every Java-enabled browser, so you don't have to worry about it—Java applets just automatically run. For more general Java applications, you'll need to have the interpreter installed on your system to run that Java program. Right now, you can get the Java interpreter as part of your development environment, or if you buy a Java program, you'll get it with that package. In the future, however, the Java bytecode interpreter will most likely come with every new operating system—buy a Windows machine, and you'll get Java for free.

Why go through all the trouble of adding this extra layer of the bytecode interpreter? Having your Java programs in bytecode form means that instead of being specific to any one system, your programs can be run on any platform and any operating or window system as long as the Java interpreter is available. This capability of a single binary file to be executable across platforms is crucial to what makes applets work because the World Wide Web itself is also platform independent. Just as HTML files can be read on any platform, so can applets be executed on any platform that has a Java-enabled browser.

The disadvantage of using bytecodes is in execution speed. Because system-specific programs run directly on the hardware for which they are compiled, they run significantly faster than Java bytecodes, which must be processed by the interpreter. For many basic Java programs, speed may not be an issue. If you write programs that require more execution speed than the Java interpreter can provide, you have several solutions available to you, including being able to link native code into your Java program or using special tools (called just-in-time compilers) to convert your Java bytecodes into native code and speed up their execution. Note that by using any of these solutions, you lose the portability that Java bytecodes provide. You'll learn about each of these mechanisms on Day 20, "Using Native Methods and Libraries."

Java Is Object Oriented

To some, the object-oriented programming (OOP) technique is merely a way of organizing programs, and it can be accomplished using any language. Working with a real object-oriented language and programming environment, however, enables you to take full advantage of object-oriented methodology and its capabilities for creating flexible, modular programs and reusing code.

Many of Java's object-oriented concepts are inherited from C++, the language on which it is based, but it borrows many concepts from other object-oriented languages as well. Like most object-oriented programming languages, Java includes a set of class libraries that provide basic data types, system input and output capabilities, and other utility functions. These basic libraries are part of the standard Java environment, which also includes simple libraries, form networking, common Internet protocols, and user interface toolkit functions. Because these class libraries are written in Java, they are portable across platforms as all Java applications are.

You'll learn more about object-oriented programming and Java tomorrow.

Java Is Easy to Learn

In addition to its portability and object orientation, one of Java's initial design goals was to be small and simple, and therefore easier to write, easier to compile, easier to debug, and, best of all, easy to learn. Keeping the language small also makes it more robust because programmers have fewer chances to make mistakes that are difficult to fix. Despite its size and simple design, however, Java still has a great deal of power and flexibility.

Java is modeled after C and C++, and much of the syntax and object-oriented structure are borrowed from the latter. If you're familiar with C++, learning Java will be particularly easy for you because you have most of the foundation already. (In fact, you may find yourself skipping through the first week of this book fairly rapidly. Go ahead; I won't mind.)

Although Java looks similar to C and C++, most of the more complex parts of those languages have been excluded from Java, making the language simpler without sacrificing much of its power. You won't find pointers in Java, nor will you find pointer arithmetic. Strings and arrays are real objects in Java. Memory management is automatic. To an experienced programmer, these omissions may be difficult to get used to, but to beginners or programmers who have worked in other languages, they make the Java language far easier to learn.

Although Java's design makes it easier to learn than other programming languages, working with a programming language is still a great deal more complicated than, say, working in HTML. If you have no programming language background at all, you may find Java difficult to understand and to grasp. But don't be discouraged! Learning programming is a valuable skill for the Web and for computers in general, and Java is a terrific language to start out with.

Getting Started Programming in Java

Enough background! For the second half of this day, let's actually dive into simple Java programming and create two Java programs: a standalone Java application and an applet that you can view in a Java-enabled browser. Although both these programs are extremely simple, they will give you an idea of what a Java program looks like and how to compile and run it.

Getting a Java Development Environment

To write Java programs, you will, of course, need a Java development environment. (Although browsers such as Netscape allow you to play Java applets, they don't let you write them. For that, you'll need a separate tool.) Sun's JDK, which is available for downloading at the JavaSoft Web site (http://www.javasoft.com/) and included on the CD for this book, will do just fine. However, despite the JDK's popularity, it is not the easiest development tool to use. If you're used to using a graphical user interface–based development tool with an integrated editor and debugger, you'll most likely find the JDK's command-line interfaces rather primitive. Fortunately, the JDK is not the only tool in town.

As I mentioned earlier, a number of third-party development environments (called integrated development environments, or IDEs) are also available for developing in Java. They include Sun's Java Workshop for Solaris, Windows NT, and Windows 95 (you can get more information about it at http://www.sun.com/developer-products/java/); Symantec's Café for Windows 95, Windows NT, and Macintosh (http://cafe.symantec.com/); Microsoft's Visual J++ for Windows 95 and Windows NT (http://www.microsoft.com/visualj/); and Natural Intelligence's Roaster (http://www.natural.com/pages/products/roaster/index.html). All are commercial programs, but you might be able to download trial or limited versions of these programs to try them out.

> **NOTE**
>
> I find the graphical development environments far easier to use than the standard JDK. If you have the money and the time to invest in one of these tools, I highly recommend you do so. It'll make your Java development experience much more pleasant.

Installing the JDK and Sample Files

Sun's 1.1 JDK for Solaris and Windows is included as part of the CD-ROM that comes with this book. If you're on a Macintosh, the JDK is also available on the CD, but it's the 1.02 version. (There isn't a Mac version of the 1.1 JDK yet.) Also on the CD-ROM are all the code examples from this book—a great help if you don't want to type them all in again. To install either the JDK or the sample files (or both), use one of the following procedures:

> **NOTE**
>
> If you don't have access to a CD-ROM drive, you can also get access to these files over the World Wide Web. You can download the JDK itself from http://www.javasoft.com/products/JDK/1.1/index.html and install it per the instructions on those pages. If you're on a Mac and you want to use the 1.1 features of the JDK, you might also want to check that page periodically to see if a 1.1 JDK has been released.
>
> The sample files from this book are available on the Web site for this book: http://www.lne.com/Web/Java1.1/.
>
> If you download the JDK and source files, as opposed to getting them off the CD-ROM, make sure you read the section "Configuring the JDK" to make sure everything is set up right.

WINDOWS Sun's JDK runs on Windows 95 and Windows NT. It does not run on Windows 3.x.

To install the JDK or the sample files on Windows, run the Setup program on the CD-ROM (double-clicking the CD icon will do this automatically). By default, the package will be installed into C:/JDK1.1; you can install it anywhere on your hard disk that you'd like. You'll be given options to install the JDK, the sample files, and various other extra files; choose the options you want and those files will be installed.

If you've installed the JDK, note the file called `classes.zip` in the directory `JDK\lib`. You do not need to unzip this file.

MACINTOSH Sun's JDK for Macintosh runs on System 7 (MacOS) for 68KB or Power Mac.

To install the JDK or the sample files on the Macintosh, uncompress the original `bin` or `hqx` file to your hard drive, and then double-click the installation program. By default, the package will be installed into the folder Java on your hard disk; you can install it anywhere on your disk that you'd like. You'll be given options to install the JDK, the sample files, and various other extra files; choose the options you want and those files will be installed.

SOLARIS Sun's JDK for Solaris runs on Solaris 2.3, 2.4, and 2.5, as well as the x86 version of Solaris.

The CD-ROM for this book contains the JDK in the `JDK/1NTESOL/jdk1_1-beta4-solaris-x86.sh` or `JDK/SPARCSOL/jdk1_1-solaris2-sparc.sh` directory, depending on your system. To find the specific installation nuances for your particular version of Solaris, check the JavaSoft Web site at:

    http:/www.javasoft.com/products/jdk/1.1/installation-solaris2.html

The sample files are also contained on the CD-ROM in `source/source.tar`. Create a directory where the sample files will live (for example, a directory called `javasamples` in your home directory), copy the `source.tar.` file there, and then use the `tar` command to extract it, like this:

```
mkdir ~/javasamples
cp /cdrom/source/source.tar
```

Configuring the JDK

If you've installed the JDK using the setup programs from the CD-ROM, chances are good that it has been correctly configured for you. However, because most common problems with Java result from configuration errors, I recommend that you double-check your configuration to make sure everything is right. And if you've installed the JDK from a source other than the CD-ROM, you'll definitely want to read this section to make sure you're all set up.

 The JDK needs two important modifications to your `autoexec.bat` file so that it works correctly: The `JDK1.1\bin` directory must be in your execution path, and you must have the `CLASSPATH` variable set up.

Edit your `autoexec.bat` file using your favorite editor (Notepad will do just fine). Look for a line that looks something like this:

```
PATH C:\WINDOWS;C:\WINDOWS\COMMAND;C:\DOS; ...
```

Somewhere in that line you should see an entry for the JDK; if you installed the JDK from the CD-ROM, the line will look something like this (the dots are there to indicate that some other stuff may appear on this line):

```
PATH C:\WINDOWS; ... C:\JDK1.1\BIN; ...
```

If you cannot find any reference to JDK\BIN or JAVA\BIN in your `PATH`, you'll need to add it. Simply include the full pathname to your JDK installation to the end of that line, starting with `C:` and ending with `BIN`; for example, `C:\JAVA\BIN` or `C:\Java\JDK1.1\BIN`.

The second thing you'll need to add to the `autoexec.bat` file (if it isn't already there) is a `CLASSPATH` variable. Check for a line that looks something like this:

```
SET CLASSPATH=C:\TEACHY~1\JDK1.1\lib\classes.zip;.;
```

The `CLASSPATH` variable may also have other entries in it for Netscape or Internet Explorer, but the one you're most interested in is a reference to the `classes.zip` file in the JDK, and to the current directory (.). If your `autoexec.bat` file does not include either of these locations, add a line to the file that contains both these things (the preceding line will work just fine).

After saving your `autoexec.bat` file, you'll need to restart Windows for the changes to take effect.

MACINTOSH The JDK for Macintosh should need no further configuration after installation.

SOLARIS To configure the JDK for Solaris, all you need to do is add the java/bin or jdk/bin directory to your execution path. Usually a line something like this in your .cshrc, .login, or .profile files will work:

```
set path= (~/java/bin/ $path)
```

This line assumes that you've installed the JDK (as the directory java) into your home directory; if you've installed it somewhere else, you'll want to substitute that pathname.

Make sure you use the source command with the name of the appropriate file to ensure that the changes take effect (or log out and log back in again):

```
source ~/.login
```

Creating a Java Application

Now let's actually get to work. Start by creating a simple Java application: the classic Hello World example that many programming language books use to begin.

Java applications are different from Java applets. Applets, as you have learned, are Java programs that are downloaded over the World Wide Web and executed by a Web browser on the reader's machine. Applets depend on a Java-enabled browser so that they can run.

Java applications, however, are more general programs written in the Java language. Java applications don't require a browser to run; in fact, Java can be used to create all the kinds of applications that you would normally use a more conventional programming language to create.

NEW TERM Java applications are standalone Java programs that do not require a Web browser to run. Java applications are more general-purpose programs like those you would find on any computer.

A single Java program can be an applet or an application, or both, depending on how you write that program and the capabilities that program uses. Throughout this first week as you learn the Java language, you'll be writing mostly applications; then you'll apply what you've learned to write applets in Week 2. If you're eager to get started with applets, be patient. Everything that you learn while you're creating simple Java applications will apply to creating applets, and starting with the basics before moving onto the hard stuff is best. You'll be creating plenty of applets in Week 2.

Creating the Source File

As with all programming languages, your Java source files are created in a plain text editor, or in an editor that can save files in plain ASCII without any formatting characters. On UNIX, emacs, pico, and vi will work; on Windows, Notepad or DOS Edit are both text editors that will work (although I prefer to use the shareware TextPad). On the Macintosh, SimpleText (which comes with your Mac) or the shareware BBedit will work. If you're using a development environment like Café or Roaster, it'll have its own built-in text editor you can use.

NOTE

> If you're using Windows to do your Java development, you may have to make sure Windows understands the .java file extension before you start; otherwise, your text editor may insist on giving all your files a .txt extension. The easiest way to do this is to type the file name with double quotes ("HelloWorld.java"). An even better solution, however, is to go to any Windows Explorer window, choose View | Options | File Types, choose New Type, and add Java Source File and .java to the Description of Type and Associated Extension boxes, respectively.

Fire up your editor of choice, and enter the Java program shown in Listing 1.1. Type this program, as shown, in your text editor. Be careful that all the parentheses, braces, and quotation marks are there and that you've used all the correct upper- and lowercase letters.

NOTE

> You can also find the code for these examples on the CD-ROM as part of the sample code. However, actually typing in these first few short examples is a good idea so that you get a feel for what Java code actually looks like.

TYPE   **Listing 1.1. Your first Java application.**

```
1: class HelloWorld {
2:     public static void main (String args[]) {
3:         System.out.println("Hello World!");
4:     }
5: }
```

The number before each line is part of the listing and not part of the program. I included the numbers so that I can refer to specific line numbers when I explain what's going on in the program. Do not include them in your own file.

After you finish typing in the program, save the file somewhere on your disk with the name HelloWorld.java. This name is very important. Java source files must have the same name as the class they define (including the same upper- and lowercase letters), and they must have the extension .java. Here, the class definition has the name HelloWorld, so the filename must be HelloWorld.java. If you name your file something else (even something like helloworld.java or Helloworld.java), you won't be able to compile it. Make absolutely certain the name is HelloWorld.java.

You can save your Java files anywhere you like on your disk, but I like to have a central directory or folder to keep them all in. For the examples in this chapter, I've put my files into a directory called TYJtests (short for Teach Yourself Java Tests).

Compiling and Running the Source File

Now you're ready to compile the file. If you're using the JDK, you can use the instructions for your computer system contained in the next few pages. If you're using a graphical development environment, you will most likely have a button or option to compile the file (check with the documentation that came with your program).

 To compile the Java source file, you'll use the command-line Java compiler that comes with the JDK. To run the compiler, you'll need to first start up a DOS shell. In Windows 95, the DOS shell is under the Programs menu (it's called MS-DOS Prompt).

From inside DOS, change directories to the location where you've saved your HelloWorld.java file. I put mine into the directory TYJtests, so to change directories, I'd use this command:

```
CD C:\TYJtests
```

After you change to the right directory, use the javac command as follows, with the name of the file as you saved it in Windows (javac stands for Java compiler). Note that you have to make sure you type all the same upper- and lowercase characters here as well:

```
javac HelloWorld.java
```

NOTE

I've emphasized using the original filename because after you're inside the DOS shell, you might notice that your nice long filenames have been truncated to old-style 8.3 names and that, in fact, HelloWorld.java actually shows up as HELLOW~1.jav. Don't panic; this is simply a side effect of Windows 95 and how it manages long filenames. Ignore the fact that the file appears to be HELLOW~1.jav, and just use the filename you originally used when you saved the file.

Figure 1.4 shows what I've done in the DOS shell, so you can make sure you're following along.

Figure 1.4.

Compiling Java in the DOS shell.

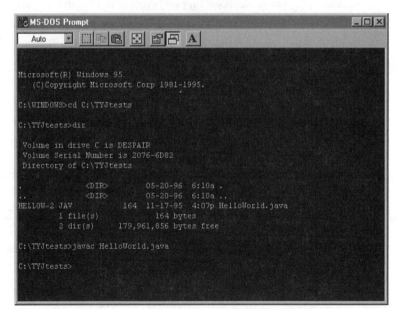

If all goes well, you'll end up with a file called HelloWorld.class (or at least that's what it'll be called if you look at it outside the DOS shell; from inside DOS its called HELLOW~1.cla). It's your Java bytecode file. If you get any errors, go back to your original source file and make sure you typed it exactly as it appears in Listing 1.1 with the same upper- and lowercase. Also make sure the filename has exactly the same upper- and lowercase as the name of the class (that is, both should be HelloWorld).

Once you have a class file, you can run that file using the Java bytecode interpreter. The Java interpreter is called simply java, and you run it from the DOS shell as you did javac. Run your Hello World program like this from the command line, with all the same upper- and lowercase (and note that the argument to the java program does not have a .class extension):

```
java HelloWorld
```

If your program was typed and compiled correctly, you should get the phrase Hello World! printed to your screen as a response. Figure 1.5 shows how I did it.

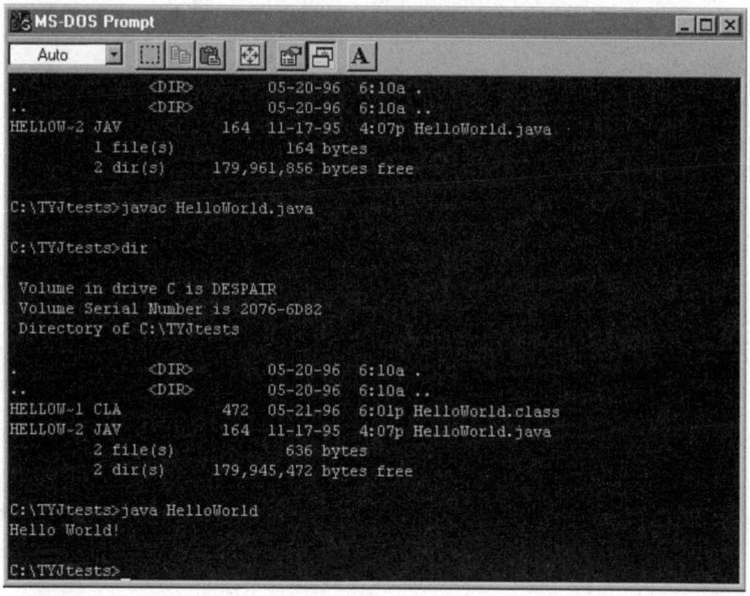

Figure 1.5.

Running Java applications in the DOS shell.

```
MS-DOS Prompt                                              _ □ ✕

Auto   ▼   🔲 🖹 🖺 🔳 🖼 🖨 A

.                    <DIR>         05-20-96  6:10a .
..                   <DIR>         05-20-96  6:10a ..
HELLOW~2 JAV              164  11-17-95  4:07p HelloWorld.java
        1 file(s)              164 bytes
        2 dir(s)      179,961,856 bytes free

C:\TYJtests>javac HelloWorld.java

C:\TYJtests>dir

 Volume in drive C is DESPAIR
 Volume Serial Number is 2076-6D82
 Directory of C:\TYJtests

.                    <DIR>         05-20-96  6:10a .
..                   <DIR>         05-20-96  6:10a ..
HELLOW~1 CLA             472  05-21-96  6:01p HelloWorld.class
HELLOW~2 JAV             164  11-17-95  4:07p HelloWorld.java
        2 file(s)              636 bytes
        2 dir(s)      179,945,472 bytes free

C:\TYJtests>java HelloWorld
Hello World!

C:\TYJtests>_
```

NOTE

Remember, the Java compiler and the Java interpreter are different things. You use the Java compiler (javac) for your Java source files to create .class files, and you use the Java interpreter (java) to actually run your class files.

MACINTOSH The JDK for the Mac comes with an application called Java Compiler. To compile your Java source file, simply drag and drop it on top of the Java Compiler icon. The program will compile your Java file and, if no errors occur, create a file called HelloWorld.class in the same folder as your original source file.

TIP

Putting an alias for Java Compiler on the desktop allows you to easily drag and drop Java source files.

If you get any errors, go back to your original source file and make sure you typed it exactly as it appears in Listing 1.1, with the same upper- and lowercase. Also make sure the filename has exactly the same upper- and lowercase as the name of the class (that is, both should be HelloWorld).

After you successfully generate a `HelloWorld.class` file, simply double-click it to run it. The application Java Runner, part of the Mac JDK, will start, and the program will ask you for command-line arguments. Leave that screen blank and click OK. A window labeled stdout will appear with the message `Hello World!`. Figure 1.6 shows that window.

Figure 1.6.

Running Java applications on the Mac using Java Runner.

```
┌──────────────────────── stdout ────────────────────────┐
│ Hello World!                                            │
│                                                         │
│                                                         │
│                                                         │
│                                                         │
│                                                         │
└─────────────────────────────────────────────────────────┘
```

That's it! Keep in mind as you work that you use the Java Compiler application to compile your `.java` files into `.class` files, which you can then run using Java Runner.

SOLARIS To compile the Java source file in Solaris, you'll use the command-line Java compiler that comes with the JDK. From a UNIX command line, cd to the directory that contains your Java source file. I put mine in the directory TYJtests, so to change directories, I'd use this command:

```
cd ~/TYJtests
```

After you're in the right directory, use the `javac` command with the name of the file, like this:

```
javac HelloWorld.java
```

If all goes well, you'll end up with a file called `HelloWorld.class` in the same directory as your source file. That's your Java bytecode file. If you get any errors, go back to your original source file and make sure you typed it exactly as it appears in Listing 1.1, with the same upper- and lowercase letters. Also make sure the filename has exactly the same upper- and lowercase letters as the name of the class (that is, both should be HelloWorld).

After you have a class file, you can run that file using the Java bytecode interpreter. The Java interpreter is called simply `java`, and you run it from the command line as you did `javac`, like this (and note that the argument to the Java program does not have a .class extension):

```
java HelloWorld
```

If your program was typed and compiled correctly, you should get the phrase `Hello World!` printed to your screen as a response. Figure 1.7 shows a listing of all the commands I used to get to this point (the part with `[desire]~[1]` is my system prompt).

Figure 1.7.

Compiling and running a Java application on Solaris.

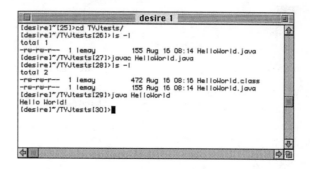

```
                          desire 1
[desire]~[25]>cd TYJtests/
[desire]~/TYJtests[26]>ls -l
total 1
-rw-rw-r--   1 lemay          155 Aug 16 08:14 HelloWorld.java
[desire]~/TYJtests[27]>javac HelloWorld.java
[desire]~/TYJtests[28]>ls -l
total 2
-rw-rw-r--   1 lemay          472 Aug 16 08:16 HelloWorld.class
-rw-rw-r--   1 lemay          155 Aug 16 08:14 HelloWorld.java
[desire]~/TYJtests[29]>java HelloWorld
Hello World!
[desire]~/TYJtests[30]>█
```

NOTE

> Remember that the Java compiler and the Java interpreter are different things. You use the Java compiler (`javac`) for your Java source files to create `.class` files, and you use the Java interpreter (`java`) to actually run your class files.

Creating a Java Applet

Creating applets is different from creating a simple application. Java applets run and are displayed inside a Web page with other page elements, and therefore have special rules for how they behave. Because of these special rules for applets, creating an applet may in many cases be more complex than creating an application.

For example, to create a simple Hello World applet, instead of merely being able to print a message as a set of characters, you have to make space for your message on the Web pages and then use special font and graphics operations to paint the message to the screen.

NOTE

> Actually, you can run a plain Java application as an applet, but the `Hello World` message will print to a special window or to a log file, depending on how the browser has its output set up. You'll learn more about this next week.

Creating the Source File

In this example, you'll create a simple Hello World applet, place it inside a Web page, and view the result. As with the Hello World application, you'll first create the source file in a plain text editor. Listing 1.2 shows the code for the example.

Listing 1.2. The Hello World applet.

```
1: import java.awt.Graphics;
2:
3: public class HelloWorldApplet extends java.applet.Applet {
4:
5:     public void paint(Graphics g) {
6:         g.drawString("Hello world!", 5, 25);
7:     }
8:}
```

Save that file just as you did the Hello World application, with the filename exactly the same as the name of the class. In this case the class name is HelloWorldApplet, so the filename you save it to would be HelloWorldApplet.java. As with the application, I put the file in a directory called TYJch01, but you can save it anywhere you like.

Compiling the Source File

The next step is to compile the Java applet file. Despite the fact that this is an applet, you compile the file exactly the same way you did the Java application, using one of the following procedures:

 From inside a DOS shell, cd to the directory containing your applet source file, and use the javac command to compile it (watch those upper- and lowercase letters):

```
javac HelloWorldApplet.java
```

 Drag and drop the HelloWorldApplet.java file onto the Java Compiler icon.

SOLARIS From a command line, cd to the directory containing your applet source file and use the javac command to compile it:

```
javac HelloWorldApplet.java
```

Including the Applet in a Web Page

If you've typed the file correctly, you should end up with a file called HelloWorldApplet.class in the same directory as your source file. That's your Java applet file; to have the applet run inside a Web page, you must refer to that class file inside the HTML code for that page by using the <APPLET> tag. Listing 1.3 shows a simple HTML file you can use.

 Listing 1.3. The HTML with the applet in it.

```
1: <HTML>
2: <HEAD>
```

```
3: <TITLE>Hello to Everyone!</TITLE>
4: </HEAD><BODY>
5: <P>My Java applet says:
6: <APPLET CODE="HelloWorldApplet.class" WIDTH=150 HEIGHT=25>
7: </APPLET>
8: </BODY>
9: </HTML>
```

You'll learn more about <APPLET> later in this book, but here are two things to note about it:

☐ Use the CODE attribute to indicate the name of the class that contains your applet, here HelloWorldApplet.Class.

☐ Use the WIDTH and HEIGHT attributes to indicate the size of the applet on the page. The browser uses these values to know how big a chunk of space to leave for the applet on the page. Here, a box 150 pixels wide and 25 pixels high is created.

Save the HTML file in the same directory as your class file, with a descriptive name and an .html extension (for example, you might name your HTML file the same name as your applet—HelloWorldApplet.html).

NOTE

As I mentioned earlier about the Java source files, your text editor may insist on naming your HTML files with a .txt extension if Windows does not understand what the .html extension is used for. Choose View | Options | File Types from any Windows Explorer window to add a new file type for HTML files to solve this problem.

Now you're ready for the final test—actually viewing the result of running your applet. To view the applet, you need one of the following:

☐ A browser that supports Java applets, such as Netscape 2.0 or Internet Explorer 3.0. If you're running on the Macintosh, you'll need Netscape 3.0 or later. If you're running on Windows 95 or NT, you'll need the 32-bit version of Netscape. And if you're using Internet Explorer, you'll need the 3.0 beta 5 or later (the final version will do just fine).

☐ The appletviewer application, which is part of the JDK. The appletviewer is not a Web browser and won't let you see the entire Web page, but it's acceptable for testing to see how an applet will look and behave if nothing else is available.

☐ An applet viewer or runner tool that comes with your development environment.

If you're using a Java-enabled browser such as Netscape to view your applet files, you can choose File | Open File to navigate to the HTML file containing the applet (make sure you open the HTML file and not the class file). In Internet Explorer, choose File | Open and then select Browse to find the file on your disk. You don't need to install anything on a Web server yet; all this works on your local system. Note that the Java applet may take awhile to start up after the page appears to be done loading; be patient. Figure 1.8 shows the result of running the applet in Netscape.

Figure 1.8.

The applet running in Netscape.

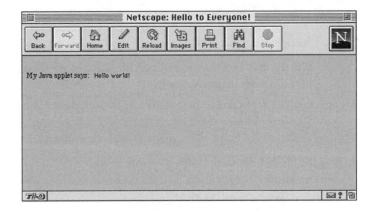

If you don't have a Web browser with Java capabilities built into it (or if you want to test applets written for Java 1.1), you can use the JDK's appletviewer program to view your Java applet.

To run the appletviewer in Windows or Solaris versions of the JDK, cd to the directory where your HTML and class files are contained, and use the appletviewer command with the name of the HTML file you just created:

```
appletviewer HelloWorldApplet.html
```

The appletviewer will show you only the applet itself, not the HTML text around the applet.

Troubleshooting

If you've run into any problems with the preceding examples, this section can help. The following are some of the most common problems and how to fix them:

☐ Bad command or filename or Command not found

These errors result when you do not have the JDK's bin directory in your execution path, or the path to that directory is wrong. On Windows, double-check your autoexec.bat file; on UNIX, check the system file with your path commands in it (.cshrc, .login, .profile, or some similar file).

☐ `javac: invalid argument`

Make sure the name of the file you're giving to the `javac` command is exactly the same name as the file. In particular, in the DOS shell you want to use the Windows filename with a `.java` extension, not the DOS equivalent (`HELLOW~1.jav`, for example).

☐ `Warning: public class HelloWorldApplet must be defined in a file called HelloWorldApplet.java`

This error most often happens if a mismatch occurs between the name of the class as defined in the Java file itself (the name following the word class) and the name of the java source file. Both the filenames must match, including upper- and lowercase letters (this particular error implies that the filename had lowercase letters). Rename either the filename or the class name, and this error will go away.

☐ `Insufficient-memory errors`

The JDK is not the most efficient user of memory. If you're getting errors about memory, consider exiting larger programs before compiling or running your Java programs, turn on virtual memory, or install more RAM.

☐ Other code errors

If you cannot compile the Java source files because of other errors I haven't mentioned here, be sure that you've typed them in exactly as they appear, including all upper- and lowercase letters. Java is case sensitive, meaning that upper- and lowercase letters are treated differently, so you will need to make sure that everything is capitalized correctly. If all else fails, try comparing your source files to the files on the CD-ROM.

Summary

Today you got a basic introduction to the Java language and its goals and features. Java is a programming language, similar to C or C++, in which you can develop a wide range of programs. One of the more common uses for Java is in creating applets for Java-enabled Web browsers. Applets are Java programs that are downloaded and run as part of a Web page. Applets can create animation, games, interactive programs, and other multimedia effects on Web pages.

Java's strengths lie in its portability—both at the source and at the binary level, in its object-oriented design—and in its simplicity. Each of these features helps make applets possible, but they also make Java an excellent language for writing more general-purpose programs that do not require a Java-enabled browser to run. These general-purpose Java programs are called applications.

To end this day, you experimented with an example of an applet and an example of an application, getting a feel for the differences between the two and how to create, compile, and run Java programs—or, in the case of applets, how to include them in Web pages. From here, you now have the foundation to create more complex applications and applets. Onward to Day 2, "Object-Oriented Programming and Java!"

Q&A

Q **I know a lot about HTML but not much about computer programming. Can I still write Java programs?**

A If you have no programming experience whatsoever, you most likely will find programming Java significantly more difficult than programming HTML. However, Java is an excellent language to learn programming with, and if you patiently work through the examples and the exercises in this book, you should be able to learn enough to get started with Java.

Q **What's the relationship between JavaScript and Java?**

A They have the same first four letters.

A common misconception in the Web world is that Java and JavaScript have more in common than they actually do. Java is the general-purpose programming language that you'll learn about in this book; you use it to create applets. JavaScript is a Netscape-invented scripting language that looks sort of like Java; with it you can do various nifty things in Web pages. They are independent languages, used for different purposes. If you're interested in JavaScript programming, you'll want to pick up another book, such as *Teach Yourself JavaScript in a Week* or *Laura Lemay's Web Workshop: JavaScript*, both also available from Sams.net Publishing.

Q **I'm really confused about the difference between Java 1.02 and 1.1. This book is supposed to be on Java 1.1, but you're telling me that 1.02 is more popular, and that few browsers support 1.1. Which version am I supposed to use?**

A Java 1.1 is still very new, and because of that there's going to be a bit of a transition period between the older, more popular 1.02 and the newer version. As time goes on, 1.1 will become more and more widely supported and the confusion will go away.

The general rule is that if you write code to conform to the 1.02 API, it'll compile and run anywhere—even in the 1.1 version of the JDK. If you use features of 1.1, however, you're limiting your code such that it will only compile and run in a 1.1 environment. Depending on how you intend to use Java, you'll need to decide whether or not to use the 1.1 features. (For applets, it's probably a good idea to stick with 1.02 for now; for applications, you have more flexiblity.)

You won't really need to worry about this for a bit. Most of the Java basics are exactly the same between the two versions; it's only as we delve deeper into the JDK that the differences become important. I'll point out 1.1 features as they appear.

Q According to today's lesson, Java applets are downloaded via a Java-enabled browser such as Netscape and run on the reader's system. Isn't that an enormous security hole? What stops someone from writing an applet that compromises the security of my system—or worse, that damages my system?

A Sun's Java team has thought a great deal about the security of applets within Java-enabled browsers and has implemented several checks to make sure applets cannot do nasty things:

- [ ] Java applets cannot read or write to the disk on the local system.

- [ ] Java applets cannot execute any programs on the local system.

- [ ] Java applets cannot connect to any machines on the Web except for the server from which they are originally downloaded.

Note that some of these restrictions may be allowed in some browsers or may be turned on in the browser configuration. However, you cannot expect any of these capabilities to be available.

In addition, the Java compiler and interpreter check both the Java source code and the Java bytecodes to make sure that the Java programmer has not tried any sneaky tricks (for example, overrunning buffers or stack frames).

These checks obviously cannot stop every potential security hole (no system can promise that!), but they can significantly reduce the potential for hostile applets. You'll learn more about security issues for applets on Day 8, "Java Applet Basics," and in greater detail on Day 21, "Under the Hood."

Q You've mentioned Solaris, Windows, and Macintosh in this chapter. What about other operating systems?

A If you use a flavor of UNIX other than Solaris, chances are good that the JDK has been ported to your system. Here are some examples:

- [ ] SGI's version of the JDK can be found at `http://www.sgi.com/Products/cosmo/cosmo_instructions.html`.

- [ ] Information about Java for Linux can be found at `http://www.blackdown.org/java-linux/`.

- [ ] IBM has ported the JDK to OS/2 and AIX. Find out more from `http://www.ncc.hurley.ibm.com/javainfo/`.

- [ ] OSF is porting the JDK to HP/UX, Unixware, Sony NEWS, and Digital UNIX. See `http://www.osf.org/mall/web/javaport.htm`.

    (Thanks to Elliote Rusty Harold's Java FAQ at `http://www.sunsite.unc.edu/javafaq/javafaq/html` for this information.)

Q **I'm using Notepad on Windows to edit my Java files. The program insists on adding a .txt extension to all my files, regardless of what I name them (so I always end up with files like HelloWorld.java.txt). Short of renaming them before I compile them, what else can I do to fix this problem?**

A Although you can rename the files just before you compile them, that can get to be a pain, particularly when you have a lot of files. The problem here is that Windows doesn't understand the .java extension (you may also have this problem with HTML's .html extension as well).

To fix this problem, go into any Windows Explorer window and choose View|Options|File Types. From the panel that appears, select New Type. Enter Java Source Files in the Description of Type box and .java into the Associated Extension box. Then click OK. Do the same with HTML files if you need to, and click OK again. You should now be able to use Notepad (or any other text editor) to create and save Java and HTML files.

An easier method, but one you have to remember each time, is to save your files with double-quotes around the file name—for example, "HelloWorld.java".

Q **Where can I learn more about Java and find applets and applications to play with?**

A You can read the rest of this book! Here are some other places to look for Java information and Java applets:

☐ The Java home page at http://www.java.sun.com/ is the official source for Java information, including information about the JDK, about the upcoming 1.1 release, and about developer tools such as the Java Workshop, as well as extensive documentation.

☐ Gamelan, at http://www.gamelan.com/, is a repository of applets and Java information, organized into categories. If you want to play with applets or applications, you should look here.

☐ For Java discussion, check out the comp.lang.java newsgroups, including comp.lang.java.programmer, comp.lang.java.tech, comp.lang.java.advocacy, and so on. (You'll need a Usenet newsreader to access these newsgroups.)

Day 2

Object-Oriented Programming and Java

by Laura Lemay

Object-oriented programming (OOP) is one of the biggest programming ideas of recent years, and you might worry that you must spend years learning all about object-oriented programming methodologies and how they can make your life easier than The Old Way of programming. It all comes down to organizing your programs in ways that echo how things are put together in the real world.

Today you'll get an overview of object-oriented programming concepts in Java and how they relate to how you structure your own programs:

☐ What classes and objects are and how they relate to each other

☐ The two main parts of a class or object: its behaviors and its attributes

☐ Class inheritance and how inheritance affects the way you design your programs

☐ Some information about packages and interfaces

If you're already familiar with object-oriented programming, much of today's lesson will be old hat to you. You may want to skim it and go to a movie today instead. Tomorrow, you'll get into more specific details.

Thinking in Objects: An Analogy

Consider, if you will, Legos. Legos, for those who do not spend much time with children, are small plastic building blocks in various colors and sizes. They have small round bits on one side that fit into small round holes on other Legos so that they fit together snugly to create larger shapes. With different Lego parts (Lego wheels, Lego engines, Lego hinges, Lego pulleys), you can put together castles, automobiles, giant robots that swallow cities, or just about anything else you can imagine. Each Lego part is a small object that fits together with other small objects in predefined ways to create other larger objects. That is roughly how object-oriented programming works: putting together smaller elements to build larger ones.

Here's another example. You can walk into a computer store and, with a little background and often some help, assemble an entire PC computer system from various components: a motherboard, a CPU chip, a video card, a hard disk, a keyboard, and so on. Ideally, when you finish assembling all the various self-contained units, you have a system in which all the units work together to create a larger system with which you can solve the problems you bought the computer for in the first place.

Internally, each of those components may be vastly complicated and engineered by different companies with different methods of design. But you don't need to know how the component works, what every chip on the board does, or how, when you press the A key, an *A* gets sent to your computer. As the assembler of the overall system, each component you use is a self-contained unit, and all you are interested in is how the units interact with each other. Will this video card fit into the slots on the motherboard, and will this monitor work with this video card? Will each particular component speak the right commands to the other components it interacts with so that each part of the computer is understood by every other part? Once you know what the interactions are between the components and can match the interactions, putting together the overall system is easy.

What does this have to do with programming? Everything. Object-oriented programming works in exactly this same way. Using object-oriented programming, your overall program is made up of lots of different self-contained components (objects), each of which has a specific role in the program and all of which can talk to each other in predefined ways.

Objects and Classes

Object-oriented programming is modeled on how, in the real world, objects are often made up of many kinds of smaller objects. This capability of combining objects, however, is only one very general aspect of object-oriented programming. Object-oriented programming provides several other concepts and features to make creating and using objects easier and more flexible, and the most important of these features is classes.

When you write a program in an object-oriented language, you don't define actual objects. You define classes of objects, where a *class* is a template for multiple objects with similar features. Classes embody all the features of a particular set of objects. For example, you might have a Tree class that describes the features of all trees (has leaves and roots, grows, creates chlorophyll). The Tree class serves as an abstract model for the concept of a tree—to reach out and grab, or interact with, or cut down a tree you have to have a concrete instance of that tree. Of course, once you have a tree class, you can create lots of different *instances* of that tree, and each different tree instance can have different features (short, tall, bushy, drops leaves in autumn), while still behaving like and being immediately recognizable as a tree (see Figure 2.1).

Figure 2.1.

The Tree *class and several* Tree *instances.*

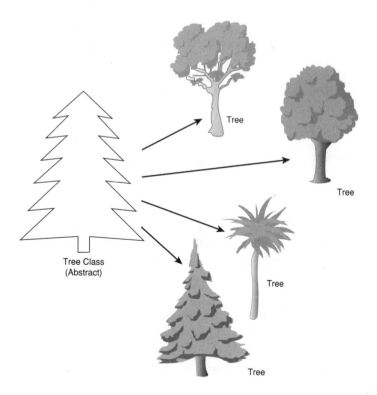

Tree Class
(Abstract)

Tree

Tree

Tree

Tree

NEW TERM A *class* is a generic template for a set of objects with similar features.

An *instance* of a class is another word for an actual object. If class is the general (generic) representation of an object, an instance is its concrete representation. So what, precisely, is the difference between an instance and an object? Nothing, really. Object is the more general term, but both instances and objects are the concrete representation of a class. In fact, the terms instance and object are often used interchangeably in OOP lingo. An instance of a tree and a tree object are both the same thing.

NEW TERM An *instance* is the specific concrete representation of a class. Instances and objects are the same thing.

What about an example closer to the sort of things you might want to do in Java programming? You might create a class for the user interface element called a button. The Button class defines the features of a button (its label, its size, its appearance) and how it behaves. (Does it need a single-click or a double-click to activate it? Does it change color when it's clicked? What does it do when it's activated?) After you define the Button class, you can then easily create instances of that button—that is, button objects—that all take on the basic features of the button as defined by the class, but may have different appearances and behavior based on what you want that particular button to do. By creating a Button class, you don't have to keep rewriting the code for each individual button you want to use in your program, and you can reuse the Button class to create different kinds of buttons as you need them in this program and in other programs.

> **TIP**
>
> If you're used to programming in C, you can think of a class as sort of creating a new composite data type by using struct and typedef. Classes, however, can provide much more than just a collection of data, as you'll discover in the rest of today's lesson.

When you write a Java program, you design and construct a set of classes. Then when your program runs, instances of those classes are created and discarded as needed. Your task, as a Java programmer, is to create the right set of classes to accomplish what your program needs to accomplish.

Fortunately, you don't have to start from the very beginning: The Java environment comes with a standard set of classes (called a *class library*) that implements a lot of the basic behavior you need—not only for basic programming tasks (classes to provide basic math functions, arrays, strings, and so on), but also for graphics and networking behavior. In many cases, the Java class libraries may be enough so that all you have to do in your Java program is create a single class that uses the standard class libraries. For complicated Java programs, you may have to create a whole set of classes with defined interactions between them.

 A *class library* is a collection of classes intended to be reused repeatedly in different programs. The standard Java class libraries contain quite a few classes for accomplishing basic programming tasks in Java.

Attributes and Behavior

Every class you write in Java has two basic features: attributes and behavior. In this section, you'll learn about each one as it applies to a theoretical simple class called Motorcycle. To finish up this section, you'll create the Java code to implement a representation of a motorcycle.

Attributes

Attributes are the individual things that differentiate one object from another and determine the appearance, state, or other qualities of that object. Let's create a theoretical class called Motorcycle. A motorcycle class might include the following attributes and have these typical values:

- ☐ Color: red, green, silver, brown
- ☐ Style: cruiser, sport bike, standard
- ☐ Make: Honda, BMW, Bultaco

Attributes of an object can also include information about its state; for example, you could have features for engine condition (off or on) or current gear selected.

Attributes are defined in classes by variables. Those variables' types and names are defined in the class, and each object can have its own values for those variables. Because each instance of a class can have different values for its variables, these variables are often called *instance variables*.

 An *instance variable* defines the attributes of the object. Instance variables' types and names are defined in the class, but their values are set and changed in the object.

Instance variables may be initially set when an object is created and stay constant throughout the life of the object, or they may be able to change at will as the program runs. Change the value of the variable and you change an object's attributes.

In addition to instance variables, there are also class variables, which apply to the class itself and to all its instances. Unlike instance variables, whose values are stored in the instance, class variables' values are stored in the class itself. You'll learn about class variables later on this week, and more specifics about instance variables tomorrow.

Behavior

A class's behavior determines how an instance of that class operates; for example, how it will "react" if asked to do something by another class or object or if its internal state changes. Behavior is the only way objects can do anything to themselves or have anything done to them. For example, to go back to the theoretical Motorcycle class, here are some behaviors that the Motorcycle class might have:

- ☐ Start the engine
- ☐ Stop the engine
- ☐ Speed up
- ☐ Change gear
- ☐ Stall

To define an object's behavior, you create *methods*, a set of Java statements that accomplish some task. Methods look and behave just like functions in other languages but are defined and accessible solely inside a class. Java does not have functions defined outside classes (as C++ does).

NEW TERM   *Methods* are functions defined inside classes that operate on instances of those classes.

While methods can be used solely to operate on an individual object, methods are also used between objects to communicate with each other. A class or an object can call methods in another class or object to communicate changes in the environment or to ask that object to change its state.

Just as there are instance and class variables, there are also instance and class methods. Instance methods (which are so common that they're usually just called methods) apply and operate on an instance of a class; class methods apply and operate on the class itself. You'll learn more about class methods later on this week.

Creating a Class

Up to this point, today's lesson has been pretty theoretical. In this section, you'll create a working example of the Motorcycle class so that you can see how instance variables and methods are defined in a class in Java. You'll also create a Java application that creates a new instance of the Motorcycle class and shows its instance variables.

I'm not going to go into a lot of detail about the actual syntax of this example. Don't worry too much about it if you're not really sure what's going on; it will become clear to you later on this week. All you really need to worry about in this example is understanding the basic parts of this class definition.

2

Ready? Let's start with a basic class definition. Open the text editor you've been using to create Java source code and enter the following (remember, upper- and lowercase matters):

```
class Motorcycle {

}
```

Congratulations! You've now created a class. Of course, it doesn't do very much at the moment, but that's a Java class at its very simplest.

First, let's create some instance variables for this class—three of them, to be specific. Just below the first line, add the following three lines:

```
String make;
String color;
boolean engineState = false;
```

Here you've created three instance variables: Two, make and color, can contain String objects (a string is the generic term for a series of characters; String, with a capital *S*, is part of that standard class library mentioned earlier). The third, engineState, is a boolean variable that refers to whether the engine is off or on; a value of false means that the engine is off, and true means that the engine is on. Note that boolean is lowercase *b*.

NEW TERM   A *boolean* is a value of either true or false.

TECHNICAL NOTE

boolean in Java is a real data type that can have the values true or false. Unlike in C, booleans are not numbers. You'll hear about this again tomorrow so that you won't forget.

Now let's add some behavior (methods) to the class. There are all kinds of things a motorcycle can do, but to keep things short, let's add just one method—a method that starts the engine. Add the following lines below the instance variables in your class definition:

```
void startEngine() {
    if (engineState == true)
        System.out.println("The engine is already on.");
    else {
```

```
          engineState = true;
          System.out.println("The engine is now on.");
      }
  }
```

The startEngine() method tests to see whether the engine is already running (in the part engineState == true) and, if it is, merely prints a message to that effect. If the engine isn't already running, it changes the state of the engine to true (turning the engine on) and then prints a message. Finally, because the startEngine() method doesn't return a value, its definition includes the word void at the beginning. (You can also define methods to return values; you'll learn more about method definitions on Day 6, "Creating Classes and Applications in Java.")

TIP

> Here and throughout this book, whenever I refer to the name of a method, I'll add empty parentheses to the end of the name (for example, as I did in the first sentence of the previous paragraph: "The startEngine() method..." This is a convention used in the programming community at large to indicate that a particular name is a method and not a variable. The parentheses are silent.

With your methods and variables in place, save the program to a file called Motorcycle.java (remember that you should always name your Java source files the same names as the class they define). Listing 2.1 shows what your program should look like so far.

TYPE **Listing 2.1. The Motorcycle.java file.**

```
 1:class Motorcycle {
 2:
 3: String make;
 4: String color;
 5: boolean engineState = false;
 6:
 7: void startEngine() {
 8:     if (engineState == true)
 9:         System.out.println("The engine is already on.");
10:     else {
11:         engineState = true;
12:         System.out.println("The engine is now on.");
13:     }
14: }
15:}
```

TIP

The indentation of each part of the class isn't important to the Java compiler. Using some form of indentation, however, makes your class definition easier for you and other people to read. The indentation used here, with instance variables and methods indented from the class definition, is the style used throughout this book. The Java class libraries use a similar indentation. You can choose any indentation style that you like.

Before you compile this class, let's add one more method just below the startEngine() method (that is, between lines 14 and 15). The showAtts() method is used to print the current values of all the instance variables in an instance of your Motorcycle class. Here's what it looks like:

```
void showAtts() {
    System.out.println("This motorcycle is a "
        + color + " " + make);
    if (engineState == true)
        System.out.println("The engine is on.");
    else System.out.println("The engine is off.");
}
```

The showAtts() method prints two lines to the screen: the make and color of the motorcycle object and whether the engine is on or off.

Now you have a Java class with three instance variables and two methods defined. Save that file again, and compile it using one of the following methods:

NOTE

After this point, I'm going to assume you know how to compile and run Java programs. I won't repeat this information after this.

 WINDOWS From inside a DOS shell, CD to the directory containing your Java source file, and use the javac command to compile it:

```
javac Motorcycle.java
```

 MACINTOSH Drag and drop the Motorcycle.java file onto the Java Compiler icon.

 SOLARIS From a command line, CD to the directory containing your Java source file, and use the javac command to compile it:

```
javac Motorcycle.java
```

When you run this little program using the java or Java Runner programs, you'll get an error. Why? When you run a compiled Java class directly, Java assumes that the class is an application and looks for a main() method. Because we haven't defined a main() method inside the class, the Java interpreter (java) gives you an error something like one of these two errors:

```
In class Motorcycle: void main(String argv[]) is not defined
Exception in thread "main": java.lang.UnknownError
```

To do something with the Motorcycle class—for example, to create instances of that class and play with them—you're going to need to create a separate Java applet or application that uses this class or add a main() method to this one. For simplicity's sake, let's do the latter. Listing 2.2 shows the main() method you'll add to the Motorcycle class. You'll want to add this method to your Motorcycle.java source file just before the last closing brace (}), underneath the startEngine() and showAtts() methods.

TYPE **Listing 2.2. The main() method for Motorcycle.java.**

```
 1: public static void main (String args[]) {
 2:     Motorcycle m = new Motorcycle();
 3:     m.make = "Yamaha RZ350";
 4:     m.color = "yellow";
 5:     System.out.println("Calling showAtts...");
 6:     m.showAtts();
 7:     System.out.println("--------");
 8:     System.out.println("Starting engine...");
 9:     m.startEngine();
10:     System.out.println("--------");
11:     System.out.println("Calling showAtts...");
12:     m.showAtts();
13:     System.out.println("--------");
14:     System.out.println("Starting engine...");
15:     m.startEngine();
16:}
```

With the main() method in place, the Motorcycle class is now an official application, and you can compile it again and this time it'll run. Here's how the output should look:

OUTPUT
```
Calling showAtts...
This motorcycle is a yellow Yamaha RZ350
The engine is off.
--------
Starting engine...
The engine is now on.
--------
Calling showAtts...
This motorcycle is a yellow Yamaha RZ350
The engine is on.
--------
Starting engine...
The engine is already on.
```

ANALYSIS The contents of the main() method are all going to look very new to you, so let's go through it line by line so that you at least have a basic idea of what it does (you'll get details about the specifics of all of this tomorrow and the day after).

The first line declares the main() method. The first line of the main() method always looks like this; you'll learn the specifics of each part later this week.

Line 2, `Motorcycle m = new Motorcycle();`, creates a new instance of the Motorcycle class and stores a reference to it in the variable m. Remember, you don't usually operate directly on classes in your Java programs; instead, you create objects from those classes and then call methods in those objects.

Lines 3 and 4 set the instance variables for this Motorcycle object: The make is now a Yamaha RZ350 (a very pretty motorcycle from the mid-1980s), and the color is yellow.

Lines 5 and 6 call the showAtts() method, defined in your Motorcycle object. (Actually, only 6 does; 5 just prints a message that you're about to call this method.) The new motorcycle object then prints out the values of its instance variables—the make and color as you set in the previous lines—and shows that the engine is off.

Line 7 prints a divider line to the screen; this is just for prettier output.

Line 9 calls the startEngine() method in the motorcycle object to start the engine. The engine should now be on.

Line 11 prints the values of the instance variables again. This time, the report should say the engine is now on.

Line 15 tries to start the engine again, just for fun. Because the engine is already on, this should print the message The engine is already on.

 Listing 2.3 shows the final Motorcycle class, in case you've been having trouble compiling and running the one you've got (and remember, this example and all the examples in this book are available on the CD that accompanies the book):

TYPE **Listing 2.3. The final version of Motorcycle.java.**

```
1: class Motorcycle {
2:
3:     String make;
4:     String color;
5:     boolean engineState;
6:
7:     void startEngine() {
8:         if (engineState == true)
9:             System.out.println("The engine is already on.");
10:        else {
```

continues

Listing 2.3. continued

```
11:             engineState = true;
12:             System.out.println("The engine is now on.");
13:         }
14:     }
15:
16:     void showAtts() {
17:         System.out.println("This motorcycle is a "
18:             + color + " " + make);
19:         if (engineState == true)
20:             System.out.println("The engine is on.");
21:         else System.out.println("The engine is off.");
22:     }
23:
24:     public static void main (String args[]) {
25:         Motorcycle m = new Motorcycle();
26:         m.make = "Yamaha RZ350";
27:         m.color = "yellow";
28:         System.out.println("Calling showAtts...");
29:         m.showAtts();
30:       System.out.println("------");
31:         System.out.println("Starting engine...");
32:         m.startEngine();
33:         System.out.println("------");
34:         System.out.println("Calling showAtts...");
35:         m.showAtts();
36:         System.out.println("------");
37:         System.out.println("Starting engine...");
38:         m.startEngine();
39:     }
40:}
```

Inheritance, Interfaces, and Packages

Now that you have a basic grasp of classes, objects, methods, variables, and how to put them all together in a Java program, it's time to confuse you again. Inheritance, interfaces, and packages are all mechanisms for organizing classes and class behaviors. The Java class libraries use all these concepts, and the best class libraries you write for your own programs will also use these concepts.

Inheritance

Inheritance is one of the most crucial concepts in object-oriented programming, and it has a very direct effect on how you design and write your Java classes. Inheritance is a powerful mechanism that means when you write a class you only have to specify how that class is different from some other class; inheritance will give you automatic access to the information contained in that other class.

With inheritance, all classes—those you write, those from other class libraries that you use, and those from the standard utility classes as well—are arranged in a strict hierarchy (see Figure 2.2). Each class has a superclass (the class above it in the hierarchy), and each class can have one or more subclasses (classes below that class in the hierarchy). Classes further down in the hierarchy are said to *inherit from* classes further up in the hierarchy.

Figure 2.2.

A class hierarchy.

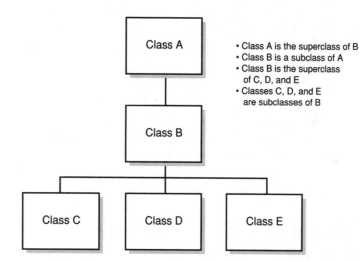

- Class A is the superclass of B
- Class B is a subclass of A
- Class B is the superclass of C, D, and E
- Classes C, D, and E are subclasses of B

Subclasses inherit all the methods and variables from their superclasses—that is, in any particular class, if the superclass defines behavior that your class needs, you don't have to redefine it or copy that code from some other class. Your class automatically gets that behavior from its superclass, that superclass gets behavior from its superclass, and so on all the way up the hierarchy. Your class becomes a combination of all the features of the classes above it in the hierarchy.

NEW TERM *Inheritance* is a concept in object-oriented programming where all classes are arranged in a strict *hierarchy*. Each class in the hierarchy has *superclasses* (classes above it in the hierarchy) and any number of *subclasses* (classes below it in the hierarchy). Subclasses inherit attributes and behavior from their superclasses.

At the top of the Java class hierarchy is the class Object; all classes inherit from this one superclass. Object is the most general class in the hierarchy; it defines behavior inherited by all the classes in Java. Each class further down in the hierarchy adds more information and becomes more tailored to a specific purpose. In this way, you can think of a class hierarchy as defining very abstract concepts at the top of the hierarchy and those ideas becoming more concrete the farther down the chain of superclasses you go.

Most of the time when you write new Java classes, you'll want to create a class that has all the information some other class has, plus some extra information. For example, you may want a version of a `Button` with its own built-in label. To get all the `Button` information, all you have to do is define your class to inherit from `Button`. Your class will automatically get all the behavior defined in `Button` (and in `Button`'s superclasses), so all you have to worry about are the things that make your class different from `Button` itself. This mechanism for defining new classes as the differences between them and their superclasses is called *subclassing*.

Subclassing involves creating a new class that inherits from some other class in the class hierarchy. Using subclassing, you only need to define the differences between your class and its parent; the additional behavior is all available to your class through inheritance.

NEW TERM *Subclassing* is the process of creating a new class that inherits from some other already-existing class.

What if your class defines an entirely new behavior and isn't really a subclass of another class? Your class can also inherit directly from `Object`, which still allows it to fit neatly into the Java class hierarchy. In fact, if you create a class definition that doesn't indicate its superclass in the first line, Java automatically assumes you're inheriting from `Object`. The `Motorcycle` class you created in the previous section inherited from `Object`.

Creating a Class Hierarchy

If you're creating a larger set of classes for a very complex program, it makes sense for your classes not only to inherit from the existing class hierarchy, but also to make up a hierarchy themselves. This may take some planning beforehand when you're trying to figure out how to organize your Java code, but the advantages are significant once it's done:

☐ When you develop your classes in a hierarchy, you can factor out information common to multiple classes in superclasses, and then reuse that superclass's information over and over again. Each subclass gets that common information from its superclass.

☐ Changing (or inserting) a class further up in the hierarchy automatically changes the behavior of its subclasses—no need to change or recompile any of the lower classes because they get the new information through inheritance and not by copying any of the code.

For example, let's go back to that `Motorcycle` class and pretend you created a Java program to implement all the features of a motorcycle. It's done, it works, and everything is fine. Now, your next task is to create a Java class called `Car`.

`Car` and `Motorcycle` have many similar features—both are vehicles driven by engines. Both have transmissions, headlamps, and speedometers. So your first impulse may be to open your `Motorcycle` class file and copy over a lot of the information you already defined into the new class `Car`.

A far better plan is to factor out the common information for Car and Motorcycle into a more general class hierarchy. This may be a lot of work just for the classes Motorcycle and Car, but once you add Bicycle, Scooter, Truck, and so on, having common behavior in a reusable superclass significantly reduces the amount of work you have to do overall.

Let's design a class hierarchy that might serve this purpose. Starting at the top is the class Object, which is the root of all Java classes. The most general class to which a motorcycle and a car both belong might be called Vehicle. A vehicle, generally, is defined as a thing that propels someone from one place to another. In the Vehicle class, you define only the behavior that enables someone to be propelled from point a to point b, and nothing more.

Below Vehicle? How about two classes: PersonPoweredVehicle and EnginePoweredVehicle? EnginePoweredVehicle is different from Vehicle because it has an engine, and the behaviors might include stopping and starting the engine, having certain amounts of gasoline and oil, and perhaps the speed or gear in which the engine is running. Person-powered vehicles have some kind of mechanism for translating people motion into vehicle motion—pedals, for example. Figure 2.3 shows what you have so far.

Figure 2.3.

The basic vehicle hierarchy.

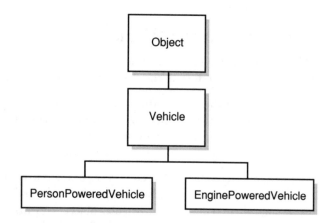

Now let's become even more specific. With EnginePoweredVehicle, you might have several classes: Motorcycle, Car, Truck, and so on. Or you can factor out still more behavior and have intermediate classes for TwoWheeled and FourWheeled vehicles, with different behaviors for each (see Figure 2.4).

Finally, with a subclass for the two-wheeled engine-powered vehicles, you can have a class for motorcycles. Alternatively, you could additionally define scooters and mopeds, both of which are two-wheeled engine-powered vehicles but have different qualities from motorcycles.

Figure 2.4.

Two-wheeled and four-wheeled vehicles.

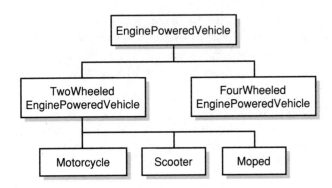

Where do qualities such as make or color come in? Wherever you want them to go—or, more usually, where they fit most naturally in the class hierarchy. You can define the make and color on `Vehicle`, and all the subclasses will have those variables as well. The point to remember is that you have to define a feature or a behavior only once in the hierarchy; it's automatically reused by each subclass.

How Inheritance Works

How does inheritance work? How is it that instances of one class can automatically get variables and methods from the classes further up in the hierarchy?

For instance variables, when you create a new instance of a class, you get a "slot" for each variable defined in the current class and for each variable defined in all its superclasses. In this way, all the classes combine to form a template for the current object, and then each object fills in the information appropriate to its situation.

Methods operate similarly: New objects have access to all the method names of its class and its superclasses, but method definitions are chosen dynamically when a method is called. That is, if you call a method on a particular object, Java first checks the object's class for the definition of that method. If it's not defined in the object's class, it looks in that class's superclass, and so on up the chain until the method definition is found (see Figure 2.5).

Things get complicated when a subclass defines a method that has the same signature (name, number, and type of arguments) as a method defined in a superclass. In this case, the method definition that is found first (starting at the bottom and working upward toward the top of the hierarchy) is the one that is actually executed. Therefore, you can intentionally define a method in a subclass that has the same signature as a method in a superclass, which then "hides" the superclass's method. This is called *overriding* a method. You'll learn all about methods on Day 7, "More About Methods."

Figure 2.5.

How methods are located.

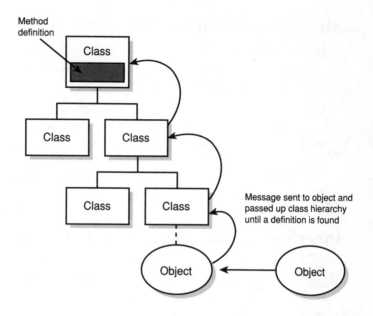

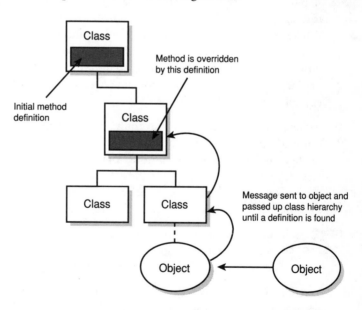

NEW TERM   *Overriding* a method is creating a method in a subclass that has the same signature (name, number, and type of arguments) as a method in a superclass. That new method then hides the superclass's method (see Figure 2.6).

Figure 2.6.

Overriding methods.

Single and Multiple Inheritance

Java's form of inheritance, as you learned in the previous sections, is called *single inheritance*. Single inheritance means that each Java class can have only one superclass (although any given superclass can have multiple subclasses).

In other object-oriented programming languages, such as C++, classes can have more than one superclass, and they inherit combined variables and methods from all those classes. This is called *multiple inheritance*. Multiple inheritance can provide enormous power in terms of being able to create classes that factor just about all imaginable behavior, but it can also significantly complicate class definitions and the code to produce them. Java makes inheritance simpler by being only singly inherited.

Interfaces, Packages, and Inner Classes

There are two remaining concepts to discuss here: packages and interfaces. Both are advanced topics for implementing and designing groups of classes and class behavior. You'll learn about both interfaces and packages on Day 16, "Packages, Interfaces, and Inner Classes," but they are worth at least introducing here.

Recall that each Java class has only a single superclass, and it inherits variables and methods from that superclass and all its superclasses. Although single inheritance makes the relationship between classes and the functionality those classes implement easy to understand and to design, it can also be somewhat restrictive—in particular, when you have similar behavior that needs to be duplicated across different "branches" of the class hierarchy. Java solves this problem of shared behavior by using the concept of interfaces, which collect method names into one place and then allow you to add those methods as a group to the various classes that need them. Note that interfaces contain only method names and interfaces (arguments, for example), not actual definitions.

Although a single Java class can have only one superclass (due to single inheritance), that class can also implement any number of interfaces. By implementing an interface, a class provides method implementations (definitions) for the method names defined by the interface. If two very disparate classes implement the same interface, they can both respond to the same method calls (as defined by that interface), although what each class actually does in response to those method calls may be very different.

 An *interface* is a collection of method names, without definitions, that can be added to classes to provide additional behavior not included with those methods the class defined itself or inherited from its superclasses.

You don't need to know very much about interfaces right now. You'll learn more as the book progresses, so if all this is very confusing, don't panic!

The final new Java concept for today is packages. *Packages* in Java are a way of grouping together related classes and interfaces in a single library or collection. Packages enable modular groups of classes to be available only if they are needed and eliminate potential conflicts between class names in different groups of classes.

You'll learn all about packages, including how to create and use them, in Week 3. For now, there are only a few things you need to know:

☐ The class libraries in the Java Developer's Kit are contained in a package called java. The classes in the java package are guaranteed to be available in any Java implementation and are the *only* classes guaranteed to be available across different implementations. The java package itself contains other packages for classes that define the language, the input and output classes, some basic networking, the window toolkit functions, and classes that define applets. Classes in other packages (for example, classes in the sun or netscape packages) may be available only in specific implementations.

☐ By default, your Java classes have access to only the classes in java.lang (the base language package inside the java package). To use classes from any other package, you have to either refer to them explicitly by package name or import them into your source file.

☐ To refer to a class within a package, list all the packages that class is contained in and the class name, all separated by periods (.). For example, take the Color class, which is contained in the awt package (awt stands for Abstract Windowing Toolkit). The awt package, in turn, is inside the java package. To refer to the Color class in your program, you use the notation java.awt.Color.

Creating a Subclass

To finish up today, let's create a class that is a subclass of another class and override some methods. You'll also get a basic feel for how packages work in this example.

Probably the most typical instance of creating a subclass, at least when you first start programming in Java, is creating an applet. All applets are subclasses of the class Applet (which is part of the java.applet package). By creating a subclass of Applet, you automatically get all the behavior from the window toolkit and the layout classes that enable your applet to be drawn in the right place on the page and to interact with system operations, such as keypresses and mouse clicks.

In this example, you'll create an applet similar to the Hello World applet from yesterday, but one that draws the Hello string in a larger font and a different color. To start this example, let's first construct the class definition itself. Let's go to your text editor, and enter the following class definition:

```
public class HelloAgainApplet extends java.applet.Applet {

}
```

Here, you're creating a class called `HelloAgainApplet`. Note the part that says extends `java.applet.Applet`—that's the part that says your applet class is a subclass of the `Applet` class. Note that because the `Applet` class is contained in the `java.applet` package, you don't have automatic access to that class, and you have to refer to it explicitly by package and class name.

The other part of this class definition is the `public` keyword. Public means that your class is available to the Java system at large once it is loaded. Most of the time you need to make a class `public` only if you want it to be visible to all the other classes in your Java program, but applets, in particular, must be declared to be public. (You'll learn more about `public` classes in Week 3.)

A class definition with nothing in it doesn't really have much of a point; without adding or overriding any of its superclasses' variables or methods, there's no reason to create a subclass at all. Let's add some information to this class, inside the two enclosing braces, to make it different from its superclass.

First, add an instance variable to contain a `Font` object:

```
Font f = new Font("TimesRoman", Font.BOLD, 36);
```

The `f` instance variable now contains a new instance of the class `Font`, part of the `java.awt` package. This particular `Font` object is a Times Roman font, boldface, 36 points high. In the previous Hello World applet, the font used for the text was the default font: 12-point Times Roman. Using a `Font` object, you can change the font of the text you draw in your applet.

By creating an instance variable to hold this font object, you make it available to all the methods in your class. Now let's create a method that uses it.

When you write applets, there are several "standard" methods defined in the applet superclasses that you will commonly override in your applet class. These include methods to initialize the applet, to make it start running, to handle operations such as mouse movements or mouse clicks, or to clean up when the applet stops running. One of those standard methods is the `paint()` method, which actually displays your applet onscreen. The default definition of `paint()` doesn't do anything—it's an empty method. By overriding `paint()`, you tell the applet just what to draw on the screen. Here's a definition of `paint()`:

```
public void paint(Graphics g) {
    g.setFont(f);
    g.setColor(Color.red);
    g.drawString("Hello again!", 5, 40);
}
```

There are two things to know about the paint() method. First, note that this method is declared public, just as the applet itself was. The paint() method is actually public for a different reason—because the method it's overriding is also public. If a superclass's method is defined as public, your override method also has to be public, or you'll get an error when you compile the class.

Second, note that the paint() method takes a single argument: an instance of the Graphics class. The Graphics class provides platform-independent behavior for rendering fonts, colors, and behavior for drawing basic lines and shapes. You'll learn a lot more about the Graphics class in Week 2, when you create more extensive applets.

Inside your paint() method, you've done three things:

☐ You've told the graphics object that the default drawing font will be the one contained in the instance variable f.

☐ You've told the graphics object that the default color is an instance of the Color class for the color red.

☐ Finally, you've drawn your "Hello Again!" string onto the screen, at the x and y positions of 5 and 25. The string will be rendered in the new font and color.

For an applet this simple, this is all you need to do. Here's what the applet looks like so far:

```
public class HelloAgainApplet extends java.applet.Applet {

  Font f = new Font("TimesRoman",Font.BOLD,36);

  public void paint(Graphics g) {
    g.setFont(f);
    g.setColor(Color.red);
    g.drawString("Hello again!", 5, 40);
  }
}
```

If you've been paying close attention, you'll notice that something is wrong with this example up to this point. If you don't know what it is, try saving this file (remember, save it to the same name as the class: HelloAgainApplet.java) and compiling it. You should get a bunch of errors similar to this one:

```
HelloAgainApplet.java:7: Class Graphics not found in type declaration.
```

Why are you getting these errors? Because the classes you're referring to in this class, such as Graphics and Font, are part of a package that isn't available by default. Remember that the only package you have access to automatically in your Java programs is java.lang. You referred to the Applet class in the first line of the class definition by referring to its full package name (java.applet.Applet). Further on in the program, however, you referred to all kinds of other classes as if they were available. The compiler catches this and tells you that you don't have access to those other classes.

There are two ways to solve this problem: Refer to all external classes by full package name or import the appropriate class or package at the beginning of your class file. Which one you choose to do is mostly a matter of choice, although if you find yourself referring to a class in another package lots of times, you may want to import it to cut down on the amount of typing.

In this example, you'll import the classes you need. There are three of them: Graphics, Font, and Color. All three are part of the java.awt package. Here are the lines to import these classes. These lines go at the top of your program, before the actual class definition:

```
import java.awt.Graphics;
import java.awt.Font;
import java.awt.Color;
```

TIP

You also can import an entire package of public classes by using an asterisk (*) in place of a specific class name. For example, to import all the classes in the awt package, you can use this line:

```
import java.awt.*;
```

Now, with the proper classes imported into your program, HelloAgainApplet.java should compile cleanly to a class file. Listing 2.4 shows the final version to double-check.

TYPE   **Listing 2.4. The final version of HelloAgainApplet.java.**

```
1:import java.awt.Graphics;
2:import java.awt.Font;
3:import java.awt.Color;
4:
5:public class HelloAgainApplet extends java.applet.Applet {
6:
7:  Font f = new Font("TimesRoman",Font.BOLD,36);
8:
9:  public void paint(Graphics g) {
10:    g.setFont(f);
11:    g.setColor(Color.red);
12:    g.drawString("Hello again!", 5, 40);
13:  }
14:}
```

To test it, create an HTML file with the <APPLET> tag as you did yesterday. Here's an HTML file to use:

```
<HTML>
<HEAD>
```

```
<TITLE>Another Applet</TITLE>
</HEAD>
<BODY>
<P>My second Java applet says:
<BR><APPLET CODE="HelloAgainApplet.class" WIDTH=200 HEIGHT=50>
</APPLET>
</BODY>
</HTML>
```

For this HTML example, your Java class file is in the same directory as this HTML file. Save the file to `HelloAgainApplet.html` and fire up your Java-enabled browser or the Java applet viewer. Figure 2.7 shows the result you should be getting (the `"Hello Again!"` string is red).

Figure 2.7.

The HelloAgain *applet.*

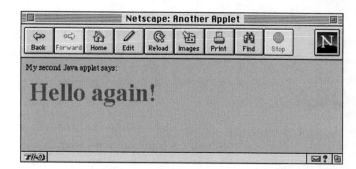

Summary

If this is your first encounter with object-oriented programming, a lot of the information in this lesson is going to seem really theoretical and overwhelming. Fear not—the further along in this book you get, and the more Java classes and applications you create, the easier it is to understand.

One of the biggest hurdles of object-oriented programming is not necessarily the concepts; it's their names. OOP has lots of jargon surrounding it. To summarize today's material, here's a glossary of terms and concepts you learned today:

class: A template for an object, which contains variables and methods representing behavior and attributes. Classes can inherit variables and methods from other classes.

class method: A method defined in a class, which operates on the class itself and can be called via the class or any of its instances.

class variable: A variable that is "owned" by the class and all its instances as a whole and is stored in the class.

instance: The same thing as an object; each object is an instance of some class.

instance method: A method defined in a class, which operates on an instance of that class. Instance methods are usually called just *methods*.

instance variable: A variable that is owned by an individual instance and whose value is stored in the instance.

interface: A collection of abstract behavior specifications that individual classes can then implement.

object: A concrete instance of some class. Multiple objects that are instances of the same class have access to the same methods, but often have different values for their instance variables.

package: A collection of classes and interfaces. Classes from packages other than java.lang must be explicitly imported or referred to by full package name.

subclass: A class lower in the inheritance hierarchy than its parent, the superclass. When you create a new class, it's often called *subclassing*.

superclass: A class further up in the inheritance hierarchy than its child, the subclass.

Q&A

Q Methods are effectively functions that are defined inside classes. If they look like functions and act like functions, why aren't they called functions?

A Some object-oriented programming languages do call them functions (C++ calls them member functions). Other object-oriented languages differentiate between functions inside and outside a body of a class or object, where having separate terms is important to understanding how each works. Because the difference is relevant in other languages and because the term method is now in such common use in object-oriented technology, Java uses the word as well.

Q I understand instance variables and methods, but not the idea of class variables and methods.

A Most everything you do in a Java program will be with objects. Some behaviors and attributes, however, make more sense if they are stored in the class itself rather than in the object. For example, to create a new instance of a class, you need a method that is defined and available in the class itself. (Otherwise, how can you create an object? You need an object to call the method, but you don't have an object yet.) Class variables, on the other hand, are often used when you have an attribute whose value you want to share with all the instances of a class.

Most of the time, you'll use instance variables and methods. You'll learn more about class variables and methods later this week.

Day 3

Java Basics

by Laura Lemay

Already this week you've learned about Java programming in very broad terms—what a Java program and an executable look like, and how to create simple classes. For the remainder of this week, you're going to get down to details and deal with the specifics of what the Java language looks like.

Today you won't define any classes or objects or worry about how any of them communicate inside a Java program. Rather, you'll draw closer and examine simple Java statements—the basic things you can do in Java within a method definition such as main().

Today you'll learn about the following:

- [ ] Java statements and expressions
- [ ] Variables and data types
- [ ] Comments
- [ ] Literals

☐ Arithmetic

☐ Comparisons

☐ Logical operators

NOTE

> Java looks a lot like C++, and—by extension—like C. Much of the syntax will be familiar to you if you're used to working in these languages. If you're an experienced C or C++ programmer, you may want to pay special attention to the technical notes (such as this one), because they provide information about the specific differences between these and other traditional languages and Java.

Statements and Expressions

A statement indicates the simplest tasks you can accomplish in Java; a statement forms a single Java operation. All the following are simple Java statements:

```
int i = 1;
import java.awt.Font;
System.out.println("This motorcycle is a "+ color + " " + make);
m.engineState = true;
```

Statements sometimes return values—for example, when you add two numbers together or test to see whether one value is equal to another. These kinds of statements are called *expressions*. You'll learn about them later today.

White space in Java statements, as with C, is unimportant. A statement can be contained on a single line or on multiple lines, and the Java compiler will be able to read it just fine. The most important thing to remember about Java statements is that each one ends with a semicolon (;). Forget the semicolon, and your Java program won't compile.

Java also has compound statements, or *blocks*, which can be placed wherever a single statement can. Block statements are surrounded by braces ({}). You'll learn more about blocks on Day 5, "Arrays, Conditionals, and Loops."

Variables and Data Types

Variables are locations in memory in which values can be stored. Each one has a name, a type, and a value. Before you can use a variable, you have to declare it. After it is declared, you can then assign values to it (you can also declare and assign a value to a variable at the same time, as you'll learn in this section).

Java actually has three kinds of variables: instance variables, class variables, and local variables.

Instance variables, as you learned yesterday, are used to define the attributes of a particular object. Class variables are similar to instance variables, except their values apply to all that class's instances (and to the class itself) rather than having different values for each object.

Local variables are declared and used inside method definitions, for example, for index counters in loops, as temporary variables, or to hold values that you need only inside the method definition itself. They can also be used inside blocks, which you'll learn about on Day 5. After the method (or block) finishes executing, the variable definition and its value cease to exist. Use local variables to store information needed by a single method and instance variables to store information needed by multiple methods in the object.

Although all three kinds of variables are declared in much the same way, class and instance variables are accessed and assigned in slightly different ways from local variables. Today you'll focus on variables as used within method definitions; tomorrow you'll learn how to deal with instance and class variables.

NOTE

Unlike other languages, Java does not have global variables—that is, variables that are global to all parts of a program. Instance and class variables can be used to communicate global information between and among objects. Remember that Java is an object-oriented language, so you should think in terms of objects and how they interact rather than in terms of programs.

Declaring Variables

To use any variable in a Java program, you must first declare it. Variable declarations consist of a type and a variable name:

```
int myAge;
String myName;
boolean isTired;
```

Variable definitions can go anywhere in a method definition (that is, anywhere a regular Java statement can go), although they are most commonly declared at the beginning of the definition before they are used:

```
public static void main ( String args[] )
{
    int count;
    String title;
    boolean isAsleep;
    ...
}
```

You can string together variable names of the same type on one line:

```
int x, y, z;
String firstName, LastName;
```

You can also give each variable an initial value when you declare it:

```
int myAge, mySize, numShoes = 28;
String myName = "Laura";
boolean isTired = true;
int a = 4, b = 5, c = 6;
```

If multiple variables appear on the same line with only one initializer (as in the first of the preceding examples), the initial value applies only to the last variable in the declaration. You can also group individual variables and initializers on the same line using commas, as with the last example here.

Local variables must be given values before they can be used (your Java program will not compile if you try to use an unassigned local variable). For this reason, you should always give initial values to all your local variables. Instance and class variable definitions do not have this restriction; instead, their initial value depends on the type of the variable: null for instances of classes, 0 for numeric variables, '\0' for characters, and false for booleans.

Notes on Variable Names

Variable names in Java can start with a letter, an underscore (_), or a dollar sign ($). They cannot start with a number. After the first character, your variable names can include any letter or number. Symbols, such as %, *, @, and so on, are often reserved for operators in Java, so be careful when using symbols in variable names.

In addition, the Java language uses the Unicode character set. Unicode is a character set definition that not only offers characters in the standard ASCII character set, but also includes several thousand other characters for representing most international alphabets. You therefore can use accented characters and other glyphs as legal characters in variable names, as long as they have a Unicode character number above 00C0.

WARNING

The Unicode specification is a two-volume set of lists of thousands of characters. If you don't understand Unicode, or don't think you have a use for it, just using plain numbers and letters in your variable names is safest. You'll learn more about Unicode later.

Finally, note that the Java language is case sensitive, which means that uppercase letters are different from lowercase letters. The variable X is therefore different from the variable x, and a rose is not a Rose is not a ROSE. Keep this point in mind as you write your own Java programs and as you read Java code other people have written.

By convention, Java variables have meaningful names, often made up of several words combined. The first word is lowercase, but all following words have an initial uppercase letter:

```
button theButton;
long reallyBigNumber;
boolean currentWeatherStateOfPlanetXShortVersion;
```

Variable Types

In addition to the variable name, each variable declaration must have a type, which defines what values that variable can hold. The variable type can be one of three things:

☐ One of the eight primitive data types

☐ The name of a class or interface

☐ An array

You'll learn how to declare and use array variables on Day 5; this lesson focuses on the primitive and class types.

Primitive Types

The eight primitive data types handle common types for integers, floating-point numbers, characters, and boolean values (true or false). They're called *primitive* because they're built into the system and are not actual objects, which makes them more efficient to use. Note that these data types are machine-independent, which means that you can rely on their sizes and characteristics to be consistent across your Java programs.

Each of the four Java integer types has a different range of values (as listed in Table 3.1). All are signed, which means they can hold either positive or negative numbers. Which type you choose for your variables depends on the range of values you expect that variable to hold; if a value becomes too big for the variable type, it is silently truncated.

Table 3.1. Integer types.

Type	Size	Range
byte	8 bits	−128 to 127
short	16 bits	−32,768 to 32,767
int	32 bits	−2,147,483,648 to 2,147,483,647
long	64 bits	−9,223,372,036,854,775,808 to 9,223,372,036,854,775,807

Floating-point numbers are used for numbers with a decimal part. Java floating-point numbers are compliant with IEEE 754 (an international standard for defining floating-point numbers and arithmetic). You'll find two floating-point types: `float` (32 bits, single precision) and `double` (64 bits, double precision).

The `char` type is used for individual characters. Because Java uses the Unicode character set, the `char` type has 16 bits of precision, unsigned.

Finally, the `boolean` type can have one of two values: `true` or `false`. Note that unlike in other C-like languages, `boolean` is not a number, nor can it be treated as one. All tests of `boolean` variables should test for `true` or `false`.

Note that all the primitive types are in lowercase. Be careful when you use them in your programs that you do use the lowercase, because there are also classes with the same names (and an initial capital letter) that have different behavior. For example, the primitive type `boolean` is different from the `Boolean` class. You'll learn more about these special classes and what they're used for on Day 4, "Working with Objects."

Class Types

In addition to the eight primitive data types, variables in Java can also be declared to hold an instance of a particular class:

```
String LastName;
Font basicFont;
OvalShape myOval;
```

Each of these variables can hold instances of the named class or of any of its subclasses. The latter is useful when you want a variable to be able to hold different instances of related classes. For example, say you have a set of fruit classes—`Apple`, `Pear`, `Strawberry`, and so on—all of which inherit from the general class `Fruit`. If you declare a variable of type `Fruit`, that variable can then hold instances of any of the `Fruit` classes. Declaring a variable of type `Object` means that variable can hold any object.

 NOTE
Java does not have a `typedef` statement (as in C and C++). To declare new types in Java, you declare a new class; then variables can be declared to be of that class's type.

Assigning Values to Variables

Once a variable has been declared, you can assign a value to that variable by using the assignment operator =, like this:

```
size = 14;
tooMuchCaffeine = true;
```

Comments

Java has three kinds of comments: two for regular comments in source code and one for the special documentation system javadoc.

The symbols /* and */ surround multi-line comments, as in C or C++. All text between the two delimiters is ignored:

```
/* I don't know how I wrote this next part; I was working
really late one night and it just sort of appeared. I
suspect the code elves did it for me. It might be wise
not to try and change it.
*/
```

These comments cannot be nested; that is, you cannot have a comment inside a comment.

Double-slashes (//) can be used for a single line of comment. All the text up to the end of the line is ignored:

```
int vices = 7; // are there really only 7 vices?
```

The final type of comment begins with /** and ends with */. The contents of these special comments are used by the javadoc system, but are otherwise used identically to the first type of comment. javadoc is used to generate API documentation from the code. You won't learn about javadoc in this book; you can find out more information from the documentation that comes with Sun's JDK or from the Java home page (http://java.sun.com).

Literals

A *literal* is a programming language term that essentially means that what you type is what you get. For example, if you type 4 in a Java program, you automatically get an integer with the value 4. If you type 'a', you get a character with the value a. Literals are used to indicate simple values in your Java programs.

NEW TERM   A *literal* is a simple value where "what you type is what you get." Numbers, characters, and strings are all examples of literals.

Literals may seem intuitive most of the time, but Java has some special cases of literals for different kinds of numbers, characters, strings, and boolean values.

Number Literals

Java has several integer literals. The number 4, for example, is a decimal integer literal of type int (although you can assign it to a variable of type byte or short because it's small enough to fit into those types). A decimal integer literal larger than an int is automatically of type long. You also can force a smaller number to a long by appending an L or l to that number (for example, 4L is a long integer of value 4). Negative integers are preceded by a minus sign—for example, -45.

Integers can also be expressed as octal or hexadecimal: A leading 0 indicates that a number is octal—for example, 0777 or 0004. A leading 0x (or 0X) means that it is in hex (0xFF, 0XAF45). Hexadecimal numbers can contain regular digits (0–9) or upper- or lowercase hex digits (a–f or A–F).

Floating-point literals usually have two parts: the integer part and the decimal part—for example, 5.77777. A floating-point literal results in a floating-point number of type double, regardless of the precision of the number. You can force the number to the type float by appending the letter f (or F) to that number—for example, 2.56F.

You can use exponents in floating-point literals, using the letter e or E followed by the exponent (which can be a negative number): 10e45 or .36E-2.

Boolean Literals

Boolean literals consist of the keywords true and false. These keywords can be used anywhere you need a test or as the only possible values for boolean variables.

Character Literals

Character literals are expressed by a single character surrounded by single quotation marks: 'a', '#', '3', and so on. Characters are stored as 16-bit Unicode characters. Table 3.2 lists the special codes that can represent nonprintable characters as well as characters from the Unicode character set. The letter d in the octal, hex, and Unicode escapes represents a number or a hexadecimal digit (a–f or A–F).

Table 3.2. Character escape codes.

Escape	Meaning
\n	Newline
\t	Tab
\b	Backspace
\r	Carriage return
\f	Formfeed
\\	Backslash
\'	Single quotation mark
\"	Double quotation mark
\ddd	Octal
\xdd	Hexadecimal
\udddd	Unicode character

NOTE   C and C++ programmers should note that Java does not include character codes for \a (bell) or \v (vertical tab).

String Literals

A combination of characters is a string. Strings in Java are instances of the class String. Strings are not simply arrays of characters as they are in C or C++, although they do have many array-like characteristics. Because string objects are real objects in Java, they have methods that enable you to combine, test, and modify strings very easily.

String literals consist of a series of characters inside double quotation marks:

```
"Hi, I'm a string literal."
"" //an empty string
```

Strings can contain character constants such as newline, tab, and Unicode characters:

```
"A string with a \t tab in it"
"Nested strings are \"strings inside of\" other strings"
"This string brought to you by Java\u2122"
```

In the last example here, the Unicode code sequence \u2122 produces a trademark symbol (™).

NOTE

Just because you can represent a character using a Unicode escape does not mean your computer can display that character—the computer or operating system you're running may not support Unicode, or the font you're using may not have a glyph (picture) for that character. All that Unicode escapes in Java provide is a way to encode Unicode characters for systems that support Unicode. Note that Java 1.02 was more limited in this respect than Java 1.1 is; in Java 1.1 you can display any Unicode character as long as there is a glyph for that character.

For more information about Unicode, visit the Unicode home page at `http://unicode.org`.

When you use a string literal in your Java program, Java automatically creates an instance of the class `String` for you with the value you give it. Strings are unusual in this respect; the other literals do not behave in this way (none of the primitive data types are actual objects), and usually creating a new object involves explicitly creating a new instance of a class. You'll learn more about strings, the `String` class, and the things you can do with strings later today and tomorrow.

Expressions and Operators

An expression is the simplest form of statement in Java that actually accomplishes something. All expressions, when evaluated, return a value (other statements don't necessarily do so). Arithmetic and tests for equality and magnitude are common examples of expressions. Because they return a value, you can assign that result to a variable or test that value in other Java statements.

Most of the expressions in Java use operators. Operators are special symbols for things like arithmetic, various forms of assignment, increment and decrement, and logical operations.

 Expressions are statements that return a value.

 Operators are special symbols that are commonly used in expressions.

Arithmetic

Java has five operators for basic arithmetic, as shown in Table 3.3.

Table 3.3. Arithmetic operators.

Operator	Meaning	Example
+	Addition	3 + 4
-	Subtraction	5 - 7
*	Multiplication	5 * 5
/	Division	14 / 7
%	Modulus	20 % 7

Each operator takes two operands, one on either side of the operator. The subtraction operator (-) can also be used to negate a single operand.

Integer division results in an integer. Because integers don't have decimal fractions, any remainder is ignored. The expression 31 / 9, for example, results in 3 (9 goes into 31 only 3 times).

Modulus (%) gives the remainder once the operands have been evenly divided. For example, 31 % 9 results in 4 because 9 goes into 31 three times, with 4 left over.

Note that the result type of most arithmetic operations involving integers is an int regardless of the original type of the operands (shorts and bytes are both automatically converted to int). If either or both operands are of type long, the result is of type long. If one operand is an integer and another is a floating-point number, the result is a floating point. (If you're interested in the details of how Java promotes and converts numeric types from one type to another, you may want to check out the Java Language Specification on Sun's official Java Web site at http://java.sun.com/; that's more detail than I want to cover here.)

Listing 3.1 is an example of simple arithmetic in Java.

TYPE **Listing 3.1. Simple arithmetic.**

```
1: class ArithmeticTest {
2: public static void main (String args[]) {
3:     short x = 6;
4:     int y = 4;
5:     float a = 12.5f;
6:     float b = 7f;
7:
8:     System.out.println("x is " + x + ", y is " + y);
9:     System.out.println("x + y = " + (x + y));
10:    System.out.println("x - y = " + (x - y));
11:    System.out.println("x / y = " + (x / y));
12:    System.out.println("x % y = " + (x % y));
13:
```

continues

Listing 3.1. continued

```
14:       System.out.println("a is " + a + ", b is " + b);
15:       System.out.println("a / b = " + (a / b));
16: }
17: }
```

OUTPUT
```
x is 6, y is 4
x + y = 10
x - y = 2
x / y = 1
x % y = 2
a is 12.5, b is 7
a / b = 1.78571
```

In this simple Java application (note the main() method), you initially define four variables in lines 3 through 6: x and y, which are integers (type int), and a and b, which are floating-point numbers (type float). Keep in mind that the default type for floating-point literals (such as 12.5) is double, so to make sure these numbers are of type float, you have to use an f after each one (lines 5 and 6).

The remainder of the program merely does some math with integers and floating-point numbers and prints out the results.

I want to mention one other element of this program: the method System.out.println(). You've seen this method on previous days, but you haven't really learned exactly what it does. The System.out.println() method merely prints a message to the standard output of your system—to the screen, to a special window, or maybe just to a special log file, depending on your system and the development environment you're running. The System.out.println() method takes a single argument—a string—but you can use + to concatenate multiple values into a single string, as you'll learn later today.

NOTE

While we're talking about math, there are two other Java features worth mentioning. The first is the Math class, which provides many common mathematical operations such as square root, absolute value, cosine, and so on. You'll learn a little more about Math tomorrow in Day 4, "Working with Objects." The second feature is specific to Java 1.1: the BigDecimal and BigInteger classes. These classes provide mechanisms for storing and operating on extremely large numbers (sometimes called "bignums") which may be too big for the standard Java primitive types. If you're interested in the big number classes, see the API documentation for the java.math package.

More About Assignment

Variable assignment is a form of expression; in fact, because one assignment expression results in a value, you can string them together like this:

```
x = y = z = 0;
```

In this example, all three variables now have the value 0.

The right side of an assignment expression is always evaluated before the assignment takes place. Expressions such as x = x + 2 therefore do the right thing; 2 is added to the value of x, and then that new value is reassigned to x. In fact, this sort of operation is so common that Java includes several operators to create a shorthand version, borrowed from C and C++. Table 3.4 shows these shorthand assignment operators.

Table 3.4. Assignment operators.

Expression	Meaning
x += y	x = x + y
x -= y	x = x - y
x *= y	x = x * y
x /= y	x = x / y

NOTE

Technically, the shorthand assignment and longhand expressions are not exactly equivalent, particularly in cases where x and y may themselves be complicated expressions and your code relies on side effects of those expressions. In most instances, however, they are functionally equivalent. For more information about very complicated expressions, evaluation order, and side effects, you might want to consult the Java Language Specification.

Incrementing and Decrementing

As in C and C++, the ++ and -- operators are used to increment or decrement a variable's value by 1. For example, x++ increments the value of x by 1, just as if you had used the expression x = x + 1. Similarly x-- decrements the value of x by 1. (Unlike C and C++, Java allows x to be floating point.)

These increment and decrement operators can be prefixed or postfixed; that is, the ++ or --can appear before or after the value it increments or decrements. For simple increment or decrement expressions, which one you use isn't overly important. In complex assignments in which you are assigning the result of an increment or decrement expression, which one you use does make a difference.

Consider, for example, the following two expressions:

```
y = x++;
y = ++x;
```

These two expressions yield very different results because of the difference between prefix and postfix. When you use postfix operators (x++ or x--), y gets the value of x before x is changed; using prefix, the value of x is assigned to y after the change has occurred. Listing 3.2 is a Java example of how all this works.

TYPE **Listing 3.2. Test of prefix and postfix increment operators.**

```
1: class PrePostFixTest {
2:
3: public static void main (String args[]) {
4:      int x = 0;
5:      int y = 0;
6:
7:      System.out.println("x and y are " + x + " and " + y );
8:      x++;
9:      System.out.println("x++ results in " + x);
10:     ++x;
11:     System.out.println("++x results in " + x);
12:     System.out.println("Resetting x back to 0.");
13:     x = 0;
14:     System.out.println("------------");
15:     y = x++;
16:     System.out.println("y = x++ (postfix) results in:");
17:     System.out.println("x is " + x);
18:     System.out.println("y is " + y);
19:     System.out.println("------------");
20:
21:     y = ++x;
22:     System.out.println("y = ++x (prefix) results in:");
23:     System.out.println("x is " + x);
24:     System.out.println("y is " + y);
25:     System.out.println("------------");
26:
27:  }
28:}
```

OUTPUT
```
x and y are 0 and 0
x++ results in 1
++x results in 2
Resetting x back to 0.
- - - - - - - - - - - -
y = x++ (postfix) results in:
x is 1
y is 0
- - - - - - - - - - - -
y = ++x (prefix) results in:
x is 2
y is 2
- - - - - - - - - - - -
```

In the first part of this example, you increment x alone using both prefix and postfix increment operators. In each, x is incremented by 1 each time. In this simple form, using either prefix or postfix works the same way.

In the second part of this example, you use the expression y = x++, in which the postfix increment operator is used. In this result, the value of x is incremented after that value is assigned to y. Hence the result: y is assigned the original value of x (0), and then x is incremented by 1.

In the third part, you use the prefix expression y = ++x. Here, the reverse occurs: x is incremented before its value is assigned to y. Because x is 1 from the previous step, its value is incremented (to 2), and then that value is assigned to y. Both x and y end up being 2.

NOTE

> Technically, this description is not entirely correct. In reality, Java always completely evaluates all expressions on the right of an expression before assigning that value to a variable, so the concept of "assigning x to y before x is incremented" isn't precisely right. Instead, Java takes the value of x and "remembers" it, evaluates (increments) x, and then assigns the original value of x to y. Although in most simple cases this distinction may not be important, for more complex expressions with side effects, it may change the behavior of the expression overall. See the Language Specification for many more details about expression evaluation in Java.

Comparisons

Java has several expressions for testing equality and magnitude. All these expressions return a boolean value (that is, true or false). Table 3.5 shows the comparison operators.

Table 3.5. Comparison operators.

Operator	Meaning	Example
==	Equal	x == 3
!=	Not equal	x != 3
<	Less than	x < 3
>	Greater than	x > 3
<=	Less than or equal to	x <= 3
>=	Greater than or equal to	x >= 3

Logical Operators

Expressions that result in boolean values (for example, the comparison operators) can be combined by using logical operators that represent the logical combinations AND, OR, XOR, and logical NOT.

For AND combinations, use either the & or && operator. The entire expression will be true only if both expressions on either side of the operator are true; if either expression is false, the entire expression is false. The difference between the two operators is in expression evaluation. Using &, both sides of the expression are evaluated regardless of the outcome. Using &&, if the left side of the expression is false, the entire expression is assumed to be false (the value of the right side doesn't matter), so the expression returns false, and the right side of the expression is never evaluated. (This is often called a "short-circuited" expression.)

For OR expressions, use either | or ||. OR expressions result in true if either or both of the expressions on either side is also true; if both expression operands are false, the expression is false. As with & and &&, the single | evaluates both sides of the expression, regardless of the outcome, and || is short-circuited: If the left expression is true, the expression returns true, and the right side is never evaluated.

In addition, you can use the XOR operator ^, which returns true only if its operands are different (one true and one false, or vice versa) and false otherwise (even if both are true).

In general, only the && and || are commonly used as actual logical combinations. The operators &, |, and ^ are more commonly used for bitwise logical operations.

For NOT, use the ! operator with a single expression argument. The value of the NOT expression is the negation of the expression; if x is true, !x is false.

Bitwise Operators

Finally, here's a short summary of the bitwise operators in Java. Most of these expressions are inherited from C and C++ and are used to perform operations on individual bits in integers. This book does not go into bitwise operations; it's an advanced topic covered better in books on C or C++. Table 3.6 summarizes the bitwise operators.

Table 3.6. Bitwise operators.

Operator	Meaning
&	Bitwise AND
|	Bitwise OR
^	Bitwise XOR
<<	Left shift
>>	Right shift
>>>	Zero fill right shift
~	Bitwise complement
<<=	Left shift assignment (x = x << y)
>>=	Right shift assignment (x = x >> y)
>>>=	Zero fill right shift assignment (x = x >>> y)
x &= y	AND assignment (x = x & y)
x |= y	OR assignment (x = x | y)
x ^= y	XOR assignment (x = x ^ y)

Operator Precedence

Operator precedence determines the order in which expressions are evaluated. This precedence, in some cases, can determine the overall value of the expression. For example, consider the following expression:

```
y = 6 + 4 / 2
```

Depending on whether the 6 + 4 expression or the 4 / 2 expression is evaluated first, the value of y can end up being 5 or 8. Because operator precedence determines the order in which expressions are evaluated, you can predict the outcome of an expression. In general, increment and decrement are evaluated before arithmetic, arithmetic expressions are evaluated before comparisons, and comparisons are evaluated before logical expressions. Assignment expressions are evaluated last.

Table 3.7 shows the specific precedence of the various operators in Java. Operators further up in the table are evaluated first; operators on the same line have the same precedence and are evaluated left to right based on how they appear in the expression itself. For example, given that same expression y = 6 + 4 / 2, you now know, according to this table, that division is evaluated before addition, so the value of y will be 8.

Table 3.7. Operator precedence.

Operator	Notes
. [] ()	Parentheses (()) are used to group expressions; dot (.) is used for access to methods and variables within objects and classes (discussed tomorrow); square brackets ([ ]) are used for arrays (this operator is discussed later in the week)
++ -- ! ~ instanceof	The instanceof operator returns true or false based on whether the object is an instance of the named class or any of that class's subclasses (discussed tomorrow)
new (type) expression	The new operator is used for creating new instances of classes; () in this case is for casting a value to another type (you'll learn about both of these tomorrow)
* / %	Multiplication, division, modulus
+ -	Addition, subtraction
<< >> >>>	Bitwise left and right shift
< > <= >=	Relational comparison tests
== !=	Equality
&	AND
^	XOR
|	OR
&&	Logical AND
||	Logical OR
? :	Shorthand for if...then...else (discussed on Day 5)
= += -= *= /= %= ^=	Various assignments
&= |= <<= >>= >>>=	More assignments

You can always change the order in which expressions are evaluated by using parentheses around the expressions that you want to evaluate first. You can nest parentheses to make sure expressions evaluate in the order you want them to (the innermost parenthetic expression is evaluated first). The following expression results in a value of 5, because the 6 + 4 expression is evaluated first, and then the result of that expression (10) is divided by 2:

```
y = (6 + 4) / 2
```

Parentheses also can be useful in cases in which the precedence of an expression isn't immediately clear—in other words, they can make your code easier to read. Adding parentheses doesn't hurt, so if they help you figure out how expressions are evaluated, go ahead and use them.

String Arithmetic

One special expression in Java is the use of the addition operator (+) to create and concatenate strings. In most of the examples shown today and in earlier lessons, you've seen lots of lines that looked something like this:

```
System.out.println(name + " is a " + color + " beetle");
```

The output of that line (to the standard output) is a single string, with the values of the variables (name and color) inserted in the appropriate spots in the string. So what's going on here?

The + operator, when used with strings and other objects, creates a single string that contains the concatenation of all its operands. If any one of the operands in string concatenation is not a string, it is automatically converted to a string, allowing you to easily create these sorts of output lines.

NOTE

> An object or type can be converted to a string if you implement the method toString(). All objects have a default string representation, but most classes override toString() to provide a more meaningful printable representation.

String concatenation makes lines such as the preceding one especially easy to construct. To create a string, just add all the parts together—the descriptions plus the variables—and print to the standard output, to the screen, to an applet, or anywhere.

The += operator, which you learned about earlier, also works for strings. For example, consider the following expression:

```
myName += " Jr.";
```

This expression is equivalent to

```
myName = myName + " Jr.";
```

just as it would be for numbers. In this case, it changes the value of myName, which might be something like John Smith, to have a Jr. at the end (John Smith Jr.).

Summary

As you've learned in the preceding two lessons, a Java program is made up primarily of classes and objects. Classes and objects, in turn, are made up of methods and variables, and methods are made up of statements and expressions. You've learned about these last two today: the basic building blocks that enable you to create classes and methods and build them up to a full-fledged Java program.

Today you learned about variables, how to declare them and assign values to them; literals for easily creating numbers, characters, and strings; and operators for arithmetic, tests, and other simple operations. With this basic syntax, you can move on tomorrow to learning about working with objects and building simple, useful Java programs.

To finish up this summary, Table 3.8 is a list of all the operators you learned about today so that you can refer back to them.

Table 3.8. Operator summary.

Operator	Meaning
+	Addition
-	Subtraction
*	Multiplication
/	Division
%	Modulus
<	Less than
>	Greater than
<=	Less than or equal to
>=	Greater than or equal to
==	Equal
!=	Not equal
&&	Logical AND
||	Logical OR

3

Operator	Meaning
!	Logical NOT
&	AND
|	OR
^	XOR
<<	Left shift
>>	Right shift
>>>	Zero fill right shift
~	Complement
=	Assignment
++	Increment
- -	Decrement
+=	Add and assign
-=	Subtract and assign
*=	Multiply and assign
/=	Divide and assign
%=	Modulus and assign
&=	AND and assign
|=	OR and assign
<<=	Left shift and assign
^=	XOR and assign
>>=	Right shift and assign
>>>=	Zero fill right shift and assign

Q&A

Q I didn't see any way to define constants.

A You can't create local constants in Java; you can create only constant instance and class variables. You'll learn how to do this tomorrow.

Q What happens if you assign an integer value to a variable that is too large for that variable to hold?

A Logically, you would think that the variable is just converted to the next larger type, but this isn't what happens. What does happen is called *overflow*. In this situation, if a number becomes too big for its variable, that number wraps around to the smallest possible negative number for that type and starts counting upward toward zero again.

Because overflow can result in some very confusing (and wrong) results, make sure that you declare the right integer type for all your numbers. If there's a chance a number will overflow its type, use the next larger type instead.

Q How can you find out the type of a given variable?

A If you're using any of the primitive types (`int`, `float`, `boolean`, and so on), you can't. If you care about the type, you can convert the value to some other type by using casting. (You'll learn about this subject tomorrow.)

If you're using class types, you can use the `instanceof` operator, which you'll learn more about tomorrow.

Q Why does Java have all these shorthand operators for arithmetic and assignment? It's really hard to read that way.

A The syntax of Java is based on C++, and therefore on C. One of C's implicit goals is the capability of doing very powerful tasks with a minimum of typing. Because of this, shorthand operators, such as the wide array of assignments, are common.

No rule says you have to use these operators in your own programs, however. If you find your code to be more readable using the long form, no one will come to your house and make you change it.

Q You covered simple math in the section about using operators. I'm assuming that Java has ways of doing more complex math operations?

A You assume correctly. A special class in the `java.lang` package, called `java.lang.Math`, has a number of methods for exponential, trigonometric, and other basic math operations. In fact, because you call these methods using the `Math` class itself, these are prime examples of class methods. You'll learn more about this subject tomorrow.

Day 4

Working with Objects

by Laura Lemay

Let's start today's lesson with an obvious statement: Because Java is an object-oriented language, you're going to be dealing with a lot of objects. You'll create them, modify them, move them around, change their variables, call their methods, combine them with other objects—and, of course, develop classes and use your own objects in the mix.

Today, therefore, you'll learn all about the Java object in its natural habitat. Today's topics include

☐ Creating instances of classes

☐ Testing and modifying class and instance variables in your new instance

☐ Calling methods in that object

☐ Casting (converting) objects and other data types from one class to another

☐ Other odds and ends about working with objects

☐ An overview of the Java class libraries

Creating New Objects

When you write a Java program, you define a set of classes. As you learned on Day 2, "Object-Oriented Programming and Java," classes are templates for objects; for the most part, you merely use the class to create instances and then work with those instances. In this section, therefore, you'll learn how to create a new object from any given class.

Remember strings from yesterday? You learned that using a string literal—a series of characters enclosed in double-quotes—creates a new instance of the class String with the value of that string.

The String class is unusual in that respect—although it's a class, there's an easy way to create instances of that class using a literal. The other classes don't have that shortcut; to create instances of those classes you have to do so explicitly by using the new operator.

Note   What about the literals for numbers and characters? Don't they create objects, too? Actually, they don't. The primitive data types for numbers and characters create numbers and characters, but for efficiency, they aren't actually objects. You can put object wrappers around them if you need to treat them like objects (you'll learn how to do this in "Casting and Converting Objects and Primitive Types").

Using new

To create a new object, you use the new operator with the name of the class you want to create an instance of, then parentheses after that. The following examples create new instances of the classes String, Random, and Motorcycle, and store those new instances in variables of the appropriate types:

```
String str = new String();

Random r = new Random();

Motorcycle m2 = new Motorcycle();
```

The parentheses are important; don't leave them off. The parentheses can be empty (as in these examples), in which case the most simple, basic object is created; or the parentheses can contain arguments that determine the initial values of instance variables or other initial qualities of that object:

```
Date dt = new Date(90, 4, 1, 4, 30);

Point pt = new Point(0,0);
```

The number and type of arguments you can use inside the parentheses with new are defined by the class itself using a special method called a constructor (you'll learn more about constructors later today). If you try and create a new instance of a class with the wrong number or type of arguments (or if you give it no arguments and it needs some), then you'll get an error when you try to compile your Java program.

Here's an example of creating several different types of objects using different numbers and types of arguments. The Date class, part of the java.util package, creates objects that represent the current date. Listing 4.1 is a Java program that shows three different ways of creating a Date object using new.

TYPE **Listing 4.1. Laura's Date program.**

```
 1: import java.util.Date;
 2:
 3: class CreateDates {
 4:
 5:     public static void main(String args[]) {
 6:         Date d1, d2, d3;
 7:
 8:         d1 = new Date();
 9:         System.out.println("Date 1: " + d1);
10:
11:         d2 = new Date(71, 7, 1, 7, 30);
12:         System.out.println("Date 2: " + d2);
13:
14:         d3 = new Date("April 3 1993 3:24 PM");
15:         System.out.println("Date 3: " + d3);
16:     }
17: }
```

OUTPUT
```
Date 1: Tue Feb 13 09:36:56 PST 1996
Date 2: Sun Aug 01 07:30:00 PDT 1971
Date 3: Sat Apr 03 15:24:00 PST 1993
```

ANALYSIS In this example, three different Date objects are created using different arguments to the class listed after new. The first instance (line 8) uses new Date() with no arguments, which creates a Date object for today's date (the first line of the output shows a sample; your output will, of course, read the current date and time for you).

The second Date object you create in this example has five integer arguments. The arguments represent a date: year, month, day, hours, and minutes. And, as the output shows, this creates a Date object for that particular date: Sunday, August 1, 1971, at 7:30 a.m.

NOTE

Java numbers months starting from 0. So although you might expect the seventh month to be July, month 7 in Java is indeed August.

The third version of Date takes one argument, a string, representing the date as a text string. When the Date object is created, that string is parsed, and a Date object with that date and time is created (see the third line of output). The date string can take many different formats; see the API documentation for the Date class (part of the java.util package) for information about what strings you can use.

What new Does

When you use the new operator, the new instance of the given class is created, and memory is allocated for it. In addition (and most importantly), a special method defined in the given class is called to initialize the object and set up any initial values it needs. This special method is called a constructor. Constructors are special methods, defined in classes, that create and initialize new instances of classes.

Constructors are special methods that initialize a new object, set its variables, create any other objects that object needs, and generally perform any other operations the object needs to initialize itself.

Multiple constructor definitions in a class can each have a different number or type of arguments—then, when you use new, you can specify different arguments in the argument list, and the right constructor for those arguments will be called. That's how each of those different versions of new that you used in the CreateDates class can create different Date objects.

When you create your own classes, you can define as many constructors as you need to implement that class's behavior. You'll learn how to create constructors on Day 7, "More About Methods."

A Note on Memory Management

Memory management in Java is dynamic and automatic. When you create a new object in Java, Java automatically allocates the right amount of memory for that object in the heap. You don't have to allocate any memory for any objects explicitly; Java does it for you.

What happens when you're finished with that object? How do you de-allocate the memory that object uses? The answer, again, is that memory management is automatic. Once you're done with an object, you reassign all the variables that might hold that object and remove it from any arrays, thereby making the object unusable. Java has a garbage collector that looks for unused objects and reclaims the memory that those objects are using. You don't have to do any explicit freeing of memory; you just have to make sure you're not still holding onto an object you want to get rid of. You'll learn more specific details about the Java garbage collector and how it works on Day 21, "Under the Hood."

 A *garbage collector* is a special tool built into the Java environment that looks for unused objects. If it finds any, it automatically removes those objects and frees the memory those objects were using.

Accessing and Setting Class and Instance Variables

Now you have your very own object, and that object may have class or instance variables defined in it. How do you work with those variables? Easy! Class and instance variables behave in exactly the same ways as the local variables you learned about yesterday; you just refer to them slightly differently than you do regular variables in your code.

Getting Values

To get to the value of an instance variable, you use an expression in what's called dot notation. With dot notation, the reference to an instance or class variable has two parts: the object on the left side of the dot and the variable on the right side of the dot.

 Dot notation is an expression used to get at instance variables and methods inside a given object.

For example, if you have an object assigned to the variable myObject, and that object has a variable called var, you refer to that variable's value like this:

```
myObject.var;
```

This form for accessing variables is an expression (it returns a value), and both sides of the dot can also be expressions. This means that you can nest instance variable access. If that var instance variable itself holds an object and that object has its own instance variable called state, you could refer to it like this:

```
myObject.var.state;
```

Dot expressions are evaluated left to right, so you start with myObject's variable var, which points to another object with the variable state. You end up with the value of that state variable after the entire expression is done evaluating.

Changing Values

Assigning a value to that variable is equally easy—just tack an assignment operator on the right side of the expression:

```
myObject.var.state = true;
```

Listing 4.2 is an example of a program that tests and modifies the instance variables in a Point object. Point is part of the java.awt package and refers to a coordinate point with an x and a y value.

TYPE | **Listing 4.2. The TestPoint Class.**

```
 1: import java.awt.Point;
 2:
 3: class TestPoint {
 4: public static void main(String args[]) {
 5:     Point thePoint = new Point(10,10);
 6:
 7:     System.out.println("X is " + thePoint.x);
 8:     System.out.println("Y is " + thePoint.y);
 9:
10:     System.out.println("Setting X to 5.");
11:     thePoint.x = 5;
12:     System.out.println("Setting Y to 15.");
13:     thePoint.y = 15;
14:
15:     System.out.println("X is " + thePoint.x);
16:     System.out.println("Y is " + thePoint.y);
17:
18:   }
19:}
```

OUTPUT
```
X is 10
Y is 10
Setting X to 5.
Setting Y to 15.
X is 5
Y is 15
```

ANALYSIS In this example, you first create an instance of Point where X and Y are both 10 (line 5). Lines 7 and 8 print out those individual values, and you can see dot notation at work there. Lines 10 through 13 change the values of those variables to 5 and 15, respectively. Finally, lines 15 and 16 print out the values of X and Y again to show how they've changed.

Class Variables

Class variables, as you've already learned, are variables that are defined and stored in the class itself. Their values, therefore, apply to the class and to all its instances.

With instance variables, each new instance of the class gets a new copy of the instance variables that class defines. Each instance can then change the values of those instance variables without affecting any other instances. With class variables, there is only one copy of that variable. Every instance of the class has access to that variable, but there is only one value. Changing the value of that variable changes it for all the instances of that class.

You define class variables by including the static keyword before the variable itself. You'll learn more about this on Day 6, "Creating Classes and Applications in Java." For example, take the following partial class definition:

```
class FamilyMember {
    static String surname = "Johnson";
    String name;
    int age;
    ...
}
```

Instances of the class FamilyMember each have their own values for name and age. But the class variable surname has only one value for all family members. Change surname, and all the instances of FamilyMember are affected.

To access class variables, you use the same dot notation as you do with instance variables. To get or change the value of the class variable, you can use either the instance or the name of the class on the left side of the dot. Both of the lines of output in this example print the same value:

```
FamilyMember dad = new FamilyMember();
System.out.println("Family's surname is: " + dad.surname);
System.out.println("Family's surname is: " + FamilyMember.surname);
```

Because you can use an instance to change the value of a class variable, it's easy to become confused about class variables and where their values are coming from (remember that the value of a class variable affects all the instances). For this reason, it's a good idea to use the name of the class when you refer to a class variable—it makes your code easier to read and strange results easier to debug.

Calling Methods

Calling a method is similar to referring to an object's instance variables: Method calls to objects also use dot notation. The object itself whose method you're calling is on the left side of the dot; the name of the method and its arguments are on the right side of the dot:

```
myObject.methodOne(arg1, arg2, arg3);
```

Note that all calls to methods must have parentheses after them, even if that method takes no arguments:

```
myObject.methodNoArgs();
```

If the method you've called returns an object that itself has methods, you can nest methods as you would variables. This next example calls the getName() method, which is defined in the object returned by the getClass() method, which was defined in myObject. Got it?

```
myObject.getClass().getName();
```

You can combine nested method calls and instance variable references as well (in this case you're calling the methodTwo() method, which is defined in the object stored by the var instance variable, which in turn is part of the myObject object):

```
myObject.var.methodTwo(arg1, arg2);
```

System.out.println(), the method you've been using through the book this far to print out bits of text, is a great example of nesting variables and methods. The System class (part of the java.lang package) describes system-specific behavior. System.out is a class variable that contains an instance of the class PrintStream that points to the standard output of the system. PrintStream instances have a println() method that prints a string to that output stream.

Listing 4.3 shows an example of calling some methods defined in the String class. Strings include methods for string tests and modification, similar to what you would expect in a string library in other languages.

TYPE **Listing 4.3. Several uses of String methods.**

```
 1: class TestString {
 2:
 3:     public static void main(String args[]) {
 4:         String str = "Now is the winter of our discontent";
 5:
 6:         System.out.println("The string is: " + str);
 7:         System.out.println("Length of this string: "
 8:                 + str.length());
 9:         System.out.println("The character at position 5: "
10:                 + str.charAt(5));
11:         System.out.println("The substring from 11 to 17: "
12:                 + str.substring(11, 17));
13:         System.out.println("The index of the character d: "
14:                 + str.indexOf('d'));
15:         System.out.print("The index of the beginning of the ");
16:         System.out.println("substring \"winter\": "
17:                 + str.indexOf("winter"));
18:         System.out.println("The string in upper case: "
19:                 + str.toUpperCase());
20:     }
21: }
```

```
The string is: Now is the winter of our discontent
Length of this string: 35
The character at position 5: s
The substring from positions 11 to 17: winter
The index of the character d: 25
The index of the beginning of the substring "winter": 11
The string in upper case: NOW IS THE WINTER OF OUR DISCONTENT
```

ANALYSIS In line 4, you create a new instance of `String` by using a string literal (this way is easier than using `new` and then putting the characters in individually). The remainder of the program simply calls different string methods to do different operations on that string:

☐ Line 6 prints the value of the string we created in line 4: `"Now is the winter of our discontent"`.

☐ Line 7 calls the `length()` method in the new `String` object. This string has 35 characters.

☐ Line 9 calls the `charAt()` method, which returns the character at the given position in the string. Note that string positions start at `0`, so the character at position `5` is `s`.

☐ Line 11 calls the `substring()` method, which takes two integers indicating a range and returns the substring at those starting and ending points. The `substring()` method can also be called with only one argument, which returns the substring from that position to the end of the string.

☐ Line 13 calls the `indexOf()` method, which returns the position of the first instance of the given character (here, `'d'`).

☐ Line 15 shows a different use of the `indexOf()` method, which takes a string argument and returns the index of the beginning of that string.

☐ Finally, line 19 uses the `toUpperCase()` method to return a copy of the string in all uppercase.

Class Methods

Class methods, like class variables, apply to the class as a whole and not to its instances. Class methods are commonly used for general utility methods that may not operate directly on an instance of that class, but fit with that class conceptually. For example, the `String` class contains a class method called `valueOf()`, which can take one of many different types of arguments (integers, booleans, other objects, and so on). The `valueOf()` method then returns a new instance of `String` containing the string value of the argument it was given. This method doesn't operate directly on an existing instance of `String`, but getting a string from another object or data type is definitely a `String`-like operation, and it makes sense to define it in the `String` class.

Class methods can also be useful for gathering general methods together in one place (the class). For example, the Math class, defined in the java.lang package, contains a large set of mathematical operations as class methods—there are no instances of the class Math, but you can still use its methods with numeric or boolean arguments. For example, the class method Math.max() takes two arguments and returns the larger of the two. You don't need to create a new instance of Math; just call the method anywhere you need it, like this:

```
in biggerOne = Math.max(x, y);
```

To call a class method, you use dot notation as you do with instance methods. As with class variables, you can use either an instance of the class or the class itself on the left side of the dot. However, for the same reasons noted in the discussion on class variables, using the name of the class for class methods makes your code easier to read. The last two lines in this example produce the same result (the string "5"):

```
String s, s2;
s = "foo";
s2 = s.valueOf(5);
s2 = String.valueOf(5);
```

References to Objects

As you work with objects, one important thing going on behind the scenes is the use of references to those objects. When you assign objects to variables, or pass objects as arguments to methods, you are passing references to those objects, not the objects themselves or copies of those objects.

An example should make this clearer. Examine Listing 4.4, which shows a simple example of how references work.

TYPE   **Listing 4.4. A references example.**

```
 1: import java.awt.Point;
 2:
 3: class ReferencesTest {
 4:     public static void main (String args[]) {
 5:         Point pt1, pt2;
 6:         pt1 = new Point(100, 100);
 7:         pt2 = pt1;
 8:
 9:         pt1.x = 200;
10:         pt1.y = 200;
11:         System.out.println("Point1: " + pt1.x + ", " + pt1.y);
12:         System.out.println("Point2: " + pt2.x + ", " + pt2.y);
13:     }
14: }
```

OUTPUT   Point1: 200, 200
              Point2: 200, 200

ANALYSIS In the first part of this program, you declare two variables of type Point (line 5),
create a new Point object to pt1 (line 6), and finally, assign the value of pt1 to pt2
(line 7).

Now, here's the challenge. After changing pt1's x and y instance variables in lines 9 and 10,
what will pt2 look like?

As you can see, pt2's x and y instance variables were also changed, even though you never
explicitly changed them. When you assign the value of pt1 to pt2, you actually create a
reference from pt2 to the same object to which pt1 refers (see Figure 4.1). Change the object
that pt2 refers to, and you also change the object that pt1 points to, because both are references
to the same object.

NOTE   If you actually do want pt1 and pt2 to point to separate objects, you
              should use new Point() for both lines to create separate objects.

Figure 4.1.

References to objects.

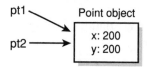

The fact that Java uses references becomes particularly important when you pass arguments
to methods. You'll learn more about this later today, but keep these references in mind.

**TECHNICAL
NOTE**   There are no explicit pointers or pointer arithmetic in Java as there are
              in C-like languages—just references. However, with these references,
              and with Java arrays, you have most of the capabilities that you have
              with pointers without the confusion and lurking bugs that explicit
              pointers can create.

Casting and Converting Objects and Primitive Types

Sometimes in your Java programs you may have a value stored somewhere that is the wrong type for what you want to do with it. Maybe it's an instance of the wrong class, or perhaps it's a `float` and you want it to be an `int`. To convert the value of one type to another, you use casting. Casting is a programming term that means, effectively, converting a value or an object from one type to another. The result of a cast is a new value or object; casting does not change the original object or value.

NEW TERM   *Casting* converts the value of an object or primitive type into another type.

Although the concept of casting is a simple one, the rules for what types in Java can be converted to what other types are complicated by the fact that Java has both primitive types (`int`, `float`, `boolean`), and object types (`String`, `Point`, `Window`, and so on). There are three forms of casts and conversions to talk about in this section:

☐ Casting between primitive types: `int` to `float` or `float` to `double`

☐ Casting between object types: an instance of a class to an instance of another class

☐ Converting primitive types to objects and then extracting primitive values back out of those objects

Casting Primitive Types

Casting between primitive types allows you to "convert" the value of one type to another primitive type—for example, to assign a number of one type to a variable of another type. Casting between primitive types most commonly occurs with the numeric types; boolean values cannot be cast to any other primitive type.

Often, if the type you are casting to is "larger" than the type of the value you're converting, you may not have to use an explicit cast. You can often automatically treat a byte or a character as an `int`, for example, or an `int` as a `long`, an `int` as a `float`, or anything as a `double` automatically. In most cases, because the larger type provides more precision than the smaller, no loss of information occurs when the value is cast. The exception is casting integers to floating-point values; casting an `int` or a `long` to a `float` or a `long` to a `double` may cause some loss of precision.

To convert a large value to smaller type, you must use an explicit cast, because converting that value may result in a loss of precision. Explicit casts look like this:

```
(typename)value
```

In this form, *typename* is the name of the type you're converting to (for example: `short`, `int`, `float`, `boolean`), and *value* is an expression that results in the value you want to convert. So, for example, in this expression the value of x is divided by the value of y and the result is cast to an `int`:

```
(int) (x / y);
```

Note that because the precedence of casting is higher than that of arithmetic, you have to use parentheses here; otherwise, the value of x would be cast first and then divided by y (which might very well be a very different result).

Casting Objects

Instances of classes can also be cast to instances of other classes, with one restriction: The class of the object you're casting and the class you're casting it to must be related by inheritance; that is, you can cast an object only to an instance of its class's sub- or superclass—not to any random class.

Analogous to converting a primitive value to a larger type, some objects may not need to be cast explicitly. In particular, because subclasses contain all the same information as their superclass, you can use an instance of a subclass anywhere a superclass is expected. For example, suppose you have a method that takes two arguments: one of type `Object`, and one of type `Number`. You don't have to pass instances of those particular classes to that method. For the `Object` argument, you can pass any subclass of `Object` (any object, in other words), and for the `Number` argument you can pass in any instance of any subclass of `Number` (`Integer`, `Boolean`, `Float`, and so on); you don't have to explicitly convert them first. Additionally, if you have a variable defined as class Object or Number, you could assign objects of those classes or any of their superclasses to that variable as is.

What about the reverse case? Can you use an object of a superclass where a subclass is expected? The answer is yes, as long as the two classes are related by inheritance. There is a catch, however: Remember that subclasses contain more information (methods and variables) than their superclasses. So although you can use superclass objects in place of subclass objects, those superclass objects may not have all the information they need to be used in that context. If you have an operation that calls methods in objects of class Integer, using an object of class Number won't define those Integer methods. You'll get errors if you try to call methods that that object doesn't have.

To use superclass objects where subclass objects are expected, you need an explicit cast. You won't lose any information in the cast, but you will gain all the methods and variables the subclass defines. To cast an object to another class, you use the same operation that you used for base types:

```
(classname)object
```

In this case, `classname` is the name of the class you want to cast the object to, and `object` is a reference to the object you're casting. Note that casting creates a reference to the old object of the type `classname`; the old object still continues to exist as it did before.

Here's a (fictitious) example of a cast of an instance of the class GreenApple to an instance of the class Apple (where GreenApple is theoretically a subclass of Apple with more information to define the apple as green):

```
Apple a = new Apple();
GreenApple aGreen = new GreenApple();
a = aGreen;  // no cast needed for upward use
aGreen = (GreenApple)a; // must cast Apple to GreenApple explicitly
```

In addition to casting objects to classes, you can also cast objects to interfaces—but only if that object's class or one of its superclasses actually implements that interface. Casting an object to an interface means that you can call one of that interface's methods even if that object's class does not actually implement that interface. You'll learn more about interfaces in Week 3.

Converting Primitive Types to Objects and Vice Versa

Now you know how to cast a primitive type to another primitive type and how to cast between classes. How can you cast one to the other?

You can't! Primitive types and objects are very different things in Java and you can't automatically cast or convert between the two. However, the java.lang package includes several special classes that correspond to each primitive data type: Integer for ints, Float for floats, Boolean for booleans, and so on. Note that the class names have an initial capital letter, and the primitive types are lowercase. Java treats these names very differently, so don't confuse them, or your methods and variables won't behave the way you expect.

Using class methods defined in these classes, you can create an object-equivalent for all the primitive types using new. The following line of code creates an instance of the Integer class with the value 35:

```
Integer intObject = new Integer(35);
```

Once you have actual objects, you can treat those values as objects. Then, when you want the primitive values back again, there are methods for that as well—for example, the intValue() method extracts an int primitive value from an Integer object:

```
int theInt = intObject.intValue();  // returns 35
```

See the Java API documentation for these special classes for specifics on the methods for converting primitives to and from objects.

NOTE

In Java 1.0 there are special type classes for Boolean, Character, Double, Float, Integer, and Long. Java 1.1 adds classes for Byte and Short, as well as a special wrapper class for Void. The latter classes are used primarily for object reflection.

Odds and Ends

This section is a catchall for other information about working with objects, particularly the following:

☐ Comparing objects

☐ Finding out the class of any given object

☐ Testing to see whether an object is an instance of a given class

Comparing Objects

Yesterday you learned about operators for comparing values: equals, not equals, less than, and so on. Most of these operators work only on primitive types, not on objects. If you try to use other values as operands, the Java compiler produces errors.

The exception to this rule is with the operators for equality: == (equal) and != (not equal). These operators, when used with objects, test whether the two operands refer to exactly the same object in memory.

What should you do if you want to be able to compare instances of your class and have meaningful results? You have to implement special methods in your class, and you have to call those methods using those method names.

TECHNICAL NOTE

Java does not have the concept of operator overloading—that is, the ability to redefine the behavior of the built-in operators using methods in your own classes. The built-in operators remain defined only for numbers.

A good example of this is the String class. It is possible to have two strings, two independent objects in memory with the same values—that is, the same characters in the same order. According to the == operator, however, those two String objects will not be equal, because, although their contents are the same, they are not the same object.

The String class, therefore, defines a method called equals() that tests each character in the string and returns true if the two strings have the same values. Listing 4.5 illustrates this.

TYPE **Listing 4.5. A test of string equality.**

```
 1: class EqualsTest {
 2: public static void main(String args[]) {
 3:         String str1, str2;
 4:         str1 = "she sells sea shells by the sea shore.";
 5:         str2 = str1;
 6:
 7:      System.out.println("String1: " + str1);
 8:       System.out.println("String2: " + str2);
 9:       System.out.println("Same object? " + (str1 == str2));
10:
11:      str2 = new String(str1);
12:
13:      System.out.println("String1: " + str1);
14:       System.out.println("String2: " + str2);
15:       System.out.println("Same object? " + (str1 == str2));
16:       System.out.println("Same value? " + str1.equals(str2));
17:    }
18:  }
```

OUTPUT
```
String1: she sells sea shells by the sea shore.
String2: she sells sea shells by the sea shore.
Same object? true
String1: she sells sea shells by the sea shore.
String2: she sells sea shells by the sea shore.
Same object? false
Same value? true
```

ANALYSIS The first part of this program (lines 3 through 5) declares two variables (str1 and str2), assigns the literal she sells sea shells by the sea shore. to str1, and then assigns that value to str2. As you learned earlier when we talked about object references, now str1 and str2 point to the same object, and the equality test at line 9 proves that.

In the second part, you create a new string object with the same value as str1 and assign str2 to that new string object. Now you have two different string objects in str1 and str2, both with the same value. Testing them to see whether they're the same object by using the == operator (line 15) returns the expected answer (false—they are not the same object in memory), as does testing them using the equals() method (line 16) (true—they have the same values).

TECHNICAL NOTE Why can't you just use another literal when you change str2, rather than using new? String literals are optimized in Java—if you create a string using a literal, and then use another literal with the same characters, Java knows enough to give you the first String object back. Both strings are the same objects—to create two separate objects you have to go out of your way.

Determining the Class of an Object

Want to find out the class of an object? Here's the way to do it for an object assigned to the variable `obj`:

```
String name = obj.getClass().getName();
```

What does this do? The `getClass()` method is defined in the `Object` class, and as such is available for all objects. The result of that method is a `Class` object (where `Class` is itself a class), which has a method called `getName()`. `getName()` returns a string representing the name of the class.

Another test that might be useful to you is the `instanceof` operator. `instanceof` has two operands: an object on the left and the name of a class on the right. The expression returns `true` or `false` based on whether the object is an instance of the named class or any of that class's subclasses:

```
"foo" instanceof String // true
Point pt = new Point(10, 10);
pt instanceof String // false
```

The `instanceof` operator can also be used for interfaces; if an object implements an interface, the `instanceof` operator with that interface name on the right side returns `true`. You'll learn all about interfaces in Week 3.

Inspecting Classes and Methods with Reflection

One of the improvements made to the Java language with the 1.1 release is the introduction of reflection, which also is called introspection. Under any name, reflection enables one Java class—such as a program you write—to learn details about any other class.

Through reflection, a Java program can load a class it knows nothing about, find out the variables, methods, and constructors of that class, and work with them.

This might make more sense if you see an example of it right off the bat. Listing 4.6 is a short Java application named `SeeMethods`.

TYPE **Listing 4.6. The full text of `SeeMethods.java`.**

```
1: import java.lang.reflect.*;
2: import java.util.Random;
3:
4: class SeeMethods {
```

continues

Listing 4.6. continued

```
 5:     public static void main(String[] argumentss)  {
 6:         Random rd = new Random();
 7:         Class className = rd.getClass();
 8:         Method[] methods = className.getMethods();
 9:         for (int i = 0; i < methods.length; i++) {
10:             System.out.println("Method: " + methods[i]);
11:         }
12:     }
13: }
```

This program uses the java.lang.reflect.* group of classes, which provide information about the attributes, methods, and constructor methods of any class.

The SeeMethods application creates a Random object in line 6, and then uses reflection to display all of the public methods that are a part of the class. Listing 4.7 shows the output of the application.

Listing 4.7. The output of the SeeMethods application.

```
 1: Method: public final native java.lang.Class java.lang.Object.getClass()
 2: Method: public native int java.lang.Object.hashCode()
 3: Method: public boolean java.lang.Object.equals(java.lang.Object)
 4: Method: public java.lang.String java.lang.Object.toString()
 5: Method: public final native void java.lang.Object.notify()
 6: Method: public final native void java.lang.Object.notifyAll()
 7: Method: public final native void java.lang.Object.wait(long)
 8: Method: public final void java.lang.Object.wait(long,int)
 9: Method: public final void java.lang.Object.wait()
10: Method: public synchronized void java.util.Random.setSeed(long)
11: Method: public void java.util.Random.nextBytes(byte[])
12: Method: public int java.util.Random.nextInt()
13: Method: public long java.util.Random.nextLong()
14: Method: public float java.util.Random.nextFloat()
15: Method: public double java.util.Random.nextDouble()
16: Method: public synchronized double java.util.Random.nextGaussian()
```

By using reflection, the SeeMethods application can learn every method of the Random class and all methods that it inherited from superclasses of Random. Each line of the listing shows the following information about a method:

☐ Whether or not it's public

☐ What type of object or variable the method returns

☐ Whether the method is from the current class or one of its superclasses

☐ The name of the method

☐ The type of objects and variables used as arguments when calling the method

The SeeMethods application could be done with any class of objects—change line 6 of SeeMethods.java to create a different object and take a look at its innards.

Reflection is most commonly used by tools such as class browsers and debuggers as a way to learn more about the class of objects being browsed or debugged. It also is needed with JavaBeans, where the ability for one object to query another object about what it can do (and then ask it to do something) is useful to building larger applications. You'll learn more about JavaBeans during Day 14, "Neworking, Advanced APIs, and Miscellaneous Tidbits."

The java.lang.reflect package includes the following classes:

☐ Field, for managing and finding out information about class and instance variables

☐ Method, for managing class and instance methods

☐ Constructor, for managing the special methods for creating new instances of classes

☐ Array, for managing arrays

☐ Modifier, for decoding modifier information about classes, variables and methods (which is described on Day 15, "Modifiers").

In addition, there will be a number of new methods available in a class of objects called Class that helps tie together the various reflection classes.

Reflection is an advanced feature that you might not be readily using in your programs. It becomes most useful when you're working on object serialization, JavaBeans, and other more sophisticated Java programming.

The Java Class Library

To finish up today, let's look at the Java class library. Actually, you've had some experience with some of the Java classes already, so they shouldn't seem that strange.

The Java class library provides the set of classes that are guaranteed to be available in any commercial Java environment (for example, in any Java development environment or in browsers such as Netscape). Those classes are in the java package and include all the classes you've seen so far in this book, plus a whole lot more classes you'll learn about later on in this book (and more you may not learn about at all).

The Java Development Kit comes with documentation for all of the Java class library, which includes descriptions of each class's instance variables, methods, constructors, interfaces, and so on. You can get to this documentation (called the Java Application Programmer's

Interface, or API) via the Web at http://java.sun.com:80/products/JDK/CurrentRelease/api/packages.html. A shorter summary of the Java API is in Appendix C as well. Exploring the Java class library and its methods and instance variables is a great way to figure out what Java can and cannot do, as well as how it can become a starting point for your own development.

Here are the class packages that are part of the Java class library:

☐ java.lang—Classes that apply to the language itself, including the Object class, the String class, and the System class. It also contains the special classes for the primitive types (Integer, Character, Float, and so on). You'll get at least a glance at most of the classes in this package in this first week.

☐ java.util—Utility classes, such as Date, as well as simple collection classes, such as Vector and Hashtable.

☐ java.io—Input and output classes for writing to and reading from streams (such as standard input and output) and for handling files. Day 19, "Java Streams and I/O," describes the classes in this package.

☐ java.net—Classes for networking support, including Socket and URL (a class to represent references to documents on the World Wide Web). You'll learn a little about networking on Day 14.

☐ java.awt—This is the Abstract Windowing Toolkit. It contains classes to implement graphical user interface features, including classes for Window, Menu, Button, Font, CheckBox, and so on. It also includes mechanisms for managing system events and for processing images (in the java.awt.Image package). You'll learn all about the AWT in Week 2.

☐ java.applet—Classes to implement Java applets.

In addition to the Java classes, your development environment may also include additional classes that provide other utilities or functionality. Although these classes may be useful, because they are not part of the standard Java library, they may not be available to other people trying to run your Java program unless you explicitly include those classes with your program. This is particularly important for applets, because applets are expected to be able to run on any platform, using any Java-enabled browser. Only classes inside the java package are guaranteed to be available on all browsers and Java environments.

Summary

Objects, objects everywhere. Today, you've learned all about how to deal with objects: how to create them, how to find out and change the values of their variables, and how to call their methods. You have also learned how to copy and compare them and how to convert them into other objects. Finally, you have learned a bit about the Java class libraries—which give you a whole slew of classes to play with in your own programs.

You now have the fundamentals of how to deal with most simple things in the Java language. All you have left are arrays, conditionals, and loops, which you'll learn about tomorrow. Then you'll learn how to define and use classes in Java applications on Day 6, and launch directly into applets next week. With just about everything you do in your Java programs, you'll always come back to objects.

Q&A

Q **I'm confused about the differences between objects and the primitive data types, such as `int` and `boolean`.**

A The primitive types in the language (`byte`, `short`, `int`, `long`, `float`, `double`, `boolean`, and `char`) represent the smallest things in the language. They are not objects, although in many ways they can be handled like objects—they can be assigned to variables and passed in and out of methods. Most of the operations that work exclusively on objects, however, will not work with primitive types.

Objects are instances of classes and, as such, are usually much more complex data types than simple numbers and characters, often containing numbers and characters as instance or class variables.

Q **No pointers in Java? If you don't have pointers, how are you supposed to do something like linked lists, where you have a pointer from one nose to another so you can traverse them?**

A Java doesn't have no pointers at all; it has no *explicit* pointers. Object references are, effectively, pointers. So to create something like a linked list, you would create a class called `Node`, which would have an instance variable also of type `Node`. Then to link together node objects all you need to do is assign a node object to the instance variable of the object just before it in the list. Because object references are pointers, linked lists set up this way will behave as you would expect them to.

Q **In the section on calling methods, you had examples of calling a method with a different number of arguments each time—and it gave a different kind of result. How is that possible?**

A That's called *method overloading*. Overloading means that the same method can have different behavior based on the arguments it's called with—and the number and type of arguments can vary. When you define methods in your own classes, you define separate method signatures with different sets of arguments and different definitions. When a method is called, Java figures out which definition to execute based on the number and type of arguments with which you called it.

You'll learn all about this on Day 6.

Q **No operator overloading in Java? Why not? I thought Java was based on C++, and C++ has operator overloading.**

A Java was indeed based on C++, but it was also designed to be simple, so many of C++'s features have been removed. The argument against operator overloading is that because the operator can be defined to mean anything; it makes it very difficult to figure out what any given operator is doing at any one time. This can result in entirely unreadable code. When you use a method, you know it can mean many things to many classes, but when you use an operator you would like to know that it always means the same thing. Given the potential for abuse, the designers of Java felt it was one of the C++ features that was best left out.

4

Day 5

Arrays, Conditionals, and Loops

by Laura Lemay

Although you could write Java programs using what you've learned so far, those programs would be pretty dull. Much of the good stuff in Java or in any programming language results when you have arrays to store values in and control-flow constructs (loops and conditionals) to execute different bits of a program based on tests. Today, you'll find out about the following:

- ☐ Arrays, one of the most useful objects in Java, which enable you to collect objects or primitive types into an easy-to-manage list

- ☐ Block statements, for grouping together related statements

- ☐ `if` and `switch`, for conditional tests

- ☐ `for` and `while` loops, for iteration or repeating a statement or statements multiple times

Arrays

Arrays in Java, as in other languages, are a way to store collections of items into a single unit. The array has some number of *slots*, each of which holds an individual item. You can add and delete items to those slots as needed. Unlike in other languages, however, arrays in Java are actual objects that can be passed around and treated just like other objects.

 An *array* is a collection of items. Each slot in the array can hold an object or a primitive value. Arrays in Java are objects that can be treated just like other objects in the language.

Arrays can contain any type of element value (primitive types or objects), but you can't store different types in a single array. You can have an array of integers or an array of strings or an array of arrays, but you can't have an array that contains, for example, both strings and integers.

To create an array in Java, you use three steps:

1. Declare a variable to hold the array.
2. Create a new array object and assign it to the array variable.
3. Store things in that array.

Declaring Array Variables

The first step in creating an array is creating a variable that will hold the array, just as you would any other variable. Array variables indicate the type of object the array will hold (just as they do for any variable) and the name of the array, followed by empty brackets ([ ]). The following are all typical array variable declarations:

```
String difficultWords[];

Point hits[];

int temps[];
```

An alternate method of defining an array variable is to put the brackets after the type instead of after the variable. They are equivalent, but this latter form is often much more readable. So, for example, these three declarations could be written like this:

```
String[] difficultWords;

Point[] hits;

int[] temps;
```

Creating Array Objects

The second step is to create an array object and assign it to that variable. There are two ways to do this:

- ☐ Using new
- ☐ Directly initializing the contents of that array

The first way is to use the new operator to create a new instance of an array:

```
String[] names = new String[10];
```

That line creates a new array of Strings with 10 slots (sometimes called elements). When you create a new array object using new, you must indicate how many slots that array will hold. This line does not put actual String objects in the slots—you'll have to do that later.

Array objects can contain primitive types such as integers or booleans, just as they can contain objects:

```
int[] temps = new int[99];
```

When you create an array object using new, all its slots are initialized for you (0 for numeric arrays, false for boolean, '\0' for character arrays, and null for objects). You can then assign actual values or objects to the slots in that array. You can also create an array and initialize its contents at the same time. Instead of using new to create the new array object, enclose the elements of the array inside braces, separated by commas:

```
String[] chiles = { "jalapeno", "anaheim", "serrano",
    "habanero", "thai" };
```

TECHNICAL NOTE

> Note that the Java keyword null refers to a null object (and can be used for any object reference). It is not equivalent to zero or the '\0' character as the NULL constant is in C.

Each of the elements inside the braces must be of the same type and must be the same type as the variable that holds that array (the Java compiler will complain if they're not). An array the size of the number of elements you've included will be automatically created for you. This example creates an array of String objects named chiles that contains five elements.

Accessing Array Elements

Once you have an array with initial values, you can test and change the values in each slot of that array. To get at a value stored within an array, use the array subscript expression ([ ]):

```
myArray[subscript];
```

The myArray part of this expression is a variable holding an array object, although it can also be an expression that results in an array. The subscript part of the expression, inside the brackets, specifies the number of the slot within the array to access. Array subscripts start with 0, as they do in C and C++. So, an array with 10 elements has 10 array slots accessed using subscript 0 to 9.

Note that all array subscripts are checked when your Java program is run to make sure that they are inside the boundaries of the array (greater than or equal to 0 but less than the array's length). Unlike in C, it is impossible in Java to access or assign a value to an array slot outside the boundaries of the array (thereby avoiding a lot of the common problems and bugs that result from overrunning the bounds of an array in C-like languages). Note the following two statements, for example:

```
String[] arr = new String[10];
arr[10] = "eggplant";
```

A program with that last statement in it produces an error at that line when you try to run it. (Actually, to be more technically correct, it throws an exception. You'll learn more about exceptions on Day 18, "Multithreading.") The array stored in arr has only 10 slots numbered from 0; the element at subscript 10 doesn't exist.

If the array subscript is calculated at runtime (for example, as part of a loop) and ends up outside the boundaries of the array, the Java interpreter also produces an error.

How can you keep from accidentally overrunning the end of an array in your own programs? You can test for the length of the array in your programs using the length instance variable—it's available for all array objects, regardless of type:

```
int len = arr.length // returns 10
```

However, just to reiterate: The length of the array is 10, but its subscript can only go up to 9. Arrays start numbering from 0. Whenever you work with arrays, keep this in mind and subtract 1 from the length of the array to get its largest element.

Changing Array Elements

To assign an element value to a particular array slot, merely put an assignment statement after the array access expression:

```
myarray[1] = 15;
sentence[0] = "The";
sentence[10] = sentence[0];
```

An important thing to note is that an array of objects in Java is an array of references to those objects (similar in some ways to an array of pointers in C or C++). When you assign a value to a slot in an array, you're creating a reference to that object, just as you do for a plain variable. When you move values around inside arrays (as in that last line), you just reassign the reference; you don't copy the value from one slot to another. Arrays of primitive types such as ints or floats do copy the values from one slot to another.

Arrays of references to objects, as opposed to the objects themselves, are particularly useful because you can have multiple references to the same objects both inside and outside arrays. For example, you can assign an object contained in an array to a variable and refer to that same object by using either the variable or the array position.

Got it? Arrays are pretty simple to create and modify, but they provide an enormous amount of functionality for Java. You'll find yourself running into arrays a lot the more you use Java.

To finish up the discussion on arrays, here's a simple program that shows how to create, initialize, modify, and examine parts of an array. Listing 5.1 has the code.

TYPE **Listing 5.1. Various simple array operations.**

```
 1: class ArrayTest {
 2:
 3:     String[] firstNames = { "Dennis", "Grace", "Bjarne", "James" };
 4:     String[] lastNames = new String[firstNames.length];
 5:
 6:     void printNames() {
 7:       int i = 0;
 8:       System.out.println(firstNames[i]
 9:           + " " + lastNames[i]);
10:       i++;
11:       System.out.println(firstNames[i]
12:          + " " + lastNames[i]);
13:       i++;
14:       System.out.println(firstNames[i]
15:           + " " + lastNames[i]);
16:       i++;
```

continues

Listing 5.1. continued

```
17:       System.out.println(firstNames[i]
18:           + " " + lastNames[i]);
19:     }
20:
21:     public static void main (String args[]) {
22:       ArrayTest a = new ArrayTest();
23:         a.printNames();
24:         System.out.println("----------");
25:         a.lastNames[0] = "Ritchie";
26:         a.lastNames[1] = "Hopper";
27:       a.lastNames[2] = "Stroustrup";
28:         a.lastNames[3] = "Gosling";
29:         a.printNames();
30:     }
31:}
```

OUTPUT

```
Dennis null
Grace null
Bjarne null
James null
----------
Dennis Ritchie
Grace Hopper
Bjarne Stroustrup
James Gosling
```

ANALYSIS This somewhat verbose example shows you how to create and use arrays. The class we've created here, ArrayTest, has two instance variables that hold arrays of String objects. The first, called firstNames, is declared and initialized in the same line (line 3) to contain four strings. The second instance variable, lastNames, is declared and created in line 4, but no initial values are placed in the slots. Note also that we created the lastNames array to have exactly the same number of slots as the firstNames array by using the firstNames.length variable as the initial array index. The length instance variable on array objects returns the number of slots in the array.

The ArrayTest class also has two methods: printNames() and main(). printNames(), defined in lines 6 through 19, is a utility method that does nothing but go through the firstNames and lastNames arrays sequentially, printing the values of each slot, one name per line. Note that the array index we've defined here (i) is initially set to 0 because Java array slots all start numbering from 0.

Finally, there is main(), which performs the actual actions of this example. The main() method here does four things:

5

☐ Line 22 creates an initial instance of `ArrayTest`, so we can set and modify its instance variables and call its methods.

☐ Line 23 calls `printNames()` to show what the object looks like initially. The result is the first four lines of the output; note that the `firstNames` array was initialized, but the values in `lastNames` are all `null`. If you don't initialize an array when you declare it, the values of the initial slots will be empty (or, actually, `null` for object arrays, `0` for numbers, and `false` for booleans).

☐ Lines 25 through 28 set the values of each of the slots in the `lastNames` array to actual strings.

☐ Finally, line 29 calls `printNames()` once again to show that the `lastNames` array is now full of values, and each first and last name prints as you would expect. The results are shown in the last four lines of the output.

NOTE

Who are the people in this example? They're inventors of computer programming languages. Dennis Ritchie is the inventor of C, Bjarne Stroustrup did C++, Grace Hopper is credited with COBOL, and, finally, James Gosling is the principal designer of Java.

One other note I should make about Listing 5.1 is that it's a terrible example of programming style. Usually when you deal with arrays you do not hard code the number of elements into the code as we have here; instead, you use a loop to go through each element of the array in turn. This makes the code a lot shorter and, in many cases, easier to read. You'll learn about loops later in this section, and we'll rewrite this example so that it works more flexibly.

Multidimensional Arrays

One last thing to note about arrays before we move on to the rest of this lesson is about multidimensional arrays. Java does not directly support multidimensional arrays. However, you can declare and create an array of arrays (and those arrays can contain arrays, and so on, for however many dimensions you need) and access the arrays as you would C-style multidimensional arrays:

```
int coords[][] = new int[12][12];
coords[0][0] = 1;
coords[0][1] = 2;
```

Block Statements

Before we launch into the last two-thirds of this lesson, let's take a small detour into a topic I haven't mentioned a whole lot up to this point (but that will be important later on): block statements.

A block statement is simply a group of Java statements surrounded by braces ({}). You've seen blocks a whole lot already; you've used a block statement to contain the variables and methods in a class definition, and inside that block you've also used blocks to hold the body of a method definition. The opening brace opens the block, and the closing brace closes the nearest closing block. Easy, right?

You can also use blocks even further, inside method definitions. The rule is that you can use a block anywhere a single statement would go. Each statement inside the block is then executed sequentially.

 A *block statement* is a group of individual Java statements enclosed in braces ({}). You can put a block statement anywhere a single statement can go.

So what's the difference between using a group of individual statements and using a block? The block creates a new local variable scope for the statements inside it. This means that you can declare and use local variables inside a block, and those variables will cease to exist after the block is finished executing. For example, here's a block inside a method definition that declares a new variable y. You cannot use y outside the block in which it's declared:

```
void testblock() {
    int x = 10;
    { // start of block
      int y = 50;
      System.out.println("inside the block:");
      System.out.println("x:" + x);
      System.out.println("y:" + y);
    } // end of block
}
```

Blocks are not usually used in this way—alone in a method definition, with random variable declarations inside them. You've mostly seen blocks up to this point surrounding class and method definitions, but another very common use of block statements is in the control flow constructs you'll learn about in the remainder of today's lesson.

if Conditionals

The if conditional statement is used when you want to execute different bits of code based on a simple test. if conditions are nearly identical to if statements in C: They contain the keyword if, followed by a boolean test, followed by either a single statement or a block statement to execute if the test is `true`. Here's a simple example that prints the message `x is smaller than y` only if the value of x is less than the value of y:

```
if (x < y)
    System.out.println("x is smaller than y");
```

An optional `else` keyword provides the alternative statement to execute if the test is `false`:

```
if (x < y)
    System.out.println("x is smaller than y");
else System.out.println("y is bigger");
```

 NEW TERM The `if` *conditional* executes different bits of code based on the result of a single boolean test.

TECHNICAL NOTE

> The difference between `if` conditionals in Java and C or C++ is that the test must return a boolean value (`true` or `false`). Unlike in C, the test cannot return an integer.

Using `if`, you can only include a single statement as the code to execute after the test (in this case, the `System.out.println()` method for each one). But because a block can appear anywhere a single statement can, if you want to do more than just one thing (as you usually will), you can enclose those statements inside a block:

```
if (engineState == true )
    System.out.println("Engine is already on.");
else {
    System.out.println("Now starting Engine.");
    if (gasLevel >= 1)
        engineState = true;
    else System.out.println("Low on gas! Can't start engine.");
}
```

This example uses the test (`engineState == true`). For boolean tests of this type, a common shortcut is merely to include the first part of the expression rather than explicitly test its value against `true` or `false`. Because it's a boolean variable, it automatically returns `true` or `false` all by itself, so you don't have to explicitly test it for that value. Here's a shorter version of the previous code, with the test replaced with the shorthand version:

```
if (engineState)
    System.out.println("Engine is on.");
else System.out.println("Engine is off.");
```

Listing 5.2 shows another simple example—this one in full application form. The `Peeper` class contains one utility method called `peepMe()`, which tests a value to see if it's even. If it is, it prints `Peep!` to the screen.

Type   **Listing 5.2. The** `Peeper` **class.**

```
1: class Peeper {
2:
3:    void peepMe(int val) {
4:       System.out.println("Value is "
5:          + val + ". ");
6:       if (val % 2 == 0)
7:          System.out.println("Peep!");
8:    }
9:
10:    public static void main (String args[]) {
11:       Peeper p = new Peeper();
12:
13:       p.peepMe(1);
14:       p.peepMe(2);
15:        p.peepMe(54);
16:       p.peepMe(77);
17:      p.peepMe(1346);
18:    }
19: }
```

Output
```
Value is 1.
Value is 2.
Peep!
Value is 54.
Peep!
Value is 77.
Value is 1346.
Peep!
```

Analysis   The heart of the Peeper class is the peepMe() method (lines 3 through 8), where values are tested and an appropriate message is printed. Unlike the methods you've defined in previous examples, note that the definition of peepMe() includes a single integer argument (see line 3). The peepMe() method starts by printing out the value that was passed to it. Then that argument is tested, using an if conditional, to see if it's an even number. (The modulus test, as you'll remember from Day 3, "Java Basics," returns the remainder of the division of its operands. So if the remainder of a number divided by 2 is 0, it's an even number.) If the number is even, Peep! is printed (you'll learn more about defining methods with arguments tomorrow).

We'll use a main() method, as always, in this application to create a new instance of Peeper and test it, calling the peepMe() method repeatedly with different values. In the output, only the values that are even get a Peep! message.

5

The Conditional Operator

An alternative to using the if and else keywords in a conditional statement is to use the *conditional operator*, sometimes called the *ternary operator* (*ternary* means three; the conditional operator has three parts).

The conditional operator is an expression, meaning that it returns a value (unlike the more general if, which can only result in a statement or block being executed). The conditional operator is most useful for very short or simple conditionals and looks like this:

```
test ? trueresult : falseresult;
```

test is a boolean expression that returns true or false, just like the test in the if statement. If the test is true, the conditional operator returns the value of *trueresult*; if it's false, it returns the value of *falseresult*. For example, the following conditional tests the values of x and y, returns the smaller of the two, and assigns that value to the variable smaller:

```
int smaller = x < y ? x : y;
```

The conditional operator has a very low precedence; that is, it's usually evaluated only after all its subexpressions are evaluated. The only operators lower in precedence are the assignment operators. See the precedence chart in Day 3's lesson for a refresher on precedence of all the operators.

switch **Conditionals**

A common programming practice in any language is to test a variable against some value, and if it doesn't match that value, to test it again against a different value, and if it doesn't match that one to make yet another test, and so on until it matches with the right result. Using only if statements, this can become unwieldy, depending on how it's formatted and how many different options you have to test. For example, you might end up with a set of if statements like this or longer:

```
if (oper == '+')
  addargs(arg1, arg2);
else if (oper == '-')
   subargs(arg1, arg2);
else if (oper == '*')
   multargs(arg1, arg2);
else if (oper == '/')
   divargs(arg1, arg2);
```

This form of if statement is called a *nested* if because each else statement in turn contains yet another if, and so on, until all possible tests have been made.

5

Many languages have a shorthand version of the nested `if` that is (somewhat) easier to read and allows you to group the tests and actions. Called a `switch` or `case` statement, in Java it's called `switch` and behaves as it does in C:

```
switch (test) {
    case valueOne:
      resultOne;
      break;
    case valueTwo:
      resultTwo;
      break;
    case valueThree:
      resultThree;
      break;
    ...
    default: defaultresult;
}
```

In the `switch` statement, the *test* (a variable or expression that evaluates to a `byte`, `char`, `short`, or `int`) is compared with each of the case values (`valueOne`, `valueTwo`, and so on) in turn. If a match is found, the statement (or statements) after the test is executed. If no match is found, the `default` statement is executed. The `default` is optional, so if there isn't a match in any of the cases and `default` doesn't exist, the `switch` statement completes without doing anything.

Note that the significant limitation of the `switch` in Java is that the tests and values can be only simple primitive types (and then only primitive types that are automatically castable to `int`). You cannot use larger primitive types (`long`, `float`), strings, or other objects within a `switch`, nor can you test for any relationship other than simple equality. This limits the usefulness of `switch`; nested `if`s can work for any kind of test on any type.

Here's a simple example of a `switch` statement similar to the nested `if` shown earlier:

```
switch (oper) {
    case '+':
        addargs(arg1, arg2);
        break;
    case '-':
        subargs(arg1, arg2);
        break;
    case '*':
        multargs(arg1, arg2);
        break;
    case '/':
        divargs(arg1, arg2);
        break;
 }
```

There are two things to be aware of in this example: The first is that after each case, you can include a single result statement or as many as you need. Unlike with `if`, you don't need to surround multiple statements with braces for it to work. The second thing to note about this example is the break statement included at the end of every case. Without the explicit break, once a match is made, the statements for that match (*and also* all the statements further down in the switch for all the other cases) are executed until a break or the end of the switch is found. In some cases, this may be exactly what you want to do, but in most cases, you'll want to make sure to include the break so that only the statements you want to be executed are actually executed (break, which you'll learn about in the section "Breaking Out of Loops," stops execution at the current point and jumps to the code outside of the next closing bracket (})).

One handy use of allowing a switch to continue processing statements after a match is found occurs when you want multiple values to match to the same statements. In this instance, you can use multiple case lines with no result, and the switch will execute the first statement it finds. For example, in the following switch statement, the string "x is an even number." is printed if x has a value of 2, 4, 6, or 8. All other values of x print the string "x is an odd number.":

```
switch (x) {
    case 2:
    case 4:
    case 6:
    case 8:
        System.out.println("x is an even number.");
        break;
    default: System.out.println("x is an odd number.");
}
```

Listing 5.3 shows yet another example of a switch. This class, called NumberReader, converts integer values to their actual English word equivalents using a method called convertIt().

TYPE **Listing 5.3. The NumberReader class.**

```
 1: class NumberReader {
 2:
 3:     String convertNum(int val) {
 4:         switch (val) {
 5:             case 0: return "zero ";
 6:             case 1: return "one ";
 7:           case 2: return "two ";
 8:             case 3: return "three ";
 9:             case 4: return "four ";
10:           case 5: return "five ";
11:           case 6: return "six ";
12:           case 7: return "seven ";
13:             case 8: return "eight ";
14:             case 9: return "nine ";
15:             default: return " ";
16:         }
17:     }
18:
```

continues

Listing 5.3. continued

```
19:     public static void main (String args[]) {
20:       NumberReader n = new NumberReader();
21:       String num = n.convertNum(4) + n.convertNum(1)  + n.convertNum(5);
22:       System.out.println("415 converts to " + num);
23:   }
24:}
```

OUTPUT   `415 converts to four one five`

ANALYSIS The heart of this example is, of course, the main `switch` statement in the middle of the `convertNum()` method in lines 4 through 16. This `switch` statement takes the integer argument that was passed into `convertNum()` and, when it finds a match, returns the appropriate string value. (Note that this method is defined to return a string as opposed to the other methods you've defined up to this point, which didn't return anything. You'll learn more about this tomorrow.)

So where are the `break` statements? You don't need them here because you're using `return` instead. `return` is similar to `break` except that it breaks out of the entire method definition and returns a single value. Again, you'll learn more about this tomorrow when you learn all about how to define methods.

At this point, you've probably seen enough `main()` methods to know what's going on, but let's run through this one quickly.

Line 20 creates a new instance of the `NumberReader` class.

Line 21 defines a string called `num` that will be the concatenation of the string values of three numbers. Each number is converted using a call to the `convertNum()` method.

Finally, line 22 prints out the result.

for **Loops**

The `for` loop, as in C, repeats a statement or block of statements until a condition is matched. `for` loops are frequently used for simple iterations in which you repeat a block of statements a certain number of times and then stop, but you can use `for` loops for just about any kind of loop.

The `for` loop in Java looks roughly like this:

```
for (initialization; test; increment) {
    statements;
}
```

The start of the for loop has three parts:

☐ `initialization` is an expression that initializes the start of the loop. If you have a loop index variable to keep track of how many times the loop has occurred, this expression might declare and initialize it—for example, `int i = 0`. Variables that you declare in this part of the for loop are local to the loop itself; they cease existing after the loop is finished executing.

☐ `test` is the test that occurs before each pass of the loop. The test must be a boolean expression or function that returns a boolean value—for example, `i < 10`. If the test is `true`, the loop executes. Once the test is `false`, the loop stops executing.

☐ `increment` is any expression or function call. Commonly, the increment is used to change the value of the loop index to bring the state of the loop closer to returning `false` and completing.

The statement part of the for loop is the statements that are executed each time the loop iterates. Just as with `if`, you can only include one statement, although a block will work just fine as well.

Remember the example in the section on arrays where I said that iterating over the contents of an array is usually done with a loop? Here's an example of a for loop that does just that—it initializes all the values of a `String` array to null strings:

```
String strArray[] = new String[10]; \\ the array
int i; // loop index

for (i = 0; i < strArray.length; i++)
    strArray[i] = "";
```

In this example, the variable I keeps track of the number of times the loop has occurred; it also makes a convenient index for the array itself. Here, we start the for loop with an index of I. The test for when the for loop will end is whether the current index is less than the length of the array (once the index is bigger than the array, you should stop), and the increment is simply to add 1 to the index each time. Then, for every loop you can put a null string (`""`) into the array at the given slot.

Any of the parts of the for loop can be empty statements; that is, you can simply include a semicolon with no expression or statement, and that part of the for loop will be ignored. Note that if you do use a null statement in your for loop, you may have to initialize or increment any loop variables or loop indices yourself elsewhere in the program.

You can also have an empty statement for the body of your for loop, if everything you want to do is in the first line of that loop. For example, here's one that finds the first prime number higher than 4000 (it calls a method called `notPrime()`, which will theoretically have a way of figuring that out):

5

```
for (i = 4001; notPrime(i); i += 2)
    ;
```

Note that a common mistake in C that also occurs in Java is to accidentally put a semicolon after the first line of the `for` loop:

```
for (i = 0; i < 10; i++);
    System.out.println("Loop!");
```

Because the first semicolon ends the loop with an empty statement, the loop doesn't actually do anything. The `println()` function will be printed only once because it's actually outside the `for` loop entirely. Be careful not to make this mistake in your own Java programs.

To finish up `for` loops, let's rewrite that example with the names from the array section. The original example is long and repetitive and only works with an array four elements long. This version, shown in Listing 5.4, is shorter and more flexible (but it returns the same output).

TYPE   **Listing 5.4. A modified array test with loops.**

```
 1: class NamesLoop {
 2:
 3:    String[] firstNames = { "Dennis", "Grace", "Bjarne", "James" };
 4:    String[] lastNames = new String[firstNames.length];
 5:
 6:    void printNames() {
 7:      for (int i = 0; i < firstNames.length; i++)
 8:          System.out.println(firstNames[i] + " " + lastNames[i]);
 9:    }
10:
11:    public static void main (String args[]) {
12:       NamesLoop a = new NamesLoop();
13:        a.printNames();
14:        System.out.println("----------");
15:        a.lastNames[0] = "Ritchie";
16:        a.lastNames[1] = "Hopper";
17:      a.lastNames[2] = "Stroustrup";
18:        a.lastNames[3] = "Gosling";
19:
20:        a.printNames();
21:}
22:}
```

OUTPUT
```
Dennis null
Grace null
Bjarne null
James null
----------
Dennis Ritchie
Grace Hopper
Bjarne Stroustrup
James Gosling
```

ANALYSIS The only difference between this example and Listing 5.1 is in the printNames() method. Instead of going through the array slots one by one, this example uses a for loop to iterate through the array one slot at a time, stopping at the last element in the array. Using a more general-purpose loop to iterate over an array allows you to use printNames() for any array of any size and still have it print all the elements.

while **and** do **Loops**

Finally, there are while and do loops. while and do loops, like for loops, repeat the execution of a block of Java code until a specific condition is met. Whether you use a for, a while, or a do loop is mostly a matter of your programming style.

while and do loops are exactly the same as in C and C++ except that their test conditions must be booleans.

while **Loops**

The while loop is used to repeat a statement or block of statements as long as a particular condition is true. while loops look like this:

```
while (condition) {
    bodyOfLoop;
}
```

The condition is a boolean test as it is in the if and for constructions. If the test returns true, the while loop executes the statements in bodyOfLoop and then tests the condition again, repeating until the condition is false. I've shown the while loop here with a block statement because it's most commonly used, although you can use a single statement in place of the block.

Listing 5.5 shows an example of a while loop that copies the elements of an array of integers (in array1) to an array of floats (in array2), casting each element to a float as it goes. The one catch is that if any of the elements in the first array is 0, the loop will immediately exit at that point.

TYPE Listing 5.5. while **loops to copy array elements.**

```
1: class CopyArrayWhile {
2:   public static void main (String args[]) {
3:       int[] array1 = { 5, 7, 3, 6, 0, 3, 2, 1 };
4:       float[] array2 = new float[array1.length];
5:
6:       System.out.print("array1: [ ");
```

continues

Listing 5.5. continued

```
 7:          for (int i = 0; i < array1.length; i++) {
 8:              System.out.print(array1[i] + " ");
 9:          }
10:          System.out.println("]");
11:
12:          System.out.print("array2: [ ");
13:          int count = 0;
14:          while ( count < array1.length && array1[count] != 0) {
15:                  array2[count] = (float) array1[count];
16:                  System.out.print(array2[count++] + " ");
17:          }
18:          System.out.println("]");
19:      }
20:}
```

OUTPUT
```
array1: [ 5 7 3 6 0 3 2 1 ]
array2: [ 5.0 7.0 3.0 6.0 ]
```

ANALYSIS   I've done all the work in main() to make things shorter. Here's what's going on:

Lines 3 and 4 declare the arrays; array1 is an array of ints, which I've initialized to some suitable numbers. array2, or floats, is the same length as array1, but doesn't have any initial values.

Lines 6 through 10 are for output purposes; they simply iterate through array1 using a for loop to print out its values.

Lines 13 through 17 are where the interesting stuff happens. This bunch of statements both assigns the values of array2 (converting the numbers to floats along the array) and prints it out at the same time. We start with a count variable, which keeps track of the array index elements. The test in the while loop keeps track of the two conditions for existing the loop, where those two conditions are running out of elements in array1 or encountering a 0 in array1 (remember, that was part of the original description of what this program does). We can use the logical conditional && to keep track of the test; remember that && makes sure both conditions are true before the entire expression is true. If either one is false, the expression returns false and the loop exits.

So what goes on in this particular example? The output shows that the first four elements in array1 were copied to array2, but there was a 0 in the middle that stopped the loop from going any further. Without the 0, array2 should end up with all the same elements as array1.

Note that if the while loop's test is initially false the first time it is tested (for example, if the first element in that first array is 0), the body of the while loop will never be executed. If you need to execute the loop at least once, you can do one of two things:

☐ Duplicate the body of the loop outside the `while` loop.

☐ Use a `do` loop (which is described in the following section).

The `do` loop is considered the better solution of the two.

do...while **Loops**

The `do` loop is just like a `while` loop, except that `do` executes a given statement or block until the condition is `false`. The main difference is that `while` loops test the condition before looping, making it possible that the body of the loop will never execute if the condition is `false` the first time it's tested. `do` loops run the body of the loop at least once before testing the condition. `do` loops look like this:

```
do {
    bodyOfLoop;
} while (condition);
```

Here, the `bodyOfLoop` part is the statements that are executed with each iteration. It's shown here with a block statement because it's most commonly used that way, but you can substitute the braces for a single statement as you can with the other control-flow constructs. The condition is a boolean test. If it returns `true`, the loop is run again. If it returns `false`, the loop exits. Keep in mind that with `do` loops, the body of the loop executes at least once.

Listing 5.6 shows a simple example of a `do` loop that prints a message each time the loop iterates (10 times, for this example):

TYPE   **Listing 5.6. A simple do loop.**

```
 1: class DoTest {
 2:    public static void main (String args[]) {
 3:       int x = 1;
 4:
 5:       do {
 6:          System.out.println("Looping, round " + x);
 7:          x++;
 8:       } while (x <= 10);
 9:    }
10: }
```

OUTPUT
```
Looping, round 1
Looping, round 2
Looping, round 3
Looping, round 4
Looping, round 5
Looping, round 6
Looping, round 7
Looping, round 8
Looping, round 9
Looping, round 10
```

5

Breaking Out of Loops

In all the loops (for, while, and do), the loop ends when the condition you're testing for is met. What happens if something odd occurs within the body of the loop and you want to exit the loop early? For that, you can use the break and continue keywords.

You've already seen break as part of the switch statement; it stops execution of the switch, and the program continues. The break keyword, when used with a loop, does the same thing—it immediately halts execution of the current loop. If you've nested loops within loops, execution picks up in the next outer loop; otherwise, the program merely continues executing the next statement after the loop.

For example, take that while loop that copied elements from an integer array into an array of floats until the end of the array or until a 0 is reached. You can instead test for that latter case inside the body of the while and then use a break to exit the loop:

```
int count = 0;
while (count < array1.length) {
    if (array1[count] == 0) {
        break;
    }
    array2[count] = (float) array1[count++];
}
```

continue is similar to break except that instead of halting execution of the loop entirely, the loop starts over at the next iteration. For do and while loops, this means that the execution of the block starts over again; for for loops, the increment and test expressions are evaluated and then the block is executed. continue is useful when you want to special-case elements within a loop. With the previous example of copying one array to another, you can test for whether the current element is 0 and restart the loop if you find it so that the resulting array will never contain zero. Note that because you're skipping elements in the first array, you now have to keep track of two different array counters:

```
int count1 = 0;
int count2 = 0;
while (count < array1.length) {
    if (array1[count1] == 0)  {
        continue;
            count1++
    }
    array2[count2++] = (float)array1[count1++];
}
```

Labeled Loops

Both break and continue can have an optional label that tells Java where to break to. Without a label, break jumps outside the nearest loop (to an enclosing loop or to the next statement outside the loop), and continue restarts the enclosing loop. Using labeled breaks and continues, you can break to specific points outside nested loops or continue a loop outside the current loop.

To use a labeled loop, add the label before the initial part of the loop, with a colon between them. Then, when you use break or continue, add the name of the label after the keyword itself:

```
out:
    for (int i = 0; i <10; i++) {
        while (x < 50) {
            if (i * x == 400)
                break out;
            ...
        }
        ...
    }
```

In this snippet of code, the label out labels the outer loop. Then, inside both the for and the while loops, when a particular condition is met, a break causes the execution to break out of both loops and continue executing any code after both loops.

Here's another example: The program shown in Listing 5.7 contains a nested for loop. Inside the innermost loop, if the summed values of the two counters is greater than 4, both loops exit at once.

TYPE **Listing 5.7. A labeled loop example.**

```
 1: class LabelTest {
 2:     public static void main (String arg[]) {
 3:
 4:       foo:
 5:       for (int i = 1; i <= 5; i++)
 6:         for (int j = 1; j <= 3; j++) {
 7:             System.out.println("i is " + i + ", j is " + j);
 8:             if (( i + j) > 4)
 9:             break foo;
10:         }
11:       System.out.println("end of loops");
12:     }
13:}
```

OUTPUT
```
i is 1, j is 1
i is 1, j is 2
i is 1, j is 3
i is 2, j is 1
i is 2, j is 2
i is 2, j is 3
end of loops
```

5

As you can see, the loop iterated until the sum of i and j was greater than 4, and then both loops exited back to the outer block and the final message was printed.

Summary

Today you have learned about three main topics that you'll most likely use quite often in your own Java programs: arrays, conditionals, and loops.

You have learned how to declare an array variable, create and assign an array object to that variable, and access and change elements within that array.

Conditionals include the if and switch statements, with which you can branch to different parts of your program based on a boolean test.

Finally, you have learned about the for, while, and do loops, each of which enable you to execute a portion of your program repeatedly until a given condition is met.

Now that you've learned the small stuff, all that's left is to go over the bigger issues of declaring classes and creating methods within which instances of those classes can communicate with each other by calling methods. Get to bed early tonight, because tomorrow is going to be a wild ride.

Q&A

Q If arrays are objects, and you use new to create them, and they have an instance variable length, where is the Array class? I didn't see it in the Java class libraries.

A Arrays are implemented kind of weirdly in Java. The Array class is constructed automatically when your Java program runs; Array provides the basic framework for arrays, including the length variable. Additionally, each primitive type and object has an implicit subclass of Array that represents an array of that class or object. When you create a new array object, it may not have an actual class, but it behaves as if it does.

Q When you create an array, you have to give it the number of slots that the array has. What happens if you get halfway through your program and you've run out of slots in the array? Does the array get bigger automatically?

A No, arrays stay the same size throughout their existence. And, as I noted in the part of this lesson on arrays, you cannot access slots outside the bounds of the array, so adding extra elements to a full array will cause an error.

So what do you do if an array is full? You have to do it the hard way: Create a new array that's bigger than the initial one and copy all the elements from the old array to the new.

Optionally, you can use a data structure other than an array if you expect to have widely varying numbers of elements in the array. The Vector class, part of the java.util package, is a growable collection you can use in place of an array.

Q Does Java have gotos?

A The Java language defines the keyword goto, but it is not currently used for anything. In other words, no—Java does not have gotos.

Q I declared a variable inside a block statement for an if. When the if was done, the definition of that variable vanished. Where did it go?

A In technical terms, block statements form a new lexical scope. What this means is that if you declare a variable inside a block, it's only visible and usable inside that block. When the block finishes executing, all the variables you declared go away.

It's a good idea to declare most of your variables in the outermost block in which they'll be needed—usually at the top of a block statement. The exception might be very simple variables, such as index counters in for loops, where declaring them in the first line of the for loop is an easy shortcut.

Q Why can't you use switch with strings?

A Strings are objects, and switch in Java works only for the primitive types byte, char, short, and int. To compare strings, you have to use nested ifs, which enable more general expression tests, including string comparison.

Q It seems to me that a lot of for loops could be written as while loops, and vice versa.

A True. The for loop is actually a special case of while that enables you to iterate a loop a specific number of times. You could just as easily do this with a while and then increment a counter inside the loop. Either works equally well. This is mostly just a question of programming style and personal choice.

5

Day 6

Creating Classes and Applications in Java

by Laura Lemay

In just about every lesson up to this point you've been creating Java applications—writing classes, creating instance variables and methods, and running those applications to perform simple tasks. Also up to this point, you've focused either on the very broad (general object-oriented theory) or the very minute (arithmetic and other expressions). Today you'll pull it all together and learn how and why to create classes by using the following basics:

- ☐ The parts of a class definition
- ☐ Declaring and using instance variables
- ☐ Defining and using methods
- ☐ Creating Java applications, including the `main()` method and how to pass arguments to a Java program from a command line

Defining Classes

Defining classes is pretty easy; you've seen how to do it a bunch of times in previous lessons. To define a class, use the `class` keyword and the name of the class:

```
class MyClassName {
...
}
```

By default, classes inherit from the `Object` class. If this class is a subclass of another specific class (that is, inherits from another class), use `extends` to indicate the superclass of this class:

```
class myClassName extends mySuperClassName {
...
}
```

NOTE

As of Java 1.1 you now have the ability to nest a class definition inside other classes—a useful construction when you're defining "adapter classes" that implement an interface. The flow of control from the inner class then moves automatically to the outer class. For more details (beyond this sketchy description), see Day 16, "Packages, Interfaces, and Inner Classes."

Creating Instance and Class Variables

A class definition with nothing in it is pretty dull; usually, when you create a class, you have something you want to add to make that class different from its superclasses. Inside each class definition are declarations and definitions for variables, methods, or both—for the class *and* for each instance. In this section, you'll learn all about instance and class variables; the next section talks about methods.

Defining Instance Variables

On Day 3, "Java Basics," you learned how to declare and initialize local variables—that is, variables inside method definitions. Instance variables, fortunately, are declared and defined in almost exactly the same way as local variables; the main difference is their location in the class definition. Variables are considered instance variables if they are declared outside a method definition. Customarily, however, most instance variables are defined just after the first line of the class definition. For example, Listing 6.1 shows a simple class definition for the class `Bicycle`, which inherits from the class `PersonPoweredVehicle`. This class definition contains five instance variables:

☐ `bikeType`—The kind of bicycle this bicycle is—for example, `Mountain` or `Street`

☐ `chainGear`—The number of gears in the front

☐ `rearCogs`—The number of minor gears on the rear axle

☐ `currentGearFront` and `currentGearRear`—The gear the bike is currently in, both front and rear

TYPE **Listing 6.1. The `Bicycle` class.**

```
1: class Bicycle extends PersonPoweredVehicle {
2:     String bikeType;
3:     int chainGear;
4:     int rearCogs;
5:     int currentGearFront;
6:     int currentGearRear;
7: }
```

Constants

A *constant variable* or *constant* is a variable whose value never changes (which may seem strange given the meaning of the word *variable*). Constants are useful for defining shared values for all the methods of an object—for giving meaningful names to object-wide values that will never change. In Java, you can create constants only for instance or class variables, not for local variables.

NEW TERM A *constant* is a variable whose value never changes.

To declare a constant, use the `final` keyword before the variable declaration and include an initial value for that variable:

```
final float pi = 3.141592;
final boolean debug = false;
final int maxsize = 40000;
```

TECHNICAL NOTE

The only way to define constants in Java is by using the `final` keyword. Neither the C and C++ constructs for `#define` nor `const` are available in Java, although the `const` keyword is reserved to prevent you from accidentally using it.

6

Constants can be useful for naming various states of an object and then testing for those states. For example, suppose you have a test label that can be aligned left, right, or center. You can define those values as constant integers:

```
final int LEFT = 0;
final int RIGHT = 1;
final int CENTER = 2;
```

The variable alignment is then also declared as an int:

```
int alignment;
```

Then, later in the body of a method definition, you can either set the alignment:

```
this.alignment = CENTER;
```

or test for a given alignment:

```
switch (this.alignment) {
    case LEFT: // deal with left alignment
            ...
            break;
    case RIGHT: // deal with right alignment
            ...
            break;
    case CENTER: // deal with center alignment
            ...
            break;
}
```

Class Variables

As you have learned in previous lessons, class variables are global to a class and to all that class's instances. You can think of class variables as being even more global than instance variables. Class variables are good for communicating between different objects with the same class, or for keeping track of global states among a set of objects.

To declare a class variable, use the static keyword in the class declaration:

```
static int sum;
static final int maxObjects = 10;
```

Creating Methods

Methods, as you learned on Day 2, "Object-Oriented Programming and Java," define an object's behavior—what happens when that object is created and the various operations that object can perform during its lifetime. In this section, you'll get a basic introduction to method definition and how methods work; tomorrow, you'll go into more detail about advanced things you can do with methods.

Defining Methods

Method definitions have four basic parts:

- [ ] The name of the method
- [ ] The type of object or primitive type the method returns
- [ ] A list of parameters
- [ ] The body of the method

NOTE

> To keep things simple today, I've left off two optional parts of the method definition: a modifier such as `public` or `private`, and the `throws` keyword, which indicates the exceptions a method can throw. You'll learn about these parts of a method definition in Week 3, "Advanced Java."

The first three parts of the method definition form what's called the method's *signature* and indicate the most important information about the method itself.

In other languages, the name of the method (or function, subroutine, or procedure) is enough to distinguish it from other methods in the program. In Java, you can have different methods that have the same name but a different return type or argument list, so all these parts of the method definition are important. This is called *method overloading*, and you'll learn more about it tomorrow.

NEW TERM A method's *signature* is a combination of the name of the method, the type of object or primitive data type this method returns, and a list of parameters.

Here's what a basic method definition looks like:

```
returntype methodname(type1 arg1, type2 arg2, type3 arg3..) {
    ...
}
```

The `returntype` is the type of value this method returns. It can be one of the primitive types, a class name, or `void` if the method does not return a value at all.

Note that if this method returns an array object, the array brackets can go either after the return type or after the parameter list; because the former way is considerably easier to read, it is used in the examples today (and throughout this book):

```
int[] makeRange(int lower, int upper) {...}
```

The method's parameter list is a set of variable declarations, separated by commas, inside parentheses. These parameters become local variables in the body of the method, whose values are the objects or values of primitives passed in when the method is called.

6

Inside the body of the method, you can have statements, expressions, method calls to other objects, conditionals, loops, and so on—everything you've learned about in the previous lessons.

If your method has a real return type (that is, it has not been declared to return void), somewhere inside the body of the method you need to explicitly return a value. Use the return keyword to do this. Listing 6.2 shows an example of a class that defines a makeRange() method. makeRange() takes two integers—a lower bound and an upper bound—and creates an array that contains all the integers between those two boundaries (inclusive).

 Listing 6.2. The RangeClass class.

```
 1: class RangeClass {
 2:     int[] makeRange(int lower, int upper) {
 3:         int arr[] = new int[ (upper - lower) + 1 ];
 4:
 5:         for (int i = 0; i < arr.length; i++) {
 6:             arr[i] = lower++;
 7:         }
 8:         return arr;
 9:     }
10:
11:     public static void main(String arg[]) {
12:         int theArray[];
13:         RangeClass theRange = new RangeClass();
14:
15:         theArray = theRange.makeRange(1, 10);
16:         System.out.print("The array: [ ");
17:         for (int i = 0; i < theArray.length; i++) {
18:             System.out.print(theArray[i] + " ");
19:         }
20:         System.out.println("]");
21:     }
22:
23: }
```

OUTPUT The array: [1 2 3 4 5 6 7 8 9 10]

ANALYSIS The main() method in this class tests the makeRange() method by creating a range where the lower and upper boundaries of the range are 1 and 10, respectively (see line 6), and then uses a for loop to print the values of the new array.

The this Keyword

In the body of a method definition, you may want to refer to the current object—the object in which the method is contained in the first place—to refer to that object's instance variables or to pass the current object as an argument to another method. To refer to the current object in these cases, you can use the `this` keyword. `this` can be used anywhere the current object might appear—in dot notation to refer to the object's instance variables, as an argument to a method, as the return value for the current method, and so on. Here's an example:

```
t = this.x;            // the x instance variable for this object
this.myMethod(this);   // call the myMethod method, defined in
                       // this class, and pass it the current
                       // object
return this;           // return the current object
```

In many cases, you may be able to omit the `this` keyword entirely. You can refer to both instance variables and method calls defined in the current class simply by name; the `this` is implicit in those references. So the first two examples could be written like this:

```
t = x            // the x instance variable for this object
myMethod(this)   // call the myMethod method, defined in this
                 // class
```

NOTE

> Omitting the `this` keyword for instance variables depends on whether there are variables of the same name declared in the local scope. See the next section for more details on variable scope.

Keep in mind that because `this` is a reference to the current *instance* of a class, you should only use it inside the body of an instance method definition. Class methods—that is, methods declared with the static keyword—cannot use `this`.

Variable Scope and Method Definitions

When you declare a variable, that variable always has a limited scope. Variable scope determines where that variable can be used. Variables with a local scope, for example, can only be used inside the block in which they were defined. Instance variables have a scope that extends to the entire class so they can be used by any of the methods within that class.

NEW TERM   *Variable scope* determines where a variable can be used.

When you refer to a variable within your method definitions, Java checks for a definition of that variable first in the current scope (which may be a block, for example, inside a loop), then in the outer scopes up to the current method definition. If that variable is not a local variable, Java then checks for a definition of that variable as an instance or class variable in the current class, and then, finally, in each superclass in turn.

Because of the way Java checks for the scope of a given variable, it is possible for you to create a variable in a lower scope such that a definition of that same variable "hides" the original value of that variable. This can introduce subtle and confusing bugs into your code.

For example, note the small Java program in Listing 6.3.

TYPE **Listing 6.3. A variable scope example.**

```
 1: class ScopeTest {
 2:     int test = 10;
 3:
 4:     void printTest () {
 5:         int test = 20;
 6:         System.out.println("test = " + test);
 7:     }
 8:
 9:     public static void main (String args[]) {
10:         ScopeTest st = new ScopeTest();
11:         st.printTest();
12:     }
13: }
```

ANALYSIS In this class, you have two variables with the same name and definition: The first, an instance variable, has the name `test` and is initialized to the value `10`. The second is a local variable with the same name, but with the value `20`. Because the local variable hides the instance variable, the `println()` method will print that `test` is `20`.

The easiest way to get around this problem is to make sure you don't use the same names for local variables as you do for instance variables. Another way to get around this particular problem, however, is to use `this.test` to refer to the instance variable, and just `test` to refer to the local variable. By referring explicitly to the instance variable by its object scope you avoid the conflict.

A more insidious example of this variable naming problem occurs when you redefine a variable in a subclass that already occurs in a superclass. This can create very subtle bugs in your code—for example, you may call methods that are intended to change the value of an instance variable, but that change the wrong one. Another bug might occur when you cast an object from one class to another—the value of your instance variable may mysteriously change (because it was getting that value from the superclass instead of from your class). The best way to avoid this behavior is to make sure that when you define variables in a subclass you're aware of the variables in each of that class's superclasses and you don't duplicate what is already there.

Passing Arguments to Methods

When you call a method with object parameters, the variables you pass into the body of the method are passed by reference, which means that whatever you do to those objects inside the method affects the original objects as well. This includes arrays and all the objects that arrays contain; when you pass an array into a method and modify its contents, the original array is affected. (Note that primitive types are passed by value.)

Listing 6.4 is an example to demonstrate how this works.

TYPE   **Listing 6.4. The `PassByReference` class.**

```
 1: class PassByReference {
 2:     int onetoZero(int arg[]) {
 3:         int count = 0;
 4:
 5:         for (int i = 0; i < arg.length; i++) {
 6:             if (arg[i] == 1) {
 7:                 count++;
 8:                 arg[i] = 0;
 9:             }
10:         }
11:         return count;
12:     }
13:     public static void main (String arg[]) {
14        int arr[] = { 1, 3, 4, 5, 1, 1, 7 };
15:         PassByReference test = new PassByReference();
16:         int numOnes;
17:
18:         System.out.print("Values of the array: [ ");
19:         for (int i = 0; i < arr.length; i++) {
20:             System.out.print(arr[i] + " ");
21:         }
22:         System.out.println("]");
23:
24          numOnes = test.onetoZero(arr);
25:         System.out.println("Number of Ones = " + numOnes);
26:         System.out.print("New values of the array: [ ");
27:         for (int i = 0; i < arr.length; i++) {
28:             System.out.print(arr[i] + " ");
29:         }
30:         System.out.println("]");
31:     }
32:}
```

OUTPUT   Values of the array: [1 3 4 5 1 1 7]
Number of Ones = 3
New values of the array: [0 3 4 5 0 0 7]

ANALYSIS   Note the method definition for the onetoZero() method in lines 2 to 12, which takes a single array as an argument. The onetoZero() method does two things:

☐ It counts the number of 1s in the array and returns that value.

☐ If it finds a 1, it substitutes a 0 in its place in the array.

6

The `main()` method in the `PassByReference` class tests the use of the `onetoZero()` method. Let's go over the `main()` method line by line so that you can see what is going on and why the output shows what it does.

Lines 14 through 16 set up the initial variables for this example. The first one is an array of integers; the second one is an instance of the class `PassByReference`, which is stored in the variable test. The third is a simple integer to hold the number of ones in the array.

Lines 18 through 22 print out the initial values of the array; you can see the output of these lines in the first line of the output.

Line 24 is where the real work takes place; this is where you call the `onetoZero()` method, defined in the object test, and pass it the array stored in `arr`. This method returns the number of ones in the array, which you'll then assign to the variable `numOnes`.

Got it so far? Line 25 prints out the number of 1s (that is, the value you got back from the `onetoZero()` method). It returns 3, as you would expect.

The last bunch of lines print out the array values. Because a reference to the array object is passed to the method, changing the array inside that method changes that original copy of the array. Printing out the values in lines 27 through 30 proves this—that last line of output shows that all the 1s in the array have been changed to 0s.

Class Methods

Just as you have class and instance variables, you also have class and instance methods, and the differences between the two types of methods are analogous. Class methods are available to any instance of the class itself and can be made available to other classes. Therefore, some class methods can be used anywhere, regardless of whether an instance of the class exists.

For example, the Java class libraries include a class called `Math`. The `Math` class defines a whole set of math operations that can be used in any program or the various number types:

```
float root = Math.sqrt(453.0);
System.out.print("The larger of x and y is " + Math.max(x, y));
```

To define class methods, use the `static` keyword in front of the method definition, just as you would create a class variable. For example, the max class method might have a signature like this:

```
static int max(int arg1, int arg2) { ... }
```

Java supplies "wrapper" classes for each of the primitive data types—for example, classes for `Integer`, `Float`, and `boolean`. Using class methods defined in those classes, you can convert to and from objects and primitive types. For example, the `parseInt()` class method in the `Integer` class takes a string and a radix (base) and returns the value of that string as an integer:

```
int count = Integer.parseInt("42", 10) // returns 42
```

Most methods that operate on a particular object, or that affect that object, should be defined as instance methods. Methods that provide some general utility but do not directly affect an instance of that class are better declared as class methods.

Creating Java Applications

Now that you know how to create classes, objects, and class and instance variables and methods, all that's left is to put it together into something that can actually run—in other words, to create a Java application.

Applications, to refresh your memory, are Java programs that run on their own. Applications are different from applets, which require a Java-enabled browser to view them. Much of what you've been creating up to this point have been Java applications; next week you'll dive into how to create applets. (Applets require a bit more background in order to get them to interact with the browser and draw and update with the graphics system. You'll learn all of this next week.)

A Java application consists of one or more classes and can be as large or as small as you want it to be. Although all the Java applications you've created up to this point do nothing but output some characters to the screen or to a window, you can also create Java applications that use windows, graphics, and user interface elements, just as applets do (you'll learn how to do this next week). The only thing you need to make a Java application run, however, is one class that serves as the "jumping-off" point for the rest of your Java program. If your program is small enough, it may need only the one class.

The jumping-off class for your application needs only one thing: a `main()` method. When you run your compiled Java class (using the Java interpreter), the `main()` method is the first thing that gets called. None of this should be much of a surprise to you at this point; you've been creating Java applications with `main()` methods all along.

The signature for the `main()` method always looks like this:

```
public static void main(String args[]) {...}
```

Here's a run-down of the parts of the `main()` method:

6

☐ `public` means that this method is available to other classes and objects. The `main()` method must be declared `public`. You'll learn more about `public` and `private` methods in Week 3.

☐ `static` means that this is a class method.

☐ `void` means that the `main()` method doesn't return anything.

☐ `main()` takes one parameter: an array of strings. This argument is used for command-line arguments, which you'll learn about in the next section.

The body of the `main()` method contains any code you need to get your application started: initializing variables or creating instances of any classes you may have declared.

When Java executes the `main()` method, keep in mind that `main()` is a class method—the class that holds it is not automatically instantiated when your program runs. If you want to treat that class as an object, you have to instantiate it in the `main()` method yourself (all the examples up to this point have done this).

Helper Classes

Your Java application can have only one class, or, in the case of most larger programs, it may be made up of several classes, where different instances of each class are created and used while the application is running. You can create as many classes as you want for your program, and as long as they are in the same directory or listed in your CLASSPATH, Java will be able to find them when your program runs. Note, however, that only the one jumping-off class, only the class you use with the Java bytecode interpreter, needs a `main()` method. Remember, `main()` is used only so that Java can start up the program and create an initial object; after that, the methods inside the various classes and objects take over. Although you can include `main()` methods in helper classes, they will be ignored when the program actually runs.

Java Applications and Command-Line Arguments

Because Java applications are standalone programs, it's useful to be able to pass arguments or options to a program to determine how the program is going to run, or to enable a generic program to operate on many different kinds of input. Command-line arguments can be used for many different purposes—for example, to turn on debugging input, to indicate a filename to read or write from, or for any other information that you might want your Java program to know.

Passing Arguments to Java Programs

How you pass arguments to a Java application varies based on the platform you're running Java on. On Windows and UNIX, you can pass arguments to the Java program via the command line; in the Macintosh, the Java Runner gives you a special window to type those arguments in.

 To pass arguments to a Java program on Windows or Solaris, append them to the command line when you run your Java program:

```
java Myprogram argumentOne 2 three
```

 To pass arguments to a Java program on the Macintosh, double-click the compiled Java class file. The Java Runner will start up, and you'll get the dialog box shown in Figure 6.1.

Figure 6.1.

Java Runner arguments.

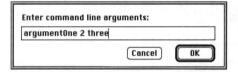

Enter your arguments, separated by spaces, into this box.

In these examples, you've passed three arguments to your program: argumentOne, the number 2, and three. Note that a space separates arguments, so if you use the phrase Java is cool as your arguments, you'll get three of them.

To group arguments, surround them with double-quotes. So, for example, the argument "Java is cool" produces one argument for your program to deal with. The double-quotes are stripped off before the argument gets to your Java program.

Handling Arguments in Your Java Program

How does Java handle arguments? It stores them in an array of strings, which is passed to the main() method in your Java program. Remember the signature for main():

```
public static void main (String args[]) {...}
```

Here, args is the name of the array of strings that contains the list of arguments. You can actually call it anything you want.

Inside your main() method, you can then handle the arguments your program was given by iterating over the array of arguments and handling those arguments any way you want. For example, Listing 6.5 is a really simple class that prints out the arguments it gets, one per line.

6

TYPE **Listing 6.5. The EchoArgs class.**

```
1: class EchoArgs {
2:     public static void main(String args[]) {
3:         for (int i = 0; i < args.length; i++) {
4:             System.out.println("Argument " + i + ": " + args[i]);
5:         }
6:     }
7: }
```

The following is some sample input and output from this program:

INPUT `java EchoArgs 1 2 3 jump`

OUTPUT
```
Argument 0: 1
Argument 1: 2
Argument 2: 3
Argument 3: jump
```

INPUT `java EchoArgs "foo bar" zap twaddle 5`

OUTPUT
```
Argument 0: foo bar
Argument 1: zap
Argument 2: twaddle
Argument 3: 5
```

Note how the arguments are grouped in the second input example; putting quotes around foo bar causes that argument to be treated as one unit inside the argument array.

TECHNICAL NOTE
> The array of arguments in Java is not analogous to argv in C and UNIX. In particular, arg[0], the first element in the array of arguments, is the first command-line argument after the name of the class—*not* the name of the program as it would be in C. Be careful of this as you write your Java programs.

An important thing to note about the arguments you pass into a Java program is that those arguments will be stored in an array of strings. This means that any arguments you pass to your Java program are strings stored in the argument array. To treat them as non-strings, you'll have to convert them to whatever type you want them to be.

For example, suppose you have a very simple Java program called SumAverage that takes any number of numeric arguments and returns the sum and the average of those arguments. Listing 6.6 shows a first pass at this program. Don't try compiling this one; just look at the code and see if you can figure out what it does.

Listing 6.6. A first try at the SumAverage class.

```
 1: class SumAverage {
 2:     public static void main (String args[]) {
 3:         int sum = 0;
 4:
 5:         for (int i = 0; i < args.length; i++) {
 6:             sum += args[i];
 7:         }
 8:
 9:         System.out.println("Sum is: " + sum);
10:         System.out.println("Average is: " +
11:             (float)sum / args.length);
12:     }
13: }
```

At first glance, this program seems rather straightforward—a for loop iterates over the array of arguments, summing them, and then the sum and the average are printed out as the last step.

What happens when you try and compile this? You get an error similar to this one:

```
SumAverage.java:6: Incompatible type for +=.
Can't convert java.lang.String to int.
    sum += args[i];
```

You get this error because the argument array is an array of strings. Even though you passed integers into the program from the command line, those integers were converted to strings before they were stored in the array. To be able to sum those integers, you have to convert them back from strings to integers. There's a class method for the Integer class, called parseInt, that does just this. If you change line 6 to use that method, everything works just fine:

```
sum += Integer.parseInt(args[i]);
```

Now, compiling the program produces no errors and running it with various arguments returns the expected results. For example, java SumAverage 1 2 3 returns the following output:

```
Sum is: 6
Average is: 2.0
```

Summary

Today you put together everything you've come across in the preceding days of this week about how to create Java classes and use them in Java applications. This includes the following:

6

☐ Instance and class variables, which hold the attributes of the class and its instances. You have learned how to declare them, how they are different from regular local variables, and how to declare constants.

☐ Instance and class methods, which define a class's behavior. You have learned how to define methods, including the parts of a method's signature, how to return values from a method, how arguments are passed in and out of methods, and how to use the this keyword to refer to the current object.

☐ Java applications—all about the main() method and how it works, as well as how to pass arguments into a Java application from a command line.

Q&A

Q **I tried creating a constant variable inside a method and I got a compiler error when I tried it. What was I doing wrong?**

A You can create only constant (final) class or instance variables; local variables cannot be constant.

Q **static and final are not exactly the most descriptive words for creating class variables, class methods, and constants. Why not use class and const?**

A static comes from Java's C++ heritage; C++ uses the static keyword to retain memory for class variables and methods (and, in fact, they aren't called class methods and variables in C++: static member functions and variables are more common terms).

final, however, is new. final is used in a more general way for classes and methods to indicate that those things cannot be subclassed or overridden. Using the final keyword for variables is consistent with that behavior. final variables are not quite the same as constant variables in C++, which is why the const keyword is not used.

Q **In my class, I have an instance variable called origin. I also have a local variable called origin in a method, which, because of variable scope, gets hidden by the local variable. Is there any way to get hold of the instance variable's value?**

A The easiest way is not to name your local variables the same names as your instance variables. If you feel you must, you can use this.origin to refer to the instance variable and origin to refer to the local variable.

Q **I want to pass command-line arguments to an applet. How do I do this?**

A You're writing applets already? Been skipping ahead, have you? The answer is that you use HTML attributes to pass arguments to an applet, not the command line (you don't have a command line for applets). You'll learn how to do this next week.

Q I wrote a program to take four arguments, but if I give it too few arguments, it crashes with a runtime error.

A Testing for the number and type of arguments your program expects is up to you in your Java program; Java won't do it for you. If your program requires four arguments, test that you have indeed been given four arguments, and return an error message if you haven't.

6

Day 7

More About Methods

by Laura Lemay

Methods are arguably the most important part of any object-oriented language. Whereas classes and objects provide the framework, and class and instance variables provide a way of holding that class's or object's attributes, the methods actually provide an object's behavior and define how that object interacts with other objects in the system.

Yesterday you learned a little about defining methods. With what you learned yesterday, you could create lots of Java programs, but you'd be missing some of the features of methods that make them really powerful and that make your objects and classes more efficient and easier to understand. Today you'll learn about these additional features, including the following:

☐ Overloading methods—that is, creating methods with multiple signatures and definitions but with the same name

☐ Creating constructor methods—methods that enable you to initialize objects to set up their initial state when created

□ Overriding methods—creating a different definition for a method that has been
        defined in a superclass

□ Using finalizer methods—a way for an object to clean up after itself before it is
        removed from the system

Creating Methods with the Same Name, Different Arguments

Yesterday you learned how to create methods with a single name and a single signature. Methods in Java can also be overloaded—that is, you can create methods that have the same name, but different signatures and different definitions. Method overloading allows instances of your class to have a simpler interface to other objects (no need for entirely different methods with different names that do essentially the same thing) and to behave differently based on the input to that method. For example, an overloaded `draw()` method could be used to draw just about anything, whether it were a circle or a point or an image. The same method name, with different arguments, could be used for all cases.

When you call a method in an object, Java matches up the method name and the number and type of arguments to choose which method definition to execute.

 Method overloading is creating multiple methods with the same name but with different signatures and definitions. Java uses the number and type of arguments to choose which method definition to execute.

To create an overloaded method, all you need to do is create several different method definitions in your class, all with the same name, but with different parameter lists (either in number or type of arguments). Java allows method overloading as long as each parameter list is unique for the same method name.

Note that Java differentiates overloaded methods based on the number and type of parameters to that method, not on the method's return type. That is, if you try to create two methods with the same name and same parameter list, but different return types, you'll get a compiler error. Also, the variable names you choose for each parameter to the method are irrelevant—all that matters is the number and the type.

Here's an example of creating an overloaded method. Listing 7.1 shows a simple class definition for a class called `MyRect`, which defines a rectangular shape. The `MyRect` class has four instance variables to define the upper-left and lower-right corners of the rectangle: `x1`, `y1`, `x2`, and `y2`.

NOTE

Why did I call it MyRect instead of just Rectangle? The java.awt package has a class called Rectangle that implements much of this same behavior. I called this class MyRect to prevent confusion between the two classes.

TYPE **Listing 7.1. The MyRect class.**

```
1: class MyRect {
2:     int x1 = 0;
3:     int y1 = 0;
4:     int x2 = 0;
5:     int y2 = 0;
6: }
```

NOTE

Don't try to compile this example yet. Actually, it'll compile just fine, but it won't run because it doesn't (yet) have a main() method. When you're finished building this class definition, the final version can be compiled and run.

When a new instance of the MyRect class is initially created, all its instance variables are initialized to 0. Let's define a buildRect() method that takes four integer arguments and "resizes" the rectangle to have the appropriate values for its corners, returning the resulting rectangle object (note that because the arguments have the same names as the instance variables, you have to make sure to use this to refer to them):

```
MyRect buildRect(int x1, int y1, int x2, int y2) {
    this.x1 = x1;
    this.y1 = y1;
    this.x2 = x2;
    this.y2 = y2;
    return this;
}
```

What if you want to define a rectangle's dimensions in a different way—for example, by using Point objects rather than individual coordinates? You can overload buildRect() so that its parameter list takes two Point objects (note that you'll also need to import the java.awt.Point class at the top of your source file so Java can find it):

```
MyRect buildRect(Point topLeft, Point bottomRight) {
    x1 = topLeft.x;
    y1 = topLeft.y;
```

7

```
    x2 = bottomRight.x;
    y2 = bottomRight.y;
    return this;
}
```

Perhaps you want to define the rectangle using a top corner and a width and height. You can do that, too. Just create a different definition for buildRect():

```
MyRect buildRect(Point topLeft, int w, int h) {
    x1 = topLeft.x;
    y1 = topLeft.y;
    x2 = (x1 + w);
    y2 = (y1 + h);
    return this;
}
```

To finish up this example, let's create a method—called printRect()—to print out the rectangle's coordinates, and a main() method to test it all (just to prove that this does indeed work). Listing 7.2 shows the completed class definition with all its methods: three buildRect() methods, one printRect(), and one main().

TYPE   **Listing 7.2. The complete MyRect class.**

```
 1:import java.awt.Point;
 2:
 3:class MyRect {
 4:    int x1 = 0;
 5:    int y1 = 0;
 6:    int x2 = 0;
 7:    int y2 = 0;
 8:
 9:    MyRect buildRect(int x1, int y1, int x2, int y2) {
10:        this.x1 = x1;
11:        this.y1 = y1;
12:        this.x2 = x2;
13:        this.y2 = y2;
14:        return this;
15:    }
16:
17:    MyRect buildRect(Point topLeft, Point bottomRight) {
18:        x1 = topLeft.x;
19:        y1 = topLeft.y;
20:        x2 = bottomRight.x;
21:        y2 = bottomRight.y;
22:        return this;
23:    }
24:
25:    MyRect buildRect(Point topLeft, int w, int h) {
26:        x1 = topLeft.x;
27:        y1 = topLeft.y;
28:        x2 = (x1 + w);
29:        y2 = (y1 + h);
30:        return this;
31:    }
32:
```

```
33:    void printRect(){
34:        System.out.print("MyRect: <" + x1 + ", " + y1);
35:        System.out.println(", " + x2 + ", " + y2 + ">");
36:    }
37:
38:    public static void main(String args[]) {
39:        MyRect rect = new MyRect();
40:
41:        System.out.println("Calling buildRect with coordinates 25,25,
           ➥50,50:");
42:         rect.buildRect(25, 25, 50, 50);
43:         rect.printRect();
44:        System.out.println("----------");
45:
46:        System.out.println("Calling buildRect w/points (10,10), (20,20):");
47:        rect.buildRect(new Point(10,10), new Point(20,20));
48:        rect.printRect();
49:        System.out.println("----------");
50:
51:        System.out.print("Calling buildRect w/1 point (10,10),");
52:        System.out.println(" width (50) and height (50):");
53:
54:         rect.buildRect(new Point(10,10), 50, 50);
55:         rect.printRect();
56:        System.out.println("----------");
57:    }
58: }
```

OUTPUT

```
Calling buildRect with coordinates 25,25 50,50:
MyRect: <25, 25, 50, 50>
----------
Calling buildRect w/points (10,10), (20,20):
MyRect: <10, 10, 20, 20>
----------
Calling buildRect w/1 point (10,10), width (50) and height (50):
MyRect: <10, 10, 60, 60>
----------
```

As you can see from this example, all the buildRect() methods work based on the arguments
with which they are called. You can define as many versions of a method as you need to in
your own classes to implement the behavior you need for that class.

Constructor Methods

In addition to regular methods, you can also define constructor methods in your class
definition. Constructor methods are used to initialize new objects when they're created.
Unlike regular methods, you can't call a constructor method by calling it directly; instead,
constructor methods are called by Java automatically when you create a new object. As you
learned on Day 4, "Working with Objects," when you use new, Java does three things:

7

☐ Allocates memory for the new object

☐ Initializes that object's instance variables, either to their initial values or to a default (0 for numbers, null for objects, false for booleans, '\0' for characters)

☐ Calls the class's constructor method (which may be one of several methods)

NEW TERM *Constructor methods* are special methods that are called automatically by Java to initialize a new object.

If a class doesn't have any special constructor methods defined, you'll still end up with a new object, but you might have to set its instance variables or call other methods that the object needs to initialize itself. All the examples you've created up to this point have behaved like this.

By defining constructor methods in your own classes, you can set initial values of instance variables, call methods based on those variables or on other objects, or calculate initial properties of your object. You can also overload constructors, as you would regular methods, to create an object that has specific properties based on the arguments you give in the new expression.

Basic Constructors

Constructors look a lot like regular methods, with two basic differences:

☐ Constructors always have the same name as the class.

☐ Constructors don't have a return type.

For example, Listing 7.3 shows a simple class called Person. The constructor method for Person takes two arguments: a string object representing a person's name and an integer for the person's age.

TYPE **Listing 7.3. The Person class.**

```
1: class Person {
2:     String name;
3:     int age;
4:
5:     Person(String n, int a) {
6:         name = n;
7:         age = a;
8:     }
9:
10:    void printPerson() {
11:        System.out.print("Hi, my name is " + name);
12:        System.out.println(". I am " + age + " years old.");
13:    }
14:
15:    public static void main (String args[]) {
```

```
16:        Person p;
17:        p = new Person("Laura", 20);
18:        p.printPerson();
19:        System.out.println("--------");
20:        p = new Person("Tommy", 3);
21:        p.printPerson();
22:        System.out.println("--------");
23:    }
24:}
```

OUTPUT
```
Hi, my name is Laura. I am 20 years old.
--------
Hi, my name is Tommy. I am 3 years old.
--------
```

The person class has three methods: The first is the constructor method, defined in lines 5 to 8, which initializes the class's two instance variables based on the arguments to new. The Person class also includes a method called printPerson() so that the object can "introduce" itself, and a main() method to test each of these things.

Calling Another Constructor

Some constructors you write may be supersets of other constructors defined in your class; that is, they might have the same behavior plus a little bit more. Rather than duplicating identical behavior in multiple constructor methods in your class, it makes sense to be able to just call that first constructor from inside the body of the second constructor. Java provides a special syntax for doing this. To call a constructor defined on the current class, use the this keyword as if it were a method name, with the arguments just after it, like this:

```
this(arg1, arg2, arg3...);
```

The arguments to this() are, of course, the arguments to the constructor.

Overloading Constructors

Like regular methods, constructors can also take varying numbers and types of parameters, enabling you to create your object with exactly the properties you want it to have, or for it to be able to calculate properties from different kinds of input.

For example, the buildRect() methods you defined in the MyRect class earlier today would make excellent constructors because they're initializing an object's instance variables to the appropriate values. So, for example, instead of the original buildRect() method you had defined (which took four parameters for the coordinates of the corners), you could create a constructor instead. Listing 7.4 shows a new class, MyRect2, that has all the same functionality of the original MyRect, except with overloaded constructor methods instead of the overloaded buildRect() method. The output shown at the end is also the same output as for the previous MyRect class; only the code to produce it has changed.

TYPE   **Listing 7.4. The** `MyRect2` **class (with constructors).**

```
 1: import java.awt.Point;
 2:
 3: class MyRect2 {
 4:     int x1 = 0;
 5:     int y1 = 0;
 6:     int x2 = 0;
 7:     int y2 = 0;
 8:
 9:     MyRect2(int x1, int y1, int x2, int y2) {
10:         this.x1 = x1;
11:         this.y1 = y1;
12:         this.x2 = x2;
13:         this.y2 = y2;
14:     }
15:
16:     MyRect2(Point topLeft, Point bottomRight) {
17:         x1 = topLeft.x;
18:         y1 = topLeft.y;
19:         x2 = bottomRight.x;
20:         y2 = bottomRight.y;
21:     }
22:
23:     MyRect2(Point topLeft, int w, int h) {
24:         x1 = topLeft.x;
25:         y1 = topLeft.y;
26:         x2 = (x1 + w);
27:         y2 = (y1 + h);
28:     }
29:
30:     void printRect() {
31:         System.out.print("MyRect: <" + x1 + ", " + y1);
32:         System.out.println(", " + x2 + ", " + y2 + ">");
33:     }
34:
35:     public static void main(String args[]) {
36:         MyRect2 rect;
37:
38:         System.out.println("Calling MyRect2 with coordinates 25,25 50,50:");
39:         rect = new MyRect2(25, 25, 50,50);
40:         rect.printRect();
41:         System.out.println("----------");
42:
43:         System.out.println("Calling MyRect2 w/points (10,10), (20,20):");
44:         rect= new MyRect2(new Point(10,10), new Point(20,20));
45:         rect.printRect();
46:         System.out.println("----------");
47:
48:         System.out.print("Calling MyRect2 w/1 point (10,10)");
49:         System.out.println(" width (50) and height (50):");
50:         rect = new MyRect2(new Point(10,10), 50, 50);
51:         rect.printRect();
52:         System.out.println("----------");
53:
54:     }
55: }
```

OUTPUT
```
Calling MyRect2 with coordinates 25,25 50,50:
MyRect: <25, 25, 50, 50>
- - - - - - - - - -
Calling MyRect2 w/points (10,10), (20,20):
MyRect: <10, 10, 20, 20>
- - - - - - - - - -
Calling MyRect2 w/1 point (10,10), width (50) and height (50):
MyRect: <10, 10, 60, 60>
- - - - - - - - - -
```

Overriding Methods

When you call an object's method, Java looks for that method definition in the class of that object, and if it doesn't find a match with the right signature, it passes the method call up the class hierarchy until a definition is found. Method inheritance means that you can use methods in subclasses without having to duplicate the code.

However, there may be times when you want an object to respond to the same methods but have different behavior when that method is called. In this case, you can override that method. Overriding a method involves defining a method in a subclass that has the same signature as a method in a superclass. Then, when that method is called, the method in the subclass is found and executed instead of the one in the superclass.

Creating Methods That Override Existing Methods

To override a method, all you have to do is create a method in your subclass that has the same signature (name, return type, and parameter list) as a method defined by one of your class's superclasses. Because Java executes the first method definition it finds that matches the signature, this effectively "hides" the original method definition. Here's a simple example; Listing 7.5 shows a simple class with a method called printMe(), which prints out the name of the class and the values of its instance variables.

TYPE **Listing 7.5. The PrintClass class.**

```
 1: class PrintClass {
 2:     int x = 0;
 3:     int y = 1;
 4:
 5:     void printMe() {
 6:         System.out.println("x is " + x + ", y is " + y);
 7:         System.out.println("I am an instance of the class " +
 8:             this.getClass().getName());
 9:     }
10: }
```

7

Listing 7.6 shows a class called PrintSubClass that is a subclass of (extends) PrintClass. The only difference between PrintClass and PrintSubClass is that the latter has a z instance variable.

TYPE **Listing 7.6. The** PrintSubClass **class.**

```
1: class PrintSubClass extends PrintClass {
2:     int z = 3;
3:
4:     public static void main(String args[]) {
5:         PrintSubClass obj = new PrintSubClass();
6:         obj.printMe();
7:     }
8: }
```

 OUTPUT
```
x is 0, y is 1
I am an instance of the class PrintSubClass
```

In the main() method of PrintSubClass, you create a PrintSubClass object and call the printMe() method. Note that PrintSubClass doesn't define this method, so Java looks for it in each of PrintSubClass's superclasses—and finds it, in this case, in PrintClass. Unfortunately, because printMe() is still defined in PrintClass, it doesn't print the z instance variable.

NOTE

> There's an important feature of PrintClass I should point out: It doesn't have a main() method. It doesn't need one; it isn't an application. PrintClass is simply a utility class for the PrintSubClass class, which is an application and therefore has a main() method. Only the class that you're actually executing the Java interpreter on needs a main() method.

Now, let's create a third class. PrintSubClass2 is nearly identical to PrintSubClass, but you override the printMe() method to include the z variable. Listing 7.7 shows this class.

TYPE **Listing 7.7. The** PrintSubClass2 **class.**

```
1: class PrintSubClass2 extends PrintClass {
2:     int z = 3;
3:
4:     void printMe() {
5:         System.out.println("x is " + x + ", y is " + y +
6:                 ", z is " + z);
```

```
 7:          System.out.println("I am an instance of the class " +
 8:              this.getClass().getName());
 9:      }
10:
11:      public static void main(String args[]) {
12:          PrintSubClass2 obj = new PrintSubClass2();
13:          obj.printMe();
14:      }
15: }
```

Now when you instantiate this class and call the `printMe()` method, the version of `printMe()` you defined for this class is called instead of the one in the superclass `PrintClass` (as you can see in this output):

```
x is 0, y is 1, z is 3
I am an instance of the class PrintSubClass2
```

Calling the Original Method

Usually, there are two reasons why you want to override a method that a superclass has already implemented:

☐ To replace the definition of that original method completely

☐ To augment the original method with additional behavior

You've already learned about the first one; by overriding a method and giving that method a new definition, you've hidden the original method definition. But sometimes you may just want to add behavior to the original definition rather than erase it altogether. This is particularly useful where you end up duplicating behavior in both the original method and the method that overrides it; by being able to call the original method in the body of the overridden method, you can add only what you need.

To call the original method from inside a method definition, use the `super` keyword to pass the method call up the hierarchy:

```
void myMethod (String a, String b) {
    // do stuff here
    super.myMethod(a, b);
    // maybe do more stuff here
}
```

The `super` keyword, somewhat like the `this` keyword, is a placeholder for this class's superclass. You can use it anywhere you can use `this`, but to refer to the superclass rather than to the current class.

For example, Listing 7.8 shows the two different `printMe()` methods used in the previous example.

7

TYPE   **Listing 7.8. The `printMe()` methods.**

```
1: // from PrintClass
2: void printMe() {
3:         System.out.println("x is " + x + ", y is " + y);
4:         System.out.println("I am an instance of the class" +
5:                 this.getClass().getName());
6:     }
7: }
8:
9: //from PrintSubClass2
10:     void printMe() {
11:         System.out.println("x is " + x + ", y is " + y + ", z is " + z);
12:         System.out.println("I am an instance of the class " +
13:                 this.getClass().getName());
14:     }
```

Rather than duplicating most of the behavior of the superclass's method in the subclass, you can rearrange the superclass's method so that additional behavior can easily be added:

```
// from PrintClass
void printMe() {
    System.out.println("I am an instance of the class" +
                this.getClass().getName());
    System.out.println("x is " + x);
    System.out.println("y is " + y);
}
```

Then, in the subclass, when you override `printMe()`, you can merely call the original method and then add the extra stuff:

```
// From PrintSubClass2
void printMe() {
    super.printMe();
    System.out.println("z is " + z);
}
```

Here's the output of calling `printMe()` on an instance of the subclass:

OUTPUT
```
I am an instance of the class PrintSubClass2
X is 0
Y is 1
Z is 3
```

Overriding Constructors

Because constructors have the same name as the current class, you cannot technically override a superclass's constructors. If you want a constructor in a subclass with the same number and type of arguments as in the superclass, you'll have to define that constructor in your own class.

However, when you create your constructors you will almost always want to call your superclass's constructors to make sure that the inherited parts of your object get initialized the way your superclass intends them to be. By explicitly calling your superclasses constructors in this way you can create constructors that effectively override or overload your superclass's constructors.

To call a regular method in a superclass, you use the form super.methodname(arguments). Because with constructors you don't have a method name to call, you have to use a different form:

```
super(arg1, arg2, ...);
```

Note that Java has a specific rule for the use of super(): It must be the very first thing in your constructor definition. If you don't call super() explicitly in your constructor, Java will do it for you—using super() with no arguments.

Similar to using this(...) in a constructor, super(...) calls a constructor method for the immediate superclass with the appropriate arguments (which may, in turn, call the constructor of its superclass, and so on). Note that a constructor with that signature has to exist in the superclass in order for the call to super() to work. The Java compiler will check this when you try to compile the source file.

Note that you don't have to call the constructor in your superclass that has exactly the same signature as the constructor in your class; you only have to call the constructor for the values you need initialized. In fact, you can create a class that has constructors with entirely different signatures from any of the superclass's constructors.

Listing 7.9 shows a class called NamedPoint, which extends the class Point from Java's awt package. The Point class has only one constructor, which takes an x and a y argument and returns a Point object. NamedPoint has an additional instance variable (a string for the name) and defines a constructor to initialize x, y, and the name.

TYPE   **Listing 7.9. The NamedPoint class.**

```
 1: import java.awt.Point;
 2: class NamedPoint extends Point {
 3:     String name;
 4:
 5:     NamedPoint(int x, int y, String name) {
 6:         super(x,y);
 7:         this.name = name;
 8:     }
 9:     public static void main (String arg[]) {
10:         NamedPoint np = new NamedPoint(5, 5, "SmallPoint");
11:         System.out.println("x is " + np.x);
12:         System.out.println("y is " + np.y);
13:         System.out.println("Name is " + np.name);
14:     }
15:}
```

7

OUTPUT
```
x is 5
y is 5
name is SmallPoint
```

The constructor defined here for NamedPoint (lines 5 through 8) calls Point's constructor method to initialize Point's instance variables (x and y). Although you can just as easily initialize x and y yourself, you may not know what other things Point is doing to initialize itself, so it's always a good idea to pass constructors up the hierarchy to make sure everything is set up correctly.

Finalizer Methods

Finalizer methods are almost the opposite of constructor methods; whereas a constructor method is used to initialize an object, finalizer methods are called just before the object is garbage-collected and its memory reclaimed.

The finalizer method is named simply finalize(). The Object class defines a default finalizer method, which does nothing. To create a finalizer method for your own classes, override the finalize() method using this signature:

```
protected void finalize() throws Throwable {
    super.finalize();
}
```

NOTE

> The throws Throwable part of this method definition refers to the errors that might occur when this method is called. Errors in Java are called *exceptions*; you'll learn more about them on Day 17, "Exceptions." For now, all you need to do is include these keywords in the method definition.

Inside the body of that finalize() method, include any cleaning up you want to do for that object. You can also call super.finalize() to allow your class's superclasses to finalize your object, if necessary (it's a good idea to do so just to make sure that everyone gets a chance to deal with the object if they need to).

You can always call the finalize() method yourself at any time; it's just a plain method like any other. However, calling finalize() does not trigger an object to be garbage-collected. Only removing all references to an object will cause it to be marked for deleting.

Finalizer methods are best used for optimizing the removal of an object—for example, by removing references to other objects, by releasing external resources that have been acquired (for example, external files), or for other behaviors that may make it easier for that object to be removed. In most cases, you will not need to use finalize() at all. See Day 21, "Under the Hood," for more about garbage collection and finalize().

Summary

Today you have learned all kinds of techniques for using, reusing, defining, and redefining methods. You have learned how to overload a method name so that the same method can have different behaviors based on the arguments with which it's called. You've learned about constructor methods, which are used to initialize a new object when it's created. You have learned about method inheritance and how to override methods that have been defined in a class's superclasses. Finally, you have learned about finalizer methods, which can be used to clean up after an object just before that object is garbage-collected and its memory reclaimed.

Congratulations on completing your first week of *Teach Yourself Java in 21 Days*! Starting next week, you'll apply everything you've learned this week to writing Java applets and to working with more advanced concepts in putting together Java programs and working with the standard Java class libraries.

Q&A

Q I created two methods with the following signatures:

```
int total(int arg1, int arg2, int arg3) {...}
float total(int arg1, int arg2, int arg3) {...}
```

The Java compiler complains when I try to compile the class with these method definitions. But their signatures are different. What have I done wrong?

A Method overloading in Java works only if the parameter lists are different—either in number or type of arguments. Return type is not relevant for method overloading. Think about it—if you had two methods with exactly the same parameter list, how would Java know which one to call?

Q Can I overload overridden methods (that is, can I create methods that have the same name as an inherited method, but a different parameter list)?

A Sure! As long as parameter lists vary, it doesn't matter whether you've defined a new method name or one that you've inherited from a superclass.

7

Developing Applets

WEEK

2

Developing Applets

Day 8

Java Applet Basics

by Laura Lemay

Much of Java's current popularity has come about because of Java-enabled World Wide Web browsers and their support for applets—Java programs that run on Web pages and can be used to create dynamic, interactive Web sites. Applets, as noted at the beginning of this book, are written in the Java language and can be viewed in a Web browser that supports Java. Learning how to create applets is most likely the reason you bought this book, so let's waste no more time.

Last week, you focused on learning about the Java language itself, and most of the little programs you created were Java applications. This week, now that you have the basics down, you'll move on to creating and using applets, which includes a discussion of many of the classes in the standard Java class library.

Today you'll start with the basics:

☐ Reviewing differences between Java applets and applications

☐ Getting started with applets: the basics of how an applet works and how to create your own simple applets

- [ ] Including an applet on a Web page by using the <APPLET> tag, including the various features of that tag
- [ ] Passing parameters to applets
- [ ] Storing applets and related files in a compressed archive for faster download
- [ ] Setting up applets that can be trusted to run without any security restrictions

How Applets and Applications Are Different

Although you explored the differences between Java applications and Java applets in the early part of this book, let's review them.

In short, Java applications are standalone Java programs that can be run by using just the Java interpreter, for example, from a command line. Most everything you've used up to this point in the book has been a Java application, albeit a simple one.

Java applets, however, are run from inside a World Wide Web browser. A reference to an applet is embedded in a Web page using a special HTML tag. When a reader, using a Java-enabled browser, loads a Web page with an applet in it, the browser downloads that applet from a Web server and executes it on the local system (the one the browser is running on). (The Java interpreter is built into the browser and runs the compiled Java class file from there.)

Because Java applets run inside a Java browser, they have access to the structure the browser provides: an existing window, an event-handling and graphics context, and the surrounding user interface. Java applications can also create this structure (allowing you to create graphical applications), but they don't require it (you'll learn how to create Java applications that use applet-like graphics and user interface (UI) features on Day 14, "Other Miscellaneous Tidbits").

Note that a single Java program can be written to operate as both a Java application and a Java applet. Although you use different procedures and rules to create applets and applications, none of those procedures or rules conflict with each other. The features specific to applets are ignored when the program runs as an application, and vice versa. Keep this point in mind as you design your own applets and applications.

One final significant difference between Java applets and applications—probably the biggest difference—is the set of restrictions placed on how applets can operate in the name of security. Given the fact that Java applets can be downloaded from any site on the World Wide Web and run on a client's system, Java-enabled browsers and tools limit what can be done to prevent a rogue applet from causing system damage or security breaches. Without these restrictions in place, Java applets could be written to contain viruses or Trojan horses (programs that seem friendly but do some sort of damage to the system), or be used to compromise the security of the system that runs them. The restrictions on applets include the following:

- ☐ Applets can't read or write to the reader's file system, which means they cannot delete files or test to see what programs you have installed on the hard drive.

- ☐ Applets can't communicate with any network server other than the one that had originally stored the applet, to prevent the applet from attacking another system from the reader's system.

- ☐ Applets can't run any programs on the reader's system. For UNIX systems, this restriction includes forking a process.

- ☐ Applets can't load programs native to the local platform, including shared libraries such as DLLs.

All these rules are true for Java applets running Netscape Navigator or Microsoft Internet Explorer. Other Java-enabled browsers or tools may allow you to configure the level of security you want—for example, the appletviewer tool in the JDK allows you to set an access control list for which directories an applet can read or write. However, as an applet developer, you can safely assume that most of your audience is going to be viewing your applets in a browser that implements the strictest rules for what an applet can do. Java applications have none of these restrictions.

Java 1.1 introduces a way for a Web user to trust an applet so that it can run without restriction on the user's system, just like an application. This method is described later today.

NOTE

> The security restrictions imposed on applets are sometimes called "the sandbox" (as in applets are only allowed to play in the sandbox and can go no further).

In addition to the applet restrictions listed, Java itself includes various forms of security and consistency checking in the Java compiler and interpreter for all Java programs to prevent unorthodox use of the language (you'll learn more about this issue on Day 21, "Under the Hood"). This combination of restrictions and security features makes it more difficult for a rogue Java applet to do damage to the client's system.

WARNING

These restrictions prevent all the traditional ways of causing damage to a client's system, but you cannot possibly be absolutely sure that a clever programmer cannot somehow work around these restrictions, violate privacy, use CPU resources, or just plain be annoying. Sun has asked the Net at large to try to break Java's security and to create an applet that can work around the restrictions imposed on it. In fact, several problems have been unearthed and fixed, usually relating to loading classes and to connecting to unauthorized sites. You'll learn about more issues in Java security on Day 21.

Applets in Java 1.02 Versus Java 1.1

Up to this point in the book, we haven't dealt very much with the differences between Java 1.02 and Java 1.1. That's about to change. For the next week, those differences will become very important, as many of them determine how you write your applets and how those applets will be distributed.

Java 1.1 is designed such that if you use none of the new features and stick to a 1.02 API, your programs will continue to run in a 1.02 environment. After you use a feature specific to Java 1.1, however, your applet or application will only run in a 1.1 environment.

For applets, that means that if you use 1.1 features you (or your users) can only run that applet in a browser that supports 1.1. At the time I'm writing this, Netscape has announced support for Java 1.1 in its Communicator product, but there is not yet a working version available. Neither Netscape 3.0 nor Microsoft Internet Explorer 3.0 will run applets written using Java 1.1 features.

If you intend to use Java 1.1 features in your applets, you can test those applets using the Sun appletviewer program that comes with the 1.1 JDK (and is available on the CD that comes with this book). If, by the time you're reading this, there are 1.1 browsers available, you can go ahead and use them for testing.

Keep in mind, however, that the Web itself contains a number of different kinds of browsers. Just because a 1.1 browser is available doesn't mean that your readers will all be running that browser. To keep older browsers in mind, you may want to provide multiple applets (for 1.1 and 1.02), write your applets to catch for missing methods in 1.02, or stick with the 1.02 API for a while longer to allow for 1.1 to catch on a bit more. If you're working on an intranet where you can be sure all your readers are using 1.1, this precaution isn't necessary.

Version 1.1 features are flagged throughout this book, so if you're already used to working in Java 1.02, you can tell which features are different in the newer version. In addition, a

8

number of method names have changed from 1.02 to 1.1. You can still use the old methods, but when you compile your programs, you'll get warnings about deprecated methods. Change over to the 1.1 API, and the warnings will disappear.

As part of the JDK, Sun provides a script for converting programs written to the old API to support the new API. The script is written in UNIX SED, so it works best on a UNIX system, although if you have a Windows environment that supports UNIX tools, you may be able to make it work there as well. The script simply replaces old methods with new methods; it will not add new features or rewrite the structure of your program.

For more information on converting your 1.02 programs to the new 1.1 API, see the page at

```
http://www.javasoft.com:80/products/jdk/1.1/docs/guide/awt/HowToUpgrade.html
```

Creating Applets

For the most part, all the Java programs you've created up to this point have been Java applications—simple programs with a single main() method that create objects, set instance variables, and run methods. Today and in the next few days, you'll be creating applets exclusively, so you will need a good grasp of how an applet works, the sorts of features an applet has, and where to start when you first create your own applets.

To create an applet, you create a subclass of the class Applet. The Applet class, part of the java.applet package, provides much of the behavior your applet needs to work inside a Java-enabled browser. Applets also take strong advantage of Java's Abstract Windowing Toolkit (AWT), which provides behavior for creating graphical user interface (GUI)-based applets and applications: drawing to the screen; creating windows, menu bars, buttons, check boxes, and other UI elements; and managing user input such as mouse clicks and keypresses. The AWT classes are part of the java.awt package.

Java's Abstract Windowing Toolkit (AWT) provides classes and behavior for creating GUI-based applications in Java. Applets make use of many of the capabilities in the AWT.

Although your applet can have as many additional "helper" classes as it needs, the main applet class actually triggers the execution of the applet. That initial applet class always has a signature like this:

```
public class myClass extends java.applet.Applet {
    ...
}
```

Note the public keyword. Java requires that your applet subclass be declared public. Again, this is true only of your main applet class; any helper classes you create do not necessarily need to be public. Public, private, and other forms of access control are described on Day 15, "Modifiers."

When a Java-enabled browser encounters your applet in a Web page, it loads your initial applet class over the network, as well as any other helper classes that first class uses, and runs the applet using the browser's built-in bytecode interpreter. Unlike with applications, where Java calls the main() method directly on your initial class, when your applet is loaded, Java creates an instance of the applet class, and a series of special applet methods are called on that instance. Different applets that use the same class use different instances, so each one can behave differently from the other applets running in the same browser.

Major Applet Activities

To create a basic Java application, your class has to have one method, main(), with a specific signature. Then, when your application runs, main() is found and executed, and from main() you can set up the behavior that your program needs to run. Applets are similar but more complicated—and, in fact, applets don't need a main() method at all. Applets have many different activities that correspond to various major events in the life cycle of the applet— for example, initialization, painting, and mouse events. Each activity has a corresponding method, so when an event occurs, the browser or other Java-enabled tool calls those specific methods.

The default implementations of these activity methods do nothing; to provide behavior for an event you must override the appropriate method in your applet's subclass. You don't have to override all of them, of course; different applet behavior requires different methods to be overridden.

You'll learn about the various important methods to override as the week progresses, but, for a general overview, here are five of the most important methods in an applet's execution: initialization, starting, stopping, destroying, and painting.

Initialization

Initialization occurs when the applet is first loaded (or reloaded), similarly to the main() method in applications. The initialization of an applet might include reading and parsing any parameters to the applet, creating any helper objects it needs, setting up an initial state, or loading images or fonts. To provide behavior for the initialization of your applet, override the init() method in your applet class:

```
public void init() {
    ...
}
```

Starting

After an applet is initialized, it is started. *Starting* is different from initialization because it can happen many different times during an applet's lifetime, whereas initialization happens only once. Starting can also occur if the applet was previously stopped. For example, an applet is stopped if the reader follows a link to a different page, and it is started again when the reader returns to this page. To provide startup behavior for your applet, override the `start()` method:

```
public void start() {
   ...
}
```

Functionality that you put in the `start()` method might include creating and starting up a thread to control the applet, sending the appropriate messages to helper objects, or in some way telling the applet to begin running. You'll learn more about starting applets on Day 10, "Animation, Images, Threads, and Sound."

Stopping

Stopping and starting go hand in hand. Stopping occurs when the reader leaves the page that contains a currently running applet, or you can stop the applet yourself by calling `stop()`. By default, when the reader leaves a page, any threads the applet had started will continue running. You'll learn more about threads on Day 10. By overriding `stop()`, you can suspend execution of these threads and then restart them if the applet is viewed again:

```
public void stop() {
   ...
}
```

Destroying

Destroying sounds more violent than it is. Destroying enables the applet to clean up after itself just before it is freed or the browser exits—for example, to stop and remove any running threads, close any open network connections, or release any other running objects. Generally, you won't want to override `destroy()` unless you have specific resources that need to be released—for example, threads that the applet has created. To provide clean-up behavior for your applet, override the `destroy()` method:

```
public void destroy() {
   ...
}
```

TECHNICAL NOTE

How is `destroy()` different from `finalize()`, which was described on Day 7, "More About Methods?" First, `destroy()` applies only to applets. Using `finalize()` is a more general-purpose way for a single object of any type to clean up after itself.

Painting

Painting is the way an applet actually draws something on the screen, be it text, a line, a colored background, or an image. Painting can occur many thousands of times during an applet's life cycle (for example, after the applet is initialized, if the browser is placed behind another window on the screen and then brought forward again, if the browser window is moved to a different position on the screen, or perhaps repeatedly, in the case of animation). You override the `paint()` method if your applet needs to have an actual appearance on the screen (that is, most of the time). The `paint()` method looks like this:

```
public void paint(Graphics g) {
    ...
}
```

Note that unlike the other major methods in this section, `paint()` takes an argument, an instance of the class `Graphics`. This object is created and passed to paint by the browser, so you don't have to worry about it. However, you will have to make sure that the `Graphics` class (part of the `java.awt` package) gets imported into your applet code, usually through an `import` statement at the top of your Java file:

```
import java.awt.Graphics;
```

A Simple Applet

Way back on Day 2, "Object-Oriented Programming and Java," you created a simple applet called `HelloAgainApplet` (this was the one with the big red `Hello Again`). There, you created and used that applet as an example of creating a subclass. Let's go over the code for that applet again, this time looking at it slightly differently in light of the things you just learned about applets. Listing 8.1 shows the code for that applet.

TYPE **Listing 8.1. The `HelloAgainApplet` applet.**

```
1:  import java.awt.Graphics;
2:  import java.awt.Font;
3:  import java.awt.Color;
4:
5:  public class HelloAgainApplet extends java.applet.Applet {
6:
```

```
7:      Font f = new Font("TimesRoman", Font.BOLD, 36);
8:
9:      public void paint(Graphics g) {
10:         g.setFont(f);
11:         g.setColor(Color.red);
12:         g.drawString("Hello again!", 5, 40);
13:     }
14: }
```

This applet implements the `paint()` method, one of the major methods described in the preceding section (actually, it overrides the default implementation of `paint()`, which does nothing). Because the applet doesn't actually do much (it just prints a couple words to the screen), and it doesn't really have anything to initialize, you don't need a `start()`, `stop()`, `init()`, or `destroy()` method.

The `paint()` method is the place where the real work of this applet (what little work goes on) really occurs. The `Graphics` object passed into the `paint()` method holds the graphics state for the applet—that is, the current features of the drawing surface, such as foreground and background colors or clipping area. Lines 10 and 11 set up the font and color for this graphics state (here, the font object held in the `f` instance variable and a `Color` object representing the color red).

Line 12 draws the string `"Hello Again!"` by using the current font and color at the position `5, 40`. Note that the `0` point for `x, y` is at the top left of the applet's drawing surface, with positive y moving downward, so `50` is actually at the bottom of the applet. Figure 8.1 shows how the applet's bounding box and the string are drawn on the page.

Figure 8.1.
Drawing the applet.

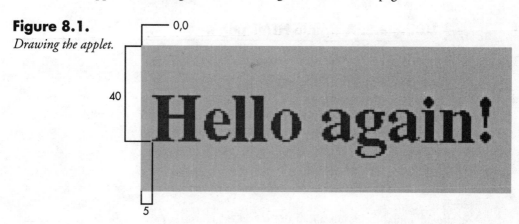

If you've been following along with all the examples up to this point, you might notice that something appears to be missing in this class: a `main()` method. As I mentioned in the section on the differences between applets and applications, applets don't need a `main()` method. If you implement the right applet methods in your class (`init()`, `start()`, `stop()`, `paint()`, and so on), your applet just seamlessly works without needing an explicit jumping-off point.

Including an Applet on a Web Page

After you create a class or classes that contain your applet and compile them into class files as you would any other Java program, you have to create a Web page that will hold that applet by using the HTML language. You use a special HTML tag for including applets in Web pages; Java-enabled browsers use the information contained in that tag to locate the compiled class files and execute the applet itself. In this section, you'll learn about how to put Java applets in a Web page and how to serve those files to the Web at large.

NOTE

The following section assumes that you have at least a passing understanding of writing HTML pages. If you need help in this area, you might find the book *Teach Yourself Web Publishing with HTML 3.2 in 14 Days* useful. It is also from Sams.net Publishing and also by Laura Lemay, the author of much of this book.

The `<APPLET>` Tag

To include an applet on a Web page, use the `<APPLET>` tag. `<APPLET>` is a special extension to HTML for including applets in Web pages. Listing 8.2 shows a simple example of a Web page with an applet included in it.

TYPE **Listing 8.2. A simple HTML page.**

```
 1: <HTML>
 2: <HEAD>
 3: <TITLE>This page has an applet on it</TITLE>
 4: </HEAD>
 5: <BODY>
 6: <P>My second Java applet says:
 7: <BR><APPLET CODE="HelloAgainApplet.class" WIDTH=200 HEIGHT=50>
 8: Hello Again!
 9: </APPLET>
10: </BODY>
11: </HTML>
```

You should note three points about the `<APPLET>` tag in this page:

☐ The CODE attribute indicates the name of the class file that contains this applet, including the `.class` extension. In this case, the class file must be in the same directory as this HTML file. To indicate applets are in a specific directory, use CODEBASE, described later today.

☐ WIDTH and HEIGHT are required and are used to indicate the bounding box of the applet—that is, how big a box to draw for the applet on the Web page. Be sure you set WIDTH and HEIGHT to be an appropriate size for the applet; depending on the browser, if your applet draws outside the boundaries of the space you've given it, you may not be able to see or get to those parts of the applet outside the bounding box.

☐ The text between the <APPLET> and </APPLET> tags is displayed by browsers that do not understand the <APPLET> tag (which includes most browsers that are not Java aware). Because your page may be viewed in many different kinds of browsers, including some sort of alternate text or HTML tags, here is a good idea so that readers of your page who don't have Java will see something other than a blank line. For example, you might show just an image or some other element. Here, you include a simple statement that says Hello Again!.

Note that the <APPLET> tag, like the <IMG> tag itself, is not a paragraph, so it should be enclosed inside a more general text tag, such as <P> or one of the heading tags (<H1>, <H2>, and so on).

Testing the Result

Now with a class file and an HTML file that refers to your applet, you should be able to load that HTML file into your Java-enabled browser from your local disk (in Netscape, choose File I Open File; in Internet Explorer, choose File I Open and then choose Browse to find the right file on your disk). The browser loads and parses your HTML file, and then loads and executes your applet class.

If you don't have a Java-enabled browser, tools often come with your development environment to help you test applets. In the JDK, the appletviewer application will test your applets. You won't see the Web page the applet is running on, but you can figure out if the applet is indeed running the way you expect it to.

Figure 8.2 shows the HelloAgainApplet applet running in Netscape.

Figure 8.2.

The HelloAgain- Applet *applet.*

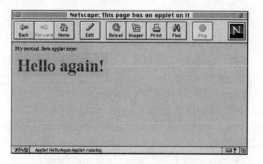

Making Java Applets Available to the Web

After you have an applet and an HTML file, and you've verified that everything is working correctly on your local system, the last step is to make that applet available to the World Wide Web at large so that anyone with a Java-enabled browser can view that applet.

Java applets are served by a Web server the same way that HTML files, images, and other media are. You don't need special server software to make Java applets available to the Web; you don't even need to configure your server to handle Java files. If you have a Web server up and running or space on a Web server available to you, all you have to do is move your HTML and compiled class files to that server, as you would any other file.

If you don't have a Web server, you have to rent space on one or set one up yourself. (Web server setup and administration, as well as other facets of Web publishing in general, are outside the scope of this book.)

More About the `<APPLET>` Tag

In its simplest form, by using CODE, WIDTH, and HEIGHT, the `<APPLET>` tag merely creates a space of the appropriate size and then loads and runs the applet in that space. The `<APPLET>` tag, however, does include several attributes that can help you better integrate your applet into the overall design of your Web page.

NOTE   The attributes available for the `<APPLET>` tag are almost identical to those for the HTML `<IMG>` tag.

ALIGN

The ALIGN attribute defines how the applet will be aligned on the page. This attribute can have one of nine values: LEFT, RIGHT, TOP, TEXTTOP, MIDDLE, ABSMIDDLE, BASELINE, BOTTOM, or ABSBOTTOM.

In the case of ALIGN=LEFT and ALIGN=RIGHT, the applet is placed at the left or right margin of the page, respectively, and all text following that applet flows in the space to the right or left of that applet. The text will continue to flow in that space until the end of the applet, or you can use a line break tag (`<BR>`) with the CLEAR attribute to start the left line of text below that applet. The CLEAR attribute can have one of three values: CLEAR=LEFT starts the text at the next clear left margin, CLEAR=RIGHT does the same for the right margin, and CLEAR=ALL starts the text at the next line where both margins are clear.

For example, here's a snippet of HTML code that aligns an applet against the left margin, has some text flowing alongside it, and then breaks at the end of the paragraph so that the next bit of text starts below the applet:

```
<P><APPLET CODE="HelloAgainApplet.class" WIDTH=200 HEIGHT=50
ALIGN=LEFT>Hello Again!</APPLET>
To the left of this paragraph is an applet. It's a
simple, unassuming applet, in which a small string is
printed in red type, set in 36 point Times bold.
<BR CLEAR=ALL>
<P>In the next part of the page, we demonstrate how
under certain conditions, styrofoam peanuts can be
used as a healthy snack.
```

Figure 8.3 shows how this applet and the text surrounding it might appear in a Java-enabled browser (I've lightened the default page background so you can see where the applet begins and the background ends).

Figure 8.3.
An applet aligned left.

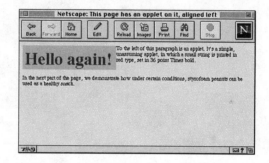

For smaller applets, you might want to include your applet within a single line of text. To do so, you can use one of the following seven values for ALIGN that determine how the applet is vertically aligned with the text:

☐ ALIGN=TEXTTOP aligns the top of the applet with the top of the tallest text in the line.

☐ ALIGN=TOP aligns the applet with the topmost item in the line (which may be another applet, or an image, or the top of the text).

☐ ALIGN=ABSMIDDLE aligns the middle of the applet with the middle of the largest item in the line.

☐ ALIGN=MIDDLE aligns the middle of the applet with the middle of the baseline of the text.

☐ ALIGN=BASELINE aligns the bottom of the applet with the baseline of the text. ALIGN=BASELINE is the same as ALIGN=BOTTOM, but ALIGN=BASELINE is a more descriptive name.

☐ ALIGN=ABSBOTTOM aligns the bottom of the applet with the lowest item in the line (which may be the baseline of the text or another applet or image).

Figure 8.4 shows the various alignment options, where the line is an image and the arrow is a small applet.

Figure 8.4.

Applet alignment options.

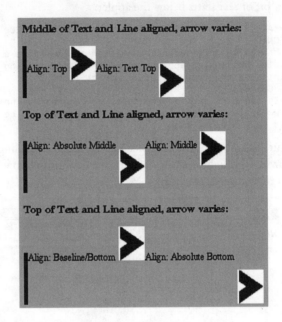

HSPACE **and** VSPACE

The HSPACE and VSPACE attributes are used to set the amount of space, in pixels, between an applet and its surrounding text. HSPACE controls the horizontal space (the space to the left and right of the applet). VSPACE controls the vertical space (the space above and below). For example, here's that sample snippet of HTML with vertical space of 50 and horizontal space of 10:

```
<P><APPLET CODE="HelloAgainApplet.class" WIDTH=300 HEIGHT=200
ALIGN=LEFT VSPACE=50 HSPACE=10>Hello Again!</APPLET>
To the left of this paragraph is an applet. It's a
simple, unassuming applet, in which a small string is
printed in red type, set in 36 point Times bold.
<BR CLEAR=ALL>
<P>In the next part of the page, we demonstrate how
under certain conditions, styrofoam peanuts can be
used as a healthy snack.
```

The result in a typical Java browser might look like that in Figure 8.5.

Figure 8.5.

*Vertical and
horizontal space.*

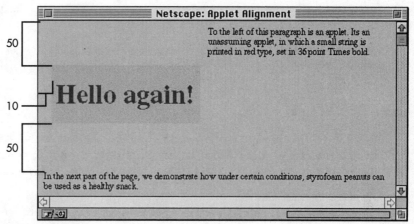

CODE **and** CODEBASE

The final two attributes to note in <APPLET> are CODE and CODEBASE. Unlike the other attributes, neither of them has anything to do with the applet's appearance on the page; these two refer to the actual location of the Java applet file so that the Java-enabled browser can find it.

CODE is used to indicate the name of the class file that holds the current applet. If CODE is used alone in the <APPLET> tag, the class file is searched for in the same directory as the HTML file that references it. Note that class filenames used in CODE have the .class extension; this is different from the Java command-line interpreter, which doesn't use the extension.

If you want to store your class files in a different directory on your Web server than that of your HTML files, you have to tell the browser where to find those class files. To do so, you use CODEBASE. CODE contains only the name of the class file; CODEBASE contains an alternative pathname (actually a URL or relative pathname) where classes are contained. For example, if you store your class files in a directory called classes, which is in the same directory as your HTML files, CODEBASE is the following:

```
<APPLET CODE="MyClass.class" CODEBASE="classes"
WIDTH=100 HEIGHT=100></APPLET>
```

If you store all your Java classes in some central location, you can also use a URL in CODEBASE:

```
<APPLET CODE="MyClass.class" CODEBASE="http://myserver.com/javaclasses"
WIDTH=100 HEIGHT=100></APPLET>
```

What if your class files are actually stored on an entirely different server altogether? You can use that URL in CODEBASE as well:

```
<APPLET CODE="MyClass.class" CODEBASE="http://www.joesserver.com/javaclasses"
WIDTH=100 HEIGHT=100></APPLET>
```

Java Archives

The standard way of placing a Java applet on a Web page is to use <APPLET> to indicate the primary class file of the applet. A Java-enabled browser will then download and run the applet. Any other classes and other files needed by the applet are downloaded from the Web server.

The problem with running applets in this way is that every single file an applet needs—be it another helper class, image, audio file, text file, or anything else—is a separate connection the browser has to make to the server. Because a fair amount of time is needed just to make the connection itself, connecting this way can increase the amount of time it takes to download your applet and everything it needs.

The solution to this problem is a Java archive, or JAR file. A Java archive is a collection of Java classes and other files packaged into a single file. By using a Java archive, the browser makes only one connection to the server rather than several. By reducing the number of files the browser has to load from the server, you can download and run your applet that much faster. Java archives may also be compressed, making the overall file size smaller and therefore faster to download as well (although it may take some time on the browser side for the files to be decompressed before they can run).

Java 1.1 includes support for JAR files; the JDK includes a tool called jar that can pack files into Java archives and also unpack them. JAR files can be compressed using the zip format or packed without using compression. The following command packs all of a directory's class and GIF image files into a single Java archive called Animate.jar:

```
jar cf Animate.jar *.class *.gif
```

The argument cf specifies two command-line options that can be used when running the jar program. The c option indicates that a Java archive file should be created, and f indicates that the name of the archive file will follow as one of the next arguments. Run jar without any arguments to see a list of options that can be used.

8

After you create a Java archive, the ARCHIVES attribute is used with the `<APPLET>` tag to show where the archive can be found. You can use Java archives with an applet with tags such as the following:

```
<applet code="Animate.class" archives="Animate.jar" width=460 height=160>
</applet>
```

This tag specifies that an archive called `Animate.jar` contains files used by the applet. Browsers and browsing tools that support JAR files will look inside the archive for files that are needed as the applet runs.

WARNING

> Although a Java archive can contain class files, the ARCHIVES attribute does not remove the need for the CODE attribute. A browser still needs to know the name of the applet's main class file in order to load it.

Other Archival Formats

Before Java's developers introduced the JAR file format, both Netscape and Microsoft offered their own archival solutions. They do not offer some of the advantages of Java archives, but they have the benefit of working with Java-enabled browsers that do not yet support Java 1.1.

Current versions of Netscape's Web browsers support the use of zip archives with the ARCHIVE attribute, but they can be used only for class files, not images or other types of files that an applet might need. Within Netscape, you can use the ARCHIVE attribute to indicate the name of the archive, like this:

```
<APPLET CODE="MyApplet.class" ARCHIVE="appletstuff.zip" WIDTH=100 HEIGHT=100>
</APPLET>
```

The archive itself is an uncompressed zip file. Standard zip files, which use some form of compression to make the file smaller, are not recognized. Also, helper classes may be contained inside or outside the zip file; Netscape browsers will look in either place. The ARCHIVE attribute is ignored by browsers or applet viewers that may run across this Web page.

Microsoft Internet Explorer recognizes a third type of archive format for the delivery of Java applets: the CAB file. CAB is short for cabinet, and it's a way to group files together and compress them for faster delivery over the Web.

Cabinet archives are created with a tool from Microsoft called CABarc. It currently is available for free download from the following address:

```
http://www.microsoft.com/workshop/java/cab-f.htm
```

Using CABarc, you can compress all class files and other files needed by an applet into a single archive, which has the .cab file extension. To specify this archive, a parameter called cabbase is used with the <PARAM> tag in HTML, and the value of cabbase is set to the name of the .cab file. The following is an example:

```
<APPLET CODE="DanceFever.class" WIDTH=200 HEIGHT=450>
<PARAM NAME="cabbase" VALUE="DanceFever.cab">
</APPLET>
```

Like the ARCHIVE attribute, the cabbase parameter will be ignored by Web browsers that do not support its use.

Netscape and Microsoft's Java archival features were introduced prior to the release of Java 1.1, so they work on the current editions of these companies' Web browsers and perhaps others. If you use either solution, you ought to store both the archive and the individual files that comprise the archive on your Web server. This way, everyone with a Java-enabled browser will be able to use the applet.

Using Digital Signatures to Identify Applets

One of the fundamental assumptions of Java's applet security strategy is that you can't trust anyone on the World Wide Web. Such thinking might sound cynical, but what it means in practice is this: Java security assumes that someone might try to write malicious applets, so it prevents anything malicious from being attempted. As a result, any language feature that has potential for abuse has been blocked from use in applets.

Java 1.1 makes it possible for applets to do everything that a Java application can do—but only if they come from a trusted applet provider and are digitally signed to verify their authenticity. A *digital signature* is an encrypted file or files that accompany a program indicating exactly who it came from. Users, armed with the knowledge of who produced a program, can decide whether that group or individual should be trusted. People who are familiar with ActiveX controls will recognize this system—it's similar to how ActiveX programs are made available on World Wide Web pages.

Future versions of the JDK will make it possible to establish different levels of security other than complete trust (an applet can do anything) or no trust (an applet can't do anything that might be damaging).

For now, all applets will be fully restricted unless a user goes through the process of manually establishing that a programmer is trustworthy.

8

Because none of the commonly available Web browsers support JDK 1.1's new security model yet, the procedure for signing applets and offering these programs to users is still in an early stage of development. This section is based on the tools that have been made available to date and JavaSoft documentation on how the process will work.

You might find understanding the applet-trusting process easier if you use these three fictional entities: an applet developer called Fishhead Software, a Java industry group called Signatures 'R' Us, and a Web user named Gilbert.

Fishhead Software offers a game applet on its Web site that saves high scores and other information on the user's hard drive. This capability isn't possible normally with an applet—disk access is a definite no-no. For the game to be playable, Fishhead must digitally sign the applet and enable users to establish Fishhead as a trusted programmer.

This process has five steps:

1. Fishhead Software uses javakey, a tool that comes with the JDK, to create two encrypted files called a *public key* and a *private key*. Together, these keys are an electronic "ID card" that fully identifies the company. Fishhead makes sure its private key is hidden from anyone else. It can—and should—make its public key available to anyone as a partial form of ID.

2. Fishhead Software needs an entity that can verify who it is. It sends its public key and a descriptive file about Fishhead Software to an independent group that Java users are likely to trust—Signatures 'R' Us.

3. Signatures 'R' Us checks out Fishhead Software to see that it's a legitimate group with the same public key that was sent to Signatures 'R' Us. When Fishhead passes muster, Signatures 'R' Us creates a new encrypted file called a *certificate*. It is sent back to Fishhead.

4. Fishhead creates a Java archive file that contains its game applet and all related files. With a public key, private key, and a certificate, Fishhead Software can now use the jar tool to digitally sign the archive file.

5. Fishhead puts the signed archive on the Web site along with a way to download its public key.

Following this process is all that Fishhead Software needs to do to make the applet available to anyone who trusts the company enough to run it over the Web. One of the people who decides to trust Fishhead is a Web user named Gilbert, who has a Java 1.1-enabled browser.

His process is simpler:

1. Gilbert realizes that he can't run Fishhead's new game applet without establishing the company as a trustworthy programmer. He downloads Fishhead's public key.
2. Deciding that Fishhead is an organization he can trust, Gilbert uses javakey along with Fishhead's public key to add the company to his system's list of trusted programmers.

Now Gilbert can play Fishhead's game applet to his heart's content. It can do anything on his system that a Java application could. This means that malicious or unintentionally damaging code can be executed on Gilbert's system, but this is also true of any software that he could install and run on his computer. The advantage of a digital signature is that the programmers are clearly identified. Ask yourself how many virus writers would distribute their work under any kind of system that provided a trail of digital crumbs leading straight to their house.

One aspect of the new Java security model you might be unclear about is why you have a public key and a private key. If they can be used together to identify someone, how can the public key alone be used as an ID for Fishhead?

A public key and a private key are a matched set. Because they fully identify Fishhead Software, that entity is the only one that has access to both keys. Otherwise, someone else could pretend to be Fishhead, and no one could tell it was a fake. If Fishhead protects its private key, it protects its identity and reputation.

When Signatures 'R' Us uses a public key to verify Fishhead's identity, its main function is to make sure the public key really belongs to the company. Because public keys can be given to anyone, Fishhead can make its public key available on its Web site. As part of its certification process, Signatures 'R' Us could download this public key and compare it to the one it received. The certifying group acts as a substitute of sorts for the private key, verifying that the public key is legitimate. The certificate that is issued is linked to the public key, which can be used only with Fishhead's private key.

Anyone can issue a certificate for a public key using the javakey tool—Fishhead Software could even certify itself. However, doing so would make it much harder for users to trust the company than if a well-established, independent certification group was used.

Working together, the public key, private key, and certificate can create a reliable digital signature for a Java archive. JavaSoft documentation for javakey, jar applet signing, and other new security features are available from the following Web address:

```
http://www.javasoft.com/products/JDK/1.1/docs/guide/security
```

Passing Parameters to Applets

With Java applications, you pass parameters to your main() routine by using arguments on the command line or, for Macintoshes, in the Java Runner's dialog box. You can then parse those arguments inside the body of your class, and the application acts accordingly, based on the arguments it is given.

Applets, however, don't have a command line. How do you pass in different arguments to an applet? Applets can get different input from the HTML file that contains the <APPLET> tag through the use of applet parameters. To set up and handle parameters in an applet, you need these two pieces:

- ☐ A special parameter tag in the HTML file
- ☐ Code in your applet to parse those parameters

Applet parameters come in two parts: a parameter name, which is simply a name you pick, and a value, which is the actual value of that particular parameter. So, for example, you can indicate the color of text in an applet by using a parameter with the name color and the value red. You can determine an animation's speed using a parameter with the name speed and the value 5.

In the HTML file that contains the embedded applet, you indicate each parameter using the <PARAM> tag, which has two attributes for the name and the value, called (surprisingly enough) NAME and VALUE. The <PARAM> tag goes inside the opening and closing <APPLET> tags:

```
<APPLET CODE="MyApplet.class" WIDTH=100 HEIGHT=100>
<PARAM NAME=font VALUE="TimesRoman">
<PARAM NAME=size VALUE="36">
A Java applet appears here.</APPLET>
```

This particular example defines two parameters to the MyApplet applet: one whose name is font and whose value is TimesRoman, and one whose name is size and whose value is 36.

Parameters are passed to your applet when it is loaded. In the init() method for your applet, you can then get hold of those parameters by using the getParameter() method. getParameter() takes one argument—a string representing the name of the parameter you're looking for—and returns a string containing the corresponding value of that parameter. (Like arguments in Java applications, all the parameter values are strings.) To get the value of the font parameter from the HTML file, you might have a line such as this in your init() method:

```
String theFontName = getParameter("font");
```

NOTE

The names of the parameters as specified in `<PARAM>` and the names of the parameters in `getParameter()` must match identically, including having the same case. In other words, `<PARAM NAME="Geraldo">` is different from `<PARAM NAME="geraldo">`. If your parameters are not being properly passed to your applet, make sure the parameter cases match.

Note that if a parameter you expect has not been specified in the HTML file, `getParameter()` returns `null`. Most often, you will want to test for a `null` parameter in your Java code and supply a reasonable default:

```
if (theFontName == null)
theFontName = "Courier"
```

Keep in mind that `getParameter()` returns strings—if you want a parameter to be some other object or type, you have to convert it yourself. To parse the `size` parameter from that same HTML file and assign it to an integer variable called `theSize`, you might use the following lines:

```
int theSize;
String s = getParameter("size");
if (s == null)
theSize = 12;
else theSize = Integer.parseInt(s);
```

Get it? Not yet? Let's create an example of an applet that uses this technique. You'll modify the `Hello Again` applet so that it says hello to a specific name, for example, `"Hello Kukla"` or `"Hello Fran"`. The name is passed into the applet through an HTML parameter.

Start by copying the original `HelloAgainApplet` class and calling it `MoreHelloAgain`, as shown in Listing 8.3.

TYPE **Listing 8.3. The `MoreHelloAgain` applet.**

```
 1:import java.awt.Graphics;
 2:import java.awt.Font;
 3:import java.awt.Color;
 4:
 5:public class MoreHelloApplet extends java.applet.Applet {
 6:
 7:    Font f = new Font("TimesRoman", Font.BOLD, 36);
 8:
 9:    public void paint(Graphics g) {
10:        g.setFont(f);
11:        g.setColor(Color.red);
12:        g.drawString("Hello Again!", 5, 40);
13:    }
14:}
```

The first thing you need to add to this class is a place to hold the name of the person you're saying hello to. Because you'll need that name throughout the applet, add an instance variable for the name, just after the variable for the font in line 7:

```
String name;
```

To set a value for the name, you have to get that parameter from the HTML file. The best place to handle parameters to an applet is inside an init() method. The init() method is defined similarly to paint() (public, with no arguments, and a return type of void). When you test for a parameter, make sure that you test for a value of null. The default, in this case, if a name isn't indicated, is to say hello to "Laura". Add the init() method in between your instance variable definitions and the definition for paint(), just before line 9:

```
public void init() {
name = getParameter("name");
if (name == null)
    name = "Laura";
}
```

Now that you have the name from the HTML parameters, you'll need to modify it so that it's a complete string—that is, to tack the word Hello with a space onto the beginning, and an exclamation point onto the end. You could make this change in the paint() method just before printing the string to the screen, but that would mean creating a new string every time the applet is painted. It would be much more efficient to do it just once, right after getting the name itself, in the init() method. Add this line to the init() method just before the last brace:

```
name = "Hello " + name + "!";
```

And now, all that's left is to modify the paint() method to use the new name parameter. The original drawString() method looked like this:

```
g.drawString("Hello Again!", 5, 40);
```

To draw the new string you have stored in the name instance variable, all you need to do is substitute that variable for the literal string:

```
g.drawString(name, 5, 40);
```

Listing 8.4 shows the final result of the MoreHelloApplet class. Compile it so that you have a class file ready.

TYPE   **Listing 8.4. The MoreHelloApplet class.**

```
1:  import java.awt.Graphics;
2:  import java.awt.Font;
3:  import java.awt.Color;
4:
```

continues

Listing 8.4. continued

```
5:   public class MoreHelloApplet extends java.applet.Applet {
6:
7:       Font f = new Font("TimesRoman", Font.BOLD, 36);
8:       String name;
9:
10:      public void init() {
11:          name = getParameter("name");
12:          if (name == null)
13:              name = "Laura";
14:
15:          name = "Hello " + name + "!";
16:      }
17:
18:      public void paint(Graphics g) {
19:          g.setFont(f);
20:          g.setColor(Color.red);
21:          g.drawString(name, 5, 40);
22:      }
23: }
```

Now let's create the HTML file that contains this applet. Listing 8.5 shows a new Web page for the MoreHelloApplet applet.

TYPE   **Listing 8.5. The HTML file for the MoreHelloApplet applet.**

```
1:  <HTML>
2:  <HEAD>
3:  <TITLE>Hello!</TITLE>
4:  </HEAD>
5:  <BODY>
6:  <P>
7:  <APPLET CODE="MoreHelloApplet.class" WIDTH=200 HEIGHT=50>
8:  <PARAM NAME=name VALUE="Bonzo">
9:  Hello to whoever you are!
10: </APPLET>
11: </BODY>
12: </HTML>
```

Note the <APPLET> tag, which points to the class file for the applet and has the appropriate width and height (200 and 50). Just below it (line 8) is the <PARAM> tag, which you use to pass in the value for the name. Here, the NAME parameter is simply name, and the VALUE is the string "Bonzo".

Loading up this HTML file in Netscape Navigator produces the result shown in Figure 8.6.

Figure 8.6.

The result of using MoreHelloApplet *the first time.*

Let's try a second example. Remember that in the code for MoreHelloApplet, if no name is specified in a parameter, the default is the name Laura. Listing 8.6 creates an HTML file with no parameter tag for name.

TYPE **Listing 8.6. Another HTML file for the MoreHelloApplet applet.**

```
 1: <HTML>
 2: <HEAD>
 3: <TITLE>Hello!</TITLE>
 4: </HEAD>
 5: <BODY>
 6: <P>
 7: <APPLET CODE="MoreHelloApplet.class" WIDTH=200 HEIGHT=50>
 8: Hello to whoever you are!
 9: </APPLET>
10: </BODY>
11: </HTML>
```

Here, because no name was supplied, the applet uses the default, and the result is what you might expect, as you can see in Figure 8.7.

Figure 8.7.

The result of using MoreHelloApplet *the second time.*

Summary

Applets are probably the most common use of the Java language today. They are more complicated than many Java applications because they are executed and drawn inline within Web pages, but they can access the graphics, user interface, and event structure provided by the Web browser itself. Today you learned the basics of creating applets, including the following points:

☐ All applets you develop using Java inherit from the Applet class, which is part of the java.applet package. The Applet class provides basic behavior for how the applet will be integrated with and react to the browser and various forms of input from that browser and the person running it. By subclassing Applet, you have access to all that behavior.

☐ Applets have five main methods, which are used for the basic activities an applet performs during its life cycle: init(), start(), stop(), destroy(), and paint(). Although you don't need to override all these methods, they are the most common methods you'll see repeated in many of the applets you'll create in this book and in other sample programs.

☐ To run a compiled applet class file, you include it in an HTML Web page by using the <APPLET> tag. When a Java-capable browser comes across <APPLET>, it loads and runs the applet described in that tag. To publish Java applets on the World Wide Web alongside HTML files, you don't need special server software; any plain old Web server will do just fine.

☐ To speed up downloading of an applet as it loads on a Web page, you can consider three possible solutions: Java archive files, which work for Java 1.1-enabled browsers and can compress all files an applet requires into a single archive; Netscape Navigator's zip archives, which work only for class files and do not handle any compression; and Microsoft's Cabinet files, which work like Java's archive files for current Internet Explorer users.

☐ Java 1.1 makes it possible to digitally sign applets so that users can elect to run them without any security restrictions. This capability involves the use of the javakey tool to create and use encrypted public key, private key, and certificate files, and the jar tool to digitally sign a Java archive.

☐ Unlike applications, applets do not have a command line on which to pass arguments, so those arguments must be passed into the applet through the HTML file that contains it. You indicate parameters in an HTML file by using the <PARAM> tag inside the opening and closing <APPLET> tags. <PARAM> has two attributes: NAME for the name of the parameter and VALUE for its value. Inside the body of your applet (usually in init()), you can then gain access to those parameters using the getParameter() method.

Q&A

Q If I can't read or write files or run programs on the system the applet is running on, doesn't that mean I basically can't do anything other than simple animation and flashy graphics? How can I save state in an applet? How can I create, say, a word processor or a spreadsheet as a Java applet?

A For everyone who doesn't believe that Java is secure enough, you can find someone who believes that Java's security restrictions are too severe for just these reasons. Yes, Java applets are limited because of the security restrictions. But, given the possibility for abuse, I believe that erring on the side of being more conservative is better as far as security is concerned.

Through digitally signed applets, more sophisticated features can be offered on Web pages than were possible prior to Java 1.1. The trade-off is that users must trust the applet publisher, and only time will tell how effective this security system is at balancing the safety of a user's system with the desire to run fully featured applets.

Q I noticed in my documentation that the `<APPLET>` tag also has a `NAME` attribute. You didn't discuss it here.

A `NAME` is used when you have multiple applets on a page that need to communicate with each other. You'll learn about this attribute on Day 11, "Managing Simple Events and Interactivity."

Q Lots of the applet examples I've seen on the Web have an `init()` method that does nothing to call a `resize()` method with the same values as in the `<APPLET>` tag's `WIDTH` and `HEIGHT`. I asked a friend about that, and he said that you have to have `resize()` in there to make sure the applet's the right size. You don't mention `resize()`.

A The call to the `resize()` method in `init()` is left over from the early days of applets when you did need `resize()` to set the initial size of the applet. These days, only the `WIDTH` and `HEIGHT` attributes do that; calling `resize()` isn't necessary.

Q I'm using Netscape 2.0 on Windows, and I can't put text and an applet next to each other, as you described in the section on `ALIGN`. What am I doing wrong?

A Nothing. Netscape 2.0 on Windows has a bug that prevents `ALIGN` from working right on Windows. Upgrade to Netscape 3.0 or higher and the problem will go away.

Q I have an applet that takes parameters and an HTML file that passes it those parameters. But when my applet runs, all I get are null values. What's going on here?

A Do the names of your parameters (in the NAME attribute) match exactly with the names you're testing for in getParameter()? They must be exact, including case, for the match to be made. Make sure also that your <PARAM> tags are inside the opening and closing <APPLET> tags and that you haven't misspelled anything.

Q **Because applets don't have a command line or a stdout stream, how can you do simple debugging output like System.out.println() in an applet?**

A You can. Depending on your browser or other Java-enabled environment, you may have a console window where debugging output (the result of System.out.println()) appears, or it may be saved to a log file (Netscape has a Java Console under the Options menu; Internet Explorer uses a Java log file that you must enable by choosing Options | Advanced). You can continue to print messages using System.out.println() in your applets—just remember to remove them after you're done so that they don't confuse your actual readers!

Day 9

Graphics, Fonts, and Color

by Laura Lemay

Knowing the basics of how applets work is only the first step. The next step is to become familiar with the capabilities Java gives you for drawing to the screen, updating the screen dynamically, managing mouse and keyboard events, and creating user interface elements. You'll perform all these tasks this week. You'll start today with how to draw to the screen—that is, how to produce lines and shapes with the built-in graphics primitives, how to print text using fonts, and how to use and modify color in your applets. Today you'll learn, specifically, the following:

☐ How the graphics system works in Java: the Graphics class, the coordinate system used to draw to the screen, and how applets paint and repaint

☐ How to use the Java graphics primitives, including drawing and filling lines, rectangles, ovals, and arcs

☐ How to create and use fonts, including how to draw characters and strings and how to find out the metrics of a given font for better layout

☐ All about color in Java, including the Color class, setting the foreground (drawing) and background colors for your applet, and using the color scheme of your computer's windowing system

NOTE

Today and for the rest of this week, you'll get an introduction to many of the classes that make up the Java class libraries, in particular the classes in the java.awt package. Keep in mind, however, that I have the space to give you only an introduction to these classes; many other capabilities that you can use in your own programs are available to you in these classes, depending on what you're trying to accomplish. After you finish this book (and perhaps after each of these lessons), you'll want to familiarize yourself with the classes themselves and what they can do. Be sure to check out the Java API documentation for more details; you can find that API documentation on the JavaSoft Web site at http://www.javasoft.com/products/JDK/1.1/docs/.

The Graphics **Class**

With the basic graphics capabilities built into Java's class libraries, you can draw lines, shapes, characters, and images to the screen inside your applet. Most of the graphics operations in Java are methods defined in the Graphics class. You don't have to create an instance of Graphics to draw something in your applet; in your applet's paint() method (which you learned about yesterday), you are given a Graphics object. By drawing on that object, you draw onto your applet and the results appear onscreen.

The Graphics class is part of the java.awt package, so if your applet does any painting (as it usually will), make sure you import that class at the beginning of your Java file:

```
import java.awt.Graphics;

public class MyClass extends java.applet.Applet {
    ...
}
```

The Graphics Coordinate System

To draw an object on the screen, you call one of the drawing methods available in the Graphics class. All the drawing methods have arguments representing endpoints, corners, or starting locations of the object as values in the applet's coordinate system—for example, a line starts at the point 10,10 and ends at the point 20,20.

Java's coordinate system has the origin (0,0) in the top-left corner. Positive x values are to the right and positive y values are downward. All pixel values are integers; there are no partial or fractional pixels. Figure 9.1 shows how you might draw a simple square by using this coordinate system.

Figure 9.1.

The Java graphics coordinate system.

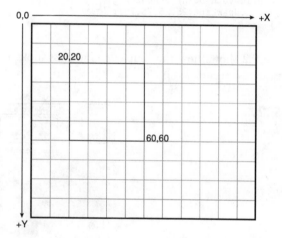

Java's coordinate system is different from that of many painting and layout programs, which have their x and y in the bottom left. If you're not used to working with this upside-down graphics system, getting familiar with it may take some practice.

Drawing and Filling

The Graphics class provides a set of simple built-in graphics primitives for drawing, including lines, rectangles, polygons, ovals, and arcs.

NOTE

Bitmap images, such as GIF files, can also be drawn by using the Graphics class. You'll learn about these images tomorrow.

Lines

To draw straight lines, use the drawLine() method. drawLine() takes four arguments: the x and y coordinates of the starting point and the x and y coordinates of the ending point. So, for example, the following MyLine class draws a line from the point 25,25 to the point 75,75. Note that the drawLine() method is defined in the Graphics class (as are all the other graphics methods you'll learn about today). Here you're using that method for the current graphics context stored in the variable g:

```java
import java.awt.Graphics;

public class MyLine extends java.applet.Applet {
    public void paint(Graphics g) {
        g.drawLine(25,25,75,75);
    }
}
```

Figure 9.2 shows how the simple MyLine class looks in a Java-enabled browser such as Netscape Navigator.

Figure 9.2.

Drawing lines.

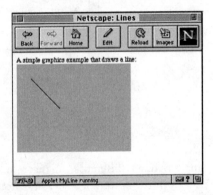

Rectangles

The Java graphics primitives provide not just one, but three kinds of rectangles:

☐ Plain rectangles

☐ Rounded rectangles, which are rectangles with rounded corners

☐ Three-dimensional rectangles, which are drawn with a shaded border

For each of these rectangles, you can choose from two methods: one that draws the rectangle in outline form and one that draws the rectangle filled with color.

To draw a plain rectangle, use either the drawRect() or fillRect() methods. Both take four arguments: the x and y coordinates of the top-left corner of the rectangle and the width and height of the rectangle to draw. For example, the following class (`MyRect`) draws two squares: The left one is an outline and the right one is filled. Figure 9.3 shows the result.

```java
import java.awt.Graphics;

public class MyRect extends java.applet.Applet {
    public void paint(Graphics g) {
        g.drawRect(20,20,60,60);
        g.fillRect(120,20,60,60);
    }
}
```

Figure 9.3.

Rectangles.

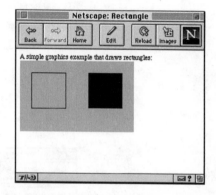

Rounded rectangles are, as you might expect, rectangles with rounded corners. The `drawRoundRect()` and `fillRoundRect()` methods to draw rounded rectangles are similar to those for regular rectangles except that rounded rectangles have two extra arguments for the width and height of the angle of the corners. Those two arguments determine how far along the edges of the rectangle the arc for the corner will start; the first for the angle along the horizontal plane, the second for the vertical. Larger values for the angle width and height make the overall rectangle more rounded; values equal to the width and height of the rectangle itself produce a circle. Figure 9.4 shows some examples of rounded corners.

The following is a `paint()` method inside a class called `MyRRect` that draws two rounded rectangles: one as an outline with a rounded corner 10 pixels square; the other, filled, with a rounded corner 20 pixels square. Figure 9.5 shows the resulting squares.

```java
import java.awt.Graphics;

public class MyRRect extends java.applet.Applet {
    public void paint(Graphics g) {
        g.drawRoundRect(20,20,60,60,10,10);
        g.fillRoundRect(120,20,60,60,20,20);
    }
}
```

Figure 9.4.
Rounded corners.

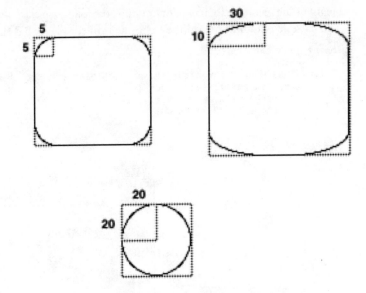

Figure 9.5.
Rounded rectangles.

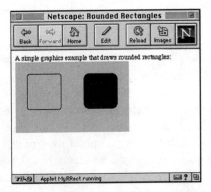

Polygons

Polygons are shapes with an unlimited number of sides. To draw a polygon, you need a set of x and y coordinates. The polygon is then drawn as a set of straight lines from the first point to the second, the second to the third, and so on.

As with rectangles, you can draw an outline or a filled polygon (using the `drawPolygon()` and `fillPolygon()` methods, respectively). You also have a choice of how you want to indicate the list of coordinates—either as arrays of x and y coordinates or as an instance of the `Polygon` class.

Using the first way of drawing polygons, the `drawPolygon()` and `fillPolygon()` methods take three arguments:

- ☐ An array of integers representing x coordinates
- ☐ An array of integers representing y coordinates
- ☐ An integer for the total number of points

The x and y arrays should, of course, have the same number of elements.

The following is an example of drawing a polygon's outline using this method. Figure 9.6 shows the result.

```java
import java.awt.Graphics;

public class MyPoly extends java.applet.Applet {
    public void paint(Graphics g) {
        int exes[] = { 39,94,97,142,53,58,26 };
        int whys[] = { 33,74,36,70,108,80,106 };
        int pts = exes.length;

        g.drawPolygon(exes,whys,pts);
    }
}
```

Figure 9.6.

A polygon.

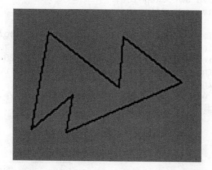

Note that Java automatically closes the polygon. If you want to leave the shape incomplete for an unfilled polygon, you have to use the `drawPolyline()` method described at the end of this section.

WARNING

The fact that Java automatically closes the polygon represents a change from prior versions of the Java language. Under version 1.02, you had to repeat the starting point to make the `drawPolygon()` method close the polygon, and `fillPolygon()` automatically closed the polygon. The `drawPolyline()` method is newly introduced with Java 1.1.

The second way of calling drawPolygon() and fillPolygon() is to use a Polygon object to store the individual points of the polygon. The Polygon class is useful if you intend to add points to the polygon or if you're building the polygon on-the-fly. Using the Polygon class, you can treat the polygon as an object rather than have to deal with individual arrays.

To create a Polygon object, you can either first create an empty polygon

```
Polygon poly = new Polygon();
```

or create a polygon from a set of points using integer arrays, as in the previous example:

```
int exes[] = { 39,94,97,142,53,58,26 };
int whys[] = { 33,74,36,70,108,80,106 };
int pts = exes.length;
Polygon poly = new Polygon(exes,whys,pts);
```

After you have a Polygon object, you can add points to the polygon as you need to:

```
poly.addPoint(20,35);
```

Then, to draw the polygon, just use the polygon object as an argument to drawPolygon() or fillPolygon(). Here's that previous example, rewritten this time with a Polygon object. You'll also fill this polygon rather than just drawing its outline. Figure 9.7 shows the output.

```
import java.awt.Graphics;
import java.awt.Polygon;

public class MyPoly2 extends java.applet.Applet {
    public void paint(Graphics g) {
        int exes[] = { 39,94,97,142,53,58,26 };
        int whys[] = { 33,74,36,70,108,80,106 };
        int pts = exes.length;
        Polygon poly = new Polygon(exes,whys,pts);
        g.fillPolygon(poly);
    }
}
```

Figure 9.7.

Another polygon.

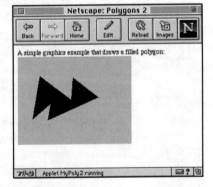

The drawPolyLine() method, which is used to draw unclosed polygons, works exactly like the first polygon-drawing example of this section. You specify two integer arrays that contain the x and y coordinates of each point and another integer to specify the number of points.

The following example draws an incomplete polygon. Figure 9.8 shows the result.

```java
import java.awt.Graphics;

public class MyPoly3 extends java.applet.Applet {
    public void paint(Graphics g) {
        int exes[] = { 39,94,97,142,53,58,26 };
        int whys[] = { 33,74,36,70,108,80,106 };
        int pts = exes.length;

        g.drawPolyline(exes,whys,pts);
    }
}
```

Figure 9.8.

An incomplete polygon.

Ovals

You use ovals to draw ellipses or circles. Ovals are just like rectangles with overly rounded corners. You draw them using four arguments: the x and y of the top corner, and the width and height of the oval itself. Note that because you're drawing an oval, the starting point is some distance to the left and up from the actual outline of the oval itself. Again, if you think of it as a rectangle, placing it is easier.

As with the other drawing operations, the drawOval() method draws an outline of an oval, and the fillOval() method draws a filled oval.

The following example draws two ovals—a circle and an ellipse. Figure 9.9 shows how these two ovals appear onscreen.

```java
import java.awt.Graphics;
```

```
public class MyOval extends java.applet.Applet {
    public void paint(Graphics g) {
    g.drawOval(20,20,60,60);
    g.fillOval(120,20,100,60);
    }
}
```

Figure 9.9.

A circle and an ellipse.

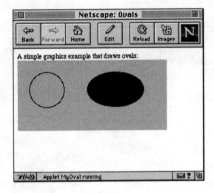

Arcs

Of all the shapes you can construct using methods in the `Graphics` class, arcs are the most complex to construct, which is why I saved them for last. An arc is a part of an oval; in fact, the easiest way to think of an arc is as a section of a complete oval. Figure 9.10 shows some arcs.

Figure 9.10.

Arcs.

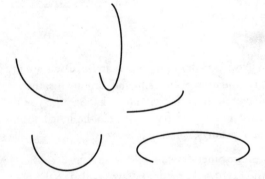

The `drawArc()` method takes six arguments: the starting corner, the width and height, the angle at which to start the arc, and the degrees to draw it before stopping. Once again, you have a `drawArc` method to draw the arc's outline and the `fillArc()` method to fill the arc. Filled arcs are drawn as if they were sections of a pie; instead of joining the two endpoints, both endpoints are joined to the center of the circle.

The important point to understand about arcs is that you're actually formulating the arc as an oval and then drawing only some of that. The starting corner and width and height are not the starting point and width and height of the actual arc as drawn on the screen; they're the width and height of the full ellipse of which the arc is a part. These first points determine the size and shape of the arc; the last two arguments (for the degrees) determine the starting and ending points.

Let's start with a simple arc, a C shape on a circle, as shown in Figure 9.11.

Figure 9.11.
A C arc.

To construct the method to draw this arc, you first think of it as a complete circle. Then you find the x and y coordinates and the width and height of that circle. These four values are the first four arguments to the `drawArc()` or `fillArc()` methods. Figure 9.12 shows how to get those values from the arc.

Figure 9.12.
Constructing a circular arc.

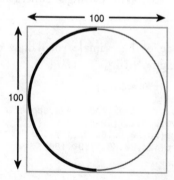

To get the last two arguments, think in degrees around the circle, going counterclockwise. Zero degrees is at 3 o'clock, 90 degrees is at 12 o'clock, 180 at 9 o'clock, and 270 at 6 o'clock. The start of the arc is the degree value of the start of the arc. In this example, the starting point is the top of the C at 90 degrees; `90` therefore is the fifth argument.

The sixth and last argument is another degree value indicating how far around the circle to sweep and the direction to go in (it's not the ending degree angle, as you might think). In this case, because you're going halfway around the circle, you're sweeping 180 degrees—and 180 is therefore the last argument in the arc. The important part is that you're sweeping 180 degrees counterclockwise, which is in the positive direction in Java. If you're drawing a backwards C, you sweep 180 degrees in the negative direction, and the last argument is -180. See Figure 9.13 for the final illustration of how this works.

Figure 9.13.

Arcs on circles.

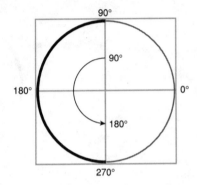

> **NOTE**
>
> It doesn't matter which side of the arc you start with. Because the shape of the arc has already been determined by the complete oval it's a section of, starting at either endpoint will work.

Here's the code for this example; you'll draw an outline of the C and a filled C to its right, as shown in Figure 9.14.

```java
import java.awt.Graphics;

public class MyOval extends java.applet.Applet {
    public void paint(Graphics g) {
    g.drawArc(20,20,60,60,90,180);
    g.fillArc(120,20,60,60,90,180);
    }
}
```

Using circles is an easy way to visualize arcs on circles; arcs on ellipses are slightly more difficult. Let's go through this same process to draw the arc shown in Figure 9.15.

Figure 9.14.
Two circular arcs.

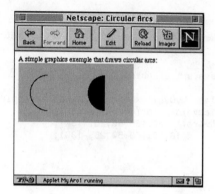

Figure 9.15.
An elliptical arc.

Like the arc on the circle, this arc is a piece of a complete oval, in this case, an elliptical oval. By completing the oval that this arc is a part of, you can get the starting points and the width and height arguments for the drawArc() or fillArc() method (see Figure 9.16).

Figure 9.16.
Arcs on ellipses.

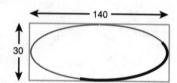

Then all you need is to figure out the starting angle and the angle to sweep. This arc doesn't start on a nice boundary such as 90 or 180 degrees, so you'll need some trial and error. This arc starts somewhere around 25 degrees and then sweeps clockwise about 130 degrees (see Figure 9.17).

Figure 9.17.
Starting and ending points.

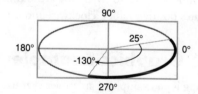

With all portions of the arc in place, you can write the code. Here's the Java code for this arc, both drawn and filled (note in the filled case how filled arcs are drawn as if they were pie sections):

```java
import java.awt.Graphics;

public class MyOval extends java.applet.Applet {
    public void paint(Graphics g) {
    g.drawArc(10,20,150,50,25,-130);
    g.fillArc(10,80,150,50,25,-130);
    }
}
```

Figure 9.18 shows the two elliptical arcs.

Figure 9.18.

Two elliptical arcs.

To summarize, here are the steps to take to construct arcs in Java:

1. Think of the arc as a slice of a complete oval.

2. Construct the full oval with the starting point and the width and height (it often helps to draw the full oval on the screen to get an idea of the right positioning).

3. Determine the starting angle for the beginning of the arc.

4. Determine how far to sweep the arc and in which direction (counterclockwise indicates positive values, clockwise indicates negative).

A Simple Graphics Example

The following is an example of an applet that uses many of the built-in graphics primitives to draw a rudimentary shape. In this case, it's a lamp with a spotted shade (or a sort of cubist mushroom, depending on your point of view). Listing 9.1 has the complete code for the lamp; Figure 9.19 shows the resulting applet.

TYPE   **Listing 9.1. The Lamp class.**

```
1: import java.awt.*;
2:
3: public class Lamp extends java.applet.Applet {
4:
5:     public void paint(Graphics g) {
6:         // the lamp platform
7:         g.fillRect(0,250,290,290);
8:
9:         // the base of the lamp
10:         g.drawLine(125,250,125,160);
11:         g.drawLine(175,250,175,160);
12:
13:         // the lamp shade, top and bottom edges
14:         g.drawArc(85,157,130,50,-65,312);
15:         g.drawArc(85,87,130,50,62,58);
16:
17:         // lamp shade, sides
18:         g.drawLine(85,177,119,89);
19:         g.drawLine(215,177,181,89);
20:
21:         // dots on the shade
22:         g.fillArc(78,120,40,40,63,-174);
23:         g.fillOval(120,96,40,40);
24:         g.fillArc(173,100,40,40,110,180);
25:     }
26: }
```

Figure 9.19.

The Lamp *applet.*

Copying and Clearing

After you've drawn a few things on the screen, you may want to move them around or clear the entire applet. The Graphics class provides methods for doing both these things.

The copyArea() method copies a rectangular area of the screen to another area of the screen. copyArea() takes six arguments: the x and y of the top corner of the rectangle to copy, the width and the height of that rectangle, and the distance in the x and y directions to which to copy it. For example, this line copies a square area 100 pixels on a side 100 pixels directly to its right:

```
g.copyArea(0,0,100,100,100,0);
```

To clear a rectangular area, use the clearRect() method. clearRect(), which takes the same four arguments as the drawRect() and fillRect() methods, fills the given rectangle with the current background color of the applet (you'll learn how to set the current background color later today).

To clear the entire applet, you can use the size() method, which returns a Dimension object representing the width and height of the applet. You can then get to the actual values for width and height by using the width and height instance variables:

```
g.clearRect(0,0,size().width,size().height);
```

Text and Fonts

Using the Graphics class, you can also print text on the screen, in conjunction with the Font class (and, sometimes, the FontMetrics class). The Font class represents a given font—its name, style, and point size—and FontMetrics gives you information about that font (for example, the actual height or width of a given character) so that you can precisely lay out text in your applet.

Note that the text here is drawn to the screen once and intended to stay there. You'll learn about entering text from the keyboard later this week.

Creating Font Objects

To draw text to the screen, first you need to create an instance of the Font class. Font objects represent an individual font—that is, its name, style (bold, italic), and point size. Font names are strings representing the family of the font, for example, "TimesRoman", "Courier", or "Helvetica". Font styles are constants defined by the Font class; you can get to them using class variables—for example, Font.PLAIN, Font.BOLD, or Font.ITALIC. Finally, the point size is the size of the font, as defined by the font itself; the point size may or may not be the height of the characters.

To create an individual font object, use these three arguments to the Font class's new constructor:

```
Font f = new Font("TimesRoman", Font.BOLD, 24);
```

This example creates a font object for the Times Roman Bold font, in 24 points. Note that as with most Java classes, you have to import the java.awt.Font class before you can use it.

NOTE   Font styles are actually integer constants that can be added to create combined styles; for example, Font.BOLD + Font.ITALIC produces a font that is both bold and italic.

The fonts you have available to you in your applets depend on which fonts are installed on the system where the applet is running. If you pick a font for your applet and that font isn't available on the current system, Java will substitute a default font. You can get an array of the names of the current fonts available in the system using this bit of code:

```
String[] fontslist = this.getToolkit().getFontList();
```

From this list, you can then often intelligently decide which fonts you want to use in your applet. For best results, however, sticking with standard fonts such as "TimesRoman", "Helvetica", and "Courier" is a good idea.

Drawing Characters and Strings

With a font object in hand, you can draw text on the screen using the methods drawChars() and drawString(). First, though, you need to set the current font to your font object using the setFont() method.

The current font is part of the graphics state that is kept track of by the Graphics object on which you're drawing. Each time you draw a character or a string to the screen, Java draws that text in the current font. To change the font of the text, therefore, first change the current font. The following paint() method creates a new font, sets the current font to that font, and draws the string "This is a big font.", at the point 10,100:

```
public void paint(Graphics g) {
    Font f = new Font("TimesRoman", Font.PLAIN, 72);
    g.setFont(f);
    g.drawString("This is a big font.", 10, 100);
}
```

This code should all look familiar to you; this is how the Hello World and Hello Again applets throughout this book were produced.

The latter two arguments to drawString() determine the point where the string will start. The x value is the start of the leftmost edge of the text; y is the baseline for the entire string.

Similar to drawString() is the drawChars() method that, instead of taking a string as an argument, takes an array of characters. drawChars() has five arguments: the array of characters, an integer representing the first character in the array to draw, another integer for the last character in the array to draw (all characters between the first and last are drawn), and the x and y for the starting point. Most of the time, drawString() is more useful than drawChars().

Listing 9.2 shows an applet that draws several lines of text in different fonts; Figure 9.20 shows the result.

TYPE **Listing 9.2. Many different fonts.**

```
 1: import java.awt.Font;
 2: import java.awt.Graphics;
 3:
 4: public class ManyFonts extends java.applet.Applet {
 5:
 6:     public void paint(Graphics g) {
 7:         Font f = new Font("TimesRoman", Font.PLAIN, 18);
 8:         Font fb = new Font("TimesRoman", Font.BOLD, 18);
 9:         Font fi = new Font("TimesRoman", Font.ITALIC, 18);
10:         Font fbi = new Font("TimesRoman", Font.BOLD + Font.ITALIC, 18);
11:
12:         g.setFont(f);
13:         g.drawString("This is a plain font", 10, 25);
14:         g.setFont(fb);
15:         g.drawString("This is a bold font", 10, 50);
16:         g.setFont(fi);
17:         g.drawString("This is an italic font", 10, 75);
18:         g.setFont(fbi);
19:         g.drawString("This is a bold italic font", 10, 100);
20:     }
21:
22: }
```

Figure 9.20.

The output of the ManyFonts *applet.*

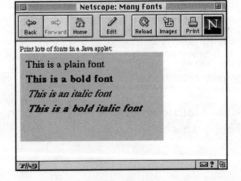

Finding Out Information About a Font

Sometimes you may want to make decisions in your Java program based on the qualities of the current font—for example, its point size and the total height of its characters. You can find out some basic information about fonts and font objects by using simple methods on `Graphics` and on the `Font` objects. Table 9.1 shows some of these methods.

Table 9.1. Font methods.

Method Name	In Object	Action
getFont()	Graphics	Returns the current font object as previously set by setFont()
getName()()	Font	Returns the name of the font as a string
getSize()()	Font	Returns the current font size (an integer)
getStyle()()	Font	Returns the current style of the font (styles are integer constants: 0 is plain, 1 is bold, 2 is italic, 3 is bold italic)
isPlain()()	Font	Returns true or false if the font's style is plain
isBold()()	Font	Returns true or false if the font's style is bold
isItalic()()	Font	Returns true or false if the font's style is italic

For more detailed information about the qualities of the current font (for example, the length or height of given characters), you need to work with font metrics. The `FontMetrics` class describes information specific to a given font: the leading between lines, the height and width of each character, and so on. To work with these sorts of values, you create a `FontMetrics` object based on the current font by using the applet method `getFontMetrics()`:

```
Font f = new Font("TimesRoman", Font.BOLD, 36);
FontMetrics fmetrics = getFontMetrics(f);
g.setFont(f);
```

Table 9.2 shows some of the information you can find using font metrics. All these methods should be called on a `FontMetrics` object.

Table 9.2. Font metrics methods.

Method Name	Action
stringWidth(String)	Given a string, returns the full width of that string, in pixels
charWidth(char)	Given a character, returns the width of that character
getAscent()	Returns the ascent of the font, that is, the distance between the font's baseline and the top of the characters

continues

Table 9.2. continued

Method Name	Action
getDescent()	Returns the descent of the font, that is, the distance between the font's baseline and the bottoms of the characters (for characters such as p and q that drop below the baseline)
getLeading()	Returns the leading for the font, that is, the spacing between the descent of one line and the ascent of another line
getHeight()	Returns the total height of the font, which is the sum of the ascent, descent, and leading value

As an example of the sorts of information you can use with font metrics, Listing 9.3 shows the Java code for an applet that automatically centers a string horizontally and vertically inside an applet. The centering position is different depending on the font and font size; by using font metrics to find out the actual size of a string, you can draw the string in the appropriate place. Figure 9.21 shows the result (which is less interesting than if you actually compile and experiment with various applet and font sizes).

TYPE **Listing 9.3. Centering a string.**

```
 1: import java.awt.Font;
 2: import java.awt.Graphics;
 3: import java.awt.FontMetrics;
 4:
 5: public class Centered extends java.applet.Applet {
 6:
 7:     public void paint(Graphics g) {
 8:         Font f = new Font("TimesRoman", Font.PLAIN, 36);
 9:         FontMetrics fm = getFontMetrics(f);
10:         g.setFont(f);
11:
12:         String s = "This is how the world ends.";
13:         int xstart = (size().width - fm.stringWidth(s)) / 2;
14:         int ystart = size().height / 2;
15:
16:         g.drawString(s, xstart, ystart);
17:     }
18:}
```

9

Figure 9.21.

The centered text.

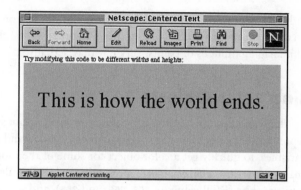

Note the `size()` method in lines 13 and 14, which returns the width and height of the overall applet area as a `Dimension` object. You can then get to the individual width and height using the `width` and `height` instance variables of that `Dimension`, here by chaining the method call and the variable name. Getting the current applet size in this way is a better idea than hard coding the size of the applet into your code; this code works equally well with an applet of any size.

Note also that the line of text, as shown in Figure 9.21, isn't precisely vertically centered in the applet bounding box. This example centers the baseline of the text inside the applet; using the `getAscent()` and `getDescent()` methods from the `FontMetrics` class (to get the number of pixels from the baseline to the top of the characters and the number of pixels from the baseline to the bottom of the characters), you can figure out exactly the middle of the line of text.

Color

Drawing black lines and text on a gray background is all very nice, but being able to use different colors is much nicer. Java provides methods and behaviors for dealing with color in general through the `Color` class, and also provides methods for setting the current foreground and background colors so that you can draw with the colors you created.

Java's abstract color model uses 24-bit color, wherein a color is represented as a combination of red, green, and blue values. Each component of the color can have a number between `0` and `255`. `0,0,0` is black, `255,255,255` is white, and Java can represent millions of colors between as well.

Java's abstract color model maps onto the color model of the platform Java is running on, which usually has only 256 or fewer colors from which to choose. If a requested color in a color object is not available for display, the resulting color may be mapped to another or dithered, depending on how the browser viewing the color implemented it, and depending on the platform on which you're running. In other words, although Java gives the capability of managing millions of colors, very few may actually be available to you in real life.

Using Color Objects

To draw an object in a particular color, you must create an instance of the Color class to represent that color. The Color class defines a set of standard color objects, stored in class variables, to quickly get a color object for some of the more popular colors. For example, Color.red returns a Color object representing red (RGB values of 255, 0, and 0), Color.white returns white (RGB values of 255, 255, and 255), and so on. Table 9.3 shows the standard colors defined by variables in the Color class.

Table 9.3. Standard colors.

Color Name	RGB Value
Color.white	255,255,255
Color.black	0,0,0
Color.lightGray	192,192,192
Color.gray	128,128,128
Color.darkGray	64,64,64
Color.red	255,0,0
Color.green	0,255,0
Color.blue	0,0,255
Color.yellow	255,255,0
Color.magenta	255,0,255
Color.cyan	0,255,255
Color.pink	255,175,175
Color.orange	255,200,0

If the color you want to draw in is not one of the standard Color objects, fear not. You can create a Color object for any combination of red, green, and blue, as long as you have the values of the color you want. Just create a new color object:

```
Color c = new Color(140,140,140);
```

This line of Java code creates a Color object representing a dark gray. You can use any combination of red, green, and blue values to construct a Color object.

Alternatively, you can create a `Color` object using three floats from `0.0` to `1.0`:

```
Color c = new Color(0.55,0.55,0.55);
```

Testing and Setting the Current Colors

To draw an object or text using a color object, you have to set the current color to be that color object, just as you have to set the current font to the font in which you want to draw. Use the `setColor()` method (a method for `Graphics` objects) to do this:

```
g.setColor(Color.green);
```

After you set the current color, all drawing operations will occur in that color.

In addition to setting the current color for the graphics context, you can also set the background and foreground colors for the applet itself by using the `setBackground()` and `setForeground()` methods. Both of these methods are defined in the `java.awt.Component` class, which `Applet`—and therefore your classes—automatically inherits.

The `setBackground()` method sets the background color of the applet, which is usually a light gray (to match the default background of the browser). It takes a single argument, a `Color` object:

```
setBackground(Color.white);
```

The `setForeground()` method also takes a single color as an argument, and it affects everything that has been drawn on the applet, regardless of the color in which it has been drawn. You can use `setForeground()` to change the color of everything in the applet at once rather than have to redraw everything:

```
setForeground(Color.black);
```

In addition to the `setColor()`, `setForeground()`, and `setBackground()` methods, corresponding get methods enable you to retrieve the current graphics color, background, or foreground. These methods are `getColor()` (defined in `Graphics` objects), `getForeground()` (defined in `Applet`), and `getBackground()` (also in `Applet`). You can use these methods to choose colors based on existing colors in the applet:

```
setForeground(g.getColor());
```

A Simple Color Example

Listing 9.4 shows the code for an applet that fills the applet's drawing area with square boxes, each of which has a randomly chosen color in it. This code is written so that it can handle any size of applet and automatically fill the area with the right number of boxes.

TYPE   **Listing 9.4. Random color boxes.**

```
1:  import java.awt.Graphics;
2:  import java.awt.Color;
3:
4:  public class ColorBoxes extends java.applet.Applet {
5:
6:      public void paint(Graphics g) {
7:          int rval, gval, bval;
8:
9:          for (int j = 30; j < (size().height -25); j += 30)
10:             for (int i = 5; i < (size().width -25); i += 30) {
11:                 rval = (int)Math.floor(Math.random() * 256);
12:                 gval = (int)Math.floor(Math.random() * 256);
13:                 bval = (int)Math.floor(Math.random() * 256);
14:
15:                 g.setColor(new Color(rval,gval,bval));
16:                 g.fillRect(i, j, 25, 25);
17:                 g.setColor(Color.black);
18:                 g.drawRect(i-1, j-1, 25, 25);
19:             }
20:     }
21: }
```

The two for loops are the heart of this example; the first one draws the rows, and the second draws the individual boxes within each row. When a box is drawn, the random color is calculated first, and then the box is drawn. A black outline is drawn around each box because some of them tend to blend into the background of the applet. Because this paint method generates new colors each time the applet is painted, you can regenerate the colors by moving the window around or by covering the applet's window with another one (or by reloading the page). Figure 9.22 shows the final applet (although given that this picture is black and white, you can't get the full effect of the multicolored squares).

Figure 9.22.

The random colors applet.

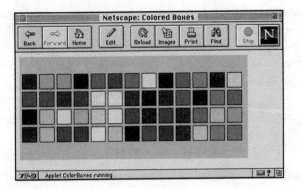

Using Standard System Colors (Java 1.1 only)

One of the features added with Java version 1.1 is the ability to use the system's color scheme—the colors that the user has chosen for the desktop, windows, and other elements of the screen display.

You use these colors by referring to variables of the `SystemColor` class, which is part of the `java.awt` package of classes. You can use `SystemColor` variables with methods that designate a current color in the same way `Color` variables are used.

The following statement chooses the system's desktop color—defined by `SystemColor.desktop`—as the current background:

```
setBackground(SystemColor.desktop);
```

These colors do not represent a specific RGB value, unlike the `Color` variables, because they can be changed by the user at any time. Table 9.4 lists some of the 26 system colors that you can use in your programs. You might not need to use many of them until you start creating your own graphical user interfaces for programs. However, using them is a good way to personalize a program to the colors that users find easiest to work with.

Table 9.4. System colors.

System Color	What It Colors
`SystemColor.activeCaption`	The bar atop an active window
`SystemColor.activeCaptionBorder`	The thin edge of an active window
`SystemColor.activeCaptionText`	The text in an active window
`SystemColor.inactiveCaption`	The bar atop an inactive window
`SystemColor.inactiveCaptionBorder`	The thin edge of an inactive window
`SystemColor.inactiveCaptionText`	The text in an inactive window
`SystemColor.desktop`	The desktop's background
`SystemColor.window`	The background of windows such as folders
`SystemColor.windowText`	The text in windows such as folders
`SystemColor.textHighlight`	The area surrounding selected text (such as for a cut-and-paste operation)
`SystemColor.textHighlightText`	The selected text

Listing 9.5 shows a short applet that uses some of the system colors displayed as text or rectangles. Load the program several times with the appletviewer tool after changing your system's color scheme.

TYPE   **Listing 9.5. The full text of** `SysColor.java`.

```
 1: import java.awt.Graphics;
 2: import java.awt.SystemColor;
 3:
 4: public class SysColor extends java.applet.Applet {
 5:
 6:     public void init() {
 7:         setBackground(SystemColor.window);
 8:     }
 9:
10:     public void paint(Graphics g) {
11:         g.setColor(SystemColor.windowText);
12:         g.drawString("Window text is this color", 20, 50);
13:         g.setColor(SystemColor.activeCaption);
14:         g.fillRect(5, 58, 180, 19);
15:         g.setColor(SystemColor.activeCaptionText);
16:         g.drawString("Active caption colors", 20, 70);
17:         g.setColor(SystemColor.inactiveCaption);
18:         g.fillRect(5, 78, 180, 19);
19:         g.setColor(SystemColor.inactiveCaptionText);
20:         g.drawString("Inactive caption colors", 20, 90);
21:     }
22: }
```

Though it definitely loses something in translation to black-and-white, Figure 9.23 shows what the `SysColor` applet looks like if you load it into a Web page using appletviewer.

Figure 9.23.

The SysColor *applet running under appletviewer.*

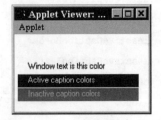

Summary

You present something on the screen by painting inside your applet: shapes, graphics, text, or images. Today you learned the basics of how to paint, including how to use the graphics primitives to draw rudimentary shapes and how to use fonts and font metrics to draw text.

You also learned how to use Color objects to change the color of what you're drawing on the screen and 1.1 SystemColor class to make your programs match the colors chosen for a user's system. This foundation in painting enables you to do animation inside an applet (which basically involves just painting repeatedly to the screen) and to work with images. You'll learn about these topics tomorrow.

Q&A

Q **In all the examples you show and in all the tests I've made, the graphics primitives, such as drawLine() and drawRect(), produce lines that are one pixel wide. How can I draw thicker lines?**

A In the current state of the Java Graphics class, you can't; no methods exist for changing the default line width. If you really need a thicker line, you have to draw multiple lines one pixel apart to produce that effect.

Q **I want to draw a line of text with a boldface word in the middle. I understand that I need two font objects—one for the regular font and one for the bold one—and that I'll need to reset the current font in between. The problem is that drawString() requires an x and a y position for the start of each string, and can't find anything that refers to "current point." How can I figure out where to start the boldface word?**

A Java's text display capabilities are fairly primitive. Java has no concept of the current point, so you'll have to figure out yourself where the end of one string was so that you can begin the next string. The stringWidth() methods can help you with this problem, both to find out the width of the string you just drew and to add the space after it.

Q **I tried out the applet that draws boxes with random colors, but each time it draws, a lot of the boxes are the same color. If the colors are truly random, why is it doing this?**

A Two reasons. The first is that the random number generator I used in that code (from the Math class) isn't a very good random number generator; in fact, the documentation for that method says as much. For a better random number generator, use the Random class from the java.util package.

The second, more likely, reason is that not enough colors are available in your browser or on your system to draw all the colors that the applet is generating. If your system can't produce the wide range of colors available using the Color class, or if the browser has allocated too many colors for other things, you may end up with duplicate colors in the boxes, depending on how the browser and the system have been written to handle that situation. Usually, your applet won't use quite so many colors, so you won't run into this problem quite so often.

Q **I noticed that in addition to drawRect() and drawRoundRect(), there's also a drawWRoundRect() method. You don't talk about this one. Why?**

A The draw3DRect() method, as you might expect, draws a 3D style rectangle. Or at least it would, if Java allowed line widths of greater than one pixel. In the current Java state, the 3D rectangles don't look very 3D at all, so I omitted that method from this chapter.

Q **I have a tiled background on my Web page. I can create images with transparent backgrounds so that the tiled page background shows through. Can I create transparent applets?**

A Under Java 1.1, you cannot make the applet background transparent so that the Web page shows through. For applets, your best bet is to use a single-color background and set your applet's background to be that color or some other complementary color.

Another idea if you use a tiled image for the page background is to import that image and draw it as the background for your applet (you'll learn about images tomorrow). However, if you use that mechanism, the edges of the tile are unlikely to match up exactly because you can't determine exactly where an applet will appear on a page. Unfortunately, a good workaround doesn't appear to be available for this problem.

Day 10

Animation, Images, Threads, and Sound

by Laura Lemay

The first Java program that many people saw was simple animation on a World Wide Web page. Spinning heads, dancing headlines, and other effects were completely novel when Java was first introduced in late 1995.

Those kinds of animation effects take just a few methods to implement in Java, but those methods form the basis for any Java applet that updates the screen dynamically—such as animation, changing tables of data, and other programs.

Animation in Java is accomplished by using interrelated parts of the Abstract Windowing Toolkit (AWT). Today you'll learn the fundamentals of animation in Java: how the various parts of the system work together so you can create moving figures and dynamically updated applets.

Creating animation is fun and easy to do in Java, but there's only so much you can do with the built-in Java methods for lines, fonts, and colors. For really interesting animation, you have to provide your own images for each frame of the animation—and having sounds is nice as well.

During the day, you'll explore the following topics:

☐ How to create animation in Java—the paint() and repaint() methods, starting and stopping dynamic applets, and how to use and override these methods in your own applets

☐ Threads—what they are and how they can make your applets more well-behaved with other applets and with other parts of the AWT

☐ Reducing the common problem of flickering animation with techniques such as double-buffering

☐ Using bitmap images such as GIF or JPEG files—getting them from the server, loading them into Java, displaying them in your applet, and using them in animation

☐ Using sounds—getting them and playing them at the appropriate times

Creating Animation in Java

Animation in Java involves two basic steps: constructing a frame of animation, and then asking Java to paint that frame. You repeat these steps as necessary to create the illusion of movement. The basic, static graphical applets that you created yesterday taught you how to accomplish the first part; all that's left is how to tell Java to paint a frame.

Painting and Repainting

The paint() method, as you learned yesterday, is called whenever an applet needs to be painted—when the applet is initially drawn, when the window containing it is moved, or when another window is moved from over it. You can also, however, ask Java to repaint the applet at a time you choose. So, to change the appearance of what is on the screen, you construct the image or "frame" you want to paint, and then ask Java to paint this frame. If you do this repeatedly, and fast enough, you get animation inside your Java applet. That's all there is to it.

Where does all this take place? Not in the paint() method itself. All paint() does is put dots on the screen. In other words, paint() is responsible only for the current frame of the animation. The real work of changing what paint() does, of modifying the frame for an animation, actually occurs somewhere else in the definition of your applet.

In that "somewhere else," you construct the frame (set variables for paint() to use, create Color or Font or other objects that paint() will need), and then call the repaint() method. repaint() is the trigger that causes Java to call paint() and your frame to get drawn.

TECHNICAL NOTE

When you call repaint()— and therefore paint()—you're not immediately drawing to the screen as you do in other windowing or graphics toolkits. Instead, repaint() is a request for Java to repaint your applet as soon as possible. If too many repaint() requests are made in a short amount of time, the system might only call repaint() once for all of them. Usually, the delay between the call and the actual repaint is negligible. However, for very tight loops, the AWT may combine several calls to repaint() into one. Keep this in mind as you create your own animation.

10

Starting and Stopping an Applet's Execution

Remember start() and stop() from Day 8, "Java Applet Basics?" These are the methods that trigger your applet to start and stop running. You didn't use start() and stop() yesterday because the applets on that day did nothing except paint once. With animation and other Java applets that are actually processing and running over time, you'll need to make use of start() and stop() to trigger the start of your applet's execution, and to stop it from running when you leave the page that contains that applet. For many applets, you'll want to override start() and stop() for just this reason.

The start() method triggers the execution of the applet. You can either do all the applet's work inside that method, or you can call other object's methods in order to do so. Usually, start() is used to create and begin execution of a thread so the applet can run in its own time.

On the other hand, stop() suspends an applet's execution so when you move off the page on which the applet is displaying, it doesn't keep running and using up system resources. Most of the time when you create a start() method, you should also create a corresponding stop().

The Missing Link: Threads

There's one more part to the animation mix that you'll have to know about, and that's threads. I'm going to discuss threads in more detail on Day 18, "Multithreading," but for now, here's the basic idea: Anything you do in a Java program that runs continually and takes up a lot of processing time should run in its own thread. Animation is one of these things.

To accomplish animation in Java, therefore, you use the start() method to start a thread, and then do all your animation processing inside the thread's run() method. This allows the animation to run on its own without interfering with any other parts of the program.

Threads are a very important part of Java and of programming Java. The larger your Java programs get and the more things they do, the more likely it is that you'll want to use threads. Depending on your experience with operating systems and with environments within those systems, you may or may not have run into the concept of threads, so let's start from the beginning.

First, the analogy. A group of students is on a bus on a field trip somewhere. To pass the time, the teachers are leading a sing-along. As the trip progresses, the students sing one song, then when that song is done, they sing another song. While different parts of the bus could sing different songs, it wouldn't sound very good, so the singing of one song monopolizes the time until it's done, at which time another song can start.

Now let's say you have two buses; both are on the same route to the field trip, both are going at the same speed, and both are full of students singing songs. But the songs being sung by the students in the second bus don't interfere with the songs being sung in the first bus; in this way you can get twice as many songs sung in the same amount of time by singing them in parallel.

Threads are like that. In a regular single-threaded program, the program starts executing, runs its initialization code, calls methods or procedures, and continues running and processing until it's complete or until the program is exited. That program runs in a single thread—it's the one bus with all the students.

Multithreading, as in Java, means that several different parts of the same program can run at the same time, in parallel, without interfering with each other. Multiple threads, each running by itself, are like multiple buses with different things going on in each bus.

Using threads in Java, you can create parts of an applet (or application) that run in their own threads, and those parts will happily run all by themselves without interfering with anything else. Depending on how many threads you have, you may eventually tax the system so much that all of them will run slower, but all of them will still run independently.

Even if you don't use lots of them, using threads in your applets is a good Java programming practice. The general rule of thumb for well-behaved applets: Whenever you have any bit of processing that is likely to continue for a long time (such as an animation loop, or a bit of code that takes a long time to execute), put it in a thread.

Writing Applets with Threads

Creating applets that use threads is very easy. In fact, many of the basic things you need to do to use threads are just boilerplate code that you can copy and paste from one applet to another. Because it's so easy, there's almost no reason not to use threads in your applets, given the benefits.

There are four modifications you need to make to create an applet that uses threads:

☐ Change the signature of your applet class to include the words implements Runnable.

☐ Include an instance variable to hold the applet's thread object.

☐ Create a start() method that does nothing but create a thread and start it running.

☐ Create a stop() method that stops the thread.

☐ Create a run() method that contains the actual code that controls the applet.

The first change is to the first line of your class definition. You've already got something like this:

```
public class MyAppletClass extends java.applet.Applet {
    ...
}
```

You need to change it to the following:

```
public class MyAppletClass extends java.applet.Applet implements Runnable {
    ...
}
```

What does this do? It includes support for the Runnable interface in your applet. If you think way back to Day 2, "Object-Oriented Programming and Java," you'll remember that interfaces are a way to collect method names common to different classes, which can then be mixed in and implemented inside different classes that need to implement that behavior. Here, the Runnable interface defines the behavior your applet needs in order to run a thread; in particular, it gives you a default definition for the run() method. By implementing Runnable, you tell others that they can call the run() method on your instances.

The second step is to add an instance variable to hold this applet's thread. Call it anything you like; it's a variable of the type Thread (Thread is a class in java.lang, so you don't have to import it):

```
Thread runner;
```

Third, add a start() method or modify the existing one so that it does nothing but create a new thread and start it running. Here's a typical example of a start() method:

```
public void start() {
    if (runner == null) {
        runner = new Thread(this);
        runner.start();
    }
}
```

If you modify start() to do nothing but spawn a thread, where does the code that drives your applet go? It goes into a new method, run(), which looks like this:

```
public void run() {
    // what your applet actually does
}
```

Your run() method actually overrides the default version of run(), which you get when you include the Runnable interface with your applet. run() is one of those standard methods, like start() and paint(), that you override in your own classes to get standard behavior.

run() can contain anything you want to run in the separate thread: initialization code, the actual loop for your applet, or anything else that needs to run in its own thread. You also can create new objects and call methods from inside run(), and they'll run inside that thread. The run() method is the real heart of your applet.

Finally, now that you have threads running and a start() method to start them, you should add a stop() method to suspend execution of that thread (and therefore whatever the applet is doing at the time) when the reader leaves the page. stop(), like start(), is usually something along these lines:

```
public void stop() {
    if (runner != null) {
        runner.stop();
        runner = null;
    }
}
```

The stop() method here does two things: It stops the thread from executing and also sets the thread's variable runner to null. Setting the variable to null makes the Thread object it previously contained available for garbage collection so that the applet can be removed from memory after a certain amount of time. If the reader comes back to this page and this applet, the start() method creates a new thread and starts up the applet once again.

And that's it! Four basic modifications, and now you have a well-behaved applet that runs in its own thread.

10

Putting It Together

Explaining how to do Java animation is more of a task than actually showing you how it works in code. An example will help make the relationship between all these methods clearer.

Listing 10.1 shows a sample applet that uses basic applet animation techniques to display the date and time and constantly update it every second, creating a very simple animated digital clock (a frame from that clock is shown in Figure 10.1).

NOTE

> This applet is written to use the GregorianCalendar class from the 1.1 JDK. You can accomplish the same functions in 1.02 using the more limited (and less international) Date class.

10

Figure 10.1.
Output of the
DigitalClock
applet using
appletviewer.

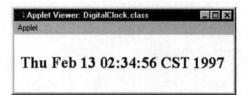

Thu Feb 13 02:34:56 CST 1997

This applet uses the paint(), repaint(), start(), and stop() methods. It also uses threads.

TYPE **Listing 10.1. The full text of DigitalClock.java.**

```
 1: import java.awt.Graphics;
 2: import java.awt.Font;
 3: import java.util.Calendar;
 4: import java.util.GregorianCalendar;
 5:
 6: public class DigitalClock extends java.applet.Applet
 7:     implements Runnable {
 8:
 9:     Font theFont = new Font("TimesRoman",Font.BOLD,24);
10:     GregorianCalendar theDate;
11:     Thread runner;
12:
13:     public void start() {
14:         if (runner == null) {
15:             runner = new Thread(this);
16:             runner.start();
17:         }
18:     }
19:
```

continues

Listing 10.1. continued

```
20:     public void stop() {
21:         if (runner != null) {
22:             runner.stop();
23:             runner = null;
24:         }
25:     }
26:
27:     public void run() {
28:         while (true) {
29:             repaint();
30:             try { Thread.sleep(1000); }
31:             catch (InterruptedException e) { }
32:         }
33:     }
34:
35:     public void paint(Graphics g) {
36:         theDate = new GregorianCalendar();
37:         g.setFont(theFont);
38:         g.drawString("" + theDate.getTime(), 10, 50);
39:     }
40: }
```

Animation is a good example of the kind of task that needs its own thread. Consider the endless while() loop in the DigitalClock applet. If you didn't use threads, while() would run in the default Java system thread, which is also responsible for handling painting the screen, dealing with user input like mouse clicks, and keeping everything internally up-to-date. Unfortunately, however, if you run that while() loop in the main system thread, it will monopolize all Java's resources and prevent anything else—including painting—from happening. You'd never actually see anything on the screen because Java would be sitting and waiting for the while() loop to finish before it did anything else.

We'll look at this applet from the perspective of the actual animation parts in this section, and deal with the parts that manage threads afterward.

Lines 9 and 10 define two basic instance variables: theFont and theDate, which hold objects representing the current font and the current date, respectively. You'll learn more about these later.

The start() and stop() methods here start and stop a thread; the bulk of the applet's work goes on in the run() method (lines 27 to 33).

Inside run() is where the animation actually takes place. Note the while loop inside this method (beginning with the statement on line 28); given that the test (true) always returns true, the loop never exits. A single animation frame is constructed inside that while loop.

The first thing that happens in the loop is that the `repaint()` statement is called in line 29 to repaint the applet. Lines 30 and 31, as complicated as they look, do nothing except pause for 1000 milliseconds (1 second) before the loop repeats. The `sleep()` method there, part of the `Thread` class, is what causes the applet to pause. Without a specific `sleep()` method, the applet would run as fast as it possibly could. The `sleep()` method controls exactly how fast the animation takes place. The `try` and `catch` stuff around it enables Java to manage errors if they occur. `try` and `catch` handle exceptions and are described on Day 17, "Exceptions."

On to the `paint()` method in lines 34 through 37. Here, a new instance of the `GregorianCalendar` class is created to hold the current date and time—note that it was specifically imported in line 4. This new `GregorianCalendar` object is assigned to the `theDate` instance variable.

In line 37, the current font is set using the value of the variable `theFont` and the date itself is displayed to the screen—note that you have to call the `getTime()` method of `GregorianCalendar` to display the date and time as a string. Every time that `paint()` is called, a new `theDate` object is created that holds the current date and time.

Let's look at the lines of this applet that create and manage threads. First, look at the class definition itself in lines 6 and 7—note that the class definition includes the `Runnable` interface. Any classes you create that use threads must include `Runnable`.

Line 11 defines a third instance variable for this class called runner of type `Thread`, which will hold the thread object for this applet.

Lines 13 through 25 define the boilerplate `start()` and `stop()` methods that do nothing except create and destroy threads. These method definitions can essentially be exactly the same from class to class because all they do is set up the infrastructure for the thread itself.

And, finally, the bulk of your applet's work goes on inside the `run()` method in lines 27 through 33.

Reducing Animation Flickering

If you've been following along with this lesson and trying the examples as you go rather than reading this book on an airplane or in the bathtub, you may have noticed that when the digital clock program runs, every once in a while there's an annoying flickering in the animation. (Not that there's anything wrong with reading this book in the bathtub, but you won't see the flickering if you do that, so just trust me—there's flickering.) This isn't a mistake or an error in the program; in fact, that flickering is a side effect of creating animation in Java. Because it is really annoying, you'll learn how to reduce flickering in this part of today's lesson so that your animations run cleaner and look better on the screen.

Flickering and How to Avoid It

Flickering is caused by the way Java paints and repaints each frame of an applet. At the beginning of today's lesson, you learned that when you call the repaint() method, repaint() calls paint(). That's not precisely true. A call to paint() does indeed occur in response to a repaint(), but what actually happens is the following:

1. The call to repaint() results in a call to the method update().

2. The update() method clears the screen of any existing contents (in essence, fills it with the current background color), and then calls paint().

3. The paint() method then draws the contents of the current frame.

It's step 2, the call to update(), that causes animation flickering. Because the screen is cleared between frames, the parts of the screen that don't change alternate rapidly between being painted and being cleared—hence, flickering.

There are two major ways to avoid flickering in your Java applets:

☐ Override update() either not to clear the screen at all, or to clear only the parts of the screen you've changed.

☐ Override both update() and paint(), and use double-buffering.

If the second way sounds complicated, that's because it is. Double-buffering involves drawing to an offscreen graphics surface and then copying that entire surface to the screen. Because it's more complicated, we'll explore that one a little later. First, let's cover the easier solution: overriding update().

How to Override update()

The cause of flickering lies in the update() method. To reduce flickering, therefore, override update(). Here's what the default version of update() does (comes from the Component class, is part of the AWT, and is one of the superclasses of the applet class. You'll learn more about it on Day 12, "Creating User Interfaces with AWT"):

```
public void update(Graphics g) {
    g.setColor(getBackground());
    g.fillRect(0, 0, width, height);
    g.setColor(getForeground());
    paint(g);
}
```

Basically, update() clears the screen (or, to be exact, fills the applet's bounding rectangle with the background color), sets things back to normal, and then calls paint(). When you override update(), you have to keep these two things in mind and make sure that your version of update() does something similar. In the next two sections, you'll work through some examples of overriding update() in different cases to reduce flickering.

Solution One: Don't Clear the Screen

The first solution to reduce flickering is not to clear the screen at all. This works only for some applets, of course. Here's an example of an applet of this type. The ColorSwirl applet prints a single string to the screen ("All the Swirly Colors"), but that string is presented in different colors that fade into each other dynamically. This applet flickers terribly when it's run. Listing 10.2 shows the initial source for this applet and Figure 10.2 shows the result.

TYPE **Listing 10.2. The full text of** ColorSwirl.java.

```
 1: import java.awt.Graphics;
 2: import java.awt.Color;
 3: import java.awt.Font;
 4:
 5: public class ColorSwirl extends java.applet.Applet
 6:     implements Runnable {
 7:
 8:     Font f = new Font("TimesRoman", Font.BOLD, 48);
 9:     Color colors[] = new Color[50];
10:     Thread runner;
11:
12:     public void start() {
13:         if (runner == null) {
14:             runner = new Thread(this);
15:             runner.start();
16:         }
17:     }
18:
19:     public void stop() {
20:         if (runner != null) {
21:             runner.stop();
22:             runner = null;
23:         }
24:     }
25:
26:     public void run() {
27:
28:         // initialize the color array
29:         float c = 0;
30:         for (int i = 0; i < colors.length; i++) {
31:             colors[i] =
32:             Color.getHSBColor(c, (float)1.0,(float)1.0);
33:             c += .02;
34:         }
35:
36:         // cycle through the colors
37:         int i = 0;
38:         while (true) {
39:             setForeground(colors[i]);
40:             repaint();
41:
42:             i++;
```

continues

10

Listing 10.2. continued

```
43:                    try { Thread.sleep(200); }
44:                    catch (InterruptedException e) { }
45:                    if (i == colors.length ) i = 0;
46:            }
47:        }
48:
49:        public void paint(Graphics g) {
50:            g.setFont(f);
51:            g.drawString("Look to the Cookie!", 15, 50);
52:        }
53: }
```

Figure 10.2.

Output of the
ColorSwirl *applet*
using appletviewer.

There are three things to note about this applet that might look strange to you:

- ☐ Line 9 defines an instance variable colors, which is an array of 50 elements. When the applet starts, the first thing you do in the run() method (in lines 28 through 34) is to fill up that array with Color objects. By creating all the colors beforehand, you can then just draw text in that color, one at a time; it's easier to precompute all the colors at once (and, in fact, this for loop might make more sense in an init() method because it only needs to happen once). Note that I arbitrarily picked the number 50 for the number of colors we'll be using; we could just as easily cycle through 20 or 250 colors.

- ☐ To create the different color objects, we used a method in the Color class called getHSBColor(), rather than just using new with various RGB values. The getHSBColor() class method creates a Color object based on values for hue, saturation, and brightness, rather than the standard red, green, and blue. HSB is simply a different way of looking at colors, and by incrementing the hue value and keeping saturation and brightness constant, you can create a range of colors without having to know the RGB for each one. If you don't understand this, don't worry about it; it's just a quick and easy way to create the color array.

- ☐ To create the animation, the applet cycles through the array of colors, setting the foreground color to each color object in turn and calling repaint(). When it gets to the end of the array, it starts over again (line 45), so the process repeats over and over ad infinitum.

Now that you understand what the applet does, let's fix the flickering. Flickering here results because each time the applet is painted, there's a moment where the screen is cleared. Instead of the text cycling neatly from red to a nice pink to purple, it's going from red to gray, to pink to gray, to purple to gray, and so on—not very nice-looking at all.

Because the screen clearing is all that's causing the problem, the solution is easy: Override update() and remove the part where the screen gets cleared. It doesn't really need to get cleared anyhow, because nothing is changing except the color of the text. With the screen clearing behavior removed from update(), all update needs to do is call paint(). Here's what the update() method looks like in this applet (you'll want to add it after the paint() method after line 51):

```
public void update(Graphics g) {
    paint(g);
}
```

With that—one small three-line addition—no more flickering. Wasn't that easy?

NOTE

If you're following along with the examples on the CD, the first version of ColorSwirl.java can be found in a FirstColorSwirl folder, and the second version can be found in the SecondColorSwirl folder.

Retrieving and Using Images

Basic image handling in Java is easy. The Image class in the java.awt package provides abstract methods to represent common image behavior, and special methods defined in Applet and Graphics give you everything you need to load and display images in your applet as easily as drawing a rectangle. In this section, you'll learn how to get and draw images in your Java applets.

Getting Images

To display an image in your applet, you first must load that image over the World Wide Web into your Java program. Images are stored as separate files from your Java class files, so you have to tell Java where to find them.

The Applet class provides a method called getImage(), which loads an image and automatically creates an instance of the Image class for you. To use it, all you have to do is import the `java.awt.Image` class into your Java program, and then give `getImage()` the URL of the image you want to load. There are two ways of doing the latter step:

☐ The `getImage()` method with a single argument (an object of type `URL`) retrieves the image at that URL.

☐ The `getImage()` method with two arguments: the base URL (also an `URL` object) and a string representing the path or filename of the actual image (relative to the base).

Although the first way may seem easier (just plug in the URL as an `URL` object), the second is more flexible. Remember, because you're compiling Java files, if you include a hard-coded URL of an image and then move your files around to a different location, you have to recompile all your Java files.

The latter form, therefore, is usually the one to use. The `Applet` class also provides two methods that will help with the base URL argument to `getImage()`:

☐ The `getDocumentBase()` method returns an URL object representing the directory of the HTML file that contains this applet. So, for example, if the HTML file is located at `http://www.myserver.com/htmlfiles/javahtml/`, `getDocumentBase()` returns an URL pointing to that path.

☐ The `getCodeBase()` method returns a string representing the directory in which this applet is contained—which may or may not be the same directory as the HTML file, depending on whether the `CODEBASE` attribute in `<APPLET>` is set or not.

Whether you use `getDocumentBase()` or `getCodeBase()` depends on whether your images are relative to your HTML files or relative to your Java class files. Use whichever one applies better to your situation. Note that either of these methods is more flexible than hard-coding an URL or pathname into the `getImage()` method; using either `getDocumentBase()` or `getCodeBase()` enables you to move your HTML files and applets around and still allow Java to find your images. (This assumes, of course, that you move the class files and the images around together. If you move the images somewhere else and leave the class files where they are, you'll have to edit and recompile your source.)

Here are a few examples of `getImage()`, to give you an idea of how to use it. This first call to `getImage()` retrieves the file at that specific URL (`http://www.server.com/files/image.gif`). If any part of that URL changes, you have to recompile your Java applet to take into account the new path:

```
Image img = getImage(
new URL("http://www.server.com/files/image.gif"));
```

In the following form of `getImage()`, the `image.gif` file is in the same directory as the HTML files that refer to this applet:

```
Image img = getImage(getDocumentBase(), "image.gif")
```

In this similar form, the file `image.gif` is in the same directory as the applet itself:

```
Image img = getImage(getCodeBase(), "image.gif")
```

If you have lots of image files, it's common to put them into their own subdirectory. This form of `getImage()` looks for the file `image.gif` in the directory `images`, which, in turn, is in the same directory as the Java applet:

```
Image img = getImage(getCodeBase(), "images/image.gif")
```

If `getImage()` can't find the file indicated, it returns null. `drawImage()` on a null image will simply draw nothing. Using a null image in other ways will probably cause an error.

NOTE

> Currently, Java supports images in the GIF and JPEG formats. Other image formats may be available later; however, for now, your images should be in either GIF or JPEG.

10

Drawing Images

All that stuff with `getImage()` does nothing except go off and retrieve an image and stuff it into an instance of the `Image` class. Now that you have an image, you have to do something with it.

TECHNICAL NOTE

> Actually, the loading of images is internally a lot more complex than this. When you retrieve an image using `getImage()`, that method actually spawns a thread to load the image and returns almost immediately with your `Image` object. This gives your program the illusion of almost instantaneously having the image there ready to use. It may take some time, however, for the actual image to download and decompress, which may cause your image applets to draw with only partial images, or for the image to be drawn on the screen incrementally as it loads (all the examples in this chapter work like this). You can control how you want your applet to behave given a partial image (for example, if you want it to wait until it's all there before displaying it) by taking advantage of the `ImageObserver` interface. You'll learn more about `ImageObserver` later in this lesson in the section "A Note About Image Observers."

The most likely thing you're going to want to do with an image is display it as you would a rectangle or a text string. The Graphics class provides two methods to do just this, both called drawImage().

The first version of drawImage() takes four arguments: the image to display, the x and y positions of the top-left corner, and this:

```
public void paint() {
    g.drawImage(img, 10, 10, this);
}
```

This first form does what you would expect it to: It draws the image in its original dimensions with the top-left corner at the given x and y positions. The second form of drawImage() takes six arguments: the image to draw, the x and y coordinates of the top-left corner, a width and height of the image bounding box, and this. If the width and height arguments for the bounding box are smaller or larger than the actual image, the image is automatically scaled to fit. By using those extra arguments, you can squeeze and expand images into whatever space you need them to fit in (keep in mind, however, that there may be some image degradation from scaling it smaller or larger than its intended size).

One helpful hint for scaling images is to find out the size of the actual image that you've loaded, so you can then scale it to a specific percentage and avoid distortion in either direction. Two methods defined for the Image class can give you that information: getWidth() and getHeight(). Both take a single argument, an instance of ImageObserver, which is used to track the loading of the image (more about this later). Most of the time, you can use just this as an argument to either getWidth() or getHeight().

If you stored the ladybug image in a variable called bugimg, for example, this line returns the width of that image, in pixels:

```
theWidth = bugimg.getWidth(this);
```

TECHNICAL NOTE

Here's another case where, if the image isn't loaded all the way, you may get different results. Calling getWidth() or getHeight() before the image has fully loaded will result in values of -1 for each one. Tracking image loading with image observers can help you keep track of when this information appears.

Listing 10.3 shows another use of the ladybug image, this time scaled several times to different sizes (Figure 10.3 shows the result).

Figure 10.3.

Output of the
LadyBug *applet using*
appletviewer.

TYPE **Listing 10.3. The full text of** LadyBug.java.

```
1: import java.awt.Graphics;
2: import java.awt.Image;
3:
4: public class LadyBug extends java.applet.Applet {
5:
6:     Image bugimg;
7:
8:     public void init() {
9:         bugimg = getImage(getCodeBase(),
10:             "images/ladybug.gif");
11:     }
12:
13:     public void paint(Graphics g) {
14:         int iwidth = bugimg.getWidth(this);
15:         int iheight = bugimg.getHeight(this);
16:         int xpos = 10;
17:
18:         // 25 %
19:         g.drawImage(bugimg, xpos, 10,
20:             iwidth / 4, iheight / 4, this);
21:
22:         // 50 %
23:         xpos += (iwidth / 4) + 10;
24:         g.drawImage(bugimg, xpos , 10,
25:             iwidth / 2, iheight / 2, this);
26:
27:         // 100%
28:         xpos += (iwidth / 2) + 10;
29:         g.drawImage(bugimg, xpos, 10, this);
30:
31:         // 150% x, 25% y
32:         g.drawImage(bugimg, 10, iheight + 30,
33:             (int)(iwidth * 1.5), iheight / 4, this);
34:     }
35: }
```

10

A Note About Image Observers

I've been steadfastly ignoring mentioning that last argument to drawImage(): the mysterious this, which also appears as an argument to getWidth() and getHeight(). Why is this argument used? Its official use is to pass in an object that functions as an ImageObserver (that is, an object that implements the ImageObserver interface). Image observers are used to watch the progress of how far along an image is in the loading process and to make decisions when the image is only fully or partially loaded. So, for example, your applet could pause until all the images are loaded and ready, or display a "loading" message, or do something else while it was waiting.

The Applet class, from which your applet inherits, contains a default behavior for image observation (which it inherits from the Component superclass) that should work in the majority of cases—hence, the this argument to drawImage(), getWidth(), and getHeight(). The only reason you'll want to use an alternate argument in its place is if you want more control over what your applet will do in cases where an image may only be partially loaded, or if tracking lots of images loading asynchronously.

Modifying Images

In addition to the basics of handling images described in this section, the java.awt.image package provides more classes and interfaces that enable you to modify images and their internal colors, or to create bitmap images by hand.

Creating Animation Using Images

Creating animation with images is much the same as creating animation with fonts, colors, or shapes—you use the same methods and the same procedures for painting, repainting, and reducing flickering that you learned about earlier in this chapter. The only difference is that you have a stack of images to flip through rather than a set of painting methods.

Probably the best way to show you how to use images for animation is simply to walk through an example. Here's an extensive one of an animation of a small cat called Neko.

An Example: Neko

Neko is a small Macintosh animation/game written and drawn by Kenji Gotoh in 1989. "Neko" is Japanese for "cat," and the animation is of a small kitten that chases the mouse pointer around the screen, sleeps, scratches, and generally acts cute. The Neko program has since been ported to just about every possible platform, as well as rewritten as a popular screen saver.

10

For this example, you'll implement a small animation based on the original Neko graphics. Unlike the original Neko the cat, which was autonomous (it could "sense" the edges of the window and turn and run in a different direction), this applet merely causes Neko to run in from the left side of the screen, stop in the middle, yawn, scratch its ear, sleep a little, and then run off to the right.

NOTE

This is by far the largest of the applets discussed so far in this book, and if I either print it here and then describe it, or build it up line by line, you'll be here for days. Instead, I'm going to describe the parts of this applet independently, and I'm going to leave out the basics—the stuff you learned earlier about starting and stopping threads, what the run() method does, and so on. All the code is printed later today so that you can put it all together.

Step 1: Collect Your Images

Before you begin writing Java code to construct an animation, you should have all the images that form the animation itself. For this version of Neko, there are nine of them (the original has 36), as shown in Figure 10.4.

Figure 10.4.
The images for the
Neko *applet.*

NOTE

The Neko images, as well as the source code for this applet, are available on the CD.

For this example I've stored these images in a directory called, appropriately, images. Where you store your images isn't all that important, but you should take note of where you've put them because you'll need that information later on when you load your images.

Step 2: Organize and Load the Images in Your Applet

Now, on to the applet. The basic idea here is that you have a set of images and you display them one at a time, rapidly, so that they give the appearance of movement. The easiest way to manage this in Java is to store the images in an array of class Image, and then to have a special variable to keep track of the current image. As you iterate over the slots in the array (using a `for` loop), you can change the value of the current image each time.

For the `Neko` applet, you'll create instance variables to implement both these things: an array to hold the images, called `nekopics`, and a variable of type `Image` called `currentimg`, to hold the current image being displayed:

```
Image nekopics[] = new Image[9];
Image currentimg;
```

Here the image array has nine slots, as the Neko animation has nine images. If you have a larger or smaller set of images, you'll have a different number of slots.

TECHNICAL NOTE

> The `java.util` class contains a class (`HashTable`) that implements a hash table. For large numbers of images, a hash table is faster to find and retrieve images from than an array is. Because there's a small number of images here, and because arrays are better for fixed-length, repeating animation, I'll use an array here.

Because the Neko animation draws the cat images in different positions on the screen, you'll also want to keep track of the current x and y positions so that the various methods in this applet know where to start drawing. The y stays constant for this particular applet (Neko runs left to right at the same y position), but the x may vary. Let's add two instance variables for those two positions:

```
int xpos;
int ypos = 50;
```

Now, on to the body of the applet. During the applet's initialization, you'll read in all the images and store them in the nekopics array. This is the sort of operation that works especially well in an `init()` method.

Given that you have nine images with nine different filenames, you could do a separate call to `getImage()` for each one. You can save at least a little typing, however, by creating a local array of the file names (`nekosrc`, an array of strings) and then use a for loop to iterate over each one and load them in turn. Here's the `init()` method for the Neko applet that loads all the images into the nekopics array:

```
public void init() {

    String nekosrc[] = { "right1.gif", "right2.gif",
        "stop.gif", "yawn.gif", "scratch1.gif",
        "scratch2.gif","sleep1.gif", "sleep2.gif",
        "awake.gif" };
```

```
        for (int i=0; i < nekopics.length; i++) {
            nekopics[i] = getImage(getCodeBase(),
                "images/" + nekosrc[i]);
        }
    }
```

Note here in the call to getImage() that the directory these images are stored in (the images directory) is included as part of the path.

Step 3: Animate the Images

With the images loaded, the next step is to start animating the bits of the applet. You do this inside the applet's thread's run() method. In this applet, Neko does five main things:

☐ Runs in from the left side of the screen

☐ Stops in the middle and yawns

☐ Scratches four times

☐ Sleeps

☐ Wakes up and runs off to the right side of the screen

Although you could animate this applet by merely painting the right image to the screen at the right time, it makes more sense to write this applet so that many of Neko's activities are contained in individual methods. This way, you can reuse some of the activities (the animation of Neko running, in particular) if you want Neko to do things in a different order.

Let's start by creating a method to make Neko run. Because you're going to be using this one twice, making it generic is a good plan. Let's create a nekorun() method, which takes two arguments: the x position to start, and the x position to end. Neko then runs between those two positions (the y remains constant).

```
void nekorun(int start, int end) {
    ...
}
```

There are two images that represent Neko running; to create the running effect, you need to alternate between those two images (stored in positions 0 and 1 of the image array), as well as move them across the screen. The moving part is a simple for loop between the start and end arguments, setting the x position to the current loop value. Swapping the images means merely testing to see which one is active at any turn of the loop and assigning the other one to the current image. Finally, at each new frame, you'll call repaint() and sleep() for a bit to pause the animation.

Actually, given that during this animation there will be a lot of pausing of various intervals, it makes sense to create a utility method that does just that—pause for a given amount of time.

10

The pause() method, therefore, takes one argument, a number of milliseconds. Here's its definition:

```
void pause(int time) {
    try { Thread.sleep(time); }
    catch (InterruptedException e) { }
}
```

Back to the nekorun() method. To summarize, nekorun() iterates from the start position to the end position. For each turn of the loop, it sets the current x position, sets currentimg to the right animation frame, calls repaint(), and pauses. Got it? Here's the definition of nekorun:

```
void nekorun(int start, int end) {
    for (int i = start; i < end; i+=10) {
        xpos = i;
        // swap images
        if (currentimg == nekopics[0])
            currentimg = nekopics[1];
        else currentimg = nekopics[0];
        repaint();
        pause(150);
    }
}
```

Note that in that second line you increment the loop by 10 pixels. Why 10 pixels and not, say, 5 or 8? The answer is determined mostly through trial and error to see what looks right. Ten seems to work best for the animation. When you write your own animation, you have to play with both the distances and the sleep times until you get an animation you like. Speaking of repaint(), let's skip over to that paint() method, which paints each frame. Here the paint() method is trivially simple; all paint() is responsible for is painting the current image at the current x and y positions. All that information is stored in instance variables. However, we do want to make sure that the images actually exist before we draw them (the images might be in the process of loading). To catch this and make sure we don't try drawing an image that isn't there (resulting in all kinds of errors), we'll test to make sure currentimg isn't null before calling drawImage() to paint the image:

```
public void paint(Graphics g) {
    if (currentimg != null)
        g.drawImage(currentimg, xpos, ypos, this);
}
```

Now let's back up to the run() method, where the main processing of this animation is happening. You've created the nekorun() method; in run() you'll call that method with the appropriate values to make Neko run from the left edge of the screen to the center:

```
// run from one side of the screen to the middle
nekorun(0, size().width / 2);
```

The second major thing Neko does in this animation is stop and yawn. You have a single frame for each of these things (in positions 2 and 3 in the array), so you don't really need a separate method to draw them. All you need to do is set the appropriate image, call `repaint()`, and pause for the right amount of time. This example pauses for a second each time for both stopping and yawning—again, using trial and error. Here's the code:

```
// stop and pause
currentimg = nekopics[2];
repaint();
pause(1000);

// yawn
currentimg = nekopics[3];
repaint();
pause(1000);
```

Let's move on to the third part of the animation: Neko scratching. There's no horizontal movement for this part of the animation. You alternate between the two scratching images (stored in positions 4 and 5 of the image array). Because scratching is a distinct action, however, let's create a separate method for it.

The `nekoscratch()` method takes a single argument: the number of times to scratch. With that argument, you can iterate, and then, inside the loop, alternate between the two scratching images and repaint each time:

```
void nekoscratch(int numtimes) {
    for (int i = numtimes; i > 0; i—) {
        currentimg = nekopics[4];
        repaint();
        pause(150);
        currentimg = nekopics[5];
        repaint();
        pause(150);
    }
}
```

Inside the run method, you can then call `nekoscratch()` with an argument of (4):

```
// scratch four times
nekoscratch(4);
```

Onward! After scratching, Neko sleeps. Again, you have two images for sleeping (in positions 6 and 7 of the array), which you'll alternate a certain number of times. Here's the `nekosleep()` method, which takes a single number argument, and animates for that many "turns":

```
void nekosleep(int numtimes) {
    for (int i = numtimes; i > 0; i—) {
        currentimg = nekopics[6];
        repaint();
        pause(250);
        currentimg = nekopics[7];
        repaint();
        pause(250);
    }
}
```

Call `nekosleep()` in the `run()` method like this:

```
// sleep for 5 "turns"
nekosleep(5);
```

Finally, to finish off the applet, Neko wakes up and runs off to the right side of the screen. The waking up image is the last image in the array (position 8), and you can reuse the nekorun method to finish:

```
// wake up and run off
currentimg = nekopics[8];
repaint();
pause(500);
nekorun(xpos, size().width + 10);
```

Step 4: Finish Up

There's one more thing left to do to finish the applet. The images for the animation all have white backgrounds. Drawing those images on the default applet background (a medium gray) means an unsightly white box around each image. To get around the problem, merely set the applet's background to white at the start of the `run()` method:

```
setBackground(Color.white);
```

Got all that? There's a lot of code in this applet, and a lot of individual methods to accomplish a rather simple animation, but it's not all that complicated. The heart of it, as in the heart of all forms of animation in Java, is to set up the frame and then call `repaint()` to enable the screen to be drawn.

Note that you don't do anything to reduce the amount of flickering in this applet. It turns out that the images are small enough, and the drawing area also small enough, that flickering is not a problem for this applet. It's always a good idea to write your animation to do the simplest thing first, and then add behavior to make it run cleaner.

To finish up this section, Listing 10.4 shows the complete code for the Neko applet.

TYPE   **Listing 10.4. The full text of `Neko.java`.**

```
 1: import java.awt.Graphics;
 2: import java.awt.Image;
 3: import java.awt.Color;
 4:
 5: public class Neko extends java.applet.Applet
 6:     implements Runnable {
 7:
 8:     Image nekopics[] = new Image[9];
 9:     Image currentimg;
10:     Thread runner;
```

```
11:     int xpos;
12:     int ypos = 50;
13:
14:     public void init() {
15:         String nekosrc[] = { "right1.gif", "right2.gif",
16:             "stop.gif", "yawn.gif", "scratch1.gif",
17:             "scratch2.gif","sleep1.gif", "sleep2.gif",
18:             "awake.gif" };
19:
20:         for (int i=0; i < nekopics.length; i++) {
21:             nekopics[i] = getImage(getCodeBase(),
22:             "images/" + nekosrc[i]);
23:         }
24:     }
25:
26:     public void start() {
27:         if (runner == null) {
28:             runner = new Thread(this);
29:             runner.start();
30:         }
31:     }
32:
33:     public void stop() {
34:         if (runner != null) {
35:             runner.stop();
36:             runner = null;
37:         }
38:     }
39:
40:     public void run() {
41:         setBackground(Color.white);
42:
43:         // run from one side of the screen to the middle
44:         nekorun(0, size().width / 2);
45:
46:         // stop and pause
47:         currentimg = nekopics[2];
48:         repaint();
49:         pause(1000);
50:
51:         // yawn
52:         currentimg = nekopics[3];
53:         repaint();
54:         pause(1000);
55:
56:         // scratch four times
57:         nekoscratch(4);
58:
59:         // sleep for 5 "turns"
60:         nekosleep(5);
61:
62:         // wake up and run off
63:         currentimg = nekopics[8];
64:         repaint();
65:         pause(500);
66:         nekorun(xpos, size().width + 10);
```

continues

Listing 10.4. continued

```
67:        }
68:
69:        void nekorun(int start, int end) {
70:            for (int i = start; i < end; i += 10) {
71:                xpos = i;
72:                // swap images
73:                if (currentimg == nekopics[0])
74:                    currentimg = nekopics[1];
75:                else currentimg = nekopics[0];
76:                    repaint();
77:                pause(150);
78:            }
79:        }
80:
81:
82:        void nekoscratch(int numtimes) {
83:            for (int i = numtimes; i > 0; i--) {
84:                currentimg = nekopics[4];
85:                repaint();
86:                pause(150);
87:                currentimg = nekopics[5];
88:                repaint();
89:                pause(150);
90:            }
91:        }
92:
93:        void nekosleep(int numtimes) {
94:            for (int i = numtimes; i > 0; i--) {
95:                currentimg = nekopics[6];
96:                repaint();
97:                pause(250);
98:                currentimg = nekopics[7];
99:                repaint();
100:               pause(250);
101:           }
102:       }
103:
104:       void pause(int time) {
105:           try { Thread.sleep(time); }
106:           catch (InterruptedException e) { }
107:       }
108:
109:       public void paint(Graphics g) {
110:           if (currentimg != null)
111:               g.drawImage(currentimg, xpos, ypos, this);
112:       }
113: }
```

Retrieving and Using Sounds

Java has built-in support for playing sounds in conjunction with running animation or for sounds on their own. In fact, support for sound, like support for images, is built into the Applet and AWT classes, so using sound in your Java applets is as easy as loading and using images.

Currently, the only sound format that Java supports is Sun's AU format, sometimes called m-law format. AU files tend to be smaller than sound files in other formats, but the sound quality is not very good. If you're especially concerned with sound quality, you may want your sound clips to be references in the traditional HTML way (as links to external files) rather than included in a Java applet.

The simplest way to retrieve and play a sound is through the play() method, part of the Applet class and therefore available to you in your applets. The play() method is similar to the getImage() method in that it takes one of two forms:

□ play() with one argument, a URL object, loads and plays the given audio clip at that URL.

□ play() with two arguments, one a base URL and one a pathname, loads and plays that audio file. The first argument can most usefully be either a call to getDocumentBase() or getCodeBase().

For example, the following line of code retrieves and plays the sound meow.au, which is contained in the audio directory. The audio directory, in turn, is located in the same directory as this applet:

```
play(getCodeBase(), "audio/meow.au");
```

The play() method retrieves and plays the given sound as soon as possible after it is called. If it can't find the sound, you won't get an error; you simply won't get any audio when you expect it.

If you want to play a sound repeatedly, start and stop the sound clip, or run the clip as a loop (play it over and over), things are then slightly more complicated—but not much more so. In this case, you use the applet method getAudioClip() to load the sound clip into an instance of the class AudioClip (part of java.applet—don't forget to import it) and then operate directly on that AudioClip object.

Suppose, for example, that you have a sound loop that you want to play in the background of your applet. In your initialization code, you can use this line to get the audio clip:

```
AudioClip clip = getAudioClip(getCodeBase(),
"audio/loop.au");
```

Then, to play the clip once, use the play() method:

```
clip.play();
```

To stop a currently playing sound clip, use the stop() method:

```
clip.stop();
```

To loop the clip (play it repeatedly), use the loop() method:

```
clip.loop();
```

If the getAudioClip() method can't find the sound you indicate, or can't load it for any reason, it returns null. It's a good idea to test for this case in your code before trying to play the audio clip, because trying to call the play(), stop(), and loop() methods on a null object will result in an error (actually, an exception).

In your applet, you can play as many audio clips as you need; all the sounds you use will mix together properly as they are played by your applet.

Note that if you use a background sound—a sound clip that loops repeatedly—that sound clip will not stop playing automatically when you suspend the applet's thread. This means that even if your reader moves to another page, the first applet's sounds will continue to play. You can fix this problem by stopping the applet's background sound in your stop() method:

```
public void stop() {
    if (runner != null) {
        if (bgsound != null)
        bgsound.stop();
        runner.stop();
        runner = null;
    }
}
```

Listing 10.5 shows a simple framework for an applet that plays two sounds: The first, a background sound called loop.au, plays repeatedly. The second, a horn honking (beep.au), plays every five seconds. (I won't bother giving you a picture of this applet because it doesn't actually display anything other than a simple string to the screen.)

TYPE   **Listing 10.5. The full text of AudioLoop.java applet.**

```
1: import java.awt.Graphics;
2: import java.applet.AudioClip;
3:
4: public class AudioLoop extends java.applet.Applet
5:     implements Runnable {
6:
7:     AudioClip bgsound;
8:     AudioClip beep;
9:     Thread runner;
```

```
10:
11:    public void start() {
12:        if (runner == null) {
13:            runner = new Thread(this);
14:            runner.start();
15:        }
16:    }
17:
18:    public void stop() {
19:        if (runner != null) {
20:            if (bgsound != null) bgsound.stop();
21:            runner.stop();
22:            runner = null;
23:        }
24:    }
25:
26:    public void init() {
27:        bgsound = getAudioClip(getCodeBase(),"audio/loop.au");
28:        beep = getAudioClip(getCodeBase(), "audio/beep.au");
29:    }
30:
31:    public void run() {
32:        if (bgsound != null) bgsound.loop();
33:        while (runner != null) {
34:            try { Thread.sleep(5000); }
35:            catch (InterruptedException e) { }
36:            if (beep != null) beep.play();
37:        }
38:    }
39:
40:    public void paint(Graphics g) {
41:        g.drawString("Playing Sounds....", 10, 10);
42:    }
43: }
```

There are only a few things to note about this applet. First, note the init() method in lines 26 to 29, which loads both the loop.au and the beep.au sound files. We've made no attempt here to make sure these files actually load as expected, so the possibility exists that the bgsound and beep instance variables may end up with the null values if the file cannot load. In that case, we won't be able to call start(), stop(), or any other methods, so we should make sure we test for that elsewhere in the applet.

And we have tested for null several places here, particularly in the run() method in lines 32 and 36. These lines start the sounds looping and playing, but only if the values of the bgsound and beep variables are something other than null.

Finally, note line 20, which explicitly turns off the background sound if the thread is also being stopped. Because background sounds do not stop playing even when the thread has been stopped, you have to explicitly stop them here.

More About Flickering: Double-Buffering

Earlier, you learned a simple way to reduce flickering in Java animation. A second, more complex but often more useful way of controlling animation flicker is called double-buffering.

With double-buffering, you create a second surface (offscreen, so to speak), do all your painting to that offscreen surface, and then draw the whole surface at once onto the actual applet (and onto the screen) at the end—rather than drawing to the applet's actual graphics surface. Because all the work actually goes on behind the scenes, there's no opportunity for interim parts of the drawing process to appear accidentally and disrupt the smoothness of the animation.

 Double-buffering is the process of doing all your drawing to an offscreen buffer and then displaying that entire screen at once. It's called double-buffering because there are two drawing buffers and you switch between them.

Double-buffering isn't always the best solution. If your applet is suffering from flickering, try overriding update() and drawing only portions of the screen first; that may solve your problem. Double-buffering is less efficient than regular buffering and also takes up more memory and space, so in some cases it may not be the optimal solution. In terms of nearly eliminating animation flickering, however, double-buffering works exceptionally well.

Creating Applets with Double-Buffering

To create an applet that uses double-buffering, you need two things: an offscreen image to draw on and a graphics context for that image. Those two together mimic the effect of the applet's drawing surface: the graphics context (an instance of Graphics) to provide the drawing methods, such as drawImage() (and drawString()), and the Image to hold the dots that get drawn.

There are four major steps to adding double-buffering to your applet. First, your offscreen image and graphics context need to be stored in instance variables so that you can pass them to the paint() method. Declare the following instance variables in your class definition:

```
Image offscreenImage;
Graphics offscreenGraphics;
```

Second, during the initialization of the applet, you'll create an Image and a Graphics object and assign them to these variables (you have to wait until initialization so you know how big they're going to be). The createImage() method gives you an instance of Image, which you can then send the getGraphics() method in order to get a new Graphics context for that image:

```
offscreenImage = createImage(size().width,
size().height);
offscreenGraphics = offscreenImage.getGraphics();
```

Now, whenever you have to draw to the screen (usually in your `paint()` method), rather than drawing to paint's graphics, draw to the offscreen graphics. For example, to draw an image called `img` at position 10,10, use this line:

```
offscreenGraphics.drawImage(img, 10, 10, this);
```

Finally, at the end of your paint method, after all the drawing to the offscreen image is done, add the following line to place the offscreen buffer on to the real screen:

```
g.drawImage(offscreenImage, 0, 0, this);
```

Of course, you most likely will want to override `update()` so that it doesn't clear the screen between paintings:

```
public void update(Graphics g) {
    paint(g);
}
```

Let's review those four steps:

1. Add instance variables to hold the image and graphics contexts for the offscreen buffer.

2. Create an image and a graphics context when your applet is initialized.

3. Do all your applet painting to the offscreen buffer, not the applet's drawing surface.

4. At the end of your `paint()` method, draw the offscreen buffer to the real screen.

A Note on Disposing Graphics Contexts

If you make extensive use of graphics contexts in your applets or applications, be aware that those contexts will often continue to stay around after you're done with them, even if you no longer have any references to them. Graphics contexts are special objects in the AWT that map to the native operating system; Java's garbage collector cannot release those contexts by itself. If you use multiple graphics contexts or use them repeatedly, you'll want to explicitly get rid of those contexts once you're done with them.

Use the `dispose()` method to explicitly clean up a graphics context. A good place to put this might be in the applet's `destroy()` method (which you learned about on Day 8, "Java Applet Basics"; it was one of the primary applet methods, along with `init()`, `start()`, and `stop()`):

```
public void destroy() {
    offscreenGraphics.dispose();
}
```

10

An Example: Checkers

Here's another example of a simple animation. In this applet, called Checkers, a red oval (a checker piece) moves from a black square to a white square, as if on a checkerboard. At the end of its movement it returns to the starting position and moves again. Listing 10.6 shows the code for a first pass try at this applet, and Figure 10.5 shows the applet itself.

TYPE   **Listing 10.6. The Checkers applet.**

```
 1: import java.awt.Graphics;
 2: import java.awt.Color;
 3:
 4: public class Checkers extends java.applet.Applet implements Runnable {
 5:
 6:     Thread runner;
 7:     int xpos;
 8:
 9:     public void start() {
10:       if (runner == null); {
11:         runner = new Thread(this);
12:         runner.start();
13:       }
14:     }
15:
16:     public void stop() {
17:       if (runner != null) {
18:         runner.stop();
19:         runner = null;
20:       }
21:     }
22:
23:     public void run() {
24:       while (true) {
25:         for (xpos = 5; xpos <= 105; xpos+=4) {
26:           repaint();
27:           try { Thread.sleep(100); }
28:           catch (InterruptedException e) { }
29:         }
30:       xpos=5;
31:       }
32:     }
33:
34:     public void update(Graphics g) {
35:
36:     }
37:
38:     public void paint(Graphics g) {
39:       // Draw background
40:       g.setColor(Color.black);
41:       g.fillRect(0,0,100,100);
42:       g.setColor(Color.white);
43:       g.fillRect(100,0,100,100);
44:
```

10

```
45:      // Draw checker
46:      g.setColor(Color.red);
47:      g.fillOval(xpos,5,90,90);
48:  }
49: }
```

Figure 10.5.

The Checkers *applet.*

ANALYSIS Here's a quick run-through of what this applet does: An instance variable, xpos, keeps track of the current starting position of the checker. (Because it moves horizontally, the y stays constant and only the x changes; we don't need to keep track of the y position.) In the run() method, you change the value of x and repaint, waiting 100 milliseconds between each move. The checker then appears to move from the left side of the screen to the right, resetting back at its original position after it hits the right side of the screen.

In the actual paint() method, the background squares are painted (one black and one white), and then the checker is drawn at its current position.

This applet, like the ColorSwirl applet, also has a terrible flicker. However, simply overriding update() as we did here isn't enough to fix it, as parts of the screen are erased and redrawn as the checker moves across the screen. The flicker in this applet results because of the background being drawn first and then the checker being drawn on top of it.

You could modify this applet such that paint() only redraws what's been changed using clipRect() to try to minimize the flicker, but that strategy involves keeping track of old and new positions of the checker, and doesn't do a whole lot of good. A better solution in this case is to use double-buffering, which eliminates the flickering altogether. Fortunately, adding double-buffering to this example is easy. First, add the instance variables for the offscreen image and its graphics context:

```
Image offscreenImg;
Graphics offscreenG;
```

Second, add an init method to initialize the offscreen buffer:

```
public void init() {
    offscreenImg = createImage(size().width, size().height);
    offscreenG = offscreenImg.getGraphics();
}
```

Third, modify the paint() method to draw to the offscreen buffer instead of to the main graphics buffer:

```
public void paint(Graphics g) {
    // Draw background
    offscreenG.setColor(Color.black);
    offscreenG.fillRect(0, 0, 100, 100);
    offscreenG.setColor(Color.white);
    offscreenG.fillRect(100, 0, 100, 100);

    // Draw checker
    offscreenG.setColor(Color.red);
    offscreenG.fillOval(xpos, 5, 90, 90);

    g.drawImage(offscreenImg, 0, 0, this);
}
```

Finally, in the applet's destroy() method, explicitly dispose of the graphics context stored in offscreenG:

```
public void destroy() {
    offscreenG.dispose();
}
```

Listing 10.7 shows the final code for the Checkers applet (Checkers2.java), which includes double-buffering.

TYPE   **Listing 10.7. The full text of Checkers2.java.**

```
 1: import java.awt.Graphics;
 2: import java.awt.Color;
 3: import java.awt.Image;
 4:
 5: public class Checkers2 extends java.applet.Applet implements Runnable {
 6:
 7:    Thread runner;
 8:    int xpos;
 9:    Image offscreenImg;
10:    Graphics offscreenG;
11:
12:    public void init() {
13:        offscreenImg = createImage(this.size().width, this.size().height);
14:        offscreenG = offscreenImg.getGraphics();
15:    }
16:
17:    public void start() {
18:        if (runner == null); {
19:            runner = new Thread(this);
20:            runner.start();
21:        }
22:    }
23:
```

10

```
24:   public void stop() {
25:      if (runner != null) {
26:        runner.stop();
27:        runner = null;
28:      }
29:   }
30:
31:   public void run() {
32:      while (true) {
33:        for (xpos = 5; xpos <= 105; xpos+=4) {
34:          repaint();
35:          try { Thread.sleep(100); }
36:          catch (InterruptedException e) { }
37:        }
38:        xpos = 5;
39:      }
40:   }
41:
42:   public void update(Graphics g) {
43:      paint(g);
44:   }
45:
46:   public void paint(Graphics g) {
47:      // Draw background
48:      offscreenG.setColor(Color.black);
49:      offscreenG.fillRect(0,0,100,100);
50:      offscreenG.setColor(Color.white);
51:      offscreenG.fillRect(100,0,100,100);
52:
53:      // Draw checker
54:      offscreenG.setColor(Color.red);
55:      offscreenG.fillOval(xpos,5,90,90);
56:
57:      g.drawImage(offscreenImg,0,0,this);
58:   }
59:
60:   public void destroy() {
61:      offscreenG.dispose();
62:   }
63: }
```

Summary

Congratulations on getting through Day 10! This day was a bit rough; you've learned a lot, and it all might seem overwhelming. You learned about a plethora of methods to use and override—start(), stop(), paint(), repaint(), run(), and update()—and you got a basic foundation in creating and using threads. You also learned about using images in your applets—locating them, loading them, and using the drawImage() method to display and animate them.

An animation technique that you now can use is double-buffering, which virtually eliminates flickering in your animation at some expense of animation efficiency and speed. Using images and graphics contexts, you can create an offscreen buffer to draw to, the result of which is then displayed to the screen at the last possible moment.

You learned how to use sounds, which can be included in your applets any time you need them—at specific moments or as background sounds that can be repeated while the applet executes. You learned how to locate, load, and play sounds using both the play() and the getAudioClip() methods.

Q&A

Q **Why all the indirection with paint(), repaint(), update(), and all that? Why not have a simple paint() method that puts stuff on the screen when you want it there?**

A The Java AWT enables you to nest drawable surfaces within other drawable surfaces. When a paint() takes place, all the parts of the system are redrawn, starting from the outermost surface and moving downward into the most nested one. Because the drawing of your applet takes place at the same time everything else is drawn, your applet doesn't get any special treatment. Your applet will be painted when everything else is painted. Although with this system you sacrifice some of the immediacy of instant painting, it enables your applet to coexist with the rest of the system more cleanly.

Q **When an applet uses threads, I have to tell the thread to start and it starts, or tell it to stop and it stops? That's it? I don't have to test anything in my loops or keep track of its state? It just stops?**

A It just stops. When you put your applet into a thread, Java can control the execution of your applet much more readily. By causing the thread to stop, your applet just stops running, and then resumes when the thread starts up again. Yes, it's all automatic. Neat, isn't it?

Q **In the Neko program, you put the image loading into the init() method. It seems to me that it might take Java a long time to load all those images, and because init() isn't in the main thread of the applet, there's going to be a distinct pause there. Why not put the image loading at the beginning of the run() method instead?**

A There are sneaky things going on behind the scenes. The getImage() method doesn't actually load the image; in fact, it returns an Image object almost instantaneously, so it isn't taking up a large amount of processing time during initialization. The image data that getImage() points to isn't actually loaded until the image is needed. This way, Java doesn't have to keep enormous images around in memory if the program is going to use only a small piece. Instead, it can just keep a reference to that data and retrieve what it needs later.

Q I compiled and ran the Neko applet. Something weird is going on; the animation starts in the middle and drops frames. It's as if only some of the images have loaded when the applet is run.

A That's precisely what's going on. Because image loading doesn't actually load the image right away, your applet may be merrily animating blank screens while the images are still being loaded. Depending on how long it takes those images to load, your applet may appear to start in the middle, to drop frames, or to not work at all.

There are three possible solutions to this problem. The first is to have the animation loop (that is, start over from the beginning once it stops). Eventually, the images will load and the animation will work correctly. The second solution, and not a very good one, is to sleep for a while before starting the animation, to pause while the images load. The third, and best solution, is to use image observers to make sure no part of the animation plays before its images have loaded. Check out the documentation for the ImageObserver interface for details.

Q I wrote an applet to do a background sound using the `getAudioClip()` and `loop()` methods. The sound works great, but it won't stop. I've tried suspending the current thread and killing the thread altogether, but the sound goes on.

A I mentioned this as a small note in the section on sounds; background sounds don't run in the main thread of the applet, so if you stop the thread, the sound keeps going. The solution is easy—in the same method where you stop the thread, also stop the sound, like this:

```
runner.stop();  //stop the thread
bgsound.stop(); //also stop the sound
```

10

Day 11

Managing Simple Events and Interactivity

by Laura Lemay

Java events are part of the Java Abstract Windowing Toolkit (AWT) package. An event is the way that the AWT communicates to you, as the programmer, and to other Java AWT components that something has happened. That something can be input from the user (mouse movements or clicks, keypresses), changes in the system environment (a window opening or closing, the window being scrolled up or down), or a host of other things that might, in some way, affect the operation of the program. By catching those events in your Java program, your program can react to user input and change its behavior based on that input.

Today I'll cover both the 1.02 and 1.1 event models. For the first half of this lesson, we'll focus primarily on the older model; for the second half, we'll move to 1.1 and I'll show you how to convert your old code so that it uses the new model. More specifically, today you'll cover the following subjects:

☐ A general introduction to events (Start here, regardless of the event model you'll be using.)

☐ Handling mouse clicks in the 1.02 event model

☐ Handling mouse movements in the 1.02 event model

☐ Handling keyboard actions in the 1.02 event model

☐ Graduating to the 1.1 event model: why it was needed, how it works, and how to convert your old programs to the new model

☐ Mouse and keyboard events in the 1.1 event model

Tomorrow you'll learn how to combine the basic knowledge of events you learned here with other AWT components to create a complete user interface for your applet.

A Unified Theory of Events

Let's start with a general description of events, the kinds of events you can use in your programs, and how event handling works in both the 1.02 and 1.1 event models. Regardless of which of the event models you intend to use, read this section for a general overview.

What Are Events?

An event, as I mentioned earlier, is generated in response to just about anything that occurs during the life cycle of an applet or an application. Every movement of the mouse, every button click, every keypress, any actions on user interface elements, any operations on windows—all of these things generate events. This means that as your Java program is running, a swarm of events is going by, like objects on a conveyor belt. In fact, in Java, events are indeed objects; they're instances of a particular event class.

In your applet code, you don't have to deal with all the events that might possibly occur; that would be no fun at all. In fact, you aren't even allowed to touch several events; instead, the operating system or the Java environment handles many of them for you. Painting, for example, is an event that you don't have to deal with; all you have to do is tell the AWT what you want painted when it gets to your part of the window.

You can intercept a set of events, however, and you may be interested in dealing with them in your programs. If the user clicks the mouse somewhere inside your applet or presses a key, you may want to do something in response to that event. That's what AWT event management is for; it's like standing in front of the conveyor belt, waiting for the right object to come by, and plucking that object off the conveyor belt to do something with it. And if an event that you don't care about occurs, you can just safely ignore that event (leave it on the conveyor belt); either some other part of the system will deal with it, or it will eventually disappear.

The following are the events that you can deal with in your own programs:

☐ Mouse clicks: mouse down (button pressed), mouse up (button released), or mouse clicked (pressed and released in the same location)

☐ Mouse movements: generic mouse pointer movements, the pointer entering or exiting a part of your program, and mouse drags (pointer motions that occur with the button held down)

☐ Keypresses: key pressed, key released, and key typed (pressed and released)

☐ User interface events: buttons clicked, scroll bars scrolled up and down, pop-up menus popped up, and so on

☐ Window events: window opened, window closed, and window exited

Today you'll learn how to manage mouse and keyboard events (the first three bullets). As you learn more about how to create and use AWT user interface elements in the next few days, you'll learn how to manage the user interface and window events as well.

The Two Event Models

Events are generated and flow through the system in roughly the same way, regardless of whether you're using the 1.02 or the 1.1 event models in your code. The two models differ in how you receive and process those events.

NOTE

This section contains a general conceptual view of how events work. If this section leaves you more confused than when you began, don't panic; the code examples later in this lesson will help make the information more concrete.

In the 1.02 event model, all the events that occur during the life cycle of your Java program flow through that program and are handled by a method called handleEvent(). The basic version of the handleEvent() method, defined in java.awt.Component (which the applet class inherits from), calls several default methods for different events: mouseDown(), mouseUp(), keyDown(), and so on. To handle an event in your applet, all you have to do is override a specific event method. Then, when that event occurs, your method is called. So, for example, if you override the mouseDown() method in your applet to print a message of some sort, when a mouse down event occurs inside your applet, that message will be printed. That's it.

In the 1.1 event model, the flow of events—and how you handle them in your programs—is very different. The 1.1 event model has the concept of an *event listener*. Different listeners are responsible for handling a specific set of events; for example, you would define a mouse listener for mouse events or a key listener for keyboard events.

Inside your applet, you "register" the listener as being interested in those events (you can use special methods for doing just that). After a listener is registered, only those events that the applet is listening for will pass through that applet, and the listener object is actually responsible for handling those events once they occur.

Which Model Should You Use?

Which event model you use in your own applications depends on the environment your program will run in. As I write this lesson, the vast majority of browsers and Java virtual machines are compatible only with the 1.02 event model (and the 1.02 JDK). If your applet will run primarily in these environments, you'll want to stick with the 1.02 model. (In fact, the 1.1 model will not work in the 1.02 environments.)

You can also use the 1.02 model inside a 1.1 environment; 1.1 is designed to be backward compatible with the old model. If you find 1.02 to be much easier to understand and implement (as will usually be the case), you can probably go ahead and use it for a while longer.

If you're working exclusively for the Java 1.1 environment, and you're implementing a larger application or one that uses JavaBeans, you should be using the 1.1 event model.

Even if you continue to use the 1.02 event model, becoming familiar with and porting your programs to the 1.1 model is probably a good idea as soon as support for it becomes more widespread. Eventually, the 1.02 model will stop being supported by Java. The 1.1 model is more flexible in the long run and more easily maintained for larger programs.

With all that general background behind us, let's get down to brass tacks and dig into some real event-handling code. In the next three sections, you'll work with the 1.02 event model to handle mouse clicks, mouse movements, and keypresses. If you're interested in dealing with the 1.1 event model exclusively, you can read these sections for kicks if you want to, or you can skip ahead to "Moving Up to the 1.1 Event Model." There will not be a pop quiz.

Handling Mouse Clicks in the 1.02 Model

One of the most common events in your applet that you might be interested in is a mouse click. Mouse-click events occur when your user clicks the mouse somewhere in the body of your applet. You can intercept mouse clicks to do simple things—for example, to toggle the sound on and off in your applet, to move to the next slide in a presentation, or to clear the screen and start over. Or you can use mouse clicks in conjunction with mouse movements to perform more complex motions inside your applet.

Mouse Down and Mouse Up Events

When you click the mouse once, the 1.02 AWT generates two separate events: a mouse down event when the mouse button is pressed and a mouse up event when the button is released. Why two individual events for a single mouse action? Because you may want to do different things for the "down" and the "up." For example, look at a pull-down menu. The mouse down extends the menu, and the mouse up selects an item (with mouse drags between—but you'll learn about that one later). If you have only one event for both actions (mouse up and mouse down), you cannot implement that sort of user interaction.

Handling mouse events in your applet is easy—all you have to do is override the right method definition in your applet. That method will be called when that particular event occurs. Here's an example of the method signature for a mouse down event:

```
public boolean mouseDown(Event evt, int x, int y) {
...
}
```

The mouseDown() method (and the mouseUp() method as well) takes three parameters: the event itself and the x and y coordinates where the mouse down or mouse up event occurred.

The evt argument is an instance of the class Event. All system events generate an instance of the Event class, which contains information about where and when the event took place, the kind of event it is, and other information that you might want to know about this event. Sometimes having a handle to that Event object is useful, as you'll discover later in this section.

The x and the y coordinates of the event, as passed in through the x and y arguments to the mouseDown() method, are particularly nice to know because you can use them to determine precisely where the mouse click took place. So, for example, if the mouse down event were over a graphical button, you could activate that button. Note that you can get to the x and y coordinates inside the Event object itself; in this method, they're passed in as separate variables to make them easier to deal with.

Here's a simple method that prints out information about a mouse down event when it occurs:

```
public boolean mouseDown(Event evt, int x, int y) {
   System.out.println("Mouse down at " + x + "," + y);
   return true;
}
```

By including this method in your applet, every time your user clicks the mouse inside your applet, this message will be printed. The AWT system calls each of these methods when the actual event takes place.

 NOTE

> Unlike with Java applications, where System.out.println() outputs to the screen, the output that appears in applets varies from system to system and browser to browser. Netscape has a special window called the Java console that must be visible for you to see the output. Internet Explorer logs Java output to a separate file. Check with your environment to see where Java output from applets is sent.

Note that this method, unlike the other system methods you've studied this far, returns a boolean value instead of not returning anything (void). This information will become important tomorrow when you create user interfaces and then manage input to these interfaces. Having an event-handler method return true or false determines whether a given component can intercept an event or whether it needs to pass it on to the enclosing component. The general rule is that if your method intercepts and does something with the event, it should return true. If, for any reason, the method doesn't do anything with that event, it should return false so that other components in the system can have a chance to see that event. In most of the examples in today's lesson, you'll be intercepting simple events, so most of the methods here will return true. Tomorrow you'll learn about nesting components and passing events up the component hierarchy.

The second half of the mouse click is the mouseUp() method, which is called when the mouse button is released. To handle a mouse up event, add the mouseUp() method to your applet: mouseUp() looks just like mouseDown():

```
public boolean mouseUp(Event evt, int x, int y) {
....
}
```

An Example: Spots

In this section, you'll create an example of an applet that implements the 1.02 event model to handle mouse events—mouse down events in particular. The Spots applet starts with a blank screen and then sits and waits. When you click the mouse on that screen, a blue dot is drawn. You can place up to 10 dots on the screen. Figure 11.1 shows the Spots applet.

Figure 11.1.
The Spots *applet.*

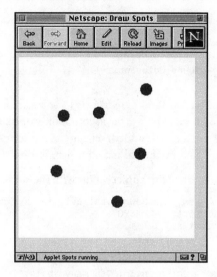

Let's start from the beginning and build this applet, starting from the initial class definition:

```
import java.awt.Graphics;
import java.awt.Color;
import java.awt.Event;

public class Spots extends java.applet.Applet {

final int MAXSPOTS = 10;
int xspots[] = new int[MAXSPOTS];
int yspots[] = new int[MAXSPOTS];
int currspots = 0;

}
```

This class uses three other AWT classes: Graphics, Color, and Event. The last class, Event, needs to be imported in any applets that use events. The class has four instance variables: a constant to determine the maximum number of spots that can be drawn, two arrays to store the x and y coordinates of the spots that have already been drawn, and an integer to keep track of the number of the current spot.

NOTE

The Event class doesn't include the implements Runnable words in its definition. As you'll see later as you build this applet, it also doesn't have a run() method. Why not? Because it doesn't actually do anything on its own—all it does is wait for input and then do stuff when input happens. The applet doesn't need threads if it isn't actively doing something all the time.

Let's start by adding the init() method, which does only one thing, set the background color to white:

```
public void init() {
    setBackground(Color.white);
}
```

You set the background here in init(), instead of in paint() as you have in past examples, because you need to set the background only once. Because paint() will be called repeatedly each time a new spot is added, setting the background in the paint() method unnecessarily slows down that method. Putting it here is a much better idea.

The main action of this applet occurs with the mouseDown() method, so let's add that one now:

```
public boolean mouseDown(Event evt, int x, int y) {
    if (currspots < MAXSPOTS) {
        addspot(x,y);
        return true;
    }
    else {
        System.out.println("Too many spots.");
        return false;
    }
}
```

When the mouse click occurs, the mouseDown() method tests to see whether there are fewer than 10 spots. If so, it calls the addspot() method (which you'll write soon) and returns true (the mouse down event was intercepted and handled). If not, it just prints an error message and returns false. What does addspot() do? It adds the coordinates of the spot to the arrays that store the coordinates, increments the currspots variable, and then calls repaint():

```
void addspot(int x, int y) {
    xspots[currspots] = x;
    yspots[currspots] = y;
    currspots++;
    repaint();
}
```

You may be wondering why you have to keep track of all the past spots in addition to the current spot. It's because of repaint(): Each time you paint the screen, you have to paint all the old spots in addition to the newest spot. Otherwise, each time you paint a new spot, the older spots are erased.

Now, on to the paint() method:

```
public void paint(Graphics g) {
    g.setColor(Color.blue);
    for (int i = 0; i < currspots; i++) {
        g.fillOval(xspots[i] -10, yspots[i] - 10, 20, 20);
    }
}
```

Inside paint(), you just loop through the spots you've stored in the xspots and yspots arrays, painting each one (actually, painting them a little to the right and upward so that the spot is painted around the mouse pointer rather than below and to the right).

That's it! That's all you need to create an applet that handles mouse clicks. Everything else is handled for you. You have to add the appropriate behavior to mouseDown() or mouseUp() to intercept and handle that event. Listing 11.1 shows the full text for the Spots applet.

TYPE **Listing 11.1. The Spots applet.**

```
1: import java.awt.Graphics;
2: import java.awt.Color;
3: import java.awt.Event;
4:
5: public class Spots extends java.applet.Applet {
6:
7:     final int MAXSPOTS = 10;
8:     int xspots[] = new int[MAXSPOTS];
9:     int yspots[] = new int[MAXSPOTS];
10:     int currspots = 0;
11:
12:     public void init() {
13:         setBackground(Color.white);
14:     }
15:
16:     public boolean mouseDown(Event evt, int x, int y) {
17:         if (currspots < MAXSPOTS) {
18:             addspot(x,y);
19:             return true;
20:         }
21:         else {
22:             System.out.println("Too many spots.");
23:             return false;
24:         }
25:     }
26:
27:     void addspot(int x,int y) {
28:         xspots[currspots] = x;
29:         yspots[currspots] = y;
30:         currspots++;
31:         repaint();
32:     }
33:
34:     public void paint(Graphics g) {
35:         g.setColor(Color.blue);
36:         for (int i = 0; i < currspots; i++) {
37:             g.fillOval(xspots[i] - 10, yspots[i] - 10, 20, 20);
38:         }
39:     }
40: }
```

11

Double-Clicks

What if the mouse event you're interested in is more than a single mouse click? What if you want to track double- or triple-clicks? The Java Event class provides a variable called clickCount for tracking this information. clickCount is an integer representing the number of consecutive mouse clicks that have occurred (where "consecutive" is usually determined by the operating system or the mouse hardware). If you're interested in multiple mouse clicks in your applets, you can test this value in the body of your mouseDown() method, like this:

```
public boolean mouseDown(Event evt, int x, int y) {
    switch (evt.clickCount) {
        case 1:  // single-click
        case 2:  // double-click
        case 3:  // triple-click
        ....
    }
}
```

Handling Mouse Movements in the 1.02 Model

Every time the mouse is moved a single pixel in any direction, a mouse move event is generated, one for each pixel. So moving the mouse from one side of the applet to the other can result in hundreds of events. You'll discover two kinds of distinct mouse movement events in the AWT: mouse drags, where the movement occurs with the mouse button pressed down, and plain mouse movements, where the mouse button isn't pressed. In addition, mouse enter and mouse exit events are generated each time the mouse enters or exits your applet or any portion of that applet. (In case you're wondering why you might need to know this information, it's more useful on AWT components that you might put inside an applet. You'll learn more about the AWT tomorrow.)

For each of these events, special methods intercept the events, just as the mouseDown() and mouseUp() methods intercept mouse clicks.

Mouse Drag and Mouse Move Events

To intercept and manage mouse movement events in the 1.02 event model, use the mouseDrag() and mouseMove() methods.

The mouseMove() method, for handling plain mouse pointer movements without the mouse button pressed, looks much like the mouse click methods:

```
public boolean mouseMove(Event evt, int x, int y) {
    ...
}
```

The mouseDrag() method handles mouse movements made with the mouse button pressed down (a complete dragging movement consists of a mouse down event, a series of mouse drag events for each pixel the mouse is moved, and a mouse up event when the button is released). The mouseDrag() method looks like this:

```
public boolean mouseDrag(Event evt, int x, int y) {
    ...
}
```

Note that for both the mouseMove() and mouseDrag() methods, the arguments for the x and y coordinates are the *new* location of the mouse, not its starting location.

Mouse Enter and Mouse Exit Events

The mouseEnter() and mouseExit() methods are called when the mouse pointer enters or exits an applet or a portion of that applet. Both mouseEnter() and mouseExit() have signatures similar to the mouse click methods. They have three arguments: the event object and the x and y coordinates of the point where the mouse entered or exited the applet. The following examples show the signatures for mouseEnter() and mouseExit():

```
public boolean mouseEnter(Event evt, int x, int y) {
    ...
}

public boolean mouseExit(Event evt, int x, int y) {
    ...
}
```

An Example: Drawing Lines

Examples always help to make concepts more concrete. In this section, you'll create an applet that enables you to draw straight lines on the screen by dragging from the startpoint to the endpoint. Figure 11.2 shows the applet at work.

As you did with the Spots applet (on which this applet is based), let's start with the basic definition and work our way through it, adding the appropriate methods to build the applet. Here's a simple class definition for the Lines applet, with a number of initial instance variables and a simple init() method:

```
import java.awt.Graphics;
import java.awt.Color;
import java.awt.Event;
import java.awt.Point;

public class Lines extends java.applet.Applet {

final int MAXLINES = 10;
Point starts[] = new Point[MAXLINES]; // starting points
```

```
Point ends[] = new Point[MAXLINES];     // ending points
Point anchor;     // start of current line
Point currentpoint; // current end of line
int currline = 0; // number of lines

public void init() {
    setBackground(Color.white);
}
}
```

Figure 11.2.

Drawing lines.

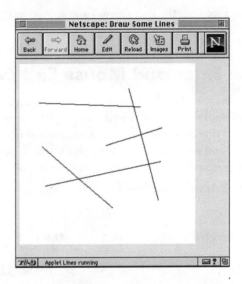

This applet has a few more initial variable things than the Spots applet. Unlike Spots, which keeps track of individual integer coordinates, the Lines applet keeps track of Point objects. Points represent an x and a y coordinate, encapsulated in a single object. To deal with points, you import the Point class (java.awt.Point) and set up a bunch of instance variables that hold points:

☐ The starts array holds points representing the starts of lines already drawn.

☐ The ends array holds the endpoints of those same lines.

☐ anchor holds the starting point of the line currently being drawn.

☐ currentpoint holds the current endpoint of the line currently being drawn.

☐ currline holds the current number of lines (to make sure you don't go over MAXLINES, and to keep track of which line in the array to access next).

Finally, the init() method, as in the Spots applet, sets the background of the applet to white.

11

The three main events this applet deals with are mouseDown(), to set the anchor point for the current line; mouseDrag(), to animate the current line as it's being drawn; and mouseUp(), to set the ending point for the new line. Given that you have instance variables to hold each of these values, you merely have to plug the right variables into the right methods. Here's mouseDown(), which sets the anchor point (but only if you haven't exceeded the maximum number of lines):

```
public boolean mouseDown(Event evt, int x, int y) {
    if (currline < MAXLINES) {
        anchor = new Point(x,y);
        return true;
    }
    else {
        System.out.println("Too many lines.");
        return false;
    }
}
```

While the mouse is being dragged to draw the line, the applet animates the line being drawn. As you drag the mouse around, the new line moves with it from the anchor point to the tip of the mouse. The mouseDrag() event contains the current point each time the mouse moves, so use that method to keep track of the current point (and to repaint for each movement so the line "animates"). Note that if you've exceeded the maximum number of lines, you won't want to do any of this work. Here's the mouseDrag() method to do all those jobs:

```
public boolean mouseDrag(Event evt, int x, int y) {
    if (currline < MAXLINES) {
        currentpoint = new Point(x,y);
        repaint();
        return true;
    }
    else return false;
    }
```

The new line doesn't get added to the arrays of old lines until the mouse button is released. Here's mouseUp(), which tests to make sure you haven't exceeded the maximum number of lines before calling the addline() method (described next):

```
public boolean mouseUp(Event evt, int x, int y) {
    if (currline < MAXLINES) {
        addline(x,y);
        return true;
    }
    else return false;
}
```

In the addline() method, the arrays of starting and ending points get updated, and the applet is repainted to take the new line into effect:

```
void addline(int x,int y) {
    starts[currline] = anchor;
    ends[currline] = new Point(x,y);
```

```
        currline++;
        currentpoint = null;
        anchor = null;
        repaint();
    }
```

Note that in this method you also set currentpoint and anchor to null. Why? Because the current line you were drawing is over. By setting these variables to null, you can test for that value in the paint() method to see whether you need to draw a current line.

Painting the applet means drawing all the old lines stored in the starts and ends arrays, as well as drawing the current line in progress (whose endpoints are in anchor and currentpoint, respectively). To show the animation of the current line, draw it in blue. Here's the paint() method for the Lines applet:

```
public void paint(Graphics g) {
    // Draw existing lines
        for (int i = 0; i < currline; i++) {
        g.drawLine(starts[i].x, starts[i].y,
        ends[i].x, ends[i].y);
    }

    // Draw current line
    g.setColor(Color.blue);
    if (currentpoint != null)
    g.drawLine(anchor.x, anchor.y,
    currentpoint.x, currentpoint.y);
}
```

In paint(), when you're drawing the current line, you test first to see whether currentpoint is null. If it is, the applet isn't in the middle of drawing a line, so it doesn't have any reason to try drawing a line that doesn't exist. By testing for currentpoint (and by setting currentpoint to null in the addline() method), you can paint only what you need. That's it—just 60 lines of code and a few basic methods, and you have a basic drawing application in your Web browser. Listing 11.2 shows the full text of the Lines applet so that you can put the pieces together.

TYPE   Listing 11.2. The Lines applet.

```
1: import java.awt.Graphics;
2: import java.awt.Color;
3: import java.awt.Event;
4: import java.awt.Point;
5:
6: public class Lines extends java.applet.Applet {
7:
8:      final int MAXLINES = 10;
9:      Point starts[] = new Point[MAXLINES]; // starting points
10:     Point ends[] = new Point[MAXLINES];    // endingpoints
11:     Point anchor;     // start of current line
12:     Point currentpoint; // current end of line
13:     int currline = 0; // number of lines
```

```
14:
15:    public void init() {
16:        setBackground(Color.white);
17:    }
18:
19:    public boolean mouseDown(Event evt, int x, int y) {
20:        if (currline < MAXLINES) {
21:            anchor = new Point(x,y);
22:            return true;
23:        }
24:       else  {
25:          System.out.println("Too many lines.");
26:          return false;
27:        }
28:     }
29:
30:    public boolean mouseUp(Event evt, int x, int y) {
31:        if (currline < MAXLINES) {
32:            addline(x,y);
33:            return true;
34:        }
35:        else return false;
36:    }
37:
38:    public boolean mouseDrag(Event evt, int x, int y) {
39:        if (currline < MAXLINES) {
40:            currentpoint = new Point(x,y);
41:            repaint();
42:            return true;
43:        }
44:        else return false;
45:    }
46:
47:    void addline(int x,int y) {
48:        starts[currline] = anchor;
49:        ends[currline] = new Point(x,y);
50:        currline++;
51:        currentpoint = null;
52:        anchor = null;
53:        repaint();
54:    }
55:
56:    public void paint(Graphics g) {
57:
58:        // Draw existing lines
59:        for (int i = 0; i < currline; i++) {
50:            g.drawLine(starts[i].x, starts[i].y,
51:                ends[i].x, ends[i].y);
52:        }
53:
54:        // draw current line
55:        g.setColor(Color.blue);
56:        if (currentpoint != null)
57:            g.drawLine(anchor.x,anchor.y,
58:                currentpoint.x,currentpoint.y);
59:    }
60:}
```

11

Handling Keyboard Events in the 1.02 Event Model

A keyboard event is generated whenever a user presses a key on the keyboard. By using keyboard events, you can get hold of the values of the keys the user pressed to perform an action or merely to get character input from the users of your applet.

The `keyDown()` and `keyUp()` Methods

To capture a keyboard event in the 1.02 event model, use the `keyDown()` method:

```
public boolean keyDown(Event evt, int key) {
...
}
```

The keys generated by key down events (and passed into `keyDown()` as the key argument) are integers representing Unicode character values, which include alphanumeric characters, function keys, tabs, returns, and so on. To use them as characters (for example, to print them), you need to cast them to characters:

```
currentchar = (char)key;
```

Here's a simple example of a `keyDown()` method that does nothing but print the key you just typed in both its Unicode and character representations (it can be fun to see which key characters produce which values):

```
public boolean keyDown(Event evt, int key) {
System.out.println("ASCII value: " + key);
System.out.println("Character: " + (char)key);
return true;
}
```

As with mouse clicks, each key down event also has a corresponding key up event. To intercept key up events, use the `keyUp()` method:

```
public boolean keyUp(Event evt, int key)  {
...\
}
```

Default Keys

The Event class provides a set of class variables that refer to several standard nonalphanumeric keys, such as the arrow and function keys. If your applet's interface uses these keys, you can provide more readable code by testing for these names in your `keyDown()` method rather than testing for their numeric values (and your code is also more likely to work across different platforms if you use these variables). For example, to test whether the up arrow was pressed, you might use the following snippet of code:

```
if (key == Event.UP) {
...
}
```

Because the values these class variables hold are integers, you also can use the switch statement to test for them.

Table 11.1 shows the standard Event class variables for various keys and the actual keys they represent.

Table 11.1. Standard keys defined by the Event class.

Class Variable	Represented Key
Event.HOME	Home key
Event.END	End key
Event.PGUP	Page Up key
Event.PGDN	Page Down key
Event.UP	Up arrow
Event.DOWN	Down arrow
Event.LEFT	Left arrow
Event.RIGHT	Right arrow
Event.F1	F1 key
Event.F2	F2 key
Event.F3	F3 key
Event.F4	F4 key
Event.F5	F5 key
Event.F6	F6 key
Event.F7	F7 key
Event.F8	F8 key
Event.F9	F9 key
Event.F10	F10 key
Event.F11	F11 key
Event.F12	F12 key

An Example: Entering, Displaying, and Moving Characters

Let's look at an applet that demonstrates keyboard events in the 1.02 event model. With this applet, you type a character, and that character is displayed in the center of the applet window. You then can move that character around on the screen with the arrow keys. Typing another character at any time changes the character as it's currently displayed. Figure 11.3 shows an example.

Figure 11.3.

The Keys *applet.*

 NOTE

To get the Keys applet to work, you might have to click it once with the mouse for the keys to show up. This way, you can make sure the applet has the keyboard focus (that is, that it's actually listening when you type characters on the keyboard).

This applet is actually less complicated than the previous applets you've used. This one has only three methods: `init()`, `keyDown()`, and `paint()`. The instance variables are also simpler because the only things you need to keep track of are the x and y positions of the current character and the values of that character itself. Here's the initial class definition:

```
import java.awt.Graphics;
import java.awt.Event;
import java.awt.Font;
import java.awt.Color;

public class Keys extends java.applet.Applet {
```

```
char currkey;
int currx;
int curry;
}
```

Let's start by adding an init() method. Here, init() is responsible for three tasks: setting the background color, setting the applet's font (here, 36-point Helvetica bold), and setting the beginning position for the character (the middle of the screen, minus a few points to nudge it up and to the right).

```
public void init() {
currx = (size().width / 2) - 8;
curry = (size().height / 2) - 16;
setBackground(Color.white);
setFont(new Font("Helvetica", Font.BOLD, 36));
}
```

Because this applet's behavior is based on keyboard input, most of the work of the applet takes place in the keyDown() method:

```
public boolean keyDown(Event evt, int key) {
    switch (key) {
        case Event.DOWN:
            curry += 5;
            break;
        case Event.UP:
            curry -= 5;
            break;
        case Event.LEFT:
            currx -= 5;
            break;
        case Event.RIGHT:
            currx += 5;
            break;
        default:
            currkey = (char)key;
    }
    repaint();
    return true;
}
```

In the center of the keyDown() applet is a switch statement that tests for different key events. If the event is an arrow key, the appropriate change is made to the character's position. If the event is any other key, the character itself is changed (that's the default part of the switch). The method finishes up with a repaint() and returns true.

The paint() method here is almost trivial; just display the current character at the current position. However, note that when the applet starts up, it has no initial character and nothing to draw, so you have to take that point into account. The currkey variable is initialized to 0, so you paint the applet only if currkey has an actual value:

```
public void paint(Graphics g) {
    if (currkey != 0) {
```

```
        g.drawString(String.valueOf(currkey), currx,curry);
    }
}
```

Listing 11.3 shows the complete source code for the Keys applet.

TYPE   **Listing 11.3. The Keys applet.**

```
1: import java.awt.Graphics;
2: import java.awt.Event;
3: import java.awt.Font;
4: import java.awt.Color;
5:
6: public class Keys extends java.applet.Applet {
7:
8:     char currkey;
9:     int currx;
10:    int curry;
11:
12:     public void init() {
13:         currx = (size().width / 2) -8;   // default
14:         curry = (size().height / 2) -16;
15:
16:         setBackground(Color.white);
17:         setFont(new Font("Helvetica",Font.BOLD,36));
18:     }
19:
20:     public boolean keyDown(Event evt, int key) {
21:         switch (key) {
22:         case Event.DOWN:
23:             curry += 5;
24:             break;
25:         case Event.UP:
26:             curry -= 5;
27:             break;
28:         case Event.LEFT:
29:             currx -= 5;
30:             break;
31:         case Event.RIGHT:
32:             currx += 5;
33:             break;
34:         default:
35:             currkey = (char)key;
36:         }
37:
38:         repaint();
39:         return true;
40:     }
41:
42:     public void paint(Graphics g) {
43:         if (currkey != 0) {
44:             g.drawString(String.valueOf(currkey), currx,curry);
45:         }
46:     }
47: }
```

Testing for Modifier Keys and Multiple Mouse Buttons

Shift, Control (Ctrl), and Meta are modifier keys. They don't generate key events themselves, but when you get an ordinary mouse or keyboard event, you can test to see whether these modifier keys were held down when the event occurred. Sometimes it may be obvious—shifted alphanumeric keys produce different key events than unshifted ones, for example. For other events, however—mouse events in particular—you may want to handle an event with a modifier key held down differently from a regular version of that event.

NOTE

> The Meta key is commonly used on UNIX systems; it's usually mapped to Alt on PC keyboards and Command (apple) on Macintoshes.

The Event class provides three methods for testing whether a modifier key is held down: shiftDown(), metaDown(), and controlDown(). All return boolean values based on whether that modifier key is indeed held down. You can use these three methods in any of the event-handling methods (mouse or keyboard) by calling them on the event object passed into that method:

```
public boolean mouseDown(Event evt, int x, int y ) {
   if (evt.shiftDown())
   // handle shift-click
   else if controlDown()
   /// handle control-click
   else // handle regular click
}
```

One other significant use of these modifier key methods is to test for which mouse button generated a particular mouse event on systems with two or three mouse buttons. By default, in the 1.02 event model, mouse events (such as mouse down and mouse drag) are generated regardless of which mouse button is used. However, Java events internally map left and middle mouse actions to Meta and Control (Ctrl) modifier keys, respectively, so testing for the key tests for the mouse button's action. By testing for modifier keys, you can find out which mouse button was used and execute different behavior for those buttons than you would use for the left button. Use an if statement to test each case, like this:

```
public boolean mouseDown(Event evt, int x, int y ) {
if (evt.metaDown())
// handle a right-click
else if (evt.controlDown())
// handle a middle-click
else // handle a regular click
}
```

Note that because this mapping from multiple mouse buttons to keyboard modifiers happens automatically, you don't have to do a lot of work to make sure your applets or applications work on different systems with different kinds of mouse devices. Because left-button or right-button mouse clicks map to modifier key events, you can use the actual modifier keys on systems with fewer mouse buttons to generate exactly the same results. So, for example, holding down the Ctrl key and clicking the mouse on Windows or holding the Control key on the Macintosh is the same as clicking the middle button on a three-button mouse; holding down the Command (apple) key and clicking the mouse on the Mac is the same as clicking the right button on a two- or three-button mouse.

Consider, however, that the use of different mouse buttons or modifier keys may not be immediately obvious if your applet or application runs on a system with fewer buttons than you're used to working with. Consider restricting your interface to a single mouse button or to providing help or documentation to explain the use of your program in this case.

The Generic 1.02 Event Handler: handleEvent()

The default methods you've learned about today for handling basic events in applets are actually called by a generic event-handler method called handleEvent(). By using the handleEvent() method, the 1.02 AWT generically deals with events that occur between application components and events based on user input.

In the default handleEvent() method, basic events are processed and the methods you learned about today are called. To handle events other than those mentioned here (for example, events for scroll bars or for other user interface elements—which you'll learn about on Day 12, "Creating User Interfaces with AWT"), to change the default event handling behavior, or to create and pass around your own events, you need to override handleEvent() in your own Java programs. The handleEvent() method looks like this:

```
public boolean handleEvent(Event evt) {
    ...
}
```

To test for specific events, examine the id instance variable of the Event object that gets passed in to handleEvent(). The event ID is an integer, but fortunately the Event class defines a whole set of event IDs as class variables whose names you can test for in the body of handleEvent(). Because these class variables are integer constants, a switch statement works particularly well. For example, here's a simple handleEvent() method to print out debugging information about mouse events:

```
public boolean handleEvent(Event evt) {
    switch (evt.id) {
```

```
    case Event.MOUSE_DOWN:
        System.out.println("MouseDown: " +
        evt.x + "," + evt.y);
        return true;
    case Event.MOUSE_UP:
        System.out.println("MouseUp: " +
        evt.x + "," + evt.y);
        return true;
    case Event.MOUSE_MOVE:
        System.out.println("MouseMove: " +
        evt.x + "," + evt.y);
        return true;
    case Event.MOUSE_DRAG:
        System.out.println("MouseDrag: " +
        evt.x + "," + evt.y);
        return true;
    default:
        return false;
    }
}
```

You can test for the following keyboard events:

☐ Event.KEY_PRESS is generated when a key is pressed (the same as the keyDown()
method).

☐ Event.KEY_RELEASE is generated when a key is released.

☐ Event.KEY_ACTION and Event.KEY_ACTION_RELEASE are generated when an "action"
key (a function key, an arrow key, Page Up, Page Down, or Home) is pressed or
released.

You can test for these mouse events:

☐ Event.MOUSE_DOWN is generated when the mouse button is pressed (the same as the
mouseDown() method).

☐ Event.MOUSE_UP is generated when the mouse button is released (the same as the
mouseUp() method).

☐ Event.MOUSE_MOVE is generated when the mouse is moved (the same as the
mouseMove() method).

☐ Event.MOUSE_DRAG is generated when the mouse is moved with the button pressed
(the same as the mouseDrag() method).

☐ Event.MOUSE_ENTER is generated when the mouse enters the applet (or a component
of that applet). You can also use the mouseEnter() method.

☐ Event.MOUSE_EXIT is generated when the mouse exits the applet. You can also use
the mouseExit() method.

In addition to these events, the Event class has a whole suite of methods for handling events
in 1.02 AWT components. You'll learn more about these events tomorrow.

11

Note that if you override handleEvent() in your class, none of the default event-handling methods you learned about today will get called unless you explicitly call them in the body of handleEvent(). So be careful if you decide to override this event. The best way to get around this problem is to test for the event you're interested in, and if that event isn't it, call super.handleEvent() so that the superclass that defines handleEvent() can process things. Here's an example:

```
public boolean handleEvent(Event evt) {
   if (evt.id == Event.MOUSE_DOWN) {
      // process the mouse down
      return true;
   } else
     return super.handleEvent(evt);
}
```

Also, note that like the individual methods for individual events, handleEvent() also returns a boolean value. The value you return here is particularly important; if you pass handling of the event to another method, you must return false (the method you call will return true or false itself). If you handle the event in the body of this method, return true. If you pass the event up to a superclass, that method will return true or false; you don't have to return it yourself.

Moving Up to the 1.1 Event Model

Now that you've learned how to deal with mouse and keyboard events in the old JDK 1.02 event model, you can start from scratch and relearn everything in the new 1.1 JDK model. As I mentioned earlier in this lesson, you don't necessarily have to move to the new model right this moment if you're not working exclusively in a 1.1 environment. Eventually, though, you'll have to convert your code, so at least familiarizing yourself with the new 1.1 model is a good idea so that you'll be prepared.

In reality, a lot of what you learned about the 1.02 event model still applies to the new model. A mouse down is still a mouse down. The only differences are in how events propagate through the system and in how you program your applet to handle those events.

In this section, you'll look at the new model, why it was needed, and how it works. You'll also convert the Lines applet from the old model into the new so that you can get an idea how it works.

What's Wrong with the Old Model?

Why are do two models exist in the first place? What was so awful about the old 1.02 event model that it had to be changed so drastically?

Nothing is inherently bad about the old event model; it's simple and easy to learn (as you probably discovered), and it works well for smaller Java applications such as applets that may have only a few user interface elements and process only a few events. However, once you start creating bigger, more complex applications, which may have hundreds of events that need to be processed in different ways, the old model starts to become unwieldy and its limitations become apparent. The old model also makes it difficult to develop the kind of component-based system that JavaBeans provides.

The new 1.1 event model fixes several limitations to the 1.02 model. The first limitation is the problem of handleEvent(). As you learned in "The Generic 1.02 Event Handler" section, the handleEvent() method is used to process all the events that could possibly be useful to your applet. That's not a very useful way of processing events. The 1.1 model fixes this limitation by sending events to the applet only if the applet has expressed an interest in those events; this process makes for less work by the applet to handle events.

The second limitation in the 1.02 event model is in how events are represented. In 1.02, all events are instances of the Event class. An event ID identifies the kind of event the object is. To decide what to do in the event, you have to use a huge switch statement inside handleEvent() to decide what kind of event you're using, and then either deal with it there or pass off control to a method such as mouseDown(). Even then, what happens if you have multiple events with the same ID, but they're generated by different UI elements (for example, different buttons inside the applet)? More switch statements or if...else clauses need to be developed and maintained. The larger the program grows, the more complex the event-handling code becomes, and the more easily bugs can be introduced. The 1.1 model fixes this problem by separating events into classes, and by having separate listeners deal with separate classes of events. It distributes the logic into manageable chunks, each of which can be separately maintained.

The third problem with 1.02 is that of inheritance. To add event behavior to an AWT object in the 1.02 event model, you must subclass that object to override handleEvent() or one of its utility methods such as mouseDown(). This isn't as important with mouse and keyboard events, as you've already subclassed the applet class to add other behavior besides events.

Consider the button, a UI element you'll learn about tomorrow. The button has an appearance and a functionality; all it really needs from you is information telling it what to do when the button is clicked. With the old model, the only way to add that functionality is to subclass the Button class. For each button in your interface, you'll therefore have to create either a subclass for each one (and deal with a plethora of buttons) or create a single button subclass with a particularly large event method that switches off the name of the button to try to decide what to do. This solution is inelegant, particularly if you subscribe to the good object-oriented design theory that subclassing should occur only when you're making significant reusable changes to a class. The 1.1 model neatly avoids this problem by moving the event code to a separate class altogether, which can then be used and reused by multiple generic button objects or changed independently of the UI itself.

11

So now that you understand why the old model isn't such a good idea, let's approach what the new 1.1 event model looks like and how you use it.

How the New Model Works

The biggest difference between the old 1.02 event model and the new 1.1 event model is that event processing is separated into two main parts. The first part is the object that receives a given event—which can be your applet or a part of that applet such as a button.

The second, more important part, is the event listener. The listener represents a certain set of events—you can have a mouse listener, or a key listener, or a scrolling listener, for example—and is responsible for doing something in response to these specific events. When you create a listener, you put your event code into that listener.

The event receiver and the listener are tied together via listener *registration*. To register a listener with your program, you use a special method in your applet code that says "this listener will process these events." In the older model, your applet (the event receiver) received *all* the events the system generated. In this new model, your applet will receive only those events that have a listener registered. This way, the process is more efficient for both the overall system and for your applet itself, as it doesn't have to constantly test every event that goes by.

Figure 11.4 shows the differences between the 1.02 and 1.1 event models. Note that in the 1.02 model all events are handled by your applet; in the 1.1 model events are more distributed.

The third part that makes this model work is that the events themselves are different in the old and new event models. As I mentioned earlier, in the 1.02 model, all events were instances of the Event class. In the 1.1 model, a whole package full of events is available in the java.awt.events package, with different classes representing different kinds of events. This makes events much more object-oriented, allows them to inherit event information from event superclasses, and allows events to be passed only to listeners and listener code that are interested in dealing with that kind of event.

If you remember back to the introduction, I used the concept of the conveyor belt to explain how events work. In the 1.02 model, you, as the applet, stand by the conveyor belt and watch all the events go by, examining each one to see if it is useful to you. In the 1.1 event model, you have multiple conveyor belts with different kinds of events, and you, the applet, have assistants (listeners) that stand by those conveyor belts for you to deal with events.

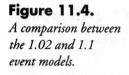

Figure 11.4.

A comparison between the 1.02 and 1.1 event models.

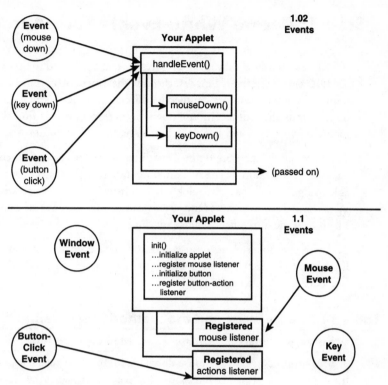

Using the 1.1 Event Model

Got it? Now let's write some code. When you're using the new event model in your applets or applications, you should follow these three basic steps:

☐ Decide which events your applet is interested in, and match those event types to listeners.

☐ Create the code for that listener (and the code to process the event).

☐ Register the listener with that applet.

You'll work through each of these steps in turn so that you can get a feel for the process. In "An Example: Converting Lines," you'll convert an applet that uses the old event model into one that uses the new event model so you can get an idea of how the process really works.

Step 1: Decide Which Events Your Applet Will Use

The first step is to figure out what events your applet will use. You actually had to do this with the 1.02 event model as well, and figure out which method to use (`mouseDown()`, `keyDown()`, `handleEvent()`). In the 1.1 model, though, the process is a bit more explicit. In the 1.1 event model, different events are handled by different listeners, which include different methods. So if your applet will use mouse down events, you have to find the listener that supports mouse down events and has a method to handle those events.

The different listeners are defined by different interfaces contained in the `java.awt.event` package. If you examine the API documentation or the source for these interfaces, you'll be able to figure out relatively quickly which listener interfaces go with which events and the methods in those interfaces (and as you learn about more events tomorrow and the next day, I'll go over the different listeners you can use).

Today you've focused on mouse and keyboard events. For these events, you have three listener interfaces. Table 11.2 shows the events and methods that the three mouse and keyboard listeners contain.

Table 11.2. Interfaces and the methods they define.

Listener Interface	Events	Method Definition
MouseListener	mouse down	public void mousePressed(MouseEvent e)
	mouse up	public void mouseReleased(MouseEvent e)
	mouse enter	public void mouseEntered(MouseEvent e)
	mouse exit	public void mouseExited(MouseEvent e)
	mouse clicks	public void mouseClicked(MouseEvent e) (a mouse click is a press followed by a release in the same location)
MouseMotionListener	mouse move	public void mouseMoved(MouseMotionEvente)
	mouse drag	public void mouseDragged(MouseMotionEvent e)
KeyListener	key down	public void keyReleased(KeyEvent e)
	key up	public void keyPressed(KeyEvent e)
	key typed	public void keyTyped(KeyEvent e) (a key typed is a key down followed by the same key up)

Mark down the listener names you'll need for your applet or application; you'll need them in the next step. Don't worry about the methods right now (except to note that their names and signatures are different from those in 1.02); you'll deal with them in the next step.

Step 2: Implement the Interface

The next step, now that you know the event listeners that will handle your events, is to actually create the listener. The listener will contain the code you write for handling specific events.

An event listener is technically defined as a class that implements one or more listener interfaces. Yesterday, you learned how to add the Runnable interface to your classes; the process for listeners is just like that. When you create a listener class, that class will include the keyword implements in the definition, along with the name of the specific listener type for the events that class handles.

When you create a listener, you can either create a brand-new class that handles the events for your main applet, or you can modify your applet so that it is its own listener. The former is more elegant in terms of design and a better idea if you've got a larger program with lots of events. The latter method is a quick way to convert old event code into new or to create simple applets like the ones you've been creating in this lesson.

Creating a Separate Listener Class

To create a separate listener class, you can either implement the interfaces you picked in the previous step, or you can use a shorthand method: You can define your listener class to inherit from an event adapter. The adapters are classes in the java.awt.event package, one for each listener interface, which provide stub methods for that interface. To create a listener class, all you have to do is define the class so that it extends the appropriate interface and then override the methods for the events you want to handle. For the mouse and keyboard event listeners, you can choose from three corresponding adapters: MouseAdapter (implements MouseListener), MouseMotionAdapter (implements MouseMotionListener), and KeyAdapter (implements KeyListener).

To create a listener class for mouse events, then, here's a basic class definition:

```
import java.awt.event.*;

class MyMouseListenerClass extends MouseAdapter {

public void mousePressed(MouseEvent e) {
    // handle mouse down events
}

public void mouseReleased(MouseEvent e) {
    // handle mouse up events
}
}
```

Don't forget to import the java.awt.event package at the beginning of the class so that it can find the MouseAdapter class. You also should import any other classes you need to implement the listener.

This particular example overrides the mousePressed() and mouseReleased() methods, which are defined in the MouseListener interface (implemented as stubs in the MouseAdapter class) and handle mouse down and mouse up events, respectively. Note that although the MouseAdapter class (and the MouseListener interface) also contains methods for mouseEntered and mouseExit(), you're not interested in them, so you can ignore them altogether.

Creating a Listener Applet

Instead of creating separate listener classes, you can also create an applet that is its own listener. Nothing is wrong with creating such an applet; in fact, in many cases, doing so is the easiest and fastest way to convert an applet that uses the 1.02 event model to the 1.1 model.

To create an applet that is also a listener, you must modify the applet so that it implements the appropriate listener interface, by following these steps:

1. Make sure you import java.awt.event.*.
2. Add the implements keyword to the class definition followed by the listener interfaces you're interested in.
3. Fill in method stubs for the interface.
4. Add event processing code to the appropriate methods.

Modifying the class definition is the easy part. Here's an example that uses the MouseListener and KeyListener interfaces:

```
public class MyApplet extends java.applet.Applet
    implements MouseListener,KeyListener {

...
}
```

Substitute the names of the listener interfaces that you're interested in; you don't have to include listeners for events you don't care about.

Now, add stubs for the methods in that interface. The basic rule of interfaces, which you'll learn more about on Day 16, "Packages, Interfaces, and Inner Classes," is that after you decide to implement an interface, you must create methods definitions for all the methods in that interface. For the Runnable interface, this task is easy. This interface has only one method: run(). For the event listeners, you may have two or three or more methods to implement.

Don't panic. To satisfy the rule, all you have to do is add stub methods for each of the methods in the interface (which is exactly what the listener adapters do, actually). They don't have to actually contain any code. Then you can go back and add actual code to the methods you actually care about.

Let's pick an example. Say you're implementing the MouseListener interface. You can find out the signatures from the API documentation for the MouseListener interface, or you can look at the source code that came with your JDK and copy and paste the method stubs from the MouseAdapter class. In either case, the MouseListener interface contains five methods, and the stubs for those methods you'll add to your class would look like this:

```
public void mouseClicked(MouseEvent e) {}
public void mousePressed(MouseEvent e) {}
public void mouseReleased(MouseEvent e) {}
public void mouseEntered(MouseEvent e) {}
public void mouseExited(MouseEvent e) {}
```

After you add the stubs, the last step is simply to fill in the code for the methods you're actually interested in dealing with. For example, if all you care about is mouse down events, fill in your event code in the mousePressed() method. You can leave the others empty.

Step 3: Register the Listener

You're almost there. The last step, now that you have a listener class or you've modified your applet to be its own listener, is to link the two together and let the system know that you want to receive events. You do so by "registering" the listener with the object that will receive the method so that the two can be linked together.

You use special methods to register listeners. These methods are defined by the Component class or its subclasses, and are available to all AWT components including applets. For every listener type is a listener registration method; you'll learn about these methods as you learn different types of events. For the three kinds of listeners covered here, the methods are

- ☐ addMouseListener()
- ☐ addMouseMotionListener()
- ☐ addKeyListener()

All three methods take a single argument: an object that implements the appropriate interface. So, if you implement your listeners in different classes, you create an instance of that listener class and then pass it into the right method, like this:

```
ml = new MyMouseListenerClass();
addMouseListener(ml);
```

 NOTE

> The example I'm using here of having a separate listener class is overly vague. Much of the time your separate listener class will also need a reference back to the event receiver or applet so that it can modify that object based on an event. Tomorrow you'll go over a more detailed example of using separate listener classes.

If you've modified your applet to be its own listener, use `this` as the argument to the listener registration method:

```
addMouseListener(this);
```

Listener registration typically takes place in the `init()` method of your applet, as it's a task that should happen when the program starts up. After the listener has been registered, your applet will start receiving events, and the listener can process them.

TECHNICAL NOTE

You can register multiple listener objects of the same type to the same applet. Perhaps you have three key listener classes to handle different keyboard events, and you don't feel like packing all that code into the same class. However, be forewarned that if you do decide to register objects this way, the AWT does not guarantee that your listener classes will receive the event in any reliable order (order of registration does not matter). If you're concerned about the order of your listeners, a much better idea is to register only one class per applet (or component) and then chain the listeners together in the order you want them to process the event.

Converting 1.02 Event Code to 1.1

Converting applets or applications that use the older event model is not very difficult. In many cases, you can simply add a few lines of code, and copy and paste the code into the right place to make it work. Here's a checklist of things you'll need to do to get new events working as fast as possible (you'll work through an example in the next section):

- [ ] Add imports `java.awt.events.*` to the list of imported packages at the top of the page.
- [ ] Determine which listeners you'll be using for your events. Add an `implements` keyword to the class definition followed by the names of those interfaces.
- [ ] Create method stubs for each of the methods in each interface. You can get the stubs from the source code or the API documentation for the interface.
- [ ] Copy the appropriate code from older 1.02 methods into the new methods. Delete all old 1.02-style methods.
- [ ] Remove all `return` statements (the new methods do not have return values).
- [ ] If your old method code referred to `x` and `y`, note that the new methods do not have those variables. You can get to these values using the `getX()` and `getY()` methods, defined in the event object passed in as an argument to the method.

☐ Note any other differences. The section "Mouse and Keyboard Events in the 1.1 Event Model," later in this lesson, contains some points to watch out for with mouse and keyboard events. Tomorrow you'll look at the differences for various other components.

An Example: Converting Lines

Earlier in this lesson, you created an applet called Lines that let you draw 10 lines on the screen. Let's convert that applet into one that uses the 1.1 event model.

The first step is to figure out which listener interfaces you need. A quick look back at Listing 11.2 shows that the old Lines applet uses mouse down, mouse up, and mouse drag events. The first two are in the MouseListener interface; the latter one is in MouseMotionListener. You'll have to implement both of these interfaces to intercept all three events.

Start, then, with a basic class definition that includes those interfaces. Note that I've also added an import line for the java.awt.event package here:

```
import java.awt.Graphics;
import java.awt.Color;
import java.awt.Point;
import java.awt.event.*;

public class LinesNew extends java.applet.Applet
    implements MouseListener,MouseMotionListener {

    ...
}
```

The next step is to add stubs for every method that both MouseListener and MouseMotionListener defines. They have six methods altogether; here I've copied and pasted their definitions from MouseAdapter and MouseMotionAdapter:

```
public void mouseMoved(MouseEvent e) {
}
public void mouseDragged(MouseEvent e) {
)
public void mousePressed(MouseEvent e) {
)
public void mouseReleased(MouseEvent e) {
)
public void mouseClicked(MouseEvent e) {
}
public void mouseEntered(MouseEvent e) {
}
public void mouseExited(MouseEvent e) {
}
```

Now that you've satisfied the requirements of implementing the interface, you can add the event code to actually make the applet do something. You've already got old-style mouseDown(), mouseUp(), and mouseDrag() methods from the old version of this applet. These old methods correspond to the mousePressed(), mouseReleased(), and mouseDragged() methods in the new model. To convert these methods, you'll simply copy and paste the code from the old methods to the new and delete the old methods. You can also remove all return statements; the new methods do not have return values so you don't need to care what they return. The new methods will look like this:

```
public void mousePressed(MouseEvent e) {
    if (currline < MAXLINES)
        anchor = new Point(x,y);
    else
        System.out.println("Too many lines.");
}

public void mouseReleased(MouseEvent e) {
    if (currline < MAXLINES)
        addline(x,y);
}

public void mouseDragged(MouseEvent e) {
    if (currline < MAXLINES) {
        currentpoint = new Point(x,y);
        repaint();
    }
}
```

Copying and pasting the old event code to the new event methods may work with no changes, but you usually need to watch out for one thing (two things, actually). The old-style event methods had three arguments: the event object and the x and y coordinates of the mouse event. The new mouse methods do not have these arguments, so all references you made to x and y in the old code (three of them here, one in each method) will have to be changed.

Fortunately, the event object (an instance of MouseEvent) passed in here has methods for getting ahold of the x and y values: getX() and getY(). So each time you see a reference to x, replace it with e.getX(), and every time you see a y, replace it with e.getY(), like this:

```
anchor = new Point(e.getX(),e.getY());
```

Easy, right? You have only two steps left to finish converting this applet. The first is not to forget the rest of the code that makes up this applet: the instance variables and the methods for addline() and paint(). I won't duplicate them here because they're identical to the old applet.

The last step is to register the listener so that the applet can receive events and the event methods can be called at the right time. You'll put listener administration inside the init() method for the applet and use two methods to do it: addMouseListener() and addMouseMotionListener(). Because you used two listener types, you have to use both listener registrations. Each listener must be registered.

The arguments to the listener registration methods are the listeners themselves. Here, you've converted the applet into a listener, so you can use the this argument to both methods:

```
public void init() {
   setBackground(Color.white);

   addMouseListener(this);
   addMouseMotionListener(this);
}
```

With the listener registered, you're done! You can compile the applet under the 1.1 JDK, and it'll work with the new 1.1 event model. Note that, as I mentioned earlier, the 1.1 event model will *not* work in 1.02 environments, so make sure you're running a browser or viewer that supports 1.1.

Listing 11.4 shows the complete source code for the LinesNew applet, the converted version of the original Lines applet.

TYPE **Listing 11.4. The LinesNew applet.**

```
1: import java.awt.Graphics;
2: import java.awt.Color;
3: import java.awt.Point;
4: import java.awt.event.*;
5:
6: public class LinesNew extends java.applet.Applet
7:    implements MouseListener,MouseMotionListener {
8:
9:      final int MAXLINES = 10;
10:     Point starts[] = new Point[MAXLINES]; // starting points
11:     Point ends[] = new Point[MAXLINES];    // ending points
12:     Point anchor;     // start of current line
13:     Point currentpoint; // current end of line
14:     int currline = 0; // number of lines
15:
16:     public void init() {
17:         setBackground(Color.white);
18:         // register event listeners
19:         addMouseListener(this);
20:         addMouseMotionListener(this);
21:     }
22:
23:// needed to satisfy listener interfaces
24:     public void mouseMoved(MouseEvent e) {}
25:     public void mouseClicked(MouseEvent e) {}
26:     public void mouseEntered(MouseEvent e) {}
27:     public void mouseExited(MouseEvent e) {}
28:
29:// same as mouseDown
30:     public void mousePressed(MouseEvent e) {
31:         if (currline < MAXLINES)
32:             anchor = new Point(e.getX(),e.getY());
```

continues

Listing 11.4. continued

```
33:       else
34:           System.out.println("Too many lines.");
35:    }
36:
37:// same as mouseUp
38:    public void mouseReleased(MouseEvent e) {
39:        if (currline < MAXLINES)
40:            addline(e.getX(),e.getY());
41:    }
42:
43:// same as mouseDrag
44:    public void mouseDragged(MouseEvent e) {
45:        if (currline < MAXLINES) {
46:            currentpoint = new Point(e.getX(),e.getY());
47:            repaint();
48:        }
49:    }
50:
51:    void addline(int x,int y) {
52:        starts[currline] = anchor;
53:        ends[currline] = new Point(x,y);
54:        currline++;
55:        currentpoint = null;
56:        anchor = null;
57:        repaint();
58:    }
59:
60:    public void paint(Graphics g) {
61:        // Draw existing lines
62:        for (int i = 0; i < currline; i++) {
63:            g.drawLine(starts[i].x, starts[i].y,
64:                   ends[i].x, ends[i].y);
65:        }
66:        // draw current line
67:        g.setColor(Color.blue);
68:        if (currentpoint != null)
69:            g.drawLine(anchor.x,anchor.y,
70:                   currentpoint.x,currentpoint.y);
71:    }
72:}
```

Mouse and Keyboard Events in the 1.1 Event Model

In the preceding sections, you learned the basics of the new 1.1 event model and how to convert the simple applets you created in the first part of this lesson. In this section, I'll give you a quick rundown of the changes between 1.02 and 1.1 in the mouse and keyboard events themselves and how you handle them.

In the 1.02 event model, all mouse and keyboard events were instances of the Event class. In 1.1, they are split into the MouseEvent, MouseMotionEvent, and KeyEvent classes, all three of which inherit from InputEvent, and are contained in the java.awt.event package. This separation of events into different classes changes how you'll handle specific mouse and keyboard events in your own classes.

Mouse Clicks and Mouse Movements

Mouse events are defined by two classes: MouseEvent and MouseMotionEvent. The listener interfaces for these events are defined in MouseListener and MouseMotionListener. Thus, you can find the following differences between 1.02 and 1.1 for mouse events:

☐ The mouseDown() method is now mousePressed().

☐ The mouseUp() method is now mouseReleased().

☐ The mouseDrag() method is now mouseDragged().

☐ The mouseMove() method is now mouseMoved().

☐ The mouseEnter() method is now mouseEntered().

☐ The mouseExit() method is now mouseExited().

☐ A new method, mouseClicked(), is generated in response to a mouse click event, which is defined as a mouse down followed by a mouse up in the same location. No 1.02 equivalent exists.

Note that none of the 1.1 mouse methods have x and y as arguments (as many of the old 1.02 methods did). To refer to the x and y position of the mouse click or drag, you'll have to use the getX() and getY() methods, defined by the event object itself. You saw an example in the Spots applet.

To handle double- and triple-clicks, use the getClickCount() method in MouseEvent instead of the 1.02 model's clickCount instance variable. The result is the same.

Handling clicks with modifier keys or multiple mouse buttons operates the same way it does in 1.02 (as I noted previously in "Testing for Modifier Keys and Multiple Mouse Buttons"): middle and left mouse buttons are mapped to the Control and Meta keys, respectively. The metaDown() and controlDown() methods of 1.02 are now called isMetaDown() and isControlDown() and are defined in InputListener (which makes them available to both mouse and key listeners).

Keypresses

Keypress events are now defined by the KeyEvent class, a subclass of InputEvent, and should be handled in your programs with KeyListener. Thus, you find the following changes from 1.02 to 1.1:

11

☐ The `keyDown()` method is now `keyPressed()`.

☐ The `keyUp()` method is now `keyReleased()`.

☐ The concept of the key action and key released action events in 1.02, for handling the presses and released of "action" keys, no longer exists. The `isActionKey()` method, defined by `KeyEvent`, will tell you if a given key is an action key.

☐ The new `keyTyped()` method is called in response to a key typed method, which is defined as the same key pressed and released.

You can test for modifier keys (Shift, Control, Alt, Meta) using methods defined by `InputEvent` (and available to both mouse and key events): `isShiftDown()`, `isControlDown()`, `isAltDown()`, and `isMetaDown()`. All four methods return the boolean `true` or `false` values.

To handle special keys such as function, Page Up, Page Down, and so on, you can use *virtual keys*. Virtual keys are class variables defined by the `KeyEvent` class. These keys represent just about any key on any keyboard you can think of (they're similar to the class variables for special keys defined in 1.02's `Event` class, but more general purpose). You can test for them in your code using the `getKeyCode()` method (defined by `KeyEvent`) and then testing it against a special value, for example:

```
if (e.getKeyCode() == KeyEvent.VK_PAGE_DOWN) {
    // handle a page down key
}
```

Because different keyboards may generate different numeric values for different keys, testing for the values of the virtual keys is a better idea than testing for hard-coded values. Each Java implementation on a specific platform will generate the right virtual keys for each key. Note, however, that not all keyboards will have all the keys that another platform has, and Java makes no attempt to map between them for different platforms.

The full list of virtual keys is available in the API documentation for the `KeyEvent` class. Table 11.3 shows a partial list.

Table 11.3. A partial list of virtual keys.

Class Variable	Represented Key
VK_CLEAR	Clear key
VK_DOWN	Down arrow
VK_END	End key
VK_ESCAPE	Escape (Esc) key
VK_F1 through VK_F12	Function keys
VK_HELP	Help key
VK_HOME	Home key

Class Variable	Represented Key
VK_INSERT	Insert (Ins) Key
VK_LEFT	Left arrow
VK_NUMPAD0 through VK_NUMPAD9	Numbers on the number pad
VK_PAGE_DOWN	Page Down (PgDn) key
VK_PAGE_UP	Page Up (PgUp) key
VK_PAUSE	Pause key
VK_PRINTSCREEN	Print screen (PrtScrn) key
VK_RIGHT	Right arrow
VK_UP	Up arrow

Summary

Events are the way your program responds to things that happen while it's running, usually when the user uses the mouse or the keyboard or interacts with the elements in your applet or application. In this lesson, you got a basic understanding of how events work, and you learned how to deal with events in both the older 1.02 and newer 1.1 versions of the AWT event system.

Handling events in the 1.02 Java's Abstract Windowing Toolkit is easy. Most of the time all you need to do is stick the right method in your applet code, and your applet intercepts and handles that event at the right time. The methods you learned about in this lesson included mouseUp() and mouseDown() for mouse clicks, mouseMove() and mouseDrag() for mouse movements, mouseEnter() and mouseExit() for when the mouse enters and exits the applet area, and keyDown() and keyUp() for when a key on the keyboard is pressed. You also learned about the handleEvent() method, the "parent" of the individual event methods and the mechanism for capturing events that may not have individual methods to override.

For Java 1.1, the event model has changed. How events are handled and how you manage them in your code is quite different. With the 1.1 event model, your applet receives an event only if that applet has registered a listener for that event. Listeners, in turn, are classes that implement a listener interface for a set of events and process those events when they are received. You can create separate listener classes, or you can create an applet that also behaves as a listener for its own events. In the latter half of this lesson, you learned about listeners and events in the new 1.1 event model, as well as how to convert your code from the old event model to the new one.

11

Q&A

Q In the Spots applet, the spot coordinates are stored in arrays, which have a limited size. How can I modify this applet so that it will draw an unlimited number of spots?

A You can do one of a couple things.

The first is to test, in your addspot() method, whether the number of spots has exceeded MAXSPOTS. Then create a bigger array, copy the elements of the old array into that bigger array (using the System.arraycopy() method), and reassign the x and y arrays to that new, bigger array.

The second is to use the Vector class. Vector, part of the java.util package, implements an array that is automatically growable—sort of like a linked list is in other languages. The disadvantage of Vector is that to put something into Vector, it has to be an actual object. You'll therefore have to cast integers to Integer objects and then extract their values from Integer objects to treat them as integers again. The Vector class allows you to access and change elements in the Vector just as you can in an array (by using method calls rather than array syntax). Check it out.

Q What's a Meta key?

A It's popular in UNIX systems and often mapped to Alt on most keyboards (Command on Macs). Because Shift and Control (Ctrl) are more popular and wide-spread, basing your interfaces on those modifier keys, if you can, is probably a good idea.

Q I looked at the API for the Event class (in the 1.02 model), and many more event types are listed there than the ones you mention today.

A Yes. The Event class defines many different kinds of events, both for general user input, such as the mouse and keyboard events you learned about here, and also events for managing changes to the state of user interface components, such as windows and scroll bars. Tomorrow you'll learn about these other events.

Q Adapter classes, as I understand them, implement the various methods in the event listeners as stubs. You can then extend these classes to create new listeners. If these adapter classes are so useful, why can't you just inherit from them in your applet?

A Your applet already has a superclass: java.applet.Applet. And in Java, unlike in other languages, you cannot have multiple superclasses. So unless you're creating separate listener classes, the adapters are useless to you. You'll have to use the raw interfaces instead.

Q Why do you have to create stub methods in your applet class when you implement a listener interface? That seems really silly. Why can't you just override the methods that you need?

A The key here is that you're not overriding them, you're actually creating their initial implementations. You'll learn more about interfaces on Day 16, but the main rule to follow is that the interface provides a set of method definitions. When you add the `implements` interface words to your class definition, you're promising to support *all* the methods in that interface, not just the few that you need. So you are responsible for making sure you define all those methods.

As I mentioned previously, however, to satisfy that rule, you just need to make sure the methods exist; they don't have to do anything. Hence, the method stubs.

Q **What's the difference between creating a listener as a separate class or creating an applet that is also a listener? Does one have any advantage over the other?**

A When you create a listener as a separate class, you can use the adapter classes as superclasses, and then only override the methods that you care about, which means there are fewer stub methods cluttering up your classes. Separate Listener classes also have the advantage of being separately compiled, so if you want to change your applet's or object's reaction to an event, you can just change it in the listener and recompile that listener without having to recompile the whole program. And, finally, with listeners in separate classes, if any one listener becomes too huge, you can break up the behavior into multiple listener classes, register them all, and then maintain them separately.

Using an applet as a listener, however, is slightly easier to do, uses slightly less code, and is easier to convert to from older applet code. You might want to get used to dealing with the applet as listener model for a while before getting into creating separate listener classes.

Q **I've got an applet with both key listeners and old-style `mouseDown()` methods in it. The keyboard events are working, but the mouse events are being ignored. What's going on here?**

A As I mentioned early in this lesson, you can use either the 1.02 event model or the 1.1 model, but you can't mix them. You'll have to convert those old `mouseDown()` methods into mouse listener methods for them to work.

Day 12

Creating User Interfaces with the AWT

by Laura Lemay

For the past four days, you've concentrated on creating applets that do simple tasks: display text, play an animation or a sound, or interact with the user. When you get past that point, however, you may want to start creating more complex applets that behave like real applications embedded in a Web page—applets that start to look like real GUI applications with buttons, menus, text fields, and other elements.

This sort of real work in Java applets and applications is what Java's Abstract Windowing Toolkit, or AWT, was designed for. You've actually been using the AWT all along, as you might have guessed from the classes you've been importing. The Applet class and most of the classes you've been using this week are all integral parts of the AWT. In addition, you can use the AWT in standalone applications, so everything you've learned so far this week can still be used. If you find the framework of the Web browser too limiting, you can take your AWT background and start writing full-fledged Java applications.

The AWT provides the following:

☐ A full set of user-interface (UI) widgets and other components, including windows, menus, buttons, check boxes, text fields, scroll bars, and scrolling lists

☐ Support for UI containers, which can contain other embedded containers or UI widgets

☐ An event system for managing system and user events among parts of the AWT (actually, as you learned yesterday, different versions of the AWT provide different events systems)

☐ Mechanisms for laying out components in a way that enables platform-independent UI design

The AWT is a big topic, and if I were to cover it in one day, it would be a very long day indeed. So I'll split it up into two days: today you'll learn the basics, including learning about a number of simple AWT components, how to put them into applets, how to arrange them using layout managers, and how to add events to them to handle input from your user.

Tomorrow you'll finish up the AWT, and you'll learn more about components as well as break out of the applet framework to create windows, dialogs, and full-fledged AWT applications.

An AWT Overview

The basic idea behind the AWT is that a graphical Java program is a set of nested components, starting from the outermost window all the way down to the smallest UI component. Components can include elements you can actually see on the screen, such as windows, menu bars, buttons, and text fields, and they can also include containers, which in turn can contain other components. Figure 12.1 shows how a sample page in a Java browser might include several different components, all of which are managed through the AWT.

Figure 12.1.

AWT components.

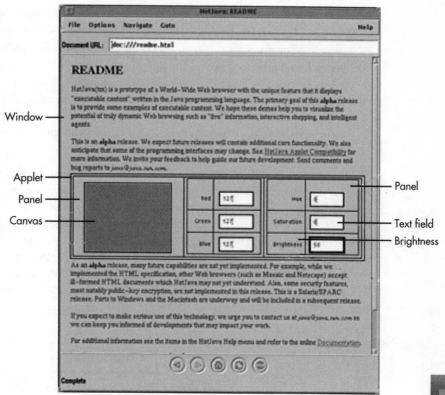

This nesting of components within containers within other components creates a hierarchy of components, from the smallest check box inside an applet to the overall window on the screen. The hierarchy of components determines the arrangement of items on the screen and inside other items, the order in which they are painted, and (in the 1.02 version of the AWT) how events are passed from one component to another.

The following are the major components you can work with in the AWT:

☐ Containers. Containers are generic AWT components that can contain other components, including other containers. The most common form of container is the panel, which represents a container that can be displayed onscreen. Applets are a form of panel (in fact, the Applet class is a subclass of the Panel class).

☐ Canvases. A canvas is a simple drawing surface. Although you can draw on panels (as you've been doing all along), canvases are good for painting images or performing other graphics operations.

☐ UI components. These components can include buttons, lists, simple pop-up menus, check boxes, test fields, and other typical elements of a user interface.

☐ Window construction components. These components include windows, frames, menu bars, and dialog boxes. They are listed separately from the other UI components because you'll use them less often—particularly in applets. In applets, the browser provides the main window and menu bar, so you don't have to use these components. Your applet may create a new window, however, or you may want to write your own Java application that uses these components. (You'll learn about them tomorrow.)

The classes inside the java.awt package are written and organized to mirror the abstract structure of containers, components, and individual UI components. Figure 12.2 shows some of the class hierarchy that makes up the main classes in the AWT. The root of most of the AWT components is the class Component, which provides basic display and event-handling features. The classes Container, Canvas, TextComponent, and many of the other UI components inherit from Component. Inheriting from the Container class are objects that can contain other AWT components—the Panel and Window classes, in particular. Note that the java.applet.Applet class, even though it lives in its own package, inherits from Panel, so your applets are an integral part of the hierarchy of components in the AWT system.

Figure 12.2.

A partial AWT class hierarchy.

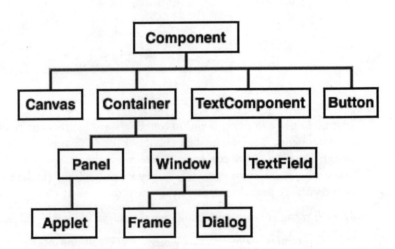

A graphical user interface-based application that you write with the AWT can be as complex as you like, with dozens of nested containers and components inside each other. The AWT was designed so that each component can play its part in the overall AWT system without needing to duplicate or keep track of the behavior of other parts in the system.

In addition to the components, the AWT also includes a set of layout managers. Layout managers determine how the various components are arranged when they are displayed onscreen, and their various sizes relative to each other. Because Java applets and applications that use the AWT can run on different systems with different displays, different fonts, and different resolutions, you cannot just stick a particular component at a particular spot on the window. Layout managers help you create UI layouts that are dynamically arranged and that can be displayed anywhere the applet or application might be run.

The Basic User Interface Components

One of the neat things about applets is that because they are already AWT containers (by virtue of their inheritance), you can start adding other AWT components to them right away without having to know a lot about the more complicated parts of the AWT. So let's start by doing just that; in this section you'll learn about six of the basic UI components in the AWT: labels, buttons, check boxes, radio buttons, choice menus, and text fields and the basics of how to create and use them.

Note that for this section, I'll focus on the components as far as their appearance and use go. Later in this lesson, I'll show you how to add event behavior to these components.

NOTE For the most part, these components remain unchanged between Java 1.02 and 1.1. However, some methods and constructors were renamed in 1.1. I've noted them where they've changed. The old versions will continue to work in Java 1.1, but you'll get "deprecated" warnings when you try to compile your programs.

12

How to Add Components to Your Applet

For any of the UI components you'll learn about in this lesson (or in the next lesson as well), the procedure for creating that component is the same: first you create it, and then you add it to the applet or panel that holds it, at which point it is displayed on the screen. To add a component to a panel (such as your applet), you use the add() method:

```
public void init() {
    Button b = new Button("OK");
    add(b);
}
```

Here the add() method refers to the current applet; in other words, it means "add this element to me." You can also add elements to other panels and containers, nesting components within other components. You'll look more closely at that subject tomorrow.

Note that adding a component to a panel or applet says nothing about the position of that component on the screen. That position depends on the layout manager the panel is defined to have. To make things simple for now, in these examples I've used a couple different kinds of layouts, depending on which makes the applet look better. You'll learn more about panels and layouts in the next section.

Labels

The simplest form of UI component is the label, which is, effectively, a text string that you can use to label other UI components. You cannot edit labels; they just label other components on the screen.

The advantages that a label has over an ordinary text string (that you'd draw using drawString() in the paint() method) are as follow:

☐ You don't have to redraw labels yourself in paint(). Labels are an AWT element, and the AWT keeps track of drawing them for you.

☐ Labels follow the layout of the panel in which they're contained and can be aligned with other UI components. Panel layout is determined by the layout manager, which you'll learn about later, in the section "Panels and Layout."

NEW TERM A *label* is an uneditable text string that acts as a description for other AWT components.

To create a label, use one of the following constructors:

☐ Label() creates an empty label, with its text aligned left.

☐ Label(String) creates a label with the given text string, also aligned left.

☐ Label(String, int) creates a label with the given text string and the given alignment. The available alignment numbers are stored in class variables in Label, making them easier to remember: Label.RIGHT, Label.LEFT, and Label.CENTER.

You can change the label's font with the setFont() method, either called on the label itself to change the individual label, or on the enclosing component to change all the labels. Here's some simple code to create a few labels in Helvetica Bold. Figure 12.3 shows how these labels look onscreen.

This code uses the `setLayout()` method to create a new layout manager. Don't worry about that line right now; you'll learn more about layout managers in the next section.

```java
import java.awt.*;

public class LabelTest extends java.applet.Applet {

    public void init() {
        setFont(new Font ("Helvetica", Font.BOLD, 14));
        setLayout(new GridLayout(3,1));
        add(new Label("aligned left", Label.LEFT));
        add(new Label("aligned center", Label.CENTER));
        add(new Label("aligned right", Label.RIGHT));
    }
}
```

Figure 12.3.

Three labels with various alignments.

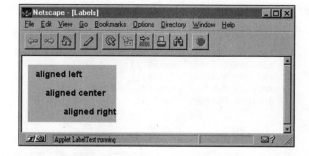

After you have a new `Label` object, you can use methods defined in the `Label` class to get and set various attributes of it, as shown in Table 12.1.

Table 12.1. Label methods.

Method	Action
`getText()`	Returns a string containing this label's text
`setText(String)`	Changes the text of this label
`getAlignment()`	Returns an integer representing the alignment of this label: 0 is `Label.LEFT` 1 is `Label.CENTER` 2 is `Label.RIGHT`
`setAlignment(int)`	Changes the alignment of this label to the given integer; use the class variables listed in the `getAlignment()` method

12

Buttons

The second user interface component to explore is the button. Buttons are simple UI components that trigger some action in your interface when they are pressed. For example, a calculator applet might have buttons for each number and operator, or a dialog box might have buttons for OK and Cancel.

 A *button* is a UI component that, when "pressed" (selected) with the mouse, triggers some action.

To create a button, use one of the following constructors:

☐ `Button()` creates an empty button with no label.

☐ `Button(String)` creates a button with the given string as a label.

After you create a Button object, you can get the value of the button's label by using the `getLabel()` method and set the label using the `setLabel(String)` method.

You can use the following code to create some simple buttons, as shown in Figure 12.4:

```
public class ButtonTest extends java.applet.Applet {

    public void init() {
        add(new Button("Rewind"));
        add(new Button("Play"));
        add(new Button("Fast Forward"));
        add(new Button("Stop"));
    }
}
```

Figure 12.4.

Four buttons in Netscape.

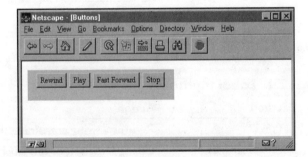

Check Boxes

Check boxes are user-interface components that have two states: on and off (or checked and unchecked, selected and unselected, true and false, and so on). Unlike buttons, check boxes usually don't trigger direct actions in a UI, but instead are used to indicate optional features of some other action.

Check boxes can be used in two ways:

☐ Nonexclusive—Given a series of check boxes, any of them can be selected.

☐ Exclusive—Given a series, only one check box can be selected at a time.

The latter kind of check boxes are called radio buttons or check box groups, and are described in the next section.

 Check boxes are UI components that can be selected or deselected (checked or unchecked) to provide options.

Nonexclusive check boxes can be checked or unchecked independently of other check boxes.

Exclusive check boxes, sometimes called *radio buttons*, exist in groups; only one in the group can be checked at one time.

Nonexclusive check boxes can be created by using the Checkbox class. You can create a check box using one of the following constructors:

☐ Checkbox() creates an empty check box, unselected.

☐ Checkbox(String) creates a check box with the given string as a label.

☐ Checkbox(String, boolean) (Java 1.1 *only*) creates a check box that is either selected or deselected based on whether the boolean argument is true or false, respectively.

☐ Checkbox(String, null, boolean) (Java 1.02 *only*) creates a check box that is either selected or deselected based on whether the boolean argument is true or false, respectively. (The null is used as a placeholder for a group argument. Only radio buttons have groups, as you'll learn in the next section.)

 NOTE

In Java 1.1, the Checkbox(String, null, boolean) constructor has been deprecated (it still exists, but you're not supposed to use it). To create a preselected check box in Java 1.1, use the Checkbox(String, boolean) constructor. To create a check box with a group, you can use a 1.1 version of this constructor with the last two arguments reversed. See the next section for details.

12

You can generate a few simple check boxes (only the Underwear box is selected), as shown in Figure 12.5, using the following code. (Note that the fourth checkbox uses the 1.1 constructor; to modify this code for 1.02, add a null between the two arguments.)

```
import java.awt.*;

public class CheckboxTest extends java.applet.Applet {

    public void init() {
        setLayout(new FlowLayout(FlowLayout.LEFT));
        add(new Checkbox("Shoes"));
        add(new Checkbox("Socks"));
        add(new Checkbox("Pants"));
        add(new Checkbox("Underwear", true));
        add(new Checkbox("Shirt"));
    }
}
```

Figure 12.5.

Five check boxes, one selected.

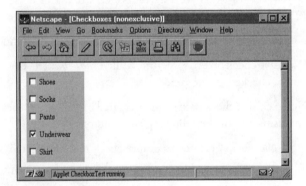

Table 12.2 lists some of the check box methods.

Table 12.2. Check box methods.

Method	Action
getLabel()	Returns a string containing this check box's label
setLabel(String)	Changes the text of the check box's label
getState()	Returns true or false, based on whether the check box is selected
setState(boolean)	Changes the check box's state to selected (true) or unselected (false)

12

Radio Buttons

Radio buttons have the same appearance as check boxes (and, in fact, are also created from the Checkbox class), but only one in a series can be selected at a time. To create a series of radio buttons, first create an instance of CheckboxGroup:

```
CheckboxGroup cbg = new CheckboxGroup();
```

Then create and add the individual radio buttons from the CheckBox class. You can do so in two ways, depending on whether or not you're using Java 1.1:

☐ For Java 1.02, use Checkbox(String, CheckboxGroup, boolean) to create a radio button with the a string label, the name of the check box group you just created, and true or false whether this radio button should be selected or deselected.

☐ For Java 1.1, use Checkbox(String, boolean, CheckboxGroup), where the arguments are the same as for the 1.02 version, except that the last two have been reversed.

Here are two radio buttons, added to the cbg check box group using Java 1.02:

```
add(new Checkbox("Yes", cbg, true);
add(new Checkbox("No", cbg, false);
```

Here are the same check boxes added using Java 1.1:

```
add(new Checkbox("Yes", true, cbg);
add(new Checkbox("No", false, cbg);
```

Note that because groups of radio buttons, by definition, can have only one button selected at a time, the last true button to be added to the group will be the one selected by default. If you create a set of buttons with none selected, then they will initially all appear unselected, and the first choice the user makes will become the default.

Here's a simple example of a set of radio buttons created in Java 1.1. (To convert this example to 1.02, reverse the last two arguments for each Checkbox constructor.) The results are shown in Figure 12.6.

```
import java.awt.*;

public class CheckboxGroupTest extends java.applet.Applet {

    public void init() {
        setLayout(new FlowLayout(FlowLayout.LEFT));
        CheckboxGroup cbg = new CheckboxGroup();

        add(new Checkbox("Red", false, cbg,));
        add(new Checkbox("Blue", false, cbg));
        add(new Checkbox("Yellow", false, cbg));
        add(new Checkbox("Green", true, cbg));
        add(new Checkbox("Orange", false, cbg));
        add(new Checkbox("Purple", false, cbg));
    }
}
```

12

Figure 12.6.

*Six radio buttons
(exclusive check
boxes), one selected.*

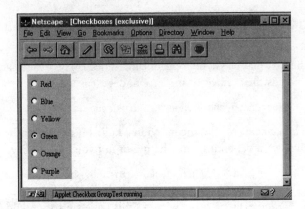

All the check box methods shown in Table 12.2 in the previous section can be used with the radio buttons as well. In addition, you can use the getCheckboxGroup() and setCheckboxGroup() methods (defined in the Checkbox() class) to access and change the group of any given check box.

Finally, the getCurrent() and setCurrent(Checkbox) methods, defined in CheckboxGroup, can be used to get or set the currently selected check box.

Choice Menus

The choice menu is a more complex UI component than labels, buttons, or check boxes. Choice menus are pop-up (or pull-down) lists of items from which you can select an item. The menu then displays that choice on the screen. The function of a choice menu is the same across platforms, but its actual appearance may vary from platform to platform.

NOTE

The terminology here is slightly wrong. Choice menus are closer to multiple-choice lists than they are to actual pop-up menus. In fact, Java 1.1 has an actual Popup menu component, which is a much better component for creating menu behavior. You'll learn about pop-up menus tomorrow.

Note that choice menus can have only one item selected at a time. If you want to be able to choose multiple items from the menu, use a scrolling list instead (you'll learn more about scrolling lists tomorrow).

12

New Term   *Choice menus* are pop-up lists of items from which you can choose one item.

To create a choice menu, first create an instance of the `Choice` class and then add individual items to that object. In Java 1.02, use the `addItem()` method with a string to add an item to the list. In Java 1.1, use the `add()` method with a string instead. Here's a choice menu with three items, built in Java 1.02:

```
Choice c = new Choice();
c.addItem("Green");
c.addItem("Red");
c.addItem("Blue");
```

Here's the same menu, built in Java 1.1:

```
Choice c = new Choice();
c.add("Green");
c.add("Red");
c.add("Blue");
```

After you build the choice menu, add the entire thing to the panel using `add()` in the usual way.

Here's a simple program (using 1.1 code) that builds a choice menu of fruits. Figure 12.7 shows the result (with the list pulled down).

```
import java.awt.*;

public class ChoiceTest extends java.applet.Applet {

    public void init() {
        Choice c = new Choice();
        c.add("Apples");
        c.add("Oranges");
        c.add("Strawberries");
        c.add("Blueberries");
        c.add("Bananas");
        add(c);
    }
}
```

12

Figure 12.7.

A choice menu.

Even after your choice menu has been added to a panel, you can continue to add items to that menu with the addItem() method. Table 12.3 shows some other methods that may be useful in working with choice menus.

Table 12.3. Choice menu methods.

Method	Action
getItem(int)	Returns the string item at the given position (items inside a choice begin at 0, just like arrays)
countItems()	Returns the number of items in the menu (Java 1.02 only; use getItemCount() in 1.1)
getItemCount()	Returns the number of items in the menu (Java 1.1 only)
getSelectedIndex()	Returns the index position of the item that's selected
getSelectedItem()	Returns the currently selected item as a string
select(int)	Selects the item at the given position
select(String)	Selects the item with the given string

Text Fields

Unlike the UI components up to this point, which only enable you to select among several options to perform an action, text fields allow you to enter and edit text. Text fields are generally only a single line and do not have scroll bars; text areas, which you'll learn about later today, are better for larger amounts of text.

Text fields are different from labels in that they can be edited; labels are good for just displaying text, text fields for getting text input from the user.

NEW TERM   *Text fields* provide an area where you can enter and edit a single line of text.

To create a text field, use one of the following constructors:

☐ TextField() creates an empty text field that is 0 characters wide (it will be resized by the current layout manager).

☐ TextField(int) creates an empty text field. The integer argument indicates the minimum number of characters to display. Use this method only for Java 1.02; it has been replaced in 1.1 with TextField(String, int).

☐ TextField(String) creates a text field initialized with the given string. The field will be automatically resized by the current layout manager.

12

☐ `TextField(String, int)` creates a text field some number of characters wide (the integer argument) containing the given string. If the string is longer than the width, you can select and drag portions of the text within the field, and the box will scroll left or right.

The following line creates a text field 30 characters wide with the string `"Enter Your Name"` as its initial content:

```
TextField tf = new TextField("Enter Your Name", 30);
add(tf);
```

TIP Text fields include only the editable field itself. You usually need to include a label with a text field to indicate what belongs in that text field.

You can also create a text field that obscures the characters typed into it—for example, for password fields. To do so, first create the text field itself; then use the `setEchoCharacter()` method in Java 1.02 or the `setEchoChar()` method in Java 1.1 to set the character that is echoed on the screen. Here is an example for 1.02:

```
TextField tf = new TextField(30);
tf.setEchoCharacter('*');
```

Here's the same thing in Java 1.1:

```
TextField tf = new TextField(30);
tf.setEchoChar('*');
```

Using the following Java 1.1 code, you can create three text boxes (and labels), as shown in Figure 12.8:

```
import java.awt.*;

public class TextFieldTest extends java.applet.Applet {
    public void init() {
        setLayout(new GridLayout(3,2,5,15));
        add(new Label("Enter your Name"));
        add(new TextField("your name here", 45));
        add(new Label("Enter your phone number"));
        add(new TextField(12));
        add(new Label("Enter your password"));
        TextField t = new TextField(20);
        t.setEchoChar('*'); // 1.1 only!  Use setEchoCharacter() for 1.02
        add(t);
    }
```

12

Figure 12.8.

Three text fields to allow input from the user.

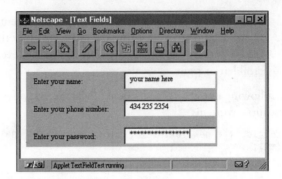

The text in the first field ("your name here") was initialized in the code; I typed the text in the remaining two boxes just before taking the screen shot shown in Figure 12.8.

Text fields inherit from the class TextComponent and have a whole suite of methods, both inherited from that class and defined in their own class, that may be useful to you in your Java programs. Table 12.4 shows a selection of those methods.

Table 12.4. Text field methods.

Method	Action
getText()	Returns the text that this text field contains (as a string)
setText(String)	Puts the given text string into the field
getColumns()	Returns the width of this text field
select(int, int)	Selects the text between the two integer positions (positions start from 0)
selectAll()	Selects all the text in the field
isEditable()	Returns true or false based on whether the text is editable
setEditable(boolean)	true (the default) enables text to be edited; false freezes the text
getEchoChar()	Returns the character used for masking input
setEchoCharacter(char)	Set the character used for masking input (1.02 only)
setEchoChar(char)	Set the character used for masking input (1.1 only)
echoCharIsSet()	Returns true or false based on whether the field has an echo (masking) character set

Panels and Layout

AWT panels can contain UI components or other panels. The question now is how those components are actually arranged and displayed onscreen.

In other windowing systems, UI components are often arranged using hard-coded pixel measurements—put a text field at the position 10,30, for example—the same way you used the graphics operations to paint squares and ovals on the screen. Because Java is cross-platform, however, your AWT UI design may be displayed on many different window systems on many different screens and with many different kinds of fonts with different font metrics. Therefore, you need a more flexible method of arranging components on the screen so that a layout that looks nice on one platform isn't a jumbled, unusable mess on another.

For just this purpose, Java has layout managers, insets, and hints that each component can provide to help dynamically lay out the screen.

Layout Managers: An Overview

The actual appearance of the AWT components on the screen is usually determined by two factors: how those components are added to the panel that holds them (either the order or through arguments to add()) and the layout manager that panel is currently using to lay out the screen. The layout manager determines how portions of the screen will be sectioned and how components within that panel will be placed.

NEW TERM The *layout manager* determines how AWT components are dynamically arranged on the screen.

Each panel on the screen can have its own layout manager. By nesting panels within panels, and using the appropriate layout manager for each one, you can often arrange your UI to group and arrange components in a way that is functionally useful and that looks good on a variety of platforms and windowing systems. You'll learn about nesting panels in a later section.

The AWT provides five basic layout managers: FlowLayout, GridLayout, BorderLayout, CardLayout, and GridBagLayout. To create a layout manager for a given panel, create an instance of that layout manager and then use the setLayout() method for that panel. This example sets the layout manager of the entire enclosing applet panel:

```
public void init() {
   setLayout(new FlowLayout());
}
```

Setting the default layout manager, like creating user-interface components, is best done during the applet's initialization, which is why it's included here.

12

After the layout manager is set, you can start adding components to the panel. The order in which components are added or the arguments you use to add those components is often significant, depending on which layout manager is currently active. Read on for information about the specific layout managers and how they present components within the panel to which they apply.

The following sections describe the five basic Java AWT layout managers.

The `FlowLayout` Class

The `FlowLayout` class is the most basic of layouts. Using flow layout, components are added to the panel one at a time, row by row. If a component doesn't fit onto a row, it's wrapped onto the next row. The flow layout also has an alignment, which determines the alignment of each row. By default, each row is centered.

 Flow layout arranges components from left to right in rows. The rows are aligned left, right, or centered.

To create a basic flow layout with a centered alignment, use the following line of code in your panel's initialization (because this is the default panel layout, you don't need to include this line if that is your intent):

```
setLayout(new FlowLayout());
```

With the layout set, the order in which you add elements to the layout determines their position. The following code creates a simple row of six buttons in a centered flow layout. Figure 12.9 shows the result.

```
import java.awt.*;

public class FlowLayoutTest extends java.applet.Applet {

    public void init() {
        setLayout(new FlowLayout());
        add(new Button("One"));
        add(new Button("Two"));
        add(new Button("Three"));
        add(new Button("Four"));
        add(new Button("Five"));
        add(new Button("Six"));
    }
}
```

Figure 12.9.

Six buttons, arranged using a flow layout manager.

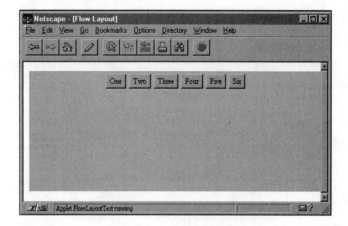

To create a flow layout with an alignment other than centered, add the FlowLayout.RIGHT or FlowLayout.LEFT class variable as an argument:

```
setLayout(new FlowLayout(FlowLayout.LEFT));
```

You can also set horizontal and vertical gap values by using flow layouts. The gap is the number of pixels between components in a panel; by default, the horizontal and vertical gap values are three pixels, which can be very close indeed. Horizontal gap spreads out components to the left and to the right; vertical gap spreads them to the top and bottom of each component. Add integer arguments to the flow layout constructor to increase the gap. You can add a gap of 30 points in the horizontal and 10 in the vertical directions, as follows. Figure 12.10 shows the result.

```
setLayout(new FlowLayout(FlowLayout.LEFT, 30, 10));
```

Figure 12.10.

Flow layout with a gap of 10 points.

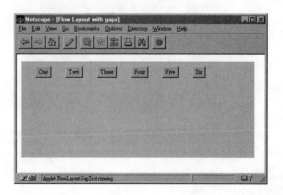

12

Grid Layouts

Grid layouts offer more control over the placement of components inside a panel. Using a grid layout, you portion off the display area of the panel into rows and columns. Each component you then add to the panel is placed in a cell of the grid, starting from the top row and progressing through each row from left to right (here the order of calls to the add() method are relevant to how the screen is laid out).

To create a grid layout, indicate the number of rows and columns you want the grid to have when you create a new instance of the GridLayout class. Here's a grid layout with three rows and two columns. Figure 12.11 shows the result.

```
import java.awt.*;

public class GridLayoutTest extends java.applet.Applet {

    public void init() {
        setLayout(new GridLayout(3,2);
        add(new Button("One"));
        add(new Button("Two"));
        add(new Button("Three"));
        add(new Button("Four"));
        add(new Button("Five"));
        add(new Button("Six"));
    }
}
```

Figure 12.11.

Six buttons, displayed using a grid layout of three rows and two columns.

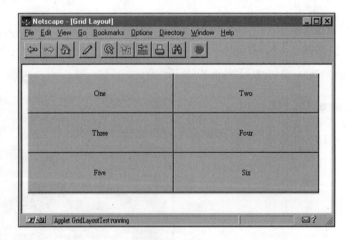

Grid layouts can also have a horizontal and vertical gap between components. To create gaps, add the pixel values:

```
setLayout(new GridLayout(3, 3, 10, 30));
```

Figure 12.12 shows a grid layout with a 10-pixel horizontal gap and a 30-pixel vertical gap.

Figure 12.12.
A grid layout with horizontal and vertical gaps.

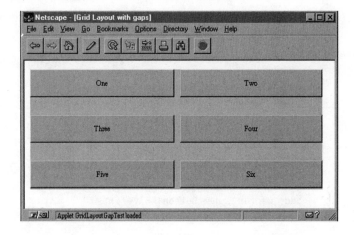

Border Layouts

Border layouts behave differently from flow and grid layouts. When you add a component to a panel that uses a border layout, you indicate its placement as a geographic direction: north, south, east, west, or center. (See Figure 12.13.) The components around all the edges are laid out with as much size as they need; the component in the center, if any, gets any space left over.

Figure 12.13.
Where components go in a border layout.

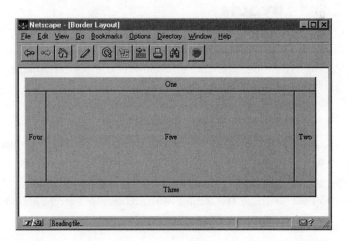

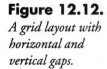

To use a border layout, you create it as you do the other layouts; then you add the individual components with a special add() method that has two arguments. The first argument is a string indicating the position of the component within the layout, and the second is the component to add:

```
add("North", new TextField("Title", 50));
```

You can also use this form of add() for the other layout managers; the string argument will be ignored if it's not needed.

Here's the code to generate the border layout shown in Figure 12.13:

```
import java.awt.*;

public class BorderLayoutTest extends java.applet.Applet {

    public void init() {
        setLayout(new BorderLayout());
        add("North", new Button("One"));
        add("East", new Button("Two"));
        add("South", new Button("Three"));
        add("West", new Button("Four"));
        add("Center", new Button("Five"));
    }
}
```

Border layouts can also have horizontal and vertical gaps. Note that the north and south components extend all the way to the edge of the panel, so the gap will result in less vertical space for the east, west, and center components. To add gaps to a border layout, include those pixel values in the constructor as with the other layout managers:

```
setLayout(new BorderLayout(10, 10));
```

Card Layouts

Card layouts behave much differently from the other layouts. When you add components to one of the other layout managers, all those components appear on the screen at once. Card layouts are used to produce slide shows of components, one at a time. If you've ever used the HyperCard program on the Macintosh, or seen dialog boxes on windows with several different tabbed pages, you've worked with the same basic idea.

When you create a card layout, the components you add to the outer panel will be other container components—usually other panels. You can then use different layouts for those individual cards so that each screen has its own look.

NEW TERM *Cards*, in a card layout, are different panels added one at a time and displayed one at a time. If you think of a card file, you'll get the idea; only one card can be displayed at once, but you can switch between cards.

When you add each card to the panel, you can give it a name. Then, to flip between the container cards, you can use methods defined in the CardLayout class to move to a named card, move forward or back, or move to the first card or to the last card. Typically, you'll have a set of buttons that call these methods to make navigating the card layout easier.

The following two simple snippets of code create a card layout containing three cards:

```
setLayout(new CardLayout());
//add the cards
Panel one = new Panel()
add("first", one);
Panel two = new Panel()
add("second", two);
Panel three = new Panel()
add("third", three);

// move around
show(this, "second"); //go to the card named "second"
show(this, "third");   //go to the card named "third"
previous(this);        //go back to the second card
first(this);           // go to the first card
```

Grid Bag Layouts

I've saved grid bag layouts for last because although they are the most powerful way of managing AWT layout, they are also extremely complicated.

Using one of the other four layout managers, getting the exact layout you want can sometimes be difficult without doing a lot of nesting of panels within panels. Grid bags provide a more general-purpose solution. Like grid layouts, grid bag layouts allow you to arrange your components in a grid-like layout. However, grid bag layouts also allow you to control the span of individual cells in the grid, the proportions between the rows and columns, and the arrangement of components inside cells in the grid.

To create a grid bag layout, you actually use two classes: GridBagLayout, which provides the overall layout manager, and GridBagConstraints, which defines the properties of each component in the grid—its placement, dimensions, alignment, and so on. The relationship between the grid bag, the constraints, and each component defines the overall layout.

In its most general form, creating a grid bag layout involves the following steps:

1. Creating a GridBagLayout object and defining it as the current layout manager, as you would any other layout manager

2. Creating a new instance of GridBagConstraints

3. Setting up the constraints for a component

4. Telling the layout manager about the component and its constraints

5. Adding the component to the panel

The following simple code sets up the layout and then creates constraints for a single button. (Don't worry about the various values for the constraints; I'll cover them later in this section.)

```
// set up layout
```

12

```
GridBagLayout gridbag = new GridBagLayout();
GridBagConstraints constraints = new GridBagConstraints();
setLayout(gridbag);

// define constraints for the button
Button b = new Button("Save");
constraints.gridx = 0;
constraints.gridy = 0;
constraints.gridwidth = 1;
constraints.gridheight = 1;
constraints.weightx = 30;
constraints.weighty = 30;
constraints.fill = GridBagConstraints.NONE;
constraints.anchor = GridBagConstraints.CENTER;

// attach constraints to layout, add button
gridbag.setConstraints(b, constraints);
add(b);
```

By far, the most tedious part of this process is setting up the constraints for each component. (As you can see from this example, you have to set all the constraints for every component you want to add to the panel.) In addition to the tedium, constraints aren't all that easy to understand; they have many different values (many of which are interrelated) which means that changing one may have strange effects on others.

Given the numerous constraints, it helps to have a plan and to deal with each kind of constraint one at a time. I like to follow five steps in this process. Let's walk through each of them.

Step One: Design the Grid

The first place to start in the grid bag layout is on paper. Sketching out your UI design beforehand—before you write even a single line of code—will help enormously in the long run with trying to figure out where everything goes. So put your editor aside for a second, pick up a piece of paper and a pencil, and build the grid.

Figure 12.14 shows the panel layout you'll be building in this example. Figure 12.15 shows the same layout with a grid imposed on top of it. Your layout will have a grid similar to this one, with rows and columns forming individual cells.

Figure 12.14.

A grid bag layout.

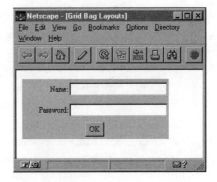

Figure 12.15.

The grid bag layout from Figure 12.14, with grid imposed.

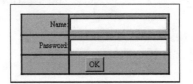

As you draw your grid, keep in mind that each component must have its own cell. You cannot put more than one component into the same cell. The reverse is not true, however; one component can span multiple cells in the x or y directions (as in the OK button in the bottom row, which spans two columns). In Figure 12.15, note that the labels and text fields have their own grids and that the button spans two column cells.

While you're still working on paper, something that will help you later is to label the cells with their x and y coordinates. They aren't pixel coordinates; rather, they're cell coordinates. The top-left cell is 0,0. The next cell to the right of it in the top row is 1,0. The cell to the right of that one is 2,0. Moving to the next row, the leftmost cell is 1,0, the next cell in the row is 1,1, and so on. Label your cells on the paper with these numbers; you'll need them later when you do the code for this example. Figure 12.16 shows the numbers for each of the cells in this example.

Figure 12.16.

The grid bag layout from Figure 12.14, with cell coordinates.

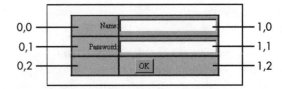

12

Step Two: Create the Grid in Java

Now go back to Java and start implementing the layout you've just drawn on paper. Initially, you're going to focus exclusively on the layout—getting the grid and the proportions right. For that, it helps to not work with actual UI elements. I like to use buttons as placeholders for the actual elements in the layout until I can get everything set up right, and then change the buttons to the right elements.

To cut down on the amount of typing you have to do to set up all those constraints, you can start by defining a helper method that takes several values and sets the constraints for those values. buildConstraints() takes seven arguments: a GridBagConstraints object and six integers representing the GridBagConstraints instance variables gridx, gridy, gridwidth, gridheight, weightx, and weighty. You'll learn what these actually do soon; for now, here's the code to the helper method that you'll use further on in this example:

```
void buildConstraints(GridBagConstraints gbc, int gx, int gy,
int gw, int gh, int wx, int wy) {
gbc.gridx = gx;
gbc.gridy = gy;
gbc.gridwidth = gw;
gbc.gridheight = gh;
gbc.weightx = wx;
gbc.weighty = wy;
}
```

Now move on to the init() method, where all the layout actually occurs. Here's the basic method definition, where you'll define the GridBagLayout to be the initial layout manager and create a constraints object (an instance of GridBagConstraints):

```
public void init() {
GridBagLayout gridbag = new GridBagLayout();
GridBagConstraints constraints = new GridBagConstraints();
setLayout(gridbag);

constraints.fill = GridBagConstraints.BOTH;
}
```

One more small note of explanation: The last line, which sets the value of constraints.fill, will be removed (and explained) later. It's there so that the components will fill the entire cell in which they're contained, which helps you see what's going on. Add it for now, and you'll get a clearer idea of what it's for later.

Now add the button placeholders to the layout (remember, you're focusing on basic grid organization at the moment, so you'll use buttons as placeholders for the actual UI elements you'll add later). Start with a single button so you can get a feel for setting its constraints. This code will go into the init() method just after the setLayout line:

```
// Name label
buildConstraints(constraints, 0, 0, 1, 1, 100, 100);
Button label1 = new Button("Name:");
gridbag.setConstraints(label1, constraints);
add(label1);
```

These four lines set up the constraints for an object, create a new button, attach the constraints to the button, and then add it to the panel. Note that constraints for a component are stored in the GridBagConstraints object, so the component doesn't even have to exist to set up its constraints.

Now you can get down to details: Just what are the values for the constraints that you've plugged into the helper method buildConstraints()?

The first two integer arguments are the gridx and gridy values of the constraints. They are the cell coordinates of the cell that contains this component. Remember how you wrote these components down on paper in step one? With the cells nearly numbered on paper, all you have to do is plug in the right values. Note that if you have a component that spans multiple cells, the cell coordinates are those of the cell in the top-left corner.

Here this button is in the top-left corner, so its gridx and gridy (the first two arguments to buildConstraints()) are 0 and 0, respectively.

The second two integer arguments are the gridwidth and gridheight. They are not the pixel widths and heights of the cells; rather, they are the number of cells this component spans: gridwidth for the columns and gridheight for the rows. Here this component spans only one cell, so the values for both are 1.

The last two integer arguments are for weightx and weighty. They are used to set up the proportions of the rows and columns—that is, how wide or deep they will be. Weights can become very confusing, so, for now, just set both values to 100. You'll deal with weights in step three.

After the constraints have been built, you can attach them to an object using the setConstraints() method. setConstraints(),which is a method defined in GridBagLayout, takes two arguments: the component (here a button) and the constraints for that button. Finally, you can add the button to the panel.

After you've set and assigned the constraints to one component, you can reuse that GridBagConstraints object to set up the constraints for the next object. You, therefore, duplicate these four lines for each component in the grid, with different values for the buildConstraints() method. To save space, I'm just going to show you the buildConstraints() methods for the last four cells.

The second cell to add is the one that will hold the text box for the name. The cell coordinates for this one are 1,0 (second column, first row); it too spans only one cell, and the weights (for now) are also both 100:

```
buildConstraints(constraints, 1, 0, 1, 1, 100, 100);
```

The next two components, which will be a label and a text field, are nearly exactly the same as the previous two; the only difference is in their cell coordinates. The password label is at

0,1 (first column, second row), and the password text field is at 1,1 (second column, second row):

```
buildConstraints(constraints, 0, 1, 1, 1, 100, 100);
buildConstraints(constraints, 1, 1, 1, 1, 100, 100);
```

And, finally, you need the OK button, which is a component that spans two cells in the bottom row of the panel. Here the cell coordinates are the left and topmost cell where the span starts (0,2). Here, unlike the previous components, you'll set gridwidth and gridheight to be something other than 1 because this cell spans multiple columns. The gridweight is 2 (it spans two cells) and the gridheight is 1 (it spans only one row):

```
buildConstraints(constraints, 0, 2, 2, 1, 100, 100);
```

Got it? You've set the placement constraints for all the components that you'll add to the grid layout. You will also need to assign each component's constraints to the layout manager and then add each component to the panel. Figure 12.17 shows the result so far. Note that you're not concerned about exact proportions here, or about making sure everything lines up. What you should keep track of at this point is making sure the grid is working, that you have the right number of rows and columns, that the spans are correct, and that nothing strange is going on (cells in the wrong place, cells overlapping, that kind of thing).

Figure 12.17.

Grid bag layout, first pass.

Step Three: Determine the Proportions

The next step is to determine the proportions of the rows and columns in relation to other rows and columns. For example, in this case you'll want the labels (name and password) to take up less space than the text boxes. And you might want the OK button at the bottom to be only half the height of the two text boxes above it. You arrange the proportions of the cells within your layout using the weightx and weighty constraints.

The easiest way to think of weightx and weighty is that their values are either percentages of the total width and height of the panel, or 0 if the weight or height has been set by some other cell. The values of weightx and weighty for all your components, therefore, should sum to 100.

TECHNICAL NOTE

Actually, the `weightx` and `weighty` values are not percentages; they're simply proportions—they can have any value whatsoever. When the proportions are calculated, all the values in a direction are summed so that each individual value is in proportion to that total (in other words, divided into the total to actually get a percentage). Because this process is incredibly nonintuitive, I find it far easier to look at the weights as percentages and to make sure they all sum up to 100 to make sure everything is coming out right.

So which cells get values and which cells get 0? Cells that span multiple rows or columns should always be 0 in the direction they span. Beyond that, deciding is simply a question of picking a cell to have a value, and then all the other cells in that row or columns should be 0.

Let's look at the five calls to `buildConstraints()` made in the preceding step:

```
buildConstraints(constraints, 0, 0, 1, 1, 100, 100); //name
buildConstraints(constraints, 1, 0, 1, 1, 100, 100); //name text
buildConstraints(constraints, 0, 1, 1, 1, 100, 100); //password
buildConstraints(constraints, 1, 1, 1, 1, 100, 100); //password text
buildConstraints(constraints, 0, 2, 2, 1, 100, 100); //OK button
```

You'll be changing those last two arguments in each call to `buildConstraints` to be either a value or 0. Let's start with the x direction (the proportions of the columns), which is the second-to-last argument in that list.

If you look back to Figure 12.15 (the picture of the panel with the grid imposed), you'll note that the second column is much larger than the first. If you were going to pick theoretical percentages for those columns, you might say that the first is 10 percent and the second is 90 percent (I'm making a guess here; that's all you need to do as well). With these two guesses, you can assign them to cells. You don't want to assign any values to the cell with the OK button because that cell spans both columns, and percentages there wouldn't work. So add them to the first two cells, the name label and the name text field:

```
buildConstraints(constraints, 0, 0, 1, 1, 10, 100); //name
buildConstraints(constraints, 1, 0, 1, 1, 90, 100); //name text
```

And what about the values of the remaining two cells, the password label and text field? Because the proportions of the columns have already been set up by the name label and field, you don't have to reset them here. You'll give both of these cells and the one for the OK box 0 values:

```
buildConstraints(constraints, 0, 1, 1, 1, 0, 100); //password
buildConstraints(constraints, 1, 1, 1, 1, 0, 100); //password text
buildConstraints(constraints, 0, 2, 2, 1, 0, 100); //OK button
```

12

Note here that a 0 value does not mean that the cell has 0 width. These values are proportions, not pixel values. A 0 simply means that the proportion has been set somewhere else; all 0 says is "stretch it to fit."

Now that the totals of all the `weightx` constraints are 100, you can move on to the `weighty`s. Here you have three rows. Glancing over the grid you drew, it looks like the button has about 20 percent and the text fields have the rest (40 percent each). As with the x values, you have to set the value of only one cell per row (the two labels and the button), with all the other cells having a `weightx` of 0.

Here are the final five calls to `buildConstraints()` with the weights in place:

```
buildConstraints(constraints, 0, 0, 1, 1, 10, 40); //name
buildConstraints(constraints, 1, 0, 1, 1, 90, 0); //name text
buildConstraints(constraints, 0, 1, 1, 1, 0, 40); //password
buildConstraints(constraints, 1, 1, 1, 1, 0, 0); //password text
buildConstraints(constraints, 0, 2, 2, 1, 0, 20); //OK button
```

Figure 12.18 shows the result with the correct proportions.

Figure 12.18.

*Grid bag layout,
second pass.*

At this step, the goal is to try to come up with some basic proportions for how the rows and cells will be spaced on the screen. You can make some basic estimates based on how big you expect the various components to be, but chances are you're going to use a lot of trial and error in this part of the process.

Step Four: Add and Arrange the Components

With the layout and the proportions in place, you can now replace the button placeholders with actual labels and text fields. And because you set up everything already, it should all work perfectly, right? Well, almost. Figure 12.19 shows what you get if you use the same constraints as before and replace the buttons with actual components.

Figure 12.19.
*Grid bag layout,
almost there.*

This layout is close, but it's weird. The text boxes are too tall, and the OK button stretches the width of the cell.

What's missing are the constraints that arrange the components inside the cell. There are two of them: `fill` and `anchor`.

The `fill` constraint determines, for components that can stretch in either direction (such as text boxes and buttons), in which direction to stretch. `fill` can have one of four values, defined as class variables in the `GridBagConstraints` class:

☐ `GridBagConstraints.BOTH`, which stretches the component to fill the cell in both directions

☐ `GridBagConstraints.NONE`, which causes the component to be displayed in its smallest size

☐ `GridBagConstraints.HORIZONTAL`, which stretches the component in the horizontal direction

☐ `GridBagConstraints.VERTICAL`, which stretches the component in the vertical direction

NOTE

Keep in mind that this layout is dynamic. You're not going to set up the actual pixel dimensions of any components; rather, you're telling these elements in which direction they can grow given a panel that can be of any size.

By default, the `fill` constraint for all components is `NONE`. So why are the text fields and labels filling the cells? If you remember way back to the start of the code for this example, I added this line to the `init()` method:

```
constraints.fill = GridBagConstraints.BOTH;
```

Now you know what it does. For the final version of this applet, you'll want to remove that line and add `fill` values for each independent component.

The second constraint that affects how a component appears in the cell is anchor. This constraint applies only to components that aren't filling the whole cell, and it tells the AWT where inside the cell to place the component. The possible values for the anchor constraint are `GridBagConstraints.CENTER`, which aligns the component both vertically and horizontally inside the cell, or one of eight direction values: `GridBagConstraints.NORTH`, `GridBagConstraints.NORTHEAST`, `GridBagConstraints.EAST`, `GridBagConstraints.SOUTHEAST`, `GridBagConstraints.SOUTH`, `GridBagConstraints.SOUTHWEST`, `GridBagConstraints.WEST`, or `GridBagConstraints.NORTHWEST`. The default value of anchor is `GridBagConstraints.CENTER`.

You set these constraints in the same way you did all the other ones: by changing instance variables in the `GridBagConstraints` object. Here you can change the definition of `buildConstraints()` to take two more arguments (they're `int`s), or you could just set them in the body of the `init()` method. I prefer the latter way.

Be careful with defaults. Keep in mind that because you're reusing the same `GridBagConstraints` object for each component, you may have some values left over after you're done with one component. On the other hand, if a `fill` or anchor from one object is the same as the one before it, you don't have to reset that object.

For this example, I'm going to make three changes to the `fill`s and anchors of the components:

- [ ] The labels will have no `fill` and will be aligned east (so they hug the right side of the cell).
- [ ] The text fields will be filled horizontally (so they start one line high, but stretch to the width of the cell).
- [ ] The button will have no `fill` and will be center aligned.

I'm not going to show you all the code for this here; the full code for the example is at the end of this section. You can see the changes I've made there.

Step Five: Futz with It

I added this step to the list because, in my own experimentation with grid bag layouts, I found that even by following all the steps, the resulting layout usually wasn't quite right, and I needed to do a considerable amount of tinkering and playing with various values of the constraints to get it to come out right (that's what *futzing* means). There's nothing wrong with that; the goal of the preceding four steps was to get things fairly close to their final positions, not to come out with a perfect layout each and every time.

The Code

Listing 12.1 shows the complete code for the panel layout you've been building up in this section. If you had trouble following the discussion up to this point, you might find it useful to go through this code line by line to make sure you understand the various bits.

TYPE   **Listing 12.1. The panel with the final grid bag layout.**

```
1:import java.awt.*;
2:
3:public class GridBagTestFinal extends java.applet.Applet {
4:
5:   void buildConstraints(GridBagConstraints gbc, int gx, int gy,
6:        int gw, int gh,
7:        int wx, int wy) {
8:        gbc.gridx = gx;
9:        gbc.gridy = gy;
10:       gbc.gridwidth = gw;
11:       gbc.gridheight = gh;
12:       gbc.weightx = wx;
12:       gbc.weighty = wy;
14:   }
15:
16:   public void init() {
17:        GridBagLayout gridbag = new GridBagLayout();
18:        GridBagConstraints constraints = new GridBagConstraints();
19:        setLayout(gridbag);
20:
21:        // Name label
22:        buildConstraints(constraints, 0, 0, 1, 1, 10, 40);
23:        constraints.fill = GridBagConstraints.NONE;
24:        constraints.anchor = GridBagConstraints.EAST;
25:        Label label1 = new Label("Name:", Label.LEFT);
26:        gridbag.setConstraints(label1, constraints);
27:        add(label1);
28:
29:        // Name text field
30:        buildConstraints(constraints, 1, 0, 1, 1, 90, 0);
31:        constraints.fill = GridBagConstraints.HORIZONTAL;
32:        TextField tfname = new TextField();
33:        gridbag.setConstraints(tfname, constraints);
34:        add(tfname);
35:
36:        // password label
37:        buildConstraints(constraints, 0, 1, 1, 1, 0, 40);
38:        constraints.fill = GridBagConstraints.NONE;
39:        constraints.anchor = GridBagConstraints.EAST;
40:        Label label2 = new Label("Password:", Label.LEFT);
41:        gridbag.setConstraints(label2, constraints);
42:        add(label2);
43:
44:        // password text field
45:        buildConstraints(constraints, 1, 1, 1, 1, 0, 0);
```

12

continues

Listing 12.1. continued

```
46:         constraints.fill = GridBagConstraints.HORIZONTAL;
47:         TextField tfpass = new TextField();
48:         tfpass.setEchoCharacter('*');
49:         gridbag.setConstraints(tfpass, constraints);
50:         add(tfpass);
51:
52:         // OK Button
53:         buildConstraints(constraints, 0, 2, 2, 1, 0, 20);
54:         constraints.fill = GridBagConstraints.NONE;
55:         constraints.anchor = GridBagConstraints.CENTER;
56:         Button okb = new Button("OK");
57:         gridbag.setConstraints(okb, constraints);
58:         add(okb);
59:  }
60:}
```

ipadx and ipady

Before you finish up with grid bag layouts (isn't it over yet?), two more constraints deserve mentioning: ipadx and ipady. These two constraints control the padding—that is, the extra space around an individual component. By default, no components have extra space around them (which is easiest to see in components that fill their cells).

ipadx adds space to either side of the component, and ipady adds it above and below.

Insets

Horizontal and vertical gap, created when you create a new layout manager (or using ipadx and ipady in grid bag layouts), are used to determine the amount of space between components in a panel. Insets, however, are used to determine the amount of space around the panel itself. The Insets class includes values for the top, bottom, left, and right insets, which are then used when the panel itself is drawn.

NEW TERM   *Insets* determine the amount of space between the edges of a panel and that panel's components.

To include an inset for your layout, you override either the insets() or the getInsets() method in your Applet class or other panel class. For 1.02, use insets(); for 1.1, use getInsets(). They do the same thing; only the name has changed.

Inside the insets() or getInsets() method, create a new Insets object, where the constructor to the Insets class takes four integer values representing the insets on the top, left, bottom, and right of the panel. The insets() method should then return that Insets object. Here's some 1.02 code to add insets for a grid layout, 10 to the top and bottom, and 30 to the left and right. Figure 12.20 shows the inset.

```
public Insets insets() {
return new Insets(10, 30, 10, 30);
}
```

Figure 12.20.

A panel with insets of 10 pixels on the top and bottom and 30 pixels to the left and right.

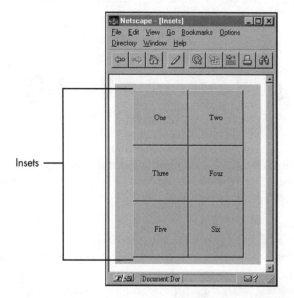

Insets

Input Focus and Mouseless Operation (1.1 only)

One of the new features of Java 1.1 is mouseless operation—that is, the ability to select or activate various AWT components without the use of a mouse. This capability is useful for systems without mice, or for "power users" who prefer to use keyboard commands instead of the mouse.

All the standard AWT components can be activated or used once they have the input focus. Input focus simply means the component that's currently being operated on, which means that component will accept key commands to operate or activate it. Only one component at a time can have the input focus, and there will usually be some visual indication that a particular component has the focus (for example, buttons have a dotted line around them).

12

After a component has the focus, you can use various keys (arrows, Return, spacbar) to operate or activate that component, although those keys may differ from platform to platform (and some platforms may not provide input focus for some elements at all).

To switch the focus from one component to another (what's called *focus traversal*), use the Tab key to move forward and the Shift-Tab key combination to move back. The order in which the focus moves from one component to another is determined by the order in which those components are added to their enclosing component. To change the focus traversal for a set of components, change the order in which you use add() to add them to a component.

A component can also specifically request the input focus using the requestFocus() method, defined in the Component class and therefore available to all AWT components.

Handling UI Events in the 1.02 Event Model

If you stopped reading today's lesson right now, you could go out and create an applet that had lots of little UI components, nicely laid out on the screen with the proper layout manager, gap, and insets. If you did stop right here, however, your applet would be really dull, because none of your UI components would actually do anything when they were pressed, typed into, or selected.

For these capabilities, you need to add code to handle events. Like the mouse and keyboard events you learned about yesterday, UI events let your applet or application react to input by the user. For AWT components, however, events are more high level; for example, buttons use action events that are triggered when the button is pressed. You don't have to worry about mouse down or mouse up or determining where the mouse down and up happened; the component handles all of that for you.

Also, as with the events you learned about yesterday, UI events are created and handled differently depending on whether you're using the 1.02 or 1.1 event models. Everything you learned yesterday about the differences between the models will continue to apply today; only the details are different. In this section, I'll describe UI events as they're managed in 1.02. In the next section, you'll learn how UI events work in 1.1.

Let's focus today on the events generated by the six basic UI components you learned about earlier. Actually, only five generate any events (labels are static). These six UI components can generate five kinds of events:

☐ Action events: The primary events for most UI components to indicate that component has been "activated." Action events are generated when a button is pressed, when a check box or radio button is selected or deselected, when a choice menu item is picked, or when the user presses Return or Enter inside a text field.

☐ List select and deselect events: These events are generated when a check box or choice menu item is selected (which also generates an action event).

☐ Got focus or lost focus events: These events can be generated by any component either in response to a mouse click or as part of focus traversal using the Tab key. Got focus means just that—the component has the input focus and can now be selected, typed into, or activated. Lost focus means that the input focus has moved to some other component.

Handling Action Events

Action events are by far the most commonly used UI event, and for that reason a special method is used to handle it, just like basic mouse and keyboard event methods you learned about yesterday.

To intercept an action event generated by any UI component, define an `action()` method in your applet or class with the following signature:

```
public boolean action(Event evt, Object arg) {
...
}
```

This `action()` method should look similar to the basic mouse and keyboard event methods. Like those methods, this one gets passed the event object that represents this event. It's also passed an extra object (in this code, the parameter arg), which can be of any class type.

What kind of object that second argument to the action method is depends on the UI component generating the action. The basic definition is that it's "any arbitrary argument," determined by the UI component itself, to pass along any extra information that might be useful for you to use in processing that action. Table 12.5 shows the extra arguments for each UI component.

Table 12.5. Action arguments for each UI component.

Component	Argument Type	Contains
Button	String	The label of the button
Check boxes	Boolean	Always true
Radio buttons	Boolean	Always true
Choice menus	String	The label of the item selected
Text fields	String	The text inside the field

12

Inside the action() method, the first thing to do is to test to see which UI component generated the action (unlike with mouse or keyboard events, where it doesn't really matter because different components can all generate actions). Fortunately, the Event object you get when action() is called contains an instance variable called target that contains a reference to the object that received the event. You can use the instanceof operator to find out which component generated the event, like this:

```
public boolean action(Event evt, Object arg) {
   if (evt.target instanceof TextField)
    return handleText(evt.target);
  else if (evt.target instanceof Choice)
    return handleChoice(arg);
 ...
    return false;
}
```

In this example, action() could have been generated by either a TextField or a choice menu; the if statements determine which one actually generated the event and call some other method (handleText() or handleChoice() here) to actually deal with it. (Neither handleText() nor handleChoice() are AWT methods. I just picked two random names to represent helper methods. It's a common practice to create these helper methods so that action() doesn't get cluttered with a lot of code.)

As with the other event methods, action() returns a boolean value. As with all the event methods, you should return true if action() itself deals with the method, or false if it passes the method on somewhere else (or ignores it). In this example, you passed control to the handleText() or handleChoice() methods, and they must return true or false, so you can return false (remember, you return true only if that method had processed the event).

Extra complications occur when you have lots of components that all have the same class— for example, a whole bunch of buttons. All of them generate actions, and all of them are instances of Button. That extra argument comes in here: you can use the labels, items, or contents of the component to determine which one generated the event, and use simple string comparisons to choose between them. (Don't forget to cast the argument to the right object.)

```
public boolean action(Event evt, Object arg) {
    if (evt.target instanceof Button) {
       String labl = (String)arg;
       if (labl.equals("OK"))
          // handle OK button
       else if (labl.equals("Cancel"))
          // handle Cancel button
       else if (labl.equals("Browse"))
          // handle Browse button
       ...
    }
```

12

NOTE What about check boxes and radio buttons? Their extra argument is always `true`, which isn't really useful for testing against. Generally, you shouldn't react to a check box or radio button when it's actually checked. Usually, check boxes and radio buttons can be selected or deselected by the user at will, and then their values are checked at some other point (for example, when a button is pressed).

If you really want your program to react to a check box or radio button as it's checked, you can use the `getLabel()` method to extract the label for the check box from inside `action()` instead of using the extra argument. (Actually, all components have some sort of method of this type; it's just easier to use when it's passed in as the extra argument.)

In the section "An Example: Background Color Switcher," you'll build a simple AWT-based applet that shows how to use the `action()` method in real life.

Handling Other Events

As I mentioned earlier, action events are by far the most common UI events that you'll deal with for the components you've learned about in this lesson. However, you can use four other events in your own programs: list select, list deselect, got focus, and lost focus.

For the got focus and lost focus events, you can use the `gotFocus()` and `lostFocus()` methods, which are used the same as `action()`. Here are their signatures:

```
public boolean gotFocus(Event evt, Object arg) {
...
}

public boolean lostFocus(Event evt, Object arg) {
...
}
```

For list select and list deselect events, no easily overrideable methods are available for use. You'll have to use `handleEvent()` for those events, like this:

```
public boolean handleEvent(Event evt) {
   if (evt.id == Event.LIST_SELECT)
      handleSelect(Event);
   else if (evt.id == Event.LIST_DESELECT)
      handleDeselect(Event);
   else return super.handleEvent(evt);
}
```

12

In this snippet of code, Event.LIST_SELECT and Event.LIST_DESELECT are the official event IDs for the list select and deselect events, and here I've simply passed control to two helper methods (handleSelect() and handleDeselect()), which are theoretically defined elsewhere. Note also the call to super.handleEvent() at the bottom; this call lets other events pass gracefully back up to the original handleEvent() method.

Handling UI events in the 1.1 Event Model

UI events did not escape the overhaul of the event model in Java 1.1; just as mouse and keyboard events are handled totally differently in the two models, so are UI events. Fortunately, because you already went through the pain of learning the new model yesterday, you should already have a good idea of what to expect.

Listeners for Basic UI Components

In 1.1, the events you can handle for the basic UI components are the same; they're just split up into different event classes (there are a couple of new ones). Each event class has a corresponding listener interface, with a set of methods to implement. Table 12.6 shows the events, the event listener classes that handles them, and the methods to deal with those events.

Table 12.6. Events, listeners, and event methods.

Event	Listener interface	Method
action	ActionListener	public void actionPerformed (ActionEvent e)
list select	ItemListener	public void itemStateChanged (ItemEvent e)
list deselect		
got focus	FocusListener	public void focusGained (FocusEvent e)
lost focus	FocusListener	public void focusLost (FocusEvent e)
text changed	TextListener	public void textValueChanged (TextEvent e)
component added	ContainerListener	public void componentAdded (ContainerListener e)
component removed	ContainerListener	public void componentRemoved (ContainerListener e)

12

The three new events listed here are for 1.1 only:

☐ The text changed event is generated when the text in a text field (or text area, which you'll learn about tomorrow) is changed in any way.

☐ The component added event is generated when you add a component to another component (such as an applet).

☐ The component removed event is generated when you remove a component from another component.

As with the mouse and keyboard events you learned about yesterday, you can create your own listeners by implementing the right interface in your applet class or by creating a separate class. Note, however, that for the listeners mentioned here, only ContainerListener and FocusListener have adapter classes (ContainerAdapter and FocusAdapter, respectively). You'll therefore have to implement the interfaces for ActionListener, ItemListener and TextListener by hand.

If you do implement a listener interface, remember that you have to implement all the methods in that interface. (Of course, because action and list events have only one method per listener, doing so is easy.)

Inside the body of your methods, you can often find out more about the event (for example, for item events, whether it was selected or deselected) by examining the event object itself. (Check the API documentation for some of the features you can find out about an event.) One of the more useful event methods is that you can get a reference to the component that received the event using the getSource() method. With that reference, you can then use the various component methods to identify the component (or modify it):

```
public void actionPerformed(ActionEvent e) {
   Button theSource = e.getSource;
   if (theSource.getLabel().equals("OK")) {
      // handle OK
   } else if (theSource.getLabel().equals("Cancel")) {
      // handle cancel
   }
}
```

Registering UI Listeners

When you're ready to register your UI listeners, you can choose from three methods: addActionListener(), addItemListener(), and addFocusListener(), which register the listeners to which they refer. As with other listeners, the init() method is the best place to put these methods, usually immediately after the code to create the component that will use that listener.

Note that unlike with mouse and keyboard methods, which were registered to the applet itself, with component listeners you have to register the listener with each specific component that will receive that event. For example, to register an action event to a button, you have to call the addActionListener() method on that button object and on every other button object in your applet. Here's a simple example, where the OKButtonAction and CancelButtonAction classes both implement ActionListener and contain the code for handling each kind of button:

```
public void init() {
    Button OKButton = new Button("OK");
    OKButtonAction ok = new OKButtonAction();
    OKButton.addActionListener(ok);

    Button CancelButton = new Button("Cancel");
    CancelButtonAction cancel = new CancelButtonAction();
    CancelButton.addActionListener(cancel);

    add(OKButton);
    add(CancelButton);
}
```

In this example, you actually have two listener classes for each button. Depending on how you feel like designing your code, you can have multiple listener classes, a single listener class for processing a whole class of events from each component, or you can put all the event processing in the applet itself. One of the nice things about the new 1.1 event model is that it lets you arrange your event code wherever you want to put it: in your main class, in a single class for all events, in separate classes for each event type, or in multiple listener classes for each and every component.

Differences Between 1.02 and 1.1 UI Events

If you're converting older Java code to the 1.1 event model, having a list of the specific changes from the old to the new is helpful.

As with mouse and keyboard events, all UI events in the 1.02 model are instances of the Event class. In the 1.1 model, action events are instances of ActionEvent, focus events (got and lost focus) are instances of FocusEvent, and list select and deselect are instances of ItemEvent.

The following are specific changes to watch for in the code:

☐ The action() method is now actionPerformed().

☐ The getFocus() method is now focusGained().

☐ The lostFocus() method is now focusLost().

For each of the new event methods, the only argument passed in is the event object; the extra argument is no longer there. In many cases, you can work around the use of the extra argument by using the getSource() method, defined on the event object, which returns an instance of the component that generated the event. You can then use whatever criteria you want to (the label or some other identifier) to decide how to proceed.

The target instance variable (defined on Event objects, which returns the component that received the event) should be replaced with getSource() for the same effect.

And, finally, you also should watch out for two new events: TextEvent, which handles the text changed event, and ContainerEvent, which handles component added and component removed events. Table 12.6 shows the listeners and methods for these new events.

An Example: Background Color Switcher

With snippets of code to work from, getting an idea of how all the parts fit together is hard. Let's fix that problem and create a simple AWT applet. Tomorrow, after you've learned more about the more complex parts of the AWT, you'll work through an even better applet, to build on everything you've learned so far.

The applet you'll build in this section, shown in Figure 12.21, doesn't do a whole lot: it uses five buttons, arranged neatly across the top of the screen, each one labeled with a color. Each button changes the background color of the applet to the label on the button.

Figure 12.21.

The Button
Actions-Test
applet.

12

In this section, you'll create two versions of this applet: one that uses the 1.02 event model and one that uses the 1.1 model. For the first step of this section, however, you'll create the UI code that both models share. That's usually the best way to approach any AWT-based applet: create the components and the layout, and make sure everything looks right before hooking up the events to actually make the applet work.

For this applet, the components and layout couldn't be any simpler. The applet contains five simple buttons, arranged at the top of the screen in a row. A flow layout works best for this arrangement and requires little work.

Here's the code for the class structure and `init()` method I created for this applet. The `FlowLayout` is centered, and each button will have 10 points between it. After that, you just need to create and add each of the buttons.

```
import java.awt.*;

public class ButtonActionsTest extends java.applet.Applet {

  Button redButton,blueButton,greenButton,whiteButton,blackButton;

  public void init() {
    setBackground(Color.white);
    setLayout(new FlowLayout(FlowLayout.CENTER, 10, 10));

    redButton = new Button("Red");
    add(redButton);
    blueButton = new Button("Blue");
    add(blueButton);
    greenButton = new Button("Green");
    add(greenButton);
    whiteButton = new Button("White");
    add(whiteButton);
    blackButton = new Button("Black");
    add(blackButton);
  }
```

At first glance, this code probably looks more verbose than it needs to be; you could argue that I really don't need all the instance variables to hold the buttons. Actually, I'm being somewhat sneaky here; because I've already created this applet, I already know the best way to write it, and the instance variables will make things easier later (you'll have to trust me). Often, as you write your own applets, you may sometimes find that the original code you wrote for the UI doesn't work well, and you have to go back and change it. There's nothing wrong with that! The more applets you write, the easier it'll become to understand how all the parts fit together.

Adding the Event Code (1.02)

At this point, finishing up the applet can take two paths: one for the 1.02 event model and one for the 1.1 model. In this section, you'll create the 1.02 version. In the next section, you'll start back at that UI framework and add the events for the 1.1 model.

Buttons, when they're pressed, result in action events. And, as you learned earlier, to handle an action event, you use the action() method. The action() method here does the following:

- ☐ It tests to make sure the target of the event is indeed a button.
- ☐ It further tests to find out exactly which button was pressed.
- ☐ It changes the background to the color named by the button.
- ☐ It calls repaint() (the action of changing the background isn't enough).

Before actually writing action(), I'm going to make one more design decision. Those last three steps are essentially identical for each button, with minor differences, so it actually makes sense to put them into their own method, which I'll call changeColor(). This will simplify the logic in action() itself.

With that decision made, the action() method itself is easy:

```
public boolean action(Event evt, Object arg) {
  if (evt.target instanceof Button) {
    changeColor((Button)evt.target);
    return true;
  } else return false;
}
```

Not much is different about this action() from the simple ones created in the section on actions. The first step is to use evt.target to make sure the component is a button, at which time you pass control to the yet-to-be-written changeColor() method and return true. If the event isn't a button, you return false.

Note the one argument to changeColor(). With this argument, you pass the actual button object that received the event to the changeColor() method. (The object in evt.target is an instance of the class Object, so it has to be cast into a Button so that you can use it as a button.) The changeColor() method will deal with it from here.

Speaking of changeColor(), let's go ahead and define that method now. The main focus of changeColor() is to decide which button was clicked. Remember that the extra argument to action() was the label of the button. Although you can use a string comparison in changeColor() to figure out which button was pressed, that solution is not the most elegant, and it ties your event code too tightly to the GUI. If you decide to change a button label, you'll have to go back and work through your event code as well. So, in this applet, you can ignore the extra argument altogether.

12

So how do you tell which button was pressed? At this point, the button instance variables come into play—the ones I told you would be useful later. The object contained in the event's target instance variable—the one you passed to changeColor()—is an instance of Button, and one of those instance variables contains a reference to that very same object. In changeColor(), you just have to compare the two to see if they're the same object, set the background, and repaint, like this:

```
void changeColor(Button b) {
    if (b == redButton) setBackground(Color.red);
    else if (b == blueButton) setBackground(Color.blue);
    else if (b == greenButton) setBackground(Color.green);
    else if (b == whiteButton) setBackground(Color.white);
    else setBackground(Color.black);

    repaint();
}
```

From the UI, a button press calls action(), action() calls changeColor(), and changeColor() sets the appropriate background. Easy! Listing 12.2 shows the final applet.

TYPE   **Listing 12.2 The final ButtonActionsTest applet (1.02 version).**

```
1: import java.awt.*;
2:
3: public class ButtonActionsTest extends java.applet.Applet {
4:
5:   Button redButton,blueButton,greenButton,whiteButton,blackButton;
6:
7:   public void init() {
8:      setBackground(Color.white);
9:      setLayout(new FlowLayout(FlowLayout.CENTER, 10, 10));
10:
11:     redButton = new Button("Red");
12:     add(redButton);
13:     blueButton = new Button("Blue");
14:     add(blueButton);
15:     greenButton = new Button("Green");
16:     add(greenButton);
17:     whiteButton = new Button("White");
18:     add(whiteButton);
19:     blackButton = new Button("Black");
20:     add(blackButton);
21:   }
22:
23:   public boolean action(Event evt, Object arg) {
24:     if (evt.target instanceof Button) {
25:        changeColor((Button)evt.target);
26:        return true;
27:     } else return false;
28:   }
29:
30:   void changeColor(Button b) {
```

12

```
31:     if (b == redButton) setBackground(Color.red);
32:     else if (b == blueButton) setBackground(Color.blue);
33:     else if (b == greenButton) setBackground(Color.green);
34:     else if (b == whiteButton) setBackground(Color.white);
35:     else setBackground(Color.black);
36:
37:     repaint();
38:   }
39:}
```

Adding the Event Code (1.1)

For this section, let's go back to the raw UI and start over again. This time you'll add the event code under the 1.1 event model. The result behaves the same; it just uses different code.

To handle button actions, you'll need to implement the ActionListener interface. In yesterday's lesson, I explained that you can either convert the applet to be its own interface, or you can create a separate class to serve as that listener. Because you did an example of the former yesterday, let's try the latter this time and create a separate listener class.

A Note on Helper Classes

Up to this point, the applets and programs you've created have had only one class, so this new step, creating multiple classes, may seem confusing. Your applet can actually have as many classes as it needs; you aren't restricted to the one class. Complex applets usually have a single applet class (which inherits from java.applet.Applet) and any number of "helper" classes. As long as the extra classes are in the same directory as your applet class, you don't have to specially import them anywhere or do anything special. You can refer to them by name, create new instances of them, set their variables, and call their methods just as if they were classes in the standard Java packages.

The second point to note about using multiple classes is where to put the source code. If you remember back to the beginning of this book, I suggested that every class definition should be contained in its own .java file, with the name of the source file the same name as the class. That habit is still a good one to get into, but it's not a technical requirement.

The real rule is that you can put as many class definitions as you want into a single source file, as long as only one of those classes is declared public (has the public keyword at the beginning of the definition). The .java file is then named after the public class. When you compile that one source file, the Java compiler will create separate .class files for each class definition in the file.

12

Some programmers prefer to work this way, to put multiple classes in a single source file so the have only one file to edit. I prefer to put each class in its own source file, because then I can easily figure out where I put everything. Having separate source files also means that you can compile only those files that have changed if your development environment supports that capability.

How you arrange your source files is up to you. You'll learn more about public classes on Day 15, "Modifiers."

Creating the Listener Class

With that note out of the way, let's create the listener class. The ActionListener doesn't have an adapter class, so you'll have to implement the interface by hand. Because the interface has only one method, this job is easy. Here's the class framework for a listener class called HandleButton:

```
import java.awt.*;
import java.awt.event.*;

public class HandleButton implements ActionListener {

    public void actionPerformed(ActionEvent e) {
    }
}
```

Pause now to consider the next step: what goes inside the actionPerformed() method? You could implement the method the same way you did for 1.02—where you have a single listener for all the buttons and then just use if-else blocks to figure out which button receives the event. Or you could do something even more interesting and efficient, which takes full advantage of the new event model and the fact that you've got this extra listener class.

Instead of creating one listener object, registering that one listener for all the buttons, and then using if-else to decide which button has the event, why can't you create multiple listener objects from this one class, each of which handles the specific event for the specific button? I'm not talking about creating separate listener classes for each button (RedHandleButton, GreenHandleButton, and so on). Instead, you can create a single HandleButton class that is generic enough that you can customize it for each button that needs to use it. You can actually perform that customization when you create and register the listener in the main applet.

Here's how to use this method. HandleButton is its own class and has all the basic features of classes you learned about last week. The first thing it needs to operate correctly is a pointer back to the applet to which it's registered so that it can actually change the background. So, add an instance variable to the HandleButton class for the applet class (note that the type is the class created for the applet, not the generic Applet class):

```
ButtonActionsTest theApplet;
```

Second, if this class is going to be generic to handle all the button events, the only real difference between one listener object and another is the color to change the background to. That color makes a perfect attribute, so add an instance variable for the color, like this:

```
Color theColor;
```

So now you have a class with two instance variables. How do those variables get set? One of the best ways to initialize variables in a class is to create a constructor for them and pass in values for those instance variables when the object is created. Remember constructors from Day 5, "Arrays, Conditionals, and Loops"? Here's one that'll work fine for this class:

```
HandleButton(ButtonActionsTest a, Color c) {
    theApp = a;
    theColor = c;
}
```

You're almost there. The last step is to fill in the contents of the `actionPerformed()` method. If each listener object, attached to each button, already knows the applet to change and the color to change it to (from the values of its instance variables), then it doesn't need to do any testing. It needs to perform only two tasks: set the background and call `repaint`. You can call those methods on the applet object:

```
public void actionPerformed(ActionEvent e) {
    theApp.setBackground(theColor);
    theApp.repaint();
}
```

Creating and Registering the Listeners

`HandleButton` is done; it's a generic action listener that will be customized and registered to each of the buttons. Now move back to the `ButtonActionsTest` applet to finish doing just that.

Inside `init()` for the applet are a set of lines that create the buttons and add them to the applet. To create and register the listeners, you have to add a couple more lines for each button.

Start with a temporary variable to hold the listener object. That variable is of type `HandleButton` (the listener class just created):

```
HandleButton he;
```

First button: the red button. You've already created the button in this line:

```
redButton = new Button("Red");
```

Now create an instance of `HandleButton` to handle that red button. The constructor defined for `HandleButton` takes two arguments: the applet and an instance of `Color`. We can use it to refer to the applet and `Color.red` for a `Color` object representing red:

```
he = new HandleButton(this, Color.red);
```

12

Then you can simply register that listener to the button and add it to the applet:

```
redButton.addActionListener(he);
add(redButton);
```

You'll do the same thing with the next button, the blue one. For this button, create a different instance of `HandleButton`, and initialize it with a blue object, register it, and add the button to the applet:

```
blueButton = new Button("Blue");
he = new HandleButton(this, Color.blue);
blueButton.addActionListener(he);
add(blueButton);
```

Continuing down the line, you'll perform precisely the same process for the other three buttons, eventually ending up with five button objects in the applet, each one with its own listener object to handle its events. Then, when a given button is selected, the event is passed to the object responsible for that button, which already has the right color in its `theColor` instance variable, so it can go ahead and change the color. The applet itself has nothing but GUI code in it; all the behavior is in the listener class. Two classes, each of which can be independently modified to add more buttons or change the behavior. Neat, huh?

I should note here that I decided to implement this applet in this somewhat-more-complex way with multiple listener objects simply to make a point about how listener objects can work. You could have just as easily created this applet such that you had only one listener object registered to all five buttons, and that the implementation of `HandleButton` had a set of `if-else`'s to figure out which button triggered the event. You would have fewer objects floating around, but each event would take a little longer because of the test. See the trade-off here.

But one of the advantages of the new 1.1 event model is the ability to have different listener objects handling events for different components, and as you create more and more complex programs, you may find that this kind of organization makes more sense. Keep it in mind for the future.

Listing 12.3 shows the final code for the `ButtonActionsTest` applet, and Listing 12.4 shows the `HandleButton` code.

TYPE **Listing 12.3. The `ButtonActionsTest` applet (1.1 version).**

```
1: import java.awt.*;
2:
3: public class ButtonActionsTest extends java.applet.Applet {
4:
5:    Button redButton,blueButton,greenButton,whiteButton,blackButton;
6:
7:    public void init() {
```

```
8:      setBackground(Color.white);
9:      setLayout(new FlowLayout(FlowLayout.CENTER, 10, 10));
10:
11:     HandleButton he;
12:
13:     redButton = new Button("Red");
14:     he = new HandleButton(this, Color.red);
15:     redButton.addActionListener(he);
16:     add(redButton);
17:     blueButton = new Button("Blue");
18:     he = new HandleButton(this, Color.blue);
19:     blueButton.addActionListener(he);
20:     add(blueButton);
21:     greenButton = new Button("Green");
22:     he = new HandleButton(this, Color.green);
23:     greenButton.addActionListener(he);
24:     add(greenButton);
25:     whiteButton = new Button("White");
26:     he = new HandleButton(this, Color.white);
27:     whiteButton.addActionListener(he);
28:     add(whiteButton);
29:     blackButton = new Button("Black");
30:     he = new HandleButton(this, Color.black);
31:   blackButton.addActionListener(he);
32:   add(blackButton);
33: }
34:}
```

TYPE **Listing 12.4. The `HandleButton` class.**

```
1: import java.awt.*;
2:import java.awt.event.*;
3:
4:public class HandleButton implements ActionListener {
5:
6:      Color theColor;
7:      ButtonActionsTest theApp;
8:
9:      HandleButton(ButtonActionsTest a, Color c) {
10:         theApp = a;
11:         theColor = c;
12:     }
13:
14:     public void actionPerformed(ActionEvent e) {
15:         theApp.setBackground(theColor);
16:         theApp.repaint();
17:     }
18:}
```

12

Summary

The Java Abstract Windowing Toolkit, or AWT, is a package of Java classes and interfaces for creating full-fledged access to a window-based graphical user interface system, with mechanisms for graphics display, event management, text and graphics primitives, user-interface components, and cross-platform layout. Applets are also an integral part of the AWT.

Today you got your first major taste of building user interfaces for your applets using the AWT, by learning about six basic UI components (labels, buttons, check boxes, radio buttons, choice menus, and text fields). In addition, you learned about layout managers, which allow you to place components on the screen in a way that lets them be reformatted depending on the platform and window system that's running your applet. And, finally, you added events to your components in both 1.02 and 1.1 models, to let the GUI you've built actually respond to user input.

Exhausted yet? There's a lot more yet to come. Tomorrow you'll learn about the other half of the AWT, including still more components, how to nest components within other components, and how to create dialogs and windows that let you create full-fledged AWT applications that run on the desktop itself.

Q&A

Q I really dislike working with layout managers; they're either too simplistic or too complicated (grid bag layout). Even with a whole lot of tinkering, I can never get my applets to look like I want them to. All I want to do is define the sizes of my components and put them at an x and y position on the screen. Can I do this?

A I'm going to tell you how, but not without a lecture.

Java applications and the AWT were designed in such a way that the same graphical user interface could run equally well on different platforms and with different resolutions, different fonts, different screen sizes, and so on. Relying on pixel coordinates in this case is a really bad idea. Variations from one platform to another or even from one Java environment to another on the same platform can mess up your careful layouts such that you can easily have components overlapping or obscuring each other, the edges of your applet cut off, or other layout disasters. Just using an example, I found significant differences in the layout of the same applet running in the JDK's appletviewer and in Netscape, both on Windows 95, side by side. Can you guarantee that your applet will always be run in precisely the same environment as the one in which you designed it? Layout managers, by dynamically placing elements on the screen, get around these problems. I'm not saying that your applet may end up looking not quite right on any platform—but at least it's usable on any platform. New versions of the AWT promise to offer better layout and UI design controls.

Still not convinced? Well, then, to make a component a specific size and to place it at a particular position, use a null layout manager and the reshape() method:

```
setLayout(null);
Button myButton (new Button("OK");
mybutton.reshape(10, 10, 30, 15);
```

You can find out more about reshape() in the Component class.

Q I was exploring the AWT classes, and I saw this subpackage called peer. References to the peer classes are also sprinkled throughout the API documentation. What do peers do?

A Peers are responsible for the platform-specific parts of the AWT. For example, when you create a Java AWT window, you have an instance of the Window class that provides generic window behavior, and then you have an instance of a class implementing WindowPeer that creates the very specific window for that platform— a motif window under X Window, a Macintosh-style window under the Macintosh, or a Windows 95 window under Windows 95. These "peer" classes also handle communication between the window system and the Java window itself. By separating the generic component behavior (the AWT classes) from the actual system implementation and appearance (the peer classes), you can focus on providing behavior in your Java application and let the Java implementation deal with the platform-specific details.

Q That example you did at the end with the action listeners for each button color seemed like a whole lot of overkill. I get the idea, and I see why separating the listener code into a separate class is a neat idea, but it didn't seem necessary for such a simple applet.

A It wasn't. In fact, for an applet that small and simple I'd take the short track and just do something similar to the 1.02 model—make the applet into its own listener and use if-else to figure out which button received the event. However, my point in creating the applet in that way was to show how you can entirely separate your GUI layout (the "look" of the applet) from the code to handle the events (the "feel" of the applet). When you start creating larger and larger applications, this ability to separate out the event code into different classes and to reuse the code through object-oriented design will become more and more important.

12

Q I have a new button class I defined to look different from the standard AWT button objects in 1.02. I'd like to implement callbacks on this button (that is, to execute an arbitrary function when the button is pressed), but I can't figure out how to get Java to execute an arbitrary method. In C++, I'd just have a pointer to a function. In Smalltalk, I'd use perform:. How can I do this in Java?

A You can't do this in Java 1.02.; button actions are executed from an action() event, which must be contained in the same class as the button. You'll need to subclass your button class each time you want to create different behavior for that button. This is one of the reasons the 1.1 Java event model was created; creating your own components is much easier and more efficient when the event code isn't tied too closely to the GUI code.

Day **13**

Advanced User Interfaces with the AWT

by Laura Lemay

Although adding individual simple components to an applet is fun, working with the AWT begins to become more fun when you move into the more advanced parts of the toolkit and building more sophisticated interfaces and programs. Today you'll build on everything you learned yesterday about components, layout managers, and UI events, and I'll introduce you to several new concepts in the AWT:

☐ Nesting components within other components

☐ More UI components to play with: text areas, scrolling lists, scrolling panes, scroll bars and sliders, canvases, and cursors

☐ How components work and the various things you can do to them

☐ Windows, frames, and dialog boxes

☐ Menus

☐ Creating standalone AWT applications (no browser needed)

In addition to all these fascinating topics, right in the middle of this lesson you'll work through a complex applet example that uses multiple components, classes, and layouts and will give you a feel about how to put a complex applet together.

Nesting Components

Let's start with something easy. Yesterday you learned about how to add components to an applet, where the applet's layout manager determined how these components would be arranged inside the applets. An applet is a form of panel, which in turn is a form of container. This inheritance hierarchy is what allows you to put objects inside an applet.

You aren't limited to putting individual components inside an applet, though. AWT panels, of which an applet is one, can contain other panels, and you can nest panels as far as you need to. Each panel has its own layout manager, which means you can create different layouts for different parts of the overall applet area, isolate background and foreground colors and fonts to individual parts of an applet, and manage the design of your UI components individually and in distinct groups. The more complex the layout of your applet, the more likely you're going to want to use nested panels.

Nested Panels

Panels, as you've already learned, are components that can be actually displayed onscreen; Panel's superclass Container provides the generic behavior for holding other components inside it. The Applet class, from which your applets all inherit, is a subclass of Panel. To nest other panels inside an applet, you merely create a new panel component and add it to the applet, just as you would add any other UI component:

```
setLayout(new GridLayout(1, 2, 10, 10));
Panel panel1 = new Panel();
Panel panel2 = new Panel();
add(panel1);
add(panel2);
```

You can then set up an independent layout for these subpanels and add AWT components to them (including still more subpanels) by calling the add() method in the appropriate panel:

```
panel1.setLayout(new FlowLayout());
panel1.add(new Button("Up"));
panel1.add(new Button("Down"));
```

Although you can do all this in a single class, figuring out which panel you're adding a component to is sometimes difficult. It's a common design practice in applets and applications that make heavy use of subpanels to factor out the layout and behavior of the subpanels into separate classes and then to communicate between the panels with methods. You'll look at an extensive example in today's lesson in the section "A Complete Example: RGB-to-HSB Converter."

Nested Panels and the 1.02 Event Model

When you create applets with nested panels, these panels form a hierarchy from the outermost panel (the applet, usually) all the way down to the innermost UI component. This hierarchy is important to how each component in the interface interacts with other components; for example, the component hierarchy determines the order in which these components are painted to the screen. More importantly, however, the component hierarchy also affects event handling in 1.02, particularly for low-level input events such as mouse and keyboard events.

Events in the 1.02 event model are received by the innermost component in the component hierarchy and passed up the chain to the applet's panel (or to the root window in Java applications). Suppose, for example, that you have an applet with a subpanel that can handle mouse events, and the panel contains a button. Clicking the button means that the button receives the event before the panel does; if the button isn't interested in the mouseDown(), the event is passed to the panel, which can then process it or pass it further up the hierarchy.

For these reasons, your event-handling methods in the 1.02 event model must return a true or false boolean value. This value determines how the event moves from one component to another in the hierarchy. A true value means that the event is "consumed"—that the current component has processed the event and that no one else should see it. A false return value means that the event should pass upward in the hierarchy so that someone else can see it. The AWT relies on these return values to make sure events are handled, which is why they are so important to get right (and the difficulty of getting them right is one of the reasons that the 1.1 event model uses a different mechanism altogether).

 NOTE

The effect of events passing from one component to the next in the hierarchy is true of the 1.02 event model *only*. In 1.1, the component hierarchy, although it still exists, does not determine how events are handled. Listener registration has replaced the hierarchy-based event dispatch mechanism.

13

More UI Components

After you master the basic UI components and how to add them to panels, organize their layout, and manage their events, you can add still more UI components to your interface. In this section, you'll learn about six more components you can use in your applets for applications to create different user interface elements: text areas, scrolling lists, scroll bars, canvases, and cursors.

Text Areas

Text areas are like text fields, except they have more functionality for handling large amounts of text. Because text fields are limited in size and don't scroll, they are better for one-line responses and simple data entry. Text areas can be any given width and height and have scroll bars by default, so you can deal with larger amounts of text more easily.

 Text areas are larger, scrollable text-entry components. Whereas text fields provide only one line of text, text areas can hold any amount of editable text.

To create a text area, use one of the following constructors:

- [ ] `TextArea()` creates an empty text area (the text area will be automatically resized based on the layout manager).
- [ ] `TextArea(int, int)` creates an empty text area with the given number of rows and columns (characters). This method has been replaced in 1.1 with `TextArea(String, int, int)`.
- [ ] `TextArea(String)` creates a text area displaying the given string, which will be sized according to the current layout manager.
- [ ] `TextArea(String, int, int)` creates a text area displaying the given string and with the given dimensions.
- [ ] `TextArea(String, int, int, int)`, which is new in Java 1.1, creates a text area with the given text and dimensions. The last integer argument is one of four values indicating the status of the scroll bars; it can take one of the following four class variables. (The default is for both horizontal and vertical scroll bars to be displayed.)

  `TextArea.SCROLLBARS_BOTH` displays both horizontal and vertical scroll bars.

  `TextArea.SCROLLBARS_HORIZONTAL_ONLY` displays only horizontal scroll bars.

  `TextArea.SCROLLBARS_VERTICAL_ONLY` displays only vertical scroll bars.

  `TextArea.SCROLLBARS_NONE` displays neither horizontal nor vertical scroll bars.

You can generate a simple text area using the following code (which works under both 1.02 and 1.1). The results are shown in Figure 13.1.

```java
import java.awt.*;

public class TextAreaTest extends java.applet.Applet {

    public void init() {
        String str =
        "Once upon a midnight dreary, while I pondered, weak and weary,\n" +
        "Over many a quaint and curious volume of forgotten lore,\n" +
        "While I nodded, nearly napping, suddenly there came a tapping,\n" +
        "As of some one gently rapping, rapping at my chamber door.\n" +
        "\"'Tis some visitor,\" I muttered, \"tapping at my chamber door-\n" +
        "Only this, and nothing more.\"\n\n";
        // more text deleted for space

        add(new TextArea(str));
    }
}
```

Figure 13.1.

A text area.

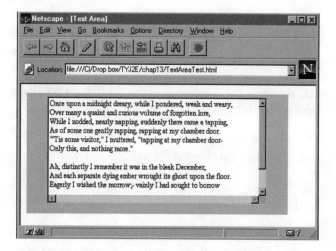

Both text areas and text fields inherit from the TextComponent class, so a lot of the behavior for text fields (particularly getting and setting text and selections) is usable on text areas as well (refer to Table 12.4). Text areas also have a number of their own methods that you may find useful. Table 13.1 shows a sampling of these methods.

13

Table 13.1. Text area methods.

Method	Action
getColumns()	Returns the width of the text area, in characters or columns
getRows()	Returns the number of rows in the text area (not the number of rows of text that the text area contains)
insertText(String, int)	Inserts the string at the given position in the text (text positions start at 0) (1.02 only; replaced in 1.1 by insert())
insert(String, int)	Inserts the string at the given position in the text (text positions start at 0) (1.1 only)
replaceText(String, int, int)	Replaces the text between the given integer positions with the new string (1.02 only; replaced in 1.1 by replace())
replace(String, int, int)	Replaces the text between the given integer positions with the new string (1.1 only)

Text areas have the same events as text fields. For 1.02, that simply means got focus and lost focus events; 1.1 also has text changed events.

For 1.02, you can use the gotFocus() and lostFocus() methods to trap focus events:

```
public boolean gotFocus(Event evt, Object arg) {
...
}

public boolean lostFocus(Event evt, Object arg) {
...
}
```

For the 1.1 event model, implement the focusGained() or focusLost() methods, part of the FocusListener interface, to intercept focus events. Use the addFocusListener() method to register a focus listener to a test area.

For the new text changed event, you'll need to implement the TextListener interface, which contains the method textValueChanged(). Use addTextListener() to register that listener to a text area.

Scrolling Lists

Remember the choice menu, a pop-up menu from which you could choose one of several different items? A scrolling list is functionally similar to a choice menu in that it lets you pick several options from a list, but scrolling lists differ in two significant ways:

☐ Scrolling lists do not pop up when selected. They're displayed as a list from which you can choose one or more items. If the number of items is larger than the list box, a scroll bar is automatically provided so that you can see the other items.

☐ You can choose more than one item in the list (if the list has been defined to allow this capability).

 Scrolling lists provide a menu of items that can be selected or deselected. Unlike choice menus, scrolling lists are not pop-up menus and can be defined to allow multiple selections.

To create a scrolling list, create an instance of the List class and then add individual items to that list. The List class has these constructors:

☐ List() creates an empty scrolling list that enables only one selection at a time.

☐ List(int) creates a scrolling list with the given number of items displayed (1.1 only).

☐ List(int, boolean) creates a scrolling list with the given number of visible lines on the screen. (You're not limited as to the number of actual items you can add to the list.) The boolean argument indicates whether this list enables multiple selections (true) or not (false).

After you create a List object, you add items to it in one of two ways, depending on whether you're using 1.02 or 1.1. For 1.02, use the addItem() method to add items to the list. For 1.1, use add(). Both methods take a single argument, a String, which indicates the name of the item.

Here's a scrolling list with two items from 1.02:

```
List theList = new List();
theList.addItem("night");
theList.addItem("day");
```

Here's the same list in 1.1:

```
List theList = new List();
theList.add ("night");
theList.add ("day");
```

After creating the list and adding items to it, add the entire list object to the component that will hold it. This example from 1.02 creates a list five items high and allows multiple selections. The result of this code is shown in Figure 13.2.

13

```
import java.awt.*;

public class ListsTest extends java.applet.Applet {

    public void init() {
        List lst = new List(5, true);
        // for 1.1, change addItem to add
        lst.addItem("Hamlet");
        lst.addItem("Claudius");
        lst.addItem("Gertrude");
        lst.addItem("Polonius");
        lst.addItem("Horatio");
        lst.addItem("Laertes");
        lst.addItem("Ophelia");

        add(lst);
    }
}
```

Figure 13.2.

A scrolling list.

Table 13.2 shows some of the methods available to scrolling lists. See the API documentation for a complete set.

Table 13.2. Scrolling list methods.

Method	Action
getItem(int)	Returns the string item at the given position
countItems()	Returns the number of items in the menu (1.02 only; for 1.1, use getItemCount())
getItemCount()	Returns the number of items in the menu (1.1 only)
getSelectedIndex()	Returns the index position of the item that's selected (used for lists that allow only single selections)
getSelectedIndexes()	Returns an array of index positions (used for lists that allow multiple selections)

13

Method	Action
getSelectedItem()	Returns the currently selected item as a string
getSelectedItems()	Returns an array of strings containing all the selected items
select(int)	Selects the item at the given position

Scrolling lists generate three different kinds of events: selecting or deselecting an individual list item results in a list select or list deselect event, and double-clicking a list item results in an action event.

For the 1.02 event model, you can override the action() event to handle a list item being double-clicked. For list select and list deselect, you'll have to override handleEvent() and test for the event IDs LIST_SELECT and LIST_DESELECT.

In the 1.1 event model, action methods on a scrolling list can be handled the same way they can for any other component: by implementing actionPerformed() in the ActionListener interface and then using addActionListener() on the scrolling list to register that event listener.

For list select and deselect events, you use the itemStateChanged() method in the ItemListener interface. The ItemEvent class contains methods for getItem() and getStateChange(), which can tell you which item received the event and whether it was selected or deselected.

Scroll Bars and Sliders

Text areas, scrolling lists, and scroll panels come with their own scroll bars, which are built into these UI components and enable you to manage both the body of the area, panel, or list and its scroll bar as a single unit. You can also create individual scroll bars, or sliders, to manipulate a range of values or implement some other form of scrollable component.

Scroll bars are used to select a value between a maximum and a minimum value. To change the current value of the scroll bar, you can use the following three different parts of the scroll bar (see Figure 13.3):

13

Figure 13.3.

Scroll bar parts.

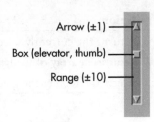

Arrow (±1) ———

Box (elevator, thumb) ———

Range (±10) ———

- [ ] Arrows on either end, which increment or decrement the values by some small unit (1 by default).

- [ ] A range in the middle, which increments or decrements the value by a larger amount (10 by default).

- [ ] A box in the middle, often called an elevator or thumb, whose position shows where in the range of values the current value is located. Moving this box with the mouse causes an absolute change in the value, based on the position of the box within the scroll bar.

Choosing any of these visual elements causes a change in the scroll bar's value; you don't have to update anything or handle any events. All you have to do is give the scroll bar a maximum and minimum, and Java will handle the rest.

NEW TERM   A *scroll bar* is a visual UI element that allows you to choose a value between some minimum and some maximum. Scroll bars are sometimes called sliders.

To create a scroll bar, you can use one of three constructors:

- [ ] `Scrollbar()` creates a scroll bar with its initial maximum and minimum values both equal to 0, in a vertical orientation.

- [ ] `Scrollbar(int)` creates a scroll bar with its initial maximum and minimum values both equal to 0. The argument represents an orientation, for which you can use the class variables `Scrollbar.HORIZONTAL` and `Scrollbar.VERTICAL`.

- [ ] `Scrollbar(int, int, int, int, int)` creates a scroll bar with the following arguments (each one is an integer, and they must be presented in this order):

  The first argument is the orientation of the scroll bar: `Scrollbar.HORIZONTAL` or `Scrollbar.VERTICAL` and `Scrollbar.VERTICAL`.

  The second argument is the initial value of the scroll bar, which should be a value between the scroll bar's maximum and minimum values.

  The third argument is the overall width (or height, depending on the orientation) of the scroll bar's box. In user-interface design, a larger box implies that a larger amount of the total range is currently showing (applies best to scrollable components such as windows and text areas).

The fourth and fifth arguments are the minimum and maximum values for the scroll bar.

Here's a simple example of a scroll bar that increments a single value in Java 1.1 (see Figure 13.4). The label to the left of the scroll bar is updated each time the scroll bar's value changes.

```java
import java.awt.*;
import java.awt.event.*;

public class SliderTest extends java.applet.Applet
  implements AdjustmentListener {
  Label l;

  public void init() {
    setLayout(new GridLayout(1,2));
    l = new Label("1", Label.CENTER);
    add(l);
    Scrollbar sb = new
            Scrollbar(Scrollbar.HORIZONTAL,0,0,1,100);
    sb.addAdjustmentListener(this);
    add(sb);
  }

  public Insets getInsets() {
    return new Insets(15,15,15,15);
  }

  public void adjustmentValueChanged(AdjustmentEvent e) {
      int v = ((Scrollbar)e.getSource()).getValue();
      l.setText(String.valueOf(v));
          repaint();
  }

}
```

Figure 13.4.

A scroll bar.

The Scrollbar class provides several methods for managing the values within scroll bars. They are listed in Table 13.3.

Table 13.3. Scrollbar **methods.**

Method	Action
getMaximum()	Returns the maximum value.
getMinimum()	Returns the minimum value.
getOrientation()	Returns the orientation of this scroll bar: 0 is Scrollbar.HORIZONTAL; 1 is Scrollbar.VERTICAL.
getValue()	Returns the scroll bar's current value.
setValue(int)	Sets the current value of the scroll bar.
setLineIncrement(int inc)	Changes the increment for how far to scroll when the endpoints of the scroll bar are selected. The default is 1. (1.02 only; replaced in 1.1 by setUnitIncrement())
setUnitIncrement(int inc)	Changes the increment for how far to scroll when the endpoints of the scroll bar are selected. The default is 1. (1.1 only)
getLineIncrement()	Returns the increment for how far to scroll when the endpoints of the scroll bar are selected. (1.02 only; replaced in 1.1 by getUnitIncrement())
getUnitIncrement(int inc)	Returns the increment for how far to scroll when the endpoints of the scroll bar are selected. (1.1 only)
setPageIncrement(int inc)	Changes the increment for how far to scroll when the inside range of the scroll bar is selected. The default is 10. (1.02 only; replaced in 1.1 by setBlockIncrement)
setBlockIncrement(int inc)	Changes the increment for how far to scroll when the inside range of the scroll bar is selected. The default is 10. (1.1 only)
getPageIncrement()	Returns the increment for how far to scroll when the inside range of the scroll bar is selected. (1.02 only; replaced in 1.1 by getBlockIncrement)
getBlockIncrement()	Returns the increment for how far to scroll when the inside range of the scroll bar is selected. (1.1 only)

If you like messing with events, you're going to love scroll bars. A whole set of events is generated and handled by different scroll bar movements only. In the 1.02 event model, you'll have to use handleEvent() for all these events. Table 13.4 shows the event IDs to look for and the motion that triggers them.

Table 13.4. Scroll bar events.

Event ID	What It Represents
SCROLL_ABSOLUTE	Generated when a scroll bar's box has been moved
SCROLL_LINE_DOWN	Generated when a scroll bar's bottom or left endpoint (button) is selected
SCROLL_LINE_UP	Generated when a scroll bar's top or right endpoint (button) is selected
SCROLL_PAGE_DOWN	Generated when the scroll bar's field below (or to the left of) the box is selected
SCROLL_PAGE_UP	Generated when the scroll bar's field above (or to the right of) the box is selected

In the 1.1 event model, scroll bar events aren't quite so much fun. All the scroll bar events are managed by the AdjustmentListener, and the method to implement is adjustment-ValueChanged(). You can use the getAdjustmentType() method in the AdjustmentEvent object to find out exactly how the scroll bar has changed.

Use addAdjustmentListener() to register the adjustment listener to the scroll bar.

Scrolling Panes (1.1 Only)

Scrolling panes were added in 1.1 in response to the complaint that creating scrolling surfaces is difficult in 1.02. (Basically, you have to link together a panel and a scroll bar—not a trivial task.) A scrolling pane is simply a container that holds a single "child" component. The scrolling pane is a "view port" to the child component; that is, if the scrolling pane is smaller than the child component, you can scroll around to see all parts of that component (see Figure 13.5). All the scrolling motion is handled by the AWT; you do not have to handle scrolling events as you would in 1.02.

Figure 13.5.

Scrolling panes.

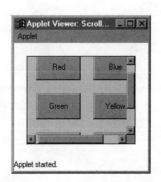

13

Scrolling panes are instances of the ScrollPane class. To create a new scrolling pane, use one of the following constructors:

☐ ScrollPane() creates a new scrolling pane. Scroll bars will be added automatically if the component inside the scrolling pane is larger than the pane itself.

☐ ScrollPane(int) creates a new scrolling pane. The integer argument determines the state of the scroll bars and can have one of three arguments: ScrollPane.SCROLLBARS_ALWAYS shows scroll bars on the scrolling pane all the time, regardless of how big the child panel is; ScrollPane.SCROLLBARS_AS_NEEDED shows scroll bars either horizontally or vertically if they are needed to see the whole of the child panel; and ScrollPane.SCROLLBARS_NEVER suppresses the use of scroll bars altogether.

After creating the ScrollPane object itself, you'll want to add a child component to that scroll pane and then add the scroll pane to its enclosing panel. Note that the scrolling pane can contain only one child component at a time.

```
ScrollPane scroller = new ScrollPane();
Panel surf = new Panel();
scroller.add(surf);
add(scroller);
```

The ScrollPane class provides several methods for managing the ScrollPane object. These methods are listed in Table 13.5.

Table 13.5. ScrollPane **methods.**

Method	Action
getScrollPosition()	Returns a Point object representing the position within the child that is displayed at the top-left corner of the pane
setScrollPosition(int, int)	Scrolls the panel to the given position within the child
setScrollPosition(Point)	Scrolls the panel to the given Point position within the child
getHAdjustable()	Returns an Adjustable object representing the state of the horizontal scroll bar
getVAdjustable()	Returns an Adjustable object representing the state of the vertical scroll bar
getViewportSize()	Returns a Dimension object representing the size of the scroll panel's view port

13

The state of the scroll bars for the scrolling pane, if any, is determined by internal objects that implement the `Adjustable` interface. To change the unit or block increment for the scroll bars, you'll want to use the `getVAdjustable` and `getHAdjustable()` methods to get an `Adjustable` object, and then use the various `Adjustable` methods—`getUnitIncrement()`, `getUnitIncrement()`, `getBlockIncrement()`, and `setBlockIncrement()`—to change the scroll bar behavior. (Scroll bars also implement the `Adjustable` interface, so these methods should be familiar.)

Scrolling panes can receive scroll bar events via the `AdjustmentListener` and container events (component added or removed) via the `ContainerListener` as well as from mouse, keyboard, and focus events.

Canvases

Although you can draw on most AWT components, such as panels, using the graphics methods you learned about on Day 10, "Animation, Images, Threads, and Sound," canvases do little except let you draw on them. They can't contain other components, but they can accept simple mouse and keyboard events, and you can create animation and display images on them. If you have a panel that doesn't need to do anything except display images or animation, a canvas would make a lighter-weight surface than a panel would.

NEW TERM A *canvas* is a simple component that you can draw on.

To create a canvas, use the `Canvas` class and add it to a panel as you would any other component:

```
Canvas can = new Canvas();
add(can);
```

Cursors

The cursor is the actual picture shown at the mouse pointer, be it an arrow, a hand, an I-beam, an hourglass, or some other icon.

Cursors, like events, vary widely depending on whether you're using Java 1.02 or 1.1. In fact, for 1.02, I should not even be talking about cursors in a section on components because they aren't components, and their use is limited primarily to Java applications running in their own windows. In 1.1, cursors are much more flexible and easy to use.

For more information about using cursors in 1.02, read on to the section on frames later in this lesson.

13

In 1.1, you can add a cursor to any component and change that cursor at any time. (Note that some components already have their own default cursors; text fields and areas, for example, change the cursor to an I-beam when you move the mouse over them.)

To add a cursor to a component or change its cursor, you'll first need to create a Cursor object. Cursor has only one constructor, Cursor(int), where the integer argument is one of a set of predefined cursor types. The cursor types you can use are listed in Table 13.6.

Table 13.6. Cursor types.

Class Variable	Cursor
Cursor.CROSSHAIR_CURSOR	A cross-hair (plus-shaped) cursor
Cursor.DEFAULT_CURSOR	The default cursor (usually a pointer or arrow)
Cursor.E_RESIZE_CURSOR	A cursor to indicate something is being resized
Cursor.HAND_CURSOR	A hand-shaped cursor (to move an object or the background)
Cursor.MOVE_CURSOR	A cursor to indicate that something is being moved
Cursor.N_RESIZE_CURSOR	The top edge of a window is being resized
Cursor.NE_RESIZE_CURSOR	The top-right corner of a window is being resized
Cursor.NW_RESIZE_CURSOR	The top-left corner of a window is being resized
Cursor.S_RESIZE_CURSOR	The bottom edge of a window is being resized
Cursor.SE_RESIZE_CURSOR	The bottom-right corner of the window is being resized
Cursor.SW_RESIZE_CURSOR	The bottom-left corner of the window is being resized
Cursor.TEXT_CURSOR	A text-entry cursor (sometimes called an I-beam)
Cursor.W_RESIZE_CURSOR	The left edge of a window is being resized
Cursor.WAIT_CURSOR	A long operation is taking place (usually an icon for a watch or an hourglass)

With a Cursor object in hand, use the setCursor() method (defined in Component, and as such available to all AWT components) to set the cursor:

```
Cursor cur = new Cursor(Cursor.HAND_CURSOR);
setCursor(cur);
```

You can also use the getCursor() component method to find out the current cursor for a component. The getCursor() method returns a Cursor object, and the Cursor method getPredefinedCursor() returns the predefined cursor type.

> Keep in mind that not all platforms use the same cursors. For example, cursors for resizing windows do not exist on Macintoshes.

Fun with Components

The Component class is the root of all the AWT objects: all the UI elements, panels, canvases, even applets. Just about everything you can display, lay out, change the color of, draw to, or interact with using events in the AWT is a component.

Components have a set of methods that allow you to modify their appearance or change their behavior. You've seen the use of a few of these methods already (setBackground(), setFont, size()), applied specifically to applets. But the methods defined in Component can be used with any component, allowing you to modify the appearance or the behavior of just about any element in your program. You can also create custom components (classes that inherit from Panel or Canvas) to make your own special AWT elements or user interface widgets.

Table 13.7 summarizes some of the methods you can use with individual components. For more methods and more about components, check out the Java API documentation for the class Component.

Table 13.7. Component methods.

Method	What It Does
getBackground()	Returns a Color object representing the component's background color.
setBackground(Color)	Sets the component's background color.
getForeground()	Returns a Color object representing the component's current foreground color.
setForeground(Color)	Sets the component's foreground color.
getFont()	Returns a Font object representing the component's current font.
setFont(Font)	Changes the component's current font.
size()	Returns a Dimension object representing the component's current size. You can then get to the individual width and height using size().width and size().height. (1.02 only; replaced in 1.1 by getSize())
getSize()	1.1 only; same as size().

continues

Table 13.7. continued

Method	What It Does
minimumSize()	The component's smallest possible size as a Dimension object. minimumSize() is usually used only by layout managers to determine how small it can draw a component; if you create a custom component, you'll want to override this method to return the minimum size of that component. (1.02 only; replaced in 1.1 by getMiniumSize())
getMinimumSize()	1.1 only; same as minimumSize().
preferredSize()	The component's preferred size (usually equal to or larger than the component's minimumSize()) as a Dimension object. (1.02 only; replaced in 1.1 by getPreferredSize())
getPreferredSize()	1.1 only; same as preferredSize().
resize(Dimension)	Changes the size of the applet to be the current size. For custom components, you'll want to also call validate() after resizing the applet so that the layout can be redrawn. (1.02 only; replaced in 1.1 by setSize())
setSize()	1.1 only; same as resize().
inside(int, int)	Returns true if the given x and y coordinates are inside the component. 1.02 only; replaced in 1.1 by contains().
contains(int, int)	1.1 only; same as inside().
hide()	Hides the component. Hidden components do not show up onscreen. (1.02 only; replaced in 1.1 by setVisible(false))
show()	Shows a component previously hidden. (1.02 only; replaced in 1.1 by setVisible(true))
setVisible(boolean)	1.1 only; replaces both show() and hide().
isVisible()	Returns true or false depending on whether this component is visible (not hidden).
disable()	Disables the component—that is, stops generating events. Disabled components cannot be pressed, selected from, typed into, and so on. (1.02 only; replaced in 1.1 by setEnabled(false))
enable()	Enables a previously disabled object. (1.02 only; replaced in 1.1 by setEnabled(true))

13

Method	What It Does
setEnabled(boolean)	1.1 only; replaces disable() and enable().
isEnabled()	Returns true or false depending on whether the component is enabled.

In addition to the specific events for each component that you've learned about throughout this lesson and the preceding one, all components can receive several other events. The first ones are the mouse and keyboard events you learned about on Day 12, "Creating User Interfaces with the AWT." In addition, ComponentListener provides a set of events that many of the methods in the Table 13.7 will generate: component moved, component resized, component hidden, component shown.

For components that are also containers, the container events component added and component removed are handled by the Container listener.

A Complete Example: RGB-to-HSB Converter

Let's take a break here from theory and smaller examples to create a larger example, using the 1.1 version of Java, that puts together much of what you've learned so far. The following sample applet demonstrates creating layouts, nesting panels, creating user-interface components, and handling events, as well as using multiple classes to put together a single applet. In short, it's the most complex applet you've created so far.

Figure 13.6 shows the applet you'll be creating in this example. The ColorTest applet enables you to pick colors based on RGB (red, green, and blue) and HSB (hue, saturation, and brightness) values.

Figure 13.6.
The ColorTest
applet.

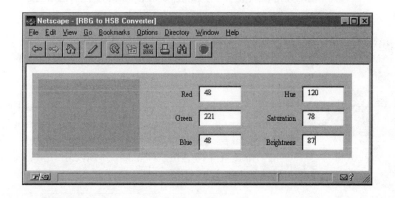

NOTE

Here's a quick summary in case you're not familiar with basic color theory: RGB color defines a color by its red, green, and blue values. Some combination of these values can produce any color in the spectrum. (Red, green, and blue are called additive colors; that's how your monitor and your TV represent different colors.)

HSB stands for hue, saturation, and brightness and is a different way of indicating color. Hue is the actual color in the spectrum you're representing (think of it as values along a color wheel). Saturation is the amount of that color: low saturation results in pastels; high-saturation colors are more vibrant and "colorful." Brightness, finally, is the lightness or darkness of the color. No brightness is black; full brightness is white.

A single color can be represented either by its RGB values or by its HSB values, and mathematical algorithms can convert between them. The ColorTest applet provides a graphical converter between the two.

The ColorTest applet has three main parts: a colored box on the left side and two groups of text fields on the right. The first group indicates RGB values; the second group, HSB. If you change any of the values in any of the text boxes, the colored box is updated to the new color, as are the values in the other group of text boxes.

This applet uses two classes:

☐ ColorTest, which inherits from Applet. It is the controlling class for the applet itself.

☐ ColorControls, which inherits from Panel. You'll create this class to represent a group of three text fields and to handle actions from them. Two instances of this class, one for the RGB values and one for the HSB ones, will be created and added to the applet.

Let's work through this example step by step because it's very complicated and can get confusing. All the code for this applet will be shown at the end of this section.

NOTE

Although I followed the 1.1 method names and 1.1 event model to create this applet, the vast majority of the code for this applet is identical for 1.02 as well (everything except the event handling, in fact). If you're still working with 1.02, you can find a version of this applet for 1.02 on the CD that comes with this book.

Designing and Creating the Applet Layout

The best way to start creating an applet that uses AWT components is to worry about the layout first and then worry about the functionality. When dealing with the layout, you should start with the outermost panel first and work inward.

Making a sketch of your UI design can help you figure out how to organize the panels inside your applet or window to best take advantage of layout and space. Paper designs are helpful even when you're not using grid bag layouts, but doubly so when you are. (You'll be using a simple grid layout for this applet.)

Figure 13.7 shows the `ColorTest` applet with a grid drawn over it so that you can get an idea of how the panels and embedded panels work.

Figure 13.7.

The `ColorTest`
applet panels and
components.

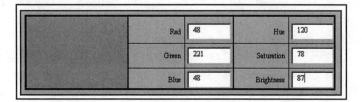

Let's start with the outermost panel—the applet itself. This panel has three parts: the color box on the left, the RGB text fields in the middle, and the HSB fields on the right.

Because the outermost panel is the applet itself, the `ColorTest` class will be the applet class and will inherit from `Applet`. You'll also import the AWT classes here. (Note that because you use so many of them in this program, just importing the entire package is easiest.)

```
import java.awt.*;
```

```
public class ColorTest extends java.applet.Applet {
...
}
```

This applet has three main elements to keep track of: the color box and the two subpanels. Each of the two subpanels refers to different things, but they're essentially the same panel and behave in the same ways. Rather than duplicate a lot of code in this class, you can take this opportunity to create another class just for the subpanels, use instances of that class in the applet, and communicate between everything using methods. In a bit, I'll define the new class called `ColorControls`.

For now, however, you know you need to keep a handle to all three parts of the applet so you can update them when they change. So let's create three instance variables: one of type `Canvas` for the color box and the other two of type `ColorControls` for the control panels:

```
ColorControls RGBcontrols, HSBcontrols;
Canvas swatch;
```

13

Now you can move onto the init() method, where all the basic initialization and layout of the applet takes place. Follow these three steps to initialize the applet:

1. Create the layout for the big parts of the panel. Although a flow layout would work, creating a grid layout with one row and three columns is a much better idea.

2. Create and initialize the three components of this applet: a canvas for the color box and two subpanels for the text fields.

3. Add these components to the applet.

Step one is the layout. Use a grid layout and a gap of 10 points to separate each of the components:

```
setLayout(new GridLayout(1, 3, 5, 15));
```

Step two is creating the components—the canvas first. You have an instance variable to hold that one. Here you'll create the canvas and initialize its background to black:

```
swatch = new Canvas();
swatch.setBackground(Color.black);
```

You need to create two instances of the as-of-yet nonexistent ColorControls panels here as well. Because you haven't created the class yet, you don't know what the constructors to that class will look like. In that case, put in some placeholder constructors here; you can fill in the details later.

```
RGBcontrols = new ColorControls(...)
HSBcontrols = new ColorControls(...);
```

Step three is adding all three components to the applet panel, like this:

```
add(swatch);
add(RGBcontrols);
add(HSBcontrols);
```

While you're working on layout, add insets for the applet: 10 points along all the edges:

```
public Insets getInsets() {
return new Insets(10, 10, 10, 10);
}
```

Got it so far? At this point, you should have three instance variables, an init() method with two incomplete constructors, and a getInsets() method in your ColorTest class. Let's move on now to creating the subpanel layout in the ColorControls class so you can fill in these constructors and finish up the layout.

Defining the Subpanels

The ColorControls class will have behavior for laying out and handling the subpanels that represent the RGB and HSB values for the color. ColorControls doesn't need to be a subclass of Applet because it isn't actually an applet; it's just a panel. Define it to inherit from Panel:

```
import java.awt.*

class ColorControls extends Panel {
...
}
```

The `ColorControls` class will need a number of instance variables so that information from the panel can get back to the applet. The first of these instance variables is a hook back up to the applet class that contains this panel. Because the outer applet class controls the updating of each panel, this panel will need a way to tell the applet that something has changed. To call a method in that applet, you need a reference to the object. So, instance variable number one is a reference to an instance of the class `ColorTest`:

```
ColorTest applet;
```

If you figure that the `applet` class is updating everything, that class will be interested in the individual text fields in this subpanel. You'll create instance variables for these text fields:

```
TextField tfield1, tfield2, tfield3;
```

Now you can move on to the constructor for this class. Because this class isn't an applet, you won't use `init()` to initialize it; instead, you'll use a constructor method. Inside the constructor you'll do much of what you did inside `init()`: create the layout for the subpanel, create the text fields, and add them to the panel.

The goal here is to make the `ColorControls` class generic enough so that you can use it for both the RGB fields and the HSB fields. These two panels differ in only one respect: the labels for the text. That's three values to get before you can create the object. You can pass these three values in through the constructors in `ColorTest`. You also need one more: the reference to the enclosing applet, which you can get from the constructor as well.

You now have four arguments to the basic constructor for the `ColorControls` class. Here's the signature for the constructor:

```
ColorControls(ColorTest parent,
String l1, String l2, String l3) {
}
```

Let's start this constructor by first setting the value of `parent` to the `applet` instance variable:

```
applet = parent;
```

Next, create the layout for this panel. You can also use a grid layout for these subpanels, as you did for the applet panel, but this time the grid will have three rows (one for each of the text field and label pairs) and two columns (one for the labels and one for the fields). Also define a 10-point gap between the components in the grid:

```
setLayout(new GridLayout(3,2,10,10));
```

13

Now you can create and add the components to the panel. First, create the text field objects (initialized to the string "0"), and assign them to the appropriate instance variables:

```
tfield1 = new TextField("0");
tfield2 = new TextField("0");
tfield3 = new TextField("0");
```

Now add these fields and the appropriate labels to the panel, using the remaining three parameters to the constructor as the text for the labels:

```
add(new Label(l1, Label.RIGHT));
add(tfield1);
add(new Label(l2, Label.RIGHT));
add(tfield2);
add(new Label(l3, Label.RIGHT));
add(tfield3);
```

You've now finished the constructor for the subpanel class ColorControls. Are you done with the layout? Not quite. You'll also add an inset around the subpanel—only on the top and bottom edges—to tinker the layout. Add the inset here as you did in the ColorTest class, using the getInsets() method:

```
public Insets getInsets() {
return new Insets(10, 10, 0, 0);
}
```

You're almost there. You have 98 percent of the basic structure in place and ready to go, but you have one step left: going back to ColorTest and fixing the placeholder constructors for the subpanel so they match the actual constructors for ColorControls.

The constructor for ColorControls that you just created now has four arguments: the ColorTest object and three labels (strings). Remember back to when you created the init() method for ColorTest. You added two placeholders for creating new ColorControls objects. You'll replace these placeholders with the correct versions now. Make sure you add the four arguments the constructor needs to work: the ColorTest object and three strings. To pass the ColorTest object to these constructors, you can use the this keyword:

```
RGBcontrols = new ColorControls(this, "Red", "Green", "Blue");
HSBcontrols = new ColorControls(this, "Hue", "Saturation", "Brightness");
```

NOTE For the initial values of all the text fields in this example, I used the number 0 (actually, the string "0"). For the color black, both the RGB and the HSB values are 0, which is why I can make this assumption. If you want to initialize the applet to some other color, you might want to rewrite the ColorControls class to use initializer values as well as to initialize labels. This way made for a shorter example.

13

Handling the Events

With the layout done, you're ready to set up event handling and updating between the various components so that when the user interacts with the applet, the applet can respond.

Text fields generate several different kinds of events, and you should make sure that each one is covered. In particular, text fields generate action events when the user enters a number and presses Return. But if the user enters a number and then presses Tab to move to the next field, or if the user uses the mouse to move to another field, neither of these motions produces an action event. They do, however, generate lost focus events if the input focus moves to some other component. In this applet, you'll handle both action and lost focus events to cover all the bases.

The parent `ColorTest` class is responsible for actually doing the updating because it keeps track of all the subpanels. Because the actual event occurs in the subpanel and its components, however, you'll need to register the event listeners in the code for that subpanel.

As with all listeners, you can either create a new class for the listener, or you can add the listener behavior to the current class. Although creating new classes would be more object-oriented, for the sake of simplicity you can add the listeners to `ColorControls` instead.

You have to implement two different listeners here: `ActionListener`, for the action events, and `FocusListener`, for the focus events. You'll add these listener interfaces to the class definition:

```
class ColorControls extends Panel
    implements FocusListener, ActionListener {
```

The next step is to add stub methods for these interfaces to the body of the class. `ActionListener` has only one method, `actionPerformed()`, but `FocusListener` has two: `focusGained()` and `focusLost()`. Here are the method signatures:

```
public void focusGained(FocusEvent e) { }
public void focusLost(FocusEvent e) { }
public void actionPerformed(ActionEvent e) { }
```

The `focusGained()` and `actionPerformed()` methods are the two you're interested in. But what do they do? The outer applet (`ColorTest`) will be responsible for doing the actual updating of everything, so all you really need to do here is tell the outer applet that things have changed (and pass along a reference to the current panel so the applet can get at the values). To make your job easy—and because I've already written this applet and know what's going to happen—you can call the method in the outer applet `update()`, and you can call it from each of the `focusLost()` and `actionPerformed()` methods. It takes one argument, `this`, for the current panel, so the outer applet can figure out what changed. Here are the listener methods with the call to `update()` in place:

13

```
public void focusLost(FocusEvent e) {
    applet.update(this);
}

public void actionPerformed(ActionEvent e) {
    if (e.getSource() instanceof TextField)
        applet.update(this);
}
```

Note the one test inside `actionPerformed()` to make sure that you're dealing with a text field. Testing isn't strictly necessary because no other action events could be generated in this applet. However, testing is a good idea anyhow.

Does this process look too easy? It is. In the next section, I'll actually define the `update()` method, and you'll wish you had stopped here.

Don't forget the last step: registering the listeners. Here you've got both focus and action listeners, and you have to register them for all three text fields on the panel. You'll add a bunch of lines to the `init()` method in `ColorControls` to perform just this task:

```
add(new Label(l1, Label.RIGHT));
tfield1.addFocusListener(this);
tfield1.addActionListener(this);
add(tfield1);
add(new Label(l2, Label.RIGHT));
tfield2.addFocusListener(this);
tfield2.addActionListener(this);
add(tfield2);
tfield3.addFocusListener(this);
tfield3.addActionListener(this);
add(new Label(l3, Label.RIGHT));
add(tfield3);
```

Updating the Result

Now comes the hard part: actually doing the updating based on the new values of whatever text field was changed. For this step, you define the `update()` method in the `ColorTest` class. This `update()` method takes a single argument: the `ColorControls` instance that contains the changed value. (You get the argument from the event methods in the `ColorControls` object.)

NOTE

Won't this `update()` method interfere with the system's `update()` method? Nope. Remember, methods can have the same name, but different signatures and definitions. Because this `update()` has a single argument of type `ColorControls`, it doesn't interfere with the other version of `update()`. Normally, all methods called `update()` should mean basically the same thing. That's not the case here, but this is only an example.

The update() method is responsible for updating all the panels in the applet. To know which panel to update, you need to know which panel changed. You can find out by testing to see whether the argument you got passed from the panel is the same as the subpanels you have stored in the RGBcontrols and HSBcontrols instance variables:

```
void update(ColorControls controlPanel) {

if (controlPanel == RGBcontrols) {  // RGB has changed, update HSB
...
} else {  // HSB has changed, update RGB
...
}
}
```

This test is the heart of the update() method. Let's start with the first case—a number has been changed in the RGB text fields. So now, based on these new RGB values, you have to generate a new Color object and update the values on the HSB panel. To reduce some typing, you can create a few local variables to hold some basic values. In particular, the values of the text fields are strings whose values you can get to using the getText() method defined in the TextField objects of the ColorControls object. Because most of the time in this method you'll want to deal with these values as integers, you can get these string values, convert them to integers, and store them in local variables (value1, value2, value3). Here's the code to take care of this job (it looks more complicated than it actually is):

```
int value1 = Integer.parseInt(controlPanel.tfield1.getText());
int value2 = Integer.parseInt(controlPanel.tfield2.getText());
int value3 = Integer.parseInt(controlPanel.tfield3.getText());
```

While you're defining local variables, you'll also need one for the new Color object:

```
Color c;
```

Now assume one of the text fields in the RGB side of the applet has changed, and add the code to the if part of the update() method. You'll need to create a new Color object and update the HSB side of the panel. That first part is easy. Given the three RGB values, you can create a new Color object using these values as arguments to the constructor:

```
c = new Color(value1, value2, value3);
```

NOTE

This part of the example isn't very robust. It assumes that the user has indeed entered integers from 0 to 255 into the text fields. A better version would test to make sure that no data-entry errors had occurred, but I was trying to keep this example small.

13

Now you'll convert the RGB values to HSB. Standard algorithms can convert an RGB-based color to an HSB color, but you don't have to go look them up. The `Color` class has a class method called `RGBtoHSB()` you can use. This method will do the work for you—or, at least, most of it. The `RGBtoHSB()` method poses two problems, however:

☐ The `RGBtoHSB()` method returns an array of the three HSB values, so you'll have to extract these values from the array.

☐ The HSB values are measured in floating-point values from `0.0` to `1.0`. I prefer to think of HSB values as integers, where the hue is a degree value around a color wheel (0 through 360), and saturation and brightness are percentages from 0 to 100.

Neither of these problems is insurmountable; you just have to add some extra lines of code. Start by calling `RGBtoHSB()` with the new RGB values you have. The return type of that method is an array of `float`s, so you'll create a local variable (`HSB`) to store the results of the `RBGtoHSB()` method. (Note that you'll also need to create and pass in an empty array of `float`s as the fourth argument to `RGBtoHSB()`.)

```
float[] HSB = Color.RGBtoHSB(value1, value2, value3, (new float[3]));
```

Now convert these floating-point values that range from `0.0` to `1.0` to values that range from `0` and `100` (for the saturation and brightness) and `0` to `360` for the hue by multiplying the appropriate numbers and reassigning the value back to the array:

```
HSB[0] *= 360;
HSB[1] *= 100;
HSB[2] *= 100;
```

Now you have the numbers you want. The last part of the update is to put these values back into the text fields. Of course, these values are still floating-point numbers, so you'll have to cast them to `int`s before turning them into strings and storing them:

```
HSBcontrols.tfield1.setText(String.valueOf((int)HSB[0]));
HSBcontrols.tfield2.setText(String.valueOf((int)HSB[1]));
HSBcontrols.tfield3.setText(String.valueOf((int)HSB[2]));
```

You're halfway there. The next part of the applet is the part that updates the RGB values when a text field on the HSB side has changed. This is the `else` in the big `if-else` that defines this method and determines what to update, given a change.

Generating RGB values from HSB values is actually easier than doing the process the other way around. A class method in the `Color` class, called `getHSBColor()`, creates a new `Color` object from three HSB values. After you have a `Color` object, you can easily pull the RGB values out of there. The catch, of course, is that `getHSBColor` takes three floating-point arguments, and the values you have are the integer values that I prefer to use. So in the call to `getHSBColor`, you'll have to cast the integer values from the text fields to `float`s and divide them by the proper conversion factor. The result of `getHSBColor` is a `Color` object. You therefore can simply assign the object to the `c` local variable so that you can use it again later:

13

```
c = Color.getHSBColor((float)value1 / 360,
(float)value2 / 100, (float)value3 / 100);
```

With the `Color` object all set, updating the RGB values involves extracting these values from that `Color` object. The `getRed()`, `getGreen()`, and `getBlue()` methods, defined in the `Color` class, will do just that job:

```
RGBcontrols.tfield1.setText(String.valueOf(c.getRed()));
RGBcontrols.tfield2.setText(String.valueOf(c.getGreen()));
RGBcontrols.tfield3.setText(String.valueOf(c.getBlue()));
```

And finally, regardless of whether the RGB or HSB value has changed, you'll need to update the color box on the left to reflect the new color. Because you have a new `Color` object stored in the variable c, you can use the `setBackground` method to change the color. Also note that `setBackground` doesn't automatically repaint the screen, so you'll want to fire off a `repaint()` as well:

```
swatch.setBackground(c);
swatch.repaint();
```

That's it! You're done. Now compile both the `ColorTest` and `ColorControls` classes, create an HTML file to load the `ColorTest` applet, and check it out.

The Complete Source Code

Listing 13.1 shows the complete source code for the applet class `ColorTest`, and Listing 13.2 shows the source for the helper class `ColorControls`. Often figuring out what's going on in an applet is easier when the code is all in one place, and you can follow the method calls and how values are passed back and forth. Start with the `init()` method in the `ColorTest` applet, and go from there.

TYPE   **Listing 13.1. The `ColorTest` applet.**

```
1:import java.awt.*;
2:
3:public class ColorTest extends java.applet.Applet {
4:  ColorControls RGBcontrols, HSBcontrols;
5:  Canvas swatch;
6:
7:  public void init() {
8:    setLayout(new GridLayout(1,3,5,15));
9:
10:    // The color swatch
11:    swatch = new Canvas();
12:    swatch.setBackground(Color.black);
13:
14:    // the subpanels for the controls
15:    RGBcontrols = new ColorControls(this, "Red", "Green", "Blue");
16:    HSBcontrols = new ColorControls(this, "Hue", "Saturation", "Brightness");
```

continues

13

Listing 13.1. continued

```
17:
18:     //add it all to the layout
19:     add(swatch);
20:     add(RGBcontrols);
21:     add(HSBcontrols);
22:   }
23:
24:   public Insets getInsets() {
25:     return new Insets(10,10,10,10);
26:   }
27:
28:   void update(ColorControls controlPanel) {
29:     Color c;
30:     // get string values from text fields, convert to ints
31:     int value1 = Integer.parseInt(controlPanel.tfield1.getText());
32:     int value2 = Integer.parseInt(controlPanel.tfield2.getText());
33:     int value3 = Integer.parseInt(controlPanel.tfield3.getText());
34:
35:     if (controlPanel == RGBcontrols) {  // RGB has changed, update HSB
36:       c = new Color(value1, value2, value3);
37:
38:       // convert RGB values to HSB values
39:       float[] HSB = Color.RGBtoHSB(value1, value2, value3, (new float[3]));
40:       HSB[0] *= 360;
41:       HSB[1] *= 100;
42:       HSB[2] *= 100;
43:
44:       // reset HSB fields
45:       HSBcontrols.tfield1.setText(String.valueOf((int)HSB[0]));
46:       HSBcontrols.tfield2.setText(String.valueOf((int)HSB[1]));
47:       HSBcontrols.tfield3.setText(String.valueOf((int)HSB[2]));
48:
49:     } else {   // HSB has changed, update RGB
50:       c = Color.getHSBColor((float)value1 / 360,
51:         (float)value2 / 100, (float)value3 / 100);
52:
53:       // reset RGB fields
54:       RGBcontrols.tfield1.setText(String.valueOf(c.getRed()));
55:       RGBcontrols.tfield2.setText(String.valueOf(c.getGreen()));
56:       RGBcontrols.tfield3.setText(String.valueOf(c.getBlue()));
57:     }
58:
59:     //update swatch
60:     swatch.setBackground(c);
61:     swatch.repaint();
62:}
63:}
```

TYPE **Listing 13.2. The `ColorControls` class.**

```
1: import java.awt.*;
2: import java.awt.event.*;
3:
```

```
 4: class ColorControls extends Panel implements FocusListener, ActionListener {
 5:   TextField tfield1, tfield2, tfield3;
 6:   ColorTest applet;
 7:
 8:   ColorControls(ColorTest parent,
 9:     String l1, String l2, String l3) {
10:
11:        // get hook to outer applet parent
12:     applet = parent;
13:
14:        //do layouts
15:     setLayout(new GridLayout(3,2,10,10));
16:
17:     tfield1 = new TextField("0");
18:     tfield2 = new TextField("0");
19:     tfield3 = new TextField("0");
20:
21:     add(new Label(l1, Label.RIGHT));
22:     tfield1.addFocusListener(this);
23:     tfield1.addActionListener(this);
24:     add(tfield1);
25:     add(new Label(l2, Label.RIGHT));
26:     tfield2.addFocusListener(this);
27:     tfield2.addActionListener(this);
28:     add(tfield2);
29:     tfield3.addFocusListener(this);
30:     tfield3.addActionListener(this);
31:     add(new Label(l3, Label.RIGHT));
32:     add(tfield3);
33:   }
34:
35: public Insets getInsets() {
36:     return new Insets(10,10,0,0);
37:   }
38:
39: public void focusGained(FocusEvent e) {}
40: public void focusLost(FocusEvent e) {
41:        applet.update(this);
42: }
43: public void actionPerformed(ActionEvent e) {
44:     if (e.getSource() instanceof TextField)
45:            applet.update(this);
46: }
47:}
```

13

Windows, Frames, and Dialog Boxes

In addition to all the graphics, events, user interface, and layout mechanisms that the AWT provides, it also provides features for creating UI elements outside the applet and browser framework including windows, frames, and dialog boxes. These features allow you to create fully featured applications either as part of your applet or independently for standalone Java applications.

The AWT Window Classes

The Java AWT classes to produce windows and dialogs inherit from a single class: Window. The Window class, which itself inherits from Container (and is therefore a standard AWT component), provides generic behavior for all window-like elements. Generally, you don't use instances of Window, however; you use instances of Frame or Dialog. Figure 13.8 shows the simple Window class hierarchy.

Figure 13.8.

The Window *class hierarchy.*

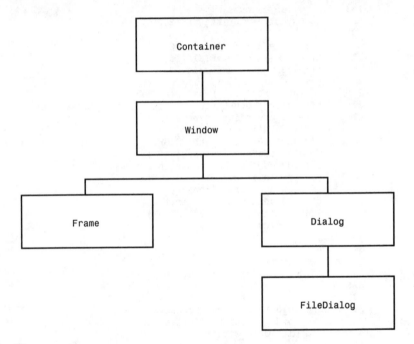

The Frame class provides a window with a title bar, close boxes, and other platform-specific window features. Frames also let you add menu bars. Dialog is a more limited form of Frame that typically doesn't have a title. FileDialog, a subclass of Dialog, provides a standard file-picker dialog box (usually only usable from inside Java applications because of security restrictions on applets).

When you want to add a new window or dialog to your applet or application, you'll create subclasses of the Frame and Dialog classes.

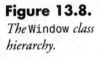

Frames

Frames are windows that are independent of an applet and of the browser that contains the applet; they are separate windows with their own titles, resize handles, close boxes, and menu bars. You can create frames for your own applets to produce windows, or you can use frames in Java applications to hold the contents of that application.

NEW TERM A *frame* is a platform-specific window with a title, a menu bar, close boxes, resize handles, and other window features.

To create a frame, use one of the following constructors:

☐ `new Frame()` creates a basic frame without a title.

☐ `new Frame(String)` creates a basic frame with the given title.

Because frames inherit from `Window`, which inherits from `Container`, which inherits from `Component`, frames are created and used much in the same way that other AWT components are created and used. Frames are containers, just like panels are, so you can add other components to them just as you would regular panels, using the `add()` method. The default layout for frames is `BorderLayout`. Here's a single example that creates a frame, sets its layout, and adds two buttons:

```
win = new Frame("My Cool Window");
win.setLayout(new BorderLayout(10, 20));
win.add("North", new Button("Start"));
win.add("Center", new Button("Move"));
```

To set a size for the new frame, use the `resize()` method with the width and height of the new frame. So, for example, this line of code resizes the window to be 100 pixels wide and 200 pixels high:

```
win.resize(100, 200);
```

Note that because different systems have different ideas of what a pixel is and different resolutions for these pixels, creating a window that is the "right" size for every platform is difficult. Windows that work fine for one may be way too large or too small for another. One way around this problem is to use the `pack()` method instead of `resize()`. The `pack()` method, which has no arguments, creates a window of the smallest possible size given the current sizes of all the components inside the window and the layout manager and insets in use. The following example creates two buttons and adds them to a window. The window will then be resized to the smallest possible window that can still hold these buttons.

```
win = new Frame("My Other Cool Window");
win.setLayout(new FlowLayout());
win.add("North", new Button("OK"));
win.add("Center", new Button("Cancel"));
win.pack();
```

13

When you initially create a window, it's invisible. You need to use the show() method to make the window appear onscreen (you can use hide() to hide it again):

```
win.show();
```

Note that when you pop up windows from inside applets, the browser may indicate in some way that the window is not a regular browser window—usually with a warning in the window itself. In Netscape, a yellow bar at the bottom of every window says Untrusted Java Window. This warning is intended to let your users know that your window comes from the applet, not from the browser itself. (Remember that the Frame class produces windows that look just like normal system windows.) The warning is to prevent you from creating a malicious applet that might, for example, ask the user for his or her password. You can't do anything to avoid this warning; it's there to stay as long as you want to use windows with applets.

Listings 13.3, 13.4, and 13.5 show the classes that make up a simple applet with a pop-up window frame. Both the applet and the window are shown in Figure 13.9. The applet has two buttons: one to show the window and one to hide the window. The window frame itself, created from a subclass I created called BaseFrame, contains a single label: This is a Window. And, finally, the class PopupActions manages the events for the buttons using the 1.1 event model. I'll refer to this basic window and applet all through this section, so the more you understand what's going on here, the easier it will be later.

NOTE In this example, I used the 1.1 event model. If you're working with 1.02, I've included an older version of this applet with the 1.02 event model on the CD for this book.

TYPE **Listing 13.3. A pop-up window.**

```
1: import java.awt.*;
2:
3: public class PopupWindow extends java.applet.Applet {
4:     Frame window;
5:     Button open, close;
6:
7:     public void init() {
8:         PopupActions handlebutton = new PopupActions(this);
9:
10:        open = new Button("Open Window");
11:        open.addActionListener(handlebutton);
12:        add(open);
13:
14:        close = new Button("Close Window");
15:        close.addActionListener(handlebutton);
```

```
16:        add(close);
17:
18:        window = new BaseFrame1("A Popup Window");
19:        window.resize(150,150);
20:        window.show();
21:    }
22:}
```

TYPE **Listing 13.4. The PopupActions class.**

```
1: import java.awt.*;
2: import java.awt.event.*;
3:
4: public class PopupActions implements ActionListener {
5:
6:    PopupWindow theApp;
7:
8:     PopupActions(PopupWindow win) {
9:        theApp = win;
10:    }
11:
12:    public void actionPerformed(ActionEvent e) {
13:        if (e.getSource() instanceof Button) {
14:
15:            if (e.getSource() == theApp.open) {
16:                if (!theApp.window.isShowing())
17:                    theApp.window.show();
18:            }
19:            else if (e.getSource() == theApp.close) {
20:                if (theApp.window.isShowing())
21:                    theApp.window.hide();
22:            }
23:        }
24:    }
25:}
```

TYPE **Listing 13.5. The BaseFrame class.**

```
1: import java.awt.*;
2: import java.awt.event.*;
3:
4: class BaseFrame1 extends Frame {
5:    String message = "This is a Window";
6:    Label l;
7:
8:    BaseFrame1(String title) {
9:        super(title);
10:        setLayout(new BorderLayout());
11:
```

13

continues

Listing 13.5. continued

```
12:     l = new Label(message, Label.CENTER);
13:     l.setFont(new Font("Helvetica", Font.PLAIN, 12));
14:     add("Center", l);
15:   }
16:
17:   public Insets getInsets() {
18:     return new Insets(20,0,25,0);
19:   }
20:}
```

Figure 13.9.

Windows.

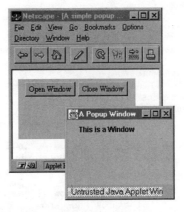

Three classes make up this example: The first, PopupWindow, is the applet class that creates and controls the pop-up window. In the init() method for this class, and in particular, in lines 10 to 16 of Listing 13.3, you add two control buttons to the applet to control the window, and then create, resize, and show the window itself.

The control in this applet occurs when one of the buttons is pressed, and the second class comes in at this point. PopupActions contains the event-handling code for these buttons, implementing ActionListener to respond to the buttons. In this class, the Open Window button simply shows the window if it's hidden (lines 15 to 18 of Listing 13.4), and hides it if it's showing (lines 19 to 21).

The pop-up window itself is a special kind of frame called BaseFrame. In this example, the frame is fairly simple; it uses a BorderLayout and displays a label in the center of the frame. Note that the initialization of the frame takes place in a constructor, not in an init() method. Because frames are regular objects and not applets, you have to initialize them in a more conventional way.

In BaseFrame's constructor, note that the first line (line 9) is a call to the constructor of BaseFrame's superclass. As you learned way back on Day 6, "Creating Classes and Applications in Java," the first step to initializing a new class is to make this call. Don't forget this step in your own classes; you never know what important things your superclass may be doing in that constructor.

Dialog Boxes

Dialog boxes are functionally similar to frames in that they pop up new windows on the screen. However, dialog boxes are intended to be used for transient windows—for example, windows that let you know about warnings, windows that ask you for specific information, and so on. Dialogs don't usually have title bars or many of the more general features that windows have (although you can create a dialog box with a title bar). They can be made nonresizable or modal (modal dialogs prevent input to any other windows on the screen until they are dismissed).

| NEW TERM | *Dialogs* are transient windows intended to alert the user to some event or to get input from the user. Unlike frames, dialogs do not generally have title bars or close boxes. |

A modal dialog prevents input to any of the other windows on the screen until that dialog is dismissed. You won't be able to bring other windows to the front or iconify a modal dialog window; you must actually dismiss the modal dialog before being able to do anything else on the system. Warnings and alerts are typically modal dialogs.

The AWT provides two kinds of dialog boxes: the Dialog class, which provides a generic dialog, and FileDialog, which produces the platform-specific file browser dialog.

Dialog Objects

Dialogs are created and used in much the same way as windows. To create a generic dialog, use one of these constructors:

- [ ] Dialog(Frame) creates an initially invisible nonmodal dialog, attached to the current frame. Use this constructor in 1.1 only.

- [ ] Dialog(Frame, boolean) creates an invisible dialog, attached to the current frame, which is either modal (true) or not (false). Use this constructor in 1.02 only; in 1.1 it has been replaced by Dialog(Frame, String, boolean).

- [ ] Dialog(Frame, String) creates an invisible nonmodal dialog with the given title.

- [ ] Dialog(Frame, String, boolean) creates an invisible dialog with the given title, which is which is either modal (true) or not (false).

The dialog window, like the frame window, is a panel on which you can lay out and draw user interface components and perform graphics operations, just as you would any other panel. Like other windows, the dialog is initially invisible, but you can show it with show() and hide it with hide().

Let's add a dialog to the example with the pop-up window. Of the three classes in this applet, BaseFrame is the only one that needs changing. Here you'll modify the class to include a Set Text button and add a new class, TextDialog, which produces a text entry dialog similar to the one shown in Figure 13.10.

13

Figure 13.10.
The Enter Text
dialog.

NOTE

In the sample code on the CD, this version of the applet is separate from the previous version. I've created a new class called `BaseFrame2` for this part of the example, a new class `PopupWindowDialog.java` to be the applet that owns this window, and `PopupActions2.java` as the class that handles the actions. Use `PopupWindowDialog.html` to view this version of the applet.

To add the dialog to the `BaseFrame` class, the changes are minor. First, you'll need an instance variable to hold the dialog because you'll be referring to it throughout this class:

```
TextDialog dl;
```

In `BaseFrame`'s constructor method, you can create the dialog (an instance of the new class `TextDialog` you'll create in a bit), assign it to the `dl` instance variable, and resize it (as shown in the next two lines of code). You don't want to show it yet because it should only appear when the Set Text button is clicked.

```
dl = new TextDialog(this, "Enter Text", true);
dl.resize(150,100);
```

Now create the Set Text button, similarly to how other buttons work, and add it to the `BorderLayout` in the `"South"` position (which puts it directly below the label).

```
Button b = new Button("Set Text");
add("South", b);
```

To get the dialog to appear at the appropriate time, you have to add event handling to this frame. I've factored the event behavior into an `ActionListener` class called `BaseFrameActions`, which is shown in Listing 13.6. This code should look familiar to you at this point, so I'm not going to explain it in great detail. The one thing to point out is that when the button is clicked, an `actionPerformed()` method calls `dl.show()` in the base frame to show the dialog.

TYPE **Listing 13.6.** BaseFrameActions.

```
 1: import java.awt.*;
 2: import java.awt.event.*;
 3:
 4: public class BaseFrameActions implements ActionListener {
 5:
 6:     BaseFrame2 theApp;
 7:
 8:     BaseFrameActions(BaseFrame2 win) {
 9:         theApp = win;
10:     }
11:
12:     public void actionPerformed(ActionEvent e) {
13:         if (e.getSource() instanceof Button)
14:             theApp.dl.show();
15:     }
16:
17:}
```

That's the end of the behavior you have to add to the pop-up window to create a dialog; the rest of the new behavior goes into the TextDialog class, the code for which is shown in Listing 13.7.

TYPE **Listing 13.7. The** TextDialog **class.**

```
 1: import java.awt.*;
 2:import java.awt.event.*;
 3:
 4: class TextDialog extends Dialog implements ActionListener {
 5:     TextField tf;
 6:     BaseFrame theFrame;
 7:
 8:     TextDialog(Frame parent, String title, boolean modal) {
 9:         super(parent, title, modal);
10:
11:         theFrame = (BaseFrame)parent;
12:         setLayout(new BorderLayout(10,10));
13:         setBackground(Color.white);
14:         tf = new TextField(theFrame.message,20);
15:         add("Center", tf);
16:
17:         Button b = new Button("OK");
18:         b.addActionListener(this);
19:         add("South", b);
20:     }
21:
22:     public Insets insets() {
23:         return new Insets(30,10,10,10);
24:     }
25:
```

13

continues

Listing 13.7. continued

```
26:  public void actionPerformed(ActionEvent e) {
27:    if (e.getSource() instanceof Button) {
28:      String label = ((Button)e.getSource()).getLabel();
29:      if (label == "OK") {
30:        hide();
31:        theFrame.l.setText(tf.getText());
32:      }
33:    }
34:  }
35:}
```

You should note a few points about this code. First, note that unlike the other two windows in this applet, the event handling is inside the class so that the dialog serves as its own listener. Sometimes portioning out the event-handling code makes sense, but sometimes just putting it all together is easier. In this case, TextDialog is a simple enough element that putting it all together seemed easier.

Despite this fact, this dialog has a lot of the same elements as the BaseFrame class. Note that the constructor for TextDialog is identical to one of the constructors for its superclass Dialog because despite the fact that TextDialog is attached to an object whose class is BaseFrame, dialogs must be attached to an actual Frame object. You can more easily make the constructor more generic and then specialize it after the superclass's constructor has been called—which is precisely what you do in lines 9 and 11 of Listing 13.7. Line 9 is the call to the superclass's constructor to hook up the dialog with the frame, and line 11 actually sets the instance variable to the specific instance of the Frame class defined in the BaseFrame class.

The remainder of the TextDialog constructor simply sets up the rest of the layout: a text field and a button in a border layout. The getInsets() method adds a few insets and, finally, the actionPerformed() method to handle the action of the dialog's OK button. The actionPerformed() method does two things: in line 30 it hides the dialog to dismiss it, and in line 31 it changes the value of the label in the parent frame to be the new value of the text.

All these classes just for a simple applet! The different windows and associated event classes make the applet complicated. At this point, though, you should feel comfortable with how each part of an applet has its own components and actions and how all the parts of the applet fit together. If you're still confused, you might want to explore the source code on the CD, starting from PopupWindowDialog, to get a better feel for how everything fits together.

Attaching Dialogs to Applets

Dialogs can be attached to frames only. To create a dialog, you have to pass an instance of the Frame class to one of the dialog's constructor methods. This implies that you cannot create dialog boxes that are attached to applets. Because applets don't have explicit frames, you cannot give the Dialog class a frame argument. Through a bit of sneaky code, however, you can get ahold of the frame object that contains that applet (often the browser or applet viewer window itself) and then use that object as the dialog's frame.

This sneaky code makes use of the getParent() method, defined for all AWT components. The getParent() method returns the object that contains this object. The parent of all AWT applications, then, must be a frame. Applets behave in this same way. By calling getParent() repeatedly, eventually you should be able to get ahold of an instance of Frame. Here's the sneaky code you can put inside your applet:

```
Object anchorpoint = getParent()
while (! (anchorpoint instanceof Frame))
anchorpoint = ((Component)anchorpoint).getParent();
```

In the first line of this code, you create a local variable, called anchorpoint, to hold the eventual frame for this applet. The object assigned to anchorpoint may be one of many classes, so declare its type to be Object.

The second two lines of this code are a while loop that calls getParent() on each different object up the chain until it gets to an actual Frame object. Note here that because the getParent() method is defined only on objects that inherit from Component, you have to cast the value of anchorpoint to Component each time for the getParent() method to work.

After the loop exits, the object contained in the anchorpoint variable will be an instance of the Frame class (or one of its subclasses). You can then create a Dialog object attached to that frame, casting anchorpoint one more time to make sure you've got a Frame object:

```
TextDialog dl = new TextDialog((Frame)anchorpoint,
"Enter Text", true);
```

File Dialog Objects

The FileDialog class provides a basic File Open/Save dialog box that enables you to access the local file system. The FileDialog class is system-independent, but depending on the platform, the standard Open File or Save File dialog is brought up.

NOTE

For applets, whether you can even use instances of FileDialog is dependent on the browser. Most browsers simply produce an error when you try. FileDialog is much more useful in standalone applications.

13

To create a file dialog, use the following constructors:

☐ `FileDialog(Frame, String)` creates a file dialog, attached to the given frame, with the given title. This form creates a dialog to load a file.

☐ `FileDialog(Frame, String, int)` also creates a file dialog, but the integer argument is used to determine whether the dialog is for loading a file or saving a file (the only difference is the labels on the buttons; the file dialog does not actually open or save anything). The possible options for the mode argument are `FileDialog.LOAD` and `FileDialog.SAVE`.

After you create a `FileDialog` instance, use `show()` to display it:

```
FileDialog fd = new FileDialog(this, "FileDialog");
fd.show();
```

When the reader chooses a file in the File dialog and dismisses it, you can then access the filename the reader chose by using the `getDirectory()` and `getFile()` methods. Both of these methods return strings indicating the values the reader chose. You can then open the file by using the stream- and file-handling methods (which you'll learn about next week) and then read from or write to that file.

Cursors (1.02 Only)

You've already learned about using cursors in the 1j1 version of the JDK, where you can define the cursor for each component you use in your applet or application. In the 1.02 version of the JDK, cursors can be added only to `frame` objects and can be changed globally for that frame only—for example, to signal wait conditions or other events happening in your program.

The `getCursorType()` and `setCursor()` methods are defined in the `Frame` class. If you can get at a `Frame` object, you can set the cursor. (You'll typically set cursors for windows, but you can also set cursors for applets using the `getParent()` method explained in the section "Attaching Dialogs to Applets"). Both of these methods use the same set of predefined cursor types listed in Table 13.6 for 1.1, except these cursors are defined by the `Frame` class instead of the `Cursor` class (the `Cursor` class doesn't exist in 1.02).

To access a particular cursor, use `FRAME.cursorname`. For example, `Frame.WAIT_CURSOR` is the default cursor for wait conditions.

Window Events

You're down to the last set of events you can handle in the AWT: the events for windows and dialogs. (In terms of events, a dialog is considered just another kind of window.) Window events result when the state of a window changes in any way: when the window is moved, resized, iconified, deiconified, moved to the front, or closed. In a well-behaved application, you'll want to handle at least some of these events—for example, to stop running threads when a window is iconified, or to clean up when the window is closed.

In the 1.02 event model, use `handleEvent()` to test for each of the events shown in Table 13.8, using the standard `switch` statement with the `id` instance variable.

Table 13.8. Window events in 1.02.

Event Name	When It Occurs
WINDOW_DESTROY	Generated when a window is destroyed using the close box or the Close menu item
WINDOW_EXPOSE	Generated when the window is brought forward from behind other windows
WINDOW_ICONIFY	Generated when the window is iconified
WINDOW_DEICONIFY	Generated when the window is restored from an icon
WINDOW_MOVED	Generated when the window is moved

In the 1.1 event model, window events generate slightly different actions, and there are more events you can use (for example, there are separate events for windows closing and when the window has fully closed). Window events in 1.1 are as follows:

☐ Window opened: This event is generated the first time a window is opened.

☐ Window activated: This event is generated when the window is brought forward or when it gains the input focus.

☐ Window deactivated: This event is generated when some other window on the screen is brought forward or gains the input focus.

☐ Window iconified: This event is generated when the window is iconified (on systems that support this capability).

☐ Window deiconified: This event is generated when the window is deiconified (on systems that support this capability).

☐ Window closing: This event is generated when the close button has been chosen or quit has been selected from a menu. You should hide or destroy the window in response to this method.

☐ Window closed: This event is generated when the window has completed closing.

A window moved event is the exception; it is treated as simply another component event (represented by the `ComponentEvent` class), and `ComponentListener` handles that one. Table 13.9 shows the events, listeners, and methods for each of the window events in 1.1.

13

Table 13.9. Window events in 1.1.

Event Name	Listener	Method
Window opened	WindowListener	public void windowOpened(WindowEvent e)
Window moved	ComponentListener	public void componentMoved (ComponentEvent e)
Window activated	WindowListener	public void windowActivated (WindowEvent e)
Window deactivated	WindowListener	public void windowDeactivated (WindowEvent e)
Window iconified	WindowListener	public void windowIconified (WindowEvent e)
Window deiconified	WindowListener	public void windowDeiconified (WindowEvent e)
Window closing	WindowListener	public void windowClosing(WindowEvent e)
Window closed	WindowListener	public void windowClosed(WindowEvent e)

To register window listeners, use the addWindowListener() method. Note that this method is available only to subclasses of Frame and Dialog, so make sure you add your listeners to the topmost windows in your applet or application.

Menus

Only one UI element in the AWT is left for me to talk about: menus. In Java 1.1, you can create two different kinds of menus: fixed menus, contained in a menu bar along the top of a window, and pop-up menus, which can appear anywhere in an application or applet. In Java 1.02, you can create only menu bar–based menus.

A menu bar is a collection of menus. A menu, in turn, contains a collection of menu items, which can have names and sometimes optional shortcuts. A pop-up menu is simply a menu that can exist outside a menu bar; it still contains menu items, and these items still behave in the same way. The AWT provides classes for all these menu elements, including MenuBar, Menu, MenuItem, and in 1.1, PopupMenu. Figure 13.11 shows the menu classes.

Figure 13.11.
The AWT menu classes.

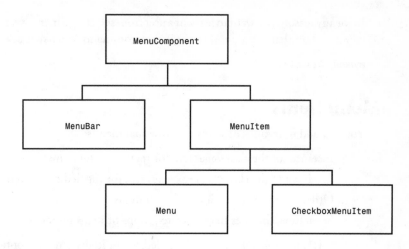

Menus and Menu Bars

A menu bar is a set of menus that appear across the top of a window. Because they are rooted to windows, you cannot create menu bars in applets (but if that applet pops up an independent window, the window can have a menu bar).

To create a menu bar for a given window, you create a new instance of the class `MenuBar`:

```
MenuBar mbar = new MenuBar();
```

To set this menu bar as the default menu for the window, you use the `setMenuBar()` method (defined in the `Frame` class):

```
window.setMenuBar(mbar);
```

You can add individual menus (File, Edit, and so on) to the menu bar by creating them and then adding them to the menu bar using `add()`. The argument to the `Menu` constructor is the name of the `Menu` as it will appear in the menu bar.

```
Menu myMenu = new Menu("File");
mbar.add(myMenu);
```

Some systems provide a special Help menu, which is drawn on the right side of the menu bar as opposed to the left side. You can indicate that a specific menu is the Help menu by using the `setHelpMenu()` method. The given menu should already be added to the menu itself before being made a Help menu.

```
Menu helpmenu = new Menu("Help");
mbar.add(helpmenu);
mbar.setHelpMenu(helpmenu);
```

13

If, for any reason, you want to prevent a user from selecting a menu, you can use the `disable()` command on that menu (and the `enable()` command to make it available again):

```
myMenu.disable();
```

Menu Items

You can add four kinds of items to individual menus:

- ☐ Instances of the class `MenuItem`, for regular menu items
- ☐ Instances of the class `CheckBoxMenuItem`, for toggled menu items
- ☐ Other menus, with their own menu items
- ☐ Separators, for lines that separate groups of items on menus

In Java 1.1, both menu items and toggled menu items can have optional menu keyboard shortcuts, which can be used in place of using the mouse to pull down the menu and select a menu item. This feature is not available using Java 1.02.

Creating Menu Items

Regular menu items are created and added to a menu using the `MenuItem` class. First, create a new instance of `MenuItem`, and then add it to the `Menu` component using the `add()` method:

```
Menu myMenu = new Menu("Tools");
myMenu.add(new MenuItem("Info"));
myMenu.add(new MenuItem("Colors"));
```

Submenus can be added simply by creating a new instance of `Menu` and adding it to the first menu. You can then add items to that menu:

```
Menu submenu = new Menu("Sizes");
myMenu.add(submenu);
submenu.add(new MenuItem("Small"));
submenu.add(new MenuItem("Medium"));
submenu.add(new MenuItem("Large"));
```

The `CheckBoxMenuItem` class creates a menu item with a check box on it, enabling the menu state to be toggled on and off. (Selecting it once makes the check box appear selected; selecting it again deselects the check box.) Create and add a check box menu item the same way you create and add regular menu items:

```
CheckboxMenuItem coords =
new CheckboxMenuItem("Show Coordinates");
myMenu.add(coords);
```

Finally, to add a separator to a menu (a line used to separate groups of items in a menu), create and add a menu item with a single dash (-) as the label. That special menu item will be drawn with a separator line. These next two lines of Java code create a separator menu item and add it to the menu `myMenu`:

```
MenuItem msep = new MenuItem("-");
myMenu.add(msep);
```

Any menu item can be disabled by using the `disable()` method and enabled again using `enable()`. Disabled menu items cannot be selected.

```
MenuItem item = new MenuItem("Fill");
myMenu.addItem(item);
item.disable();
```

Menu Item Shortcuts (Java 1.1 Only)

In Java 1.1, both menu items and check box menu items can have keyboard shortcuts, which allow you to select that menu item by using the keyboard rather than the mouse. As with using Tab for input focus between AWT components, this allows the 1.1 AWT to be operated without the mouse.

To add a menu shortcut to a menu item, you create an instance of the `MenuShortcut` class, and then pass that menu shortcut to the `MenuItem` or `CheckboxMenuItem`'s constructor. `MenuShortcut` objects can be created in one of two ways:

- [ ] `MenuShortcut(int)` creates a new shortcut with the given keycode or character as the shortcut key. (This will usually be a character.) Note that menu shortcuts can only have a single character.

- [ ] `MenuShortcut(int, boolean)` does the same as `MenuShortcut(int)` except that the boolean argument indicates whether the Shift key should be held down when the menu shortcut is selected. `True` indicates that the shortcut should be shifted; `false` is a regular shortcut.

For example, here's a menu with three menu items, each with its own keyboard shortcut:

```
Menu editMenu = new Menu("Edit");
editMenu.add(new MenuItem("Cut", new MenuShortcut('x')));
editMenu.add(new MenuItem("Copy", new MenuShortcut('c')));
editMenu.add(new MenuItem("Paste", new MenuShortcut('v')));
```

Menu shortcuts are activated in the application using a key modifier, which differs from platform to platform. On Windows and Solaris, it's Ctrl (Control); on the Macintosh it's Command (Apple). Holding down the modifier and typing the key activates the menu item. (The Shift key also needs to be held down for menu shortcuts that require it.)

After a menu shortcut has been set, a number of methods can be used to modify those shortcuts. For the `MenuItem` class, `getShortcut()`, `setShortcut()`, and `deleteShortcut()` can be used to retrieve the shortcut, change it, or delete it altogether. The `MenuBar` class also has a number of methods: `getShortcutMenuItem` returns the menu item that contains a particular shortcut; `shortcuts()` returns an `Enumeration` object with all the shortcuts in the menu bar's menus; and `deleteShortcut` deletes a particular shortcut altogether.

13

Menu Events

The act of selecting a menu item with the mouse or choosing the menu item's keyboard shortcut causes an action event to be generated, both in the 1.02 and 1.1 event models, and you can handle that event using the action() method for 1.02 or by implementing an action listener, just as you have over the last few days. For the 1.1 event model, action events should be registered to individual menu items.

In addition to action events, CheckBoxMenuItems generate list select and list deselect events, which can be handled via handleEvent() in the 1.02 event model, or by implementing ItemListener's itemStateChanged() method in the 1.1 event model.

As you process events generated by menu items and check box menu items, keep in mind that because CheckboxMenuItem is a subclass of MenuItem, you don't have to treat this menu item as a special case. You can handle this action the same way you handle other action methods.

Pop-up Menus (1.1 Only)

New to the 1.1 AWT is the pop-up menu, a new component that allows you to create menus that pop up in response to mouse down events. Different components can have different pop-up menus, thus allowing you to create context-sensitive menus. Also, because pop-up menus do not require a menu bar or a window, they can be located anywhere in an application or in an applet.

A pop-up menu is simply a special kind of menu; it can contain menu items, and each menu item can have an action event associated with it. To create a new pop-up menu, use the PopupMenu class, like this:

```
PopupMenu popmenu = new PopupMenu("Actions");
```

Add menu items to the pop-up menu just as you would for regular menus:

```
MenuItem micut = new MenuItem("Cut");
micut.addActionlistener(this);
popmenu.add(miout);
MenuItem micopy = new MenuItem("Copy");
micopy.addActionlistener(this);
popmenu.add(micopy);
MenuItem mipaste = new MenuItem("Paste");
mipaste.addActionlistener(this);
popmenu.add(mipaste);
```

After building the menu, you add it to the component using add():

```
add(popmenu);
```

Use the show() method defined in the PopupMenu class to make the pop-up menu appear at a particular position. Generally, you'll call show() in response to a mouse event.

The problem here is that different platforms use different events with which to trigger a pop-up menu. Windows pops up windows in response to a mouse up on the right button, whereas Solaris responds to a mouse down on the right button. The best way to trap for a pop-up menu is to use the `isPopupTrigger()` method inside `MouseEvent` and a component method called `processMouseEvent()`, which is used to handle mouse events in a generic way (similarly to how the `handleEvent()` method works in the 1.02 event model). In particular, this code (inside a `Component` class) will pop up the menu at the right time:

```
public void processMouseEvent(MouseEvent e) {
    if (e.isPopupTrigger())
        popup.show(e.getComponent(), e.getX(), e.getY());

    super.processMouseEvent(e);
}
```

NOTE

The `processMouseEvent()` is one of a series of generic component events that are used to implement the listener-based event model in 1.1. Most of the time you won't need to use any of these methods (all of which are defined in the `Component` class); the one case in which you might need to use them is if you're defining your own custom UI components, a task that's outside the boundaries of this book. See the API documentation for the `Component` class and the event specification at `http://www.javasoft.com:80/products/JDK/1.1/docs/guide/awt/designspec/events.html` for more details.

An Example: A Pop-up Window with Menus

To finish off this day, let's add a menu to the pop-up window applet created in the section on dialogs. You must take two steps here: creating and adding the menu, with all its menu items, to the layout of the `BaseFrame` class, and then modifying the action method in `BaseFrameActions` to deal with the menu item actions.

Start with the `BaseFrame` class and modify the layout. Listing 13.8 shows the new code, and Figure 13.12 shows the menu in action.

In the sample code on the CD, the classes you'll want to look up for this applet are `PopupWindowMenu.java`, `PopupActions2.java`, `BaseFrame3.java`, `BaseFrameActions2.java`, and `TextDialog2.java` (whew!). You can use `PopupWindowMenu.html` to view it.

13

TYPE   Listing 13.8. BaseFrame **with a menu.**

```
1:iimport java.awt.*;
2:
3:pclass BaseFrame extends Frame {
4:     String message = "This is a Window";
5:     TextDialog2 dl;
6:    Label l;
7:
8:    BaseFrame3(String title) {
9:     super(title);
10:     setLayout(new BorderLayout());
11:
12:     l = new Label(message, Label.CENTER);
13:     l.setFont(new Font("Helvetica", Font.PLAIN, 12));
14:     add("Center", l);
15:
16:     // make a dialog for this window
17:     dl = new TextDialog(this, "Enter Text", true);
18:     dl.resize(150,100);
19:
20:     Button b = new Button("Set Text");
21:     BaseFrameActions handleact = new BaseFrameActions(this);;
22:     b.addActionListener(handleact);
23:     add("South", b);
24:
25:     MenuBar mb = new MenuBar();
26:     Menu m = new Menu("Colors");
27:     MenuItem redmi = new MenuItem("Red");
28:     redmi.addActionListener(handleact);
29:     m.add(redmi);
30:     MenuItem bluemi = new MenuItem("Blue");
31:     bluemi.addActionListener(handleact);
32:     m.add(bluemi);
33:     MenuItem greenmi = new MenuItem("Green");
34:     greenmi.addActionListener(handleact);
35:     m.add(greenmi);
36:     m.add(new MenuItem("-"));
37:     CheckboxMenuItem boldmi = new CheckboxMenuItem("Bold Text");
38:     boldmi.addActionListener(handleact);
39:     m.add(boldmi);
40:     mb.add(m);
41:     setMenuBar(mb);
42:    }
43:
44:    public Insets getInsets() {
45:       return new Insets(20,0,25,0);
46:    }
47:}
```

13

Figure 13.12.

A menu.

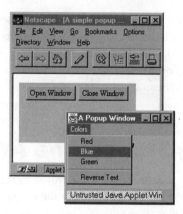

This menu has four items: one each for the colors red, blue, and green (which, when selected, change the background of the window), and one check box menu item for changing the text to boldface. All are added as part of the constructor to this class, in lines 25 to 41. In addition to creating the menu items themselves, you've also added action listeners to each of them—or rather, you've added one action listener to all of them, an instance of the class `BaseFrameActions`.

To handle the menu items themselves, you'll modify the `BaseFrameActions` class to include menu items in the `actionPerformed()` method. Previously, that method just had an entry for the Set Text button; now you'll add methods to change the label's background in response to the colors, or to change the label's font to boldface in response to the Bold Text menu item. Here's the new `actionPerformed()` method from the `BaseFrame` class:

```java
public void actionPerformed(ActionEvent e) {
    if (e.getSource() instanceof Button)
        theApp.dl.show();
    else if (e.getSource() instanceof MenuItem) {
        String label = ((MenuItem)e.getSource()).getLabel();
        if (label.equals("Red"))
            theApp.l.setBackground(Color.red);
        else if (label.equals("Blue"))
            theApp.l.setBackground(Color.blue);
        else if (label.equals("Green"))
            theApp.l.setBackground(Color.green);
        else if (label.equals("Bold Text")) {
            if (theApp.l.getFont().isPlain()) {
                theApp.l.setFont(new Font("Helvetica", Font.BOLD, 12));
            }
            else theApp.l.setFont(new Font("Helvetica", Font.PLAIN, 12));
        }
    }
}
```

13

To handle these menu items when they're chosen, test to see if the action came from a menu item (which includes the one check box menu item), and if so, test for each of the menu labels in turn. For the red, blue, and green menu items, all you need to do is set the label's background. For the Bold Text toggle, you first test to see if the text is currently plain (using the `isPlain()` method), and if so, replace it with a boldface font; otherwise, you revert to a plain font.

Creating Standalone AWT Applications

After all the space and time I've devoted to creating applets up to this point, you may be surprised that I'm sticking a description of graphical Java applications here at the end, and in a fairly small section at that. The reason is that other than a few simple lines of code and in the environment each runs in, you won't find a lot of difference between a Java applet and a graphical Java application. Everything you've learned up to this point about the AWT, including the graphics methods, animation techniques, events, UI components, and windows and dialogs, can be used the same way in Java applications as they can in applets. Applications have the advantage of being "outside the sandbox"—they have none of the security restrictions that applets have. You can do just about anything you want to with an application.

So how do you go about creating a graphical Java application? The code to create it is almost trivial. Your main application class should inherit from `Frame`. If it uses threads (for animation or other processing), it should also implement `Runnable`:

```
class MyAWTApplication extends Frame implements Runnable {
...
}
```

Inside the `main()` method for your application, you create a new instance of your class—because your class extends `Frame`, that'll give you a new AWT window that you can then resize and show as you would any AWT window.

Inside the constructor method for your class, set up the usual AWT features for a window that you might usually do in an `init()` method for an applet: Set the title, add a layout manager, create and add components such as a menu bar or other UI elements, start up a thread, and so on.

Here's an example of a very simple application:

```
import java.awt.*;

class MyAWTApplication extends Frame {

    MyAWTApplication(String title) {
        super(title);
```

```
        setLayout(new FlowLayout());
        add(new Button("OK"));
        add(new Button("Reset"));
        add(new Button("Cancel"));
    }

    public static void main(String args[]) {
        MyAWTApplication app = new MyAWTApplication("Hi!  I'm an application");
        app.resize(300,300);
        app.show();
    }
}
```

For the most part, you can use any of the methods you've learned about this week to control and manage your application. The only methods you cannot use are the ones specific to applets (that is, the ones defined in `java.applet.Applet`, which includes methods for retrieving URL information and playing audio clips). See the API documentation for that class for more details.

You should know one other difference between applications and applets: When you handle a window closing event, in addition to hiding or destroying the window, you should also call `System.exit(0)` to indicate to the system that your application has exited:

```
public void windowClosing(WindowEvent e) {
    win.hide();
    win.destroy();
    System.exit(0);
}
```

Summary

Today's lesson was long, but at this point you've learned just about everything you need to know about the practical use of the AWT. Today you learned more about the various AWT components, including text areas, scrolling lists, panes, scroll bars, canvases, and cursors. You also learned about nesting panels and components, and the various methods and events you can use with components. In the second half of this lesson, you learned about windows, dialogs, and menus, as well as how to use the AWT in standalone applications. And throughout this lesson you worked through a number of sample applets so you can get a feel for how all the parts of an applet or application fit together.

Congratulations! You're over the worst hump. Tomorrow I'll discuss some of the odds and ends in the AWT that I haven't covered here, and then you can launch into week three with some of the more advanced parts of the Java language.

13

Q&A

Q I'm trying to create a custom component that is effectively a set of buttons in a scrollable list. I'm using 1.02, and it appears the only way I can do this is to create a component that's made up of a panel and a scroll bar, and to catch the various scroll bar events and handle the scrolling myself. I can't believe I have to do all this coding to handle scrolling. Isn't there an easier way?

A Yes. Upgrade to 1.1; the ScrollPane class does exactly what you want it to. Using ScrollPane, you can just add a panel to the scrolling pane and then add buttons to that panel. All the scrolling will be handled for you. This solution is much easier and, in fact, was added to the 1.1 AWT for just the reasons you mention.

Q In the ColorTest example that converts RGB to HSB, I can't get the colored swatch to change colors. I'm using the code from the CD, and it doesn't work. What am I doing wrong?

A Are you using Internet Explorer as your browser? The applet in question works in Netscape and in the Sun appletviewer, but I hear that it doesn't work right in Explorer. I don't have an answer to the question other than for you to file a bug with Microsoft about it.

When you're in doubt about something working in one browser, one of the best things to do is to test it either in another browser that supports Java or to test it using Sun's appletviewer. When in doubt, appletviewer is the most correct implementation.

Q I really, really hate the big yellow warning that comes up in applet-based windows. It's ugly and, worse, it obscures part of my window. Is there any way to get rid of it?

A Nope, the warning is there to stay. As far as obscuring the surface of the window goes, it does indeed cut off the bottom part of the window (and menu bars, if you use them, will cut off the top). The best way to work around this problem is to use insets of 25 points to make sure all the parts of your window stay in the visible part of the window.

Q In your discussion on standalone applications, you gave me the impression that there's absolutely no difference between an applet and an application. Why is that?

13

A Both applets and applications use the same procedures inside the AWT to build components, display them, and handle events. The only differences are that applications initialize from `main()` and display in their own windows, and that applets initialize and start from `init()` and `start()` respectively. Given the vast number of similarities between applets and applications, 99 percent of what you learn regarding applets can be used with applications. And, in fact, because applets ignore the `main()` method if it happens to exist in a class, there's no reason that you can't create a single program that will run equally well as an applet and as an application.

Q **I created a standalone application, but when I click on the close box, nothing happens. What do I need to do to get my application to actually close?**

A Trap the window close event, either with `WINDOW_CLOSE` in the 1.02 event model or with the `windowClosing()` method in `WindowListener` for 1.1. In response to that event, call `hide()` the window if it may come back later, or call `destroy()` to get rid of it for good. If the window close event will result in your entire program exiting, also call `System.exit()`.

13

Day 14

Networking, Advanced APIs, and Miscellaneous Tidbits

by Laura Lemay and Michael Morrison

Here you are on the last day of the second week, and you're just about finished understanding applets and the AWT. With the information you'll learn today you can create a wide variety of applets and applications using Java. Next week's lessons provide more of the advanced stuff that you'll need if you start doing really serious work in Java.

Today, to finish up this week, we'll cover a number of very different topics, odds and ends that didn't fit anywhere else, including

☐ Tricks with applets: printing applet status messages, storing and showing applet information, creating Java-based HTML links, and communicating between applets on the same page

☐ Networking in Java: how to retrieve extra files from Web sites, some information about Java sockets, and a basic example of how to create a simple client/server application

☐ Printing from AWT applications

☐ Managing cut, copy, and paste facilities between AWT components

☐ Internationalization

☐ The Java advanced APIs: parts of the new 1.1 Java framework (including JavaBeans, RMI, JDBC, and the security framework) that are too complicated to explain in this book but that might be useful to you once you start doing advanced work in Java

Other Applet Tricks

Let's start this chapter with some small hints that don't fit in anywhere else: using showStatus() to print messages in the browser status window, providing applet information, and communicating between multiple applets on the same page.

The showStatus() Method

The showStatus() method, available in the Applet class, enables you to display a string in the status bar of the browser, which contains the applet. You can use this for printing error, link, help, or other status messages:

```
getAppletContext().showStatus("Change the color");
```

The getAppletContext() method enables your applet to access features of the browser that contains it. You already saw a use of this with links, wherein you could use the showDocument() method to tell the browser to load a page. showStatus() uses that same mechanism to print status messages.

NOTE

> showStatus() might not be supported in all browsers, so do not depend on it for your applet's functionality or interface. It is a useful way of communicating optional information to your user. If you need a more reliable method of communication, set up a label in your applet and update it to reflect changes in its message.

14

Applet Information

The AWT gives you a mechanism for associating information with your applet. Usually, there is a mechanism in the browser viewing the applet to view display information. You can use this mechanism to sign your name or your organization to your applet, or to provide contact information so that users can get hold of you if they want.

To provide information about your applet, override the `getAppletInfo()` method:

```
public String getAppletInfo() {
   return "GetRaven copyright 1995 Laura Lemay";
}
```

Creating Links Inside Applets

Because applets run inside Web pages in browsers, it's nice to be able to use the capability of that browser to load new Web pages. Java provides a mechanism to tell the browser to load a new page. You can use this mechanism, for example, to create animated image maps that, when clicked, load a new page.

To link to a new page, you create a new instance of the class URL. You saw some of this when you worked with images, but let's go over it a little more thoroughly here.

The URL class represents a uniform resource locator, a pointer to some file or object on the World Wide Web. To create a new URL, you can use one of four different constructors:

- [ ] `URL(String, String, int, String)` creates a new URL object, given a protocol (http, ftp, gopher, file), a hostname (`www.lne.com`, `ftp.netcom.com`), a port number (80 for http), and a filename or pathname.

- [ ] `URL(String, String, String)` does the same thing as the previous form, minus the port number.

- [ ] `URL(URL, String)` creates an URL, given a base path and a relative path. For the base, you can use `getDocumentBase()` for the URL of the current HTML file, or `getCodeBase()` for the URL of the Java applet class file. The relative path will be tacked onto the last directory in those base URLs (just like with images and sounds).

- [ ] `URL(String)` creates an URL object from an URL string (which should include the protocol, hostname, optional port name, and filename).

For the last one (creating an URL from a string), you have to catch a malformed URL exception, so surround the URL constructor with a `try...catch`:

```
String url = "http://www.yahoo.com/";
try { theURL = new URL(url); }
catch ( MalformedURLException e) {
   System.out.println("Bad URL: " + theURL);
}
```

14

Getting an URL object is the hard part. Once you have one, all you have to do is pass it to the browser. Do this by using this single line of code, where the URL is the URL object to link to:

```
getAppletContext().showDocument(theURL);
```

The browser that contains the Java applet with this code will then load and display the document at that URL.

Listings 14.1 and 14.2 show two classes: ButtonLink and its helper class Bookmark. ButtonLink is a simple applet that displays three buttons that represent important Web locations (the buttons are shown in Figure 14.1). Clicking on the buttons causes the document to be loaded from the locations to which those buttons refer.

NOTE

This applet must be run from inside a browser for the links to work. However, because at the time I write this no browsers support Java 1.1, that makes it difficult to test. This version of the ButtonLink class uses the 1.02 event model; a 1.1-based version is contained on the CD-ROM under the name ButtonLink1.1.java.

Figure 14.1.
Bookmark buttons.

TYPE   **Listing 14.1. Bookmark buttons (Buttonlink.java).**

```
1: // Buttonlink.java starts here
2: import java.awt.*;
3: import java.net.*;
4:
5: public class ButtonLink extends java.applet.Applet {
6:
7:     Bookmark bmlist[] = new Bookmark[3];
8:
```

14

```
 9:    public void init() {
10:        bmlist[0] = new Bookmark("Laura's Home Page",
11:            "http://www.lne.com/lemay/");
12:        bmlist[1] = new Bookmark("Gamelan",
13:            "http://www.gamelan.com");
14:        bmlist[2]= new Bookmark("Java Home Page",
15:            "http://java.sun.com");
16:
17:        setLayout(new GridLayout(bmlist.length,1, 10, 10));
18:        for (int i = 0; i < bmlist.length; i++) {
19:            add(new Button(bmlist[i].name));
20:        }
21:    }
22:
23:    public boolean action(Event evt, Object arg) {
24:        if (evt.target instanceof Button) {
25:            linkTo((String)arg);
26:            return true;
27:        }
28:        else return false;
29:    }
30:
31:    void linkTo(String name) {
32:        URL theURL = null;
33:        for (int i = 0; i < bmlist.length; i++) {
34:            if (name.equals(bmlist[i].name))
35:                theURL = bmlist[i].url;
36:        }
37:        if (theURL != null)
38:            getAppletContext().showDocument(theURL);
39:    }
40: }
```

TYPE **Listing 14.2. Bookmark buttons (Bookmark.java).**

```
 1: import java.net.URL;
 2: import java.net.MalformedURLException;
 3:
 4: class Bookmark {
 5:    String name;
 6:    URL url;
 7:
 8:    Bookmark(String name, String theURL) {
 9:        this.name = name;
10:        try { this.url = new URL(theURL); }
11:        catch ( MalformedURLException e) {
12:            System.out.println("Bad URL: " + theURL);
13:        }
14:    }
15:}
```

14

Two classes make up this applet: The first, ButtonLink, implements the actual applet itself; the second, Bookmark, is a class representing a bookmark. Bookmarks have two parts: a name and an URL.

This particular applet creates three bookmark instances (lines 10 through 15) and stores them in an array of bookmarks (this applet could be easily modified to accept bookmarks as parameters from an HTML file). For each bookmark, a button is created whose label is the value of the bookmark's name.

When the buttons are pressed, the linkTo() method is called. linkTo(), defined in lines 31 to 38, extracts the name of the button from the event, uses it to look up the actual URL from the bookmark object, and then tells the browser to load the URL referenced by that bookmark.

Communicating Between Applets

Sometimes you want to have an HTML page that has several different applets on it. To do this, all you have to do is include several different iterations of the <APPLET> tag. The browser will create different instances of your applet for each one that appears on the HTML page.

What if you want to communicate between those applets? What if you want a change in one applet to affect the other applets in some way? The best way to do this is to use the applet context to get to different applets on the same page.

NOTE Be forewarned that before you do extensive work with inter-applet communication, the mechanism described in this section is implemented differently (and often unreliably) in different browsers and different Java environments. If you need to rely on communicating between applets for your Web pages, make sure you test those applets extensively in different browsers on different platforms.

The applet context is defined in a class called, appropriately, AppletContext. To get an instance of this class for you applet, you use the getAppletContext() method. You've already seen the use of the getAppletContext() method for other uses; you can also use it to get ahold of the other applets on the page. For example, to call a method named sendMessage() on all the applets on a page (including the current applet), use the getApplets() method and a for loop that looks something like this:

```
for (Enumeration e = getAppletContext().getApplets();
    e.hasMoreElements();) {
    Applet current = (MyAppletSubclass)(e.nextElement());
    current.sendMessage();
}
```

The getApplets() method returns an Enumeration object with a list of the applets on the page. Iterating over the Enumeration object in this way enables you to access each element in the Enumeration in turn. Note that each element in the Enumeration object is an instance of the Object class; to get that applet to behave the way you want it to (and accept messages from other applets), you'll have to cast it to be an instance of your applet subclass (here, the class MyAppletSubclass).

If you want to call a method in a specific applet, it's slightly more complicated. To do this, you give your applets a name and then refer to them by name inside the body of code for that applet.

To give an applet a name, use the NAME attribute to <APPLET> in your HTML file:

```
<P>This applet sends information:
<APPLET CODE="MyApplet.class" WIDTH=100 HEIGHT=150
   NAME="sender"> </APPLET>
<P>This applet receives information from the sender:
<APPLET CODE="MyApplet.class" WIDTH=100 HEIGHT=150
   NAME="receiver"> </APPLET>
```

To get a reference to another applet on the same page, use the getApplet() method from the applet context with the name of that applet. This gives you a reference to the applet of that name. You can then refer to that applet as if it were just another object: call methods, set its instance variables, and so on. Here's some code to do just that:

```
// get ahold of the receiver applet
Applet receiver = (MyAppletSubclass)getAppletContext().getApplet("receiver");
// tell it to update itself.
receiver.update(text, value);
```

In this example, you use the getApplet() method to get a reference to the applet with the name receiver. Note that the object returned by getApplet() is an instance of the generic Applet class; you'll most likely want to cast that object to an instance of your subclass. Given the reference to the named applet, you can then call methods in that applet as if it were just another object in your own environment. Here, for example, if both applets have an update() method, you can tell the receiver to update itself by using the information the current applet has.

Naming your applets and then referring to them by using the methods described in this section enables your applets to communicate and stay in sync with each other, providing uniform behavior for all the applets on your page.

Networking in Java

Networking is the capability of making connections from your applet or application to a system over the network. Networking in Java involves classes in the java.net package, which provide cross-platform abstractions for simple networking operations, including connecting and retrieving files by using common Web protocols and creating basic UNIX-like sockets.

Used in conjunction with input and output streams (which you'll learn much more about next week), reading and writing files over the network becomes as easy as reading or writing to files on the local disk.

There are restrictions, of course. Java applets usually cannot read or write from the disk on the machine where the browser is running. Java applets cannot connect to systems other than the one on which they were originally stored. Even given these restrictions, you can still accomplish a great deal and take advantage of the Web to read and process information over the Net.

This section describes two simple ways you can communicate with systems on the Net:

- [ ] `openStream()`, a method that opens a connection to an URL and enables you to extract data from that connection
- [ ] The socket classes, `Socket` and `ServerSocket`, which enable you to open standard socket connections to hosts and read to and write from those connections

Opening Web Connections

Rather than asking the browser to just load the contents of a file, sometimes you might want to get ahold of that file's contents so that your applet can use them. If the file you want to grab is stored on the Web, and can be accessed using the more common URL forms (http, ftp, and so on), your applet can use the URL class to get it.

Note that for security reasons, applets by default can connect back only to the same host from which they originally loaded. This means that if you have your applets stored on a system called www.myhost.com, the only machine your applet can open a connection to will be that same host (and that same hostname, so be careful with host aliases). If the file the applet wants to retrieve is on that same system, using URL connections is the easiest way to get it.

This security restriction will change how you've been writing and testing applets up to this point. Because we haven't been dealing with network connections, we've been able to do all our testing on the local disk simply by opening the HTML files in a browser or with the appletviewer tool. You cannot do this with applets that open network connections. In order for those applets to work correctly, you must do one of two things:

- [ ] Run your browser on the same machine that your Web server is running on. If you don't have access to your Web server, you can often install and run a Web server on your local machine.
- [ ] Upload your class and HTML files to your Web server each time you want to test them. Then, instead of using Open File to test your applets, use the actual URL of the HTML file instead.

You'll know when you're not doing things right in regard to making sure your applet, and the connection it's opening, are on the same server. If you try to load an applet or a file from different servers, you'll get a security exception along with a lot of other scary error messages printed to your screen or to the Java console.

That said, let's move on to the methods and classes for retrieving files from the Web.

openStream()

The URL class defines a method called openStream(), which opens a network connection using the given URL (an HTTP connection for Web URLs, an FTP connection for FTP URLs, and so on) and returns an instance of the class InputStream (part of the java.io package). If you convert that stream to a DataInputStream (with a BufferedInputStream in the middle for better performance), you can then read characters and lines from that stream (you'll learn all about streams on Day 19, "Java Streams and I/O"). For example, these lines open a connection to the URL stored in the variable theURL, and then read and echo each line of the file to the standard output:

```
try {
    InputStream in = theURL.openStream();
    DataInputStream data = new DataInputStream(new BufferedInputStream(in);

    String line;
    while ((line = data.readLine()) != null) {
    System.out.println(line);
}
} catch (IOException e) {
    System.out.println("IO Error: " + e.getMessage());
}
```

NOTE　You need to wrap all those lines in a try...catch statement to catch IOExceptions generated. You'll learn more about IOExceptions and the try and catch statements on Day 17, "Exceptions."

Here's an example of an applet that uses the openStream() method to open a connection to a Web site, reads a file from that connection (Edgar Allen Poe's poem "The Raven"), and displays the result in a text area. Listing 14.3 shows the code; Figure 14.2 shows the result after the file has been read.

14

```
1: import java.awt.*;
2: import java.io.DataInputStream;
3: import java.io.BufferedInputStream;
4: import java.io.IOException;
5: import java.net.URL;
6: import java.net.URLConnection;
7: import java.net.MalformedURLException;
8:
9: public class GetRaven extends java.applet.Applet implements Runnable {
10:    URL theURL;
11:    Thread runner;
12:    TextArea ta = new TextArea("Getting text...");
13:
14:    public void init() {
15:     setLayout(new GridLayout(1,1));
16:
17:        // CHANGE THIS NEXT LINE BEFORE COMPILING!!!
18:        String url = "http://www.lne.com/Web/Java1.1/raven.txt";
19:        try { this.theURL = new URL(url); }
20:        catch ( MalformedURLException e) {
21:          System.out.println("Bad URL: " + theURL);
22:        }
23:        add(ta);
24:    }
25:
26:    public Insets insets() {
27:        return new Insets(10,10,10,10);
28:    }
29:
30:    public void start() {
31:      if (runner == null) {
32:         runner = new Thread(this);
33:         runner.start();
34:      }
35:    }
36:
37:    public void stop() {
38:      if (runner != null) {
39:         runner.stop();
40:         runner = null;
41:      }
42:    }
43:
44:    public void run() {
45:      URLConnection conn = null;
46:      DataInputStream data = null;
47:      String line;
48:     StringBuffer buf = new StringBuffer();
49:
50:      try {
51:        conn = this.theURL.openConnection();
52:        conn.connect();
53:       ta.setText("Connection opened...");
54:        data = new DataInputStream(new BufferedInputStream(
55:           conn.getInputStream()));
```

```
56:        ta.setText("Reading data...");
57:      while ((line = data.readLine()) != null) {
58:        buf.append(line + "\n");
59:      }
60:      ta.setText(buf.toString());
61:    }
62:    catch (IOException e) {
63:      System.out.println("IO Error:" + e.getMessage());
64:    }
65:}
66:}
```

Figure 14.2.

The GetRaven *class.*

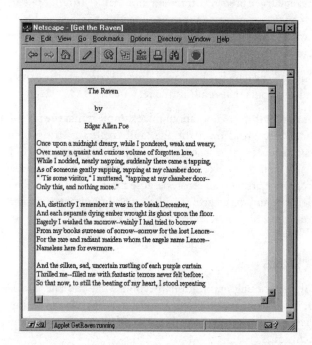

An extremely important note: If you compile this code as written, it won't work—you'll get a security exception. The reason is that this applet opens a connection to the server www.lne.com to get the file raven.txt. When you compile and run this applet, that applet isn't running on www.lne.com (unless you're me, and I already know about this problem). Before you compile this applet, make sure you change line 18 to point to a copy of raven.txt on your Web server, and install your applet and your HTML files on that same server (you can get raven.txt from the CD-ROM or from that very URL).

Alternately, you can use your browser to point to the URL http://www.lne.com/Web/Java1.1/GetRaven.html. That Web page loads this very applet and downloads the file correctly. Because both the applet and the text file are on the same server, it works just fine.

14

The init() method (lines 14 to 24) sets up the URL and the text area in which that file will be displayed. The URL could be easily passed into the applet via an HTML parameter; here, it's just hard coded for simplicity. Because it might take some time to load the file over the network, you put that routine into its own thread and use the familiar start(), stop(), and run() methods to control that thread. Inside run() (lines 44 to 64), the work takes place. Here, you initialize a bunch of variables and then open the connection to the URL (using the openStream() method in line 50). Once the connection is open, you set up an input stream in lines 51 to 55 and read from it, line by line, putting the result into an instance of StringBuffer (a string buffer is a modifiable string). I put all this work into a thread because it may take some time for the connection to open and for the file to be read—particularly across slower connections. There may be other things going on in the applet that need to take place concurrently to the file loading.

Once all the data has been read, line 60 converts the StringBuffer object into a real string and then puts that result in the text area.

One other thing to note about this example is that the part of the code that opened a network connection, read from the file, and created a string is surrounded by a try and catch statement. If any errors occur while you're trying to read or process the file, these statements enable you to recover from them without the entire program crashing (in this case, the program exits with an error, because there's little else to be done if the applet can't read the file). try and catch give you the capability of handling and recovering from errors. You'll learn more about exceptions on Day 17.

Sockets

For networking applications beyond what the URL and URLconnection classes offer (for example, for other protocols or for more general networking applications), Java provides the Socket and ServerSocket classes as an abstraction of standard TCP socket programming techniques.

NOTE

Java also provides facilities for using Datagram (UDP) sockets, but I'm not going to cover those here. See the API documentation for the java.net package if you're interested in working with datagrams.

The Socket class provides a client-side socket interface similar to standard UNIX sockets. To open a connection, create a new instance of Socket (where hostname is the host to connect to, and portnum is the port number):

```
Socket connection = new Socket(hostname, portnum);
```

If you use sockets in an applet, you are still subject to the applet security restrictions that prevent you from connecting to any system other than the same one the applet came from.

Once the socket is open, you can use input and output streams to read and write from that socket (you'll learn all about input and output streams on Day 19):

```
DataInputStream in = new DataInputStream(
new BufferedInputStream(connection.getInputStream()));
DataOutputStream out= new DataOutputStream(
new BufferedOutputStream(connection.getOutputStream()));
```

Once you're done with the socket, don't forget to close it (this also closes all the input and output streams you may have set up for that socket):

```
connection.close();
```

Server-side sockets work similarly, with the exception of the accept() method. A server socket listens on a TCP port for a connection from a client; when a client connects to that port, the accept() method accepts a connection from that client. By using both client and server sockets, you can create applications that communicate with each other over the network.

To create a server socket and bind it to a port, create a new instance of ServerSocket with the port number:

```
ServerSocket sconnection = new ServerSocket(8888);
```

To listen on that port (and to accept a connection from any clients if one is made), use the accept() method:

```
sconnection.accept();
```

Once the socket connection is made, you can use input and output streams to read from and write to the client.

In the next section, "Trivia: A Simple Socket Client and Server," we'll work through some code to implement a simple socket-based application.

Changes to Sockets for Java 1.1

In the 1.0.2 version of Java, the Socket and ServerSocket classes provide a basic abstract socket implementation. You can create new instances of these classes to make or accept connections and to pass data back and forth from a client to a server.

14

The problem comes when you try to extend or change Java's socket behavior. The `Socket` and `ServerSocket` classes in the `java.net` package are final classes, which means you cannot create subclasses of those classes (you'll learn more about finalizing classes on Day 15, "Modifiers"). To extend the behavior of the socket classes—for example, to allow network connections to work across a firewall or a proxy—you can use the abstract class `SocketImpl` and the interface `SocketImplFactory` to create a new transport-layer socket implementation. This design fits with the original goal of Java's socket classes: to allow those classes to be portable to other systems with different transport mechanisms. The problem with this mechanism is that while it works for simple cases, it prevents you from adding other protocols on top of TCP (for example, to implement an encryption mechanism such as SSL) or for having multiple socket implementations per Java runtime.

For these reasons, in Java 1.1, sockets have changed such that the `Socket` and `ServerSocket` classes are nonfinal and extendable. You can create subclasses of these classes in Java 1.1 that use either the default socket implementation or one of your own making. This allows much more flexible network capabilities in Java 1.1.

In addition, Java 1.1 has added several other new features to the `java.net` package:

☐ New options for sockets, based on BSD's socket options (for example, `TCP_NODELAY`, `IP_MULTICAST_LOOP`, `SO_BINDADDR`)

☐ Many new subclasses of the `SocketException` class, to represent network errors on a finer level of granularity than in Java 1.0.2 (for example, `NoRouteToHostException` or `ConnectException`)

For more information about all the networking changes between Java 1.02 and 1.1, see the pages at `http://java.sun.com/products/JDK/1.1/designspecs/net/index.html`.

Trivia: A Simple Socket Client and Server

To finish up the discussion on networking in Java, here's an example of a Java program that uses the Socket classes to implement a simple network-based application called Trivia.

The Trivia example works like this: The server program waits patiently for a client to connect. When a client connects, the server sends a question and waits for a response. On the other end, the client receives the question and prompts the user for an answer. The user types in an answer that is sent back to the server. The server then checks to see whether the answer is correct and notifies the user. The server follows this up by asking the client whether it wants another question. If so, the process repeats.

Designing Trivia

It's usually a good idea to perform a brief preliminary design before you start churning out code. With that in mind, let's take a look at what is required of the Trivia server and client. On the server side, you need a program that monitors a particular port on the host machine for client connections. When a client is detected, the server picks a random question and sends it to the client over the specified port. The server then enters a wait state until it hears back from the client. When it gets an answer back from the client, the server checks it and notifies the client whether it is correct or incorrect. The server then asks the client whether it wants another question, upon which it enters another wait state until the client answers. Finally, the server either repeats the process by asking another question, or it terminates the connection with the client. In summary, the server performs the following tasks:

1. Wait for a client to connect.
2. Accept the client connection.
3. Send a random question to the client.
4. Wait for an answer from the client.
5. Check the answer and notify the client.
6. Ask the client whether it wants another question.
7. Wait for an answer from the client.
8. Go back to step 3 if necessary.

The client side of this Trivia example is an application that runs from a command line (it's easier to demonstrate that way). The client is responsible for connecting to the server and waiting for a question. When it receives a question from the server, the client displays it to the user and allows the user to type in an answer. This answer is sent back to the server, and the client again waits for the server's response. The client displays the server's response to the user and allows the user to confirm whether he wants another question. The client then sends the user's response to the server and exits if the user declined any more questions. The client's primary tasks are as follows:

1. Connect to the server.
2. Wait for a question to be sent.
3. Display the question and input the user's answer.
4. Send the answer to the server.
5. Wait for a reply from the server.
6. Display the server's reply and prompt the user to confirm another question.
7. Send the user's reply to the server.
8. Go back to step 2 if necessary.

14

Implementing the Trivia Server

The heart of the Trivia example lies in the server. The Trivia server program is called
TriviaServer and is located on the CD-ROM in the file TriviaServer.java. Following are
the instance variables defined in the TriviaServer class:

```
private static final int PORTNUM = 1234;

private static final int WAITFORCLIENT = 0;

private static final int WAITFORANSWER = 1;

private static final int WAITFORCONFIRM = 2;

private String[] questions;

private String[] answers;

private ServerSocket serverSocket;

private int numQuestions;

private int num = 0;

private int state = WAITFORCLIENT;

private Random rand = new Random(System.currentTimeMillis());
```

 NOTE

I've borrowed this example from another book for the purposes of this
chapter, and some things are going to appear more complicated than
they are. In particular, don't fret too much about the fact that all those
instance variables are defined to be private; you'll learn more about that
in the next chapter.

The WAITFORCLIENT, WAITFORANSWER, and WAITFORCONFIRM variables are all state constants that
define different states the server can be in. You'll see these constants in action in a moment.
The questions and answers variables are string arrays used to store the questions and
corresponding answers. The serverSocket instance variable keeps up with the server socket
connection. numQuestions is used to store the total number of questions, while num is the
number of the current question being asked. The state variable holds the current state of the
server, as defined by the three state constants (WAITFORCLIENT, WAITFORANSWER, and
WAITFORCONFIRM). Finally, the rand variable is used to pick questions at random.

14

The `TriviaServer` constructor doesn't do much except create a `ServerSocket` rather than a `DatagramSocket`. Check it out:

```
public TriviaServer() {
super("TriviaServer");
try {
serverSocket = new ServerSocket(PORTNUM);
System.out.println("TriviaServer up and running...");
}
catch (IOException e) {
System.err.println("Exception: couldn't create socket");
System.exit(1);
}
}
```

It's the `run()` method in the `TriviaServer` class where most of the action is. The source code for the `run()` method is shown in Listing 14.4.

TYPE **Listing 14.4. The `run()` method.**

```
 1: public void run() {
 2:   Socket  clientSocket;
 3:
 4:   // Initialize the arrays of questions and answers
 5:   if (!initQnA()) {
 6:     System.err.println("Error: couldn't initialize questions and answers");
 7:     return;
 8:   }
 9:
10:   // Look for clients and ask trivia questions
11:   while (true) {
12:     // Wait for a client
13:     if (serverSocket == null)
14:       return;
15:     try {
16:       clientSocket = serverSocket.accept();
17:     }
18:     catch (IOException e) {
19:       System.err.println("Exception: couldn't connect to client socket");
20:       System.exit(1);
21:     }
22:
23:     // Perform the question/answer processing
24:     try {
25:       DataInputStream is = new DataInputStream(new
26:         BufferedInputStream(clientSocket.getInputStream()));
27:       PrintStream os = new PrintStream(new
28:         BufferedOutputStream(clientSocket.getOutputStream()), false);
29:       String inLine, outLine;
30:
31:       // Output server request
32:       outLine = processInput(null);
33:       os.println(outLine);
```

14

continues

Listing 14.4. continued

```
34:          os.flush();
35:
36:          // Process and output user input
37:          while ((inLine = is.readLine()) != null) {
38:            outLine = processInput(inLine);
39:            os.println(outLine);
40:            os.flush();
41:            if (outLine.equals("Bye."))
42:              break;
43:          }
44:
45:          // Cleanup
46:          os.close();
47:          is.close();
48:          clientSocket.close();
49:        }
50:      catch (Exception e) {
51:        System.err.println("Exception: " + e);
52:        e.printStackTrace();
53:      }
54:    }
55: }
```

The run() method first initializes the questions and answers by calling initQnA(). You'll learn about the initQnA() method in a moment. An infinite while loop is then entered that waits for a client connection. When a client connects, the appropriate I/O streams are created, and the communication is handled via the processInput() method. You'll learn about processInput() next. processInput() continually processes client responses and handles asking new questions until the client decides not to receive any more questions. This is evidenced by the server sending the string "Bye.". The run() method then cleans up the streams and client socket.

The processInput() method keeps up with the server state and manages the logic of the whole question/answer process. The source code for processInput is shown in Listing 14.5.

TYPE | **Listing 14.5. The processInput() method.**

```
1: String processInput(String inStr) {
2:    String outStr;
3:
4:    switch (state) {
5:    case WAITFORCLIENT:
6:      // Ask a question
7:      outStr = questions[num];
8:      state = WAITFORANSWER;
9:      break;
10:
```

14

```
11:   case WAITFORANSWER:
12:     // Check the answer
13:     if (inStr.equalsIgnoreCase(answers[num]))
14:       outStr = "That's correct! Want another? (y/n)";
15:     else
16:       outStr = "Wrong, the correct answer is " + answers[num] +
17:         ". Want another? (y/n)";
18:     state = WAITFORCONFIRM;
19:     break;
20:
21:   case WAITFORCONFIRM:
22:     // See if they want another question
23:     if (inStr.equalsIgnoreCase("y")) {
24:       num = Math.abs(rand.nextInt()) % questions.length;
25:       outStr = questions[num];
26:       state = WAITFORANSWER;
27:     }
28:     else {
29:       outStr = "Bye.";
30:       state = WAITFORCLIENT;
31:     }
32:     break;
33:   }
34:   return outStr;
35: }
```

The first thing to note about the processInput() method is the outStr local variable. The value of this string is sent back to the client in the run method when processInput returns. So keep an eye on how processInput uses outStr to convey information back to the client.

In FortuneServer, the state WAITFORCLIENT represents the server when it is idle and waiting for a client connection. Understand that each case statement in processInput() represents the server leaving the given state. For example, the WAITFORCLIENT case statement is entered when the server has just left the WAITFORCLIENT state. In other words, a client has just connected to the server. When this occurs, the server sets the output string to the current question and sets the state to WAITFORANSWER.

If the server is leaving the WAITFORANSWER state, it means that the client has responded with an answer. processInput() checks the client's answer against the correct answer and sets the output string accordingly. It then sets the state to WAITFORCONFIRM.

The WAITFORCONFIRM state represents the server waiting for a confirmation answer from the client. In processInput(), the WAITFORCONFIRM case statement indicates that the server is leaving the state because the client has returned a confirmation (yes or no). If the client answered yes with a y, processInput picks a new question and sets the state back to WAITFORANSWER. Otherwise, the server tells the client "Bye." and returns the state to WAITFORCLIENT to await a new client connection.

14

The questions and answers in Trivia are stored in a text file called QnA.txt, which is organized with questions and answers on alternating lines. By alternating, I mean that each question is followed by its answer on the following line, which is in turn followed by the next question. Following is a partial listing of the QnA.txt file:

```
What caused the craters on the moon?
meteorites
How far away is the moon (in miles)?
239000
How far away is the sun (in millions of miles)?
93
Is the Earth a perfect sphere?
no
What is the internal temperature of the Earth (in degrees F)?
9000
```

The initQnA() method handles the work of reading the questions and answers from the text file and storing them in separate string arrays. Listing 14.6 contains the source code for the initQnA() method.

TYPE **Listing 14.6. The initQnA() method.**

```
1: private boolean initQnA() {
2:    try {
3:      File            inFile = new File("QnA.txt");
4:      FileInputStream inStream = new FileInputStream(inFile);
5:      byte[]          data = new byte[(int)inFile.length()];
6:
7:      // Read the questions and answers into a byte array
8:      if (inStream.read(data) <= 0) {
9:        System.err.println("Error: couldn't read questions and answers");
10:       return false;
11:     }
12:
13:     // See how many question/answer pairs there are
14:     for (int i = 0; i < data.length; i++)
15:       if (data[i] == (byte)'\n')
16:         numQuestions++;
17:     numQuestions /= 2;
18:     questions = new String[numQuestions];
19:     answers = new String[numQuestions];
20:
21:     // Parse the questions and answers into arrays of strings
22:     int start = 0, index = 0;
23:     boolean isQ = true;
24:     for (int i = 0; i < data.length; i++)
25:       if (data[i] == (byte)'\n') {
26:         if (isQ) {
```

```
27:              questions[index] = new String(data, 0, start, i - start - 1);
28:              isQ = false;
29:            }
30:            else {
31:              answers[index] = new String(data, 0, start, i - start - 1);
32:              isQ = true;
33:              index++;
34:            }
35:            start = i + 1;
36:          }
37:      }
38:      catch (FileNotFoundException e) {
39:        System.err.println("Exception: couldn't find the fortune file");
40:        return false;
41:      }
42:      catch (IOException e) {
43:        System.err.println("Exception: I/O error trying to read questions");
44:        return false;
45:      }
46:
47:      return true;
48: }
```

The initQnA() method uses two arrays, and fills them with alternating strings from the QnA.txt file: first a question, then an answer, alternating until the end of the file is reached.

The only remaining method in TriviaServer is main(), and all main does is create the server object and get it started with a call to the start method:

```
public static void main(String[] args) {
TriviaServer server = new TriviaServer();
server.start();
}
```

Implementing the Trivia Client

Because the client side of the Trivia example requires the user to type in answers and receive responses back from the server, it is more straightforward to implement as a command-line application. This might not be as cute as a graphical applet, but it makes it very easy to see the communication events as they unfold. The client application is called Trivia and is located on the CD-ROM in the file Trivia.java.

The only instance variable defined in the Trivia class is PORTNUM, which defines the port number used by both the client and server. There is also only one method defined in the Trivia class: main(). The source code for the main() method is shown in Listing 14.7.

14

TYPE   **Listing 14.7. The `main()` method.**

```
1: public static void main(String[] args) {
2:    Socket           socket;
3:    DataInputStream in;
4:    PrintStream      out;
5:    String           address;
6:
7:    // Check the command-line args for the host address
8:    if (args.length != 1) {
9:      System.out.println("Usage: java Trivia <address>");
10:     return;
11:   }
12:   else
13:     address = args[0];
14:
15:   // Initialize the socket and streams
16:   try {
17:     socket = new Socket(address, PORTNUM);
18:     in = new DataInputStream(socket.getInputStream());
19:     out = new PrintStream(socket.getOutputStream());
20:   }
21:   catch (IOException e) {
22:     System.err.println("Exception: couldn't create stream socket");
23:     System.exit(1);
24:   }
25:
26:   // Process user input and server responses
27:   try {
28:     StringBuffer  str = new StringBuffer(128);
29:     String        inStr;
30:     int           c;
31:
32:     while ((inStr = in.readLine()) != null) {
33:       System.out.println("Server: " + inStr);
34:       if (inStr.equals("Bye."))
35:         break;
36:       while ((c = System.in.read()) != '\n')
37:         str.append((char)c);
38:       System.out.println("Client: " + str);
39:       out.println(str.toString());
40:       out.flush();
41:       str.setLength(0);
42:     }
43:
44:     // Cleanup
45:     out.close();
46:     in.close();
47:     socket.close();
48:   }
49:   catch (IOException e) {
50:     System.err.println("Exception: I/O error trying to talk to server");
51:   }
52: }
```

14

The first interesting thing you might notice about the main() method is that it looks for a command-line argument. The command-line argument required of the Trivia client is the address of the server, such as thetribe.com. Because this is a Java application, and not an applet, it's not enough to just connect back to the server where the applet came from—there is no default server, so you can connect to any server you want to. In the client application you'll either have to hard-code the server address or ask for it as a command-line argument. I'm not very fond of hard-coding because it requires you to recompile any time you want to change something. Hence the command-line argument!

If the server address command-line argument is valid (not null), the main() method creates the necessary socket and I/O streams. It then enters a while loop, where it processes information from the server and transmits user requests back to the server. When the server quits sending information, the while loop falls through, and the main() method cleans up the socket and streams. And that's all there is to the Trivia client!

Running Trivia

Like Fortune, the Trivia server must be running in order for the client to work. To get things started, you must first run the server by using the Java interpreter; this is done from a command line, like this:

```
java TriviaServer
```

The Trivia client is also run from a command line, but you must specify a server address as the only argument. Following is an example of running the Trivia client and connecting to the server thetribe.com:

```
java Trivia "thetribe.com"
```

After running the Trivia client and answering a few questions, you should see output similar to this:

```
Server: Is the Galaxy rotating?
yes
Client: yes
Server: That's correct! Want another? (y/n)
y
Client: y
Server: Is the Earth a perfect sphere?
no
Client: no
Server: That's correct! Want another? (y/n)
y
Client: y
Server: What caused the craters on the moon?
asteroids
```

14

```
Client: asteroids
Server: Wrong, the correct answer is meteorites. Want another? (y/n)
n
Client: n
Server: Bye.
```

Printing (Java 1.1)

A new facility in the 1.1 version of the AWT is a mechanism that allows AWT components to be printed and, for AWT-based applications, allows you to submit print jobs to the local printer in a platform-independent way.

NOTE If you're creating applets, printing is handled by the browser that contains your applet.

There are two important AWT classes that handle the ability to print AWT components (actually, one is an interface): `PrintJob` and `PrintGraphics`, both part of the `java.awt` package.

`PrintJob` is responsible for initiating, queuing, and finishing up a given print job. It's the `PrintJob` class that will initiate printing on the local system (to bring up the print dialog, if possible), find out information about the page size and resolution, and finish up once the printing is complete. To get an instance of the `PrintJob` class you first get an instance of the current toolkit, and then from there you call the `getPrintJob()` method to create a new `PrintJob` object. As arguments to the `getPrintJob()` method you'll need the parent frame to print, the name of a print job, and a properties list (if necessary). More about this later.

The second half of the printing process is the `PrintGraphics` interface, which is usually implemented in a special version of the `Graphics` object. Just as the standard graphics context allows you to paint objects on the screen, the special print graphics context allows you to print objects to a printer. To use a `PrintGraphics` object you request one using the `PrintJob` method `getGraphics()`, and then pass that object to the `print()` or `printAll()` methods, which are defined on `Component` and are, therefore, available to print an entire hierarchy of AWT components.

To print an entire AWT user interface, you'll usually call `printAll()`. The `printAll()` method, in turn, will work through the component hierarchy and call `print()` for each individual component. The default implementation of `print()` simply calls `paint()`, so what you see on the screen will be what is printed. If you want to add or override the behavior for printing, you can override `print()` to do so. Note that all the standard AWT components are printable by default, so unless you're creating your own custom components you generally won't need to do this.

In the simplest, most common case, you might create a button or menu item in your application that allows the user to print the current screen. To accomplish this, you'll use both PrintJob and a print graphics context. Listing 14.8 shows an example of how to print the current window, given a button for "Print Test".

TYPE **Listing 14.8. Queuing a Print Job.**

```
 1: public void actionPerformed(ActionEvent e) {
 2:    if (e.getSource() instanceof Button) {
 3:        PrintJob job = getToolkit().getPrintJob(this, "Print Test",
 4:            (Properties)null);
 5:        if (job != null) {
 6:            Graphics pg = job.getGraphics();
 7:            if (pg != null) {
 8:                printAll(pg);
 9:                pg.dispose();
10:            }
11:            job.end();
12:        }
13:    }
14:}
```

A lot of this code is simply boiler plate, but let's go over it so you have at least a vague idea of what's going on.

Lines 3 and 4 request a current print job from the application's current toolkit object (the toolkit object is the liaison between the cross platform parts of your application and the local window toolkit). The getPrintJob() method causes the local system to bring up a standard print dialog so your user can set any special properties for that print job. The getPrintJob() method takes three arguments:

☐ The current frame holding the screen to be printed.

☐ The name of the print job (which will appear in the local system's print queue).

☐ A Properties object representing the print job's properties. If the user changes any of the defaults in the print dialog, those properties will be stored in the Properties object you specify in this argument—you can then use that same object in later calls to PrintJob to restore those new printing properties. In this case, we're uninterested in the properties so we passed in a null object.

If the user responds to the dialog with OK or Print (anything except Cancel), you'll end up with an instance of PrintJob and printing will be all ready to go. If the user does change their mind and chooses Cancel from the dialog, you'll end up with a null object, so you'll need to test for that (as we did in line 5).

14

With the `PrintJob` object in hand the next thing to do is to get the printing graphics context. You can do that using the `getGraphics()` method (line 6). If all goes well, you'll end up with a graphics context that supports printing, which you can then pass to the `printAll()` method (line 8), which renders the page for printing. Then, finally, the `dispose()` method actually sends the page to the printer.

To finish up, call `end()` on the print job, which will clean up after the print job.

NOTE

If you're using the Beta 3 version of the 1.1 JDK on Windows, be forewarned that there's an outstanding bug where printing does not work, and this example will produce a "printing StartPage Failed" error. Newer versions of the JDK do not have this problem.

For more information about printing in the AWT, see the printing specification at `http://www.javasoft.com:80/products/JDK/1.1/docs/guide/awt/designspec/printing.html`.

Cut, Copy, and Paste (1.1 only)

In the 1.1 version of the AWT, support has been added for what is known as data transfer: the capability to cut, copy, and paste data from component to component and to other programs running on the native platform using a clipboard. Previously in the AWT, you could only copy and paste data between the components that already had basic copy and paste built into them on the native platforms (for example, text could be copied and pasted between text fields and text areas). The 1.1 version extends this capability to allow other data or objects to be transferred from one component to another.

NOTE

The concept of data transfer refers not only to cut-copy-paste, but also to drag and drop. However, only the former clipboard operations are available in the 1.1 AWT; drag and drop facilities will be added at a later time.

To be able to transfer data from one component to another, first you have to define a transferable object, and then you have to modify or create components with the capability to transfer that object.

The classes and interfaces to do this are contained in the `java.awt.datatransfer` package.

Creating Transferable Objects

A transferable object is one that can be moved from one component to another using the AWT's data transfer mechanism, and encapsulates some set of data to be transferred (for example, formatted text). More specifically, a transferable object is one that implements the Transferable interface.

When you create a transferable object, you should first decide what flavors that object will support. A *flavor* is, essentially, the format of the data that's being transferred. For example, if you copy HTML-formatted text from a browser and try to paste it in, that data could be pasted in one of several different flavors: as formatted text, as plain text, or as HTML code. Data flavors determine how the thing being copied from and the thing being pasted to negotiate how to transfer the data itself. If the source and destination of the data transfer do not support the same set of flavors, the data cannot be transferred.

Data flavors are described using MIME types, the same content negotiation mechanism used by many electronic mail programs and the World Wide Web itself. If you're unfamiliar with MIME types, RFC 1521 contains the MIME specification (which you should be able to find at any Web or FTP site that contains the various Internet RFC documents, `http://ds.internic.net/rfc/rfc1521.txt` is one example). In addition to the logical flavor name, the data flavor also has a "human-readable" flavor name, which can be translated for different international languages. Data flavors can also have a representative Java class—for example, if the data flavor is a Unicode string, the `String` class would represent that flavor. If the flavor has no class to represent it, the class `InputStream` will be used.

To create a new data flavor, you create a new instance of the `DataFlavor` class using one of these two constructors:

☐ `DataFlavor(Class, String)` creates a data flavor that represents a Java class. The `String` argument is for the human-readable flavor description. The resulting `DataFlavor` object will have a MIME type of `application/x-javaserializedobject`.

☐ `DataFlavor(String, String)` creates a data flavor that represents a MIME type, where the first argument is the MIME type and the second is the human-readable string. The class that represents this flavor will be `InputStream`.

With that data flavor object, you can query its values, or compare MIME types with other data flavor objects to negotiate how data will be transferred.

Data flavors are used by transferable objects, which are defined using the Transferable interface. A transferable object will include the data to be transferred and instances of each data flavor that represents that object. You'll also have to implement the methods `getTransferDataFlavors()`, `isDataFlavorSupported()`, and `getTransferData()` so that your transferable object can be actually negotiated and transferred (see the Transferable interface for details).

14

The class StringSelection implements a simple transferable object for transferring text strings, using both DataFlavor objects and the Transferable interface. If you're primarily concerned with copying text, StringSelection is an excellent place to start (and may be the only transferable object you need, in fact). Exploring the source for the StringSelection class will also help you figure out how transferable objects work. (You can find the source with the JDK itself, and it's also printed in the Data Transfer specification at http:// www.javasoft.com:80/products/JDK/1.1/docs/guide/awt/designspec/datatransfer.html).

Note that transferable objects are used for encapsulating data and for describing its format; they do nothing at either end to actually format that data. That's the responsibility of your program when you use the clipboard to get data from a source.

Using the Clipboard

Once you have a transferable object, you can use a clipboard to transfer that object between components and from inside Java to the native platform. Java 1.1 provides a very easy-to-use clipboard mechanism that allows you to put data on the clipboard and retrieve data from that clipboard. You can use either the single standard system clipboard, to move data to and from other programs running on the native platform, or you can use your own instances of the clipboard to create special clipboards or multiple sets of specialized clipboards.

Clipboards in Java are represented by the class Clipboard, also part of the java.awt.datatransfer package. You can get the standard system Clipboard using the getToolkit() and getSystemClipBoard() methods (as you learned in the last section, getToolkit() provides a way to access various native system capabilities), like this:

```
Clipboard clip = getToolkit().getSystemClipboard()
```

One important note for the system clipboard—currently, applets are not allowed to access the system clipboard for security reasons (there may be sensitive data contained on that clipboard). This prevents applets from being able to copy and paste anything to or from the native platform (with the exception of the capabilities which are already there such as text inside text fields and text areas). You can, however, use your own internal clipboards to copy and paste between components in an applet.

Any component that wants to use the clipboard—either to put data on the clipboard using cut or copy, or to get data from the clipboard using paste—must implement the ClipboardOwner interface. That interface has one method: lostOwnership(), which is called when some other component takes control of the clipboard.

To implement cut or copy, that is, to put data on the clipboard, perform the following steps:

1. Create an instance of your `Transferable` object to store the data to be copied.

2. Create an instance of the object that implements the `ClipboardOwner` interface (which may be the current class, or the `Transferable` object may also implement clipboard owner).

3. If you're using the system clipboard, use the `getSystemClipboard()` to get a reference to that clipboard.

3 Call the clipboard's `setContents()` method with the transferable object and the object that implements `ClipboardOwner` as arguments. With this method, your object as asserted "ownership" of the clipboard.

4. When another object takes over the clipboard, the `lostOwnership()` method will be called. You'll want to implement this method to do something when that occurs (or create an empty method if you don't care that someone else has replaced your clipboard contents).

To implement a paste operation, that is, to take data from the clipboard, complete the following steps:

1. Use the clipboard's `getContents()` method, which returns a transferable object.

2. Use the transferable object's `getTransferDataFlavors()` method to find out what flavors that transferable object supports. Determine which flavor to use.

3. Retrieve the data in the right flavor using the transferable object's `getTransferData()` method.

Here's a very simple example of an application that uses the clipboard to copy text from one text field to another (as shown in Figure 14.3). Listing 14.9 shows the code for this example.

Figure 14.3.

Testing copy and paste.

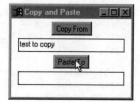

TYPE **Listing 14.9. Copy and Paste.**

```
1: import java.awt.*;
2: import java.awt.event.*;
3: import java.awt.datatransfer.*;
4:
```

continues

14

Listing 14.9. continued

```
 5: public class CopyPaste extends Frame
 6:    implements ActionListener, ClipboardOwner {
 7:    Button copy, paste;
 8:    TextField tfcopy, tfpaste;
 9:    Clipboard clip;
10:
11:    public static void main(String[] arg) {
12:       CopyPaste test = new CopyPaste();
13:       test.setSize(200,150);
14:       test.show();
15:    }
16:
17:    CopyPaste() {
18:       super("Copy and Paste");
19:       clip = getToolkit().getSystemClipboard();
20:       setLayout(new FlowLayout());
21:
22:       copy = new Button("Copy From");
23:       copy.addActionListener(this);
24:       add(copy);
25:
26:       tfcopy = new TextField("", 25);
27:       add(tfcopy);
28:
29:       paste = new Button("Paste To");
30:       paste.addActionListener(this);
31:       paste.setEnabled(false);
32:       add(paste);
33:
34:       tfpaste = new TextField("",25);
35:       add(tfpaste);
36:    }
37:
38:    public void actionPerformed(ActionEvent e) {
39:       if ((e.getSource() == copy) &&
40:          (tfcopy.getText() != null)) {
41:          String txt = tfcopy.getText();
42:          StringSelection trans = new StringSelection(txt);
43:          clip.setContents(trans,this);
44:          paste.setEnabled(true);
45:       }
46:       else if (e.getSource() == paste) {
47:          Transferable topaste = clip.getContents(this);
48:          if (topaste != null) {
49:             try {
50:                String txt = (String)topaste.getTransferData(
51:                   DataFlavor.stringFlavor);
52:                tfpaste.setText(txt);
53:                paste.setEnabled(false);
54:             }
55:             catch (Exception except) {
56:                System.out.println("Can't get data.");
57:             }
```

```
58:          }
59:       }
60:    }
61:
62:    // needed to satisfy cliboardowner inerface
63:    public void lostOwnership(Clipboard clip, Transferable contents) {
64:    }
65:}
```

Here's what's going on in this application (and note that it is an application, not an applet):

☐ The main() method (line 11) instantiates the class, sets the window size, and displays it.

☐ The constructor for the CopyPaste class sets up the layout and the components for the window. Note the call in line 19 to getSystemClipboard(), which gives us a reference to the system clipboard. Note also that the Paste To button is disabled in line 31 so that you can't paste anything unless there's something to paste.

☐ The good stuff happens when the user types something into the copy text field and clicks on the Copy From button. The actionPerformed method is called, and the first block in lines 39 through 45 is executed. That block extracts the text from the text field (line 41), creates a new transferable object from that data in line 42 (specifically, a StringSelection object), puts that object on the clipboard (line 43), and enables the Paste To button.

☐ Later on, when the Paste To button is pressed, the second half of that method is called. The first step, in line 47, is to create a new transferable object that contains the contents of the clipboard using the getContents() method

☐ If getContents() returned an object, there was something in the clipboard and we can proceed. Inside a try...catch block to catch any exceptions (usually UnknownDataFlavorExceptions, but here we'll just use any exception), we extract the string out of the transferable object (lines 50 and 51), using the getTransferData() method with the name of the data flavor (here, its the standard stringFlavor, defined by the DataFlavor class).

☐ With that text in hand, we can put it into the paste text field and disable the Paste To button once again.

☐ Note the empty definition of the lostOwnership() method in line 63; this method much be implemented to satisfy the ClipboardOwner interface, but it doesn't have to do anything. In this case, we don't care whether the application loses ownership of the clipboard—we can simply copy everything again—so we'll create an empty method here.

14

Internationalization (Java 1.1)

Internationalization is the process of creating an application, or parts of an application, that can be easily translated or used by cultures and languages other than English. Most programs—written in any programming language—are difficult to translate from one language to another. Text strings, for button labels, are often compiled into the program. Date and number formatting is often specific to English as well. For these kinds of programs, the program code usually has to be "translated" by hand by a programmer in the destination country so that the application can be understood in that country. That process of converting a program is called *localization*.

While localizing a program by translating it works well enough, it's a lot of work for the translator, and there ends up being different versions of the same program for different languages or cultures (and a lot of maintenance involved when the original program changes). It would be much easier for the translators of a program to do their job if the language and culture-specific parts of the program had been separated from other parts of that program when it was first written. With that separation, localization can mean something as simple as changing the values of a few strings.

That separation of the language and culture-specific parts of a program from the other parts is called *internationalization*, and Java 1.1 contains facilities to make it easier to create international programs. If you're working in an environment where your Java code may be used in other countries, you will most likely find yourself needing to use these facilities. It's good to think ahead each time you design a program to see when and where your code will be used.

Some parts of Java are already international—for example, the Unicode character set that Java uses allows you to represent a wide variety of international characters. Other parts, however, simply give you the ability to switch between different languages and cultures and to format data in various different ways.

Using Locales

Both internationalization and localization use the concept of a *locale* to refer to a specific set of language or cultural differences. A locale isn't necessarily a language such as French or German, although those languages are certainly locales. A locale can also imply a different culture; for example, UK English uses different number and date formatting than US English. UK English is, therefore, a locale.

When you create an international program, you'll define the current locale, and the set of locales that program supports. Then, each time the program does something that may be different in another locale—using text strings, error messages, what you print and how you print—it is based on that current locale. This architecture makes it easy to not only switch between supported locales, but also makes it easy to plug in a new locale should one be needed. Also, note that locales are not necessarily global to the entire program—different parts of the program can have different current locales.

Locales are defined in Java 1.1 by the Locale class, part of the java.util package, and each time you refer to a locale in your programs you should use instances of this class. The Locale class is simply an identifier for a specific locale, using an ISO standard mechanism for describing different locales using special codes for the country, the language, and any other variant. Table 14.1 shows the codes for various languages and countries.

Table 14.1. International Languages and Country Codes

Locale	Language	Country
da_DK	Danish	Denmark
DE_AT	German	Austria
DE_CH	German	Switzerland
DE_DE	German	Germany
el_GR	Greek	Greece
en_CA	English	Canada
en_GB	English	United Kingdom
en_IE	English	Ireland
en_US	English	United States
es_ES	Spanish	Spain
fi_FI	Finnish	Finland
fr_BE	French	Belgium
fr_CA	French	Canada
fr_CH	French	Switzerland
fr_FR	French	France
it_CH	Italian	Switzerland
it_IT	Italian	Italy
ja_JP	Japanese	Japan
ko_KR	Korean	Korea
nl_BE	Dutch	Belgium
nl_NL	Dutch	Netherlands
no_NO	Norwegian (Nynorsk)	Norway

14

continues

Table 14.1. continued

Locale	Language	Country
no_NO	B Norwegian (Bokmål)	Norway
pt_PT	Portuguese	Portugal
sv_SE	Swedish	Sweden
tr_TR	Turkish	Turkey
zh_CN	Chinese (Simplified)	China
zh_TW	Chinese(Traditional)	Taiwan

Fortunately, the `Locale` class contains several class variables which hold many of the more common locales, so often all you'll need to do is use those variables in your programs. Common locales could include `Locale.US`, `Locale.UK`, `Locale.JAPAN`, `Locale.FRENCH`, and so on (see the API documentation for the `Locale` class for details).

For each part of your program, you can figure out the current locale for yourself, or you can use the `Component` method `getLocale()` to find out what the current locale is, or `setLocale()` to set that locale (note that with `getLocale()` and `setLocale()` different components can have different locales). The default locale is `Locale.ENGLISH`.

Formatting Data Internationally

The locale object is simply a quick way of identifying a particular locale. The hard work comes when you use that locale to determine how different parts of the program will be displayed or formatted. There are two issues surrounding how locale-specific data is used:

☐ For strings and labels, there has to be a way to switch between different translations for each locale. To do this, Java provides a mechanism called *resource bundles,* which allows you to collect text strings into a single location and then dynamically select the right label.

☐ For numbers and dates, the formatting may vary from locale to locale. Java 1.1 provides a set of classes in the `java.text` package for choosing a format based on the locale. Special formatting can also be used for complex string messages, where the right values must be plugged in at runtime ("There are 15 bugs in the file `MyClass.java`," for example.)

Resource Bundles

Resource bundles are a way of organizing text strings in your program such that different strings will be used for different locales. A particular button, for example, might have a label in English, in French, in German, and so on.

Resource bundles are implemented as subclasses of the `ResourceBundle` class (part of `java.util`), and loaded into a Java program using the standard class loader. The actual filenames of the resource bundles are made up of a bundle name (for example, "labels," "messages," "errors," "menuitems," or anything else you want to use) with locale codes for the language, country, and variant, if any, appended to the name with underscores, for example, `labels_en_US` would be the filename of American English, `labels_DE` for German, or `labels_fr_CA` for Canadian French. The codes for the language, country, and variant, as in the `Locale` class, are defined by an ISO standard. To load a given bundle, you use the `ResourceBunedle.getResourceBundle()` method with the name of the bundle, the locale, and the current class loaded.

Locale-specific resources are stored within the actual bundles, and can be accessed using various methods defined by `ResourceBundle` such as `getString()`, `getObject()`, `getMenu()`, and so on.

So, for example, here's some simple code that loads a resource bundle for the current locale (using `getLocale()` to determine that locale), and then creates three buttons with labels that were stored in that bundle:

```
Locale currentLocale = getLocale();
ClassLoader loader = this.getClass().getClassLoader();
ResourceBundle labels = ResourceBundle.getResourceBundle("Labels",
    currentLocale, loader);
Button ok = new Button(labels.getString("label1"));
Button cancel = new Button(labels.getString("label2"));
```

To create a resource bundle, you create a subclass of the `ResourceBundle`, and implement the method `handleGetObject()`. Resources are generally stored as key-value pairs, and the argument to `handleGetObject()` should be the name of a key. How you store those resources in that class is up to you.

One common way to store resources might be simply as an array of key-value pairs, which makes retrieving the resources by key easy. Because this mechanism is so common, Java 1.1 provides a class to do just that: `ListResourceBundle`. To create your own resource bundles, you can just create a simple subclass of `ListResourceBundle`, define the resources as a two-dimensional array, and override the `getContents()` method to point to that array. Here's a simple example for the two buttons I used in the previous example:

```
import java.util.*;

class Labels extends ListResourceBundle {
    public Object[][] getContents() {
        return contents;
    }

    static final Object[][] contents = {
        {"label1", "OK,"},
        {"label2", "Cancel,"}
    };
}
```

14

To localize these resources, all you'd need to do is rename the class with the right locale codes, and then translate the strings "OK" and "Cancel" to the current language. The code to read the `ResourceBundle` and create the buttons will do the rest.

Note that although in this example the bundle contained strings, the `ResourceBundle` class is designed such that the values for each key can be any Java object. You could, for example, create the buttons themselves inside the resource bundle, and then simply load and use them in the main code.

International Formatting

Different locales can also determine how numbers, dates, and other messages are formatted. To handle international formatting issues, Java 1.1 provides a set of classes in the `java.text` to handle the formatting. The classes that are particularly useful are `DecimalFormat`, `DateFormat`, and `MessageFormat`.

`NumberFormat` is used to format numbers in various ways for currency, percentages, whether commas are used in thousands, positive and negative numbers, and so on.

To format a given number, you create a formatting object based on the locale and the specific format you're interested in, and then you use the `format()` method from that object to convert a value into the correctly formatted string. Here's an example for printing currency as French francs:

```
NumberFormat cfmt = NumberFormat.getDefaultCurrency(Locale.FRENCH)
System.out.println("Taxes Withheld: " + cfmt.format(taxes));
```

Date and time formatting operates in a very similar way, except the formatting class is either `DateFormat` or `SimpleDateFormat`. The latter is easier to use, and allows you to set a specific pattern, to only print, say, hours and minutes as opposed to the full date:

```
DateFormat tfmt = DateFormat.getDateFormat(
    DateFormat.DEFAULT, Locale.FRANCE);
tfmt.setPattern("hh:mm", false);
System.out.println("Time:" + fmt.format(System.currentTimeMillis()));
```

Message formatting is slightly more complex. Message formatting is used for strings which are built at runtime from several different values, for example, "Processing is 50% complete," or "There are 14 errors in the code for YourFile.java." The problem with these messages is that in different languages with different noun and pronoun order, the different values may appear in different positions in the message, which makes it difficult to simply extract the different parts of the string into a resource file.

Message formats get around this problem by using a single string with patterns to be replaced, similarly to how `printf()` works in C and C++. The message pattern can be replaced for each locale (it can be stored in a resource bundle), and the actual values can then be substituted in different orders for different patterns. Here's an example:

```
Object vals[] = new Object[3];
vals[0] = 4;
vals[1] = 56;
vals[2] = "Disk 3";
MessageFormat mfmt = new MessageFormat(
    "%0 files on %2 were processed in %1 seconds."_;
System.out.println(mfmt.format(vals, mfmt, null));
mfmt.setPattern("Disk: %2  Files: %0  Time Elapsed: %1");
System.out.println(mfmt.format(vals, mfmt, null));
```

For More Information

I've only touched on internationalization in this section; Java 1.1 contains a number of different mechanisms for handling other issues in internationalization, including sorting order for strings, character set conversions, font support for Unicode characters, and a number of other features. For more information about creating international programs, Sun has an extensive specification available for internationalization as part of the documentation for the 1.1 JDK. You can browse it online at http://www.javasoft.com:80/products/JDK/ 1.1/docs/guide/intl/index.html.

Advanced Java Topics in 1.1

When Java 1.1 was released, included were a number of advanced features for allowing Java to be used to build large-scale applications outside the framework of applets and Web browsers. These advanced features, while allowing Java and its supporting classes to become more powerful and flexible, are also extremely complex.

As you become a more sophisticated Java programmer, and particularly if you start programming Java for a living, chances are good you'll need to learn about some—or all— of these advanced features. But because this is more of an introductory book, I'm merely going to summarize what each of these advanced features are used for, instead of going into a lot of detail. Tomorrow, as you start Week 3, "Advanced Java" we'll go back to the language itself.

The advanced Java features I'll describe today are

- ☐ JavaBeans—a mechanism for developing component-based objects and connecting them together
- ☐ Java RMI (Remote Method Invocation)
- ☐ JDBC (Java Database Connections)
- ☐ Java Security

14

JavaBeans

For some time now, the software development community has been pushing the idea of reusable components. In case you've missed the hype, a component—in the generic sense, not the AWT sense—is a reusable piece of software that can be easily assembled to create applications with much greater development efficiency. This notion of reusing carefully packaged software was borrowed to some extent from the assembly-line approach that became so popular in the United States during the industrial revolution, well before the modern computer era. The idea as applied to software is to build small, reusable components once and then reuse them as much as possible, thereby streamlining the entire development process.

NEW TERM   A *software component* is a piece of software isolated into a discrete, easily reusable structure.

Although component software has its merits, fully reusable software has yet to really establish itself. This is so for a variety of reasons, not the least of which is the fact that the software industry is still very young compared to the industries carved out in the industrial revolution. It stands to reason that it should take time to iron out the kinks in the whole software-production process. (If you're like me, you'll embrace the rapid changes taking place in the software world and relish the fact that you are a part of a revolution of sorts—an information revolution. But I digress!)

Perhaps the largest difficulty component software has had to face is the wide range of disparate microprocessors and operating systems in use today. There have been a variety of reasonable attempts at component software, but they've always been limited to a specific operating system. Microsoft's VBX and OCX component architectures have had great success in the PC world, but they've done little to bridge the gap between other types of operating systems. Weighing in the amount of work required to get an inherently platform-dependent component technology running on a wide range of operating systems, it makes sense that Microsoft has focused solely on the PC market.

NOTE

Actually, Microsoft's ActiveX technology, which is based on its OCX technology, aims to provide an all-purpose component technology compatible across a wide range of platforms. However, considering the dependency of ActiveX on 32-bit Windows code, it has yet to be seen how Microsoft will solve the platform-dependency issue. Maybe they are just waiting around for everyone to switch to Windows 95/NT?

14

Prior to the explosion of the Internet, the platform-dependency issue wasn't all that big a deal. PC developers didn't necessarily care too much that their products wouldn't run on a Solaris system. Okay, some PC developers hedged their bets and ported their applications to the Macintosh platform, but most with considerable development efforts. The whole scenario changed with the operating system melting pot created by the Internet. The result was a renewed interest in developing software that everyone can use, regardless of which operating system they happen to be running. Java has been a major factor in making truly platform-independent software development a reality. However, until recently Java has not provided an answer to the issue of component software—we'll get to that in just a moment.

As if the platform-dependency issue weren't enough, some existing component technologies also suffer from having to be developed in a particular programming language or for a particular development environment. Just as platform dependency cripples components at runtime, limiting component development to a particular programming language or development environment equally cripples components at the development end. Software developers want to be able to decide for themselves which language is the most appropriate for a particular task. Likewise, developers want to be able to select the development environment that best fits their needs, rather than being forced to use one based on the constraints of a component technology. So any realistic long-term component technology must deal with both the issue of platform dependency and language dependency. This brings me to the topic at hand: JavaBeans. JavaSoft's JavaBeans technology is a component technology that answers both of these problems directly. The JavaBeans technology promises to take the component software assembly paradigm to a new level. As of this writing, the JavaBeans specification is under development with a preliminary release to follow soon after.

JavaBeans is being implemented as an architecture- and platform-independent API for creating and using dynamic Java software components. JavaBeans picks up where other component technologies have left off, using the portable Java platform as the basis for providing a complete component software solution that is readily applicable to the online world.

The Goal of JavaBeans

Following the rapid success of the Java runtime system and programming language, JavaSoft realized the importance of developing a complete component technology solution. Its answer is the JavaBeans technology, whose design goals can be summarized by the following list of requirements:

- ☐ Compact and easy to create and use
- ☐ Fully portable
- ☐ Built on the inherent strengths of Java
- ☐ Robust distributed computing mechanisms
- ☐ Support for flexible design-time component editors

14

The first requirement of JavaBeans—to be very compact—is based on the fact that the JavaBeans components will often be used in distributed environments where entire components may be transferred across a low-bandwidth Internet connection. Clearly, components must be as compact as possible to facilitate a reasonable transfer time. The second part of this goal relates to the ease with which the components are built and used. It's not such a stretch to imagine components that are easy to use, but creating a component architecture that makes it easy to build components is a different issue altogether. Existing attempts at component software have often been plagued by complex programming APIs that make it difficult for developers to create components without chronic headaches. So JavaBeans components must be not only easy to use, but also easy to develop. For you and me, this is a critical requirement because it means fewer ulcers and more time to embellish components with frilly features.

JavaBeans components are largely based on the class structure already in use with traditional Java applet programming, which is an enormous benefit to those of us heavily investing our time and energy in learning Java. JavaSoft has promised that Java applets designed around the AWT package will easily scale to new JavaBeans components. This also has the positive side effect of making JavaBeans components very compact, because Java applets are already very efficient in terms of size.

The second major goal of JavaBeans is to be fully portable; you learned the importance of this at the beginning of this lesson. JavaSoft is in the process of finalizing a JavaBeans API that defines the specific component framework for JavaBeans components. The JavaBeans API coupled with the platform-independent Java system it is based on will together comprise the platform-independent component solution alluded to earlier. As a result, developers will not need to worry about including platform-specific libraries with their Java applets. The result will be reusable components that will unify the world of computing under one happy, peaceful umbrella. (Okay, maybe that's asking a little too much—I'll settle for just being able to develop a component and have it run unmodified on any Java-supported system.)

The existing Java architecture already offers a wide range of benefits easily applied to components. One of the more important, but rarely mentioned, features of Java is its built-in class discovery mechanism, which allows objects to interact with each other dynamically. This results in a system where objects can be integrated with each other independently of their respective origins or development history. The class discovery mechanism is not just a neat feature of Java; it is a necessary requirement in any component architecture. It is fortunate for JavaBeans that this functionality is already provided by Java at no additional cost. Other component architectures have had to implement messy registration mechanisms to achieve the same result.

Another example of JavaBeans inheriting existing Java functionality is persistence, which is the capability of an object to store and retrieve its internal state. Persistence is handled automatically in JavaBeans by simply using the serialization mechanism already present in Java. Alternately, developers can create customized persistence solutions whenever necessary.

 Persistence is the capability of an object or component to store and retrieve its internal state.

 Serialization is the process of storing or retrieving information through a standard protocol.

Although not a core element of the JavaBeans architecture, support for distributed computing is a major issue with JavaBeans. Because distributed computing requires relatively complex solutions as a result of the complex nature of distributed systems, JavaBeans leverages the usage of external distributed approaches based on need. In other words, JavaBeans enables developers to use distributed computing mechanisms whenever necessary, but it doesn't overburden itself with core support for distributed computing. This may seem like the JavaBeans architects are being lazy, but, in fact, it is this very design approach that allows JavaBeans components to be very compact, because distributed computing solutions inevitably require much more overhead.

JavaBeans component developers have the option of selecting a distributed computing approach that best fits their needs. JavaSoft provides a distributed computing solution in its Remote Method Invocation (RMI) technology, but JavaBeans developers are in no way handcuffed to this solution. Other options include CORBA (Common Object Request Broker Architecture) and Microsoft's DCOM (Distributed Component Object Model), among others. The point is that distributed computing has been cleanly abstracted from JavaBeans to keep things tight while still allowing developers that require distributed support a wide range of options. The final design goal of JavaBeans deals with design-time issues and how developers build applications using JavaBeans components. The JavaBeans architecture includes support for specifying design-time properties and editing mechanisms to better facilitate visual editing of JavaBeans components. The result is that developers will be able to use visual tools to assemble and modify JavaBeans components in a seamless fashion, much the way existing PC visual tools work with components such as VBX or OCX controls. In this way, component developers specify the way in which the components are to be used and manipulated in a development environment. This feature alone will officially usher in the usage of professional visual editors and significantly boost the productivity of applications developers.

14

How JavaBeans Relates to Java

Many developers not completely familiar with the idea of software components will likely be confused by JavaBeans's relationship to Java. Hasn't Java been touted as an object-oriented technology capable of serving up reusable objects? Yes and no. Yes, Java provides a means of building reusable objects, but there are few rules or standards governing how objects interact with each other. JavaBeans builds on the existing design of Java by specifying a rich set of mechanisms for interaction between objects, along with common actions most objects will need to support, such as persistence and event handling.

The current Java component model, although not bad, is relatively limited when it comes to delivering true reusability and interoperability. At the object level, there is really no straightforward mechanism for creating reusable Java objects that can interact with other objects dynamically in a consistent fashion. The closest thing you can do in Java is to create applets and attempt to allow them to communicate with each other on a Web page, which isn't a very straightforward task. JavaBeans provides the framework by which this communication can take place with ease. Even more important is the fact that JavaBeans components can be easily tweaked via a standard set of well-defined properties. Basically, JavaBeans merges the power of full-blown Java applets with the compactness and reusability of Java AWT components, such as buttons.

JavaBeans components aren't limited to visual objects such as buttons, however. You can just as easily develop nonvisual JavaBeans components that perform some background function in concert with other components. In this way, JavaBeans merges the power of visual Java applets with nonvisual Java applications under a consistent component framework.

NOTE

A nonvisual component is any component that doesn't have visible output. When thinking of components in terms of AWT objects like buttons and menus, this may seem a little strange. However, keep in mind that a component is simply a tightly packaged program and has no specific requirement of being visual. A good example of a nonvisual component is a timer component, which fires timing events at specified intervals. Timer components are very popular in other component development environments, such as Microsoft Visual Basic.

You can use together a variety of JavaBeans components without necessarily writing any code by using visual tools. This capability to use a variety of components together regardless of their origin is an enhancement to the current Java model. You can certainly use other prebuilt objects in Java, but you must have an intimate knowledge of the object's interface.

Additionally, you must integrate the object into your code programmatically. JavaBeans components expose their own interfaces visually, providing a means to edit their properties without programming. Furthermore, using a visual editor, you can simply "drop" a JavaBeans component directly into an application without writing any code. This is an entirely new level of flexibility and reuse not previously possible in Java alone.

The JavaBeans API

Okay, I've said enough about JavaBeans from the standpoint of what it does and why it's cool. Let's focus now on some specifics regarding how all this is possible. Keep in mind that JavaBeans is ultimately a programming interface, meaning that all its features are implemented as extensions to the standard Java class library. So all the functionality provided by JavaBeans is actually implemented in the JavaBeans API. The JavaBeans API itself is a suite of smaller APIs devoted to specific functions, or services. The following is a list of the main component services in the JavaBeans API that are necessary to facilitate all the features you've been learning about today:

- ☐ GUI merging
- ☐ Persistence
- ☐ Event handling
- ☐ Introspection
- ☐ Application builder support

By understanding these services and how they work, you'll have much more insight into exactly what type of technology JavaBeans is. Each of these services is implemented in the form of smaller APIs contained within the larger JavaBeans API. The next few sections are devoted to each of these APIs and why they are necessary elements of the JavaBeans architecture.

The GUI-merging APIs provide a means for a component to merge its GUI elements with the container document, which is usually just the Web page containing the component. Most container documents have menus and toolbars that need to display any special features provided by the component. The GUI-merging APIs allow the component to add features to the container document's menu and toolbar. These APIs also define the mechanism facilitating space negotiations between components and their containers. In other words, the GUI-merging APIs also define the layout properties for components.

A container document is a document (typically HTML) containing JavaBeans components that serves as a parent for all the components it contains. Container documents typically are responsible for managing the main menu and toolbar, among other things.

14

The persistent APIs specify the mechanism by which components can be stored and retrieved within the context of a containing document. By default, components inherit the automatic serialization mechanism provided by Java. Developers are also free to design more elaborate persistence solutions based on the specific needs of their components.

The event-handling APIs specify an event-driven architecture that defines how components interact with each other. The Java AWT already includes a powerful event-handling model, which serves as the basis for the event-handling component APIs. These APIs are critical in allowing components the freedom to interact with each other in a consistent fashion.

The introspection APIs define the techniques by which components make their internal structure readily available at design time. These APIs consist of the functionality necessary to allow development tools to query a component for its internal state, including the interfaces, methods, and member variables that comprise the component. The APIs are divided into two distinct sections, based on the level at which they are being used. For example, the low-level introspection APIs allow development tools direct access to component internals, which is a function you wouldn't necessarily want in the hands of component users. This brings us to the high-level APIs. The high-level APIs use the low-level APIs to determine which parts of a component are exported for user modification. So although development tools will undoubtedly make use of both APIs, they will use the high-level APIs only when providing component information to the user.

The application builder support APIs provide the overhead necessary for editing and manipulating components at design time. These APIs are used largely by visual development tools to provide a means to visually lay out and edit components while constructing an application. The section of a component providing visual editing capabilities is specifically designed to be physically separate from the component itself. This is because standalone runtime components can be as compact as possible. In a purely runtime environment, components are transferred with only the necessary runtime component. Developers wanting to use the design-time component facilities can easily acquire the design-time portion of the component.

Had enough? Want to learn more? The JavaBeans specifications are available at the Java Web site at

```
http://www.javasoft.com:80/products/jdk/1.1/docs/guide/beans/index.html
```

Presenting JavaBeans by Michael Morrison (Sams.net Publishing, ISBN 1-57521-287-0) can also serve as a great introduction to JavaBeans and what it can do.

Security

The Java security API provides a framework for allowing Java developers to incorporate standard security mechanisms such as authentication, message digests and digital signatures into their own applications. These tools can be used to make sure that an application or its data is trustworthy, that the data hasn't been modified, and that its being used by the right people. The Java API does not, however, provide mechanisms for actual data encryption such as that provided by SSL.

Digital signatures are probably the most interesting part of the Java security API from the standpoint of the future applets, as digital signatures will eventually allow applets to break out of the security "sandbox." You've already had a glimpse at digital signatures as part of Day 8, "Java Applet Basics." As part of the Java secutity API, Java 1.1 provides the capability to generate public and private keys, to digitally sign JAR files, and to verify that a digital signature matches the key that signed it. The Java 1.1 security API does not provide an infrastructure for distributing those keys (currently you must download them by hand); this mechanism will need to be built into the browser, and the tools for the process will need to become easier to use.

A second feature of the security API is the message digest, which verifies that the data in a class or other file is unmodified from its original state. Message digests, sometimes called digital fingerprints, can be used to prevent data from being modified by other unauthorized parties (or at least letting you know that someone has modified the data) without the original author's approval. The security API provides message digests in MD2, MD5, and SHA format.

And, finally, access control lists (ACLs) can be used to control who has access to a particular class or document, and the level of access they have. An ACL for a given document describes which users or groups have access to a particular document, and precisely the kinds of permissions they have (for example, a group of users could be able to read a document, but only a few can write to it).

The Java security API consists of three packages, all under the `java.security` package:

- [ ] `java.security`: classes for handling digital signatures, message digests, key management, and tying it all together with security managers
- [ ] `java.security.acl`: classes for creating and managing ACLs
- [ ] `java.security.interfaces`: a set of interfaces for managing DSA keys

14

RMI (Remote Method Invocation)

RMI is used to create Java applications that can talk to other Java applications over a network. Or, to be more specific, RMI allows a Java application to call methods and access variables inside another Java application, which may be running in different Java environments or different systems altogether, and to pass objects back and forth over a network connection. RMI is a more sophisticated mechanism for communicating between distributed Java objects than a simple socket connection would be, because the mechanisms and protocols by which you communicate between objects are defined and standardized. You can talk to another Java program using RMI without having to know beforehand what protocol to speak to or how to speak it.

NOTE

> Another form of communicating between objects is called RPC (remote procedure calls), where you can call methods or execute procedures in other programs over a network connection. While RPC and RMI have a lot in common, the major difference is that RPC sends only procedure calls over the wire, with the arguments either passed along or described in such a way that they can be reconstructed at the either end. RMI actually passes whole objects back and forth over the Net, and is therefore better suited for a fully object-oriented distributed object model.

While the concept of RMI may bring up visions of objects all over the world merrily communicating with each other, most commonly RMI is used in a more traditional client/server situation: a single server application receives connections and requests from a number of clients. RMI is simply the mechanism by which the client and server communicate.

The RMI Architecture

The goals for RMI were to integrate a distributed object model into Java without disrupting the language or the existing objects model, and to make interacting with a remote object as easy as interacting with a local one. For example, you should be able to use remote objects in precisely the same ways as local objects (assign them to variables, pass them as arguments to methods, and so on), and calling methods in remote objects should be accomplished in the same way as local calls. In addition, however, RMI includes more sophisticated mechanisms for calling methods on remote objects to pass whole objects or parts of objects either by reference or by value, as well as additional exceptions for handling network errors that may occur while a remote operation is occurring.

To accomplish all these goals, RMI has several layers, and a single method call crosses many of these layers to get where its going (see Figure 14.4). There are actually three layers:

☐ The "stubs" and "skeletons" layers on the client and server, respectively. These layers behave as surrogate objects on each side, hiding the "remoteness" of the method call from the actual implementation classes. So, for example, in your client application you can call remote methods in precisely the same way as you call local methods; the stub object is a local surrogate for the remote object.

☐ The "Remote Reference Layer," which handles packaging of a method call and its parameters and return values for transport over the network.

☐ The transport layer, which is the actual network connection from one system to another.

Figure 14.4.

RMI Layers.

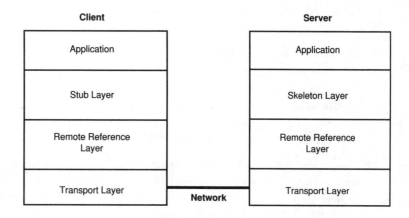

Having three layers for RMI allows each layer to be independently controlled or implemented. Stubs and skeletons allow the client and server classes to behave as if the objects they were dealing with were local, and to use exactly the same Java language features to access those objects. The Remote Reference Layer separates the remote object processing into its own layer which can then be optimized or reimplemented independently of the applications which depend on it. And, finally, the network transport later is used independently of the other two so that you can use different kinds of socket connections for RMI (TCP, UDP, or TCP with some other protocol such as SSL).

When a client application makes a remote method call, the call passes to the stub to the reference layer, which packages the arguments, if necessary, and then passes it via the network layer to the server, where the reference later on the server side unpackages the arguments and passes them to the skeleton and then to the server implementation. The return values for the method call then take the reverse trip back to the client side.

14

The packaging and passing of method arguments is one of the more interesting aspects of RMI, as objects have to be converted into something that can be passed over the network. This conversion is called serialization, and you'll learn more about it on Day 19. As long as an object can be serialized, RMI can use it as a method parameter or a return value. Serializeable objects include all the Java primitive types, remote Java objects, and any other object that implements the Serializeable interface (which includes many of the classes in the standard 1.1 JDK, such as all the AWT components).

Remote Java objects used as method parameters or return values are passed by reference, just as they would be locally. Other objects, however, are copied. Note that this behavior will affect how you write your Java programs when they use remote method calls—you cannot, for example, pass an array as an argument to a remote method, have the remote object change that array, and expect the local copy to be modified. This is different than how local objects behave, where all objects are passed as references.

Creating RMI Applications

To create an application that uses RMI, you use the classes and interfaces defined by the java.rmi packages, which includes java.rmi.server, for server-side classes; java.rmi.registry, which contains the classes for locating and registering RMI servers on a local system; and java.rmi.dgc, for garbage collection of distributed objects. The java.rmi package itself contains the general RMI interfaces, classes, and exceptions.

To implement an RMI-based client-server application, you first define an interface that contains all the methods your remote object will support. The methods in that interface must all include a throws RemoteException statement, which will handle potential network problems which may prevent the client and server from communicating.

The next step is to implement the remote interface in a server-side application, which will usually extend the UnicastRemoteObject class. Inside that class, you implement the methods in the remote interface, and also create and install a security manager for that server (to prevent random clients from connecting and making unauthorized method calls). You can, of course, configure the security manager to allow or disallow various operations. In the server application you'll also "register" the remote application, which binds it to a host and port.

On the client side, you implement a simple application that uses the remote interface, and calls methods in that interface. A class called Naming (in java.rmi) allows the client to transparently connect to the server.

With the code written, you can compile it using the standard Java compiler, but there's one other step: You'll use the rmic program to generate the stubs and skeletons layers so that RMI can actually work between the two sides of the process.

And, finally, the `rmiregistry` program is used to connect the server application to the network itself and bind it to a port so that remote connections can be made.

This is, of course, very much an oversimplification of the process you'll use to create an RMI-based application. For more information on RMI and how to use the RMI classes, a good place to start is the information on JavaSoft's Web site at

`http://www.javasoft.com:80/products/JDK/1.1/docs/guide/rmi/index.html`

JDBC (Java Database Connectivity)

JDBC, the Java Database Connectivity API, defines a structured interface to SQL (Structured Query Language) databases, which is the industry standard approach to accessing relational databases. By supporting SQL, JDBC enables developers to interact and support a wide range of databases. This means that the specifics of the underlying database platform are pretty much irrelevant when it comes to JDBC, which is very good news to Java developers.

NEW TERM   *SQL databases* are databases built on the SQL standard, which is a widely accepted standard that defines a strict protocol for accessing and manipulating data.

The JDBC API's approach to accessing SQL databases is comparable to existing database development techniques, so interacting with an SQL database using JDBC isn't all that much different than interacting with an SQL database using traditional database tools. This should give Java programmers who already have some database experience confidence that they can hit the ground running with JDBC. The JDBC API has already been widely endorsed by industry leaders, including some development-tool vendors who have announced future support for JDBC in their development products.

The JDBC API includes classes for common SQL database constructs such as database connections, SQL statements, and result sets. JDBC Java programs have the capability to use the familiar SQL programming model of issuing SQL statements and processing the resulting data. The JDBC API is largely dependent on a driver manager that supports multiple drivers connecting to different databases. JDBC database drivers can be either written entirely in Java or implemented using native methods to bridge Java applications to existing database access libraries.

JDBC also includes a bridge between JDBC and ODBC, Microsoft's common interface for accessing SQL databases. The JDBC-ODBC bridge allows JDBC drivers to be used as ODBC drivers.

14

The JDBC classes are part of Java 1.1 as the `java.sql` package, and includes classes for managing drivers, establishing connections with databases, constructing SQL queries, and dealing with the results.

JavaSoft's Web site contains extensive information and specification about JDBC at

```
http://www.javasoft.com:80/products/JDK/1.1/docs/guide/jdbc/index.html
```

Summary

Congratulations! Take a deep breath—you're finished with Week 2. This week has been full of useful information about creating applets and using the Java AWT classes to display, draw, animate, process input, and create fully fledged graphical interfaces in your applets.

Today we finished up the week by learning about applets with a number of different topics. We started with some simple applet tricks for displaying status lines, recording information about an applet itself, and for creating Web links inside applets.

Then we moved to a discussion on networking in Java, and you learned about the URL class, the `openStream()` method, and about using network sockets. We also worked through an application that creates a client and server side and interacts between them with TCP sockets.

With networking out of the way, the last part of this chapter was dedicated to Java 1.1 issues, including using clipboard operations (cut, copy, paste), and internationalizing your Java programs. Finally, we ended with an overview of some of the advanced Java APIs including JavaBeans, RMI, Security, and JDBC.

Next week, we'll get back to Java itself, and cover some of the advanced parts of the language we've only slightly touched on this week and the last, including creating public and private classes, methods and variables, packages, interfaces, using threads, exceptions, and the various I/O classes Java provides.

Q&A

Q How can I mimic an HTML form submission in a Java applet?

A Currently, applets make it difficult to do this. The best (and easiest way) is to use GET notation to get the browser to submit the form contents for you.

HTML forms can be submitted in two ways: by using the GET request, or by using POST. If you use GET, your form information is encoded in the URL itself, something like this:

```
http://www.blah.com/cgi-bin/myscript?foo=1&bar=2&name=Laura
```

Because the form input is encoded in the URL, you can write a Java applet to mimic a form, get input from the user, and then construct a new URL object with the form data included on the end. Then just pass that URL to the browser by using `getAppletContext()`, `showDocument()`, and the browser will submit the form results itself. For simple forms, this is all you need.

Q How can I do POST form submissions?

A You'll have to mimic what a browser does to send forms using POST. Open a socket to the server and send the data, which looks something like this (the exact format is determined by the HTTP protocol; this is only a subset of it):

```
POST /cgi-bin/mailto.cgi HTTP/1.0
Content-type: application/x-www-form-urlencoded
Content-length: 36

{your encoded form data here}
```

If you've done it right, you get the CGI form output back from the server. It's then up to your applet to handle that output properly. Note that if the output is in HTML, there really isn't a way to pass that output to the browser that is running your applet yet. This capability may end up in future Java releases. If you get back an URL, however, you can redirect the browser to that URL.

Q I can't get the GetRaven example to work. The errors keep mentioning security exceptions.

A The easiest way to get the GetRaven example to work is to presume that the code is correct and to view the applet on the Web at `http://www.lne.com/Web/Java1.1/GetRaven.html`. If you really want to get it to work yourself, you must do four things:

☐ Get a copy of the `raven.tx` file from the CD-ROM for this book or from `http://www.lne.com/Web/Java1.1/raven.txt`.

☐ Upload that file to a Web server. Note the URL of that file once it's available on that server

☐ Change the line in `GetRaven.java` that refers to the URL of the `raven.txt` file—line 16 in the example—to point to your version of `raven.txt`. Compile the Java class.

☐ Install the Java applet on the same Web server as the `raven.txt` file. (You'll also need to construct an HTML file to point to that applet.)

As long as both the `raven.txt` file and the applet are on the same Web server—and they are installed on a Web server, not on the local disk—everything should work. You cannot use separate servers for the applet and the class file, nor can you use file URLs. Both files must be located on a Web server.

14

Q `showStatus()` doesn't work in my browser. How can I give my readers status information?

A As you learned in the section on `showStatus()`, whether or not a browser supports `showStatus()` is up to that browser. If you must have status-like behavior in your applet, consider creating a status label in the applet itself that is updated with the information you need to present.

Q I've been trying to communicate between two applets in my Web page using the `getAppletContext()` and `getApplet()` methods. My applets keep crashing with `NullPointerException` errors. What does this mean?

A The mechanism I described for communicating between applets is how Sun and the Java class library says it's supposed to work. However, like `showStatus()`, whether or not a browser implements that mechanism, or implements it correctly, depends on that browser. Versions of Netscape before 3.0 and Internet Explorer both have strange problems with inter-applet communication.

Q The cut/copy/paste stuff in 1.1 is just fine, but I want to do drag and drop to move data from one component to another. Other than writing a lot of code myself, what can I do?

A Sun has a drag-and-drop facility planned, and it will be implementing using the same mechanism that cut/copy/paste uses. However, drag-and-drop facilities didn't make it into Java 1.1, so you'll have a wait a bit longer.

Check out the data transfer specification for more information: `http://www.javasoft.com:80/products/JDK/1.1/docs/guide/awt/designspec/datatransfer.html`.

14

Advanced Java

Day 15

Modifiers

by Laura Lemay and Charles L. Perkins

Here at the start of Week 3, you've probably grasped the basics of the Java language from Week 1, and you've applied them fairly often to create applets in Week 2. You can stop here, if you like, and go on your merry way, knowing enough Java to get by.

Week 3 extends what you already know. In this week, you'll learn more about advanced Java concepts such as access control and packages, and you'll learn techniques for structuring large programs in an efficient object-oriented way so your code can be more easily maintained and extended or, if you so choose, easily reused by other people.

Today we'll start with advanced Java language concepts for organizing and designing individual classes:

- [ ] What a modifier is and how it's used
- [ ] Controlling access to methods and variables from outside a class to better encapsulate your code
- [ ] Using a special case of controlling access to methods and variables: instance variable accessor methods
- [ ] Using `class` variables and methods to store class-specific attributes and behavior
- [ ] Finalizing classes, methods, and variables so their values or definitions cannot be subclasses or overridden
- [ ] Creating abstract classes and methods for factoring common behavior into superclasses

Modifiers

The techniques for programming you'll learn today involve different strategies and ways of thinking about how a class is organized. But the one thing all these techniques have in common is that they all use special modifier keywords in the Java language.

In Week 1, you learned how to define classes, methods, and variables in Java. Modifiers are keywords you add to those definitions to change their meaning. Classes, methods, and variables with modifiers are still classes, methods, and variables, but the modifiers change their behavior or how Java treats those elements.

 Modifiers are special language keywords that modify the definition (and the behavior) of a class, method, or variable.

 You've already learned about a few of these modifiers earlier in the book, but here we'll talk about them in detail so you can get the bigger picture of why modifiers work the way they do.

The Java language has a wide variety of modifiers, including

- [ ] Modifiers for controlling access to a class, method, or variable: `public`, `protected`, and `private`
- [ ] The `static` modifier for creating class methods and variables
- [ ] The `abstract` modifier, for creating abstract classes and methods
- [ ] The `final` modifier, for finalizing the implementations of classes, methods, and variables

☐ The synchronized and volatile modifiers, which are used for threads and which you'll learn more about on Day 18, "Multithreading"

☐ The native modifier, which is used for creating native methods, which you'll learn about on Day 21, "Under the Hood"

Some modifiers, as you can see, can apply only to classes and methods or only to methods and variables. For each of the modifiers, however, to use them you put them just previous to the class, method, or variable definition, as in the following examples:

```
public class MyApplet extends Java.applet.Applet { ... }

private boolean engineState;

static final double pi = 3.141559265

protected static final int MAXNUMELEMENTS = 128;

public static void main(String args[]) { ...}
```

The order of modifiers is irrelevant to their meaning—your order can vary and is really a matter of taste. Pick a style and then be consistent with it throughout all your classes. Here is the usual order:

```
<access> static abstract synchronized volatile final native
```

In this definition, <access> can be public, protected, or private (but no more than one of them).

All the modifiers are essentially optional; none have to appear in a declaration. Good object-oriented programming style, however, suggests adding as many as are needed to best describe the intended use of, and restrictions on, the thing you're declaring. In some special situations (inside an interface, for example, as described tomorrow), certain modifiers are implicitly defined for you, and you needn't type them—they will be assumed to be there.

Controlling Access to Methods and Variables

The most important modifiers in the language, from the standpoint of class and object design, are those that allow you to control the visibility of, and access to, variables and methods inside your classes.

Why Access Control Is Important

Why would you care about controlling access to methods and variables inside your classes? If you remember way back to the beginning of this book, I used the analogy of the PC—how you can buy different PC components and put them all together so that they interact to create a larger system.

Each component in that PC system works in a particular way and has a specific way of interacting with the other components in the system. For example, a video card plugs into your motherboard using a standard socket and plug arrangement, as does your monitor to the back of the card. And then your computer can talk the right software language through the card to get bits up on the screen.

The video card itself has a whole lot of other internal features and capabilities beyond this basic hardware and software interface. But as a user or consumer of the card, I don't need to know what every single chip does, nor do I need to touch them in order to get the card to work. Given the standard interfaces, the card figures everything out and does what it needs to do internally. And, in fact, the manufacturer of the card most likely doesn't want me to go in and start mucking with individual chips or capabilities of the card, because I'm likely to screw something up. It's best if I just stick to the defined interface and let the internal workings stay hidden.

Classes and objects are the same way. While a class may define lots of methods and variables, not all of them are useful to a consumer of that class, and some may even be harmful if they're not used in the way they were intended to be used.

Access control is about controlling visibility. When a method or variable is visible to another class, its methods can reference (call, or modify) that method or variable. Protecting those methods and instance variables limits the visibility and the use of those methods and variables (and also limits what you have to document!). As a designer of a class or an entire hierarchy of classes, therefore, it's a good idea to define what the external appearance of a class is going to be, which variables and methods will be accessible for other users of that class, and which ones are for internal use only. This is called *encapsulation* and is an important feature of object-oriented design.

NEW TERM   *Encapsulation* is the process of hiding the internal parts of an object's implementation and allowing access to that object only through a defined interface.

You may note that up to this point we haven't done very much of this in any of the examples; in fact, just about every variable and method we've created has been fairly promiscuous and had no access control whatsoever. The reason I approached the problem in this way is that it makes for simpler examples. As you become a more sophisticated programmer and create Java programs with lots of interrelated classes, you'll find that adding features such as encapsulation and protecting access to the internal workings of your classes makes for better-designed programs overall.

The Four Ps of Protection

The Java language provides four levels of protection for methods and instance variables: public, private, protected, and package (actually, the latter isn't an explicit form of Java protection, but I've included it here because it's nicely alliterative). Before applying protection levels to your own code, you should know what each form means and understand the fundamental relationships that a method or variable within a class can have to the other classes in the system.

NOTE
> You can also protect entire classes using these modifiers. But class protection applies better once you know what packages are, so we'll postpone talking about that until tomorrow.

Package Protection

The first form of protection we'll talk about is the one you've been unconsciously using all this time: what's called *package protection*. In C, there's the notion of hiding a name so that only the functions within a given source file can see it. Java doesn't have this kind of control; names will be happily found in other source files as long as Java knows where to find them. Instead of file-level protection, Java has the concept of packages, which, as you learned on Day 2, "Object-Oriented Programming and Java," and will learn a whole lot more about tomorrow, are a group of classes related by purpose or function.

Methods and variables with package protection are visible to all other classes in the same package, but not outside that package. This is the kind of protection you've been using up to this point, and it's not much protection at all. Much of the time you'll want to be more explicit when you define the protection for that class's methods and variables.

NEW TERM *Package protection*, the default level of protection, means that your methods and variables are accessible to all the other classes in the same package.

Package protection isn't an explicit modifier you can add to your method or variable definitions; instead, it's the default protection you get when you don't add any protection modifiers to those definitions.

NOTE
> You may not think you've been using packages at all up to this point, but actually, you have. In Java, if you don't explicitly put a class into a package, it'll be included in a default package that also includes all the

other classes that aren't in a specific package. While not defining a class to be in a package works for simple examples, it's better if you just create packages instead.

Private

From the default protection you get with package protection, you can either become more restrictive or more loose in how you control the visibility and access to your methods and variables. The most restrictive form of protection is `private`, which limits the visibility of methods and instance variables to the class in which they're defined. A private instance variable, for example, can be used by methods inside the same class, but cannot be seen or used by any other class or object. Private methods, analogously, can be called by other methods inside that same class, but not by any other classes. In addition, neither private variables nor private methods are inherited by subclasses.

NEW TERM *Private protection* means that your methods and variables are accessible only to other methods in the same class.

To create a private method or instance variable, add the `private` modifier to its definition:

```
class  Writer {
    private boolean writersBlock = true;
    private String mood;
    private int income = 0;

    private void getIdea(Inspiration in) {
        . . .
    }

    Book createBook(int numDays, long numPages) {
        ...
    }
}
```

In this code example, the internal data to the class `Writer` (the variables `writersBlock`, `mood`, and `income` and the method `getIdea()`) is all private. The only method accessible from outside the `Writer` class is the `createBook()` method. `createBook()` is the only thing other objects (editor objects, perhaps?) can ask the `Writer` object to do; the other bits of data are implementation details that may affect how the book is written, but don't otherwise need to be visible or accessible from other sources.

The rule of thumb for private protection is that any data or behavior internal to the class that other classes or subclasses should not be touching should be private. Judicious use of private variables and methods is how you limit the functionality of a class to only those features you want visible outside that class—as with the example of the PC components. Remember that an object's primary job is to encapsulate its data—to hide it from the world's sight and limit its manipulation. Encapsulation separates design from implementation, minimizes the amount of information one class needs to know about another to get its job done, and reduces the extent of the code changes you need to make if your internal implementation changes. Also, by separating the public interface from the private implementation, your class's interface becomes more abstract—that is, more general purpose and more easily used for other purposes. Subclasses of your class can override the more abstract behavior of your public interface with their own private implementations.

In addition to picking and choosing which methods you'll want to keep private and which will be accessible to others, a general rule of thumb is that all the instance variables in a class should be private, and you should create special nonprivate methods to get or change those variables. You'll learn more about this rule and why it's important a little later, in the section "Instance Variable Protection and Accessor Methods."

Public

The diametric opposite of private protection, and the least restrictive form of protection, is public. A method or variable that is declared with the `public` modifier is accessible to the class in which it's defined, all the subclasses of that class, all the classes in the package, and any other classes outside that package, anywhere in the entire universe of Java classes.

NEW TERM *Public protection* means that your methods and variables are accessible to other methods anywhere inside or outside the current class or package.

Indicating that a method or variable is public isn't necessarily a bad thing. Just as hiding the data that is internal to your class using `private` helps encapsulate an object, using public methods defines precisely what the interface to instances of your class is. If you expect your classes to be reused by other programmers in other programs, the methods that they'll be using to use your class should be public.

In many ways, public protection is very similar to the default package protection. Both allow methods and variables to be accessed by other classes in the same package. The difference occurs when you create packages of classes. Variables and methods with package protection can be used in classes that exist in the same package. But if someone imports your class into his own program from outside your package, those methods and variables will not be accessible unless they have been declared public. Once again, you'll learn more about packages tomorrow.

Public declarations work just like private ones; simply substitute the word `public` for `private`.

Protected

The final form of protection available in Java concerns the relationship between a class and its present and future subclasses declared inside or outside a package. These subclasses are much closer to a particular class than to any other "outside" classes for the following reasons:

☐ Subclasses usually "know" more about the internal implementation of a superclass.

☐ Subclasses are often written by you or by someone to whom you've given your source code.

☐ Subclasses frequently need to modify or enhance the representation of the data within a parent class.

To support a special level of visibility reserved for subclasses somewhat less restrictive than private, Java has an intermediate level of access between package and private called, appropriately, *protected*. Protected methods and variables are accessible to any class inside the package, as they would be if they were package protected, but those methods and variables are *also* available to any subclasses of your class that have been defined outside your package.

 Protected protection means that your methods and variables are accessible to all classes inside the package, but only to subclasses outside the package.

 In C++, the `protected` modifier means that only subclasses can access a method or variable, period. Java's meaning of protected is slightly different, also allowing any class inside the package to access those methods and variables.

Why would you need to do this? You may have methods in your class that are specific to its internal implementation—that is, not intended to be used by the general public—but that would be useful to subclasses for their own internal implementations. In this case, the developer of the subclass—be it you or someone else—can be trusted to be able to handle calling or overriding that method.

For example, let's say you had a class called `AudioPlayer`, which plays a digital audio file. `AudioPlayer` has a method called `openSpeaker()`, which is an internal method that interacts with the hardware to prepare the speaker for playing. `openSpeaker()` isn't important to anyone outside the `AudioPlayer` class, so at first glance you might want to make it private. A snippet of `AudioPlayer` might look something like this:

```
class AudioPlayer {

  private boolean openSpeaker(Speaker sp_ {
     // implementation details
  }
}
```

 15

This works fine if AudioPlayer isn't going to be subclassed. But what if you were going to create a class called StereoAudioPlayer that is a subclass of AudioPlayer? This class would want access to the openSpeaker() method so that it can override it and provide stereo-specific speaker initialization. You still don't want the method generally available to random objects (and so it shouldn't be public), but you want the subclass to have access to it—so protected is just the solution.

TECHNICAL NOTE

In versions of Java and the JDK up to 1.0.1, you could use private and protected together to create yet another form of protection that would restrict access to methods or variables solely to subclasses of a given class. As of 1.0.2, this capability has been removed from the language.

A Summary of Protection Forms

The differences between the various protection types can become very confusing, particularly in the case of protected methods and variables. Table 15.1, which summarizes exactly what is allowed where, will help clarify the differences from the least restrictive (public) to the most restrictive (private) forms of protection.

Table 15.1. Different protection schemes.

Visibility	public	protected	package	private
From the same class	yes	yes	yes	yes
From any class in the same package	yes	yes	yes	no
From any class outside the package	yes	no	no	no
From a subclass in the same package	yes	yes	yes	no
From a subclass outside the same package	yes	yes	no	no

Method Protection and Inheritance

Setting up protections in new classes with new methods is easy; you make your decisions based on your design and apply the right modifiers. When you create subclasses and override other methods, however, you have to take into account the protection of the original method.

The general rule in Java is that you cannot override a method and make the new method more private than the original method (you can, however, make it more public). More specifically, the following rules for inherited methods are enforced by Java:

- Methods declared `public` in a superclass must also be `public` in all subclasses (this, by the way, is the reason most of the applet methods are `public`).

- Methods declared `protected` in a superclass must either be `protected` or `public` in subclasses; they cannot be `private`.

- Methods declared `private` are not inherited and therefore this rule doesn't apply.

- Methods declared without protection at all (the implicit package protection) can be declared more `private` in subclasses.

Instance Variable Protection and Accessor Methods

A good rule of thumb in object-oriented programming is that unless an instance variable is constant it should almost certainly be `private`. But, I hear you say, if instance variables are private, how can they be changed from outside the class? They can't. That's precisely the point. Instead, if you create special methods that indirectly read or change the value of that instance variable, you can much better control the interface of your classes and how those classes behave. You'll learn about how to do this later in this section.

Why Nonprivate Instance Variables Are a Bad Idea

In most cases, having someone else accessing or changing instance variables inside your object isn't a good idea. Take, for example, a class called `Circle`, whose partial definition looks like this:

```
class Circle {
    int x, y, radius;

    Circle(int x, int y, int radius) {
        ...
    }

    void draw() {
        ...
    }
}
```

The `Circle` class has three instance variables: for the x and y position of the center point, and of the radius. A constructor builds the circle from those three values, and the `draw()` method draws the circle on the screen. So far, so good, right?

So let's say you have a `Circle` object created and drawn on the screen. Then some other object comes along and changes the value of `radius`. Now what? Your circle doesn't know that the radius has changed. It doesn't know to redraw itself to take advantage of the new size of the circle. Changing the value of an instance variable doesn't in itself trigger any methods. You have to rely on the same random object that changed the radius to also call the draw() method. And that overly complicates the interface of your class, making it more prone to errors.

Another example of why it's better not to make instance variables publicly accessible is that it's not possible to prevent a nonconstant instance variable from being changed. In other words, you could create a variable that you'd intended to be read-only, and perhaps your program was well mannered and didn't go about changing that variable randomly—but because the variable is there and available someone else may very well change it without understanding your methodology.

Why Accessor Methods Are a Better Idea

If all your instance variables are private, how do you give access to them to the outside world? The answer is to write special methods to read and change that variable (one for reading the value of the variable, one for changing it) rather than allowing it to be read and changed directly. These methods are sometimes called accessor methods, mutator methods (for changing the variable), or simply getters and setters.

 Accessor methods are special methods you implement to indirectly modify otherwise private instance variables.

Having a method to change a given instance variable means you can control both the value that variable is set to (to make sure it's within the boundaries you expect), as well as perform any other operations that may need to be done if that variable changes, for example, to redraw the circle.

Having two methods for reading and changing the variable also allows you to set up different protections for each. The method to read the value, for example, could be public, whereas the method to change the value can be private or protected, effectively creating a variable that's read-only except in a few cases (which is different from constant, which is read-only in all cases).

Using methods to access an instance variable is one of the most frequently used idioms in object-oriented programs. Applying it liberally throughout all your classes repays you numerous times with more robust and reusable programs.

Creating Accessor Methods

Creating accessor methods for your instance variables simply involves creating two extra methods for each variable. There's nothing special about accessor methods; they're just like any other method. So, for example, here's a modified Circle class that has three private instance variables: x, y, and radius. The public getRadius() method is used to retrieve the value of the radius variable, and the setRadius() method is used to set it (and update other parts of the class that need to be updated at the same time):

```
class Circle {
   private int x, y radius;

   public int getRadius() {
     return radius;
   }

   public int setRadius(int value) {
       radius = value;
       draw();
       doOtherStuff();
       return radius;
   }

     ....

}
```

In this modified example of the Circle class, the accessor methods for the instance variable radius have the words set and get appended with the name of the variable. This is a naming convention popular among many programmers for accessor methods, so you always know which methods do what and to which variable. To access or change the value of the instance variable, therefore, you'd just call the methods setRadius() and getRadius(), respectively:

```
theCircle.getRadius(); //get the value
theCircle.setRadius(4); //set the value (and redraw, etc)
```

Another convention for naming accessor methods is to use the same name for the methods as for the variable itself. In Java, it is legal for instance variables and methods to have the same name; Java knows from how they are used to perform the right operation. While this does make accessor methods shorter to type (no extra "set" or "get" to type at the beginning of each variable), there are two problems with using this convention:

☐ The fact that methods and variables can have the same names is a vague point in the Java specification. If someday this becomes more clarified and they cannot have the same names, you will have to change your code to fix the problem.

☐ I find that using the same name for instance variables and methods makes my code more difficult to read and understand than using a more explicit name.

Which convention you use is a question of personal taste. The most important thing is to choose a convention and stick with it throughout all your classes so that your interfaces are consistent and understandable.

Using Accessor Methods

The idea behind declaring instance variables private and creating accessor methods is so that external users of your class will be forced to use the methods you choose to modify your class's data. But the benefit of accessor methods isn't just for use by objects external to yours; they're also there for *you*. Just because you have access to the actual instance variable inside your own class doesn't mean you can avoid using accessor methods.

Consider that one of the good reasons to make instance variables private is to hide implementation details from outside your object. Protecting a variable with accessor methods means that other objects don't need to know about anything other than the accessor methods—you can happily change the internal implementation of your class without wreaking havoc on everyone who's used your class. The same is true of your code inside that class; by keeping variables separate from accessors, if you must change something about a given instance variable all you have to change are the accessor methods and not every single reference to the variable itself. In terms of code maintenance and reuse, what's good for the goose (external users of your class) is generally also good for the gander (you, as a user of your own class).

Class Variables and Methods

You learned about class variables and methods early last week, so I won't repeat a long description of them here. Because they use modifiers, however, they deserve a cursory mention.

To create a class variable or method, simply include the word static in front of the method name. The static modifier typically comes after any protection modifiers, like this:

```
public class  Circle {
    public static float  pi = 3.14159265F;

    public float  area(float r) {
        return  pi * r * r;
    }
}
```

NOTE The word static comes from C and C++. While static has a specific meaning for where a method or variable is stored in a program's runtime memory in those languages, static simply means that it's stored in the class in Java. Whenever you see the word static, remember to mentally substitute the word *class*.

Both class variables and methods can be accessed using standard dot notation with either the class name or an object on the left side of the dot. However, the convention is to always use the name of the class, to clarify that a class variable is being used, and to help the reader to know instantly that the variable is global to all instances. Here are a few examples:

```
float circumference = 2 * Circle.pi * getRadius();

float randomNumer = Math.random();
```

Class variables, for the same reasons as instance variables, can also benefit from being declared `private` and having accessor methods get or set their values.

Listing 15.1 shows a class called `CountInstances` that uses class and instance variables to keep track of how many instances of that class have been created.

Listing 15.1. The `CountInstances` class, which uses class and instance variables.

TYPE

```
 1: public class  CountInstances {
 2:    private static int    numInstances = 0;
 3:
 4:     protected static int getNumInstances() {
 5:         return numInstances;
 6:     }
 7:
 8:     private static void  addInstance() {
 9:         numInstances++;
10:     }
11:
12:    CountInstances() {
13:         CountInstances.addInstance();
14:     }
15:
16:     public static void  main(String args[]) {
17:         System.out.println("Starting with " +
18:           CountInstances.getNumInstances() + " instances");
19:         for (int  i = 0;  i < 10;   ++i)
20:             new CountInstances();
21:       System.out.println("Created " +
22:           CountInstances.getNumInstances() + " instances");
23:     }
24:}
```

OUTPUT
```
Started with 0 instances
Creates 10 instances
```

ANALYSIS
This example has a number of features, so let's go through it line by line. In line 2 we declare a `private` class variable to hold the number of instances (called `numInstances`). This is a class variable (declared `static`) because the number of instances is relevant to the class as a whole, not to any one instance. And it's private so that it follows the same rules as instance variables accessor methods.

Note the initialization of `numInstances` to `0` in that same line. Just as an instance variable is initialized when its instance is created, a class variable is initialized when its class is created.

This class initialization happens essentially before anything else can happen to that class, or its instances, so the class in the example will work as planned.

In lines 4 through 6, we created a get method for that private instance variable to get its value (getNumInstances()). This method is also declared as a class method, as it applies directly to the class variable. The getNumInstances() method is declared protected, as opposed to public, because only this class and perhaps subclasses will be interested in that value; other random classes are therefore restricted from seeing it.

Note that there's no accessor method to set the value. The reason is that the value of the variable should be incremented only when a new instance is created; it should not be set to any random value. Instead of creating an accessor method, therefore, we'll create a special private method called addInstance() in lines 8 through 10 that increments the value of numInstances by 1.

Lines 12 through 14 have the constructor method for this class. Remember, constructors are called when a new object is created, which makes this the most logical place to call addInstance() and to increment the variable.

And finally, the main() method indicates that we can run this as a Java application and test all the other methods. In the main() method we create 10 instances of the CountInstances class, reporting after we're done the value of the numInstances class variable (which, predictably, prints 10).

Finalizing Classes, Methods, and Variables

Although it's not the final modifier I'll discuss today, the final modifier is used to finalize classes, methods, and variables. Finalizing a thing effectively "freezes" the implementation or value of that thing. More specifically, here's how final works with classes, variables, and methods:

☐ When the final modifier is applied to a class, it means that the class cannot be subclassed.

☐ When applied to a variable, final means that the variable is constant.

☐ When applied to a method, final means that the method cannot be overridden by subclasses.

NEW TERM   *Finalization* (using the final modifier) freezes the implementation of a class, method, or variable.

Finalizing Classes

To finalize a class, add the `final` modifier to its definition. `final` typically goes after any protection modifiers such as `private` or `public`:

```
public final class  AFinalClass {
    . . .
}
```

You declare a class `final` for only two reasons:

- ☐ To prevent others from subclassing your class. If your class has all the capabilities it needs, and no one else should be able to extend its capabilities, then that class should be `final`.

- ☐ For better efficiency. With `final` classes you can rely on instances of only that one class (and no subclasses) being around in the system, and optimize for those instances.

The Java class library uses `final` classes extensively. Classes that have been finalized to prevent their being subclassed include `java.lang.System`, `java.net.InetAddress`, and `java.net.Socket` (although, as you learned on Day 14, " Networking, Advanced APIs, and Miscellaneous Tidbits," the latter will no longer be `final` as of Java 1.1). A good example of a class being declared `final` for efficiency reasons is `java.lang.String`. Strings are so common in Java, and so central to it that Java handles them specially.

In most cases, it will be a rare event for you to create a `final` class yourself since extendible classes are so much more useful than finalized classes, and the efficiency gains are minimal. You will, however, most likely have plenty of opportunity to be upset at certain system classes being `final` (making it more difficult to extend them).

Finalizing Variables

A finalized variable means its value cannot be changed. This is effectively a constant, which you learned about early in Week 1. To declare constants in Java, use `final` variables with initial values:

```
public class  AnotherFinalClass {
    public static final int aConstantInt    = 123;
    public final String aConstantString = "Hello world!";
}
```

Local variables (those inside blocks of code surrounded by braces, for example, in `while` or `for` loops) can't be declared `final`.

Finalizing Methods

Finalized methods are methods that cannot be overridden; that is, their implementations are frozen and cannot be redefined in subclasses.

```
public class  ClassWithFinalMethod {

    public final void  noOneGetsToDoThisButMe() {
        . . .
    }
}
```

The only reason to declare a method `final` is efficiency. Normally, method signatures and implementations are matched up when your Java program runs, not when it's compiled. Remember that when you call a method, Java dynamically checks the current class and each superclass in turn for that method's definition. Although this makes methods very flexible to define and use, it's not very fast.

If you declare a method `final`, however, the compiler can then "in-line" it (stick its definition) right in the middle of methods that call it because it "knows" that no one else can ever subclass and override the method to change its meaning. Although you might not use `final` right away when writing a class, as you tune the system later, you may discover that a few methods have to be `final` to make your class fast enough. Almost all your methods will be fine, however, just as they are.

If you use accessor methods a lot (as recommended), changing your accessor methods to be `final` can be a quick way of speeding up your class. Because subclasses will rarely want to change the definitions of those accessor methods, there's little reason those methods should not be final.

The Java class library declares a lot of commonly used methods `final` so that you'll benefit from the speed-up. In the case of classes that are already `final`, this makes perfect sense and is a wise choice. The few `final` methods declared in non-`final` classes will annoy you—your subclasses can no longer override them. When efficiency becomes less of an issue for the Java environment, many of these `final` methods can be "unfrozen" again, restoring this lost flexibility to the system.

NOTE `Private` methods are effectively `final`, as are all methods declared in a `final` class. Marking these latter methods `final` (as the Java library sometimes does) is legal, but redundant; the compiler already treats them as `final`.

It's possible to use `final` methods for some of the same security reasons you use `final` classes, but it's a much rarer event.

Abstract Classes and Methods

Whenever you arrange classes into an inheritance hierarchy, the presumption is that "higher" classes are more abstract and general, whereas "lower" subclasses are more concrete and specific. Often, as you design hierarchies of classes, you factor out common design and implementation into a shared superclass. That superclass won't have any instances; its sole reason for existing is to act as a common, shared repository for information that its subclasses use. These kinds of classes are called *abstract classes*, and you declare them using the abstract modifier. For example, the following skeleton class definition for the Fruit class declared that class to be both public and abstract:

```
public abstract class Fruit {
...
}
```

Abstract classes can never be instantiated (you'll get a compiler error if you try), but they can contain anything a normal class can contain, including class and instance variables and methods with any kind of protection or finalization modifiers. In addition, abstract classes can also contain abstract methods. An abstract method is a method signature with no implementation; subclasses of the abstract class are expected to provide the implementation for that method. Abstract methods, in this way, provide the same basic concept as abstract classes; they're a way of factoring common behavior into superclasses and then providing specific concrete uses of those behaviors in subclasses.

 Abstract classes are classes whose sole purpose is to provide common information for subclasses. Abstract classes can have no instances.

 Abstract methods are methods with signatures, but no implementation. Subclasses of the class which contains that abstract method must provide its actual implementation.

Like abstract classes, abstract methods give you the ability to factor common information into a general superclass and then reuse that class in different ways.

The opposite of abstract is concrete: Concrete classes are classes that can be instantiated; concrete methods are those that have actual implementations.

Abstract methods are declared with the abstract modifier, which usually goes after the protection modifiers but before either static or final. In addition, they have no body. Abstract methods can only exist inside abstract classes; even if you have a class full of concrete methods, with only one abstract method, the whole class must be abstract. This is because abstract methods cannot be called; they have no implementation, so calling them would produce an error. Rather than worry about special-case abstract methods inside otherwise concrete instances, it's easier just to insist that abstract methods be contained only inside abstract classes.

15

Listing 15.2 shows two simple classes. One, appropriately called MyFirstAbstractClass, has an instance variable and two methods. One of those methods, subclassesImplementMe(), is abstract. The other, doSomething(), is concrete and has a normal definition.

The second class is AConcreteSubclass, which is a subclass of MyFirstAbstractClass. It provides the implementation of subclassesImplementMe(), and inherits the remaining behavior from MyFirstAbstractClass.

NOTE

> Because both these classes are public, they must be defined in separate source files.

TYPE **Listing 15.2. Two classes: one abstract, one concrete.**

```
1:ipublic abstract class  MyFirstAbstractClass {
2:    int   anInstanceVariable;
3:p
4:       public abstract int  subclassesImplementMe(); // note no definition
5:
6:       public void  doSomething() {
7:          . . .    // a normal method
8:       }
9:}
10:
11:public class  AConcreteSubClass extends MyFirstAbstractClass {
12:    public int   subclassesImplementMe() {
13:          . . .    // we *must* implement this method here
14:    }
15:}
```

Here are some attempted uses of these classes:

```
Object  a = new MyFirstAbstractClass();     // illegal, is abstract

Object  c = new AConcreteSubClass();        // OK, a concrete subclass
```

Using an abstract class with nothing but abstract methods—that is, one that provides nothing but a template for behavior—is better accomplished in Java by using an *interface* (discussed tomorrow). Whenever a design calls for an abstraction that includes instance state and/or a partial implementation, however, an abstract class is your only choice.

Summary

Today you have learned how variables and methods can control their visibility and access by other classes via the four Ps of protection: public, package, protected, and private. You have also learned that although instance variables are most often declared private, declaring accessor methods allows you to control the reading and writing of them separately. Protection levels allow you, for example, to separate cleanly your public abstractions from their concrete representations.

You have also learned how to create class variables and methods, which are associated with the class itself, and how to declare final variables, methods, and classes to represent constants and fast or secure methods and classes.

Finally, you have discovered how to declare and use abstract classes, which cannot be instantiated, and abstract methods, which have no implementation and must be overridden in subclasses. Together, they provide a template for subclasses to fill in and act as a variant of the powerful interfaces of Java that you'll study tomorrow.

Q&A

Q Why are there so many different levels of protection in Java?

A Each level of protection, or visibility, provides a different view of your class to the outside world. One view is tailored for everyone, one for classes in your own package, another for your class and its subclasses only, one combining these last two and the final one for just within your class. Each is a logically well-defined and useful separation that Java supports directly in the language (as opposed to, for example, accessor methods, which are a convention you must follow).

Q Won't using accessor methods everywhere slow down my Java code?

A Not always. As Java compilers improve and can create more optimizations, they'll be able to make them fast automatically, but if you're concerned about speed, you can always declare accessor methods to be final, and they'll be just as fast as direct instance variable accesses.

Q Are class (static) methods inherited just like instance methods?

A No. static (class) methods are now final by default. How, then, can you ever declare a non-final class method? The answer is that you can't! Inheritance of class methods is not allowed, breaking the symmetry with instance methods.

Q Based on what I've learned, it seems like private abstract methods and final abstract methods or classes don't make sense. Are they legal?

A Nope, they're compile-time errors, as you have guessed. To be useful, abstract methods must be overridden, and abstract classes must be subclassed, but neither of those two operations would be legal if they were also private or final.

Q **What about the transient modifier? I saw that mentioned in the Java Language Specification.**

A The transient modifier is reserved by the designers of Java for use in future versions of the Java language (beyond 1.0.2 and 1.1); it will be used to create persistent object store systems (the ability to save a set of classes and objects and restore their state later on). It, like other modifiers such as byvalue, future, and generic, are not currently used but are reserved words in the language.

Q **I tried creating a private variable inside a method definition. It didn't work. What did I do wrong?**

A Nothing. All the modifiers in this chapter, when you can use them with variables, only apply to class and instance variables. Local variables—those that appear inside the body of a method or loop—cannot use any of these modifiers.

Day **16**

Packages, Interfaces, and Inner Classes

by Laura Lemay, Charles L. Perkins, and Michael Morrison

Packages and interfaces are two capabilities that allow you greater control and flexibility in designing sets of interrelated classes. Packages allow you to combine groups of classes and control which of those classes are available to the outside world; interfaces provide a way of grouping abstract method definitions and sharing them among classes that may not necessarily acquire those methods through inheritance.

Today you'll learn how to design with, use, and create your own packages and interfaces. Specific topics you'll learn about today include

☐ A discussion of designing classes versus coding classes and how to approach each

☐ What packages are and why they are useful for class design

☐ Using other people's packages in your own classes

☐ Creating your own packages

☐ What interfaces buy you in terms of code reuse and design

☐ Designing and working with interfaces

Programming in the Large and Programming in the Small

When you examine a new language feature, you should ask yourself two questions:

☐ How can I use it to better organize the methods and classes of my Java program?

☐ How can I use it while writing the actual Java code?

The first is often called programming in the large, and the second, programming in the small. Bill Joy, a founder of Sun Microsystems, likes to say that Java feels like C when programming in the small and like Smalltalk when programming in the large. What he means by that is that Java is familiar and powerful like any C-like language while you're coding individual lines, but has the extensibility and expressive power of a pure object-oriented language such as Smalltalk while you're designing.

The separation of "designing" from "coding" was one of the most fundamental advances in programming in the past few decades, and object-oriented languages such as Java implement a strong form of this separation. The first part of this separation has already been described on previous days: When you develop a Java program, first you design the classes and decide on the relationships between these classes, and then you implement the Java code needed for each of the methods in your design. If you are careful enough with both these processes, you can change your mind about aspects of the design without affecting anything but small, local pieces of your Java code, and you can change the implementation of any method without affecting the rest of the design.

As you begin to explore more advanced Java programming, however, you'll find that this simple model becomes too limiting. Today you'll explore these limitations, for programming in the large and in the small, to motivate the need for packages and interfaces. Let's start with packages.

What Are Packages?

Packages, as mentioned a number of times in this book so far, are a way of organizing groups of classes. A package contains any number of classes that are related in purpose, in scope, or by inheritance.

Why bother with packages? If your programs are small and use a limited number of classes, you may find that you don't need to explore packages at all. But the more Java programming you do, the more classes you'll find you have. And although those classes may be individually well designed, reusable, encapsulated, and with specific interfaces to other classes, you may find the need for a bigger organizational entity that allows you to group your packages.

Packages are useful for several broad reasons:

☐ They allow you to organize your classes into units. Just as you have folders or directories on your hard disk to organize your files and applications, packages allow you to organize your classes into groups so that you use only what you need for each program.

☐ They reduce problems with conflicts in names. As the number of Java classes grows, so does the likelihood that you'll use the same class name as someone else, opening up the possibility of naming clashes and errors if you try to integrate groups of classes into a single program. Packages allow you to "hide" classes so that conflicts can be avoided.

☐ They allow you to protect classes, variables, and methods in larger ways than on a class-by-class basis, as you learned yesterday. You'll learn more about protections with packages later today.

☐ They can be used to identify your classes. For example, if you implemented a set of classes to perform some purpose, you could name a package of those classes with a unique identifier that identifies you or your organization.

Although a package is most typically a collection of classes, packages can also contain other packages, forming yet another level of organization somewhat analogous to the inheritance hierarchy. Each "level" usually represents a smaller, more specific grouping of classes. The Java class library itself is organized along these lines. The top level is called java; the next level includes names such as io, net, util, and awt. The last of these has an even lower level, which includes the package image.

NOTE

By convention, the first level of the hierarchy specifies the (globally unique) name to identify the author or owner of those packages. For example, Sun Microsystems's classes, which are not part of the standard Java environment, all begin with the prefix sun. Classes that Netscape includes with its implementation are contained in the netscape package. The standard package, java, is an exception to this rule because it is so fundamental and because it might someday be implemented by multiple companies.

I'll tell you more about package-naming conventions later when you create your own packages.

Using Packages

You've been using packages all along in this book. Every time you use the `import` command, and every time you refer to a class by its full package name (`java.awt.Color`, for example), you've used packages. Let's go over the specifics of how to use classes from other packages in your own programs to make sure you've got it and to go into greater depth than we have in previous lessons.

To use a class contained in a package, you can use one of three mechanisms:

☐ If the class you want to use is in the package `java.lang` (for example, `System` or `Date`), you can simply use the class name to refer to that class. The `java.lang` classes are automatically available to you in all your programs.

☐ If the class you want to use is in some other package, you can refer to that class by its full name, including any package names (for example, `java.awt.Font`).

☐ For classes that you use frequently from other packages, you can import individual classes or a whole package of classes. After a class or a package has been imported, you can refer to that class by its class name.

What about your own classes in your own programs that don't belong to any package? The rule is that if you don't specifically define your classes to belong to a package, they're put into an unnamed default package. You can refer to those classes simply by class name from anywhere in your code.

Full Package and Class Names

To refer to a class in some other package, you can use its full name: the class name preceded by any package names. You do not have to import the class or the package to use it this way:

```
java.awt.Font f = new java.awt.Font()
```

For classes that you use only once or twice in your program, using the full name makes the most sense. If, however, you use that class multiple times, or if the package name is really long with lots of subpackages, you'll want to import that class instead to save yourself some typing.

16

The `import` Command

To import classes from a package, use the `import` command, as you've used throughout the examples in this book. You can either import an individual class, like this:

```
import java.util.Vector;
```

or you can import an entire package of classes, using an asterisk (*) to replace the individual class names:

```
import java.awt.*
```

NOTE
> Actually, to be technically correct, this command doesn't import all the classes in a package—it imports only the classes that have been declared `public`, and even then imports only those classes that the code itself refers to. You'll learn more about this in the section titled "Packages and Class Protection."

Note that the asterisk (*) in this example is not like the one you might use at a command prompt to specify the contents of a directory or to indicate multiple files. For example, if you ask to list the contents of the directory `classes/java/awt/*`, that list includes all the `.class` files and subdirectories, such as `image` and `peer`. Writing `import java.awt.*` imports all the public classes in that package, but does *not* import subpackages such as `image` and `peer`. To import all the classes in a complex package hierarchy, you must explicitly import each level of the hierarchy by hand. Also, you cannot indicate partial class names (for example, `L*` to import all the classes that begin with L). It's all the classes in a package or a single class.

The `import` statements in your class definition go at the top of the file, before any class definitions (but after the package definition, as you'll see in the next section).

So should you take the time to import classes individually or just import them as a group? It depends on how specific you want to be. Importing a group of classes does not slow down your program or make it any larger; only the classes you actually use in your code are loaded as they are needed. But importing a package does make it a little more confusing for readers of your code to figure out where your classes are coming from. Using individual `import`s or importing packages is mostly a question of your own coding style.

TECHNICAL NOTE
> Java's `import` command is not at all similar to the `#include` command in C-like languages, although they accomplish similar functions. The C preprocessor takes the contents of all the included files (and, in turn, the files they include, and so on) and stuffs them in at the spot where

> the #include was. The result is an enormous hunk of code that has far
> more lines than the original program did. Java's import behaves more
> like a linker; it tells the Java compiler and interpreter where (in which
> files) to find classes, variables, method names, and method definitions.
> It doesn't bring anything into the current Java program.

Name Conflicts

After you have imported a class or a package of classes, you can usually refer to a class name simply by its name, without the package identifier. I say "usually" because there's one case where you may have to be more explicit: when there are multiple classes with the same name from different packages.

Here's an example. Let's say you import the classes from two packages from two different programmers (Joe and Eleanor):

```
import joesclasses.*;
import eleanorsclasses.*;
```

Inside Joe's package is a class called Name. Unfortunately, inside Eleanor's package there is also a class called Name that has an entirely different meaning and implementation. You would wonder whose version of Name would end up getting used if you referred to the Name class in your own program like this:

```
Name myName = new Name("Susan");
```

The answer is neither; the Java compiler will complain about a naming conflict and refuse to compile your program. In this case, despite the fact that you imported both classes, you still have to refer to the appropriate Name class by full package name:

```
joesclasses.Name myName = new joesclasses.Name("Susan");
```

A Note About CLASSPATH and Where Classes Are Located

Before I go on to explain how to create your own packages of classes, I'd like to make a note about how Java finds packages and classes when it's compiling and running your classes.

For Java to be able to use a class, it has to be able to find it on the file system. Otherwise, you'll get an error that the class does not exist. Java uses two things to find classes: the package name itself and the directories listed in your CLASSPATH variable.

First, the package names. Package names map to directory names on the file system, so the class java.applet.Applet will actually be found in the applet directory, which in turn will be inside the java directory (java/applet/Applet.class, in other words).

Java looks for those directories, in turn, inside the directories listed in your CLASSPATH variable. If you remember back to Day 1, "An Introduction to Java Programming," when you installed the JDK, you had to set up a CLASSPATH variable to point to the various places where your Java classes live. CLASSPATH usually points to the java/lib directory in your JDK release, a class directory in your development environment if you have one, perhaps some browser-specific classes, and to the current directory. When Java looks for a class you've referenced in your source, it looks for the package and class name in each of those directories and returns an error if it can't find the class file. Most "cannot load class" errors result because of missed CLASSPATH variables.

NOTE

If you're using the Macintosh version of the JDK, you're probably wondering what I'm talking about. The Mac JDK doesn't use a CLASSPATH variable; it knows enough to be able to find the default classes and those contained in the current directory. However, if you do a lot of Java development, you may end up with classes and packages in other directories. The Java compiler contains a Preferences dialog box that lets you add directories to Java's search path.

Creating Your Own Packages

Creating your own packages is a difficult, complex process, involving many lines of code, long hours late at night with lots of coffee, and the ritual sacrifice of many goats. Just kidding. To create a package of classes, you have three basic steps to follow, which I'll explain in the following sections.

Pick a Package Name

The first step is to decide what the name of your package is going to be. The name you choose for your package depends on how you are going to be using those classes. Perhaps your package will be named after you, or perhaps after the part of the Java system you're working on (such as graphics or hardware_interfaces). If you're intending your package to be distributed to the Net at large, or as part of a commercial product, you'll want to use a package name (or set of package names) that uniquely identifies you or your organization or both.

One convention for naming packages that has been recommended by Sun is to use your Internet domain name with the elements reversed. So, for example, if Sun were following its own recommendation, its packages would be referred to using the name com.sun.java rather than just java. If your Internet domain name is fooblitzky.eng.nonsense.edu, your package name might be edu.nonsense.eng.fooblitzky (and you might add another package name onto the end of that to refer to the product or to you, specifically).

The idea is to make sure your package name is unique. Although packages can hide conflicting class names, the protection stops there. There's no way to make sure your package won't conflict with someone else's package if you both use the same package name.

By convention, package names tend to begin with a lowercase letter to distinguish them from class names. Thus, for example, in the full name of the built-in String class, java.lang.String, it's easier to separate the package name from the class name visually. This convention helps reduce name conflicts.

Create the Directory Structure

Step two in creating packages is to create a directory structure on your disk that matches the package name. If your package has just one name (mypackage), you'll only have to create a directory for that one name. If the package name has several parts, however, you'll have to create directories within directories. For the package name edu.nonsense.eng.fooblitzky, you'll need to create an edu directory and then create a nonsense directory inside edu, an eng directory inside nonsense, and a fooblitzky directory inside eng. Your classes and source files can then go inside the fooblitzky directory.

Use package to Add Your Class to a Package

The final step to putting your class inside packages is to add the package command to your source files. The package command says "this class goes inside this package," and is used like this:

```
package myclasses;
package edu.nonsense.eng.fooblitzky;
package java.awt;
```

The single package command, if any, must be the first line of code in your source file, after any comments or blank lines and before any import commands.

As mentioned before, if your class doesn't have a package command in it, that class is contained in the default package and can be used by any other class. But once you start using packages, you should make sure all your classes belong to some package to reduce the chance of confusion about where your classes belong.

Packages and Class Protection

Yesterday you learned all about the four Ps of protection and how they apply (primarily) to methods and variables and their relationship to other classes. When referring to classes and their relationship to other classes in other packages, you only have two Ps to worry about: package and public.

By default, classes have package protection, which means that the class is available to all the other classes in the same package but is not visible or available outside that package—not even to subpackages. It cannot be imported or referred to by name; classes with package protection are hidden inside the package in which they are contained.

Package protection comes about when you define a class as you have throughout this book, like this:

```
class TheHiddenClass extends AnotherHiddenClass {
...
}
```

To allow a class to be visible and importable outside your package, you'll want to give it public protection by adding the public modifier to its definition:

```
public class TheVisibleClass {
...
}
```

Classes declared as public can be imported by other classes outside the package.

Note that when you use an import statement with an asterisk, you import only the public classes inside that package. Hidden classes remain hidden and can be used only by the other classes in that package.

Why would you want to hide a class inside a package? For the same reason you want to hide variables and methods inside a class: so you can have utility classes and behavior that are useful only to your implementation, or so you can limit the interface of your program to minimize the effect of larger changes. As you design your classes, you'll want to take the whole package into consideration and decide which classes will be declared public and which will be hidden.

Listing 16.1 shows two classes that illustrate this point. The first is a public class that implements a linked list; the second is a private node of that list.

TYPE | **Listing 16.1. The public class LinkedList.**

```
1: package  collections;
2:
3: public class  LinkedList {
4:     private Node  root;
```

continues

Listing 16.1. continued

```
 5:
 6:     public  void  add(Object o) {
 7:         root = new Node(o, root);
 8:     }
 9:     . . .
10: }
11:
12: class  Node {    // not public
13:     private Object  contents;
14:     private Node    next;
15:
16:     Node(Object o, Node n) {
17:         contents = o;
18:         next     = n;
19:     }
20:     . . .
21: }
```

NOTE Notice here that I'm including two class definitions in one file. I
mentioned this briefly on Day 13, "Advanced User Interfaces with the
AWT," and it bears mentioning here as well: You can include as many
class definitions per file as you want, but only one of them can be
declared public, and that filename must have the same name as the one
public class. When Java compiles the file, it'll create separate .class
files for each class definition inside the file. In reality, I find the one-to-
one correspondence of class definition to file much more easily maintained because I don't have to go searching around for the definition of
a class.

The public LinkedList class provides a set of useful public methods (such as add()) to any
other classes that might want to use them. These other classes don't need to know about any
support classes LinkedList needs to get its job done. Node, which is one of those support
classes, is therefore declared without a public modifier and will not appear as part of the
public interface to the collections package.

NOTE Just because Node isn't public doesn't mean LinkedList won't have
access to it once it's been imported into some other class. Think of
protections not as hiding classes entirely, but more as checking the

16

permissions of a given class to use other classes, variables, and methods. When you import and use `LinkedList`, the `Node` class will also be loaded into the system, but only instances of `LinkedList` will have permission to use it.

16

One of the great powers of hidden classes is that even if you use them to introduce a great deal of complexity into the implementation of some public class, all the complexity is hidden when that class is imported or used. Thus, creating a good package consists of defining a small, clean set of public classes and methods for other classes to use, and then implementing them by using any number of hidden (package) support classes. You'll see another use for hidden classes later today.

What Are Interfaces?

Interfaces, like the abstract classes and methods you saw yesterday, provide templates of behavior that other classes are expected to implement. Interfaces, however, provide far more functionality to Java and to class and object design than do simple abstract classes and methods. The rest of this lesson explores interfaces: what they are, why they're crucial to getting the most out of the Java language for your own classes, and how to use and implement them.

The Problem of Single Inheritance

When you first begin to design object-oriented programs, the concept of the class hierarchy can seem almost miraculous. Within that single tree you can express a hierarchy of different types of objects, many simple to moderately complex relationships between objects and processes in the world, and any number of points along the axis from abstract/general to concrete/specific. The strict hierarchy of classes appears, at first glance, to be simple, elegant, and easy to use.

After some deeper thought or more complex design experience, however, you may discover that the pure simplicity of the class hierarchy is restrictive, particularly when you have some behavior that needs to be used by classes in different branches of the same tree.

Let's look at a few examples that will make the problems clearer. Way back on Day 2, "Object-Oriented Programming and Java," when you first learned about class hierarchies, we discussed the `Vehicle` hierarchy, as shown in Figure 16.1.

Figure 16.1.

The Vehicle *hierarchy.*

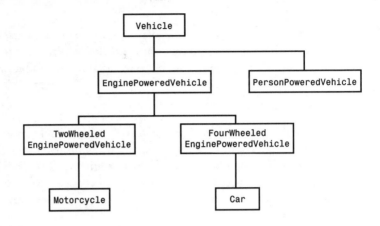

Now let's add to that hierarchy and create the classes BritishCar and BritishMotorcycle underneath Car and Motorcycle, respectively. The behavior that makes a car or motorcycle British (which might include methods for leakOil() or electricalSystemFailure()) is common to both these classes, but because they are in very different parts of the class hierarchy, you can't create a common superclass for both of them. And you can't put the British behavior further up in the hierarchy because that behavior isn't common to all motorcycles and cars. Other than physically copying the behavior between the two classes (which breaks the object-oriented programming [OOP] rules of code reuse and shared behavior), how can you create a hierarchy like this?

Let's look at an even thornier example. Say you have a biological hierarchy with Animal at the top, and the classes Mammal and Bird underneath. Things that define a mammal include bearing live young and having fur. Behavior or features of birds include having a beak and laying eggs. So far, so good, right? So how do you go about creating a class for the platypus, which has fur and a beak, and lays eggs? You'd need to combine behavior from two classes to form the Platypus class. And, because classes can have only one immediate superclass in Java, this sort of problem simply cannot be solved elegantly.

Other OOP languages include the concept of *multiple inheritance,* which solves this problem. With multiple inheritance, a class can inherit from more than one superclass and get behavior and attributes from all its superclasses at once. Using multiple inheritance, you could simply factor the common behavior of BritishCar and BritishMotorcycle into a single class (BritishThing) and then create new classes that inherit from both their primary superclass *and* the British class.

The problem with multiple inheritance is that it makes a programming language far more complex to learn, to use, and to implement. Questions of method invocation and how the class hierarchy is organized become far more complicated with multiple inheritance, and more open to confusion and ambiguity. And because one of the goals for Java was that it be simple, multiple inheritance was rejected in favor of the simpler single inheritance.

So how do you solve the problem of needing common behavior that doesn't fit into the strict class hierarchy? Java, borrowing from Objective-C, has another hierarchy altogether separate from the main class hierarchy, a hierarchy of mixable behavior classes. Then, when you create a new class, that class has only one primary superclass, but it can pick and choose different common behaviors from the other hierarchy.

This other hierarchy is the *interface hierarchy*. A Java *interface* is a collection of abstract behavior that can be mixed into any class to add to that class behavior that is not supplied by its superclasses. Specifically, a Java interface contains nothing but abstract method definitions and constants—no instance variables and no method implementations.

Interfaces are implemented and used throughout the Java class library whenever a behavior is expected to be implemented by a number of disparate classes. The Java class hierarchy, for example, defines and uses the interfaces `java.lang.Runnable`, `java.util.Enumeration`, `java.util.Observable`, `java.awt.image.ImageConsumer`, and `java.awt.image.ImageProducer`. Some of these interfaces you've seen before; others you'll see later in this book. Still others may be useful to you in your own programs, so be sure to examine the API to see what's available to you.

Abstract Design and Concrete Implementation

Throughout this book you've gotten a taste of the difference between design and implementation in object-oriented programming, where the design of a thing is its abstract representation and its implementation is the concrete counterpart of the design. You saw this with methods, where a method's signature defines how it's used, but the method implementation can occur anywhere in the class hierarchy. You saw this with abstract classes, where the class's design provides a template for behavior, but that behavior isn't implemented until further down in the hierarchy.

This distinction between the design and the implementation of a class or a method is a crucial part of object-oriented programming theory. Thinking in terms of design when you organize your classes allows you to get the big picture without being bogged down in implementation details. And having the overall design already defined when you actually start implementing allows you to concentrate on those details solely for the class you're working on. This programming version of "think globally, act locally" provides a powerful way of thinking about how your classes and your programs and your overall designs are organized and how they interrelate.

16

An interface is made up of a set of method signatures with no implementations, making it the embodiment of pure design. By mixing an interface in with your class, you're encompassing that design into your implementation. That design can then be safely included anywhere in the class hierarchy because there are no class-specific details of how an interface behaves— nothing to override, nothing to keep track of, just the name and arguments for a method.

What about abstract classes? Don't abstract classes provide this same behavior? Yes and no. Abstract classes and the abstract methods inside them do provide a separation of design and implementation, allowing you to factor common behavior into an abstract superclass. But abstract classes can, and often do, contain some concrete data (such as instance variables), and you can have an abstract superclass with both abstract and regular methods, thereby confusing the distinction.

Even a pure abstract class with only abstract methods isn't as powerful as an interface. An abstract class is simply another class; it inherits from some other class and has its place in the hierarchy. Abstract classes cannot be shared across different parts of the class hierarchy the way interfaces can, nor can they be mixed into other classes that need their behavior. To attain the sort of flexibility of shared behavior across the class hierarchy, you need an interface.

You can think of the difference between the design and the implementation of any Java class as the difference between the interface hierarchy and the design hierarchy. The singly inherited class hierarchy contains the implementations where the relationships between classes and behavior are rigidly defined. The multiply inherited mixable interface hierarchy, however, contains the design and can be freely used anywhere it's needed in the implementation. This is a powerful way of thinking about the organization of your program, and although it takes a little getting used to, it's also a highly recommended one.

Interfaces and Classes

Classes and interfaces, despite their different definitions, have an awful lot in common. Interfaces, like classes, are declared in source files, one interface to a file. Like classes, they also are compiled using the Java compiler into `.class` files. And, in most cases, anywhere you can use a class (as a data type for a variable, as the result of a cast, and so on), you can also use an interface.

Almost everywhere that this book has a class name in any of its examples or discussions, you can substitute an interface name. Java programmers often say "class" when they actually mean "class or interface." Interfaces complement and extend the power of classes, and the two can be treated almost the same. One of the few differences between them is that an interface cannot be instantiated: `new` can only create an instance of a class.

16

Implementing and Using Interfaces

Now that you've grasped what interfaces are and why they're powerful (the "programming in the large" part), let's move on to actual bits of code ("programming in the small"). There are two things you can do with interfaces: use them in your own classes and define your own. Let's start with the former.

The `implements` Keyword

To use an interface, you include the `implements` keyword as part of your class definition. You did this back on Day 11, "Managing Simple Events and Interactivity," when you learned about threads and included the `Runnable` interface in your applet definition:

```
// java.applet.Applet is the superclass
public class Neko extends java.applet.Applet
    implements Runnable {  // but it also has Runnable behavior
...
}
```

Because interfaces provide nothing but abstract method definitions, you then have to implement those methods in your own classes, using the same method signatures from the interface. Note that once you include an interface, you have to implement *all* the methods in that interface—you can't pick and choose the methods you need. By implementing an interface you're telling users of your class that you support *all* of that interface. (Note that this is another difference between interfaces and abstract classes—subclasses of the latter can pick which methods to implement or override and can ignore others.)

After your class implements an interface, subclasses of your class will inherit those new methods (and can override or overload them) just as if your superclass had actually defined them. If your class inherits from a superclass that implements a given interface, you don't have to include the `implements` keyword in your own class definition.

Let's examine one simple example—creating the new class `Orange`. Suppose you already have a good implementation of the class `Fruit` and an interface, `Fruitlike`, that represents what `Fruit`s are expected to be able to do. You want an orange to be a fruit, but you also want it to be a spherical object that can be tossed, rotated, and so on. Here's how to express it all (don't worry about the definitions of these interfaces for now; you'll learn more about them later today):

```
interface  Fruitlike {
    void  decay();
    void  squish();
    . . .
}
```

```
class  Fruit implements Fruitlike {
    private Color  myColor;
    private int    daysTilIRot;
    . . .
}

interface  Spherelike {
    void  toss();
    void  rotate();
    . . .
}

class  Orange extends Fruit implements Spherelike {
    . . .  // toss()ing may squish() me (unique to me)
}
```

Note that the class Orange doesn't have to say implements Fruitlike because, by extending Fruit, it already has! One of the nice things about this structure is that you can change your mind about what class Orange extends (if a really great Sphere class is suddenly implemented, for example), yet class Orange will still understand the same two interfaces:

```
class  Sphere implements Spherelike {    // extends Object
    private float  radius;
    . . .
}

class  Orange extends Sphere implements Fruitlike {
    . . .       // users of Orange never need know about the change!
}
```

Implementing Multiple Interfaces

Unlike the singly inherited class hierarchy, you can include as many interfaces as you need in your own classes, and your class will implement the combined behavior of all the included interfaces. To include multiple interfaces in a class, just separate their names with commas:

```
public class Neko extends java.applet.Applet
    implements Runnable, Eatable, Sortable, Observable {
...
}
```

Note that complications may arise from implementing multiple interfaces—what happens if two different interfaces both define the same method? There are three ways to solve this:

☐ If the methods in each of the interfaces have identical signatures, you implement one method in your class and that definition satisfies both interfaces.

☐ If the methods have different parameter lists, it is a simple case of method overloading; you implement both method signatures, and each definition satisfies its respective interface definition.

☐ If the methods have the same parameter lists but differ in return type, you cannot create a method that satisfies both (remember, method overloading is triggered by parameter lists, not by return type). In this case, trying to compile a class that implements both interfaces will produce a compiler error. Running across this problem suggests that your interfaces have some design flaws that might need re-examining.

16

Other Uses of Interfaces

Remember that almost everywhere that you can use a class, you can use an interface instead. So, for example, you can declare a variable to be of an interface type:

```
Runnable aRunnableObject = new MyAnimationClass()
```

When a variable is declared to be of an interface type, it simply means that any object the variable refers to is expected to have implemented that interface—that is, it is expected to understand all the methods that interface specifies. It assumes that a promise made between the designer of the interface and its eventual implementors has been kept. In this case, because aRunnableObject contains an object of the type Runnable, the assumption is that you can call aRunnableObject.run().

The important thing to realize here is that although aRunnableObject is expected to be able to have the run() method, you could write this code long before any classes that qualify are actually implemented (or even created!). In traditional object-oriented programming, you are forced to create a class with "stub" implementations (empty methods, or methods that print silly messages) to get the same effect.

You can also cast objects to an interface, just as you can cast objects to other classes. So, for example, let's go back to that definition of the Orange class, which implemented both the Fruitlike interface (through its superclass, Fruit) and the Spherelike interface. Here we'll cast instances of Orange to both classes and interfaces:

```
Orange      anOrange    = new Orange();
Fruit       aFruit      = (Fruit)anOrange;
Fruitlike   aFruitlike  = (Fruitlike)anOrange;
Spherelike  aSpherelike = (Spherelike)anOrange;

aFruit.decay();             // fruits decay
aFruitlike.squish();        //  and squish

aFruitlike.toss();          // things that are fruitlike do not toss
aSpherelike.toss();         // but things that are spherelike do

anOrange.decay();           // oranges can do it all
anOrange.squish();
anOrange.toss();
anOrange.rotate();
```

Declarations and casts are used in this example to restrict an orange's behavior to acting more like a mere fruit or sphere.

Finally, note that although interfaces are usually used to mix in behavior to other classes (method signatures), interfaces can also be used to mix in generally useful constants. So, for example, if an interface defined a set of constants, and then multiple classes used those constants, the values of those constants could be globally changed without having to modify multiple classes. This is yet another example of where the use of interfaces to separate design from implementation can make your code more general and more easily maintainable.

Creating and Extending Interfaces

After using interfaces for a while, the next step is to define your own interfaces. Interfaces look a lot like classes; they are declared in much the same way and can be arranged into a hierarchy, but there are rules for declaring interfaces that must be followed.

New Interfaces

To create a new interface, you declare it like this:

```
public interface Growable {
...
}
```

This is, effectively, the same as a class definition, with the word `interface` replacing the word `class`. Inside the interface definition you have methods and constants. The method definitions inside the interface are `public` and `abstract` methods; you can either declare them explicitly as such, or they will be turned into `public` and `abstract` methods if you do not include those modifiers. You cannot declare a method inside an interface to be either `private` or `protected`. So, for example, here's a `Growable` interface with one method explicitly declared `public` and `abstract` (`growIt()`) and one implicitly declared as such (`growItBigger()`).

```
public interface Growable {
    public abstract void growIt(); //explicity public and abstract
    void growItBigger();           // effectively public and abstract
}
```

Note that, as with abstract methods in classes, methods inside interfaces do not have bodies. Remember, an interface is pure design; there is no implementation involved.

In addition to methods, interfaces can also have variables, but those variables must be declared `public`, `static`, and `final` (making them constant). As with methods, you can explicitly define a variable to be `public`, `static`, and `final`, or it will be implicitly defined as such if you don't use those modifiers. Here's that same `Growable` definition with two new variables:

```
public interface Growable {
    public static final int increment = 10;
    long maxnum = 1000000;  // becomes public static and final

    public abstract void growIt(); //explicitly public and abstract
    void growItBigger();            // effectively public and abstract
}
```

Interfaces must have either public or package protection, just like classes. Note, however, that interfaces without the `public` modifier do not automatically convert their methods to `public` and `abstract` nor their constants to `public`. A non-public interface also has non-public methods and constants that can be used only by classes and other interfaces in the same package.

Interfaces, like classes, can belong to a package by adding a `package` statement to the first line of the class file. Interfaces can also import other interfaces and classes from other packages, just as classes can.

Methods Inside Interfaces

One trick to note about methods inside interfaces: Those methods are supposed to be abstract and apply to any kind of class, but how can you define parameters to those methods? You don't know what class will be using them!

The answer lies in the fact that you use an interface name anywhere a class name can be used, as you learned earlier. By defining your method parameters to be interface types, you can create generic parameters that apply to any class that might use this interface.

So, for example, take the interface `Fruitlike`, which defines methods (with no arguments) for `decay()` and `squish()`. There might also be a method for `germinateSeeds()`, which has one argument: the fruit itself. Of what type is that argument going to be? It can't be simply `Fruit`, because there may be a class that's `Fruitlike` (that is, implements the `Fruitlike` interface) without actually being a fruit. The solution is to declare the argument as simply `Fruitlike` in the interface:

```
public interface Fruitlike {
    public abstract germinate(Fruitlike self) {
        ...
    }
}
```

Then, in an actual implementation for this method in a class, you can take the generic `Fruitlike` argument and cast it to the appropriate object:

```
public class Orange extends Fruit {

    public germinate(Fruitlike self) {
        Orange theOrange = (Orange)self;
```

```
       . . .
    }
}
```

Extending Interfaces

As with classes, interfaces can be organized into a hierarchy. When one interface inherits from another interface, that "subinterface" acquires all the method definitions and constants that its "superinterface" defined. To extend an interface, you use the extends keyword just as you do in a class definition:

```
public interface Fruitlike extends Foodlike {
. . .
}
```

Note that, unlike classes, the interface hierarchy has no equivalent of the Object class; this hierarchy is not rooted at any one point. Interfaces can either exist entirely on their own or inherit from another interface.

Note also that, unlike the class hierarchy, the inheritance hierarchy is multiply inherited. So, for example, a single interface can extend as many classes as it needs to (separated by commas in the extends part of the definition), and the new interface will contain a combination of all its parent's methods and constants. Here's an interface definition for an interface called BusyInterface that inherits from a whole lot of other interfaces:

```
public interface BusyInterface extends Runnable, Growable, Fruitlike, Observable
{
...}
```

In multiply inherited interfaces, the rules for managing method name conflicts are the same as for classes that use multiple interfaces; methods that differ only in return type will result in a compiler error.

An Example: Enumerating Linked Lists

To finish up today's lesson, here's an example that uses packages, package protection, and defines a class that implements the Enumeration interface (part of the java.util package). Listing 16.2 shows the code.

TYPE   **Listing 16.2. Packages, classes, and interfaces.**

```
1: package  collections;
2:
3: public class  LinkedList {
4:      private Node  root;
```

16

```
 5:
 6:          . . .
 7:        public Enumeration  enumerate() {
 8:            return new LinkedListEnumerator(root);
 9:        }
10: }
11:
12: class  Node {
13:     private Object   contents;
14:     private Node     next;
15:
16:         . . .
17:     public  Object  contents() {
18:         return contents;
19:     }
20:
21:     public  Node    next() {
22:         return next;
23:     }
24: }
25:
26: class  LinkedListEnumerator implements Enumeration {
27:     private Node   currentNode;
28:
29:      LinkedListEnumerator(Node   root) {
30:         currentNode = root;
31:     }
32:
33:     public boolean  hasMoreElements() {
34:         return currentNode != null;
35:     }
36:
37:     public Object    nextElement() {
38:        Object  anObject = currentNode.contents();
39:
40:         currentNode = currentNode.next();
41:        return  anObject;
42:     }
43: }
```

Here is a typical use of the enumerator:

```
collections.LinkedList aLinkedList = createLinkedList();
java.util.Enumeration e = aLinkedList.enumerate();

while (e.hasMoreElements()) {
    Object  anObject = e.nextElement();
    // do something useful with anObject
}
```

Notice that, although you are using the Enumeration e as though you know what it is, you actually do not. In fact, it is an instance of a hidden class (LinkedListEnumerator) that you cannot see or use directly. By using a combination of packages and interfaces, the LinkedList class has managed to provide a transparent public interface to some of its most important behavior (via the already defined interface java.util.Enumeration) while still encapsulating (hiding) its two implementation (support) classes.

Handing out an object like this is sometimes called *vending*. Often the "vendor" gives out an object that a receiver can't create itself but that it knows how to use. By giving it back to the vendor, the receiver can prove it has a certain capability, authenticate itself, or do any number of useful tasks—all without knowing much about the vended object. This is a powerful metaphor that can be applied in a broad range of situations.

Inner Classes

Most Java classes are defined at the package level, meaning that each class is a member of a particular package. Even if you don't explicitly specify a package association for a class, the default package will be assumed. Classes defined at the package level are known as *top-level classes*. Prior to Java 1.1, top-level classes were the only types of classes supported. However, Java 1.1 has ushered in a more open-minded approach to class definition. Java 1.1 supports *inner classes*, which are classes that can be defined in any scope. This means that a class can be defined as a member of another class, within a block of statements, or anonymously within an expression.

Inner classes, although seemingly a minor enhancement to the Java language, actually represent a significant modification to the language. Consider the fact that inner classes are the only modification to the Java language itself in Java 1.1 and you'll start to get the picture. The rest of the Java 1.1 enhancements came in the form of new APIs. So, why bother changing the language itself for something seemingly as abstract as inner classes? The answer to this question is not exactly simple. Rather than get into a discussion that is beyond the scope of this chapter, let me sum up the need for inner classes by saying that the new Java 1.1 AWT event model specifically needed a mechanism like inner classes to function properly.

Rules governing the scope of an inner class closely match those governing variables. An inner class's name is not visible outside its scope, except in a fully qualified name, which helps in structuring classes within a package. The code for an inner class can use simple names from enclosing scopes, including class and member variables of enclosing classes, as well as local variables of enclosing blocks. In addition, you can define a top-level class as a static member of another top-level class. Unlike an inner class, a top-level class cannot directly use the instance variables of any other class. The ability to nest classes in this way allows any top-level class to provide a package style organization for a logically related group of secondary top-level classes.

NOTE The support for inner classes in Java 1.1 was provided entirely by the Java compiler and did not require any changes to the Java Virtual Machine (VM). This is a major part of the reason Java architects were willing to modify the Java language to support inner classes—because they knew it wouldn't impact the VM.

For additional information on inner classes, check out the information on Sun's web site at http://www.sun.com.

Summary

Today you have learned how packages can be used to collect and categorize classes into meaningful groups. Packages are arranged in a hierarchy, which not only better organizes your programs but allows you and the millions of Java programmers out on the Net to name and share their projects uniquely with one another.

You have also learned how to use packages, both your own and the many preexisting ones in the Java class library.

You then discovered how to declare and use interfaces, a powerful mechanism for extending the traditional single inheritance of Java's classes and for separating design inheritance from implementation inheritance in your programs. Interfaces are often used to call common (shared) methods when the exact class involved is not known. You'll see further uses of interfaces tomorrow and the day after.

Finally, you learned that packages and interfaces can be combined to provide useful abstractions, such as LinkedList, that appear simple yet are actually hiding almost all their (complex) implementation from their users. This is a powerful technique.

Q&A

Q Can you use import some.package.B* to import all the classes in that package that begin with B?

A No, the import asterisk (*) does not act like a command-line asterisk.

Q Then what exactly does `importing` with an * mean?

A Combining everything said previously, this precise definition emerges: It imports all the public classes you use in your Java code that are *directly* inside the package named, and not inside one of its subpackages. (You can import only this set of classes, or exactly one explicitly named class, from a given package.) By the way, Java only "loads" the information for a class when you actually refer to that class in your code, so the * form of `import` is no less efficient than naming each class individually.

Q Why is full multiple inheritance so complex that Java abandoned it?

A It's not so much that it is too complex, but that it makes the language overly complicated—and as you'll learn on Day 21, "Under the Hood," this can cause larger systems to be less trustworthy and thus less secure. For example, if you were to inherit from two different parents, each having an instance variable with the same name, you would be forced to allow the conflict and explain how the exact same reference to that variable name in each of your superclasses, and in you (all three), are now different. Instead of being able to call "super" methods to get more abstract behavior accomplished, you would always need to worry about which of the (possibly many) identical methods you actually wished to call in which parent. Java's run-time method dispatching would have to be more complex as well. Finally, because so many people would be providing classes for reuse on the Net, the normally manageable conflicts that would arise in your own program would be confounded by millions of users mixing and matching these fully multiply inherited classes at will. In the future, if all these issues are resolved, more powerful inheritance may be added to Java, but its current capabilities are already sufficient for 99 percent of your programs.

Q `abstract` classes don't have to implement all the methods in an interface themselves, but don't all their subclasses have to?

A Actually, no. Because of inheritance, the precise rule is that an implementation must be provided by some class for each method, but it doesn't have to be your class. This is analogous to when you are the subclass of a class that implements an interface for you. Whatever the `abstract` class doesn't implement, the first non-`abstract` class below it must implement. Then, any further subclasses need do nothing further.

Q You didn't mention callbacks. Aren't they an important use of interfaces?

A Yes, but I didn't mention them because a good example would be too bulky. Callbacks are often used in user interfaces (such as window systems) to specify what set of methods is going to be sent whenever the user does a certain set of things (such as clicking the mouse somewhere, typing, and so on). Because the user interface classes should not "know" anything about the classes using them, an interface's ability to specify a set of methods separate from the class tree is crucial in this case. Callbacks using interfaces are not as general as using, for example, the perform: method of Smalltalk, however, because a given object can request only that a user interface object "call it back" using a single method name. Suppose that object wanted two user interface objects of the same class to call it back, using different names to tell them apart? It cannot do this in Java, and it is forced to use special state and tests to tell them apart. (I warned you that it was complicated!) So although interfaces are quite valuable in this case, they are not the ideal callback facility.

16

Day **17**

Exceptions

by Charles L. Perkins and Laura Lemay

Programmers in any language endeavor to write bug-free programs, programs that never crash, programs that can handle any situation with grace and that can recover from unusual situations without causing the user any undue stress. Good intentions aside, programs like this don't exist.

In real programs, errors occur, either because the programmer didn't anticipate every situation your code would get into (or didn't have the time to test the program enough), or because of situations out of the programmer's control—bad data from users, corrupt files that don't have the right data in them, network connections that don't connect, hardware devices that don't respond, sun spots, gremlins, whatever.

In Java, these sorts of strange events that may cause a program to fail are called *exceptions*. And Java defines a number of language features to deal with exceptions, including

☐ How to handle them in your code and recover gracefully from potential problems

☐ How to tell Java and users of your methods that you're expecting a potential exception

☐ How to create an exception if you detect one

☐ How your code is limited, yet made more robust by them

NEW TERM *Exceptions* are unusual things that can happen in your Java programs outside the normal or desired behavior of that program. Exceptions include errors that could be fatal to your program but also include other unusual situations. By managing exceptions, you can manage errors and possibly work around them.

Exceptions, the Old and Confusing Way

Programming languages have long labored to solve the following common problem:

```
int  status = callSomethingThatAlmostAlwaysWorks();

if (status == FUNNY_RETURN_VALUE) {
    . . .        // something unusual happened, handle it
    switch(someGlobalErrorIndicator) {
        . . . // handle more specific problems
    }
} else {
    . . .        // all is well, go your merry way
}
```

What this bit of code is attempting to do is to run a method that should work, but might not for some unusual reason. The status might end up being some unusual return value, in which case the code attempts to figure out what happened and work around it. Somehow this seems like a lot of work to do to handle a rare case. And if the function you called returns an int as part of its normal answer, you'll have to distinguish one special integer (FUNNY_RETURN_VALUE) as an error. Alternatively, you could pass in a special return value pointer, or use a global variable to store those errors, but then problems arise with keeping track of multiple errors with the same bit of code, or of the original error stored in the global being overwritten by a new error before you have a chance to deal with it.

Once you start creating larger systems, error management can become a major problem. Different programmers may use different special values for handling errors, and may not document them overly well, if at all. You may inconsistently use errors in your own programs. Code to manage these kinds of errors can often obscure the original intent of the program, making that code difficult to read and to maintain. And, finally, if you try dealing with errors in this kludgey way, there's no easy way for the compiler to check for consistency the way it can check to make sure you called a method with the right arguments.

For all these reasons, Java has exceptions to deal with managing, creating, and expecting errors and other unusual situations. Through a combination of special language features, consistency checking at compile time, and a set of extensible exception classes, errors and other unusual conditions in Java programs can be much more easily managed. Given these features, you can now add a whole new dimension to the behavior and design of your classes, of your class hierarchy, and of your overall system. Your class and interface definitions describe how your program is supposed to behave given the best circumstances. By integrating exception handling into your program design, you can consistently describe how the program will behave when circumstances are not quite as good, and allow people who use your classes to know what to expect in those cases.

Java Exceptions

At this point in the book, chances are you've run into at least one Java exception—perhaps you mistyped a method name or made a mistake in your code that caused a problem. And chances are that your program quit and spewed a bunch of mysterious errors to the screen. Those mysterious errors are exceptions. When your program quits, it's because an exception was "thrown." Exceptions can be thrown by the system or thrown by you, and they can be caught as well (catching an exception involves dealing with it so your program doesn't crash. You'll learn more about this later). "An exception was thrown" is the proper Java terminology for "an error happened."

 Exceptions don't occur, they are *thrown*. Java throws an exception in response to an unusual situation. You can also throw your own exceptions, or *catch* an exception to gracefully manage errors.

The heart of the Java exception system is the exception itself. Exceptions in Java are actual objects, instances of classes that inherit from the class `Throwable`. When an exception is thrown, an instance of a `Throwable` class is created. Figure 17.1 shows a partial class hierarchy for exceptions.

`Throwable` has two subclasses: `Error` and `Exception`. Instances of `Error` are internal errors in the Java runtime environment (the virtual machine). These errors are rare and usually fatal; there's not much you can do about them (either to catch them or to throw them yourself), but they exist so that Java can use them if it needs to.

The class `Exception` is more interesting. Subclasses of `Exception` fall into two general groups:

☐ Runtime exceptions (subclasses of the class `RuntimeException`) such as `ArrayIndexOutofBounds`, `SecurityException`, or `NullPointerException`.

☐ Other exceptions such as `EOFException` and `MalformedURLException`.

Figure 17.1.

The exception class hierarchy.

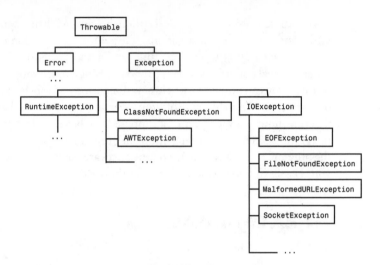

Runtime exceptions usually occur because of code that isn't very robust. An ArrayIndexOutofBounds exception, for example, should never be thrown if you're properly checking to make sure your code doesn't extend past the end of an array. NullPointerException exceptions won't happen if you don't try to reference the values of a variable that doesn't actually hold an object. If your program is causing runtime exceptions under any circumstances whatsoever, you should be fixing those problems before you even begin to deal with exception management.

The final group of exceptions is the most interesting because these are the exceptions that indicate that something very strange and out of control is happening. EOFExceptions, for example, happen when you're reading from a file and the file ends before you expect it to. MalformedURLExceptions happen when a URL isn't in the right format (perhaps your user typed it wrong). This group includes exceptions that you yourself create to signal unusual cases that may occur in your own programs.

Exceptions are arranged in a hierarchy like other classes, where the Exception superclasses are more general errors, and subclasses are more specific errors. This organization will become more important to you as you deal with exceptions in your own code.

Most of the exception classes are part of the java.lang package (including Throwable, Exception, and RuntimeException). But many of the other packages define other exceptions, and those exceptions are used throughout the class library. For example, the java.io package defines a general exception class called IOException, which is subclassed not only in the java.io package for input and output exceptions (EOFException, FileNotFoundException), but also in the java.net classes for networking exceptions such as MalFormedURLException.

17

Managing Exceptions

So now that you know what an exception is, how do you deal with them in your own code? In many cases, the Java compiler enforces exception management when you try to use methods that use exceptions; you'll need to deal with those exceptions in your own code or it simply won't compile. In this section, you'll learn about that consistency checking and how to use the `try`, `catch`, and `finally` language keywords to deal with exceptions that may or may not occur.

Exception Consistency Checking

The more you work with the Java class libraries, the more likely it is that you'll run into a compiler error (an exception!) similar to this one:

```
TestProg.java:32: Exception java.lang.InterruptedException
must be caught or it must be declared in the throws clause
of this method.
```

What on earth does that mean? In Java, a method can indicate the kinds of errors it might possibly throw. For example, methods that read from files might potentially throw IOException errors, so those methods are declared with a special modifier that indicates potential errors. When you use those methods in your own Java programs, you have to protect your code against those exceptions. This rule is enforced by the compiler itself, the same way that the compiler checks to make sure that you're using methods with the right number of arguments and that all your variable types match the thing you're assigning to them.

Why is this check in place? By having methods declare the exceptions they throw, and by forcing you to handle those exceptions in some way, the potential for fatal errors in a program occurring because you simply didn't know they could occur is minimized. You no longer have to carefully read the documentation or the code of an object you're going to use to make sure you've dealt with all the potential problems—Java does the checking for you. And, on the other side, if you define your methods so that they indicate the exceptions they can throw, then Java can tell users of your objects to handle those errors.

Protecting Code and Catching Exceptions

Let's assume that you've been happily coding and during a test compile you ran into that exception message. According to the message, you have to either catch the error or declare that your method throws it. Let's deal with the first case: catching potential exceptions.

To catch an exception, you do two things:

☐ You protect the code that contains the method that might throw an exception inside a `try` block.

☐ You test for and deal with an exception inside a `catch` block.

What `try` and `catch` effectively mean is "try this bit of code that might cause an exception. If it executes okay, go on with the program. If it doesn't, catch the exception and deal with it."

You've seen `try` and `catch` once before, when we dealt with threads. On Day 10, "Animation, Images, Threads, and Sound," you learned about an applet that created a digital clock, and the animation paused once a second using this bit of code:

```
try { Thread.sleep(1000) }
catch (InterruptedException e) {}
```

While this example uses `try` and `catch`, it's not a very good use of it. Here, the `Thread.sleep()` class method could potentially throw an exception of type `InterruptedException` (for when the thread is interrupted from running). So we've put the call to `sleep()` inside the `try` clause to catch that exception if it happens. And inside `catch` (inside the parentheses), we indicate that we're specifically looking for `InterruptedException` exceptions. The problem here is that there isn't anything inside the `catch` clause—in other words, we'll catch the exception if it happens, but then we'll drop it on the floor and pretend we didn't see it. In all but the simplest cases (such as this one, where the exception really doesn't matter), you're going to want to put something inside the braces after `catch` to try to do something responsible to clean up after the exception happens.

The part of the `catch` clause inside the parentheses is similar to the parameter list of a method definition; it contains the class of the exception to be caught and a variable name (`e` is very commonly used). Inside the body of the `catch` clause, you can then refer to the exception object, for example, to get to the detailed error message contained in the `getMessage()` method:

```
catch (InterruptedException e) {
    System.out.println("Ooops.  Error: " + e.getMessage());
}
```

Here's another example. Say you have a program that reads from a file. This program most likely uses one of the streams classes you'll learn about on Day 19, "Java Streams and I/O," but the basic idea here is that you open a connection to a file and then use the `read()` method to get data from it. What if some strange disk error happens and the `read()` method can't read anything? What if the file is truncated and has fewer bytes in it than you expected? In either of these instances, the `read()` method will throw an `IOException` which, if you didn't catch it, would cause your program to stop executing and possibly crash. By putting your `read()` method inside a `try` clause, you can then deal gracefully with that error inside `catch` to clean up after the error and return to some safe state, to patch things up enough to be able to proceed, or, if all else fails, to save as much of the current program's state as possible and to exit. This example does just that; it tries to read from the file, and catches exceptions if they happen:

```
try {
    while (numbytes <= mybuffer.length) {
        myinputstream.read(mybuffer);
        numbytes;++
    }
} catch (IOException e) {
  System.out.println("Ooops, IO Exception.  Only read " + numbytes.");
  // other cleanup code
}
```

Here, the "other cleanup code" can be anything you want it to be; perhaps you can go on with the program using the partial information you got from the file, or perhaps you want to put up a dialog saying that the file is corrupt and to let the user try to select another file or do some other operation.

Note that because the Exception classes are organized into hierarchies as other classes are, and because of the rule that you can use a subclass anywhere a superclass is expected, you can catch "groups" of exceptions and handle them with the same catch code. For example, although there are several different types of IOExceptions (EOFException, FileNotFoundException, and so on—see the java.io package for examples), by catching IOException you also catch instances of any subclass of IOException.

What if you do want to catch very different kinds of exceptions that aren't related by inheritance? You can use multiple catch clauses for a given try, like this:

```
try {
   // protected code
} catch (OneKindOfException e) {
  ...
} catch (AnotherKindOfException e2) {
  ....
} catch (YetAnotherException e3) {
  ...
} catch (StilMoreException e4) {
  ....
}
```

Note that because the scope of local variables inside catch is the same as the scope of the outer block (the method definition or a loop if you're inside one), you'll have to use different local variables for each individual catch.

Because the first catch clause that matches is executed, you can build chains such as the following:

```
try {
    someReallyExceptionalMethod();
} catch (NullPointerException n) {  // a subclass of RuntimeException
```

```
        . . .
} catch (RuntimeException r) {       // a subclass of Exception
        . . .
} catch (IOException i) {             // a subclass of Exception
        . . .
} catch (MyFirstException m) {        // our subclass of Exception
        . . .
} catch (Exception e) {               // a subclass of Throwable
        . . .
} catch (Throwable t) {
    . . . // Errors, plus anything not caught above are caught here
}
```

By listing subclasses before their parent classes, the parent catches anything it would normally catch that's also *not* one of the subclasses above it. By juggling chains like these, you can express almost any combination of tests.

The `finally` Clause

Suppose there is some action in your code that you absolutely must do, no matter what happens, whether an exception is thrown or not. Usually, this is to free some external resource after acquiring it, to close a file after opening it, or something similar. While you could put that action both inside a catch and outside it, that would be duplicating the same code in two different places. Instead, put one copy of that code inside a special optional part of the try...catch clause, called finally:

```
SomeFileClass  f = new SomeFileClass();

if (f.open("/a/file/name/path")) {
    try {
        someReallyExceptionalMethod();
    { catch (IOException e) {
        // deal with errors
    } finally {
        f.close();
    }
}
```

The finally clause is actually useful outside exceptions; you can also use it to execute cleanup code after a return, a break, or a continue inside loops. For the latter cases, you can use a try clause with a finally but without a catch clause.

Here's a fairly complex example of how this might work:

```
int  mysteriousState = getContext();

while (true) {
    System.out.print("Who ");
    try {
        System.out.print("is ");
        if (mysteriousState == 1)
```

17

```
            return;
        System.out.print("that ");
        if (mysteriousState == 2)
            break;
        System.out.print("strange ");
        if (mysteriousState == 3)
            continue;
        System.out.print("but kindly ");
        if (mysteriousState == 4)
            throw new UncaughtException();
        System.out.print("not at all ");
    } finally {
        System.out.print("amusing man?\n");
    }
    System.out.print("I'd like to meet the man");
}
System.out.print("Please tell me.\n");
```

Here is the output produced depending on the value of mysteriousState:

```
1    Who is amusing man? Please tell me.
2    Who is that amusing man? Please tell me.
3    Who is that strange amusing man? Who is that strange ....
4    Who is that strange but kindly amusing man? Please tell me.
5    Who is that strange but kindly not at all amusing man?
     I'd like to meet that man. Who is that strange ...
```

NOTE In cases 3 and 5, the output never ends until you quit the program. In 4, an error message generated by the UncaughtException is also printed.

Declaring Methods That Might Throw Exceptions

In the previous example, you learned how to deal with methods that might possibly throw exceptions by protecting code and catching any exceptions that occur. The Java compiler will check to make sure you've somehow dealt with a method's exceptions—but how did it know which exceptions to tell you about in the first place?

The answer is that the original method indicated in its signature contains the exceptions that it might possibly throw. You can use this mechanism in your own methods—in fact, it's good style to do so to make sure that other users of your classes are alerted to the errors your methods may come across.

To indicate that a method may possibly throw an exception, you use a special clause in the method definition called throws.

The throws Clause

To indicate that some code in the body of your method may throw an exception, simply add the throws keyword after the signature for the method (before the opening brace) with the name or names of the exception that your method throws:

```
public boolean myMethod (int x, int y) throws AnException {
   ...
}
```

If your method may possibly throw multiple kinds of exceptions, you can put all of them in the throws clause, separated by commas:

```
public boolean myOtherMethod (int x, int y)
  throws AnException, AnotherExeption, AThirdException {
   ...
}
```

Note that as with catch you can use a superclass of a group of exceptions to indicate that your method may throw any subclass of that exception:

```
public void YetAnotherMethod() throws IOException {
...
}
```

Keep in mind that adding a throws method to your method definition simply means that the method might throw an exception if something goes wrong, not that it actually will. The throws clause simply provides extra information to your method definition about potential exceptions and allows Java to make sure that your method is being used correctly by other people.

Think of a method's overall description as a contract between the designer of that method (or class) and the caller of the method (you can be on either side of that contract, of course). Usually, the description indicates the types of a method's arguments, what it returns, and the general semantics of what it normally does. Using throws, you add information about the abnormal things it can do as well. This new part of the contract helps to separate and make explicit all the places where exceptional conditions should be handled in your program, and that makes large-scale design easier.

Which Exceptions Should You Throw?

Once you decide to declare that your method might throw an exception, you have to decide which exceptions it might throw (and actually throw them or call a method that will throw them—you'll learn about throwing your own exceptions in the next section). In many instances, this will be apparent from the operation of the method itself. Perhaps you're creating and throwing your own exceptions, in which case you'll know exactly which exceptions to throw.

You don't really have to list all the possible exceptions that your method could throw; some exceptions are handled by the runtime itself and are so common (well, not common, but ubiquitous) that you don't have to deal with them. In particular, exceptions of either class Error or RuntimeException (or any of their subclasses) do not have to be listed in your throws clause. They get special treatment because they can occur anywhere within a Java program and are usually conditions that you, as the programmer, did not directly cause. One good example is OutOfMemoryError, which can happen anywhere, at any time, and for any number of reasons. These two kinds of exceptions are called implicit exceptions, and you don't have to worry about them.

 Implicit exceptions are exceptions that are subclasses of the classes RuntimeException and Error. Implicit exceptions are usually thrown by the Java runtime itself. You do not have to declare that your method throws them.

 You can, of course, choose to list these errors and runtime exceptions in your throws clause if you like, but the callers of your methods will not be forced to handle them; only non-runtime exceptions *must* be handled.

All other exceptions are called explicit exceptions and are potential candidates of a throws clause in your method.

Passing On Exceptions

In addition to declaring methods that throw exceptions, there's one other instance in which your method definition may include a throws clause. In this case, you want to use a method that throws an exception, but you don't want to catch that exception or deal with it. In many cases, it might make more sense for the method that calls your method to deal with that exception rather than for you to deal with it. There's nothing wrong with this; it's a fairly common occurrence that you won't actually deal with an exception, but will pass it back to the method that calls yours. At any rate, it's a better idea to pass on exceptions to calling methods than to catch them and ignore them.

Rather than using the try and catch clauses in the body of your method, you can declare your method with a throws clause such that it, too, might possibly throw the appropriate exception. Then it's the responsibility of the method that calls your method to deal with that exception. This is the other case that will satisfy the Java compiler that you have done something with a given method. Here's another way of implementing an example that reads characters from a stream:

```
public void readTheFile(String filename) throws IO Exception {
    // open the file, init the stream, etc.
    while (numbytes <= mybuffer.length) {
        myinputstream.read(mybuffer);
        numbytes;++
    }
}
```

This example is similar to the example used previously today; remember that the read()
method was declared to throw an IOException, so you had to use try and catch to use it. Once
you declare your method to throw an exception, however, you can use other methods that
also throw those exceptions inside the body of this method, without needing to protect the
code or catch the exception.

NOTE

> You can, of course, deal with other exceptions using try and catch in
> the body of your method in addition to passing on the exceptions you
> listed in the throws clause. You can also both deal with the exception in
> some way and then re-throw it so that your method's calling method
> has to deal with it anyhow. You'll learn how to throw methods in the
> next section.

throws **and Inheritance**

If your method definition overrides a method in a superclass that includes a throws clause,
there are special rules for how your overridden method deals with throws. Unlike with the
other parts of the method signature, your new method does not have to have the same set of
exceptions listed in the throws clause. Because there's a potential that your new method may
deal better with exceptions, rather than just throwing them, your subclass's method can
potentially throw fewer types of exceptions than its superclass's method definition, up to and
including throwing no exceptions at all. That means that you can have the following two class
definitions and things will work just fine:

```
public class Fruit {
    public void ripen() throws RotException {
        ...
    }
}

public class WaxFruit extends Fruit {
    public void ripen() {
        ...
    }
}
```

The converse of this rule is not true; a subclass's method cannot throw more exceptions
(either exceptions of different types or more general exception classes) than its superclass's
method.

Creating and Throwing Your Own Exceptions

There are two sides to every exception: the side that throws the exception and the side that catches it. An exception can be tossed around a number of times to a number of methods before it's caught, but eventually it'll be caught and dealt with.

But who does the actual throwing? Where do exceptions come from? Many exceptions are thrown by the Java runtime, or by methods inside the Java classes themselves. You can also throw any of the standard exceptions that the Java class libraries define, or you can create and throw your own exceptions. This section describes all these things.

17

Throwing Exceptions

Declaring that your method throws an exception is useful only to users of your method and to the Java compiler, which checks to make sure all your exceptions are being dealt with. But the declaration itself doesn't do anything to actually throw that exception should it occur; you have to do that yourself in the body of the method.

Remember that exceptions are all instances of some exception class, of which there are many defined in the standard Java class libraries. In order to throw an exception, therefore, you'll need to create a new instance of an exception class. Once you have that instance, use the throw statement to throw it (could this be any easier?). The simplest way to throw an exception is simply like this:

```
throw new ServiceNOteAvailableException();
```

TECHNICAL NOTE

> You can only throw objects that are instances of subclasses of Throwable. This is different from C++'s exceptions, which allow you to throw objects of any type.

Depending on the exception class you're using, the exception may also have arguments to its constructor that you can use. The most common of these is a string argument, which lets you describe the actual problem in greater detail (which can be very useful for debugging purposes). Here's an example:

```
throw new ServiceNotAvailableException("Exception:
    service not available, database is offline.");
```

Once an exception is thrown, the method exits immediately, without executing any other code (other than the code inside `finally`, if that clause exists) and without returning a value. If the calling method does not have a `try` or `catch` surrounding the call to your method, the program may very well exit based on the exception you threw.

Creating Your Own Exceptions

Exceptions are simply classes, just like any other class in the Java hierarchy. Although there are a fair number of exceptions in the Java class library that you can use in your own methods, there is a strong possibility that you may want to create your own exceptions to handle different kinds of errors your programs might run into. Fortunately, creating new exceptions is easy.

Your new exception should inherit from some other exception in the Java hierarchy. Look for an exception that's close to the one you're creating; for example, an exception for a bad file format would logically be an `IOException`. If you can't find a closely related exception for your new exception, consider inheriting from `Exception`, which forms the "top" of the exception hierarchy for explicit exceptions (remember that implicit exceptions, which include subclasses of `Error` and `RuntimeException`, inherit from `Throwable`).

Exception classes typically have two constructors: The first takes no arguments and the second takes a single string as an argument. In the latter case you'll want to call `super()` in that constructor to make sure the string is applied to the right place in the exception.

Beyond those three rules, exception classes look just like other classes. You can put them in their own source files and compile them just as you would other classes:

```
public class SunSpotException extends Exception {
    public SunSpotException() {}
    public SunSpotExceotion(String msg) {
        super(msg);
    }
}
```

Doing It All: Combining `throws`, `try`, and `throw`

What if you want to combine all the approaches shown so far? In your method, you'd like to handle incoming exceptions yourself, but also you'd like to pass the exception up to your caller. Simply using `try` and `catch` doesn't pass on the exception, and simply adding a `throws` clause doesn't give you a chance to deal with the exception. If you want to both manage the exception and pass it on to the caller, use all three mechanisms: the `throws` clause, the `try` statement, and by explicitly rethrowing the exception:

```
public void  responsibleExceptionalMethod() throws MyFirstException {
    MyFirstExceptionalClass  aMFEC = new MyFirstExceptionalClass();
```

```
    try {
        aMFEC.anExceptionalMethod();
    } catch (MyFirstException (m) {
        . . .            // do something responsible
        throw m;         // re-throw the exception
    }
}
```

This works because exception handlers can be nested. You handle the exception by doing something responsible with it, but decide that it is too important to not give an exception handler that might be in your caller a chance to handle it as well. Exceptions float all the way up the chain of method callers this way (usually not being handled by most of them) until at last the system itself handles any uncaught ones by aborting your program and printing an error message. In a standalone program, this is not such a bad idea; but in an applet, it can cause the browser to crash. Most browsers protect themselves from this disaster by catching all exceptions themselves whenever they run an applet, but you can never tell. If it's possible for you to catch an exception and do something intelligent with it, you should.

When and When Not to Use Exceptions

To finish up today's lesson, here's a quick summary and some advice on when to use exceptions…and when not to use them.

When to Use Exceptions

Because throwing, catching, and declaring exceptions are interrelated concepts and can be very confusing, here's a quick summary of when to do what.

If your method uses someone else's method, and that method has a throws clause, you can do one of three things:

☐ Deal with the exception using try and catch statements.

☐ Pass the exception up the calling chain by adding your own throws clause to your method definition.

☐ Do both of the above by catching the exception using catch and then explicitly rethrowing it using throw.

In cases where a method throws more than one exception, you can, of course, handle each of those exceptions differently. For example, you might catch some of those exceptions while allowing others to pass up the calling chain.

If your method throws its own exceptions, you should declare that it throws those methods using the throws clause. If your method overrides a superclass's method that has a throws clause, you can throw the same types of exceptions or subclasses of those exceptions; you cannot throw any different types of exceptions.

And, finally, if your method has been declared with a throws clause, don't forget to actually throw the exception in the body of your method using throw.

When Not to Use Exceptions

Exceptions are cool. But they aren't *that* cool. There are several cases in which you should not use exceptions, even though they may seem appropriate at the time.

First, you should not use exceptions if the exception is something that you expect and a simple test to avoid that exceptional condition would make much more sense. For example, although you can rely on an ArrayIndexOutofBounds exception to tell you when you've gone past the end of the array, a simple test of the length of the array in your code to make sure you don't get that exception in the first place is a much better idea. Or if your users are going to enter data that you need to be a letter, testing to make sure that data is a letter is a much better idea than throwing an exception and dealing with it somewhere else.

Exceptions take up a lot of processing time for your Java program. Whereas you may find exceptions stylistically interesting for your own code, a simple test or series of tests will run much faster and make your program that much more efficient. Exceptions, as I mentioned earlier, should only be used for truly exceptional cases that are out of your control.

It's also easy to get carried away with exceptions and to try to make sure that all your methods have been declared to throw all the possible exceptions that they can possibly throw. In addition to making your code more complex in general, if other people will be using your code, they'll have to deal with handling all the exceptions that your methods might throw. You're making more work for everyone involved when you get carried away with exceptions. Declaring a method to throw either few or lots of exceptions is a trade-off; the more exceptions your method potentially throws, the more complex that method is to use. Declare only the exceptions that have a reasonably fair chance of happening and that make sense for the overall design of your classes.

Bad Style Using Exceptions

When you first start using exceptions, it might be appealing to work around the compiler errors that result when you use a method that declared a throws clause. Although it is legal to add an empty catch clause or to add a throws clause to your own method (and there are appropriate reasons for doing both of these things), intentionally dropping exceptions on the floor and subverting the checks the Java compiler does for you is very bad style.

The Java exception system was designed so that if a potential error can occur, you're warned about it. Ignoring those warnings and working around them makes it possible for fatal errors to occur in your program—errors that you could have avoided with a few lines of code. And, even worse, adding throws clauses to your methods to avoid exceptions means that the users of your methods (objects further up in the calling chain) will have to deal with them. You've just made more work for someone else and made your methods more difficult to use for other people.

Compiler errors regarding exceptions are there to remind you to reflect on these issues. Take the time to deal with the exceptions that may affect your code. This extra care will richly reward you as you reuse your classes in later projects and in larger and larger programs. Of course, the Java class library has been written with exactly this degree of care, and that's one of the reasons it's robust enough to be used in constructing all your Java projects.

Summary

Today you have learned about how exceptions aid your program's design and robustness. Exceptions give you a way of managing potential errors in your programs and of alerting users of your programs that potential errors can occur. The Java class library has a vast array of exceptions defined and thrown, and also allows you to define and throw your own exceptions. Using try, catch, and finally you can protect code that may result in exceptions, catch and handle those exceptions if they occur, and execute code whether or not an exception was generated.

Handling exceptions is only half of the equation; the other half is generating and throwing exceptions yourself. Today you have learned about the throws clause, which tells users of your method that the method might throw an exception. throws can also be used to "pass on" an exception from a method call in the body of your method.

In addition to the information given by the throws clause, you learned how to actually create and throw your own methods by defining new exception classes and by throwing instances of any exception classes using throw.

And, finally, Java's reliance on strict exception handling does place some restrictions on the programmer, but you have learned that these restrictions are light compared to the rewards.

Q&A

Q I'm still not sure I understand the differences between exceptions, errors, and runtime exceptions. Is there another way of looking at them?

A Errors are caused by dynamic linking, or virtual machine problems, and are thus too low-level for most programs to care about—or be able to handle even if they did care about them. Runtime exceptions are generated by the normal execution of Java code, and although they occasionally reflect a condition you will want to handle explicitly, more often they reflect a coding mistake by the programmer and thus simply need to print an error to help flag that mistake. Exceptions that are not runtime exceptions (IOException exceptions, for example) are conditions that, because of their nature, should be explicitly handled by any robust and well-thought-out code. The Java class library has been written using only a few of these, but those few are extremely important to using the system safely and correctly. The compiler helps you handle these exceptions properly via its throws clause checks and restrictions.

Q Is there any way to "get around" the strict restrictions placed on methods by the throws clause?

A Yes. Suppose you have thought long and hard and have decided that you need to circumvent this restriction. This is almost never the case, because the right solution is to go back and redesign your methods to reflect the exceptions that you need to throw. Imagine, however, that for some reason a system class has you in a straitjacket. Your first solution is to subclass RuntimeException to make up a new, exempt exception of your own. Now you can throw it to your heart's content, because the throws clause that was annoying you does not need to include this new exception. If you need a lot of such exceptions, an elegant approach is to mix in some novel exception interfaces to your new Runtime classes. You're free to choose whatever subset of these new interfaces you want to catch (none of the normal Runtime exceptions need be caught), while any leftover (new) Runtime exceptions are (legally) allowed to go through that otherwise annoying standard method in the library.

Q I'm still a little confused by long chains of catch clauses. Can you label the previous example with which exceptions are handled by each line of code?

A Certainly. Here it is:

```
try {
    someReallyExceptionalMethod();
} catch (NullPointerException n) {
    . . . // handles NullPointerExceptions
} catch (RuntimeException r) {
    . . . // handles RuntimeExceptions
           //that are not NullPointerExceptions
} catch (IOException i) {
    . . . // handles IOExceptions
} catch (MyFirstException m) {
    . . . // handles MyFirstExceptions
} catch (Exception e) {
    . . . // handles Exceptions that are not
           // RuntimeExceptions nor IOExceptions
           // nor MyFirstExceptions
} catch (Throwable t) {
    . . . // handles Throwables that
           // are not Exceptions (i.e., Errors)
}
```

Q Given how annoying it can sometimes be to handle exceptional conditions properly, what's stopping me from surrounding any method as follows:

```
try { thatAnnoyingMethod(); } catch (Throwable t) { }
```

and simply ignoring all exceptions?

A Nothing, other than your own conscience. In some cases, you *should* do nothing, because it is the correct thing to do for your method's implementation. Otherwise, you should struggle through the annoyance and gain experience. Good style is a struggle even for the best of programmers, but the rewards are rich indeed.

17

Day 18

Multithreading

by Charles L. Perkins and Michael Morrison

One of the major features in the Java programming environment and runtime system is the multithreaded architecture shared by both. Multithreading, which is a fairly recent construct in the computer science world, is a very powerful means of enhancing and controlling program execution. Today's lesson takes a look at how the Java language supports multithreading through the use of threads. You'll learn all about the different classes that enable Java to be a threaded language, along with many of the issues surrounding the effective use of threads.

To better understand the importance of threads, imagine that you're using your favorite text editor on a large file. When it starts up, does it need to examine the entire file before it lets you begin editing? Does it need to make a copy of the file? If the file is huge, this can be a nightmare. Wouldn't it be nicer for it to show you the first page, allowing you to begin editing, and somehow (in the background) complete the slower tasks necessary for initialization? Threads allow exactly this kind of within-the-program parallelism.

Perhaps the best example of threading (or lack of it) is a Web browser. Can your browser download an indefinite number of files and Web pages at once while still enabling you to continue browsing? While these pages are downloading, can your browser download all the pictures, sounds, and so forth in parallel, interleaving the fast and slow download times of multiple Internet servers? Multithreaded browsers can do all these things by virtue of their internal usage of threads.

Today you'll learn about the following primary issues surrounding threads:

- ☐ Thread fundamentals
- ☐ How to "think multithreaded"
- ☐ How to protect your methods and variables from unintended thread conflicts
- ☐ How to create, start, and stop threads and threaded classes
- ☐ How the scheduler works in Java

Let's begin today's lesson by defining what a thread is.

Thread Fundamentals

The multithreading support in Java revolves around the concept of a thread. So what exactly is a thread? Put simply, a *thread* is a single stream of execution within a process. Okay, maybe that wasn't so simple. It might be better to start off by explaining exactly what a process is. A *process* is a program executing within its own address space. Java is a multiprocessing system, meaning that it supports many processes running concurrently in their own address spaces. You may be more familiar with the term multitasking, which describes a scenario very similar to multiprocessing. As an example, consider the variety of applications typically running at once in a graphical environment. Most Windows 95 users typically run a variety of applications together at once, such as Microsoft Word, CD Player, Windows Messaging, Volume Control, and of course Solitaire. These applications are all processes executing within the Windows 95 environment. So you can think of processes as being analogous to applications, or standalone programs; each process in a system is given its own space in memory to execute.

NEW TERM   A *process* is a program executing within its own address space.

NEW TERM   A *thread* is a single stream of execution within a process.

A thread is a sequence of code executing within the context of a process. As a matter of fact, threads cannot execute on their own; they require the overhead of a parent process to run. Within each of the processes typically running, there are no doubt a variety of threads

18

executing. For example, Word may have a thread in the background automatically checking the spelling of what is being written, while another thread may be automatically saving changes to the document. Like Word, each application (process) can be running many threads that are performing any number of tasks. The significance here is that threads are always associated with a particular process.

Judging by the fact that I've described threads and processes using Windows 95 as an example, you've probably guessed that Java isn't the first system to employ the use of threads. That's true, but Java is the first major programming language to incorporate threads at the heart of the language itself. Typically, threads are implemented at the system level, requiring a platform-specific programming interface separate from the core programming language. Because Java is presented as both a language and a runtime system, the Sun architects were able to integrate threads into both. The end result is that you are able to make use of Java threads in a standard, cross-platform fashion.

The Problem with Parallelism

If threading is so wonderful, why doesn't every system have it? Many modern operating systems have the basic primitives needed to create and run threads, but they are missing a key ingredient: The rest of their environment is not *thread safe*. A thread-safe environment is one that allows threads to safely coexist with each other peacefully. Imagine that you are a thread, one of many, and each of you is sharing some important data managed by the system. If you were managing that data, you could take steps to protect it (as you'll see later today), but the system is managing it. Now visualize a piece of code in the system that reads some crucial value, thinks about it for a while, and then adds 1 to the value:

```
if (crucialValue > 0) {
    . . .                    // think about what to do
    crucialValue += 1;
}
```

Remember that any number of threads may be calling on this part of the system at once. The disaster occurs when two threads have both executed the `if` test before either has incremented `crucialValue`. In that case, the value is clobbered by them both with the same `crucialValue += 1`, and one of the increments has been lost. This may not seem so bad on the surface, but imagine if the crucial value affects the state of the screen as it is being displayed. Now, unfortunate ordering of the threads can cause the screen to be updated incorrectly. In the same way, mouse or keyboard events can be lost, databases can be inaccurately updated, and general havoc can ensue.

This disaster is inescapable if any significant part of the system has not been written with threads in mind. Therein lies the reason why there are few mainstream threaded environments—the large effort required to rewrite existing libraries for thread safety. Luckily, Java

18

was written from scratch with this is mind, and every Java class in its library is thread safe. Thus, you now have to worry only about your own synchronization and thread-ordering problems because you can assume that the Java system will do the right thing.

Synchronized sections of code are called *critical sections*, implying that access to them is critical to the successful threaded execution of the program. Critical sections are also sometimes referred to as *atomic operations*, meaning that they appear to other threads as if they occur at once. In other words, just as an atom is a discrete unit of matter, atomic operations effectively act like a discrete operation to other threads, even though they may really contain many operations inside.

 Critical sections, or *atomic operations*, are synchronized sections of code that appear to happen "all at once"—exactly at the same time—to other threads. This results in only one thread being able to access code in a critical section at a time.

 Some readers may wonder what the fundamental problem really is. Can't you just make the ... area in the previous example smaller and smaller to reduce or eliminate the problem? Without atomic operations, the answer is no. Even if the ... took zero time, you must first look at the value of some variable to make any decision and then change something to reflect that decision. These two steps can never be made to happen at the same time without an atomic operation. Unless you're given one by the system, it's literally impossible to create your own.

Even the one line `crucialValue += 1` involves three steps: Get the current value, add one to it, and store it back. (Using `++crucialValue` doesn't help either.) All three steps need to happen "all at once" (atomically) to be safe. Special Java primitives, at the lowest levels of the language, provide you with the basic atomic operations you need to build safe, threaded programs.

Thinking Multithreaded

Getting used to threads takes a little while and a new way of thinking. Rather than imagining that you always know exactly what's happening when you look at a method you've written, you have to ask yourself some additional questions. What will happen if more than one thread calls into this method at the same time? Do you need to protect it in some way? What about your class as a whole? Are you assuming that only one of its methods is running at the same time?

Often you make such assumptions, and a local instance variable will be messed up as a result. Because common wisdom dictates that we learn from our mistakes, let's make a few mistakes and then try to correct them. First, here's the simplest case:

```java
public class ThreadCounter {
    int crucialValue;

    public void countMe() {
        crucialValue += 1;
    }

    public int howMany() {
        return crucialValue;
    }
}
```

This code shows a class used to count threads that suffers from the most pure form of the "synchronization problem": The += takes more than one step, and you may miscount the number of threads as a result. (Don't worry about how threads are created yet; just imagine that a whole bunch of them are able to call countMe(), at once, but at slightly different times.) Java allows you to fix this situation:

```java
public class SafeThreadCounter {
    int crucialValue;

    public synchronized void countMe() {
        crucialValue += 1;
    }

    public int howMany() {
        return crucialValue;
    }
}
```

The synchronized keyword tells Java to make the block of code in the method thread safe. This means that only one thread will be allowed inside this method at once, and others will have to wait until the currently running thread is finished with it before they can begin running it. This implies that synchronizing a large, long-running method is almost always a bad idea. All your threads would end up stuck at this bottleneck, waiting single file to get their turn at this one slow method.

It's even worse than you might think for unsynchronized variables. Because the compiler can keep them around in CPU registers during computations, and a thread's registers can't be seen by other threads, a variable can be updated in such a way that *no possible order* of thread updates could have produced the result. This is completely incomprehensible to the programmer, but it can happen. To avoid this bizarre case, you can label a variable volatile, meaning that you know it will be updated asynchronously by multiprocessor-like threads. Java then loads and stores it each time it's needed and does not use CPU registers.

18

> **NOTE** All variables are assumed to be thread safe unless you specifically mark them as volatile. Keep in mind that using volatile is an extremely rare event. In fact, since the 1.0.2 release, the Java API has not used volatile anywhere.

Points About Points

The method howMany() in the last example doesn't need to be synchronized because it simply returns the current value of an instance variable. A method higher in the call chain—one that uses the value returned from howMany()—may need to be synchronized, though. Listing 18.1 contains an example of a thread in need of this type of synchronization.

TYPE **Listing 18.1. The Point class.**

```
 1: public class Point {       //redefines class Point from package java.awt
 2:     private float x, y;    //OK since we're in a different package here
 3:
 4:     public float x() {         // needs no synchronization
 5:         return x;
 6:     }
 7:
 8:     public float y() {         // ditto
 9:         return y;
10:     }
11:     . . .    // methods to set and change x and y
12: }
13:
14: public class UnsafePointPrinter {
15:     public void print(Point p) {
16:         System.out.println("The point's x is " + p.x()
17:                             + " and y is " + p.y() + ".");
18:     }
19: }
```

ANALYSIS The methods analogous to howMany() are x() and y(). They need no synchronization because they just return the values of member variables. It is the responsibility of the caller of x() and y() to decide whether it needs to synchronize itself—and in this case, it does. Although the method print() simply reads values and prints them out, it reads *two* values. This means that there is a chance that some other thread, running between the call to p.x() and the call to p.y(), could have changed the value of x and y stored inside the Point p. Remember, you don't know how many other threads have a way to reach and call methods in this Point object! "Thinking multithreaded" comes down to being careful any time you make an assumption that something has *not* happened between two parts of your program (even two parts of the same line, or the same expression, such as the string + expression in this example).

TryAgainPointPrinter

You could try to make a safe version of print() by simply adding the synchronized keyword modifier to it, but instead, let's try a slightly different approach:

```
public class TryAgainPointPrinter {
    public void print(Point p) {
        float safeX, safeY;

        synchronized(this) {
            safeX = p.x();      // these two lines now
            safeY = p.y();      // happen atomically
        }
        System.out.print("The point's x is " + safeX
                                + " y is " + safeY);
    }
}
```

The synchronized statement takes an argument that says what object you would like to lock to prevent more than one thread from executing the enclosed block of code at the same time. Here, you use this (the instance itself), which is exactly the object that would have been locked by the synchronized method as a whole if you had changed print() to be like your safe countMe() method. You have an added bonus with this new form of synchronization: You can specify exactly what part of a method needs to be safe, and the rest can be left unsafe.

Notice how you took advantage of this freedom to make the protected part of the method as small as possible, while leaving the String creations, concatenations, and printing (which together take a small but finite amount of time) outside the "protected" area. This is both good style (as a guide to the reader of your code) and more efficient, because fewer threads get stuck waiting to get into protected areas.

SafePointPrinter

The astute reader, though, may still be worried by the last example. It seems as if you made sure that no one executes *your* calls to x() and y() out of order, but have you prevented the Point p from changing out from under you? If the answer is no, you still have not completely solved the problem. It turns out that you really do need the full power of the synchronized statement:

```
public class SafePointPrinter {
    public void print(Point p) {
        float safeX, safeY;
```

```
        synchronized(p) {      // no one can change p
            safeX = p.x();     // while these two lines
            safeY = p.y();     // are happening atomically
        }
        System.out.print("The point's x is " + safeX
                                    + " y is " + safeY);
    }
}
```

Now you've got it! You actually needed to protect the Point p from changes, so you lock it by providing it as the argument to your synchronized statement. Now when x() and y() are called together, they can be sure to get the current x and y of Point p, without any other thread being able to call a modifying method between. You're still assuming, however, that Point p has properly protected *itself.* You can always assume this about system classes—but *you* wrote this Point class. You can make sure it's okay by writing the only method that can change x and y inside p yourself:

```
public class  Point {
    private float x, y;

    . . .          // the x() and y() methods

    public synchronized void setXAndY(float  newX,  float  newY) {
        x = newX;
        y = newY;
    }
}
```

By making synchronized the only "set" method in Point, you guarantee that any other thread trying to grab Point p and change it out from under you has to wait. You've locked Point p with your synchronized(p) statement, and any other thread has to lock the same Point p via the implicit synchronized(this) statement that is executed when p enters setXAndY(). So at last you are thread safe.

NOTE

> By the way, if Java had some way of returning more than one value at once, you could write a synchronized getXAndY() method for Point that returns both values safely. In the current Java language, such a method could return a new, unique Point to guarantee to its callers that no one else has a copy that might be changed. This sort of trick can be used to minimize the parts of the system that need to worry about synchronization.

Protecting a Class Variable

Suppose you want a class variable to collect some information across all a class's instances:

```
public class StaticCounter {
    private static int crucialValue;

    public synchronized void countMe() {
        crucialValue += 1;
    }
}
```

Is this safe? If crucialValue were an instance variable, it would be. Because it's a class variable, however, and there is only one copy of it for all instances; you can still have multiple threads modifying it by using different *instances* of the class. (Remember that the synchronized modifier locks the this object—an instance.) Luckily, you now know the technique required to solve this:

```
public class StaticCounter {
    private static int crucialValue;

    public void countMe() {
        synchronized(getClass()) {   // can't directly name StaticCounter
            crucialValue += 1;        // the (shared) class is now locked
        }
    }
}
```

The trick is to "lock" on a different object—not on an instance of the class, but on the class itself. Because a class variable is "inside" a class, just as an instance variable is inside an instance, this shouldn't be all that unexpected. In a similar way, classes can provide global resources that any instance (or other class) can access directly by using the class name and lock by using that same class name. In the last example, crucialValue was used from within an instance of StaticCounter, but if crucialValue were declared public instead, from anywhere in the program, it would be safe to say the following:

```
synchronized(Class.forName("StaticCounter")) {
    StaticCounter.crucialValue += 1;
}
```

NOTE

> The direct use of another class's (object's) member variable is really bad style—it's used here simply to demonstrate a point quickly. StaticCounter would normally provide a countMe()-like class method of its own to do this sort of dirty work.

18

You can now begin to appreciate how much work the Java team has done for you by thinking all these hard thoughts for each and every class (and method!) in the Java class library.

Creating and Using Threads

Now that you understand the power (and the dangers) of having many threads running at once, how are those threads actually created?

WARNING

The system itself always has a few *daemon threads* running, one of which is constantly doing the tedious task of garbage collection for you in the background. There is also a main user thread that listens for events from your mouse and keyboard. If you're not careful, you can sometimes lock up this main thread. If you do, no events are sent to your program and it appears to be dead. A good rule of thumb is that whenever you're doing something that *can* be done in a separate thread, it probably *should* be. Threads in Java are relatively cheap to create, run, and destroy, so don't use them too sparingly.

Because there is a class `java.lang.Thread`, you might guess that you could create a thread of your own by subclassing it—and you are right:

```
public class MyFirstThread extends Thread { // a.k.a., java.lang.Thread
    public void run() {
        . . .                 // do something useful
    }
}
```

You now have a new type of thread called `MyFirstThread`, which does something useful when its `run()` method is called. Of course, no one has created this thread or called its `run()` method, so at this point it is just a class eager to become a thread. To actually create and run an instance of your new thread class, you write the following:

```
MyFirstThread aMFT = new MyFirstThread();
aMFT.start();    // calls our run() method
```

What could be simpler? You create a new instance of your thread class and then ask it to start running. Whenever you want to stop the thread, you do this:

```
aMFT.stop();
```

Besides responding to start() and stop(), a thread can also be temporarily suspended and later resumed:

```
Thread   t = new Thread();
t.suspend();
. . .          // do something special while t isn't running
t.resume();
```

A thread will automatically suspend() and then resume() when it's first blocked at a synchronized point and then later unblocked (when it's that thread's "turn" to run).

The Runnable Interface

This is all well and good if every time you want to create a thread you have the luxury of being able to place it under the Thread class in the single-inheritance Java class tree. But what if it more naturally belongs under some other class, from which it needs to inherit most of its implementation? The interfaces you learned about on Day 16, "Packages, Interfaces, and Inner Classes," come to the rescue:

```
public class MySecondThread extends ImportantClass implements Runnable {
    public void run() {
        . . .              // do something useful
    }
}
```

By implementing the interface Runnable, you declare your intention to run in a separate thread. In fact, the Thread class is itself an implementation of this interface, as you might expect from the design discussions on Day 16. As you also might guess from the example, the Runnable interface defines only one method: run(). As in MyFirstThread, you expect someone to create an instance of a thread and somehow call your run() method. Here's how this is accomplished using the interface approach to thread creation:

```
MySecondThread  aMST = new MySecondThread();
Thread          aThread = new Thread(aMST);
aThread.start();   // calls our run() method, indirectly
```

First, you create an instance of MySecondThread. Then, by passing this instance to the constructor creating the new thread, you make it the target of that thread. Whenever that new thread starts up, its run() method calls the run() method of the target it was given (assumed by the thread to be an object that implements the Runnable interface). When start() is called on aThread, your run() method is indirectly called. You can stop aThread with stop(). If you don't need to use the Thread object or instance of MySecondThread explicitly, here's a one-line shortcut:

```
new Thread(new MySecondThread()).start();
```

NOTE

NOTE

As you can see, the class name MySecondThread is a bit of a misnomer—
it does not descend from Thread, nor is it actually the thread that you
start() and stop(). It could have been called MySecondThreadedClass
or ImportantRunnableClass to be more clear on this point.

ThreadTester

Listing 18.2 contains a longer example of creating and using threads.

TYPE   **Listing 18.2. The SimpleRunnable class.**

```
 1: public class SimpleRunnable implements Runnable {
 2:     public void run() {
 3:         System.out.println("in thread named '"
 4:                               + Thread.currentThread().getName() + "'");
 5:     } // any other methods run() calls are in current thread as well
 6: }
 7:
 8: public class ThreadTester {
 9:     public static void main(String argv[]) {
10:         SimpleRunnable aSR = new SimpleRunnable();
11:
12:         while (true) {
13:             Thread t = new Thread(aSR);
14:
15:             System.out.println("new Thread() " + (t == null ?
16:                                                  "fail" : "succeed") + "ed.");
17:             t.start();
18:             try { t.join(); } catch (InterruptedException ignored) { }
19:                         // waits for thread to finish its run() method
20:         }
21:     }
22: }
```

NOTE

You may be worried that only one instance of the class SimpleRunnable
is created, but many new threads are using it. Don't they get confused?
Remember to separate in your mind the aSR instance (and the methods
it understands) from the various threads of execution that can pass
through it. aSR's methods provide a template for execution, and the
multiple threads created are sharing that template. Each remembers

18

where it is executing and whatever else it needs to make it distinct from the other running threads. They all share the same instance and the same methods. That's why you need to be so careful, when adding synchronization, to imagine numerous threads running rampant over each of your methods.

ANALYSIS The class method currentThread() can be called to get the thread in which a method is currently executing. If the SimpleRunnable class were a subclass of Thread, its methods would know the answer already (*it* is the thread running). Because SimpleRunnable simply implements the interface Runnable, however, and counts on someone else (ThreadTester's main()) to create the thread, its run() method needs another way to get its hands on that thread. Often, you'll be deep inside methods called by your run() method when suddenly you need to get the current thread. The class method shown in the example works, no matter where you are.

The example then calls getName() on the current thread to get the thread's name (usually something helpful, such as Thread-23) so it can tell the world in which thread run() is running. The final thing to note is the use of the method join(), which, when sent to a thread, means "I'm planning to wait forever for you to finish your run() method." You don't want to use this approach without good reason: If you have anything else important you need to get done in your thread any time soon, you can't count on how long the joined thread might take to finish. In the example, the run() method is short and finishes quickly, so each loop can safely wait for the previous thread to die before creating the next one. Here's the output produced:

```
new Thread() succeeded.
in thread named 'Thread-1'
new Thread() succeeded.
in thread named 'Thread-2'
new Thread() succeeded.
in thread named 'Thread-3'
^C
```

Incidentally, Ctrl+C was pressed to interrupt the program, because it otherwise would continue on forever.

WARNING

You can do some reasonably disastrous things with your knowledge of threads. For example, if you're running in the main thread of the system and, because you think you are in a different thread, you accidentally say the following:

```
Thread.currentThread().stop();
```

it has unfortunate consequences for your (soon-to-be-dead) program!

NamedThreadTester

If you want your threads to have particular names, you can assign them yourself by using another form of Thread's constructor:

```
public class NamedThreadTester {
    public static void main(String argv[]) {
        SimpleRunnable aSR = new SimpleRunnable();

        for (int i = 1; true; ++i) {
            Thread t = new Thread(aSR, "" + (100 - i)
                                        + " threads on the wall...");

            System.out.println("new Thread() " + (t == null ?
                                        "fail" : "succeed") + "ed.");
            t.start();
            try { t.join(); } catch (InterruptedException ignored) { }
        }
    }
}
```

This version of Thread's constructor takes a target object, as before, and a string, which names the new thread. Here's the output:

```
new Thread() succeeded.
in thread named '99 threads on the wall...'
new Thread() succeeded.
in thread named '98 threads on the wall...'
new Thread() succeeded.
in thread named '97 threads on the wall...'
^C
```

Naming a thread is one easy way to pass it some information. This information flows from the parent thread to its new child. It's also useful, for debugging purposes, to give threads meaningful names (such as network input) so that when they appear during an error—in a stack trace, for example—you can easily identify which thread caused the problem. You might also think of using names to help group or organize your threads, but Java actually provides you with a ThreadGroup class to perform this function.

The ThreadGroup class is used to manage a group of threads as a single unit. This provides you with a means to finely control thread execution for a series of threads. For example, the ThreadGroup class provides stop, suspend, and resume methods for controlling the execution of all the threads in the group. Thread groups can also contain other thread groups, allowing for a nested hierarchy of threads. Another benefit to using thread groups is that they can keep threads from being able to affect other threads, which is useful for security.

Knowing When a Thread Has Stopped

Let's imagine a different version of the last example, one that creates a thread and then hands the thread off to other parts of the program. Suppose the program would then like to know when that thread dies so that it can perform some cleanup operation. If SimpleRunnable were a subclass of Thread, you might try to catch stop() whenever it's sent—but look at Thread's declaration of the stop() method:

```
public final void stop() { . . . }
```

The final here means that you can't override this method in a subclass. In any case, SimpleRunnable is *not* a subclass of Thread, so how can this imagined example possibly catch the death of its thread? The answer is to use the following magic:

```
public class SingleThreadTester {
    public static void main(String argv[]) {
        Thread t = new Thread(new SimpleRunnable());

        try {
            t.start();
            someMethodThatMightStopTheThread(t);
        } catch (ThreadDeath aTD) {
            . . .                // do some required cleanup
            throw aTD;           // re-throw the error
        }
    }
}
```

You understand most of this magic from yesterday's lesson. All you need to know is that if the thread created in the example dies, it throws an error of class ThreadDeath. The code catches that error and performs the required cleanup. It then rethrows the error, allowing the thread to die. The cleanup code is not called if the thread exits normally (its run() method completes), but that's fine; you posited that the cleanup was needed only when stop() was used on the thread.

NOTE

Threads can die in other ways—for example, by throwing exceptions that no one catches. In these cases, stop() is never called and the previous code is not sufficient. Because unexpected exceptions can come out of nowhere to kill a thread, multithreaded programs that carefully catch and handle all their exceptions are more predictable and robust, and they're easier to debug.

Thread Scheduling

You might be wondering how any software system can be truly threaded when running on a machine with a single CPU. If there is only one physical CPU in a computer system, it's impossible for more than one machine code instruction to be executed at a time. This means that no matter how hard you try to rationalize the behavior of a multithreaded system, only one thread is really being executed at a particular time. The reality is that multithreading on a single CPU system, like the systems most of us use, is at best a good illusion. The good news is that the illusion works so well most of the time that we feel pretty comfortable in the fact that multiple threads are really running in parallel.

The illusion of parallel thread execution on a system with a single CPU is often managed by giving each thread an opportunity to execute a little bit of code at regular intervals. This approach is known as *timeslicing*, which refers to the way each thread gets a little of the CPU's time to execute code. When you speed up this whole scenario to millions of instructions per second, the whole effect of parallel execution comes across pretty well.

The general task of managing and executing multiple threads in an environment such as this is known as *scheduling*. Likewise, the part of the system that decides the real-time ordering of threads is called the *scheduler*.

Preemptive Versus Nonpreemptive

Normally, any scheduler has two fundamentally different ways of looking at its job: nonpreemptive scheduling and preemptive time slicing.

With *nonpreemptive scheduling*, the scheduler runs the current thread forever, requiring that thread to explicitly tell it when it is safe to start a different thread. With *preemptive time slicing*, the scheduler runs the current thread until it has used up a certain tiny fraction of a second, and then "preempts" it, suspends it, and resumes another thread for the next tiny fraction of a second.

Nonpreemptive scheduling is very courtly, always asking for permission to schedule, and is quite valuable in extremely time-critical real-time applications where being interrupted at the wrong moment, or for too long, could mean crashing an airplane.

However, most modern schedulers use preemptive time slicing because it generally has made writing multithreaded programs much easier. For one thing, it does not force each thread to decide exactly when it should "yield" control to another thread. Instead, every thread can just run blindly on, knowing that the scheduler will be fair about giving all the other threads their chance to run.

However, it turns out that this approach is still not the ideal way to schedule threads; you've given up a little too much control to the scheduler. The final touch many modern schedulers add is to allow you to assign each thread a priority. This creates a total ordering of all threads, making some threads more "important" than others. Being higher priority often means that a thread gets run more often or for a longer period of time, but it always means that it can interrupt other, lower-priority threads, even before their "time slice" has expired.

A good example of a low-priority thread is the garbage collection thread in the Java runtime system. Even though garbage collection is a very important function, it is not something you want hogging the CPU. Because the garbage collection thread is a low-priority thread, it chugs along in the background, freeing up memory as the processor allows it. This may result in memory being freed a little slower, but it allows more time-critical threads, such as the user input handling thread, full access to the CPU. You may be wondering what happens if the CPU stays busy and the garbage collector never gets to clean up memory. Does the runtime system run out of memory and crash? No. This brings up one of the neat aspects of threads and how they work. If a high-priority thread can't access a resource it needs, such as memory, it enters a wait state until memory becomes available. When all memory is gone, all the threads running will eventually go into a wait state, thereby freeing up the CPU to execute the garbage collection thread, which in turn frees up memory. And the circle of threaded life continues!

The current Java release (1.1) does not precisely specify the behavior of its scheduler. Threads can be assigned priorities, and when a choice is made between several threads that all want to run, the highest-priority thread wins. However, among threads that are all the same priority, the behavior is not well defined. In fact, the different platforms on which Java currently runs have different behaviors—some behaving more like a preemptive scheduler, and some more like a nonpreemptive scheduler.

NOTE

This incomplete specification of the scheduler is terribly annoying and, presumably, will be corrected in a later release. Not knowing the fine details of how scheduling occurs is perfectly all right, but not knowing whether equal-priority threads must explicitly yield or face running forever is not all right. For example, all the threads you have created so far are equal-priority threads so you don't know their basic scheduling behavior!

Testing Your Scheduler

To find out what kind of scheduler you have on your system, try out the following code:

```
public class RunnablePotato implements Runnable {
    public void run() {
```

```
        while (true)
            System.out.println(Thread.currentThread().getName());
    }
}

public class PotatoThreadTester {
    public static void main(String argv[]) {
        RunnablePotato aRP = new RunnablePotato();

        new Thread(aRP, "one potato").start();
        new Thread(aRP, "two potato").start();
    }
}
```

If your system employs a nonpreemptive scheduler, this code results in the following output:

```
one potato
one potato
one potato
. . .
```

This output will go on forever or until you interrupt the program. For a preemptive scheduler that uses time slicing, this code will repeat the line one potato a few times, followed by the same number of two potato lines, over and over:

```
one potato
one potato
...
one potato
two potato
two potato
...
two potato
. . .
```

This output will also go on forever or until you interrupt the program. What if you want to be sure the two threads will take turns, regardless of the type of system scheduler? You rewrite RunnablePotato as follows:

```
public class RunnablePotato implements Runnable {
    public void run() {
        while (true) {
            System.out.println(Thread.currentThread().getName());
            Thread.yield();   // let another thread run for a while
        }
    }
}
```

TIP

> Normally, you would have to use Thread.currentThread().yield() to get your hands on the current thread, and then call yield(). Because this pattern is so common, however, the Thread class can be used as a shortcut.

The yield() method explicitly gives any other threads that want to run a chance to begin running. (If there are no threads waiting to run, the thread that made the yield() simply continues.) In our example, there's another thread that's just *dying* to run, so when you now execute the class ThreadTester, it should output the following:

```
one potato
two potato
one potato
two potato
one potato
two potato
. . .
```

This output will be the same regardless of the type of scheduler you have.

To see whether thread priorities are working on your system, try this code:

```
public class PriorityThreadTester {
    public static void main(String argv[]) {
        RunnablePotato aRP = new RunnablePotato();
        Thread        t1  = new Thread(aRP, "one potato");
        Thread        t2  = new Thread(aRP, "two potato");

        t2.setPriority(t1.getPriority() + 1);
        t1.start();
        t2.start();   // at priority Thread.NORM_PRIORITY + 1
    }
}
```

TIP

> The values representing the lowest, normal, and highest priorities that threads can be assigned are stored in constant class members of the Thread class: Thread.MIN_PRIORITY, Thread.NORM_PRIORITY, and Thread.MAX_PRIORITY. The system assigns new threads, by default, the priority Thread.NORM_PRIORITY. Priorities in Java are currently defined in a range from 1 to 10, with 5 being normal, but you shouldn't depend on these values; use the class variables or tricks like the one shown in this example.

If one potato is the first line of output, your system does not preempt using thread priorities. Why? Imagine that the first thread (t1) has just begun to run. Even before it has a chance to print anything, along comes a higher-priority thread (t2) that wants to run as well. That higher-priority thread should preempt (interrupt) the first and get a chance to print two potato before t1 finishes printing anything. In fact, if you use the RunnablePotato class that never yield()s, t2 stays in control forever, printing two potato lines, because it's a higher priority than t1 and it never yields control. If you use the latest RunnablePotato class (with yield()), the output is alternating lines of one potato and two potato as before, but starting with two potato.

Listing 18.3 contains a good, illustrative example of how complex threads behave.

TYPE **Listing 18.3. The ComplexThread class.**

```
1: public class ComplexThread extends Thread {
2:     private int delay;
3:
4:     ComplexThread(String name, float seconds) {
5:         super(name);
6:         delay = (int) seconds * 1000;   // delays are in milliseconds
7:         start();                        // start up ourself!
8:     }
9:
10:    public void run() {
11:        while (true) {
12:            System.out.println(Thread.currentThread().getName());
13:            try {
14:                Thread.sleep(delay);
15:            } catch (InterruptedException e) {
16:                return;
17:            }
18:        }
19:    }
20:
21:    public static void main(String argv[]) {
22:        new ComplexThread("one potato",   1.1F);
23:        new ComplexThread("two potato",   1.3F);
24:        new ComplexThread("three potato", 0.5F);
25:        new ComplexThread("four",         0.7F);
26:    }
27: }
```

ANALYSIS This example combines the thread and its tester into a single class. Its constructor takes care of naming and starting itself because it is now a thread. The main() method creates new instances of its own class because the class is a subclass of Thread. The run() method is also more complicated because it now uses, for the first time, a method that can throw an unexpected exception.

The Thread.sleep() method forces the current thread to yield() and then waits for at least the specified amount of time to elapse before allowing the thread to run again. It might be interrupted by another thread, however, while it's sleeping. In such a case, it throws an InterruptedException. Now, because run() is not defined as throwing this exception, you

18

must "hide" the fact by catching and handling it yourself. Because interruptions are usually requests to stop, you should exit the thread, which you can do by simply returning from the `run()` method.

This program should output a repeating but complex pattern of four different lines, where every once in a great while you see the following:

```
. . .
one potato
two potato
three potato
four
. . .
```

You should study the pattern output to prove to yourself that true parallelism is going on inside Java programs. You may also begin to appreciate that, if even this simple set of four threads can produce such complex behavior, many more threads must be capable of producing near chaos if not carefully controlled. Luckily, Java provides the synchronization and thread-safe libraries you need to control that chaos.

Summary

Today you have learned that multithreading is desirable and powerful, but introduces many new problems—methods and variables now need to be *protected* from thread conflicts—that can lead to chaos if not carefully controlled. By "thinking multithreaded," you can detect the places in your programs that require `synchronized` statements (or modifiers) to make them thread safe. A series of `Point` examples demonstrates the various levels of safety you can achieve, and `ThreadTesters` shows how subclasses of `Thread`, or classes that implement the `Runnable` interface, are created and run to generate multithreaded programs.

You have also learned today how to use `yield()`, `start()`, `stop()`, `suspend()`, and `resume()` on your threads, and how to catch `ThreadDeath` whenever it happens. You have learned about preemptive and nonpreemptive scheduling, both with and without priorities, and how to test your Java system to see which of them your scheduler is using.

You are now armed with enough information to write the most complex of programs: multithreaded ones. As you get more comfortable with threads, you may begin to use the `ThreadGroup` class or the enumeration methods of `Thread` to get your hands on all the threads in the system and manipulate them. Don't be afraid to experiment; you can't permanently break anything, and you only learn by trying.

18

Q&A

Q If they're so important to Java, why haven't threads appeared throughout the entire book?

A Actually, they have. Every standalone program written so far has "created" at least one thread, the one in which it is running. (Of course the system created that thread for it automatically.)

Q How exactly do these threads get created and run? What about applets?

A When a simple standalone Java program starts up, the system creates a main thread, and its run() method calls your main() method to start your program—you do nothing to get that thread. Likewise, when a simple applet loads into a Java-enabled browser, a thread has already been created by the browser, and its run() method calls your init() and start() methods to start your program. In either case, a new thread of some kind was created somewhere by the Java environment itself.

Q I know the current Java release is still a little fuzzy about the scheduler's behavior, but what's the word from Sun?

A Here's the scoop, as relayed by Arthur van Hoff at Sun: The way Java schedules threads "...depends on the platform. It is usually preemptive, but not always time sliced. Priorities are not always observed, depending on the underlying implementation." This final clause gives you a hint that all this confusion is an implementation problem, and that in some future release, the design and implementation will both be clear about scheduling behavior.

Q My parallel friends tell me I should worry about something called "deadlock." Should I?

A Not for simple multithreaded programs. However, in more complicated programs, one of the biggest worries does become one of avoiding a situation in which one thread has locked an object and is waiting for another thread to finish, while that other thread is waiting for the first thread to release that same object before it can finish. That's a deadlock—both threads will be stuck forever. Mutual dependencies like this involving more than two threads can be quite intricate, convoluted, and difficult to locate, much less rectify. They are one of the main challenges in writing complex multithreaded programs.

18

Day 19

Java Streams and I/O

by Charles L. Perkins

Today you'll explore Java's streams:

- ☐ Input streams—and how to create, use, and detect the end of them— and filtered input streams, which can be nested to great effect
- ☐ Output streams, which are mostly analogous to (but the inverse of) input streams

and Java's character I/O (input/output) classes:

- ☐ Readers, which are created and used like input streams, and filtered readers, which can be nested to great effect
- ☐ Writers, which are mostly analogous to (but the inverse of) readers

You'll also learn about two stream interfaces that make the reading and writing of typed streams much easier, about how to read and write entire objects, and about several utility classes used to access the file system. Let's begin with a little history behind the invention of streams.

One of the early inventions of the UNIX operating system was the pipe. A *pipe* is an uninterpreted stream of bytes that can be used for communication between programs (or other "forked" copies of your own program), or for reading from and writing to arbitrary peripheral devices or files. By unifying many disparate ways of communicating into this single metaphor, UNIX paved the way for a whole new series of related inventions, culminating in the abstraction known as streams.

 NEW TERM   A *stream* is a path of communication between the source of some information and its destination.

This information, an uninterpreted byte stream, can come from any of the "pipe sources" previously mentioned, the computer's memory, or even from the Internet. In fact, the source and destination of a stream are completely arbitrary producers and consumers of bytes, respectively—you don't need to know about the source of the information when reading from a stream, and you don't need to know about the final destination when writing to one. That is the power of the stream abstraction.

General methods that can read from any source accept a stream argument to specify that source; general methods for writing accept a stream to specify the destination. Arbitrary *processors* (or *filters*) of data have two stream arguments. They read from the first, process the data, and write their results to the second. These processors have no idea of either the source *or* the destination of the data they are processing. Sources and destinations can vary widely: from two memory buffers on the same local computer, to the ELF transmissions to and from a submarine at sea, to the real-time data streams of a NASA probe in deep space.

By decoupling the consumption, processing, and production of data from the sources and destinations of that data, you can mix and match any combination of them at will as you write your program. In the future, when new, previously nonexistent forms of source or destination (or consumer, processor, or producer) appear, they can be used within the same framework, with no changes to your classes. In addition, new stream abstractions, supporting higher levels of interpretation "on top of" the bytes, can be written completely independently of the underlying transport mechanisms for the bytes themselves.

NOTE

In fact, one such higher-level interpretation did exactly that: The new 1.1 object serialization streams are written "on top of" the 1.0 stream mechanism. You'll learn more about serialization later today.

The foundations of this stream framework are the two abstract classes, `InputStream` and `OutputStream`. If you turn briefly to the diagram for `java.io` in Appendix B, you'll see that below these classes is a virtual cornucopia of categorized classes, demonstrating the wide range of streams in the system, but also demonstrating an extremely well-designed hierarchy of relationships between these stream classes, one well worth learning from. There's a similar tree in the diagram for `java.io-rw`, rooted at the abstract parents `Reader` and `Writer`. Let's begin with these parent classes, and work our way down these two bushy trees in parallel.

WARNING

> Because every class in today's lesson is located in package `java.io`, you'll need to either `import` each class as you use it (or use its long name, like `java.io.InputStream`), or put an `import java.io.*` statement at the start of your class.
>
> All the methods you will explore today are declared to `throw` `IOExceptions`. This new subclass of `Exception` conceptually embodies all the possible I/O errors that might occur while using Java's streams, readers, writers, and so on. (There are many subclasses of `IOException` that define more specific exceptions that can be thrown as well.) For now, it is enough to know that you must either `catch` an `IOException` or be in a method that can "pass it along," to be a well-behaved user of today's classes. (See Day 17, "Exceptions," if you've forgotten how to catch or "pass along" exceptions.)

Input Streams and Readers

The foundations for all Java's input operations are the two classes defined in the next two sections. After their definitions, you'll see the analogous classes that derive from them presented together, because these pairs of classes have nearly identical method interfaces, and you use them both in the same ways.

The abstract Classes InputStream and Reader

`InputStream` is an abstract class that defines the fundamental ways in which a destination (consumer) reads a stream of *bytes* from some source. The identity of the source, and the manner of the creation and transport of the bytes, is irrelevant. When using an input stream, you are the destination of those bytes, and that's all you need to know.

`Reader` is an abstract class that defines the fundamental ways in which a destination (consumer) reads a stream of *characters* from some source. It and all its subclasses are analogous to `InputStream` and all its subclasses, except that they use characters as their fundamental units of information instead of bytes.

19

read()

The most important method to the consumer of an input stream (or reader) is the one that reads bytes (characters) from the source. This method, read(), comes in many flavors, and each is demonstrated in an example in today's lesson.

Each of these read() methods is defined to "block" (wait) until all the input requested becomes available. Don't worry about this limitation; because of multithreading, you can do as many other things as you like while this one thread is waiting for input. In fact, it is a common idiom to assign a thread to each stream of input (and for each stream of output) that is solely responsible for reading from it (or writing to it). These input threads might then "hand off" the information to other threads for processing. This naturally overlaps the I/O time of your program with its compute time.

Here's the first form of read():

```
InputStream  s       = getAnInputStreamFromSomewhere();
Reader       r       = getAReaderFromSomewhere();
byte[]       bbuffer = new byte[1024];   // any size will do
char[]       cbuffer = new char[1024];

if (s.read(bbuffer) != bbuf.length  || r.read(cbuffer) != cbuf.length)
    System.out.println("I got less than I expected.");
```

NOTE

Unless stated otherwise, every method in the stream, reader, and writer classes that follow is used in the same way for both of the classes being discussed. For example, the preceding read() method is being used identically on both InputStreams and Readers.

Here, and throughout the rest of today's lesson, you should assume that either an import java.io.* appears before each example, or you should mentally prefix all references to java.io classes with the prefix java.io.

This form of read() attempts to fill the entire buffer given. If it cannot (usually due to reaching the end of the input stream), it returns the actual number of bytes (characters) that were read into the buffer. After that, any further invocations to read() return -1, indicating that you are at the end of the stream. Note that the if statement still works even if the stream is empty, because -1 will never equal the buffer's length.

NOTE

Don't forget that, unlike in C, the -1 case in Java is not used to indicate an error. Any I/O errors throw instances of IOException (which you're not catching yet). You learned on Day 17, that all uses of distinguished

19

> values can be replaced by the use of exceptions, and so they should. The -1 in the last example is a bit of a historical anachronism. You'll soon see a better approach to indicating end of the stream, using the class DataInputStream.

You can also read into a "slice" of your buffer by specifying the offset into the buffer, and the length desired, as arguments to the second form of read():

```
s.read(bbuffer, 100, 300);
r.read(cbuffer, 100, 300);
```

This example tries to fill in bytes (characters) 100 through 399 and behaves otherwise exactly the same as the previous read() method. In fact, in the current release, the default implementation of the first form of read() uses the second:

```
public int  read(byte[]  b) throws IOException {    /* from InputStream.java */
    return  read(b, 0, b.length);
}

public int  read(char[]  cbuf) throws IOException {     /* from Reader.java */
    return  read(cbuf, 0, cbuf.length);
}
```

Finally, the third form can read bytes (characters) one at a time:

```
InputStream   s = getAnInputStreamFromSomewhere();
InputStream   r = getAReaderFromSomewhere();
byte          b;
char          c;
int           byteOrMinus1, charOrMinus1;

while ((byteOrMinus1 = s.read()) != -1   &&   (charOrMinus1 = r.read()) != -1) {
    b = (byte) byteOrMinus1;                 c = (char) charOrMinus1;
    . . .      // process the byte b (or char c)
}
    . . .      // reached end of stream
```

NOTE

Because of the nature of integer promotion in Java in general, and because in this case the read() method returns an int, using the byte (or char) type in your code may be a little frustrating. You'll find yourself constantly having to explicitly cast the result of arithmetic expressions, or of int return values, back to your size. Because read() really should be returning a byte (or char) in this case, I feel justified in declaring and using it as such (despite the pain)—it makes the size of the data being read clearer. In cases where you feel the range of a

19

> variable is naturally limited to a byte, char, or short rather than an int, please take the time to declare it that way and pay the small price necessary to gain the added clarity. By the way, a lot of the Java class library code simply stores the result of read() in an int. This proves that even the Javasoft team is human—*everyone* makes style mistakes.

skip()

What if you want to skip over some of the bytes in a stream, or start reading a stream from other than its beginning? A method similar to read() does the trick:

```
if (s.skip(1024) != 1024   ||   r.skip(1024) != 1024)
    System.out.println("I skipped less than I expected.");
```

This skips over the next 1024 bytes (characters) in the input stream. skip() takes and returns a long integer, because streams are not required to be limited to any particular size. The default implementation of InputStream's skip() in the 1.1 release simply uses read():

```
public long  skip(long n) throws IOException {        /* from InputStream.java */
    byte[]  data = new byte[(int) n & 0xEFFFFFFF];
    return  read(data);
}
```

NOTE

> This implementation does not support large skips correctly, because its long argument is truncated to the largest possible int. (The implementation of Reader's skip() is correct—it will skip a long number of characters.) Subclasses must override this default implementation if they want to handle this properly. This won't be as trivial as you might think, because Java does not allow integer types larger than int to act as array subscripts.

available() **and** ready()

If for some reason you would like to know how many bytes are in the stream right now (or whether the reader has more characters waiting for you), you can ask:

```
if (s.available() < 1024)
    System.out.println("Too little is available right now.");
if (r.ready() != true)
    System.out.println("No characters are available right now.");
```

This tells you the number of bytes that you can read (or whether you can read any characters) without blocking. Because of the abstract nature of the source of the information, streams may or may not be able to tell you a reasonable answer to this question. For example, some streams always return 0 (or false)—that value is, in fact, the return value of the default implementation of available() (or ready()).

Unless you use specific subclasses of InputStream that you know provide a reasonable answer to this question, it's not a good idea to rely upon this method. Remember, multithreading eliminates many of the problems associated with blocking while waiting for a stream to fill again. Thus, one of the strongest rationales for the use of available() (or ready()) goes away.

mark() **and** reset()

Some streams support the notion of marking a position in the stream, and then later resetting the stream to that position to re-read the bytes (characters) there. Clearly, the stream would have to "remember" all those bytes (characters), so there is a limitation on how far apart in a stream the mark and its subsequent reset can occur. There's also a method that asks whether or not the stream supports the notion of marking at all. Here's an example:

```
InputStream   s = getAnInputStreamFromSomewhere();
Reader        r = getAReaderFromSomewhere();

if (s.markSupported()   &&   r.markSupported()) {     // supports the notion?
    . . .                                 // read the stream for a while
    s.mark(1024);     r.mark(1024);
    . . .                                 // read less than 1024 more bytes (chars)
    s.reset();        r.reset();
    . . .                                 // we can now re-read those bytes (chars)
} else {
    . . .                                 // no, do some alternative
}
```

When marking a stream, you specify the maximum number of bytes (characters) you intend to allow to pass before resetting it. This allows the stream to limit the size of its "memory." If this number of bytes (characters) goes by and you have not yet reset, the mark becomes invalid, and attempting to reset will throw an exception.

Marking and resetting a stream is most valuable when you are attempting to identify the type of the stream (or the next part of the stream), but to do so, you must consume a significant piece of it in the process. Often, this is because you have several black-box parsers that you can hand the stream to, but they will consume some (unknown to you) number of bytes (characters) before making up their mind about whether the stream is of their type. Set a large size for the read limit above, and let each parser run until it either throws an error or completes a successful parse. If an error is thrown, reset and try the next parser.

19

WARNING

Although the default implementation of `markSupported()` returns `false`, and `reset()` throws an `IOException`, for both `InputStreams` and `Readers`, `InputStream`'s `mark()` does nothing while `Reader`'s throws an `IOException`. This (unfortunately) breaks the nearly perfect symmetry that would otherwise exist between the two classes.

close()

Because you don't know what resources an open stream represents, nor how to deal with them properly when you're finished reading the stream, you should (usually) explicitly close down a stream so that it can release those resources. Of course, garbage collection via a `finalize()` method can do this for you, but what if you need to reopen that stream or those resources before they have been freed by this asynchronous process? At best, this is annoying or confusing; at worst, it introduces an unexpected, obscure, and difficult-to-track-down bug. Because you're interacting with the outside world of external resources, it's safer to be explicit about when you're finished using them:

```
InputStream   s = alwaysMakesANewInputStream();
Reader        r = alwaysMakesANewReader();

try {
    . . .      // use s (or r) to your heart's content
} finally {
    s.close();    r.close();
}
```

Get used to this idiom (using `finally`); it's a useful way to be sure something (such as closing the stream) always gets done. Of course, you're assuming that the stream is always successfully created. If this is not always the case, and `null` is sometimes returned instead, here's the correct way to be safe:

```
InputStream   s = tryToMakeANewInputStream();
Reader        r = tryToMakeAReader();

if (s != null   &&   r != null) {
    try {
        . . .
    } finally {
        s.close();    r.close();
    }
}
```

All input streams descend from the `abstract` class `InputStream`, and all readers descend from `Reader`. All share the few methods described so far. Thus, stream s (or reader r) in the previous examples could have been any of the more complex input streams (or readers) described in the next few sections.

NOTE Concrete subclasses of `InputStream` need only implement the zero-argument version (the third form) of `read()` to get all the other methods working (`InputStream` has a default implementation of `close()` that does nothing). `Reader` subclasses, however, must implement both `close()` and the three-argument version (the second form) of `read()`.

ByteArrayInputStream **and** CharArrayReader

The "inverse" of the previous `read()` examples would be to create an input stream (or reader) from an array of bytes (or characters). This is exactly what `ByteArrayInputStream` (`CharArrayReader`) does:

```
byte[]  bbuffer = new byte[1024];
char[]  cbuffer = new char[1024];

fillWithUsefulData(bbuffer);    fillWithUsefulData(cbuffer);

InputStream  s = new ByteArrayInputStream(bbuffer);
Reader       r = new CharArrayReader(cbuffer);
```

Readers of the new stream s (r) see a stream 1024 bytes (characters) long, containing the contents of the array bbuffer (cbuffer). Just as `read()` has a form that takes an offset and a length, so does this class's constructor:

```
InputStream  s = new ByteArrayInputStream(bbuffer, 100, 300);
Reader       r = new CharArrayReader(cbuffer, 100, 300);
```

Here, the stream is 300 bytes (characters) long and consists of bytes (characters) 100-399 from the array bbuffer (cbuffer).

19

NOTE Finally, you've seen your first examples of the *creation* of a stream. These new streams are attached to the simplest of all possible sources of data, an array of bytes (or characters) in the memory of the local computer.

`ByteArrayInputStreams` (`CharArrayReaders`) simply implement the standard set of methods that all input streams do. Here, however, the `available()` (`ready()`) method has a particularly simple job—it returns 1024 and 300 (true and true), respectively, for the two instances of `ByteArrayInputStream` (`CharArrayReader`) created previously, because it knows exactly how many bytes (characters) are available in those streams. Also, `markSupported()` returns `true`. Finally, invoking `reset()` without a previous `mark()` resets the stream back to the beginning of its buffer.

FileInputStream and FileReader

One of the most common uses of streams, and historically the earliest, is to attach them to files in the file system. Here, for example, is the creation of such an input stream (or reader) on a UNIX system:

```
InputStream  s = new FileInputStream("/some/path/and/fileName");
Reader       r = new FileReader("/some/path/and/fileName.utf8");
```

WARNING

> Applets attempting to open, read, or write streams based on files in the file system will cause security violations in most browsers. (Some browsers allow users to designate safe directories for reading and writing.) In the future, applets will be able to take advantage of "trusted applet" features built on top of the 1.1 `java.security` classes to gain file system access, but in the meantime, you should create applets that do not depend on files at all—for example, by using servers to hold any shared or stored information. (Stand-alone Java programs have none of these problems, of course.)

You also can create streams from a previously opened `FileDescriptor` or `File`:

```
InputStream  s = new FileInputStream(FileDescriptor.in);  /* standard input */
Reader       r = new FileReader(FileDescriptor.in);

InputStream  s = new FileInputStream(new File("/some/path/and/fileName"));
Reader       r = new FileReader(new File("/some/path/and/fileName.utf8"));
```

In all three cases, because it's based on an actual (finite length) file, the input stream (reader) created can implement `available()` (`ready()`) precisely and can `skip()` like a champ (just as `ByteArrayInputStream` and `CharArrayReader` can, by the way).

`FileReader` is actually a trivial subclass of another reader class, `InputStreamReader`, that can encapsulate any `InputStream` and turn it into a reader of characters instead. Thus, `FileReader`'s implementation consists of simply asking an `InputStreamReader` (itself) to encapsulate a `FileInputStream`:

```
public class  FileReader extends InputStreamReader {  /* from FileReader.java */
    public  FileReader(String  fileName) throws FileNotFoundException {
        super(new FileInputStream(fileName))
    }
```

```
public  FileReader(File  file) throws FileNotFoundException {
    super(new FileInputStream(file))
}
public  FileReader(FileDescriptor  fd) throws FileNotFoundException {
    super(new FileInputStream(fd))
}
}
```

In addition, `FileInputStream` (but not `FileReader`) knows a few more tricks:

```
FileInputStream  aFIS = new FileInputStream("aFileName");

FileDescriptor  myFD = aFIS.getFD();
/* aFIS.finalize(); */  // will invoke close() when automatically called by GC
```

 TIP

> To invoke `getFD()` method, you must declare the stream variable `aFIS` to be of type `FileInputStream`, because plain `InputStreams` don't know about `getFD()`.

The first is obvious: `getFD()` returns the file descriptor of the file on which the stream is based. The second, though, is an interesting shortcut that allows you to create `FileInputStreams` without worrying about closing them later. `FileInputStream`'s implementation of `finalize()`, a protected method, closes the stream. Unlike in the contrived invocation in comments, you should almost never call a `finalize()` method directly. The garbage collector invokes it for you after noticing that the stream is no longer in use, but before actually destroying the stream. Thus, you can go merrily along using the stream, never closing it, and all will be well. The system takes care of closing it (eventually).

You can get away with this because streams based on files tie up very few resources, and these resources cannot be accidentally reused before garbage collection (these were the things worried about in the previous discussion of `finalize()` and `close()`). Of course, if you were also writing to the file, you would have to be more careful. (Reopening the file too soon after writing might make it appear in an inconsistent state because the `finalize()`—and thus the `close()`—might not have happened yet.) Just because you don't have to close the stream doesn't mean you might not want to do so anyway. For clarity, or if you don't know precisely what type of an `InputStream` you were handed, you might choose to invoke `close()` yourself.

`FilterInputStream` and `FilterReader`

These "abstract" classes (only `FilterReader` is actually declared `abstract`) simply provide a "pass-through" for all the standard methods of `InputStream` (or `Reader`). They hold inside themselves another stream, by definition one further "down" the chain of filters, to which they forward all method invocations. They implement nothing new, but allow themselves to be nested:

```
InputStream        s  = getAnInputStreamFromSomewhere();
FilterInputStream  s1 = new FilterInputStream(s);
FilterInputStream  s2 = new FilterInputStream(s1);
FilterInputStream  s3 = new FilterInputStream(s2);

... s3.read() ...
```

Whenever a read is performed on the filtered stream s3, it passes along the request to s2; then s2 does the same to s1, and finally s is asked to provide the bytes. Subclasses of FilterInputStream (or FilterReader) will, of course, do some nontrivial processing of the bytes as they flow past. The rather verbose form of "chaining" in the previous example can be made more elegant:

```
s3 = new FilterInputStream(new FilterInputStream(new FilterInputStream(s)));
```

You should use this idiom in your code whenever you can. It clearly expresses the nesting of chained filters, and can easily be parsed and "read aloud" by starting at the innermost stream s and reading outward—each filter stream applying to the one within—until you reach the outermost stream s3.

NOTE

FilterReader is declared abstract, so you cannot create instances of it (as we did in the previous examples for FilterInputStream). Also, you can't arbitrarily mix the two types of filters; bytes and characters don't mix, and available() and ready() will not be passed along correctly. It would be fine, though, to say something like:

```
new FilterReaderSubclass(new InputStreamReader(new
FilterInputStream(...more FilterInputStreams...))).
```

Now let's examine each of the subclasses of FilterInputStream (and their Reader counterparts) in turn.

BufferedInputStream **and** BufferedReader

This is one of the most valuable of all streams. It implements the full complement of InputStream's (Reader's) methods, but it does so by using a buffered array of bytes (characters) that acts as a cache for future reading. This decouples the rate and the size of the "chunks" you're reading from the more regular, larger block sizes in which streams are most efficiently read (from, for example, peripheral devices, files in the file system, or the network). It also allows smart streams to read ahead when they expect that you will want more data soon.

Because the buffering of `BufferedInputStream` (`BufferedReader`) is so valuable, and it's also one of the few classes to handle `mark()` and `reset()` well, you might wish that every input stream (reader) could somehow share its valuable capabilities. Normally, because those stream classes do not implement them, you would be out of luck. Fortunately, you already saw a way that filter streams can wrap themselves "around" other streams. Suppose that you would like a buffered `FileInputStream` (`FileReader`) that can handle marking and resetting correctly. Et voilà:

```
InputStream  s = new BufferedInputStream(new FileInputStream("foo"));
Reader       r = new BufferedReader(new FileReader("foo"));
```

You have a buffered input stream based on the file `"foo"` that can `mark()` and `reset()`.

NOTE BufferedReader is not actually a subclass of `FilterReader`, but it does "nest" like one, and it implements all its methods in completely analogous ways to `BufferedInputStream`, so the parallel between the two classes holds.

In addition, `BufferedReader` has a special method to read a line of characters (ending in `'\r'`, `'\n'`, or `"\r\n"`):

```
BufferedReader  r    = new BufferedReader(new FileReader("foo"));
String          line = r.readLine();  // get the next line of input
```

Now you can begin to see the power of nesting streams. Any capability provided by a filter stream can be used by any other basic stream via nesting. Of course, any combination of these capabilities, and in any order, can be as easily accomplished by nesting the filter streams themselves.

DataInputStream

All the methods that instances of this class understand are defined in a separate interface, which both `DataInputStream` and `RandomAccessFile` (another class in `java.io`) implement. This interface is general enough that you might want to use it yourself in the classes you create. It is called `DataInput`.

The `DataInput` Interface

When you begin using streams to any degree, you'll quickly discover that byte streams are not a really helpful format into which to force all data. In particular, the primitive types of the Java language embody a rather nice way of looking at data, but with the streams you've been defining thus far in this book, you could not read data of these types. The `DataInput` interface specifies a higher-level set of methods that, when used for both reading and writing, can support a more complex, typed stream of data. Here are the set of methods this interface defines:

```
void    readFully(byte[]  bbuffer)                              throws IOException;
void    readFully(byte[]  bbuffer, int  offset, int  length)   throws IOException;
int     skipBytes(int n)                                       throws IOException;

boolean  readBoolean()          throws IOException;
byte     readByte()             throws IOException;
int      readUnsignedByte()     throws IOException;
short    readShort()            throws IOException;
int      readUnsignedShort()    throws IOException;
char     readChar()             throws IOException;
int      readInt()              throws IOException;
long     readLong()             throws IOException;
float    readFloat()            throws IOException;
double   readDouble()           throws IOException;

String   readLine()             throws IOException;
String   readUTF()              throws IOException;
```

The first three methods are simply new names for `skip()` and the first two forms of `read()` you've seen previously. Each of the next 10 methods reads in a primitive type, or its unsigned counterpart (useful for using every bit efficiently in a binary stream). These latter methods must return an integer of a wider size than you might think; because integers are signed in Java, the unsigned value does not fit in anything smaller. The final two methods read a newline-terminated (`'\r'`, `'\n'`, or `"\r\n"`) string of characters from the stream—the first in ASCII, and the second in Unicode (UTF-8) format.

Now that you know what the interface that `DataInputStream` implements looks like, let's see it in action:

```
DataInputStream  s = new DataInputStream(getNumericInputStream());

long  size = s.readLong();      // the number of items in the stream

while (size-- > 0) {
    if (s.readBoolean()) {      // should I process this item?
        int     anInteger    = s.readInt();
        int     magicBitFlags = s.readUnsignedShort();
        double  aDouble      = s.readDouble();

        if ((magicBitFlags & 0100000) != 0) {
            . . .       // high bit set, do something special
        }
        . . .       // process anInteger and aDouble
    }
}
```

Because the class implements an interface that defines all its methods, you can also use the interface directly:

```
DataInput   d = new DataInputStream(new FileInputStream("anything"));
String      line;

while ((line = d.readLine()) != null) {
    . . .       // process the line
}
```

The EOFException

One final point about most of DataInputStream's methods: When the end of the stream is reached, they throw an EOFException. This is tremendously useful and, in fact, allows you to rewrite all the kludgy uses of -1 you saw earlier today in a much nicer fashion:

```
DataInputStream   s = new DataInputStream(getAnInputStreamFromSomewhere());

try {
    while (true) {
        byte  b = (byte) s.readByte();
        . . .       // process the byte b
    }
} catch (EOFException e) {
    . . .       // reached end of stream
}
```

This works just as well for all but the last two of the read methods of DataInputStream.

WARNING

> skipBytes() does nothing at all on end of stream (except perhaps do a lot of useless looping), readLine() returns null, and readUTF() might throw a UTFDataFormatException, if it notices the problem at all. (These three methods are not the best examples of well-written Java code.)

19

LineNumberInputStream and LineNumberReader

In an editor or a debugger, line numbering is crucial. To add this valuable capability to your programs, use the filter stream LineNumberInputStream (or LineNumberReader), which keeps track of line numbers as its stream "flows through" it. It's even smart enough to remember a line number and later restore it, during a mark() and reset(). You might use this class as follows:

```
LineNumberReader        r = new LineNumberReader(new FileReader("source.utf8"));
LineNumberInputStream   aLNIS;
aLNIS = new LineNumberInputStream(new FileInputStream("source"));
```

```
DataInputStream  s = new DataInputStream(aLNIS);
String           bline, cline;

while ((bline = s.readLine()) != null   &&    (cline = r.readLine()) != null) {
    . . .   // process the lines
    System.out.println("Did byte line number: " + aLNIS.getLineNumber());
    System.out.println("Did char line number: " + r.getLineNumber());
}
```

NOTE The simpler creation of, and direct use of readLine() in, LineNumberReader's preceding code is possible because it is a subclass of BufferedReader, which defines readLine() for us. Though it is not a subclass of FilterReader, LineNumberReader does "nest" like one (just like BufferedReader), and it implements all its other methods in completely analogous ways to LineNumberInputStream, so the parallel between the two classes holds.

Here, two filter input streams are nested around the FileInputStream actually providing the data—the outer one reads lines one at a time and the inner one keeps track of the line numbers of these lines as they go by. You must explicitly name the inner filter stream, aLNIS, because if you did not, you couldn't invoke getLineNumber() on it later. Note that if you invert the order of the nested streams, reading from the DataInputStream does not cause the LineNumberInputStream to "see" the lines.

You must put any filter streams acting as "monitors" in the middle of the chain and "pull" the data from the outermost filter stream so that the data will pass through each of the monitors in turn. In the same way, buffering should occur as far inside the chain as possible, because it won't be able to do its job properly unless most of the streams that need buffering come after it in the flow. For example, here's a silly order:

```
new BufferedInputStream(new LineNumberInputStream(
        _new DataInputStream(new FileInputStream("foo"));
```

and here's a much better order:

```
new DataInputStream(new LineNumberInputStream(
        _new BufferedInputStream(new FileInputStream("foo"));
```

LineNumberInputStreams (and LineNumberReaders) can also be told to setLineNumber(), for those rare times when you know more than they do.

PushbackInputStream **and** PushbackReader

The filter stream class PushbackInputStream (PushbackReader) is commonly used in parsers, to "push back" a single byte (character) in the input (after reading it) while trying to determine what to do next—a simplified version of the mark() and reset() utility you learned about earlier. Its only addition to the standard set of InputStream methods used to be unread(), which as you might guess, pretends that it never read the byte (character) passed in as its argument, and will then give that byte (character) back as the return value of the next read(). In release 1.1, new methods for unreading a whole buffer, and a subrange of a buffer, make these three forms of unread() now the exact inverses of the three standard forms of read().

The following is a simple implementation of readLine() using this class (adapted from the implementation in DataInputStream.java):

```
public class  SimpleLineReader {
    private FilterInputStream  s;

    public  SimpleLineReader(InputStream  anIS) {
        s = new DataInputStream(anIS);
    }

    . . .    // other read() methods using stream s

    public String  readLine() throws IOException {
        char[]  buffer = new char[100];
        int      offset = 0;
        byte     thisByte;

        try {
loop:       while (offset < buffer.length) {
                switch (thisByte = (byte) s.read()) {
                    case '\n':
                        break loop;
                    case '\r':
                        byte  nextByte = (byte) s.read();

                        if (nextByte != '\n') {
                            if (!(s instanceof PushbackInputStream)) {
                                s = new PushbackInputStream(s);
                            }
                            ((PushbackInputStream) s).unread(nextByte);
                        }
                        break loop;
                    default:
                        buffer[offset++] = (char) thisByte;
                        break;
                }
            }
        } catch (EOFException e) {
            if (offset == 0)
                return null;
        }
        return String.copyValueOf(buffer, 0, offset);
    }
}
```

19

For the purpose of this example, `readLine()` is restricted to reading the first 100 characters of the line. (In this respect, it demonstrates how not to write a general-purpose line processor—you should be able to read any size line.) The example also reminds you how to break out of an outer loop, and shows you how to produce a `String` from an array of characters (in this case, from a "slice" of the array of characters). Finally, the example includes standard uses of `InputStream`'s `read()` for reading bytes one at a time, and of determining the end of the stream by enclosing it in a `DataInputStream` and catching `EOFException`.

One of the more unusual aspects of the example is the way `PushbackInputStream` is used. To be sure that `'\n'` is ignored following `'\r'` you have to "look ahead" one character; but if it is not a `'\n'`, you must push back that character. Look at the source lines starting with `if (...instaneof...)` as if you didn't know much about the stream s. The general technique used is instructive. First, you see whether s is already an instance of some kind of `PushbackInputStream`. If so, you can simply use it. If not, you enclose the current stream (whatever it is) inside a new `PushbackInputStream` and use this new stream.

The following line wants to invoke the method `unread()`. The problem is that s has a *compile-time type* of `FilterInputStream`, and thus doesn't understand that method. The previous two lines have guaranteed, however, that the run-time type of the stream in s is `PushbackInputStream`, so you can safely cast it to that type, and then safely invoke `unread()`.

NOTE

> This example was done in an unusual way for demonstration purposes. You could have simply declared a `PushbackInputStream` variable and always enclosed the `DataInputStream` in it. (Conversely, `SimpleLineReader`'s constructor could have checked whether its argument was already of the right class, the way `PushbackInputStream` did, before creating a new `DataInputStream`.) The interesting thing about this approach of "wrapping a class only when needed" is that it works for any `InputStream` you hand it, and it does additional work only if it needs to. Both of these are good general design principles.

All the subclasses of `FilterInputStream` have now been described. It's time to return to the direct subclasses of `InputStream`.

ObjectInputStream

Once you have created a large, complex network of inter-connected objects, it is often useful to be able to "save" the state of all these objects, all at once. This allows easy copying, for backup or undo/redo purposes; allows the objects to persist in a file system and later return, reconstituted and "alive" again; and allows objects to "travel together" over the Internet and arrive safely on the other side. (You can already send entire classes this way, and thus make fresh new instances on the other side, but if you want the *contents* of a local object transferred, you need something new.)

JDK 1.1 adds the new concept of *serialization*, which essentially means to take an object and safely and easily turn it into a stream and back again. `ObjectInputStream`, together with its "brother class" `ObjectOutputStream`, does exactly that. For security reasons, only objects that are declared "safe" to move between systems are allowed to be serialized; such objects are instances of classes that implement the new `Serializable` interface. Most internal system classes do not implement `Serializable`, but many of the more "informational" classes do. You can flip through Appendix B, "Class Hierarchy Diagrams," to see all the classes linked by dashed line to this new interface, and get a sense for how much of the system is serializable.

NOTE

There is also another interface, which extends `Serializable`, called `Externalizable`. It allows objects more control over exactly how they are written out and read back in. You will almost never need to use these lower-level facilities, though.

All the methods that instances of this class understand are defined in a separate interface that `ObjectInputStream` implements called `ObjectInput`.

The `ObjectInput` Interface

The `ObjectInput` interface extends the `DataInput` interface, inheriting all its methods as well as providing a single new, high-level method that supports a complex, typed stream of serialized object data:

```
Object  readObject() throws ClassNotFoundException, IOException;
```

Here's a simple example that reads such the stream produced in the "brother" example later today (in `ObjectOutputStream`):

```
FileInputStream    s   = new FileInputStream("objectFileName");
ObjectInputStream  ois = new ObjectInputStream(s);

int     i    = ois.readInt();              // uses DataInput method
String  today = (String) ois.readObject();
Date    date  = (Date)   ois.readObject();
s.close();
```

WARNING

Remember that you must always cast the results of readObject() into the class you expect before using it; even arrays will be sent as objects and must be cast into their correct compile-time types before use.

NOTE

There are many other powerful ways of using serialization (for examples, classes can come along in the stream, automatically version themselves, and so on). For more detail, read the comments in these classes or the white paper about serialization that comes with the JDK 1.1 documentation. To see some of the other classes involved in serialization, look at the diagram for java.io-objects in Appendix B.

PipedInputStream **and** PipedReader

These classes, along with their "brother" classes PipedOutputStream and PipedReader, are covered later today (they need to be understood and demonstrated together). For now, all you need to know is that each class with its brother together create a simple, two-way communication conduit between threads.

SequenceInputStream

Suppose you have two separate streams, and you would like to make a composite stream that consists of one stream followed by the other (like appending two strings together). This is exactly what SequenceInputStream was created for:

```
InputStream  s1 = new FileInputStream("theFirstPart");
InputStream  s2 = new FileInputStream("theRest");

InputStream  s  = new SequenceInputStream(s1, s2);

... s.read() ...    // reads from each stream in turn
```

You could have "faked" this example by reading each file in turn—but what if you had to hand the composite stream s to some other method that was expecting only a single InputStream? Here's an example (using s) that line-numbers the two previous files with a common numbering scheme:

```
LineNumberInputStream  aLNIS = new LineNumberInputStream(s);

... aLNIS.getLineNumber() ...
```

NOTE

Stringing together streams this way is especially useful when the streams are of unknown length and origin, and were just handed to you by someone else.

What if you want to string together more than two streams? You could try the following:

```
Vector   v = new Vector();
. . .    // set up all the streams and add each to the Vector
InputStream   s1 = new SequenceInputStream(v.elementAt(0), v.elementAt(1));
InputStream   s2 = new SequenceInputStream(s1, v.elementAt(2));
InputStream   s3 = new SequenceInputStream(s2, v.elementAt(3));
. . .
```

NOTE

A Vector is a growable array of objects that can be filled, referenced (with elementAt()), and enumerated.

However, it's much easier to use a different constructor that SequenceInputStream provides:

```
InputStream   s  = new SequenceInputStream(v.elements());
```

This takes an enumeration of all the streams you wish to combine and returns a single stream that reads through the data of each in turn.

StringBufferInputStream **and** StringReader

StringBufferInputStream (StringReader) is exactly like ByteArrayInputStream (CharArrayReader), but instead of being based on a byte (character) array, it's based on a string:

```
String       buffer = "Now is the time for all good men to come...";
InputStream  s      = new StringBufferInputStream(buffer);
Reader       r      = new StringReader(buffer);
```

All comments that were made about ByteArrayInputStream (CharArrayReader) apply here as well. (See the earlier section on those classes.)

NOTE

StringBufferInputStream is a bit of a misnomer, because this input stream is actually based on a string. It should really be called StringInputStream. Also, it handles reset() by resetting to the start of the string, and markSupported() will return false (thus it is not fully symmetric with StringReader)—these are essentially bugs (or historical hold-overs) from 1.0.

19

Output Streams and Writers

Output streams (or writers) are, in almost every case, paired with a "brother" InputStream (or Reader) that you've already learned. If an InputStream (Reader) performs a certain operation, the "brother" OutputStream (Writer) performs the inverse operation. You'll see more of what this means soon.

The abstract Classes OutputStream and Writer

OutputStream is the abstract class that defines the fundamental ways in which a source (producer) writes a stream of bytes to some destination. The identity of the destination, and the manner of the transport and storage of the bytes, is irrelevant. When using an output stream, you are the source of those bytes, and that's all you need to know.

Writer is an abstract class that defines the fundamental ways in which source (producer) writes a stream of characters to some destination. It and all its subclasses are analogous to OutputStream and all its subclasses, except that they use characters as their fundamental units of information instead of bytes.

write()

The most important method to the producer of an output stream (or writer) is the one that writes bytes (characters) to the destination. This method, write(), comes in many flavors, each demonstrated in the following examples.

NOTE

> Every one of these write() methods is defined to "block" (wait) until all the output requested has been written. You don't need to worry about this limitation—see the note under the input stream's read() method if you don't remember why.

```
OutputStream   s        = getAnOutputStreamFromSomewhere();
Writer         w        = getAWriterFromSomewhere();
byte[]         bbuffer  = new byte[1024];        // any size will do
char[]         cbuffer  = new byte[1024];

fillInData(bbuffer);    fillInData(cbuffer);    // the data we want to output
s.write(bbuffer);
w.write(cuffer);
```

You can also write a "slice" of your buffer by specifying the offset into the buffer, and the length desired, as arguments to write():

```
s.write(bbuffer, 100, 300);
w.write(cbuffer, 100, 300);
```

This writes out bytes (characters) 100 through 399, and behaves otherwise exactly the same as the previous write() method. In fact, in the current release, the default implementation of the first version of write() uses the second:

```
public void  write(byte[]  b) throws IOException {    /* from OutputStream.java
➡*/
    write(b, 0, b.length);
}

public void  write(char[]  cbuf) throws IOException {       /* from Writer.java
➡*/
    write(cbuf, 0, cbuf.length);
}
```

Finally, you can write out bytes one at a time:

```
while (thereAreMoreBytesToOutput()    &&     thereAreMoreCharsToOutput()) {
    byte  b = getNextByteForOutput();
    char  c = getNextCharForOutput();

    s.write(b);
    w.write(c);
}
```

NOTE   Writer actually has two additional methods for writing a String and for writing a slice of a String. They are used identically to the first two forms of write() just described (simply replace cbuffer with the String).

flush()

Because you don't know what an output stream (or writer) is connected to, you might be required to "flush" your output through some buffered cache to get it written (in a timely manner, or at all). OutputStream's version of this method does nothing, but it is expected that subclasses that require flushing (for example, BufferedOutputStream and PrintStream) will override this version to do something nontrivial.

close()

Just like an InputStream (or Reader), you should (usually) explicitly close down an OutputStream (Writer) so that it can release any resources it may have reserved on your behalf. (All the same notes and examples from the input stream's close() method apply here.)

All output streams descend from the abstract class OutputStream, and all writers descend from Writer. All have the previous few methods in common.

NOTE

> Concrete subclasses of OutputStream need only implement the zero-argument version of write() to get all the other methods working (OutputStream has default implementations of close() and flush() that do nothing). Writer subclasses, however, must implement close(), flush(), and the three-argument version of write().

ByteArrayOutputStream **and** CharArrayWriter

The inverse of ByteArrayInputStream (CharArrayReader), which creates an input stream from an array of bytes (characters), is ByteArrayOutputStream (CharArrayWriter), which directs an output stream into an array of bytes (characters):

```
OutputStream  s = new ByteArrayOutputStream();
Writer        w = new CharArrayWriter();

s.write(123);
w.write('\n');
. . .
```

The size of an internal byte (character) array grows as needed to store a stream of any length. You can provide an initial capacity as an aid to the class, if you like:

```
OutputStream  s = new ByteArrayOutputStream(1024 * 1024);  // 1 Megabyte
Writer        w = new CharArrayWriter(1024 * 1024);
```

NOTE

> You've just seen your first examples of the creation of an output stream (and writer). These new streams were attached to the simplest of all possible destinations of data, an array of bytes (characters) in the memory of the local computer.

Once the ByteArrayOutputStream s (or CharArrayWriter w) has been "filled," it can be output to another output stream (or writer):

```
OutputStream          anotherOutputStream = getTheOtherOutputStream();
Writer                anotherWriter       = getTheOtherWriter();
ByteArrayOutputStream s = new ByteArrayOutputStream();
CharArrayWriter       w = new CharArrayWriter();

fillWithUsefulData(s);    fillWithUsefulData(w);
s.writeTo(anotherOutputStream);
w.writeTo(anotherWriter);
```

It also can be extracted as a byte (character) array, or converted to a string:

```
byte[]   bbuffer              = s.toByteArray();
char[]   cbuffer              = w.toCharArray();
String   streamString         = s.toString();
String   writerString         = w.toString();
String   streamUnicodeString  = s.toString(upperByteValue);
```

NOTE The last method allows you to "fake" Unicode (16-bit) characters by filling in their lower bytes with ASCII and then specifying a common upper byte (usually 0) to create a (Unicode) String result.

ByteArrayOutputStreams (and CharArrayWriters) have two utility methods: One simply returns the current number of bytes (characters) stored in the internal array, and the other resets the array so that the stream can be rewritten from the beginning:

```
int   sizeOfMyByteArray = s.size();
int   sizeOfMyCharArray = w.size();

s.reset();       // s.size() would now return 0
w.reset();       // w.size() would now return 0
s.write(123);
w.write('\n');
. . .
```

NOTE There is a related writer, called StringWriter, that's a bit of an oddball—it has no Reader counterpart (has no brother), and it's almost identical to CharArrayWriter (it adds a getBuffer() that returns the String, and does not implement writeTo(), toCharArray(), or reset()). Strings and character arrays are so close in representation and use, that this class is superfluous.

FileOutputStream and FileWriter

One of the most common uses of streams is to attach them to files in the file system. Here, for example, is the creation of such an output stream (or writer) on a UNIX system:

```
OutputStream  s = new FileOutputStream("/some/path/and/fileName");
Writer        w = new FileWriter("/some/path/and/fileName.utf8");
```

19

Applets attempting to open, read, or write streams based on files in the
file system will cause security violations. See the caution under
`FileInputStream` and `FileReader` for more details.

NOTE

`FileOutputStream` (but not `FileWriter`) also has a constructor that takes
a `String` and a `boolean` that tells it whether or not it should append to
the file.

You also can create the stream from a previously opened `FileDescriptor` or `File`:

```
OutputStream  s = new FileOutputStream(FileDescriptor.out);  /* standard input
➥*/
Writer        w = new FileWriter(FileDescriptor.err);        /* standard error
➥*/
OutputStream  s = new FileOutputStream(new File("/some/path/and/fileName"));
Writer        w = new FileWriter(new File("/some/path/and/fileName.utf8"));
```

`FileWriter` is actually a trivial subclass of another writer class, `OutputStreamWriter`, that can
encapsulate any `OutputStream` and turn it into a `Writer` of characters instead. Thus,
`FileWriter`'s implementation consists of simply asking an `OutputStreamWriter` (itself) to
encapsulate a `FileOutputStream`.

`FileOutputStream` is the inverse of `FileInputStream`, and it knows the same tricks:

```
FileOutputStream  aFOS = new FileOutputStream("aFileName");

FileDescriptor  myFD = aFOS.getFD();

/* aFOS.finalize(); */  // will invoke close() when automatically called by GC
```

The first is obvious: `getFD()` simply returns the `FileDescriptor` for the file on which the
stream is based. The second, commented, contrived invocation to `finalize()` is there to
remind you that you may not have to worry about closing this type of stream—it is done for
you automatically. (See the discussion under `FileInputStream` and `FileReader` for more.)

FilterOutputStream **and** FilterWriter

These "abstract" classes (only `FilterWriter` is actually declared abstract) simply provide a
"pass-through" for all the standard methods of `OutputStream` (or `Writer`). They hold inside
themselves another stream, by definition one further "down" the chain of filters, to which

they forward all method invocations. They implement nothing new but allows themselves to be nested:

```
OutputStream        s  = getAnOutputStreamFromSomewhere();
FilterOutputStream  s1 = new FilterOutputStream(s);
FilterOutputStream  s2 = new FilterOutputStream(s1);
FilterOutputStream  s3 = new FilterOutputStream(s2);

... s3.write(123) ...
```

Whenever a write is performed on the filtered stream s3, it passes along the request to s2. Then s2 does the same to s1, and finally s is asked to output the bytes. Subclasses of FilterOutputStream, of course, do some nontrivial processing of the bytes as they flow past. This chain can be more tightly and elegantly nested—see its "brother" class, FilterInputStream for more details.

Now let's examine each of the subclasses of FilterOutputStream in turn.

BufferedOutputStream and BufferedWriter

BufferedOutputStream (BufferedWriter) is one of the most valuable of all streams. All it does is implement the full complement of OutputStream's (Writer's) methods, but it does so by using a buffered array of bytes (characters) that acts as a cache for writing. This decouples the rate and the size of the "chunks" you're writing from the more regular, larger block sizes in which streams are most efficiently written (to, for example, peripheral devices, files in the file system, or the network).

BufferedOutputStream (BufferedWriter) is one of the few classes in the Java library to implement non-trivial version of flush(), which pushes the bytes (characters) you've written through the buffer and out the other side. Because buffering is so valuable, you might wish that every output stream (or writer) could somehow be buffered. Fortunately, you can surround any output stream (or writer) in such a way as to achieve just that:

```
OutputStream  s = new BufferedOutputStream(new FileOutputStream("foo"));
Writer        w = new BufferedWriter (new FileWriter("foo.utf8"));
```

You now have a buffered output stream (writer) based on the file "foo" that can be flush()ed.

NOTE BufferedWriter is not a subclass of FilterWriter, but is "nests" as though it were. It also has an unique method called newLine() that outputs the newline character(s) appropriate to the local system on which Java is running.

Just as for filter input streams (or readers), any capability provided by a filter output stream (or writers) can be used by any other basic stream via nesting; any combination of these capabilities, in any order, can be as easily accomplished by nesting the filter streams themselves.

DataOutputStream

All the methods that instances of this class understand are defined in a separate interface, which both DataOutputStream and RandomAccessFile implement. This interface is general enough that you might want to use it in the classes you create. It is called DataOutput.

The DataOutput Interface

In cooperation with its "brother" inverse interface, DataInput, DataOutput provides a higher-level, typed-stream approach to the reading and writing of data. Rather than dealing with bytes, this interface deals with writing the primitive types of the Java language directly:

```
void   write(int i)                                      throws IOException;
void   write(byte[]  buffer)                             throws IOException;
void   write(byte[]  buffer, int  offset, int  length)   throws IOException;

void   writeBoolean(boolean b) throws IOException;
void   writeByte(int i)        throws IOException;
void   writeShort(int i)       throws IOException;
void   writeChar(int i)        throws IOException;
void   writeInt(int i)         throws IOException;
void   writeLong(long l)       throws IOException;
void   writeFloat(float f)     throws IOException;
void   writeDouble(double d)   throws IOException;

void   writeBytes(String s) throws IOException;
void   writeChars(String s) throws IOException;
void   writeUTF(String s)   throws IOException;
```

Most of these methods have counterparts in the interface DataInput.

The first three methods mirror the three forms of write() you saw previously. Each of the next eight methods write out a primitive type. The final three methods write out a string of bytes or characters to the stream: the first one as 8-bit bytes; the second, as 16-bit (binary) Unicode characters; and the last, as a special Unicode (UTF-8) stream (readable by DataInput's readUTF()).

NOTE

The unsigned read methods in DataInput have no counterparts here. You can write out the data they need via DataOutput's signed methods because they accept int arguments and also because they write out the correct number of bits for the unsigned integer of a given size as a side effect of writing out the signed integer of that same size. It is the method that reads this integer that must interpret the sign bit correctly; the writer's job is easy.

Now that you know what the interface that DataOutputStream implements looks like, let's see it in action:

```
DataOutputStream  s     = new DataOutputStream(getNumericOutputStream());
long              size = getNumberOfItemsInNumericStream();

s.writeLong(size);

for (int  i = 0;  i < size;  ++i) {
    if (shouldProcessNumber(i)) {
        s.writeBoolean(true);       // should process this item
        s.writeInt(theIntegerForItemNumber(i));
        s.writeShort(theMagicBitFlagsForItemNumber(i));
        s.writeDouble(theDoubleForItemNumber(i));
    } else
        s.writeBoolean(false);
}
```

This is the exact inverse of the example that was given for DataInput. Together, they form a pair that can communicate a particular array of structured primitive types across any stream (or "transport layer"). Use this pair as a jumping-off point whenever you need to do something similar.

In addition to the interface above, the class itself implements one (self-explanatory) utility method:

```
int  theNumberOfBytesWrittenSoFar = s.size();
```

Processing a File

One of the most common idioms in file I/O is to open a file, read and process it line-by-line, and output it again to another file. Here's a prototypical example of how that would be done in Java:

```
DataInput   aDI = new DataInputStream(new FileInputStream("source"));
DataOutput  aDO = new DataOutputStream(new FileOutputStream("dest"));
String      line;

while ((line = aDI.readLine()) != null) {
    StringBuffer  modifiedLine = new StringBuffer(line);

    . . .        // process modifiedLine in place
    aDO.writeBytes(modifiedLine.toString());
}
aDI.close();
aDO.close();
```

19

If you want to process it byte by byte, use this:

```
try {
    while (true) {
        byte  b = (byte) aDI.readByte();

        . . .           // process b in place
        aDO.writeByte(b);
    }
} finally {
    aDI.close();
    aDO.close();
}
```

Here's a cute two-liner that just copies the file:

```
try { while (true) aDO.writeByte(aDI.readByte()); }
finally { aDI.close(); aDO.close(); }
```

WARNING

Remember that many of the examples in today's lesson (and the last two) assume they appear inside a method that has `IOException` in its throws clause, so they don't have to "worry" about catching those exceptions and handling them more reasonably. Your code should be a little less cavalier.

PrintStream **and** PrintReader

You may not realize it, but you're already intimately familiar with the use of two methods of the `PrintStream` class. That's because whenever these method invocations appeared:

```
System.out.print(. . .)
System.out.println(. . .)
```

they were actually using a `PrintStream` instance located in `System`'s class variable `out` to perform the output. `System.err` is also a `PrintStream`, and `System.in` is an `InputStream`.

NOTE

On UNIX systems, these three streams will be attached to standard output, standard error, and standard input, respectively.

`PrintStream` is (uniquely) only an output stream class (it has no "brother"). `PrintWriter` is one of only two writers with this same property. Because they are usually attached to a screen output device of some kind, they provide a non-trivial implementation of `flush()`. They also provide the familiar `close()` and `write()` methods, as well as a plethora of choices for outputting the primitive types and `String`s of Java:

```
public void   write(int byteOrChar); // byte (PrintStream), char (PrintWriter)
public void   write(byte[]  buffer, int  offset, int  length); // PrintStream
public void   write(char[]  buffer, int  offset, int  length); // PrintWriter
public void   write(String  string);  // next two methods only in PrintWriter
public void   write(String  string, int  offset, int  length); // PrintWriter
public void   flush();        // (everything from here down is in both classes)
public void   close();

public void   print(Object o);
public void   print(String s);
public void   print(char[]  buffer);
public void   print(char c);
public void   print(int i);
public void   print(long l);
public void   print(float f);
public void   print(double d);
public void   print(boolean b);

public void   println(Object o);
public void   println(String s);
public void   println(char[]  buffer);
public void   println(char c);
public void   println(int i);
public void   println(long l);
public void   println(float f);
public void   println(double d);
public void   println(boolean b);

public void   println();    // output a blank line
```

PrintStream (PrintWriter) can also be wrapped around any output stream, just like a filter class (despite the fact that PrintWriter is not a subclass of FilterWriter; it "nests" like one):

```
PrintStream  s = new PrintStream(new FileOutputStream("foo"));
PrintWriter  w = new PrintWriter(new FileWriter("foo.utf8"));

s.println("Here's the first line of text in the file foo.");
w.println("Here's the first line of text in the file foo.utf8.");
```

If you provide a second argument to the constructor for PrintStream (or PrintWriter), it is a boolean that specifies whether the stream should auto-flush. If true, a flush() is sent after any newline character ('\n') is written (or for the three-argument form of write(), after a whole group of characters has been written.) PrintWriter handles auto-flush a little differently—it flushes only after one of the println(...) methods is called.

Here's a simple sample program that operates like the UNIX command cat, taking the standard input, line by line, and outputting it to the standard output:

```
import java.io.*;   // the one time today that we'll say this

public class  Cat {
    public static void  main(String argv[]) {
        DataInput   d = new DataInputStream(System.in);
        String      line;
```

```
     try {  while ((line = d.readLine()) != null)
            System.out.println(line);
        } catch (IOException  ignored) { }
      }
}
```

All the subclasses of `FilterOutputStream` have now been described. It's time to return to the direct subclasses of `OutputStream`.

ObjectOutputStream

`ObjectOutputStream`, together with its "brother class" `ObjectInputStream`, provide for the serialization of objects (see the discussion under `ObjectInputStream` for more details).

All the methods that instances of this class understand are defined in a separate interface that `ObjectOutputStream` implements, called `ObjectOutput`.

The ObjectOutput Interface

The `ObjectOutput` interface extends the `DataOutput` interface, inheriting all its methods as well as providing a single new, high-level method that supports a complex, typed stream of serialized object data:

```
void  writeObject(Object  obj) throws IOException;
```

Here's a simple example that writes the stream that's read in the "brother" example earlier today (in `ObjectInputStream`):

```
FileOutputStream    s   = new FileOutputStream("objectFileName");
ObjectOutputStream  oos = new ObjectOutputStream(s);

oos.writeInt(12345);                    // uses DataOutput method
oos.writeObject("Today");
oos.writeObject(new Date());
oos.flush();
s.close();
```

PipedOutputStream and PipedWriter

Along with `PipedInputStream` (`PipedReader`), these pairs of classes support a UNIX-pipe–like connection between two threads, implementing all the careful synchronization that allows this sort of "shared queue" to operate safely. To set up the connection:

```
PipedInputStream   sIn  = new PipedInputStream();
PipedOutputStream  sOut = new PipedOutputStream(sIn);

PipedReader  wIn  = new PipedReader();
PipedWriter  wOut = new PipedWriter(wIn);
```

One thread writes to sOut (wOut), and the other reads from sIn (wIn). By setting up two such pairs, the threads can communicate safely in both directions.

NOTE

> PipedOutputStream has both the zero-argument and three-argument form of write() implemented, while PipedWriter has only the three-argument form.

Related Classes

The other classes and interfaces in java.io supplement the streams to provide a complete I/O system. Three of them are described next.

The File class abstracts "file" in a platform-independent way. Given a filename, it can respond to queries about the type, status, and properties of a file or directory in the file system.

A RandomAccessFile is created given a filename, or a File, and a mode ("r" or "rw") for access. It combines in one class implementations of the DataInput and DataOutput interfaces, both tuned for "random access" to a file in the file system. In addition to these interfaces, RandomAccessFile provides certain traditional UNIX-like facilities, such as seek()ing to a random point in the file.

Finally, the StreamTokenizer class takes an input stream (or reader) and produces a sequence of tokens. By overriding its various methods in your own subclasses, you can create powerful lexical parsers.

You can learn more about any or all of these other classes from the full (online) API descriptions in your Java release.

19

Summary

Today, you learned about the general idea of streams and met input streams and readers based on arrays, files, objects, pipes, sequences of other streams, and string buffers, as well as input filters for buffering, reading typed data, line numbering, and pushing-back characters.

You also met the analogous "brother" output streams and writers for arrays, files, objects, and pipes, and output filters for buffering and writing typed data, and the unique output filters used for printing.

Along the way, you became familiar with the fundamental methods all streams understand (such as read() and write()), as well as the unique methods many streams add to this repertoire. You learned about catching IOExceptions—especially the most useful of them, EOFException.

Finally, the twice-useful DataInput and DataOutput interfaces formed the heart of RandomAccessFile, one of the several utility classes that round out Java's I/O facilities.

Java streams provide a powerful base on which you can build multithreaded, streaming interfaces of the most complex kinds, and the programs (such as HotJava) to interpret them. The higher-level Internet protocols and services of the future that your applets can build upon this base are limited only by your imagination.

Q&A

Q In an early read() example, you did something with the variable byteOrMinus1 that seemed a little clumsy. Isn't there a better way? If not, why recommend the cast later?

A Yes, there is something a little odd about those statements. You might be tempted to try something like this instead:

```
while ((b = (byte) s.read()) != -1) {
    . . .      // process the byte b
}
```

The problem with this shortcut occurs when read() returns the value 0xFF (0377). Since this value is signed-extended before the test gets executed, it will appear to be identical to the integer value -1 that indicates end of stream. Only saving that value in a separate integer variable, and then casting it later, will accomplish the desired result. The cast to byte is recommended in the note for orthogonal reasons— storing integer values in correctly sized variables is always good style (and besides, read() really should be returning something of byte size here and throwing an exception for end of stream).

Q What input streams in java.io actually implement mark(), reset(), and markSupported()?

A InputStream itself does—and in their default implementations, markSupported() returns false, mark() does nothing, and reset() throws an exception. The only input stream in the current release that non-trivially supports marking is BufferedInputStream, which overrides these defaults. LineNumberInputStream actually implements mark() and reset(), but even in the 1.1 release, it doesn't answer markSupported() correctly, so it looks as if it does not. The new Reader classes in 1.1 handle markSupported() correctly in all cases, and several more of them do non-trivial mark()/reset().

19

Q **Why is** `available()` **useful, even if it sometimes gives the wrong answer?**

A First, for many streams, it gives the right answer. Second, for some network streams, its implementation might be sending a special query to discover some information you couldn't get any other way (for example, the size of a file being transferred by `ftp`). If you were displaying a "progress bar" for network or file transfers, for example, `available()` will often give you the total size of the transfer, and when it does not—usually by returning `0`—it will be obvious to you (and your users).

Q **What's a good example use of the** `DataInput`/`DataOutput` **pair of interfaces?**

A One common use of such a pair is when objects want to "pickle" themselves for storage or movement over a network. Each object implements read and write methods using these interfaces, effectively converting itself to a stream that can later be reconstituted "on the other end" into a copy of the original object. This process can now be automated in 1.1 via the new object input and output streams, which use these interfaces.

19

Day **20**

Using Native Methods and Libraries

by Charles L. Perkins

Today, you'll learn all the reasons you might (or might not) want to write native methods in Java, about all of Java's built-in optimizations, and about the tricks you can use to make your programs faster. You'll also learn the procedure for creating, making headers for, and linking native methods into a dynamically loadable library. Finally, you'll learn all about the Java Native Interface.

Let's begin, however, with the reasons that you might want to implement native methods in the first place.

There are only two good reasons that you might need to declare some of your methods native, that is, implemented by a language other than Java.

The first—and by far the best reason to do so—is because you need to utilize a special capability of your computer, operating system, or legacy (non-Java) software that the Java class library does not already provide for you. Such capabilities include interfacing to new peripheral devices or plug-in cards, accessing an unusual type of networking, or using a unique, but valuable feature of your particular operating system. Two more concrete examples are acquiring real-time audio input from a microphone or using 3D "accelerator" hardware in a 3D library. Neither of these is provided to you by the current Java environment (though 3D capabilities will soon be added to Java), so you must implement them outside Java, in some other language (currently limited to C, or any language that can link with C).

The second, and often illusory, reason to implement `native` methods is speed—illusory, because you rarely need the raw speeds gained by this approach. It's even more rare to not be able to gain that speedup in other ways (as you'll see later today). Using native methods in this case takes advantage of the fact that, at present, the Java release does not perform as well as, for example, an optimized C program on some tasks. For those tasks, you can write the "needs to be fast" part (critical, inner loops, for example) in C, and still use a larger shell of Java shell classes to hide this "trick" from your users. In fact, the Java class library uses this approach for certain critical system classes to raise the overall level of efficiency in the system. As a user of the Java environment, you don't even know (or see) any side effects of this (except, perhaps, a few classes or methods that are `final` that might not be otherwise).

Disadvantages of `native` Methods

Once you decide you'd like to, or must, use `native` methods in your program, this choice will cost you dearly. Although you will gain the advantages mentioned earlier, you will lose the portability of your Java code.

Before, you had a program (or applet) that could travel to any Java environment in the world, now and forever. Any new architectures created—or new operating systems written—were irrelevant to your code. All it required was that the (tiny) Java virtual machine (or a Java-enabled browser that had one inside it) be available, and it could run anywhere, anytime—now and in the future.

Now, however, you've created a library of native code that must be linked with your program to make it work properly. The first thing you lose is the ability to "travel" as an applet; you simply can't be one! No Java-enabled browser currently in existence allows native code to be loaded with an applet, for security reasons (and these are good reasons). The Java team has struggled to place as much as possible into the `java` packages because they are the only environment you can count on as an applet. (The sun packages, shipped primarily for internal use by Sun's implementation of Java, are not standardized, and are also not always accessible by applets.)

20

NOTE

Actually, any classes that anyone writes without native code should be able to be loaded with an applet, as long as they depend only on the `java` packages. Unfortunately, a few of the sun packages contain classes that must use native code to provide functionality missing from the `java` packages. Most of these "missing pieces" from earlier sun packages have been folded back into new `java` packages in release 1.1, and some additional multimedia and sound capabilities will be added to the `java` packages in 1997. Watch `http://www.javasoft.com/` for details.

Losing the ability to travel anywhere across the Net, into any browser written now or in the future, is bad enough. What's worse, now that you can't be an applet, you have further limited yourself to only those machines that have had the Java virtual machine ported to their operating system. (Applets automatically benefit from the wider number of machines and operating systems that any Java-enabled browser is ported to, but now you do not.)

Even worse, you have usually assumed something about that machine and operating system in the implementation of your `native` methods. This often means that you have to write different *source* code for some (or all) of the machines and operating systems on which you want to be able to run. You're already forced, by using `native` methods, to produce a separate binary library for every machine and operating system pair in the world (or at least, wherever you plan to run), and you must continue to do so forever. If changing the source is also necessary, you can see that this is not a pleasant situation for you and your Java program.

NOTE

The previous discussion about virtual machine locations limiting `native` method implementations is lessened somewhat by the announcements of the last year that most operating systems will be including virtual machines in their next releases. However, Java-enabled browsers are still more quickly, more easily, and more often ported to peculiar (and new) machines.

The new JNI (explained later today in the section "The Java Native Interface") lessens the impact of `native` methods by allowing you to (usually) write only one source version of the native code, and to reuse one binary version of the native code for all operating systems running on a given machine. But it is still the case that you must have new binary versions for every different machine, and possibly a new source file as well.

20

The Illusion of Required Efficiency

If, even after the previous discussion, you must use native methods anyway, there's help for you later in today's lesson—but what if you're still thinking you need to use them for efficiency reasons?

You are in a grand tradition of programmers throughout the (relatively few) ages of computing. It is exciting, and intellectually challenging, to program within constraints. If you believe efficiency is always required, it makes your job a little more interesting—you get to consider all sorts of baroque ways to accomplish tasks, because it is the efficient way to do it. I myself was caught up in this euphoria of creativity when I first began programming, but it is creativity misapplied.

When you design your program, all that energy and creativity should be directed at the design of a tight, concise, minimal set of classes and methods that are maximally general, abstract, and reusable. (If you think that is easy, look around for a few years and see how bad most software is.) If you spend most of your programming time on thinking and rethinking these fundamental goals and how to achieve them, you are preparing for the future. A future where software is assembled as needed from small components swimming in a sea of network facilities, and anyone can write a component seen by millions (and reused in their programs) in minutes. If, instead, you spend your energy worrying about the speed your software will run right now on some computer, your work will be irrelevant after the 18 to 36 months it will take hardware to be fast enough to hide that minor inefficiency in your program.

Am I saying that you should ignore efficiency altogether? Of course not! Some of the great algorithms of computer science deal with solving hard or "impossible" problems in reasonable amounts of time—and writing your programs carelessly can lead to remarkably slow results. Carelessness, however, can as easily lead to incorrect, fragile, or non-reusable results. If you correct all these latter problems first, the resulting software will be clean, will naturally reflect the structure of the problem you're trying to solve, and thus will be amenable to "speeding up" later.

NOTE

> There are always cases where you must be fanatical about efficiency in many parts of a set of classes. The Java class library itself is such a case, as is anything that must run in real-time for some critical real-world application (such as flying a plane). Such applications are rare, however.
>
> Between JDK 1.0 and 1.1, Sun's virtual machine has, on average, gotten three times faster, and many operations are five times faster—all this in less than a year. This speedup is even larger if you run this new virtual machine on the new, faster hardware that appears each year!

20

> Thus, saying that Java is just "too slow" is not a good justification for going `native`.
>
> When speaking of a new kind of programming that must soon emerge, Bill Joy likes to invoke the four S's of Java: small, simple, safe, and secure. The "feel" of the Java language itself encourages the pursuit of clarity and the reduction of complexity. The intense pursuit of efficiency, which increases complexity and reduces clarity, is antithetical to these goals.

Once you build a solid foundation, debug your classes, and make your program (or applet) work exactly as you'd like it to, then it's time to begin optimizing it. If it's just a user interface applet, you may need to do nothing at all. The user is very slow compared to modern computers (and getting twice as slow every 18 months). The odds are that your applet is already fast enough—but suppose it isn't.

Built-In Optimizations

Your next job is to see whether your release or Java-enabled browser supports a "just-in-time" compiler, or some other native code translator or compiler. (Both the Netscape and Internet Explorer browsers have just-in-time compilers built-in.)

A just-in-time compiler translates, while a method's bytecodes are running in the Java virtual machine, each bytecode into the native binary code equivalent for the local computer, and then keeps this native code around as a cache for the next time that method is run. This trick is completely transparent to the Java code you write. You need know nothing about whether or not it's being done—your code can still "travel" anywhere, anytime. On any system with just-in-time technology in place, however, it runs a lot faster. Early testing shows that after paying a small cost the first time a method is run, this technique can achieve the speed of compiled C code.

NOTE

> More details on this technique will be presented tomorrow. As of the 1.1 release, just-in-time technology is not part of Sun's standard JDK release, but all major Java-enabled browsers and development environments already ship with just-in-time compilers built-in (and that's all that matters to you since your users will be using such environments). To see the latest performance results for browsers, look at `http://www.webfayre.com/battle.html` (or `scores.html`). Currently, JIT-based browsers range from two times faster—on complex image tasks—to 80 times faster—on simple loops—than non-JIT browsers.

20

A native code *translator* (or a tool like the experimental java2c tool discussed tomorrow) takes a whole .class file full of the bytecodes for a class and translates them, all at once, into native code (or into a portable C source code version that can be compiled by a traditional C compiler) to produce a native-method-like cached library of fast code.

NOTE
> A native code *compiler* would take the .java source for the same class and produce native code in a more traditional manner. Some versions of gcc (a compiler that is described in a Note later today) can do this. Remember, though, that the source code does not usually travel together with the bytecodes of an applet, so you cannot count on its being available.

This large cache of native code would be used whenever the class's methods are called, but only on the local computer. Your original Java code can still travel as bytecodes, and run on any other computer system. If the virtual machine were to automatically translate native code whenever it "makes sense" for a given class, this could be as transparent as just-in-time technology. Early tests of an experimental native code translator show that fully optimized C performance is achievable. (This is the best anyone can hope to do!)

So you see, even without taking any further steps to optimize your program, you may discover that for your release of Java (or your Java-enabled browser), your code is already fast enough. If it is not, remember that the world craves speed. Java will only get faster; the tools will only get better. Your code is the only permanent thing in this new world—it should be the best you can make it, with no compromises.

Simple Optimization Tricks

Suppose that these technologies aren't available to you, or they don't optimize your program far enough for your taste. You can profile your applet or program as it runs, to see in which methods it spends the most time. Once you know this crucial information, you can begin to make targeted changes to your classes.

NOTE
> Typing java -prof ClassName will produce this profile information for the class ClassName, and for all the classes that it uses. For applications, ClassName must contain main(). For applets, you usually need to profile the entire appletviewer by typing java -prof sun.applet.AppletViewer AppletTag.html. In either case, the file java.prof is created chock-full of cryptic but useful profiling data.

> In an early release (and, presumably, some later release) the javaprof tool would "pretty-print" this information into a more readable format. In release 1.1 of Java, javaprof is not included, and java -prof works, but is undocumented. (Nevertheless, java -prof is still quite useful, so don't be afraid to use it!) Check each new Java release to see if javaprof is included, and/or look on the Net for something equivalent.

TIP

> Before you begin making optimizations, you also may want to save a copy of your "clean" classes. As soon as computer speeds allow it (or a major rewrite necessitates it), you can revert to these classes, which embody the "best" implementation of your program.

First, identify the crucial few methods that take most of the time (there are almost always just a few, and often just one, that take up the majority of your program's time). If those methods contain loops, examine the inner loops to see whether they:

- ☐ call methods that can be made final
- ☐ call a group of methods that can be collapsed into a single method
- ☐ create objects that can be reused rather than created anew each loop

If you notice that a long chain of, for example, four or more method invocations is needed to reach a destination method, and this execution path is in one of the critical sections of the program, you can "short-circuit" directly to that destination method in the topmost method. This may require adding a new instance variable to reference the object for that method invocation directly. The new reference quite often violates layering or encapsulation constraints. This violation, and any other added complexity, is the price you pay for efficiency.

If, after all these tricks (and the numerous others you should try that have been collected over the years into various programming books), your Java code is still just too slow, you will have to use native methods after all.

Writing native Methods

For whatever reasons, you've decided to add native methods to your program. You've already decided which methods need to be native, and in which classes, and you're rarin' to go.

20

First, on the Java side, all you need to do is delete the method bodies (all the code between the brackets—{ and }—and the brackets themselves) of each method you picked and replace them with a single semicolon (;). Then add the modifier `native` to the method's existing modifiers. Finally, add a `static` (class) initializer to each class that now contains `native` methods to load the native code library you're about to build. (You can pick any name you like for this library.) You're done!

That's all you need to do in Java to specify a `native` method. Subclasses of any class containing your new `native` methods can still override them, and these new (Java) methods are called for instances of the new subclasses (just as you'd expect).

Unfortunately, what needs to be done in your native language environment is not so simple.

NOTE

> The following discussion assumes that C and UNIX are your language and environment. This means that a few steps may differ slightly on your system, but such differences will be outlined in the documentation on native methods in your release (and in the excellent online tutorial at `http://java.sun.com/nav/read/Tutorial/native1.1`).

The Example Class

Imagine a version of the Java environment that does not provide file I/O. Any Java program needing to use the file system would first have to write `native` methods to get access to the operating system primitives needed to do file I/O.

The following example class combines simplified versions of two actual Java library classes, `java.io.File` and `java.io.RandomAccessFile`, into a single new class, `SimpleFile`:

```
public class  SimpleFile {
    public static final  char     separatorChar = '>';
    protected             String   path;
    protected             int      fd;

    public  SimpleFile(String s) {
        path = s;
    }

    public String  getFileName() {
        int  index = path.lastIndexOf(separatorChar);

        return (index < 0) ? path : path.substring(index + 1);
    }

    public String  getPath() {
        return path;
    }
```

20

```
    public native boolean  open();
    public native void     close();
    public native int      read(byte[]  buffer, int  length);
    public native int      write(byte[]  buffer, int  length);

    static {
        System.loadLibrary("simple");  // runs when class first loaded
    }
}
```

NOTE

> The unusual separatorChar ('>') is used simply to demonstrate what an implementation might look like on some strange computer whose file system didn't use any of the more common path separator conventions. Early Xerox computers used '>' as a separator, and several existing computer systems still use strange separators today, so this is not all that farfetched.

SimpleFiles can be created and used in the usual way:

```
SimpleFile  f = new SimpleFile(">some>path>and>fileName");

f.open();
f.read(...);
f.write(...);
f.close();
```

The first thing you notice about SimpleFile's implementation is how unremarkable the first two-thirds of its Java code is! It looks just like any other class, with a class and an instance variable, a constructor, and two normal method implementations. Then there are four native method declarations. You'll recognize these, from previous discussions, as being just a normal method declaration with the code block replaced by a semicolon and the modifier native added. These are the methods you have to implement in C code later.

Finally, there is a somewhat mysterious code fragment at the very end of the class. You might recognize the general construct here as a static (class) initializer. Any code between the brackets—{ and }—is executed exactly once, when the class is first loaded into the system. You take advantage of that fact to run something you want to run only once—the loading of the native code library you'll create later today. This ties together the loading of the class itself with the loading of its native code. If either fails for some reason, the other fails as well, guaranteeing that no "half-set-up" version of the class can ever be created.

20

Generating Header Files

In order to get your hands on Java objects and data types, and to be able to manipulate them in your C code, you need to include some special .h files. Most of these will be located in your release directory under the subdirectory called include. (In particular, look at native.h in that directory, and all the headers it points to, if you're a glutton for detail punishment.)

Some of the special definitions you need must be tailored to fit your class's methods precisely. That's where the javah tool comes in.

Using javah

To generate the headers you need for your native methods, first compile SimpleFile with javac, just as you normally would. This produces a file named SimpleFile.class. This file must be fed to the javah tool, which then generates the header file you need (SimpleFile.h).

TIP

> If the class handed to javah is inside a package, it prepends the package name to the header filename (and to any uses of that class name inside the file), after replacing all the dots (.) with underscores (_) in the package's fully qualified name. If SimpleFile had been contained in a hypothetical package called acme.widgets.files, javah would have generated a header file named acme_widgets_files_SimpleFile.h, and the various uses of the class's name within it would have been renamed in a similar manner (for example, in the middle of the method names shown in the next section).

Starting with release 1.1, there are new Java native interface (described later today) header files. You should always type javah -jni, rather than simply javah, to be sure to get these new header files. When running javah, you should pass it only the class name itself, and not the full filename, which has .class on the end.

The Header File

Here's the output of javah -jni SimpleFile:

```
/* DO NOT EDIT THIS FILE - it is machine generated */
#include <jni.h>
/* Header for class SimpleFile */

#ifndef _Included_SimpleFile
#define _Included_SimpleFile
#ifdef __cplusplus
extern "C" {
#endif
/*
```

20

```
 * Class:      SimpleFile
 * Method:     open
 * Signature: ()Z
 */
JNIEXPORT jboolean JNICALL Java_SimpleFile_open
  (JNIEnv *, jobject);

/*
 * Class:      SimpleFile
 * Method:     close
 * Signature: ()V
 */
JNIEXPORT void JNICALL Java_SimpleFile_close
  (JNIEnv *, jobject);

/*
 * Class:      SimpleFile
 * Method:     read
 * Signature: ([BI)I
 */
JNIEXPORT jint JNICALL Java_SimpleFile_read
  (JNIEnv *, jobject, jbyteArray, jint);

/*
 * Class:      SimpleFile
 * Method:     write
 * Signature: ([BI)I
 */
JNIEXPORT jint JNICALL Java_SimpleFile_write
  (JNIEnv *, jobject, jbyteArray, jint);

#ifdef __cplusplus
}
#endif
#endif
```

The function definitions generated in this example are in a one-to-one correspondence with the native methods of your class, but every function has two "extra" arguments that you didn't specify. These special, initial arguments provide your function with the current thread's environment and with a pointer to the current instance (this in Java). You'll find out more about them later today.

One interesting side-effect of header file generation is the output of method descriptors, informally called method descriptions elsewhere. They are labeled "Signature:" in the preceding comments. These descriptors are quite useful. For example, they can be passed to special C functions (described later today) that allow you to invoke methods back in the Java world from C—perhaps to invoke a subclass's overriding implementation of one of your native methods. You can use javah to learn what these descriptors look like for different method arguments and return values, and then use that knowledge to invoke arbitrary Java methods from within your C code.

20

Another way to find method descriptors is via `javap`. If you have, for example, a `Test` class:

```
class Test {
    Thread thread;
    int     i;
    public static void main(String args[]) {}
    private         void aMethod() {}
}
```

After compiling it into `Test.class`, you can get its field and method descriptors by typing `javap -p -s Test`:

```
Compiled from Test.java
class Test extends java.lang.Object
    /* ACC_SUPER bit set */
{
    thread Ljava/lang/Thread;
    i I
    public static main ([Ljava/lang/String;)V
    private aMethod ()V
    <init> ()V
}
```

A method descriptor takes the form (...)X, where the X is a letter (or string) that represents the return type, and the ... contains a string that represents each of the argument's types in turn. The letter (or string) used, and the types they represent, in the examples are: [T is array of type T, Lmy/package/name/ClassName; is an object reference of type my.package.name.ClassName, B is byte, I is int, V is void, and Z is boolean.

The method `close()`, which takes no arguments and returns void, is thus represented by the string ()V, while its inverse, `open()`, that returns a boolean instead, is represented by ()Z. `read()`, which takes an array of bytes and an int as its two arguments and returns an int, is ([BI)I. Finally, `main()`, which takes an array of java.lang.Strings and returns void, is ([Ljava/lang/String;)V. (See the "Method Descriptor" section in tomorrow's lesson for more details.)

NOTE

> In order to "massage" an instance of your class gently into the land of C, you used to have to use the macro `unhand()` (as in "unhand that object!"). Both this macro, and the necessity of generating and using "stub" files, are a thing of the past as of JDK 1.1. (You'll find out what took the place of the `unhand()` macro later today.)

Creating `SimpleFile.c`

Now you can, at last, write the C code for your Java `native` methods.

The header file generated by `javah`, `SimpleFile.h`, gives you the prototypes of the four C functions you need to implement to make your native code complete. You then write some C code that provides the native facilities that your Java class needs (in this case, some low-level file I/O routines). Finally, you assemble all the C code into a new file, include a bunch of required (or useful) `.h` files, and name it `SimpleFile.c`. Here's the result:

```c
#include "SimpleFile.h"      /* for jni definitions, and our prototypes */

#include <sys/param.h>    /* for MAXPATHLEN */
#include <fcntl.h>        /* for O_RDWR and O_CREAT */

#define LOCAL_PATH_SEPARATOR  '/'    /* for UNIX */

static void  fixSeparators(char *p, JNIEnv *e, jclass jc) {
    jfieldID   jsepChF = (*e)->GetStaticFieldID(e, jc, "separatorChar", "C");
    jchar      jsepCh  = (*e)->GetStaticCharField(e, jc, jsepChF); /* errs? */

    for (; *p != '\0'; ++p)
    if (*p == (char) jsepCh)          /* casts from Java (UTF) to C char */
        *p = LOCAL_PATH_SEPARATOR;
}

JNIEXPORT jboolean JNICALL Java_SimpleFile_open(JNIEnv *e, jobject this) {
    jclass      jc      = (*e)->GetObjectClass(e, this);
    jfieldID    jpathF  = (*e)->GetFieldID(e, jc, "path", "S");
    jobject     jpath   = (*e)->GetObjectField(e, this, jpathF);
    const jbyte *jbuffer = (*e)->GetStringUTFChars(e, (jstring) jpath, NULL);
    char        buffer[MAXPATHLEN]; /* should test 1st if it ^ IS String */
    int         fd;

    strncpy(buffer, (const char *) jbuffer, MAXPATHLEN); /* now modifiable */
    (*e)->ReleaseStringUTFChars(e, (jstring) jpath, jbuffer); /* important */
    fixSeparators(buffer, e, jc);
    if ((fd = open(buffer, O_RDWR | O_CREAT, 0664)) < 0)      /* UNIX open */
    return(JNI_FALSE);   /* or, JNI's Throw() could throw an exception */
    (*e)->SetIntField(e, this, (*e)->GetFieldID(e, jc, "fd", "I"), (jint) fd);
    return(JNI_TRUE);          /* above should be checking for NULL fieldIDs */
}

JNIEXPORT void JNICALL Java_SimpleFile_close(JNIEnv *e, jobject this) {
    jclass   jc  = (*e)->GetObjectClass(e, this);
    jfieldID jfdF = (*e)->GetFieldID(e, jc, "fd", "I");

    close((int) (*e)->GetIntField(e, this, jfdF));
    (*e)->SetIntField(e, this, jfdF, (jint) -1);
}
```

20

```
static jint doIO(JNIEnv *e, jobject this, jbyteArray jarray, jint jcount,
                                            jboolean doRead) {
    jclass    jc    = (*e)->GetObjectClass(e, this);
    jfieldID  jfdF  = (*e)->GetFieldID(e, jc, "fd", "I");
    jint      jfd   = (*e)->GetIntField(e, this, jfdF);
    jbyte     *jdata = (*e)->GetByteArrayElements(e, jarray, NULL);
    jsize     jlen  = (*e)->GetArrayLength(e, jarray);
    int  numBytes = ((int) jlen < (int) jcount ? (int) jlen : (int) jcount);

    if (doRead == JNI_TRUE)
        if ((numBytes = read((int) jfd, (char *) jdata, numBytes)) == 0)
            numBytes = -1;              /* return a special error code or... */
    else
        numBytes = write((int) jfd, (char *) jdata, numBytes);
    (*e)->ReleaseByteArrayElements(e, jarray, jdata, 0); /* writes it back */
    return((jint) numBytes);  /* the number of bytes actually read/written */
}

JNIEXPORT jint JNICALL Java_SimpleFile_read(JNIEnv *e, jobject this,
                                    jbyteArray jarray, jint jcount) {
    return(doIO(e, this, jarray, jcount, JNI_TRUE));
}

JNIEXPORT jint JNICALL Java_SimpleFile_write(JNIEnv *e, jobject this,
                                    jbyteArray jarray, jint jcount) {
    return(doIO(e, this, jarray, jcount, JNI_FALSE));
}
```

NOTE

Don't worry if SimpleFile.c is incomprehensible at this point—just try to grasp the gist of it—all the strange, new functions used here are explained in "The Java Native Interface" section. You can come back here later to figure it all out when you have a deeper knowledge of them.

Once you finish writing your .c file, compile it by using your local C compiler (usually called cc or gcc) to produce an object file (SimpleFile.o on UNIX). On some systems, you need to specify special compilation flags that mean "make it relocatable and dynamically linkable."

NOTE

If you don't have a C compiler on your computer, you can always buy one. You also could get a copy of the GNU C compiler (gcc), one of the best C compilers in the world, which runs on almost every machine and operating system on the planet. The best way to get gcc is to buy the "GNU release" on CD-ROM, the profits of which go to support the Free Software Foundation. You can find both the GNU CD-ROM and the Linux CD-ROM (which includes GNU) in select places that sell software or technical books, or you can contact the F.S.F. directly. The GNU CD-ROM is a bit pricey, and, though the Linux CD-ROM is very inexpensive, if you can't afford either, or want the latest version and already own a CD-ROM, you can download the gzip file `ftp://prep.ai.mit.edu/pub/gnu/gcc-2.7.2.2.tar.gz`, which contains all 7MB of the latest gcc release. (If you'd like to make a donation to, or buy gcc or its manual from, the F.S.F., you can e-mail them at `gnu@prep.ai.mit.edu` or call 617-542-5942.)

You're now finished with all the C code that must be written (and compiled) to make your loadable native library.

A Native Library

Now you'll finally be able to tie everything together and create the native library called simple that was assumed to exist in `SimpleFile.java` at the beginning of today's lesson.

Linking It All

It's time to link everything you've done into a single library file. This looks a little different on each system that Java runs on, but here's the basic idea, in UNIX syntax:

```
cc -G SimpleFile.o -o libsimple.so
```

The `-G` flag tells the linker that you're creating a dynamically linkable library; the details differ from system to system.

NOTE

By naming the library libsimple.so, you're obeying a UNIX convention that dynamic library names should have the prefix `lib` and the suffix `.so` (on your system, these prefixes and suffixes may differ). Thus, the library named simple becomes `libsimple.so`. See your local documentation for how to create, name, and install dynamic libraries on your system, and for your release's version of `LD_LIBRARY_PATH` (mentioned in the next section).

20

Using Your Library

Now, when the Java class SimpleFile is first loaded into your program, the System class attempts to load the library named simple, which (luckily) you just created. Look back at the Java code for SimpleFile to remind yourself.

How does it locate it? It calls the dynamic linker, which consults an environment variable named LD_LIBRARY_PATH that tells it which sequence of directories to search when loading new libraries of native code. Because the current directory is in Java's load path by default, you can leave the library libsimple.so in the current directory, and it will work just fine.

The Java Native Interface (JNI)

The JNI, or Java Native Interface, is a special low-level, non-Java API that defines the interface between the virtual machine and the non-Java world. native methods can use the API to call a set of useful functions or to interact with the Java world, and non-Java programs can use a subset of it to create a Java virtual machine, attach to it, and interact with the Java world themselves.

Creation of the JNI involved all of Sun's licensees (Java partners), many of whom have virtual machine implementations of their own. Two important results of the JNI standard is that programmers can count on "driving" any virtual machine from outside in a standard way, and they can rely on a single API that will work from within all virtual machines. This last property helps to guarantee that binary native code for one virtual machine on a given type of hardware will work for all virtual machines on that type of hardware, eliminating another source of incompatibility (albeit for non-Java code only).

The JNI imposes no new burdens on the creators of virtual machine implementaions, although its users do pay a small amount of overhead when using it. This small inefficiency is well worth the benefits of learning only one virtual machine interface and then being able to use that knowledge everywhere (for example, in low-level tool building).

NOTE

> The excellent descriptions and API details in this section were para-
> phrased from the HTML version of "Native Interface Specification,
> Release 1.1" by Sheng Liang and Beth Stearns, which, along with a nice
> JNI tutorial, is at http://www.javasoft.com/products/jdk/1.1/docs/
> guide/jni. There is also a PS version available from the ftp site at ftp:/
> /ftp.javasoft.com/docs/jdk1.1/jni.ps.
>
> Of all the contributors to the JNI, Netscape's earlier JRI (Java Runtime
> Interface) had the most influence—if you know the JRI, the JNI

20

should seem quite familiar. The JNI is not binary compatible with the JRI, although a virtual machine can easily support both the JRI and the JNI.

What It Does

By programming with the JNI, your `native` methods can:

☐ create, inspect, and update Java objects (including arrays and strings)

☐ invoke Java methods

☐ catch and throw exceptions

☐ load classes and obtain class information

☐ perform runtime type checking

You can also use a subset of the JNI (the invocation API, described later today) to enable an arbitrary native application to load and access the Java virtual machine. This allows programmers to easily make their existing, non-Java applications Java-enabled without having to statically link with the virtual machine source code.

Why It Was Created

In the past, different virtual machines implementations required different native method interfaces. These different interfaces forced programmers to produce, maintain, and distribute multiple versions of native method libraries for a given platform. A standard was needed.

In addition, many of these older interfaces were based on the JDK 1.0 style of native method interface, which had two major flaws as a potential standard. First, native code accessed fields in Java objects via the elements of C `structs` directly. But *The Java Virtual Machine Specification* does not define how objects are laid out in memory, so a virtual machine is free to pick any peculiar format that might make object members non-contiguous, or have different padding between them over time. This last, at a minimum, would require the programmer to recompile their `struct` references each time the object members were rearranged by the virtual machine (ridiculous).

Second, the 1.0 native method interface depended on its conservative garbage collector—the unrestricted use of the old `unhand()` macro, for example, forced the garbage collector to conservatively scan the native stack. This uncontrolled mixture of native and non-native references made other forms of garbage collection difficult, or impossible—but any form of garbage collection must be allowed (*The Java Virtual Machine Specification* again).

20

NOTE

All native method programmers should start programming to the JNI. Although JDK 1.1 supports the old-style native method interface of 1.0, it is almost certain that future versions of the JDK will adopt a different low-level interface. Native methods relying on the old-style interface will have to be rewritten.

Despite the need for a standard, the JNI will not necessarily be the only native method interface supported by a given virtual machine. For efficiency (or to get access to some unique facility), the programmer may have to use a lower-level, virtual-machine-specific interface. Or when creating software components, some higher-level interface might be appropriate. As the Java environment and component software technologies become more mature, native methods will gradually lose their significance and the JNI will fade away in favor of these higher-level views.

How It Works

Functions in the JNI are accessed through an interface pointer. This pointer points to a per-thread JNI data structure, the first element of which must be another pointer. This new pointer points to an array of function pointers, each of which points to the actual JNI function. Every JNI function is at a predefined offset in this array of function pointers.

NOTE

Using a function pointer array, rather than hardwired functions, allows the virtual machine to easily swap multiple versions of the array (for example, one normal one for debugging). The JNI interface pointer is valid only in the current thread. A native method, therefore, should not pass the interface pointer to another thread. (Virtual machines are allowed to allocate and store other thread-specific data in the per-thread structure pointed to by the JNI interface pointer.)

All native methods get passed the JNI interface pointer as their first argument. The virtual machine passes the same interface pointer in multiple calls to a native method from the same Java thread, but native methods can be called from different threads, and thus might get passed different JNI interface pointers.

Native Method Names

The JNI performs a series of steps to derive the non-Java name for a Java native method. Some of these steps involve *name mangling*, which substitues an underscore-prefixed stings for special characters in the name (covered in detail later). The non-Java name is concatenated from the following components:

- [ ] the prefix Java_
- [ ] the mangled fully qualified class name of the class containing the native method
- [ ] an underscore ("_") separator
- [ ] the mangled native method name
- [ ] for overloaded native methods, two underscores ("__"), followed by the mangled argument descriptor of the native method

When calling a non-Java function name, the virtual machine first looks for the shortest version of the name (without the argument descriptor). It then looks for the longer name (including the argument descriptor). You need to use the longer name only when a native method is overloaded by another native method (non-native methods don't count).

Name Mangling

A simple name mangling scheme ensures that Unicode characters (and the separator "/") translate into valid non-Java function names. First, underscore ("_") substitutes for slash ("/") in fully qualified class names. Now because a name or type descriptor never begins with a number, we can use _0, ..., _9 for escape sequences:

```
Escape:     Denotes:
_0XXXX      a Unicode character XXXX.
_1          the character "_"
_2          the character ";" in descriptors
_3          the character "[" in descriptors
```

A Simple Example

We've already stated that the JNI interface pointer (type JNIEnv *) is always the first argument to native methods. The second argument is always an object reference, but exactly what it is differs for instance and class native methods. For instance methods, it's a reference to the instance itself (this). For class methods, it's a reference to the instance's class.

The remaining arguments correspond one-to-one with their regular Java counterparts, but use special JNI types in place of each Java type. Here's a simple example, for a native method called test():

```
package packageName;
class ClassName {
    native double  test(int i, String s);
    . . .
}
```

20

and here's the C (non-Java) function, with the longer version of the mangled name, that implements `test()`:

```
jdouble  Java_packageName_ClassName_test__ILjava_lang_String_2 (
                    JNIEnv  *e,      /* interface pointer */
                    jobject  this,   /* instance pointer */
                    jint     ji,     /* Java argument #1 */
                    jstring  js)     /* Java argument #2 */ {
    const jbyte  *s = (*e)->GetStringUTFChars(e, js, NULL);
    . .·.    /* do something useful with s (and ji) */
    (*e)->ReleaseStringUTFChars(e, js, s);
    return ...;
}
```

There are two calls to JNI functions in this example. The prefix ("`(*e)->`"), which precedes each call, is a necessary level of indirection to support the function pointer arrays mentioned earlier.

Referencing Java Objects

Primitive types (like `int`) are simply copied between Java and non-Java code. But Java objects, on the other hand, are passed by reference. The virtual machine must keep track of all objects that have been passed to your non-Java code, so they won't be freed by the garbage collector before you are done with them. Your non-Java code, in turn, must have a way to release these objects again when you are done.

Global and Local References

Object references in non-Java code are either *local* or *global*. Local references exist only during a non-Java function call, and are automatically freed as soon as it returns. Global references persist until they are explicitly freed. All objects passed as arguments to non-Java functions, and all objects returned from JNI functions, are local references. You can convert them to global references (via a JNI function) as needed. JNI functions accept both global and local references as object arguments, and your non-Java functions can return either as their result.

NOTE

> Though rare, you can explicitly free a local reference. You might want to do this if a long calculation follows the last use of a large object, and you don't want to wait that long to free it.
>
> To be sure you can always manually free local references, JNI functions are not allowed to create extra local references, except for the references they return as their result. Also, local references are only valid in the current thread, so don't pass them to other threads.

Accessing Java Objects and Arrays

The JNI defines special accessor functions on these local and global object references that allow you to examine and change their contents. Thus, the same non-Java function implementation works no matter how the local virtual machine represents Java objects internally (crucial to wide JNI support).

There is a small overhead in using accessor functions. But in most cases, you'll invoke `native` methods to perform non-trivial tasks that overshadow this overhead. One case in which this is not true is for array access. For this special case the JNI provides two solutions: Small sub-arrays can be copied by a single JNI function call, and with another, large arrays can be copied or "pinned" in memory temporarily while you update them.

NOTE

> Whether or not these functions have to actually copy arrays back and forth depends on internal system details. You use other JNI functions to tell the system when you are done with the "copy," and it either simply unpins the array, or it updates the original array from the copy and then frees the copy.

Accessing Fields and Methods

To access the fields and methods of Java objects, the JNI provides a two-step process that helps factor out the inefficiency of field and method lookup. First, you locate a field or method via its name and descriptor:

```
jmethodID  jtestF = (*e)->GetMethodID(jc, "test", "(ILjava/lang/String;)D");
```

Assuming that `jc` referred to the class `ClassName` from our previous example, this would gain us the method ID of the Java method `test()` defined there. Your non-Java code can then use this method ID over and over again without paying the cost of a method lookup each time:

```
jdouble  jresult = (*e)->CallDoubleMethod(jobj, jtestF, 10, jstr);
```

WARNING

> Holding a field or method ID from a class does not prevent the virtual machine from unloading that class. To be sure your field and method IDs remain valid you must either keep a global reference to the class yourself, or compute a new ID each time you need it (that is, don't hold onto it between calls).

Exceptional Conditions

Non-Java code can raise Java exceptions with the JNI, and can handle outstanding Java exceptions with it—any exceptions left unhandled are sent back into the Java world. Some JNI functions "throw" Java exceptions, but this is not the ideal way to reflect illegal arguments, and so on to non-Java code—ignoring Java exceptions will cause an invalid system state on the next JNI call, but being able to ignore some error checks is often necessary in efficient non-Java code (especially because those checks are often already done in, or handled by, the Java code surrounding the `native` method).

Thus, there are a small set of exceptions that a conforming JNI implementation must raise for certain errors. The rest of the JNI uses returned error codes (and a few other Java exceptions) to report errors. More strict JNI implementations are allowed, but these additional errors should not affect correct Java programs (which were already checking for them in Java).

Java Types

Within non-Java code, special JNI types replaces the normal Java types. For primitive types, the mapping is simple: the type `<type>` becomes the type `j<type>` (for `<type>`: `boolean`, `byte`, `char`, `short`, `int`, `long`, and `double`); `void` is the same in both worlds. This `<type>` shorthand will be used frequently from now on.

For convenience, special boolean values are defined: `JNI_FALSE` (0) and `JNI_TRUE` (1). The JNI type `jsize`, an unsigned integer type, can hold any index in the address space (that is, is at least the size of a non-Java pointer).

The JNI reference type (for objects) is called `jobject`, but it has special subtypes for classes, strings, and arrays: `jclass`, `jstring`, `jarray`. Arrays have special sub-subtypes for each primitive type of array: `j<type>Array`, plus a `jobjectArray` type for object arrays.

Field (`jfieldID`) and method (`jmethodID`) IDs are regular non-Java pointer types. A special type, `jvalue`, is used to stand for any object or primitive type, and is the non-Java union of all `j<type>s` and `jobject`.

NOTE

> JNI type descriptors used the same grammar as Java method descriptors (see the section on them tomorrow for more detail).
>
> JNI UTF-8 Unicode strings are identical to the "standard" format except that the null byte is encoded in a two-byte form (which allows C-like null termination of strings in the non-Java world), and only the 1-, 2-, and 3-byte formats are supported.

The Function Pointer Table

Each function is accessible at a fixed offset through the JNIEnv argument. The JNIEnv type is a pointer to a structure storing all JNI function pointers. It is defined in C as follows:

```
typedef const struct JNINativeInterface  *JNIEnv;
```

and the function pointer table (jump table) is defined as follows:

```
const struct JNINativeInterface ... = {
    NULL, NULL, NULL, NULL,
    GetVersion, DefineClass, FindClass,
    NULL, NULL, NULL,
    GetSuperclass, IsAssignableFrom,
    NULL,
    Throw, ThrowNew,
    ExceptionOccurred, ExceptionDescribe, ExceptionClear,
    FatalError,
    NULL, NULL,
    NewGlobalRef, DeleteGlobalRef, DeleteLocalRef,
    IsSameObject,
    NULL, NULL,
    AllocObject,
    NewObject, NewObjectV, NewObjectA,
    GetObjectClass, IsInstanceOf,
    GetMethodID,
    CallObjectMethod,  CallObjectMethodV,  CallObjectMethodA,
    CallBooleanMethod, CallBooleanMethodV, CallBooleanMethodA,
    . . .
    CallDoubleMethod,  CallDoubleMethodV,  CallDoubleMethodA,
    CallVoidMethod,    CallVoidMethodV,    CallVoidMethodA,
    CallNonvirtualObjectMethod,  CallNonvirtualObjectMethodV,  CallN...MethodA,
    CallNonvirtualBooleanMethod, CallNonvirtualBooleanMethodV, CallN...nMethodA,
    . . .
    CallNonvirtualDoubleMethod,  CallNonvirtualDoubleMethodV,  CallN...MethodA,
    CallNonvirtualVoidMethod,    CallNonvirtualVoidMethodV,    CallN...thodA,
    GetFieldID,
    GetObjectField, GetBooleanField, . . ., GetDoubleField,
    SetObjectField, SetBooleanField, . . ., SetDoubleField,
    GetStaticMethodID,
    CallStaticObjectMethod,  CallStaticObjectMethodV,  CallStaticObjectMethodA,
    CallStaticBooleanMethod, CallStaticBooleanMethodV, CallStaticBooleanMethodA,
    . . .
    CallStaticDoubleMethod,  CallStaticDoubleMethodV,  CallStaticDoubleMethodA,
    CallStaticVoidMethod,    CallStaticVoidMethodV,    CallStaticVoidMethodA,
    GetStaticFieldID,
    GetStaticObjectField, GetStaticBooleanField, . . ., GetStaticDoubleField,
    SetStaticObjectField, SetStaticBooleanField, . . ., SetStaticDoubleField,
    NewString,      GetStringLength,    GetStringChars,    ReleaseStringChars,
    NewStringUTF, GetStringUTFLength, GetStringUTFChars, ReleaseStringUTFChars,
    GetArrayLength,
    NewObjectArray,
    GetObjectArrayElement,
    SetObjectArrayElement,
    NewBooleanArray, . . ., NewDoubleArray,
    GetBooleanArrayElements,       . . ., GetDoubleArrayElements,
```

20

```
        ReleaseBooleanArrayElements, . . ., ReleaseDoubleArrayElements,
        GetBooleanArrayRegion, . . ., GetDoubleArrayRegion,
        SetBooleanArrayRegion, . . ., SetDoubleArrayRegion,
        RegisterNatives, UnregisterNatives,
        MonitorEnter, MonitorExit,
        GetJavaVM,
    };
```

NOTE

> In this example, the first three entries are reserved for future compatibility with COM. Although the JNI does make Java objects into COM objects, the JNI itself is binary compatible with COM—it uses the same jump table structure and calling convention that COM does. As soon as cross-platform support for COM is available, the JNI can become a COM interface to the Java virtual machine.
>
> In addition, a number of additional NULL entries near the beginning of the function table are reserved, so that, for example, a future class-related JNI operation can be added after FindClass, rather than at the end of the table.

The JNI Functions in Detail

In this section there will be a series of conventions for the names used to describe arguments, return values, and so on. In addition to the JNI types discussed previously, here are the new conventions:

NOTE

> The following descriptions borrow heavily from the standard JNI specification mentioned earlier, and are purposely parallel to it so when you consult it, you'll be covering familiar ground.

Version Information

```
jint GetVersion(JNIEnv *e);
```

Returns the version of the JNI, the major version number in the higher 16 bits, and the minor, in the lower 16 bits. In JDK 1.1, GetVersion() returns 0x00010001.

20

Class Operations

`jclass DefineClass(JNIEnv *e, jobject loader, const char *buf, jsize bufLen);`

Defines a class from a buffer of raw class data. `loader` is a class loader assigned to the defined class. Returns a Java class object, or `NULL` if an error occurs. Throws `ClassFormatError` if the class data does not specify a valid class.

`jclass FindClass(JNIEnv *e, const char *name);`

This function loads a locally defined class. It searches the directories and zip files specified by the `CLASSPATH` environment variable for the class with the specified `name` (a package name, delimited by "/", followed by the class name). If `name` begins with "[" (the array descriptor character), it returns an array class. Returns a class object, or `NULL` if the class cannot be found.

`jclass GetSuperclass(JNIEnv *e, jclass clazz);`

If `clazz` represents any class other than the class `java.lang.Object`, then this function returns the object that represents the superclass of the class; otherwise it returns `NULL`.

`jboolean IsAssignableFrom(JNIEnv *e, jclass clazz1, jclass clazz2);`

Determines whether an object of `clazz1` can be safely cast to `clazz2`. Returns `JNI_TRUE` if any of the following is true: Both arguments refer to the same class, the first is a subclass of the second, or the first has the second as one of its interfaces.

Exceptions

`jint Throw(JNIEnv *e, jobject obj);`

Causes a `java.lang.Throwable` object (`obj`) to be thrown. Returns zero on success; a negative value on failure.

`jint ThrowNew(JNIEnv *e, jclass clazz, const char *message);`

Constructs an exception object from the specified `clazz` with the message specified by `message` and causes that exception to be thrown. Returns zero on success; a negative value on failure.

`jobject ExceptionOccurred(JNIEnv *e);`

Determines if an exception is being thrown. The exception stays thrown until either `ExceptionClear()` is called, or the Java code handles the exception. Returns the exception object that is currently in the process of being thrown, or `NULL` if no exception is currently being thrown.

`void ExceptionDescribe(JNIEnv *e);`

Prints an exception and a backtrace of the stack to a system error reporting channel, such as stderr. This is a convenience routine provided for debugging.

```
void ExceptionClear(JNIEnv *e);
```

Clears any exception that is currently being thrown. If no exception is currently being thrown, this routine has no effect.

```
void FatalError(JNIEnv *e, char * msg);
```

Raises a fatal error and does not expect the virtual machine to recover. This function does not return.

Global and Local References

```
jobject NewGlobalRef(JNIEnv *e, jobject obj);
```

Creates a new global reference to obj (which may be a global or local reference). Global references must be explicitly disposed of by calling DeleteGlobalRef(). Returns a global reference, or NULL, if the system runs out of memory.

```
void DeleteGlobalRef(JNIEnv *e, jobject *globalRef);
```

Deletes the global reference (globalRef).

```
void DeleteLocalRef(JNIEnv *e, jobject *localRef);
```

Deletes the local reference (localRef).

Object Operations

```
jobject AllocObject(JNIEnv *e, jclass clazz);
```

Allocates a new Java object without invoking any of the constructors for the object. Returns a reference to the object. The clazz argument must not refer to an array class. Returns a Java object, or NULL if the object cannot be constructed. Throws InstantiationException if the class is an interface or an abstract class, or OutOfMemoryError if the system runs out of memory.

```
jobject NewObject(JNIEnv *e, jclass clazz, jmethodID methodID, ...);
jobject NewObjectA(JNIEnv *e, jclass clazz, jmethodID methodID, jvalue *args);
jobject NewObjectV(JNIEnv *e, jclass clazz, jmethodID methodID, va_list args);
```

Constructs a new Java object. The method ID indicates which constructor method to invoke. This ID must be obtained by calling GetMethodID() with <init> as the method name and void (V) as the return type.

These functions, and many of the functions that follow, have three forms for receiving a list of arguments of varying size:

- ☐ The arguments are placed immediately following the last fixed argument (the first, "..." form above)

- ☐ The arguments (args) are in an array of jvalues in the last argument (the second, "A" form above)

- ☐ The arguments (args) are in a va_list in the last argument (the third, "V" form above)

From now on, these will be referred to as the "usual argument conventions."

NewObject<X>() accepts these arguments, and, in turn, passes them to the Java method that the programmer wishes to invoke. Returns a Java object, or NULL if the object cannot be constructed. Throws InstantiationException if the class is an interface or an abstract class, or OutOfMemoryError if the system runs out of memory.

```
jclass GetObjectClass(JNIEnv *e, jobject obj);
```

Returns the Java class of obj.

```
jboolean IsInstanceOf(JNIEnv *e, jobject obj, jclass clazz);
```

Tests whether obj is an instance of a clazz. Returns JNI_TRUE if obj can be cast to clazz; otherwise, returns JNI_FALSE. A NULL object can be cast to any class.

```
jboolean IsSameObject(JNIEnv *e, jobject ref1, jobject ref2);
```

Tests whether two references refer to the same Java object. Returns JNI_TRUE if ref1 and ref2 refer to the same Java object, or are both NULL; otherwise, returns JNI_FALSE.

Accessing Fields of Objects

```
jfieldID GetFieldID(JNIEnv *e, jclass clazz, const char *name, const char
*desc);
```

Returns the field ID for an instance (non-static) field of a class. The field is specified by its name and descriptor. name and desc are zero-terminated UTF-8 strings. Returns a field ID, or NULL if the specified non-static field cannot be found. Throws NoSuchFieldError if the specified non-static field cannot be found, ExceptionInInitializerError if the class initializer fails due to an exception, or OutOfMemoryError if the system runs out of memory.

```
j<type> Get<Type>Field(JNIEnv *e, jobject obj, jfieldID fieldID);
void    Set<Type>Field(JNIEnv *e, jobject obj, jfieldID fieldID, j<type> value);
```

20

This family of accessor routines returns (or sets) the value of an instance (non-static) field of an object. <type> is as previously defined for primitive types, or object. <Type> has its first letter capitalized.

Calling Instance Methods

```
jmethodID GetMethodID(JNIEnv *e, jclass clazz, const char *name, const char
*desc);
```

Returns the method ID for an instance (non-static) method of a class or interface. The method may be defined in one of the clazz's super classes and inherited by clazz. The method is determined by its name and descriptor. name and desc are zero-terminated UTF-8 strings. Returns a method ID, or NULL if the operation fails. Throws NoSuchMethodError if the specified non-static method cannot be found, ExceptionInInitializerError if the class initializer fails due to an exception, or OutOfMemoryError if the system runs out of memory.

```
j<type> Call<Type>Method(JNIEnv *e, jobject obj, jmethodID methodID, ...);
j<type> Call<Type>MethodA(JNIEnv *e, jobject obj, jmethodID methodID, jvalue
*args);
j<type> Call<Type>MethodV(JNIEnv *e, jobject obj, jmethodID methodID, va_list
args);
```

This family of operations invokes an instance (non-static) method on a Java object, according to the specified method ID. When this function is used to call private methods and constructors, the method ID must be derived from the real class of obj, not from one of its super classes.

The usual argument conventions are used, and Call<Type>Method<X>() accepts these arguments and passes them to the Java method that the programmer wishes to invoke. Returns the result of calling the Java method. Throws any exceptions the Java method throws. j<type> is as previously defined for primitive types, void, or jobject. <Type> has its first letter capitalized.

```
j<type> CallNonvirtual<Type>Method(JNIEnv *e, jobject obj, jclass clazz,
                                   jmethodID methodID, ...);
j<type> CallNonvirtual<Type>MethodA(JNIEnv *e, jobject obj, jclass clazz,
                                    jmethodID methodID, jvalue
                                    *args);
j<type> CallNonvirtual<Type>MethodV(JNIEnv *e, jobject obj, jclass clazz,
                                    jmethodID methodID, va_list
                                    args);
```

This family of operations is identical to the last family except that instead of using the class of obj for dispatch, clazz is used.

Accessing Static Fields

```
jfieldID GetStaticFieldID(JNIEnv *e, jclass clazz, const char *name,
                                                   const char *desc);
```

Returns the field ID for a static field of a class. The field is specified by its name and descriptor. name and desc are zero-terminated UTF-8 strings. Returns a field ID, or NULL if the specified static field cannot be found. Throws NoSuchFieldError if the specified static field cannot be found, ExceptionInInitializerError if the class initializer fails due to an exception, or OutOfMemoryError if the system runs out of memory.

```
j<type> GetStatic<Type>Field(JNIEnv *e, jobject obj, jfieldID fieldID);
void    SetStatic<Type>Field(JNIEnv *e, jobject obj, jfieldID fieldID, j<type>
value);
```

This family of accessor routines returns (or sets) the value of a static field of an object. <type> is as previously defined for primitive types, or object. <Type> has its first letter capitalized.

Calling Static Methods

```
jmethodID GetStaticMethodID(JNIEnv *e, jclass clazz, const char *name,
                                                     const char *desc);
```

Returns the method ID for a class (static) method of a class or interface. The method is determined by its name and descriptor. name and desc are zero-terminated UTF-8 strings. Returns a method ID, or NULL if the operation fails. Throws NoSuchMethodError if the specified static method cannot be found, ExceptionInInitializerError if the class initializer fails due to an exception, or OutOfMemoryError if the system runs out of memory.

```
j<type> CallStatic<Type>Method(JNIEnv *e, jclass clazz, jmethodID methodID,
                                 ...);
j<type> CallStatic<Type>MethodA(JNIEnv *e, jclass clazz, jmethodID methodID,
                                 jvalue *args);
j<type> CallStatic<Type>MethodV(JNIEnv *e, jclass clazz, jmethodID methodID,
                                 va_list args);
```

This family of operations invokes a class (static) method on a Java clazz, according to the specified method ID. The method ID must be derived from clazz, not from one of its super classes.

The usual argument conventions are used, and CallStatic<Type>Method<X>() accepts these arguments and passes them to the Java method that the programmer wishes to invoke. Returns the result of calling the Java method. Throws any exceptions the Java method throws. j<type> is as previously defined for primitive types, void, or jobject. <Type> has its first letter capitalized.

20

String Operations

```
jstring NewString(JNIEnv *e, const jchar *unicodeChars, jsize len);
```

Constructs a new java.lang.String object from an array of Unicode characters. Returns a Java string object, or NULL if the string cannot be constructed. Throws OutOfMemoryError if the system runs out of memory.

```
jsize GetStringLength(JNIEnv *e, jstring string);
```

Returns the length (the count of Unicode characters) of a Java string.

```
const jchar *GetStringChars(JNIEnv *e, jstring string, jboolean *isCopy);
```

Returns a pointer to the array of Unicode characters of the string. This pointer is valid until ReleaseStringchars() is called. If isCopy is not NULL, then *isCopy is set to one if a copy is made, or it is set to zero if no copy is made. Returns a pointer to a Unicode string, or NULL if the operation fails.

```
void ReleaseStringChars(JNIEnv *e, jstring string, const jchar *chars);
```

Informs the virtual machine that you no longer need access to chars (the pointer returned by GetStringChars()).

```
jstring NewStringUTF(JNIEnv *e, const char *bytes, jsize length);
jsize GetStringUTFLength(JNIEnv *e, jstring string);
const jbyte *GetStringUTFChars(JNIEnv *e, jstring string, jboolean *isCopy);
void ReleaseStringUTFChars(JNIEnv *e, jstring string, const jbyte *utf);
```

Identical to the previous four functions, but for operating on UTF-8 strings—that is, C (non-Java) representable strings.

Array Operations

```
jsize GetArrayLength(JNIEnv *e, jarray array);
```

Returns the number of elements in the array.

```
jarray NewObjectArray(JNIEnv *e, jsize length, jclass elementClass, jobject
                             obj);
```

Constructs a new array holding objects of class elementClass. All elements are initially set to obj. Returns a Java array object, or NULL if the array cannot be constructed. Throws OutOfMemoryError if the system runs out of memory.

```
jobject GetObjectArrayElement(JNIEnv *e, jarray array, jsize index);
```

Returns an element of an object. Throws ArrayIndexOutOfBoundsException if index does not specify a valid index in the array.

```
void SetObjectArrayElement(JNIEnv *e, jarray array, jsize index, jobject value);
```

Sets an element of an `Object` array. Throws `ArrayIndexOutOfBoundsException` if index does not specify a valid index in the array, or `ArrayStoreException` if the class of value is not a subclass of the element class of the array.

```
j<type>Array New<Type>Array(JNIEnv *e, jsize length);
```

A family of operations to construct a new array of `<type>`s (as previously defined). Returns a Java array object, or `NULL` if the array cannot be constructed. Throws `OutOfMemoryError` if the system runs out of memory.

```
j<type> *Get<Type>ArrayElements(JNIEnv *e, j<type>Array array, jboolean
                                *isCopy);
```

A family of functions that returns the body of the array of `<type>`s (as previously defined). The result is valid until the corresponding `ReleaseScalarArrayElements()` function is called. Because the returned array may be a copy of the original Java array, changes made to the returned array will not necessarily be reflected in the original array until `ReleaseScalarArrayElements()` is called. If isCopy is not `NULL`, then `*isCopy` is set to one if a copy is made, or it is set to zero if no copy is made. Returns a pointer to the array elements, or `NULL` if the operation fails.

Regardless of how `boolean` arrays are represented in the Java VM, `GetBooleanArrayElements()` always returns a pointer to `jbooleans`, with each byte denoting an element (that is, the unpacked representation). All arrays of other types are guaranteed to be contiguous in memory.

```
void Release<Type>ArrayElements(JNIEnv *e, j<type>Array array, j<type> *elems,
                                jint mode);
```

A family of functions that inform the virtual machine that you no longer need access to elems (the pointer returned by the corresponding `GetGet<Type>ArrayElements()`). If necessary, copies back all changes made to elems to the original array. The mode argument provides information on how the array buffer should be released. mode has no effect if elems is not a copy of the elements in array. Otherwise, mode has the following impact:

```
mode:           Actions:
0               Copy back the content and free the elems buffer.
JNI_COMMIT      Copy back the content but do not free the elems buffer.
JNI_ABORT       Free the buffer without copying back the possible changes.
```

In most cases, programmers pass zero to the mode argument to ensure consistent behavior for both pinned and copied arrays. The other options give the programmer more control over memory management and must be used with extreme care.

```
void Get<Type>ArrayRegion(JNIEnv *e, j<type>Array array, jsize start, jsize len,
                          j<type> *buf);
```

20

This is a family of functions that copies a region of an array of <type>s (as previously defined) into a buffer. Throws `ArrayIndexOutOfBoundsException` if (`start + len - 1`) does not specify a valid index in the array.

```
void Set<Type>ArrayRegion(JNIEnv *e, j<type>Array array, jsize start, jsize len,
                                                              j<type> *buf);
```

This is a family of functions that copies a buffer back into a region of an array of <type>s (as previously defined). Throws `ArrayIndexOutOfBoundsException` if (`start + len - 1`) does not specify a valid index in the array.

Registering Native Methods

```
jint RegisterNatives(JNIEnv *e, jclass clazz, const JNINativeMethod *methods,
                                                              jint nMethods);
```

Registers `native` methods with the class specified by the `clazz` argument. Each `JNINativeMethod` structure (of `nMethods` total) contains the name, descriptor, and non-Java function pointer for one `native` method. Returns zero on success, a negative value on failure. Throws `NoSuchMethodError` if a specified method cannot be found or if the method is not `native`.

```
jint UnregisterNatives(JNIEnv *e, jclass clazz, const jstring *methods,
                                                              jint nMethods);
```

Unregisters `native` methods with the class specified by the `clazz` argument. Each element of the `NULL`-terminated `methods` array (of `nMethods` total) is the name of one `native` method to be unregistered. Returns zero on success, a negative value on failure.

NOTE

> The previous two functions should be used only by special low-level tools in development environments, and not by normal non-Java code.

Monitor Operations

```
jint MonitorEnter(JNIEnv *e, jobject obj);
```

Enters the monitor associated with the underlying Java object referred to by `obj`. Each Java object has a monitor associated with it. If the current thread already owns the monitor associated with `obj`, it increments a counter in the monitor indicating the number of times this thread has entered the monitor. If the monitor associated with `ref` is not owned by any thread, the current thread becomes the owner of the monitor, setting the entry count of this monitor to 1. If another thread already owns the monitor associated with `ref`, the current thread waits until the monitor is released, then tries again to gain ownership. Returns zero on success, a negative value on failure.

```
jint MonitorExit(JNIEnv *e, jobject obj);
```

The current thread must be the owner of the monitor associated with the underlying Java object referred to by obj. The thread decrements the counter indicating the number of times it has entered this monitor. If as a result the value of the counter becomes zero, the current thread releases the montior. Returns zero on success; a negative value on failure.

Java Virtual Machine Interface

```
jint GetJavaVM(JNIEnv *e, JavaVM **vm);
```

Returns the Java virtual machine interface (used in the invocation API of the next section) associated with the current thread. The result is placed at the location pointed to by the second argument, vm. Returns zero on success; a negative value on failure.

You're now done with the main JNI functions. Before we go on to the invocation API, take a break and go way back to SimpleFile.c and see if it now makes more sense than it did before (it should!). Now, take another deep breath, this next (big) section is the last.

The Invocation API

The invocation API allows you to load the Java virtual machine into any non-Java application. Thus, you can "Java-enable" applications without having to statically link with the Java virtual machine source code. Here is an example of its use:

```
#include <jni.h>                            /* where everything is defined */
. . .
JavaVM          *jvm                        /* denotes a Java Virtual Machine */
JNIEnv          *e;                         /* pointer to native method
                                               interface */
JDK1_1InitArgs  vm_args;                    /* JDK 1.1 VM initialization args.*/
. . .
JNI_GetDefaultJavaVMInitArgs(&vm_args);     /* get the default arguments */
vm_args.classpath = ...;                    /* optionally change them */
JNI_CreateJavaVM(&jvm, &e, &vm_args);       /* load and init. a Java VM */
jclass     jc  = (*e)->FindClass("Main");   /* find a class inside the VM */
jmethodID  jmID = (*e)->GetStaticMethodID(jc, "test", "(I)V");
(*e)->CallStaticVoidMethod(jc, jmID, 100);  /* invoke a method there */
(*jvm)->DestroyJavaVM();                     /* we're done */
```

This example uses three functions in the invocation API. Lets now describe them all.

20

The JNI_CreateJavaVM() function loads and initializes a Java virtual machine and returns a pointer to the JNI interface pointer. The thread that called JNI_CreateJavaVM() is considered to be the main thread. The JNI interface pointer (JNIEnv) is valid only in the current thread. Should another thread want to access the virtual machine, it must first call AttachCurrentThread() to attach itself to obtain a JNI interface pointer. Once attached, a native thread works just like an ordinary Java thread running inside a native method. The native thread remains attached until it calls DetachCurrentThread().

The main thread cannot detach itself. Instead, it must call DestroyJavaVM() to unload the entire virtual machine (and it is the only thread that can do so). The main thread must be the only user thread still running when it calls DestroyJavaVM(). User threads include both Java threads and attached native threads. This restriction exists because a Java thread or attached native thread may be holding system resources, such as locks, windows, and so on, and the DestroyJavaVM() function cannot automatically free these resources—the burden of releasing system resources held by arbitrary threads is on the programmer.

Because different Java virtual machines may use different implementation schemes, they will likely require different initialization structures. Thus, the exact content of the following initialization structures will vary among different implementations. A native application must correctly set the initialization structure depending on the particular virtual machine the application wishes to invoke. Here's the structure used by Sun's 1.1 virtual machine:

```
typedef struct JDK1_1InitArgs {
    jint         reserved0;
    void         *reserved1;
    jint         checkSource;
    jint         nativeStackSize;
    jint         javaStackSize;
    jint         minHeapSize;
    jint         maxHeapSize;
    jint         verifyMode;
    const char *classpath;
    jint         (*vprintf)(FILE *fp, const char *format, va_list args);
    void         (*exit)(jint code);
    void         (*abort)();
    jint         enableVerboseGC;
    jint         disableAsyncGC;
} JavaVMInitArgs;
```

The JavaVM type is a pointer to the invocation API function pointer array:

```
typedef const struct JNIInvokeInterface   *JavaVM;
const struct JNIInvokeInterface ... = {
    NULL, NULL, NULL,
    DestroyJavaVM,
    AttachCurrentThread, DetachCurrentThread,
};
```

NOTE   `JNI_GetDefaultJavaVMInitArgs()`, `JNI_GetCreatedJavaVMs()`, and `JNI_CreateJavaVM()` are not part of the `JavaVM` function pointer array. These functions can be called without an existing `JavaVM`.

The Functions in Detail

`void JNI_GetDefaultJavaVMInitArgs(void *vm_args);`

Returns a default configuration for the Java virtual machine. `vm_args` is a pointer to a virtual-machine-specific structure into which the default arguments will be placed.

`jint JNI_GetCreatedJavaVMs(JavaVM **vmBuf, jsize bufLen, jsize *nVMs);`

Returns all Java virtual machiness that have been created. Pointers to them are written in the buffer `vmBuf` in the order in which they were created. At most `bufLen` number of entries will be written. The total number of created virtual machines is returned in `*nVMs`. JDK 1.1 does not support creating more than one virtual machine in a single process. Returns zero on success; a negative number on failure.

`jint JNI_CreateJavaVM(JavaVM **p_vm, JNIEnv **p_env, void *vm_args);`

Loads and initializes a Java virtual machine. The current thread becomes the main thread. Sets `*p_vm` to point to the resulting `JavaVM`, and `*p_env` to the JNI interface pointer of the main thread. JDK 1.1 does not support creating more than one VM in a single process. Returns zero on success; a negative number on failure.

`jint DestroyJavaVM(JavaVM *vm);`

Unloads a Java virtual machine and reclaims its resources. Only the main thread can do this. The main thread must be the only remaining user thread when it calls `DestroyJavaVM()`. Returns zero on success; a negative number on failure. JDK 1.1 does not support unloading the virtual machine.

`jint AttachCurrentThread(JavaVM *vm, JNIEnv **p_env, void *thr_args);`

Attaches the current thread to a Java virtual machine. Sets `*p_env` to the new JNI interface pointer. Trying to attach a thread that is already attached is a no-op. A native thread cannot be attached simultaneously to two Java virtual machines. `thr_args` points to the thread attachment arguments—a structure containing nothing but padding in Sun's implementation (it requires no attach arguments). Returns zero on success; a negative number on failure.

`jint DetachCurrentThread(JavaVM *vm);`

20

Detaches the current thread from a Java virtual machine. All Java monitors held by this thread are released. All Java threads waiting for this thread to die are notified. The main thread, which is the thread that created the virtual machine, cannot be detached from the it. Instead, the main thread must call `JNI_DestroyJavaVM()`. Returns zero on success; a negative number on failure.

Summary

Today, you learned about the numerous disadvantages of using `native` methods, about the many ways that Java (and you) can make your programs run faster, and also about the often illusory need for efficiency.

You also learned the procedure for creating `native` methods, from both the Java and the C sides, in detail—by generating a header file, and by compiling and linking a full example.

Finally, you learned all about the new Java Native Interface, and its many useful functions.

After working your way through today's difficult material, you've mastered one of the most complex parts of the Java language. You now know how the Java run-time environment itself was created, and how to extend that powerful environment yourself, at its lowest levels.

As a reward, tomorrow we'll look "under the hood" to see some of the hidden power of Java, and you can just sit back and enjoy the ride.

Q&A

Q Does the Java class library need to call `System.loadLibrary()` to load the built-in classes?

A No, you won't see any `loadLibrary()` calls in the implementation of any classes in the Java class library. That's because the Java team had the luxury of being able to *statically* link most of their code into the Java environment, something that really makes sense only when you're in the unique position of providing an entire system, as they are. Your classes must *dynamically* link their libraries into an already-running copy of the Java system. This is, by the way, more flexible than static linking; it allows you to unlink old and relink new versions of your classes at any time, making updating them trivial.

Q Can I statically link my own classes into Java like the Java team did?

A Yes. You can, if you like, ask Sun Microsystems for the sources to the Java run-time environment itself, and, as long as you obey the (relatively straightforward) legal restrictions on using that code, you can relink the entire Java system plus your classes. Your classes are then statically linked into the system, but you have to give everyone who wants to use your program this special version of the Java environment (not easy to do). Sometimes, if you have strong enough requirements, this is the only way to go, but most of the time, dynamic linking is not only good enough, but preferable.

Q My applet needs some key functionality that's missing from the Java library. Given their many disadvantages, I'd like to avoid using native methods. Do I have any alternatives?

A Because it's still early in the history of Java, a valid alternative to native methods is to try to convince the Java team that your needed capability is of interest to a broad range of future Java programmers; then they may include it directly into the java packages. There are already plans to do this with many "missing" pieces of functionality (see http://java.sun.com for regular updates), so this may not be as hard a sell as you might think. Start by posting some messages to the comp.lang.java newsgroups, to be sure no one else at Sun or elsewhere is already doing it, and then see what happens. This is a young, vibrant community of enthusiasts; you are not alone.

20

Day 21

Under the Hood

by Charles L. Perkins

Today, your final day, the inner workings of the Java system will be revealed.

You'll find out all about Java's vision, Java's virtual machine, those bytecodes you've heard so much about, that mysterious garbage collector, and why you might worry about security but don't have to.

Let's begin, however, with the big picture.

The Big Picture

The Java team is very ambitious. Its ultimate goal is nothing less than to revolutionize the way software is written and distributed. It has started with the Internet, where it believes much of the interesting software of the future will live.

To achieve such an ambitious goal, a large fraction of the Internet programming community itself must be marshalled behind a similar goal and given the tools to help achieve it. The Java language, with its four S's (small, simple, safe, secure), and its flexible, Net-oriented environment, hopes to become the focal point for the rallying of this new legion of programmers.

To this end, Sun Microsystems has done something rather gutsy. What was originally a secret, tens-of-millions-of-dollars research and development project, and 100 percent proprietary, has become a free, open, and relatively unencumbered technology standard upon which anyone can build. They are literally giving it away and reserving only the rights they need to maintain and grow the standard.

NOTE As Sun's lawyers have had more time to think, the original intentions of the Java team have gotten somewhat obscured by legal details. It is still *relatively* unencumbered, but its earliest releases were completely unencumbered. Luckily, this has not gotten any worse in the latest releases.

Any truly open standard must be supported by at least one excellent, freely available "demonstration" implementation. Sun has already shipped alphas, betas, various 1.0s, and now, the 1.1 release of Java as part of its freely available Java Development Kit (JDK). Sun has also published detailed specifications for the language itself (*The Java Language Specification*) and for the virtual machine (*The Java Virtual Machine Specification*) via an Addison-Wesley book series. Finally, Sun has implemented a set of compatibility suites that other virtual machine implementations must pass to be declared fully Java compliant. These suites will try to guarantee that Java bytecodes that run here, now, will continue to run anywhere, forever.

In parallel, many universities, companies, and individuals have expressed their intention to duplicate the Java environment, based on the open API that Sun has created. There are already several non-Sun versions of the virtual machine, and almost all of the PC, Mac, and UNIX operating system companies have gone so far as to announce that compliant Java virtual machines will appear as a built-in part of the next releases of their operating systems. Thus, Java becomes a compelling language for *any* sort of software effort, and not simply for Net software.

Several university and company projects are contemplating building development environments and language compilers "on top of" Java bytecodes. In fact, several languages (other than Java) can already be compiled down to Java bytecodes, and thus sent over the Net. Java bytecodes are already a robust and widespread standard for moving executable content around on the Net, and they are rapidly becoming the universal bytecode of choice. By using these new "generic" bytecodes, it is already possible to dynamically link a class written in Lisp with other classes written in Smalltalk, Java, and several other languages, and it should soon be possible to build sophisticated cross-language development environments that allow you to mix and match languages, class by class, during development—perhaps even writing each *method* in a different language!

Why It's a Powerful Vision

One of the reasons this brilliant move on Sun's part has a real chance of success is the pent-up frustration of literally a whole generation of programmers who desperately want to share their code with one another. Right now, the computer science world is balkanized into factions at universities and companies all over the world, with hundreds of languages, dozens of them widely used, dividing and separating us all. It's the worst sort of Tower of Babel. Java hopes to build some bridges and help tear down that tower. Because it is so simple, because it's so useful for programming over the Internet, and because the Internet is so "hot" right now—this confluence of forces is propelling Java onto centerstage.

It deserves to be there. It is the natural outgrowth of ideas that, since the early 1970s inside the Smalltalk group at Xerox PARC, have lain relatively dormant in the mainstream. Smalltalk, in fact, invented the first object-oriented bytecode interpreter and pioneered many of the deep ideas that Java builds on today. Those efforts were not embraced over the intervening decades as a solution to the general problems of software, however. Today, with those problems becoming so much more obvious, and with the Net crying out for a new kind of programming, the soil is fertile to grow something stronger from those old roots, something that just might spread like wildfire. (Is it a coincidence that Java's previous internal names were Green and OAK?)

This new vision of software is one in which the Net becomes an ocean of objects, classes, and the open APIs between them. Traditional applications have vanished, replaced by skeletal frameworks like the Eiffel tower, into which any parts from this ocean can be fitted, on demand, to suit any purpose. User interfaces will be mixed and matched, built in pieces and constructed to taste, whenever the need arises, by their own users. Menus of choices will be filled by dynamic lists of all the choices available for that function, at that exact moment, across the entire ocean (of the Net).

NOTE

> The new 1.1 `java.beans` component and reflection model, along with the remote method invocation and serialization frameworks, begin to take the first baby steps into this new world. The exciting new start-up Marimba, founded by four of the original creators of Java, is taking the next steps in asynchronous, real-time use of your screen area, blurring the distinctions between application, applet, browser, desktop, and screen-saver into a wonderful new user-focused whole.

21

In such a world, software distribution is no longer an issue. Software will be everywhere and will be paid for via a plethora of new micro-accounting models, which charge tiny fractions of cents for the parts as they are assembled and used. Frameworks will come into existence to support entertainment, business, and the social (cyber-)spaces of the near future.

This is a dream that many of us have waited all our lives to be a part of. There are tremendous challenges to making it all come true, but the powerful winds of change we all feel must stir us into action, because, at last, there is a base on which to build that dream—Java.

The Java Virtual Machine

To make visions like this possible, Java must be ubiquitous. It must be able to run on any computer and any operating system—now, and in the future. In order to achieve this level of portability, Java must be very precise not only about the language itself, but about the environment in which the language lives. You can see, from earlier in the book and Appendix B, that the Java environment includes a generally useful set of packages of classes and a freely available implementation of them. This takes care of a part of what is needed, but it is crucial also to specify exactly how the run-time environment of Java behaves.

This final requirement is what has stymied many attempts at ubiquity in the past. If you base your system on any assumptions about what is "beneath" the run-time system, you lose. If you depend in any way on the computer or operating system below, you lose. Java solves this problem by inventing an abstract computer of its own and running on that.

This "virtual" machine runs a special set of "instructions" called bytecodes that are simply a stream of formatted bytes, each of which has a precise specification of exactly what each bytecode does to this virtual machine. The virtual machine is also responsible for certain fundamental capabilities of Java, such as object creation and garbage collection.

Finally, in order to be able to move bytecodes safely across the Internet, you need a bulletproof model of security—and how to maintain it—and a precise format for how this stream of bytecodes can be sent from one virtual machine to another.

Each of these requirements is addressed in today's lesson.

NOTE

This discussion blurs the distinction between the runtime and the virtual machine of Java. This is intentional but a little unconventional. Think of the virtual machine as providing all the capabilities, even those that are conventionally assigned to the runtime. This book uses the words "runtime" and "virtual machine" interchangeably. Equating the two highlights the single environment that must be created to support Java.

Much of the following description is paraphrased closely from an early "Virtual Machine Specifications" document written by Tim Lindholm, Frank Yellin, and Kathy Walrath. I thank them for the use of their excellent documentation. If you delve more deeply into the details online, you should cover some familiar ground.

In addition, the desciptions below were updated to reflect the latest published specification, *The Java Virtual Machine Specification*, by Lindholm and Yellin, Addison-Wesley, which is now the final word on these topics.

An Overview

It is worth quoting the introduction to the Java virtual machine documentation here, because it is so relevant to the vision outlined earlier:

The Java virtual machine specification has a purpose that is both like and unlike equivalent documents for other languages and abstract machines. It is intended to present an abstract, logical machine design that is free from the distraction of inconsequential details of any implementation. It does not anticipate an implementation technology, or an implementation host. At the same time it gives a reader sufficient information to allow implementation of the abstract design in a range of technologies.

However, the intent of the [...] Java project is to create a language [...] that will allow the interchange over the Internet of "executable content," which will be embodied by compiled Java code. The project specifically does not want Java to be a proprietary language and does not want to be the sole purveyor of Java language implementations. Rather, we hope to make documents like this one, and source code for our implementation, freely available for people to use as they choose.

This vision [...] can be achieved only if the executable content can be reliably shared between different Java implementations. These intentions prohibit the definition of the Java virtual machine from being fully abstract. Rather, relevant logical elements of the design have to be made sufficiently concrete to allow the interchange of compiled Java code. This does not collapse the Java virtual machine specification to a description of a Java implementation; elements of the design that do not play a part in the interchange of executable content remain abstract. But it does force us to specify, in addition to the abstract machine design, a concrete interchange format for compiled Java code.

21

The Java virtual machine specification consists of the following:

- ☐ The bytecode syntax, including opcode and operand sizes, values, and types, and their alignment and endian-ness
- ☐ The values of any identifiers (for example, type identifiers) in bytecodes or in supporting structures
- ☐ The layout of the supporting structures that appear in compiled Java code (for example, the constant pool)
- ☐ The Java .class file format

Each of these is covered today.

Despite this degree of specificity, there are still several elements of the design that remain (purposely) abstract, including the following:

- ☐ The layout and management of the run-time data areas
- ☐ The particular garbage-collection algorithms, strategies, and constraints used
- ☐ The compiler, development environment, and run-time extensions (apart from the need to generate and read valid Java bytecodes)
- ☐ Any optimizations performed, once valid bytecodes are received

These places are where the creativity of a virtual machine implementor has full rein.

The Fundamental Parts

The Java virtual machine can be divided into five fundamental pieces:

- ☐ A bytecode instruction set
- ☐ A set of registers
- ☐ A stack
- ☐ A garbage-collected heap
- ☐ An area for storing methods

Some of these might be implemented by using an interpreter, a native binary code compiler, or even a hardware chip—but all these logical, abstract components of the virtual machine must be supplied in some form in every Java system.

NOTE   The memory areas used by the Java virtual machine are not required to be at any particular place in memory, to be in any particular order, or even to use contiguous memory.

The virtual machine, and its supporting code, is often referred to as the run-time environment, and when this book refers to something being done at run-time, the virtual machine is what's doing it.

Java Bytecodes

The Java virtual machine instruction set is optimized to be small and compact. It is designed to travel across the Net, and so has traded off speed-of-interpretation for space. (Given that both Net bandwidth and mass storage speeds increase less rapidly than CPU speed, this seems like an appropriate trade-off.)

As mentioned, Java source code is "compiled" into bytecodes and stored in a .class file. On Sun's Java system, this is performed using the javac tool. It, like the Java compiler on almost all other systems, is not exactly a traditional "compiler," because javac translates source code into bytecodes, a lower-level format that cannot be run directly, but must be further interpreted by each computer. Of course, it is exactly this level of "indirection" that buys you the power, flexibility, and extreme portability of Java code.

NOTE   Quotation marks are used around the word "compiler" when talking about javac because later today you will also learn about the "just-in-time" compiler, which acts more like the back-end of a traditional compiler. The use of the same word "compiler" for these two different pieces of Java technology is unfortunate, but somewhat reasonable, because each is really one-half (either the front- or the back-end) of a more traditional compiler.

A bytecode instruction consists of a one-byte opcode that serves to identify the instruction involved and zero or more operands, each of which may be more than one byte long, that encode the parameters the opcode requires.

NOTE   When operands are more than one byte long, they are stored in big-endian order, high-order byte first. These operands must be assembled from the byte stream at run-time. For example, a 16-bit parameter appears in the stream as two bytes so that its value is first_byte * 256 + second_byte. The bytecode instruction stream is only byte-aligned, and alignment of any larger quantities is not guaranteed (except for "within" the special bytecodes lookupswitch and tableswitch, which have special alignment rules of their own).

21

A *word* embodies the abstract notion of the "natural" word size for a machine. On a "32-bit machine" it is almost always 32 bits (4 bytes) long.

 An `objectref` is an implementation-dependent pointer-like type and should be thought of as simply "a reference to an object."

 A `returnAddress` acts as an index into the bytecodes of a method and is used when returning from a subroutine call.

Bytecodes interpret data in the run-time memory areas as belonging to a fixed set of types: the primitive types you've seen several times before, consisting of several signed integer types (8-bit `byte`, 16-bit `short`, 32-bit `int`, 64-bit `long`), one unsigned integer type (16-bit `char`), and two signed floating-point types (IEEE 32-bit `float`, IEEE 64-bit `double`), the one-word reference type `objectref`, and the one-word pseudo-type `returnAddress`. Some special bytecodes (for example, the `dup` instructions), treat run-time memory areas as raw data, without regard to type. This is the exception, however, not the rule.

> The phrases "32-bit" and "one-word" in the previous paragraph refer to quite different things. Whenever an exact bit length is stated, like "32-bit `int`," it refers to the range of values that are legal for that type. However, the phrase "one-word reference type" implies only that the type must fit into one word (a storage requirement).
>
> This specification requires that a word is large enough to store a `byte`, `short`, `int`, `char`, `float`, `objectref`, `returnAddress`, or a native pointer, and that two words are large enough to store a `long` or a `double`.

These primitive types are distinguished and managed by the Java compiler, not by the Java run-time environment. These types are not "tagged" in memory, and thus cannot be distinguished at run-time. Different bytecodes are designed to handle each of the various primitive types uniquely, and the compiler carefully chooses from this palette based on its knowledge of the actual types stored in the various memory areas. For example, when adding two integers, the compiler generates an `iadd` bytecode; for adding two floats, `fadd` is generated. These two bytecodes may, in fact, perform exactly the same operation, but each implicitly describes the parameter type it requires. (You'll see all this in gruesome detail later.)

21

Registers

The registers of the Java virtual machine are just like the registers inside a "real" computer.

 Registers hold the machine's state, affect its operation, and are updated after each bytecode is executed.

The following are the Java registers:

- ☐ pc, the program counter, which indicates what bytecode is being executed
- ☐ optop, a pointer to the top of the operand stack, which is used to evaluate all arithmetic expressions
- ☐ frame, a pointer to the execution environment of the current method, which includes an activation record for this method invocation and any associated debugging information
- ☐ vars, a pointer to the first local variable of the currently executing method

The virtual machine defines these registers to be one word wide.

NOTE

Because the virtual machine is primarily stack-based, it does not use any registers for passing or receiving arguments. This is a conscious choice skewed toward bytecode simplicity and compactness. It also aids efficient implementation on register-poor architectures, which most of today's computers, unfortunately, are. Perhaps when the majority of CPUs out there are a little more sophisticated, this choice will be reexamined, though simplicity and compactness may still be reason enough!

In *The Java Virtual Machine Specification*, the pc is the only register discussed. The other registers should thus be considered unspecified internal implementation details, and are shown here simply for completeness.

By the way, the pc register is also used when the run-time handles exceptions; catch clauses are (ultimately) associated with ranges of the pc within a method's bytecodes.

21

The Stack

The Java virtual machine is stack-based. A Java stack frame is similar to the stack frame of a conventional programming language—it holds the state for a single method invocation. Frames for nested method invocations are stacked on top of this frame.

 The *stack* is used to supply parameters to bytecodes and methods, and to receive results back from them.

Each stack frame contains three (possibly empty) sets of data: the local variables for the method invocation, its execution environment, and its operand stack. The sizes of these first two are fixed at the start of a method invocation, but the operand stack varies in size as bytecodes are executed in the method.

Local variables are stored in an array of one-word slots, indexed by the register vars. Most types take up one slot in the array, but the long and double types each take up two slots.

> long and double values, stored or referenced via an index N, take up the one-word slots N and N + 1. These 64-bit values are thus not guaranteed to be two-word-aligned. Implementors are free to decide the appropriate way to divide these values among the two slots.

The execution environment in a stack frame helps to maintain the stack itself. It contains a pointer to the previous stack frame, a pointer to the local variables of the method invocation, and pointers to the stack's current "base" and "top." Additional debugging information can also be placed into the execution environment.

The operand stack, a one-word-wide first-in-first-out (FIFO) stack, is used to store the parameters and return values of most bytecode instructions. For example, the iadd bytecode expects two integers to be stored on the top of the stack. It pops them, adds them together, and pushes the resulting sum back onto the stack.

Each primitive data type has unique instructions that know how to extract, operate, and push back operands of that type. For example, long and double operands take two "slots" on the stack, and the special bytecodes that handle these operands take this into account. It is illegal for the types on the stack and the instruction operating on them to be incompatible (javac outputs bytecodes that always obey this rule).

21

NOTE

The top of the operand stack and the top of the overall Java stack are almost always the same. Thus, "the stack," refers to both stacks, collectively.

The Heap

The heap is that part of memory from which newly created instances (objects) are allocated.

The heap is often assigned a large, fixed size when the Java run-time system is started, but on systems that support virtual memory, it can grow as needed, in a nearly unbounded fashion.

Because objects are automatically garbage-collected in Java, programmers do not have to (and, in fact, cannot) manually free the memory allocated to an object when they are finished using it.

Java objects are referenced indirectly in the run-time, via objectrefs, which are a kind of indirect pointer into the heap.

Because objects are never referenced directly, parallel garbage collectors can be written that operate independently of your program, moving around objects in the heap at will. You'll learn more about garbage collection later.

The Method Area

Like the compiled code areas of conventional programming language environments, or the TEXT segment in a UNIX process, the method area stores the Java bytecodes that implement almost every method in the Java system. (Remember that some methods might be native, and thus implemented, for example, in C.) The method area also stores the symbol tables needed for dynamic linking, and any other additional information that debuggers or development environments might want to associate with each method's implementation.

The Constant Pool

Every currently loaded class has a constant pool "attached" to it. Initially created by javac, and allocated from the method area when a class is first loaded, the constants in this pool encode all the names (of variables, methods, and so forth) used by any method in the class. The class contains a count of how many constants there are and an offset that specifies how far into the class description itself the array of constants begins. These constants are typed via specially coded bytes and have a precisely defined format when they appear in the .class file for a class. Later today, a little of this file format is covered, but everything is fully specified by *The Java Virtual Machine Specification*.

21

Bytecodes in More Detail

One of the main tasks of the virtual machine is the fast, efficient execution of the Java bytecodes in methods. Unlike in the discussion yesterday about generality versus efficiency, this is a case where speed is of the utmost importance. Every Java program suffers from a slow implementation here, so the run-time must use as many "tricks" as possible to make bytecodes run fast. The only other goal (or limitation) is that Java programmers must not be able to see these tricks in the behavior of their programs. A Java run-time implementor must be extremely clever to satisfy both these goals.

The Bytecode Interpreter

A bytecode interpreter examines each opcode byte (bytecode) in a method's bytecode stream, in turn, and executes a unique action for that bytecode. This might consume further bytes for the operands of the bytecode and might affect which bytecode will be examined next. It operates like the hardware CPU in a computer, which examines memory for instructions to carry out in exactly the same manner. It is the software CPU of the Java virtual machine.

Your first, naive attempt to write such a bytecode interpreter will almost certainly be disastrously slow. The inner loop, which dispatches one bytecode each time through the loop, is notoriously difficult to optimize. In fact, smart people have been thinking about this problem, in one form or another, for more than 20 years. Luckily, they've gotten results, all of which can be applied to Java.

The final result is that the interpreter shipped in the current release of Java has an extremely fast inner loop. In fact, on even a relatively slow computer, this interpreter can perform more than 590,000 bytecodes per second! This is really quite good, because the CPU in that computer does only about 30 times better using *hardware*.

This interpreter is fast enough for most Java programs (and for those requiring more speed, they can always use `native` methods—see yesterday's discussion)—but what if a smart implementor wants to do better?

Just-in-Time Compilers

About a decade ago, a really clever trick was discovered by Peter Deutsch while trying to make Smalltalk run faster. He called it "dynamic translation" during interpretation. Sun calls it "just-in-time" compiling.

The trick is to notice that the really fast interpreter you've just written—in C, for example— already has a useful sequence of native binary code for each bytecode that it interprets: the binary code that the interpreter itself is executing. Because the interpreter has already been

21

compiled from C into native binary code, for each bytecode that it interprets, it passes through a sequence of native code instructions for the hardware CPU on which it is running. By saving a copy of each binary instruction as it "goes by," the interpreter can keep a running log of the binary code it has run to interpret a bytecode. It can just as easily keep a log of the set of bytecodes that it ran to interpret an entire method. (Actually, many of the just-in-time compilers in today's Java-enabled browsers simply use a really fast bytecode-to-native-code compiler to perform this step—less clever, but still quite fast.)

You then take the resulting log of instructions and "peephole-optimize" it, just as a smart compiler does. This eliminates redundant or unnecessary instructions from the log, and makes it look just like the optimized binary code that a good compiler might have produced.

> This is where the name compiler comes from, in "just-in-time" compiler, but it's really only the back-end of a traditional compiler—the part that does code generation. By the way, the front-end here is `javac`.

Here's where the trick comes in. The next time that method is run (in exactly the same way), the interpreter can now simply execute directly the stored log of binary native code. Because this optimizes out the inner-loop overhead of each bytecode, as well as any other redundancies between the bytecodes in a method, it can gain a factor of 10-15 in speed. In fact, an experimental version of this technology at Sun has shown that Java programs using it can run as fast as compiled C programs.

> The parenthetical in the last paragraph is needed because if anything is different about the input to the method, it takes a different path through the interpreter and must be relogged. (There are sophisticated versions of this technology that solve this, and other, difficulties.) The cache of native code for a method must be invalidated whenever the method has changed, and the interpreter must pay a small cost up front each time a method is run for the first time. However, these small bookkeeping costs are far outweighed by the amazing gains in speed possible.

21

The `java2c` Translator

Another, simpler, trick, that works well whenever you have a good, portable C compiler on each system that runs your program, is to translate the bytecodes into C and then compile the C into binary native code. If you wait until the first use of a method or class, and then perform this as an "invisible" optimization, it gains you an additional speedup over the approach outlined previously, without the Java programmer needing to know about it.

Of course, this does limit you to systems with a C compiler, but as you learned yesterday, there are extremely good, freely available C compilers. In theory, your Java code might be able to travel with its own C compiler, or know where to pull one from the Net as needed, for each new computer and operating system it faced. (Because this violates some of the rules of normal Java code movement over the Net, though, it should be used sparingly.)

If you're using Java, for example, to write a server that lives only on your computer, it might be appropriate to use Java for its flexibility in writing and maintaining the server (and for its capability of dynamically linking new Java code on-the-fly), and then to run `java2c` (or some direct-to-native-code Java compiler) by hand to translate the basic server itself entirely into native code. You'd link the Java run-time environment into that code so that your server remains a fully capable Java program, but it's now an extremely fast one.

In fact, an early experimental version of the `java2c` translator inside Sun showed that it can reach the speed of compiled and optimized C code. This is the best that you can hope to do!

NOTE
Unfortunately, as of the 1.1 release, there is still no publicly available `java2c` tool. It seems destined to remain experimental. There are various versions of direct-to-native-code Java compilers in the works outside Sun, and all of what was said above applies to them as well. Also, most of today's Java-enabled browsers effectively perform this translation as part of their version of the just-in-time compiling of bytecodes.

The Bytecodes Themselves

Let's look at a (progressively less and less) detailed description of each class of bytecodes.

For each bytecode, some brief text describes its function, and a textual "picture" of the stack, both before and after the bytecode has been executed, is shown. This text picture will look something like the following:

```
..., value1, value2 => ..., value3
```

This particular picture means that the bytecode expects two operands—value1 and value2—to be on the top of the stack, pops them both off the stack, operates on them to produce value3, and pushes value3 back onto the top of the stack. You should read each stack list ("before" on the left, "after" on the right of "=>") from right to left, with the rightmost value being the top of the stack. The . . . is read as "the rest of the stack below," which is irrelevant to the current bytecode. All operands on the stack are one word wide.

Because most bytecodes take their arguments from the stack and place their results back there, the brief text descriptions that follow only say something about the source or destination of values if they are not on the stack. For example, the description "Load integer from local variable." means that the integer is loaded onto the stack, and "Integer add." intends its integers to be taken from—and the result returned to—the stack.

Bytecodes that don't affect control flow simply move the pc onto the next bytecode that follows in sequence. Those that do affect the pc say so explicitly. Whenever you see byte1, byte2, and so forth, it refers to the first byte, second byte, and so on, that follow the opcode byte itself. After such a bytecode is executed, the pc automatically advances over these operand bytes to start the next bytecode in sequence.

The description of some bytecodes explicitly mentions various Errors or Exceptions that they might throw. In addition to these, any bytecode, at any time, is allowed (implicitly) to throw any subclass of VirtualMachineError. For example, OutOfMemoryError will most often be thrown by the array and instance creation bytecodes, and StackOverflowError will most often be thrown by the method invocation bytecodes.

NOTE The next few sections are in "reference manual style," presenting each bytecode separately in all its (often redundant) detail. Later sections begin to collapse and coalesce this verbose style into something shorter and more readable. The verbose form is shown at first because the online reference manuals will look more like it, and because it drives home the point that each bytecode "function" comes in many, nearly identical bytecodes, one for each primitive type in Java.

Pushing Constants onto the Stack

bipush   ... => ..., value

Push one-bytesigned integer. byte1 is interpreted as a signed 8-bit value. This value is sign-extended to an int and pushed onto the operand stack.

21

```
sipush          ... => ..., value
```

Push two-byte signed integer. `byte1` and `byte2` are assembled into a signed 16-bit value. This `value` is sign-extended to an `int` and pushed onto the operand stack.

```
ldc             ... => ..., item
```

Push `item` from constant pool. `byte1` is used as an unsigned 8-bit index into the constant pool of the current class. The `item` at that index is resolved and pushed onto the stack.

```
ldc_w           ... => ..., item
```

Push `item` from constant pool. `byte1` and `byte2` are used to construct an unsigned 16-bit index into the constant pool of the current class. The `item` at that index is resolved and pushed onto the stack.

```
ldc2_w          ... => ..., item.word1, item.word2
```

Push `long` or `double` from constant pool. `byte1` and `byte2` are used to construct an unsigned 16-bit index into the constant pool of the current class. The two-word constant at that index is resolved and pushed onto the stack.

```
aconst_null     ... => ..., null
```

Push the `null` object reference onto the stack.

```
iconst_m1       ... => ..., -1
```

Push the `int` -1 onto the stack.

```
iconst_<I>      ... => ..., <I>
```

Push the `int` <I> onto the stack. There are six of these bytecodes, one for each of the integers 0-5: `iconst_0`, `iconst_1`, `iconst_2`, `iconst_3`, `iconst_4`, and `iconst_5`.

```
lconst_<L>      ... => ..., <L>.word1, <L>.word2
```

Push the `long` <L> onto the stack. There are two of these bytecodes, one for each of the integers 0 and 1: `lconst_0`, and `lconst_1`.

```
fconst_<F>      ... => ..., <F>
```

Push the `float` <F> onto the stack. There are three of these bytecodes, one for each of the integers 0-2: `fconst_0`, `fconst_1`, and `fconst_2`.

```
dconst_<D>      ... => ..., <D>.word1, <D>.word2
```

Push the `double` <D> onto the stack. There are two of these bytecodes, one for each of the integers 0 and 1: `dconst_0`, and `dconst_1`.

Loading Local Variables onto the Stack

```
iload          ... => ..., value
```

Load `int` from local variable. Local variable `byte1` in the current Java frame must contain an `int`. The `value` of that variable is pushed onto the operand stack.

```
iload_<I>      ... => ..., value
```

Load `int` from local variable. Local variable `<I>` in the current Java frame must contain an `int`. The `value` of that variable is pushed onto the operand stack. There are four of these bytecodes, one for each of the integers 0-3: `iload_0`, `iload_1`, `iload_2`, and `iload_3`.

```
lload          ... => ..., value.word1, value.word2
```

Load `long` from local variable. Local variables `byte1` and `byte1 + 1` in the current Java frame must together contain a long integer. The values contained in those variables are pushed onto the operand stack.

```
lload_<L>      ... => ..., value.word1, value.word2
```

Load `long` from local variable. Local variables `<L>` and `<L> + 1` in the current Java frame must together contain a long integer. The value contained in those variables is pushed onto the operand stack. There are four of these bytecodes, one for each of the integers 0-3: `lload_0`, `lload_1`, `lload_2`, and `lload_3`.

```
fload          ... => ..., value
```

Load `float` from local variable. Local variable `byte1` in the current Java frame must contain a single precision floating-point number. The `value` of that variable is pushed onto the operand stack.

```
fload_<F>      ... => ..., value
```

Load `float` from local variable. Local variable `<F>` in the current Java frame must contain a single precision floating-point number. The value of that variable is pushed onto the operand stack. There are four of these bytecodes, one for each of the integers 0-3: `fload_0`, `fload_1`, `fload_2`, and `fload_3`.

```
dload          ... => ..., value.word1, value.word2
```

Load `double` from local variable. Local variables `byte1` and `byte1 + 1` in the current Java frame must together contain a double precision floating-point number. The value contained in those variables is pushed onto the operand stack.

```
dload_<D>      ... => ..., value.word1, value.word2
```

Load `double` from local variable. Local variables `<D>` and `<D> + 1` in the current Java frame must together contain a double precision floating-point number. The value contained in those variables is pushed onto the operand stack There are four of these bytecodes, one for each of the integers 0-3: `dload_0`, `dload1`, `dload_2`, and `dload_3`.

21

```
aload           ... => ..., objectref
```

Load object reference from local variable. Local variable byte1 in the current Java frame must contain a reference to an object. The value of that variable is pushed onto the operand stack. aload cannot be used to load a returnAddress; this asymmetry with astore is intentional.

```
aload_<A>       ... => ..., objectref
```

Load object reference from local variable. Local variable <A> in the current Java frame must contain a reference to an object. The value of that variable is pushed onto the operand stack. There are four of these bytecodes, one for each of the integers 0-3: aload_0, aload_1, aload_2, and aload_3. aload_<A> cannot be used to load a returnAddress; this asymmetry with astore_<A> is intentional.

Storing Stack Values into Local Variables

```
istore          ..., value => ...
```

Store int into local variable. value must be an int. Local variable byte1 in the current Java frame is set to value.

```
istore_<I>      ..., value => ...
```

Store int into local variable. value must be an int. Local variable <I> in the current Java frame is set to value. There are four of these bytecodes, one for each of the integers 0-3: istore_0, istore_1, istore_2, and istore_3.

```
lstore          ..., value.word1, value.word2 => ...
```

Store long into local variable. value must be a long integer. Local variables byte1 and byte1 + 1 in the current Java frame are set to value.

```
lstore_<L>      ..., value.word1, value.word2 => ...
```

Store long into local variable. value must be a long integer. Local variables <L> and <L> + 1 in the current Java frame are set to value. There are four of these bytecodes, one for each of the integers 0-3: lstore_0, lstore_1, lstore_2, and lstore_3.

```
fstore          ..., value => ...
```

Store float into local variable. value must be a single precision floating-point number. Local variable byte1 in the current Java frame is set to value.

```
fstore_<F>      ..., value => ...
```

Store float into local variable. value must be a single precision floating-point number. Local variable <F> in the current Java frame is set to value. There are four of these bytecodes, one for each of the integers 0-3: fstore_0, fstore_1, fstore_2, and fstore_3.

21

```
dstore          ..., value.word1, value.word2 => ...
```

Store `double` into local variable. `value` must be a double precision floating-point number. Local variables `byte1` and `byte1 + 1` in the current Java frame are set to `value`.

```
dstore_<D>      ..., value.word1, value.word2 => ...
```

Store `double` into local variable. `value` must be a double precision floating-point number. Local variables `<D>` and `<D> + 1` in the current Java frame are set to `value`. There are four of these bytecodes, one for each of the integers 0-3: `dstore_0`, `dstore_1`, `dstore_2`, and `dstore_3`.

```
astore          ..., objectref-or-address => ...
```

Store object reference into local variable. `objectref-or-address` must be a `returnAddress` or a reference to an object. Local variable `byte1` in the current Java frame is set to `value`. `astore` stores a `returnAddress` when implementing `finally`. `aload` cannot be used to load a `returnAddress`; this asymmetry is intentional.

```
astore_<A>      ..., objectref-or-address => ...
```

Store object reference into local variable. `objectref-or-address` must be a return address or a reference to an object. Local variable `<A>` in the current Java frame is set to `value`. There are four of these bytecodes, one for each of the integers 0-3: `astore_0`, `astore_1`, `astore_2`, and `astore_3`. `astore_<A>` stores a `returnAddress` when implementing `finally`. `aload_<A>` cannot be used to load a `returnAddress`; this asymmetry is intentional.

```
iinc            -no change-
```

Increment local variable by constant. Local variable `byte1` in the current Java frame must contain an `int`. Its value is incremented by the value `byte2`, where `byte2` is treated as a signed 8-bit quantity that is first sign-extended to an `int`.

Array Operations

```
newarray        ..., count => arrayref
```

Allocate new array. `count` must be an `int`. It represents the number of elements in the new array. `byte1` is an internal code that indicates the type of array to allocate. Possible values for `byte1` are as follows: `T_BOOLEAN` (4), `T_CHAR` (5), `T_FLOAT` (6), `T_DOUBLE` (7), `T_BYTE` (8), `T_SHORT` (9), `T_INT` (10), and `T_LONG` (11).

An attempt is made to allocate a new array of the indicated type, capable of holding `count` elements. This will be the result `arrayref`. All elements of the array are initialized to their default values. If `count` is less than zero, a `NegativeArraySizeException` is thrown.

21

```
anewarray         ..., count => arrayref
```

Allocate new array of objects. count must be an int. It represents the number of elements in the new array. byte1 and byte2 are used to construct an index into the constant pool of the current class. The item at that index is resolved. The resulting entry must be a class, array, or interface.

An attempt is made to allocate a new array of the indicated type, capable of holding count elements. This will be the result arrayref. All elements of the array are initialized to null. If count is less than zero, a NegativeArraySizeException is thrown.

NOTE

anewarray is used to create a single dimension of an array of objects. For example, the request new Thread[7] generates the following bytecodes:

```
bipush 7
anewarray <Class "java.lang.Thread">
```

anewarray can also be used to create the outermost dimension of a multidimensional array. For example, the array declaration new int[6][] generates this:

```
bipush 6
anewarray <Class "[I">
```

(See the section "Method Descriptors" for more information on strings such as "[I".)

```
multianewarray  ..., count1, [count2, ..., countN] => arrayref
```

Allocate new multidimensional array. Each count<I> must be an int. Each represents the number of elements in a dimension of the array. byte1 and byte2 are used to construct an index into the constant pool of the current class. The item at that index is resolved. The resulting entry must be an array class of one or more dimensions.

byte3 is a positive integer representing the number of dimensions being created. It must be less than or equal to the number of dimensions of the array class. byte3 is also the number of elements that are popped off the stack. All must be ints greater than or equal to zero. These are used as the sizes of the dimensions. An attempt is made to allocate a new array of the indicated class type, capable of holding count1 * count2 * ... * countN elements. This will be the result arrayref. The components of first array are initialized with subarrays of the type of the second array, and so on (except the last, if present, which is initialzed with the default values of the elements themselves). If the base class of the new array cannot be legally accessed, an IllegalAccessError is thrown. If any of the count<I> arguments on the stack is less than zero, a NegativeArraySizeException is thrown.

NOTE

> `new int[6][3][]` generates these bytecodes:
>
> ```
> bipush 6
> bipush 3
> multianewarray <Class "[[[I"> 2
> ```
>
> where only two of the three dimensions of the array are created. This is legal—the last dimension of new array is simply not initialized.
>
> When creating arrays of single dimension, it's usually more efficient to use newarray or anewarray.

```
arraylength        ..., arrayref => ..., length
```

Get length of array. `arrayref` must be a reference to an array object. The `length` of the array is determined and replaces `arrayref` on the top of the stack. If `arrayref` is `null`, a `NullPointerException` is thrown.

```
iaload             ..., arrayref, index => ..., value
laload             ..., arrayref, index => ..., value.word1, value.word2
faload             ..., arrayref, index => ..., value
daload             ..., arrayref, index => ..., value.word1, value.word2
aaload             ..., arrayref, index => ..., value
baload             ..., arrayref, index => ..., value
caload             ..., arrayref, index => ..., value
saload             ..., arrayref, index => ..., value
```

Load *<type>* from array. `arrayref` must be an array of *<type>*s. `index` must be an `int`. The *<type>* value at position number `index` in the array is retrieved and pushed onto the top of the stack. If `arrayref` is `null`, a `NullPointerException` is thrown. If `index` is not within the bounds of the array, an `ArrayIndexOutOfBoundsException` is thrown. *<type>* is, in turn, `int`, `long`, `float`, `double`, `objectref`, `byte` (or `boolean`), `char`, and `short`. *<type>*s `long` and `double` have two word values, as you've seen in previous `load` bytecodes.

```
iastore            ..., arrayref, index, value => ...
lastore            ..., arrayref, index, value.word1, value.word2 => ...
fastore            ..., arrayref, index, value => ...
dastore            ..., arrayref, index, value.word1, value.word2 => ...
aastore            ..., arrayref, index, value => ...
bastore            ..., arrayref, index, value => ...
castore            ..., arrayref, index, value => ...
sastore            ..., arrayref, index, value => ...
```

Store into *<type>* array. `arrayref` must be an array of *<type>*s, `index` must be an `int`, and `value` a *<type>*. The *<type>* value is stored at position `index` in the array. If `arrayref` is `null`, a `NullPointerException` is thrown. If `index` is not within the bounds of the array, an `ArrayIndexOutOfBoundsException` is thrown. *<type>* is, in turn, `int`, `long`, `float`, `double`, `objectref`, `byte` (or `boolean`), `char`, and `short`. *<type>*s `long` and `double` have two word values, as you've seen in previous `store` bytecodes. Trying to `aastore` an `objectref` value into an array component that is not assignment compatible with it throws an `ArrayStoreException`.

21

Stack Operations

```
nop           -no change-
```

Do nothing.

```
pop           ..., word => ...
```

Pop the top word from the stack.

```
pop2          ..., word2, word1 => ...
```

Pop the top two words from the stack.

```
dup           ..., word => ..., word, word
```

Duplicate the top word on the stack.

```
dup_x1        ..., word2, word1 => ..., word1, word2,word1
```

Duplicate the top word on the stack and insert the copy two words down in the stack.

```
dup_x2        ..., word3, word2, word1 => ..., word1, word3,word2,word1
```

Duplicate the top word on the stack and insert the copy three words down in the stack.

```
dup2          ..., word2, word1 => ..., word2, word1, word2,word1
```

Duplicate the top two words on the stack.

```
dup2_x1       ..., word3, word2, word1 => ..., word2, word1, word3,word2,word1
```

Duplicate the top two words on the stack and insert the copies two words down in the stack.

```
dup2_x2       ..., w4, w3, w2, w1 => ..., w2, w1, w4,w3,w2,w1
```

Duplicate the top two words on the stack and insert the copies three words down in the stack.

```
swap          ..., word2, word1 => ..., word1, word2
```

Swap the top two words on the stack.

Arithmetic Operations

```
iadd          ..., v1, v2 => ..., result
ladd          ..., v1.word1, v1.word2, v2.word1, v2.word2 => ..., r.word1, r.word2
fadd          ..., v1, v2 => ..., result
dadd          ..., v1.word1, v1.word2, v2.word1, v2.word2 => ..., r.word1, r.word2
```

$v1$ and $v2$ must be <type>s. The vs are added and are replaced on the stack by their <type> sum. <type> is, in turn, int, long, float, and double.

```
isub          ..., v1, v2 => ..., result
lsub          ..., v1.word1, v1.word2, v2.word1, v2.word2 => ..., r.word1, r.word2
```

```
fsub        ..., v1, v2 => ..., result
dsub        ..., v1.word1, v1.word2, v2.word1, v2.word2 => ..., r.word1, r.word2
```

v1 and v2 must be *<type>*s. v2 is subtracted from v1, and both vs are replaced on the stack by their *<type>* difference. *<type>* is, in turn, int, long, float, and double.

```
imul        ..., v1, v2 => ..., result
lmul        ..., v1.word1, v1.word2, v2.word1, v2.word2 => ..., r.word1, r.word2
fmul        ..., v1, v2 => ..., result
dmul        ..., v1.word1, v1.word2, v2.word1, v2.word2 => ..., r.word1, r.word2
```

v1 and v2 must be *<type>*s. Both vs are replaced on the stack by their *<type>* product. *<type>* is, in turn, int, long, float, and double.

```
idiv        ..., v1, v2 => ..., result
ldiv        ..., v1.word1, v1.word2, v2.word1, v2.word2 => ..., r.word1, r.word2
fdiv        ..., v1, v2 => ..., result
ddiv        ..., v1.word1, v1.word2, v2.word1, v2.word2 => ..., r.word1, r.word2
```

v1 and v2 must be *<type>*s. v2 is divided by v1, and both vs are replaced on the stack by their *<type>* quotient. An attempt to divide by zero results in an ArithmeticException being thrown. *<type>* is, in turn, int, long, float, and double.

```
irem        ..., v1, v2 => ..., result
lrem        ..., v1.word1, v1.word2, v2.word1, v2.word2 => ..., r.word1, r.word2
frem        ..., v1, v2 => ..., result
drem        ..., v1.word1, v1.word2, v2.word1, v2.word2 => ..., r.word1, r.word2
```

v1 and v2 must be *<type>*s. v2 is divided by v1, and both vs are replaced on the stack by their *<type>* remainder. An attempt to divide by zero results in an ArithmeticException being thrown. *<type>* is, in turn, int, long, float, and double.

```
ineg        ..., value => ..., result
lneg        ..., value.word1, value.word2 => ..., result.word1, result.word2
fneg        ..., value => ..., result
dneg        ..., value.word1, value.word2 => ..., result.word1, result.word2
```

value must be a *<type>*. It is replaced on the stack by its arithmetic negation. *<type>* is, in turn, int, long, float, and double.

NOTE

Now that you're familiar with the look of the bytecodes, the summaries that follow will become shorter and shorter (for space reasons). You can always get any desired level of detail from *The Virtual Machine Specification* (Lindholm and Yellin, Addison-Wesley).

21

Logical Operations

```
ishl      ..., v1, v2 => ..., result
lshl      ..., v1.word1, v1.word2, v2 => ..., r.word1, r.word2
ishr      ..., v1, v2 => ..., result
lshr      ..., v1.word1, v1.word2, v2 => ..., r.word1, r.word2
iushr     ..., v1, v2 => ..., result
lushr     ..., v1.word1, v1.word2, v2.word1, v2.word2 => ..., r.word1, r.word2
```

For types int and long: arithmetic shift-left, arithmetic shift-right, and logical shift-right.

```
iand      ..., v1, v2 => ..., result
land      ..., v1.word1, v1.word2, v2.word1, v2.word2 => ..., r.word1, r.word2
ior       ..., v1, v2 => ..., result
lor       ..., v1.word1, v1.word2, v2.word1, v2.word2 => ..., r.word1, r.word2
ixor      ..., v1, v2 => ..., result
lxor      ..., v1.word1, v1.word2, v2.word1, v2.word2 => ..., r.word1, r.word2
```

For types int and long: bitwise AND, OR, and XOR.

Conversion Operations

```
i2l       ..., value => ..., result.word1, result.word2
i2f       ..., value => ..., result
i2d       ..., value => ..., result.word1, result.word2

l2i       ..., value.word1, value.word2 => ..., result
l2f       ..., value.word1, value.word2 => ..., result
l2d       ..., value.word1, value.word2 => ..., result.word1, result.word2

f2i       ..., value => ..., result
f2l       ..., value => ..., result.word1, result.word2
f2d       ..., value => ..., result.word1, result.word2

d2i       ..., value.word1, value.word2 => ..., result
d2l       ..., value.word1, value.word2 => ..., result.word1, result.word2
d2f       ..., value.word1, value.word2 => ..., result

i2b       ..., value => ..., result
i2c       ..., value => ..., result
i2s       ..., value => ..., result
```

These bytecodes convert from a value of type <lhs> to a result of type <rhs>. <lhs> can be any of i, l, f, and d, and <rhs> any of i, l, f, d, b, c, and s, which represent int, long, float, double, byte, char, and short, respectively.

Transfer of Control

```
ifeq      ..., value => ...
ifne      ..., value => ...
iflt      ..., value => ...
ifgt      ..., value => ...
ifle      ..., value => ...
ifge      ..., value => ...
```

```
if_icmpeq    ..., value1, value2 => ...
if_icmpne    ..., value1, value2 => ...
if_icmplt    ..., value1, value2 => ...
if_icmpgt    ..., value1, value2 => ...
if_icmple    ..., value1, value2 => ...
if_icmpge    ..., value1, value2 => ...
```

Branching on ints. When value <rel> 0 is true in the first set of bytecodes or value1 <rel> value2 is true in the second set, byte1 and byte2 are used to construct a signed 16-bit offset. Execution proceeds at that offset from the address of this bytecode. Otherwise, execution proceeds at the bytecode following. <rel> is one of eq, ne, lt, gt, le, and ge, which represent equal, not equal, less than, greater than, less than or equal, and greater than or equal, respectively.

```
ifnull       ..., objectref => ...
ifnonnull    ..., objectref => ...

if_acmpeq    ..., objectref1, objectref2 => ...
if_acmpne    ..., objectref1, objectref2 => ...
```

Branching on objectrefs. When objectref is null/not null in the first set of bytecodes or objectref1 is equal/not equal to objectref2 in the second set, byte1 and byte2 are used to construct a signed 16-bit offset. Execution proceeds at that offset from the address of this bytecode. Otherwise, execution proceeds at the bytecode following.

```
lcmp         ..., v1.word1, v1.word2, v2.word1, v2.word2 => ..., result

fcmpl        ..., v1, v2 => ..., result
dcmpl        ..., v1.word1, v1.word2, v2.word1, v2.word2 => ..., result

fcmpg        ..., v1, v2 => ..., result
dcmpg        ..., v1.word1, v1.word2, v2.word1, v2.word2 => ..., result
```

v1 and v2 must be long, float, or double, respectively. They are both popped from the stack and compared. If v1 is greater than v2, the int value 1 is pushed onto the stack. If v1 is equal to v2, 0 is pushed onto the stack. If v1 is less than v2, -1 is pushed onto the stack. For floating-point, if either v1 or v2 is NaN, -1 is pushed onto the stack for the first pair of bytecodes, +1 for the second pair.

```
goto         -no change-
goto_w       -no change-
```

Branch always. byte1 and byte2 (plus byte3 and byte4 for goto_w) are used to construct a signed 16-bit (32-bit) offset. Execution proceeds at that offset from the address of this bytecode.

```
jsr          ... => ..., address
jsr_w        ... => ..., address
```

Jump subroutine. The address of the bytecode immediately following the jsr is pushed onto the stack as a returnAddress. byte1 and byte2 (plus byte3 and byte4 for jsr_w) are used to construct a signed 16-bit (32-bit) offset. Execution proceeds at that offset from the address of this bytecode.

21

```
ret          -no change-
```

Return from subroutine. Local variable byte1 in the current Java frame must contain a returnAddress. The contents of that local variable are written into the pc, and execution continues there.

NOTE

jsr pushes the returnAddress onto the stack, and ret gets it out of a local variable. This asymmetry is intentional. The jsr and ret bytecodes are used in the implementation of Java's finally keyword. Do not confuse ret with return, the bytecode described at the start of the next section.

Method Return

```
return       ... => [empty]
```

Return (void) from method. All values on the operand stack are discarded. The interpreter then returns control to the invoker of the method, making the frame of the invoker the current Java frame.

```
ireturn      ..., value => [empty]
lreturn      ..., value.word1, value.word2 => [empty]
freturn      ..., value => [empty]
dreturn      ..., value.word1, value.word2 => [empty]

areturn      ..., objectref  => [empty]
```

Return <type> (or object reference) from method. value must be a <type>. The value (or objectref) is pushed onto the stack of the previous execution environment. Any other values on the operand stack are discarded. The interpreter then returns control to the invoker of the method, making the frame of the invoker the current Java frame. <type> is, in turn, int, long, float, and double.

NOTE

The stack behavior of the "return" bytecodes may be confusing to anyone expecting the Java operand stack to be just like the C stack. Java's operand stack actually consists of a number of discontiguous segments, each corresponding to a method invocation. A return bytecode empties the Java operand stack segment corresponding to the frame of the current method invocation, but does not affect the segment of any parent invokers.

Table Jumping

```
tableswitch    ..., index => ...
```

tableswitch is a variable-length bytecode. Immediately after the tableswitch opcode, zero to three 0 bytes are inserted as padding so that the next byte begins at an offset from the start of this method that is a multiple of four. After the padding is a series of signed 4-byte quantities: default, low, high, and then (high - low + 1) further signed 4-byte offsets. These offsets are treated as a 0-based jump table.

The index must be an int. If index is less than low, or index is greater than high, default is added to the address of this bytecode. Otherwise, the (index - low)'th element of the jump table is extracted and added to the address of this bytecode. In either case, execution continues at this new address.

```
lookupswitch   ..., key => ...
```

lookupswitch is a variable-length bytecode. Immediately after the lookupswitch opcode, zero to three 0 bytes are inserted as padding so that the next byte begins at an offset from the start of this method that is a multiple of four. Immediately after the padding is a series of pairs of signed 4-byte quantities. The first pair is special; it contains the default offset and the number of pairs that follow. Each subsequent pair consists of a match and an offset.

The key on the stack must be an int. This key is compared to each of the matches. If it is equal to one of them, the corresponding offset is added to the address of this bytecode. If the key does not match any of the matches, the default offset is added to the address of this bytecode. In either case, execution continues at this new address.

NOTE The tableswitch and lookupswitch bytcodes are both used to implement the Java switch statement. The former is used for switches that are compact (have few gaps in the set of values to be matched), and the latter, for more sparse switches.

Manipulating Object Fields

```
getfield    ..., objectref => ..., value
getfield    ..., objectref => ..., value.word1, value.word2

putfield    ..., objectref, value => ...
putfield    ..., objectref, value.word1, value.word2 => ...
```

Fetch field from (or set field in) object. byte1 and byte2 are used to construct an index into the constant pool of the current class. The constant pool item will be a field reference to a class name and a field name. This item is resolved to find the field's width and offset (both in bytes).

21

For `getfield`, the `value` of the field at that offset from the start of the instance pointed to by `objectref` will replace `objectref` on the top of the stack, while for `setfield`, that field will be set to the `value` on the top of the stack. The first stack picture in each case is for one-word, and the second for two-word wide fields. These bytecodes handle both. If the specified field is `static`, an `IncompatibleClassChangeError` is thrown. If `objectref` is `null`, a `NullPointerException` is thrown.

```
getstatic        ..., => ..., value_
getstatic        ..., => ..., value.word1, value.word2

putstatic        ..., value => ...
putstatic        ..., value.word1, value.word2 => ...
```

Fetch static field from (set static field in) class. `byte1` and `byte2` are used to construct an index into the constant pool of the current class. The constant pool item will be a field reference to a static field of a class.

For `getstatic`, the `value` of that field is placed on the top of the stack, while for `setstatic`, that field will be set to have the `value` on the top of the stack. The first stack picture in each case is for one-word, and the second for two-word wide fields. These bytecodes handle both. If the specified field is not `static`, an `IncompatibleClassChangeError` is thrown.

 NOTE

> All four of these "accessor" bytecodes (and the various `invoke` bytecodes below) must perform special run-time checks if the field (method) involved has `protected` access, because that access mode requires a special relationship between the class of the current method and of the object being accessed. See *The Java Language Specification* for more details.

Method Invocation

```
invokestatic        ..., , [arg1, [arg2, ...]] => ...
```

Invoke class (`static`) method. The operand stack must contain some number of arguments. `byte1` and `byte2` are used to construct an index into the constant pool of the current class. The item at that index in the constant pool contains the complete method descriptor and class. The method descriptor is looked up in the method table of the class indicated. The method descriptor is guaranteed to exactly match one of the method descriptors in the class's method table.

The result of the lookup is a method block. The method block indicates the type of method (`native`, `synchronized`, and so on) and the number of arguments (`nargs`) expected on the operand stack. If the method is marked `synchronized`, the monitor associated with the class is entered.

The base of the local variables array for a new Java stack frame is set to point to a copy of arg1, making the supplied arguments (arg1, arg2, ...) the first nargs local variables of the new frame. The total number of local variables and other data used by the method is determined, and the base of the operand stack for this method invocation is set to the first word after them all. Finally, the pc is set to, and execution begins with, the first bytecode of the matched method (or via some implementation-dependent dispatch if it's native).

If the specified method is not static, an IncompatibleClassChangeError is thrown.

```
invokevirtual     ..., objectref, [arg1, [arg2, ...]] => ...
```

Invoke instance method based on run-time type. The operand stack must contain a reference to an object and some number of arguments. byte1 and byte2 are used to construct an index into the constant pool of the current class. The item at that index in the constant pool contains the complete method descriptor. A pointer to the object's method table is retrieved from the object reference. The method descriptor is looked up in the method table. The method descriptor is guaranteed to exactly match one of the method descriptors in the table.

The result of the lookup is an index into the method table of the named class that's used to look in the method table of the object's run-time type, where a pointer to the method block for the matched method is found. The method block indicates the type of method (native, synchronized, and so on) and the number of arguments (nargs) expected on the operand stack. If the method is marked synchronized, the monitor associated with objectref is entered.

The base of the local variables array for a new Java stack frame is set to point to a copy of objectref, making objectref and the supplied arguments (arg1, arg2, ...) the first nargs local variables of the new frame. The total number of local variables and other data used by the method is determined, and the base of the operand stack for this method invocation is set to the first word after them all. Finally, the pc is set to, and execution begins with, the first bytecode of the matched method (or via some implementation-dependent dispatch if it's native).

If the specified method is static, an IncompatibleClassChangeError is thrown. If it is abstract, an AbstractMethodError is thrown. If objectref is null, a NullPointerException is thrown.

```
invokespecial     ..., objectref, [arg1, [arg2, ...]] => ...
```

Invoke private, super, or <init> instance method with special handling. This bytecode is used to specially dispatch private, superclass, and initialization instance methods and, before JDK 1.0.2, it was otherwise identical to invokevirtual and was named invokenonvirtual. It is still identical except when the ACC_SUPER flag is set for the current class. In this case, superclass dispatches dynamically search up the superclass chain of parents, looking for the

21

closest matching method descriptor, and invoke that method. This correctly implements super from *The Java Language Specification*, and is also intuitively reasonable.

```
invokeinterface    ..., objectref, [arg1, [arg2, ...]] => ...
```

Invoke interface method. This bytecode, used to specially dispatch interface instance methods, is identical to invokevirtual except for the following points. The number of available arguments (nargs) resolved must agree with byte3 (stored there for historical reasons). byte4 must be zero (it is reserved for internal (_quick) use. The method descriptor resolved is not guaranteed to exactly match a method table entry—the table must be searched, and if a matching method is not found, an IncompatibleClassChangeError is thrown. Finally, in addition to the other errors thrown by invokevirtual, if the matching method is not public, an IllegalAccessError is thrown.

Exception Handling

```
athrow             ..., objectref => objectref
```

Throw exception or error. objectref must be a reference to an instance of Throwable (or a subclass). The current Java stack frame is searched for the most recent catch clause that handles the exception. If a matching clause is found, the pc is reset to the address indicated by it for the start of the handler code, and execution continues there (after clearing the stack and pushing objectref back onto it).

If no appropriate catch clause is found in the current stack frame, that frame is popped and objectref is rethrown, starting the process all over again in the parent frame (and making its stack look like the right side of the stack picture above). If objectref is null, then a NullPointerException is thrown instead.

Miscellaneous Object Operations

```
new                ... => ..., objectref
```

Create new object. byte1 and byte2 are used to construct an index into the constant pool of the current class. The item at that index must resolve to a class (not an array or interface). A new instance of that class is then created, and a reference (objectref) to the instance is placed on the top of the stack. Note that the instance is not fully ready for use until its <init> method is invoked. If the resolved class is abstract, an InstantiationError is thrown. If the current class cannot access the resolved class, an IllegalAccessError is thrown.

```
checkcast          ..., objectref => ..., objectref
```

Make sure object is of given type. byte1 and byte2 are used to construct an index into the constant pool of the current class. The item at that index of the constant pool must resolve to an array, class, or interface.

checkcast determines whether objectref can be cast to that array, class, or interface. (A null objectref can be cast to anything.) If objectref can be legally cast, execution proceeds at the next bytecode, and the objectref remains on the stack. If not, a ClassCastException is thrown.

```
instanceof          ..., objectref => ..., result
```

Determine whether object is of given type. byte1 and byte2 are used to construct an index into the constant pool of the current class. The item at that index of the constant pool must resolve to an array, class, or interface.

If objectref is null, the result is 0 (false). Otherwise, instanceof determines whether objectref can be legally cast to that array, class, or interface. The result is 1 (true) if it can, and 0 (false) otherwise.

NOTE
Whether or not a cast is legal is usually as simple as whether objectref is an instance of the resolved class or one of its subclasses, or is an instance of a class that implements the resolved interface. The complications come when testing arrays. See *The Java Language Specification* for more details.

Monitor Operations

```
monitorenter        ..., objectref => ...
```

Enter monitored region of code. The interpreter attempts to obtain exclusive access via a lock mechanism to objectref. If another thread already has objectref locked, the current thread waits until the objectref is unlocked. If the current thread already has objectref locked, an internal counter is incremented, and execution continues normally. If objectref has no lock on it, this bytecode obtains an exclusive lock. If objectref is null, a NullPointerException is thrown.

```
monitorexit         ..., objectref => ...
```

Exit monitored region of code. The lock on objectref is released. If this is the last lock that this thread has on that objectref (one thread is allowed to have multiple locks on a single objectref), other threads that are waiting for objectref are allowed to proceed. If objectref is null, a NullPointerException is thrown. If this thread had not locked objectref, an IllegalMonitorStateException is thrown.

21

Wide Bytecodes

```
wide            <same as modified bytecode>
```

Execute bytecode with larger index. byte1 must be the <opcode> of another bytecode that accesses a local variable in the current Java frame. <opcode> can either be iinc, or from the set iload, lload, fload, dload, aload, istore, lstore, fstore, dstore, astore, and ret. For iinc, byte4 and byte5 are used to construct a new constant to be added to the local variable. For all <opcode>s, byte2 and byte3 are used to construct the new (wider) index into the local variables. In all other ways, the modified bytecode acts the same as it would in its unmodified form.

Although the bytecode is "modified," this does not mean that somehow the original bytecode is still there. The wide bytecode takes the original bytecode's <opcode> as an operand, forming a brand new bytecode that must be treated as a unit. (For example, you cannot branch into the middle of the wide bytecode to execute the original bytecode.)

Reserved Bytecodes

```
breakpoint      -no change-
```

Call breakpoint handler. Typically, the breakpoint bytecode is used to overwrite a bytecode to force control temporarily back to a debugger prior to the effect of the overwritten bytecode. The original bytecode's operands (if any) are not overwritten, and the original bytecode is restored when the breakpoint bytecode is removed.

```
impdep1         [undefined]
impdep2         [undefined]
```

Implementation-dependent traps. Typically, these "back doors" would be used to trigger implementation-specific behaviour inside a virtual machine implementation, or would be used to interact with just-in-time compilers or sophisticated debuggers.

NOTE

None of these reserved bytecodes can appear in .class files, but are reserved simply to help the various tools that might run after .class files are loaded and executing to gracefully interact with one another.

21

The `quick` **Bytecodes**

The following discussion, straight out of the Java virtual machine documentation, shows you an example of the cleverness mentioned earlier that's needed to make a bytecode interpreter fast:

> The following set of pseudo-bytecodes, suffixed by `quick`, are all variants of standard Java bytecodes. They are used by the run-time to improve the execution speed of the bytecode interpreter. They aren't officially part of the virtual machine specification and are invisible outside a Java virtual machine implementation. However, inside that implementation they have proven to be an effective optimization.
>
> First, you should know that `javac` still generates only non-`quick` bytecodes. Second, all bytecodes that have a _quick variant reference the constant pool. When `quick` optimization is turned on, each non-`quick` bytecode (that has a _quick variant) resolves the specified item in the constant pool, signals an error if the item in the constant pool could not be resolved for some reason, turns itself into the `quick` variant of itself, and then performs its intended operation.
>
> This is identical to the actions of the non-`quick` bytecode, except for the step of overwriting itself with its `quick` variant. The `quick` variant of a bytecode assumes that the item in the constant pool has already been resolved, and that this resolution did not produce any errors. It simply performs the intended operation on the resolved item.

Thus, as your bytecodes are being interpreted, they are automatically getting faster and faster! Here are all the `quick` variants in the current Java run-time:

```
ldc_quick
ldc_w_quick
ldc2_w_quick

anewarray_quick
multinewarray_quick

getfield_quick
getfield_quick_w
getfield2_quick
putfield_quick
putfield_quick_w
putfield2_quick
getstatic_quick
getstatic2_quick
putstatic_quick
putstatic2_quick
```

21

```
invokestatic_quick
invokevirtual_quick
invokevirtual_quick_w
invokevirtualobject_quick
invokenonvirtual_quick
invokesuper_quick
invokeinterface_quick

new_quick
checkcast_quick
instanceof_quick
```

If you'd like to go back in today's lesson and look at what each of these does, you can often find the name of the original bytecode on which a quick variant is based by simply removing the quick (or quick_w) from its name. The exceptions are: invokevirtualobject_quick, which is a special variant of invokevirtual to make array (Object) methods fast; invokenonvirtual_quick and invokesuper_quick, which are variants of invokespecial, the latter of which handles the new super behaviour correctly; and getfield2_quick, setfield2_quick, getstatic2_quick, and setstatic2_quick, which represent the two-word (stack picture) variants of their original bytecodes. The quick bytecodes ending in w behave closest to the original bytecodes, while their counterparts without the w are special variants that assume smaller indices and can thus operate faster.

NOTE

Various tools (like debuggers and just-in-time compilers) may need to "recognize," or at least to ignore, special bytecodes like the quick ones. Part of new APIs in 1.1 to support this layer of interaction with the virtual machine and just the start of what promises to be a whole new layer of access to Java for the lowest-level tools.

One last note on implementing the quick optimization, regarding Sun's unusual handling of the constant pool (for detail fanatics only):

When a class is read in, an array constant_pool[] of size nconstants is created and assigned to a field in the class. constant_pool[0] is set to point to a dynamically allocated array that indicates which fields in the constant_pool have already been resolved. constant_pool[1] through constant_pool[nconstants - 1] are set to point at the "type" field that corresponds to this constant item.

When a bytecode is executed that references the constant pool, an index is generated, and constant_pool[0] is checked to see whether the index has already been resolved. If so, the value of constant_pool[index] is returned. If not, the value of constant_pool[index] is resolved to be the actual pointer or data, and overwrites whatever value was already in constant_pool[index].

The .class File Format

You won't be given the entire .class file format here, only a taste of what it's like. (You can read all about it *The Java Virtual Machine Specification*.) It's mentioned here because it is one of the parts of Java that needs to be specified carefully if all Java implementations are to be compatible with one another, and if Java byte codes are expected to travel across arbitrary networks—to and from arbitrary computers and operating systems—and yet arrive safely.

The rest of this section paraphrases, and extensively condenses, an early version of the .class documentation.

.class files are used to hold the compiled versions of both Java classes and Java interfaces. Compliant Java interpreters must be capable of dealing with all .class files that conform to the following specification.

A Java .class file consists of a stream of 8-bit bytes. All 16-bit and 32-bit quantities are constructed by reading in two or four 8-bit bytes, respectively. The bytes are joined together in big-endian order. (`java.io.DataInput`, `java.io.DataInputStream`, `java.io.DataOutput`, and `java.io.DataOutputStream` can be used to read and write class files properly.)

The class file format is presented below as a series of C-struct-like pseudostructures. However, unlike a C struct, there is no padding or alignment between pieces of the structure, each field of the structure may be of variable size, and an array may be of variable size (in this case, some field prior to the array gives the array's dimension). The types u1, u2, and u4 represent an unsigned one-, two-, or four-byte quantity, respectively.

Attributes are used at several different places in the .class format. All attributes have the following format:

```
attribute_info {
    u2 attribute_name_index;
    u4 attribute_length;
    u1 info[attribute_length];
}
```

The `attribute_name_index` is a 16-bit index into the class's constant pool; the value of `constant_pool[attribute_name_index]` is a string giving the name of the attribute. The field `attribute_length` gives the length of the subsequent information in bytes. This length does not include the six bytes needed to store `attribute_name_index` and `attribute_length`.

Certain attributes are predefined as part of the .class file specification: SourceFile, which specifies the name of the .java file which produced this .class file; ConstantValue, which holds constant (`static`) initialization values; Code, which holds information needed for a method's execution, as well as holding its bytecodes; Exceptions, which list the checked exceptions of a method; and the LineNumberTable and LocalVariableTable, which together help

21

source-level debuggers to output human-readable output. The Code, ConstantValue, and Exceptions attributes must be recognized by all .class file readers, but the rest are optional. In the future, more required and optional attributes may be added. All .class file readers are expected to skip over and ignore the information in any attributes that they do not understand.

The following pseudo-structure gives a top-level description of the format of a class file:

```
ClassFile {
    u4   magic;
    u2   minor_version
    u2   major_version
    u2   constant_pool_count;
    cp_info         constant_pool[constant_pool_count - 1];
    u2   access_flags;
    u2   this_class;
    u2   super_class;
    u2   interfaces_count;
    u2   interfaces[interfaces_count];
    u2   fields_count;
    field_info      fields[fields_count];
    u2   methods_count;
    method_info     methods[methods_count];
    u2   attributes_count;
    attribute_info  attributes[attribute_count];
}
```

Here's one of the smaller structures used:

```
method_info {
    u2   access_flags;
    u2   name_index;
    u2   descriptor_index;
    u2   attributes_count;
    attribute_info  attributes[attribute_count];
}
```

Finally, here's a sample of one of the later structures in the .class file description:

```
Code_attribute {
    u2   attribute_name_index;
    u4   attribute_length;
    u2   max_stack;
    u2   max_locals;
    u4   code_length;
    u1   code[code_length];
    u2   exception_table_length;
    {   u2   start_pc;
        u2   end_pc;
        u2   handler_pc;
        u2   catch_type;
    }   exception_table[exception_table_length];
    u2   attributes_count;
    attribute_info  attributes[attribute_count];
}
```

None of this is meant to be completely comprehensible (though you might be able to guess at what a lot of the pseudostructure members are for), but just suggestive of the sort of structures that live inside .class files. Because the compiler and run-time sources are available, you can always begin with them if you actually have to read or write .class files yourself. Thus, you don't need to have a deep understanding of the details to get started, even in that case.

Limitations

The current virtual machine and .class file format specifications place some restrictions on legal Java programs. These limitations and their implications are:

- ☐ One-word pointers, which imply that the virtual machine can usually address only 4G of memory on 32-bit machines

- ☐ Unsigned 16-bit indices into the exception, line number, and local variable tables, which limit the size of a method's bytecode implementation to 64K bytes

- ☐ Unsigned 16-bit indices into the constant pool, which limit the number of constants in a class to 64K, a limit on the overall complexity of a class

- ☐ Unsigned 16-bit sizes in max_locals and max_stack, which limit the number of local variables in a method to 64K, and the size of the operand stack to 64K words, respectively

- ☐ Unsigned 16-bit counts in fields_count and methods_count, which limit the number of fields, and methods, respectively, in a class to 64K

- ☐ Unsigned 8-bit dimension operands to multinewarray, which limit the number of dimensions in an array to 255

In addition, a valid Java method descriptor (described further in the next section) cannot require more than 255 words of method arguments. Although this means that you can have up to 255 arguments of most (one-word) types, you can have only 127 of them if they're all long or double (two-word types).

NOTE For instance methods, due to a hidden this parameter passed by the virtual machine, this limit of 255 words is reduced to 254. static methods can still use 255 words.

21

Method Descriptors

Because method descriptors are used in .class files, now is an appropriate time to explore them in the detail promised on earlier days—but they're probably most useful to you when writing the `native` methods of yesterday's lesson.

 A *descriptor* is a string representing the type of a field, a return value, a parameter, or a method.

A *field descriptor* represents the type of a class or instance variable, and is a series of characters in the following grammar:

```
<field descriptor>  := <field_type>
<field type>        := <base_type> ¦ <object_type> ¦ <array_type>
<base_type>         := B ¦ C ¦ D ¦ F ¦ I ¦ J ¦ S ¦ Z
<object_type>       := L <full/package/name/ClassName> ;
<array_type>        := [ <component_type>
<component_type>    := <field_type>
```

Here are the meanings of the base types: B (byte), C (char), D (double), F (float), I (int), J (long), S (short), and Z (boolean).

A *return descriptor* represents the return value from a method, and is a series of characters in the following grammar:

```
<return descriptor>    := <field type> ¦ V
```

The character V (void) indicates that the method returns no value. Otherwise, the descriptor indicates the type of the return value. A *parameter descriptor* represents a parameter passed to a method:

```
<parameter descriptor> := <field type>
```

Finally, a *method descriptor* represents the parameters that the method expects, and the value that it returns (<x>* means 0 or more <x>s):

```
<method_descriptor>    := (<parameter_descriptor>*) <return descriptor>
```

Let's try out the new rules: a method called `complexMethod()` in the class `my.package.name.ComplexClass` takes three arguments—a `long`, a `boolean`, and a two-dimensional array of `shorts`—and returns this. Then, `(JZ[[S)Lmy/package/name/ComplexClass;` is its method descriptor.

A method descriptor is often prefixed by the name of the method, or by its full package (using an underscore in the place of dots) and its class name followed by a slash / and the name of the method, to form a "fully-specified" method descriptor. (You saw several of these generated in stub comments yesterday.) Now, at last, you have the full story! Thus, the following:

```
my_package_name_ComplexClass/complexMethod(JZ[[S)Lmy/package/name/ComplexClass;
```

is the fully-specified method descriptor for `complexMethod()`. (Phew!)

The Garbage Collector

Decades ago, programmers in both the Lisp and the Smalltalk community realized how extremely valuable it is to be able to ignore memory deallocation. They realized that, although allocation is fundamental, deallocation is forced on the programmer by the laziness of the system—it should be able to figure out what is no longer useful, and get rid of it. In relative obscurity, these pioneering programmers developed a whole series of garbage collectors to perform this job, each getting more sophisticated and efficient as the years went by. Finally, now that the mainstream programming community has begun to recognize the value of this automated technique, Java can become the first really widespread application of the technology those pioneers developed.

The Problem

Imagine that you're a programmer in a C-like language (probably not too difficult for you, because these languages are the dominant ones right now). Each time you create something, anything, dynamically in such a language, you are completely responsible for tracking the life of this object throughout your program and mentally deciding when it will be safe to deallocate it. This can be quite a difficult (sometimes impossible) task, because any of the other libraries or methods you've called might have "squirreled away" a pointer to the object, unbeknownst to you. When it becomes impossible to know, you simply choose never to deallocate the object, or at least to wait until every library and method invocation involved has completed, which could be nearly as long.

The uneasy feeling you get when writing such code is a natural, healthy response to what is inherently an unsafe and unreliable style of programming. If you have tremendous discipline—and so does everyone who writes every library and method you call—you can, in principle, survive this responsibility without too many mishaps. But aren't you human? Aren't they? There must be some small slips in this perfect discipline due to error. What's worse, such errors are virtually undetectable, as anyone who's tried to hunt down a stray pointer problem in C will tell you. What about the thousands of programmers who don't have that sort of discipline?

21

Another way to ask this question is: Why should any programmers be forced to have this discipline, when it is entirely possible for the system to remove this heavy burden from their shoulders?

Software engineering estimates have recently shown that for every 55 lines of production C-like code in the world, there is one bug. This means that your electric razor has about 80 bugs, and your TV, 400. Soon they will have even more, because the size of this kind of embedded computer software is growing exponentially. When you begin to think of how much C-like code is in your car's engine, it should give you pause.

Many of these errors are due to the misuse of pointers, by misunderstanding or by accident, and to the early, incorrect freeing of allocated objects in memory. Java addresses both of these—the former, by eliminating explicit pointers from the Java language altogether and the latter, by including, in every Java system, a garbage collector that solves the problem.

The Solution

Imagine a run-time system that tracks each object you create, notices when the last reference to it has vanished, and frees the object for you. How could such a thing actually work?

One brute-force approach, tried early in the days of garbage collecting, is to attach a reference counter to every object. When the object is created, the counter is set to 1. Each time a new reference to the object is made, the counter is incremented, and each time such a reference disappears, the counter is decremented. Because all such references are controlled by the language—as variables and assignments, for example—the compiler can tell whenever an object reference might be created or destroyed, just as it does in handling the scoping of local variables, and thus it can assist with this task. The system itself "holds onto" a set of root objects that are considered too important to be freed. The class Object is one example of such a V.I.P. object. (V.I.O.?) Finally, all that's needed is to test, after each decrement, whether the counter has hit 0. If it has, the object is freed.

If you think carefully about this approach, you will soon convince yourself that it is definitely correct when it decides to free anything. It is so simple that you can immediately tell that it will work. The low-level hacker in you might also feel that if it's that simple, it's probably not fast enough to run at the lowest level of the system—and you'd be right.

Think about all the stack frames, local variables, method arguments, return values, and local variables created in the course of even a few hundred milliseconds of a program's life. For each of these tiny, nano-steps in the program, an extra increment—at best—or decrement, test, and deallocation—at worst—will be added to the running time of the program. In fact, the first garbage collectors were slow enough that many predicted they could never be used at all!

21

Luckily, a whole generation of smart programmers has invented a big bag of tricks to solve these overhead problems. One trick is to introduce special "transient object" areas that don't need to be reference counted. The best of these generational scavenging garbage collectors today can take less than 3 percent of the total time of your program—a remarkable feat if you realize that many other language features, such as loop overheads, can be as large or larger!

There are other problems with garbage collection. If you are constantly freeing and reclaiming space in a program, won't the heap of objects soon become fragmented, with small holes everywhere and no room to create new, large objects? Because the programmer is now free from the chains of manual deallocation, won't they create even more objects than usual?

What's worse, there is another way that this simple reference counting scheme is inefficient, in space rather than time. If a long chain of object references eventually comes full circle, back to the starting object, each object's reference count remains at least 1 forever. None of these objects will ever be freed!

Together, these problems imply that a good garbage collector must, every once in a while, step back to compact or to clean up wasted memory.

Compaction occurs when a garbage collector steps back and reorganizes memory, eliminating the holes created by fragmentation. Compacting memory is simply a matter of repositioning objects one-by-one into a new, compact grouping that places them all in a row, leaving all the free memory in the heap in one big piece.

Cleaning up the circular garbage still lying around after reference counting is called *marking and sweeping*. A mark-and-sweep of memory involves first marking every root object in the system and then following all the object references inside those objects to new objects to mark, and so on, recursively. Then, when you have no more references to follow, you "sweep away" all the unmarked objects, and compact memory as before.

The good news is that this solves the space problems you were having. The bad news is that when the garbage collector "steps back" and does these operations, a nontrivial amount of time passes during which your program is unable to run—all its objects are being marked, swept, rearranged, and so forth, in what seems like an uninterruptible procedure. Your first hint to a solution is the word "seems."

Garbage collecting can actually be done a little at a time, between or in parallel with normal program execution, thus dividing up the large time needed to "step back" into numerous so-small-you-don't-notice-them chunks of time that happen between the cracks. (Of course, years of smart thinking went into the abstruse algorithms that make all this possible!)

21

One final problem that might worry you a little has to do with these object references. Aren't these "pointers" scattered throughout your program and not just buried in objects? Even if they're only in objects, don't they have to be changed whenever the object they point to is moved by these procedures? The answer to both of these questions is a resounding yes, and overcoming them is the final hurdle to making an efficient garbage collector.

There are really only two choices. The first, brute force, assumes that all the memory containing object references needs to be searched on a regular basis, and whenever the object references found by this search match objects that have moved, the old reference is changed. This assumes that there are "hard" pointers in the heap's memory—ones that point directly to other objects. By introducing various kinds of "soft" pointers, including pointers that are like forwarding addresses, the algorithm improves greatly. Although these brute-force approaches sound slow, it turns out that modern computers can do them fast enough to be useful.

NOTE

> You might wonder how the brute-force techniques identify object references. In early systems, references were specially tagged with a "pointer bit," so they could be unambiguously located. Now, so-called conservative garbage collectors simply assume that if it looks like an object reference, it is—at least for the purposes of the mark and sweep. Later, when actually trying to update it, they can find out whether it really is an object reference or not.

The final approach to handling object references, and the one Java currently uses, is also one of the very first ones tried. It involves using 100 percent "soft" pointers. An object reference (objectref) is actually an indirect index, sometimes called an "OOP," to the real pointer, and a large object table exists to map these OOPs into the actual object reference. Although this does introduce extra overhead on almost every object reference (some of which can be eliminated by clever tricks, as you might guess), it's not too high a price to pay for this incredibly valuable level of indirection.

This indirection allows the garbage collector, for example, to mark, sweep, move, or examine one object at a time. Each object can be independently moved "out from under" a running Java program by changing only the object table entries. This not only allows the "step back" phase to happen in the tiniest steps, but it makes a garbage collector that runs literally in parallel with your program much easier to write. This is what the Java garbage collector does.

You need to be very careful about garbage collection when you're doing critical, real-time programs (such as those mentioned yesterday that legitimately require `native` methods)—but how often will your Java code be flying a commercial airliner in real-time, anyway?

Java's Parallel Garbage Collector

Java applies almost all these advanced techniques to give you a fast, efficient, parallel garbage collector. Running in a separate thread, it cleans up the Java environment of almost all trash (it is conservative), silently and in the background, is efficient in both space and time, and never steps back for more than a small amount of time. You should never need to know it's there.

By the way, if you want to force a full mark-and-sweep garbage collection to happen soon, you can do so simply by calling the `System.gc()` method. You might want to do this if you just freed up a majority of the heap's memory in circular garbage, and want it all taken away quickly. You might also call this whenever you're idle, as a hint to the system about when it would be best to come and collect the garbage. This "meta knowledge" is rarely needed by the system, however.

Ideally, you'll never notice the garbage collector, and all those decades of programmers beating their brains out on your behalf will simply let you sleep better at night—and what's wrong with that?

The Security Story

Speaking of sleeping well at night, if you haven't stepped back yet and said, "You mean Java programs will be running rampant on the Internet!?!" you better do so now, for it is a legitimate concern. In fact, it is one of the major technical stumbling blocks (the others being mostly social and economic) to achieving the dream of ubiquity and code sharing mentioned earlier in today's lesson.

Why You Should Worry

Any powerful, flexible technology can be abused. As the Net becomes mainstream and widespread, it, too, will be abused. Already, there have been many blips on the security radar screens of those of us who worry about such things, warning that (at least until today), not

21

enough attention has been paid by the computer industry (or the media) to solving some of the problems that this new world brings with it. One of the benefits of constructively solving security once and for all will be a flowering unseen before in the virtual communities of the Net; whole new economies based on people's attention and creativity will spring to life, rapidly transforming our world in new and positive ways.

The downside to all this new technology, is that we (or someone!) must worry long and hard about how to make the playgrounds of the future safe for our children, and for us. Fortunately, Java is a big part of the answer.

Why You Might Not Have To

What gives me any confidence that the Java language and environment will be safe, that it will solve the technically daunting and extremely thorny problems inherent in any good form of security, especially for networks?

One simple reason is the history of the people, and the company, that created Java. Many of them are the very smart programmers referred to throughout the book, who helped pioneer many of the ideas that make Java great and who have worked hard over the decades to make techniques such as garbage collection a mainstream reality. They are technically capable of tackling and solving the hard problems that need to be solved. In particular, from discussions with Chuck McManis and Marianne Mueller, two of Java's security gurus, I have confidence that they have thought through these hard problems deeply, and that they knows what needs to be done.

Sun Microsystems, the company, has been pushing networks as the central theme of all its software for more than a decade. Sun has the engineers and the commitment needed to solve these hard problems, because these same problems are at the very center of both its future business and its vision of the future, in which networking is the center of everything—and global networks are nearly useless without good security. For example, in late 1995, to oversee all of Sun's Net security software, Sun chose Whitfield Diffie, the man who discovered the underlying ideas on which essentially all interesting forms of modern encryption are based.

Enough on "deep background." What does the Java environment provide right now that helps me feel secure?

Java's Security Model

Java protects you against potentially nasty Java code via a series of interlocking defenses that, together, form an imposing barrier to any and all such attacks.

21

WARNING

Of course, no one can protect people from their own potential ignorance or carelessness. The kind of person who blindly downloads binary executables from an Internet browser and runs them is already in more danger than Java will ever pose.

As a user of this powerful new medium, the Internet, you should educate yourself to the possible threats this new and exciting world entails. In particular, downloading "auto running macros" or reading e-mail with "executable attachments" is just as much a threat as downloading binaries from the Net and running them.

Java does not introduce any new dangers here, but by being the first mainstream use of executable and mobile code on the Net, it is responsible for making people suddenly aware of the dangers that have always been there. Java is already, as you will soon see, much less dangerous than any of these common activities on the Net, and can be made safer still over time. Most of these other (dangerous) activities can never be made safe. So please, do not do them!

A good guideline on the Net is: Don't download anything that you plan to execute (or that will be automatically executed for you) except from someone (or some company) you know well and with whom you've had positive, personal experience. If you don't care about losing all the data on your hard drive, or don't care about your privacy, you can do anything you like, but for most of us, this rule should be law.

Fortunately, Java allows you to relax that law. You can run Java applets from anyone, anywhere, in relative safety.

Java's powerful security mechanisms act at four different levels of the system architecture. First, the Java language itself was designed to be safe, and the Java compiler ensures that source code doesn't violate these safety rules. Second, all bytecodes executed by the run-time are screened to be sure that they also obey these rules. (This layer guards against having an altered compiler produce code that violates the safety rules.) Third, the class loader ensures that classes don't violate namespace or access restrictions when they are loaded into the system. Finally, API-specific security prevents applets from doing destructive things. This final layer depends on the security and integrity guarantees from the other three layers.

Let's now examine each of these layers in turn.

21

The Language and the Compiler

The Java language and its compiler are the first line of defense. Java was designed to be a safe language.

Most other C-like languages have facilities to control access to "objects," but also have ways to "forge" access to objects (or to parts of objects), usually by (mis-)using pointers. This introduces two fatal security flaws to any system built on these languages. One is that no object can protect itself from outside modification, duplication, or "spoofing" (others pretending to be that object). Another is that a language with powerful pointers is more likely to have serious bugs that compromise security. These pointer bugs, where a "runaway pointer" starts modifying some other object's memory, were responsible for most of the public (and not-so-public) security problems on the Internet this past decade.

Java eliminates these threats in one stroke by eliminating pointers from the language altogether. There are still pointers of a kind—object references—but these are carefully controlled to be safe: they are unforgeable, and all casts are checked for legality before being allowed. In addition, powerful new array facilities in Java not only help to offset the loss of pointers, but add additional safety by strictly enforcing array bounds, catching more bugs for the programmer (bugs that, in other languages, might lead to unexpected and, thus, bad-guy-exploitable problems).

The language definition, and the compilers that enforce it, create a powerful barrier to any "nasty" Java programmer.

Because an overwhelming majority of the "Net-savvy" software on the Internet may soon be Java, its safe language definition and compilers help to guarantee that most of this software has a solid, secure base. With fewer bugs, Net software will be more predictable—a property that thwarts attacks.

Verifying the Bytecodes

What if that "nasty" programmer gets a little more determined, and rewrites the Java compiler to suit his nefarious purposes? The Java run-time, getting the lion's share of its bytecodes from the Net, can never tell whether those bytecodes were generated by a "trustworthy" compiler. Therefore, it must verify that they meet all the safety requirements.

Before running any bytecodes, the run-time subjects them to a rigorous series of tests that vary in complexity from simple format checks all the way to running a theorem prover, to make certain that they are playing by the rules. These tests verify that the bytecodes do not forge pointers, violate access restrictions, access objects as other than what they are (`InputStreams` are always used as `InputStreams`, and never as anything else), invoke methods with inappropriate parameter values or types, nor overflow the stack.

Consider the following Java code sample:

```
public class VectorTest {
    public int  array[];

    public int  sum() {
        int[]  localArray = array;
        int    sum        = 0;

        for (int  i = localArray.length; --i >= 0;  )
            sum += localArray[i];
        return sum;
    }
}
```

The bytecodes generated when this code is compiled look something like the following:

aload_0	Load this
getfield #10	Load this.array
astore_1	Store in localArray
iconst_0	Load 0
istore_2	Store in sum
aload_1	Load localArray
arraylength	Gets its length
istore_3	Store in i
A: iinc 3 -1	Subtract 1 from i
iload_3	Load i
iflt B	Exit loop if < 0
iload_2	Load sum
aload_1	Load localArray
iload_3	Load i
iaload	Load localArray[i]
iadd	Add sum
istore_2	Store in sum
goto A	Do it again
B: iload_2	Load sum
ireturn	Return it

21

NOTE

> The excellent examples and descriptions in this section of the book are paraphrased from a tremendously informative early Java security paper by Frank Yellin. The latest version of this paper is called "Low Level Security in Java" (`http://java.sun.com/sfaq/verifier.html`).

Extra Type Information and Requirements

Java bytecodes encode more type information than is strictly necessary for the interpreter. Even though, for example, the `aload` and `iload` opcodes do exactly the same thing, `aload` is always used to load an object reference and `iload` used to load an integer. Some bytecodes (such as `getfield`) include a constant pool (symbol table) reference—and that reference has even more type information. This extra type information allows the run-time system to guarantee that Java objects and data aren't illegally manipulated.

Conceptually, before and after each bytecode is executed, every slot in the stack and every local variable has some type. This collection of type information—all the slots and local variables—is called the *type state* of the execution environment. An important requirement of the Java type state is that it must be determinable statically by induction—that is, before any program code is executed. As a result, as the run-time systems reads bytecodes, each is required to have the following inductive property: given only the type state before the execution of the bytecode, the type state afterward must be fully determined.

Given "straight-line" bytecodes (no branches), and starting with a known stack state, the state of each slot in the stack is therefore always known. For example, starting with an empty stack:

`iload_1`	Load integer variable. Stack type state is I.
`iconst 5`	Load integer constant. Stack type state is II.
`iadd`	Add two integers, producing an integer. Stack type state is I.

NOTE

> Smalltalk and PostScript bytecodes do not have this restriction. Their more dynamic type behavior does create additional flexibility in those systems, but Java needs to provide a secure execution environment. It must therefore know all types at all times, in order to guarantee a certain level of security.

Another requirement made by the Java run-time is that when a set of bytecodes can take more than one path to arrive at the same point, all such paths must arrive there with exactly the same type state. This is a strict requirement, and implies, for example, that compilers cannot generate bytecodes that load all the elements of an array onto the stack. (Because each time through such a loop the stack's type state changes, the start of the loop—"the same point" in multiple paths—would have more than one type state, which is not allowed).

The Verifier

Bytecodes are checked for compliance with all these requirements, using the extra type information in a .class file, by a part of the run-time called the *verifier*. It examines each bytecode in turn, constructing the full type state as it goes, and verifies that all the types of parameters, arguments, and results are correct. Thus, the verifier acts as a gatekeeper to your run-time environment, letting in only those bytecodes that pass muster.

WARNING

> The verifier is the crucial piece of Java's security, and it depends on your having a correctly implemented (no bugs, intentional or otherwise) run-time system. As of this writing, only Sun is producing fully compliant Java run-times, and theirs are secure. In the future, however, you should be careful when downloading or buying another company's (or individual's) version of the Java run-time environment. Sun has implemented validation suites for run-times, compilers, and so forth to be sure that they are safe and correct, but they have not yet been applied to all existing implementations. In the meantime, *caveat emptor*! Your run-time is the base on which all the rest of Java's security is built, so make sure it is a good, solid, secure base.

When bytecodes have passed the verifier, they are guaranteed not to: cause any operand stack under- or overflows; use parameter, argument, or return types incorrectly; illegally convert data from one type to another (from an integer to a pointer, for example); nor access any object's fields illegally (that is, the verifier checks that the rules for public, private, package, and protected are obeyed).

As an added bonus, because the interpreter can now count on all these facts being true, it can run much faster than before. All the required checks for safety have been done up front, so it can run at full throttle. In addition, object references can now be treated as capabilities, because they are unforgeable—capabilities allow, for example, advanced security models for file I/O and authentication to be safely built on top of Java.

21

Because you can now trust that a `private` variable really is private, and that no bytecode can perform some magic with casts to extract information from it (such as your credit card number), many of the security problems that might arise in other, less safe environments simply vanish! These guarantees also make erecting barriers against destructive applets possible, and easier. Because the Java system doesn't have to worry about "nasty" bytecodes, it can reliably create other, higher levels of security for you.

The Class Loader

The class loader is another kind of gatekeeper, albeit a higher-level one. The verifier was the security of last resort. The class loader is the security of first resort.

When a new class is loaded into the system, it is placed into (lives in) one of several different "realms." In the current release, there are three possible realms: your local computer, the firewall-guarded local network on which your computer is located, and the Internet (the global Net). Each of these realms is treated differently by the class loader.

Actually, there can be as many realms as your desired level of security (or paranoia) requires. This is because the class loader is under your control. As a programmer, you can make your own class loader that implements your own peculiar brand of security. (This is a radical step: you may have to give the users of your program a whole bunch of classes—and they give you a whole lot of trust—to accomplish this.)

As a user, you can tell your Java-enabled browser, or Java system, what realm of security (of the three) you'd like it to implement for you right now, or from now on.

As a system administrator, Java has global security policies that you can set up to help guide your users to not "give away the store" (that is, set all their preferences to be unrestricted, promiscuous, "hurt me please!").

In particular, the class loader never allows a class from a "less protected" realm to replace a class from a more protected realm. The file system's I/O primitives, about which you should be very worried (and rightly so), are all defined in a local Java class, which means that they all live in the local-computer realm. Thus, no class from outside your computer (from either the supposedly trustworthy local network or from the Internet) can take the place of these classes and "spoof" Java code into using "nasty" versions of these primitives. In addition, classes in one realm cannot call upon the methods of classes in other realms, unless those classes have explicitly declared those methods public. This implies that classes from other than your local computer cannot even *see* the file system I/O methods, much less call them, unless you or the system wants them to.

In addition, every new applet loaded from the network is placed into a separate package-like namespace. This means that applets are protected even from each other! No applet can access another's methods (or variables) without its cooperation. Applets from inside the firewall can even be treated differently from those outside the firewall, if you like.

NOTE

Actually, it's all a little more complex than this. In the current release, an applet is in a package "namespace" along with any other applets from that source. This source, or origin, is most often a host (domain name) on the Internet. This special "subrealm" is used extensively in the next section. Depending on where the source is located, outside the firewall (or inside), further restrictions may apply (or be removed entirely). This model is likely to be extended in future releases of Java, providing an even finer degree of control over which classes get to do what.

The class loader essentially partitions the world of Java classes into small, protected little groups, about which you can safely make assumptions that will always be true. This type of predictability is the key to well-behaved and secure programs.

You've now seen the full lifetime of a method. It starts as source code on some computer, is compiled into bytecodes on some (possibly different) computer, and can then travel (as a .class file) into any file system or network anywhere in the world. When you run an applet in a Java-enabled browser (or download a class and run it by hand using java), the method's bytecodes are extracted from its .class file and carefully looked over by the verifier. Once they are declared safe, the interpreter can execute them for you (or a code generator can generate native binary code for them using some "just-in-time" compiler and then run that native code directly).

At each stage, more and more security is added. The final level of that security is the Java class library itself, which has several carefully designed classes and APIs that add the final touches to the security of the system.

21

The Security Manager

The SecurityManager is an abstract class that was recently added to the Java system to collect, in one place, all the security policy decisions that the system has to make as bytecodes run. You learned before that you can create your own class loader. In fact, you may not have to, because you can subclass SecurityManager to perform most of the same customizations.

An instance of some subclass of SecurityManager is always installed as the current security manager. It has complete control over which of a well-defined set of "dangerous" methods are allowed to be called by any given class. It takes the realms from the last section into account, the source (origin) of the class, and the type of the class (stand-alone, or loaded by an applet). Each of these can be separately configured to have the effect you (the programmer) like on your Java system. For non-programmers, the system provides several levels of default security policies from which you can choose.

What is this "well-defined set" of methods that are protected?

File I/O is a part of the set, for obvious reasons. In most Java-enabled browsers, applets, by default, cannot open, read, or write files at all. Java applications (and in certain Java-enabled browsers, applets) can open, read, or write files with the express permission of the user—but even then, only in certain restricted directories. (Of course, users can always be stupid about this, but that's what system administrators are for!)

Also in this protected set are the methods that create and use network connections, both incoming and outgoing.

The final members of the set are those methods that allow one thread to access, control, and manipulate other threads. (Of course, additional methods can be protected as well, by creating a new subclass of SecurityManager that handles them.)

For both file and network access, the user of a Java-enabled browser can choose between three realms (and one subrealm) of protection:

- □ *unrestricted* (allows applets to do anything)
- □ *firewall* (allows applets within the firewall to do anything)
- □ *source* (allows applets to do things only with their origin Internet host, or with other applets from there)
- □ *local* (disallows all file and network access)

For file access, the *source* subrealm is not meaningful, so it really has only three realms of protection. (As a programmer, of course, you have full access to the security manager and can set up your own peculiar criteria for granting and revoking privileges to your heart's content.)

For network access, you can imagine wanting many more realms. For example, you might specify different groups of trusted domains (companies), each of which is allowed added privileges when applets from that group are loaded. Some groups can be more trusted than others, and you might even allow groups to grow automatically by allowing existing members to recommend new members for admission. (The Java seal of approval?) The new Java 1.1 security classes allow such new, refined levels of trust to be created.

In any case, the possibilities are endless, as long as there is a secure way of recognizing the original creator of an applet.

You might think this problem has already been solved, because classes are tagged with their origin. In fact, the Java run-time goes far out of its way to be sure that that origin information is never lost—any executing method can be dynamically restricted by this information anywhere in the call chain. So why isn't this enough?

Because what you'd really like to be able to do is permanently "tag" an applet with its original creator (its true origin), and no matter where it has traveled, a browser could verify the integrity and authenticate the creator of that applet. Just because you don't know the company or individual that operates a particular server machine doesn't mean that you want to mistrust every applet stored on that machine. It's just that, currently, to be really safe, you should mistrust those applets.

If somehow those applets were irrevocably tagged with a digital signature by their creator, and that signature could also guarantee that the applet had not been tampered with, you'd be golden.

NOTE

Luckily, Sun is planning to do exactly that for Java, as soon as export restrictions can be resolved.

Here's a helpful hint of where the team would like to go, from the security documentation: "...a mechanism exists whereby public keys and cryptographic message digests can be securely attached to code fragments that not only identify who originated the code, but guarantee its integrity as well. This latter mechanism will be implemented in future releases."

In fact, the start of this new paradigm exists in the new security classes and security tools of JDK 1.1. The overall architecture to make this sort of tagging and identification commonplace doesn't exist yet on the Net, but look for these sorts of features in every new release of Java; they will be a key part of the future of the Internet!

21

One final note about security. Despite the best efforts of the Java team, there is always a trade-off between useful functionality and absolute security. For example, Java applets can create windows, an extremely useful capability, but a "nasty" applet could use this to spoof the user into typing private password information, by showing a familiar program (or operating system) window and then asking an expected, legitimate-looking question in it. (All modern releases of Java display a special banner on applet-created windows to help alleviate this problem.)

Flexibility and security can't both be maximized. Thus far on the Net, people have chosen maximum flexibility, and have lived with the minimal security the Net now provides. Let's hope that Java can help tip the scales a bit, enabling much better security, while sacrificing only a minimal amount of the flexibility that has drawn so many to the Net.

Summary

Today, you learned about the grand vision that some of us have for Java, and about the exciting future it promises.

Under the hood, the inner workings of the virtual machine, the bytecode interpreter (and all its bytecodes), the garbage collector, the class loader, the verifier, the security manager, and the powerful security features of Java were all revealed.

You now know almost enough to write a Java run-time environment of your own—but luckily, you don't have to. You can simply download the latest release of Java—or use a Java-enabled browser to enjoy most of the benefits of Java right away.

Q&A

Q I'm still a little unclear about why the Java language and compiler make the Net safer. Can't they just be "side-stepped" by nasty bytecodes?

A Yes, they can—but don't forget that the whole point of using a safe language and compiler was to make the Net as a whole safer as more Java code is written. An overwhelming majority of this Java code will be written by "honest" Java programmers, who will produce safe bytecodes. This makes the Net more predictable over time, and thus more secure.

Q I know you said that garbage collection is something I don't have to worry about, but what if I want (or need) to?

A So, you are planning to fly a plane with Java. Cool! For just such cases, there is a way to ask the Java run-time, during startup (`java -noasyncgc`), not to run garbage collection unless forced to, either by an explicit call (`System.gc()`) or by running

21

out of memory. (This can be quite useful if you have multiple threads that are messing each other up and want to "get the gc thread out of the way" while testing them.) Don't forget that turning garbage collection off means that any object you create will live a long, long time. If you're real-time, you never want to "step back" for a full gc—so be sure to reuse objects often, and don't create too many of them!

Q I like the control above; is there anything else I can do to the garbage collector?

A You can also force the `finalize()` methods of any recently freed objects to be called immediately via `System.runFinalization()`. You might want to do this if you're about to ask for some resources that you suspect might still be tied up by objects that are "gone but not forgotten" (waiting for `finalize()`). This is even rarer than starting a gc by hand, but it's mentioned here for completeness.

Q What's the last word on Java?

A Java adds much more than it can ever take away. It has always done so for me, and now, I hope it will for you, as well.

The future of the Net is filled with as-yet-undreamt horizons, and the road is long and hard, but Java is a great traveling companion.

21

APPENDIXES

Appendixes

Java Language Summary

by Laura Lemay, Michael Morrison, and Billy Barron

This appendix contains a summary or quick reference for the Java language, as described in this book.

NOTE

This is not a grammar overview, nor is it a technical overview of the language itself. It's a quick reference to be used after you already know the basics of how the language works. If you need a technical description of the language, your best bet is to visit the Java Web site (`http://java.sun.com`) and download the actual specification, which includes a full BNF grammar.

Language keywords and symbols are shown in a `monospace font`. Arguments and other parts to be substituted are in *`italic monospace`*.

Optional parts are indicated by brackets (except in the array syntax section). If there are several options that are mutually exclusive, they are shown separated by pipes (¦) like this:

```
[ public ¦ private ¦ protected ] type varname
```

Reserved Words

The following words are reserved for use by the Java language itself (some of them are reserved but not currently used). You cannot use these terms to refer to classes, methods, or variable names:

abstract	do	import	public	try
boolean	double	instanceof	return	void
break	else	int	short	volatile
byte	extends	interface	static	while
case	final	long	super	
catch	finally	native	switch	
char	float	new	synchronized	
class	for	null	this	
const	goto	package	throw	
continue	if	private	throws	
default	implements	protected	transient	

Comments

```
/* this is the format of a multiline comment */

// this is a single-line comment

/** Javadoc comment */
```

Literals

`number`	Type `int`
`number[l ¦ L]`	Type `long`
`0xhex`	Hex integer
`0Xhex`	Hex integer
`0octal`	Octal integer
`[ number ].number`	Type `double`
`number[ f ¦ f]`	Type `float`
`number[ d ¦ D]`	Type `double`
`[ + ¦ - ] number`	Signed
`numberenumber`	Exponent
`numberEnumber`	Exponent
`'character'`	Single character
`"characters"`	String
`""`	Empty string
`\b`	Backspace
`\t`	Tab
`\n`	Line feed
`\f`	Form feed
`\r`	Carriage return
`\"`	Double quote
`\'`	Single quote
`\\`	Backslash
`\uNNNN`	Unicode escape (NNNN is hex)
`true`	Boolean
`false`	Boolean

Variable Declaration

`[ byte ¦ short ¦ int ¦ long ] varname`	Integer (pick one type)
`[ float ¦ double ] varname`	Floats (pick one type)
`char varname`	Characters
`boolean varname`	Boolean
`classname varname`	Class types
`type varname, varname, varname`	Multiple variables

The following options are available only for class and instance variables. Any of these options can be used with a variable declaration:

[static] *variableDeclaration*	Class variable
[final] *variableDeclaration*	Constants
[public ¦ private ¦ protected] *variableDeclaration*	Access control

Variable Assignment

variable = value	Assignment
variable++	Postfix increment
++variable	Prefix increment
variable--	Postfix decrement
--variable	Prefix decrement
variable += value	Add and assign
variable -= value	Subtract and assign
*variable *= value*	Multiply and assign
variable /= value	Divide and assign
variable %= value	Modulus and assign
variable &= value	AND and assign
variable ¦ = value	OR and assign
variable ^= value	XOR and assign
variable <<= value	Left-shift and assign
variable >>= value	Right-shift and assign
variable <<<= value	Zero-fill, left-shift, and assign

Operators

arg + arg	Addition
arg - arg	Subtraction
*arg * arg*	Multiplication
arg / arg	Division
arg % arg	Modulus
arg < arg	Less than
arg > arg	Greater than
arg <= arg	Less than or equal to
arg >= arg	Greater than or equal to
arg == arg	Equal
arg != arg	Not equal

`arg && arg`	Logical AND
`arg ¦¦ arg`	Logical OR
`! arg`	Logical NOT
`arg & arg`	AND
`arg ¦ arg`	OR
`arg ^ arg`	XOR
`arg << arg`	Left-shift
`arg >> arg`	Right-shift
`arg >>> arg`	Zero-fill right-shift
`~ arg`	Complement
`(type)thing`	Casting
`arg instanceof class`	Instance of
`test ? trueOp : falseOp`	Tenary (if) operator

Objects

`new class();`	Create new instance
`new class(arg,arg,arg...)`	New instance with parameters
`new type(arg,arg,arg...)`	Create new instance of an anonymous class
`Primary.new type(arg,arg,arg...)`	Create new instance of an anonymous class
`object.variable`	Instance variable
`object.classvar`	Class variable
`Class.classvar`	Class variable
`object.method()`	Instance method (no args)
`object.method(arg,arg,arg...)`	Instance method
`object.classmethod()`	Class method (no args)
`object.classmethod(arg,arg,arg...)`	Class method
`Class.classmethod()`	Class method (no args)
`Class.classmethod(arg,arg,arg...)`	Class method

Arrays

NOTE The brackets in this section are parts of the array creation or access statements. They do not denote optional parts as they do in other parts of this appendix.

`type varname[]`	Array variable
`type[] varname`	Array variable
`new type[numElements]`	New array object
`new type[] {initializer}`	New anonymous array object
`array[index]`	Element access
`array.length`	Length of array

Loops and Conditionals

`if ( test) block`	Conditional
`if ( test ) block` `else block`	Conditional with `else`

`switch (test) {`
 	
    `case value : statements`
    `case value : statements`
    `...`
    `default : statement`
    `}`
	switch (only with integer or char types)

`for (initializer; test; change )`	Block `for` loop
`while ( test ) block`	while loop

`do block`
 	
`while (test)`
	do loop

`break [ label ]`	Break from loop or switch
`continue [ label ]`	Continue loop
`label:`	Labeled loops

Class Definitions

class *classname* block   Simple class definition

Any of the following optional modifiers can be added to the class definition:

[final] class *classname block*   No subclasses
[abstract] class *classname block*   Cannot be instantiated
[public] class *classname block*   Accessible outside package
class *classname* [extends   Define superclass
Superclass] *block*

class *classname* [implements   Implement one or
interfaces] *block*   more interfaces

Method and Constructor Definitions

The basic method looks like this, where *returnType* is a type name, a class name, or void:

returnType methodName() block   Basic method
returnType methodName(parameter,   Method with parameters
parameter, ...) block

Method parameters look like this:

type *parameterName*

Method variations can include any of the following optional keywords:

[abstract] *returnType methodName() block*   Abstract method
[static] *returnType methodName() block*   Class method
[native] *returnType methodName() block*   Native method
[final] *returnType methodName() block*   Final method
[synchronized] *returnType methodName() block*   Thread block
                                                          before executing

[public ¦ private ¦ protected] *returnType methodName()* Access control

Constructors look like this:

classname() block   Basic constructor
classname(parameter, parameter,   Constructor with parameters
parameter...) block

[public ¦ private ¦ protected]   Access control
classname() block

In the method/constructor body, you can use these references and methods:

`this`	Refers to current object
`classname.this`	Refers to a particular inner class object
`super`	Refers to superclass
`super.methodName()`	Calls a superclass's method
`this(...)`	Calls class's constructor
`super(...)`	Calls superclass's constructor
`type.class`	Returns the class object for the type
`return [ value ]`	Returns a value

Importing

`import package.className`	Imports specific class name
`import package.*`	Imports all classes in package
`package packagename`	Classes in this file belong to this package
`interface interfaceName`	
`[ extends anotherInterface ] block`	
`[ public ] interface`	
`interfaceName block`	
`[ abstract ] interface`	
`interfaceName block`	

Guarding

`synchronized ( object ) block`	Waits for lock on object
`try block`	Guarded statements
`catch ( exception ) block`	Executed if exception is thrown
`[ finally block ]`	Always executed
`try block`	Same as previous example (can
`[ catch ( exception ) block ]`	use optional catch or finally
`finally block`	but not both)

APPENDIX

B

Class Hierarchy Diagrams

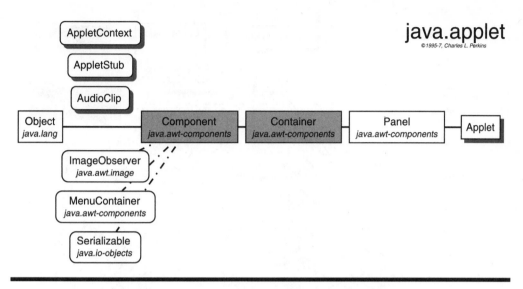

java.applet
©1995-7, Charles L. Perkins

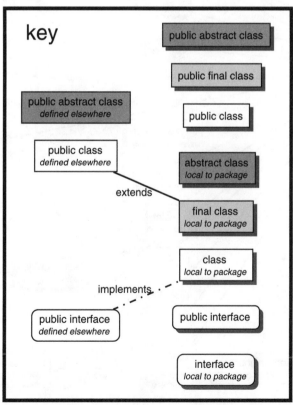

key

public abstract class

public final class

public abstract class
defined elsewhere

public class

public class
defined elsewhere

abstract class
local to package

extends

final class
local to package

class
local to package

implements

public interface
defined elsewhere

public interface

interface
local to package

java.awt
© 1995-7, Charles L. Perkins

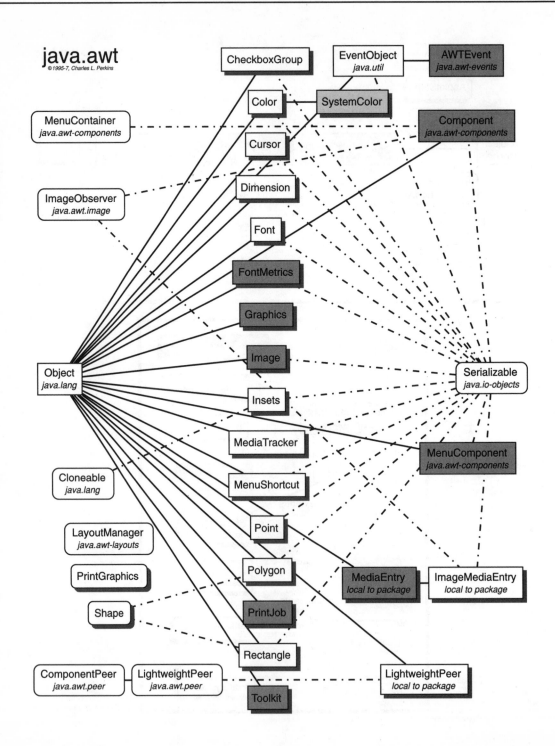

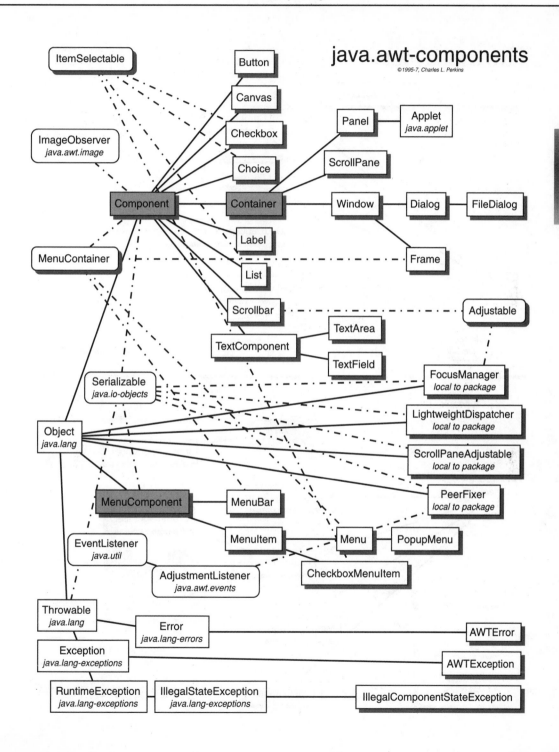

java.awt-components
©1995-7, Charles L. Perkins

java.awt-layouts

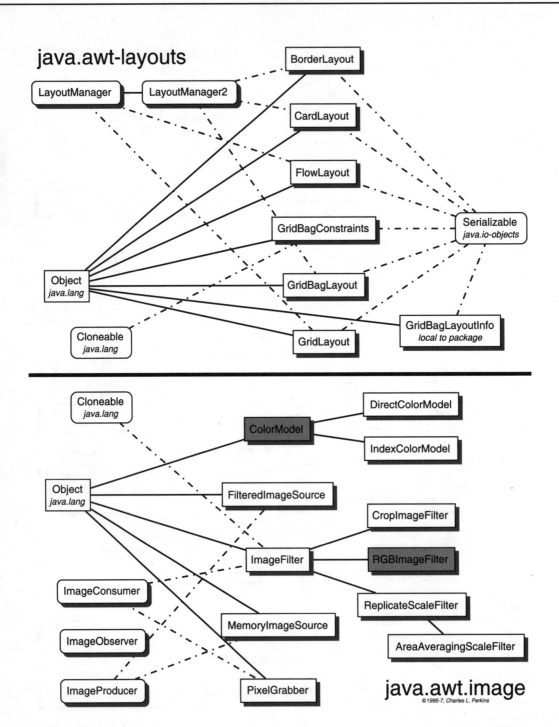

java.awt.image

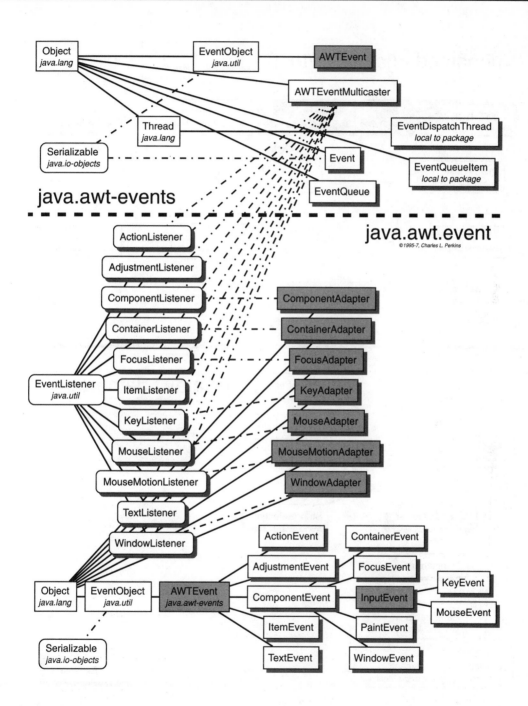

java.awt-events

java.awt.event
©1995-7, Charles L. Perkins

\<unnamed\> (java/awt/test)

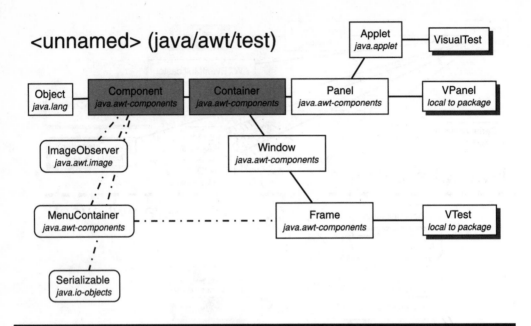

java.awt.datatransfer

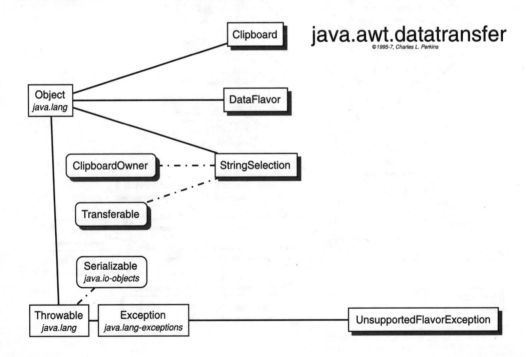

© 1995-7, Charles L. Perkins

java.awt.peer
© 1995-7, Charles L. Perkins

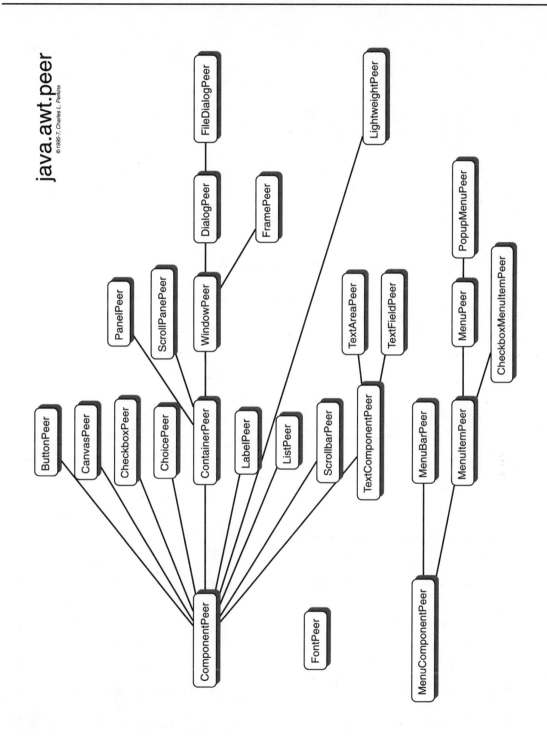

java.beans
©1995-7, Charles L. Perkins

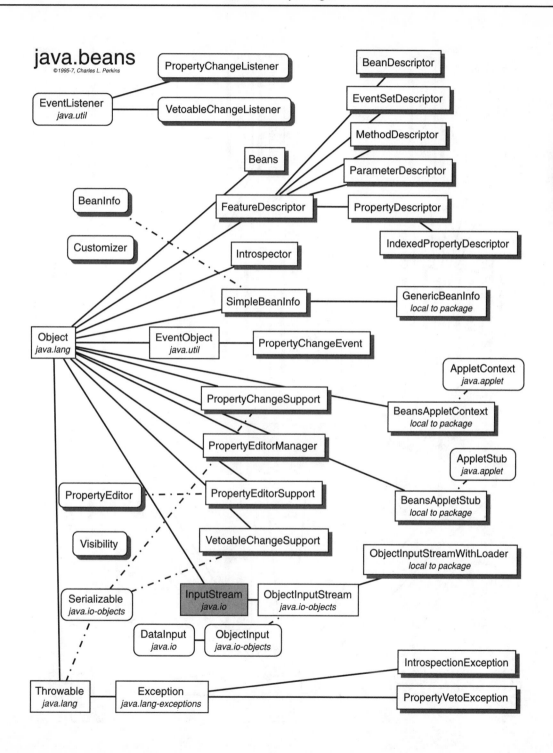

PropertyChangeListener

BeanDescriptor

EventListener
java.util

VetoableChangeListener

EventSetDescriptor

MethodDescriptor

Beans

ParameterDescriptor

BeanInfo

FeatureDescriptor

PropertyDescriptor

Customizer

IndexedPropertyDescriptor

Introspector

SimpleBeanInfo

GenericBeanInfo
local to package

Object
java.lang

EventObject
java.util

PropertyChangeEvent

AppletContext
java.applet

PropertyChangeSupport

BeansAppletContext
local to package

PropertyEditorManager

AppletStub
java.applet

PropertyEditor

PropertyEditorSupport

BeansAppletStub
local to package

Visibility

VetoableChangeSupport

ObjectInputStreamWithLoader
local to package

Serializable
java.io-objects

InputStream
java.io

ObjectInputStream
java.io-objects

DataInput
java.io

ObjectInput
java.io-objects

IntrospectionException

Throwable
java.lang

Exception
java.lang-exceptions

PropertyVetoException

B

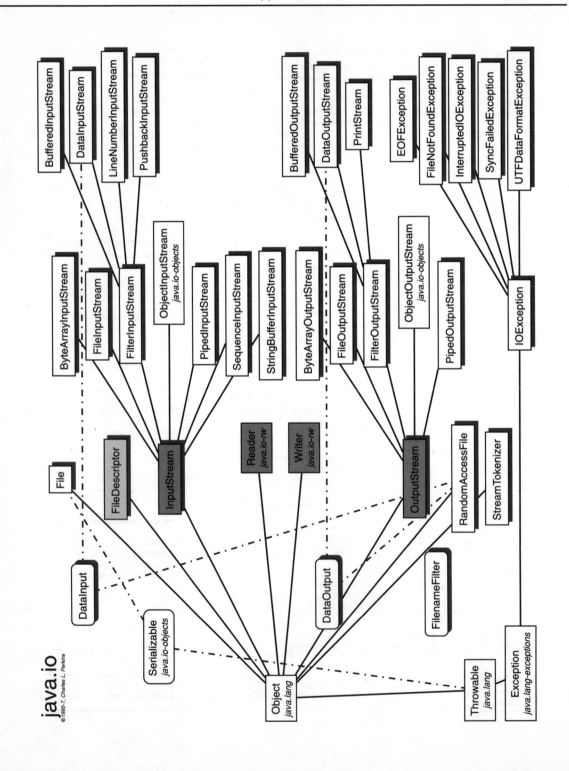

java.io
©1995-7, Charles L. Perkins

java.io-rw
©1995-7, Charles L. Perkins

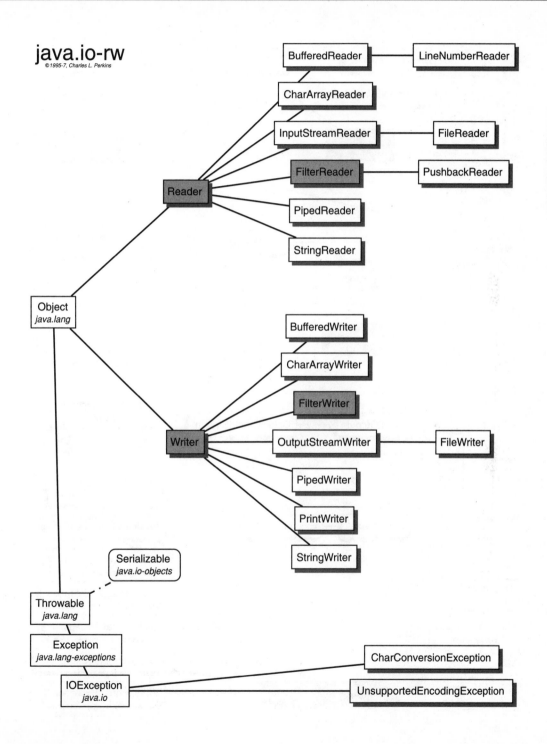

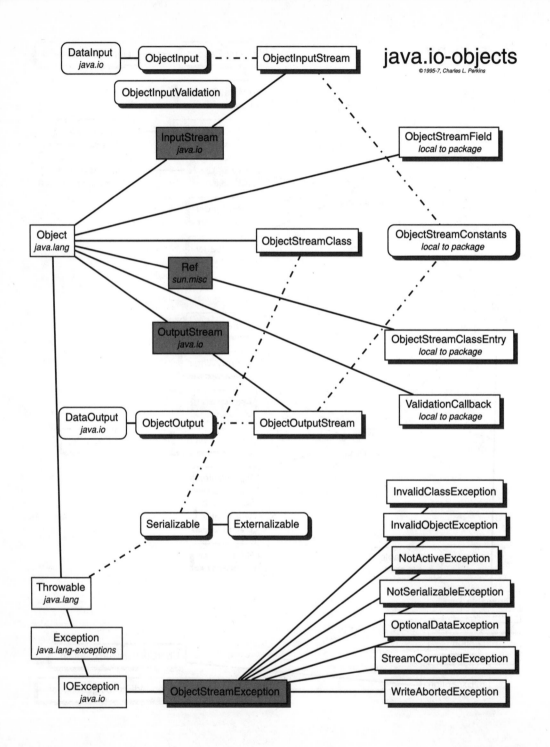

java.io-objects
©1995-7, Charles L. Perkins

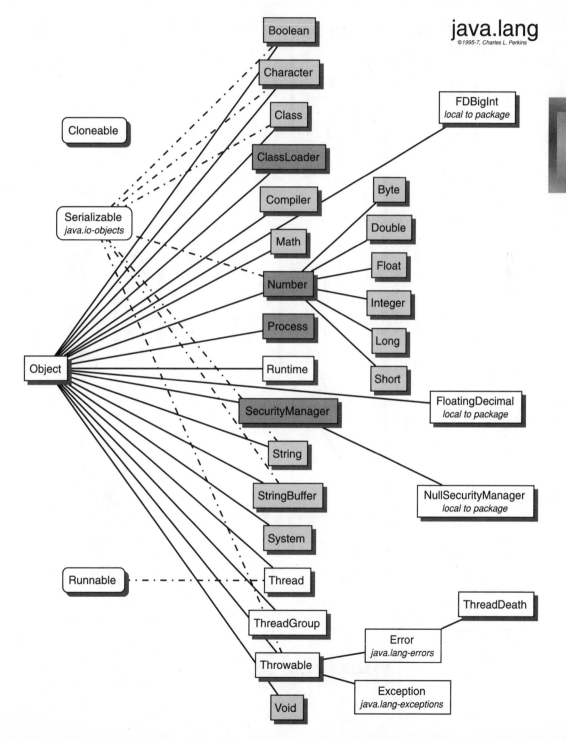

java.lang
©1995-7, Charles L. Perkins

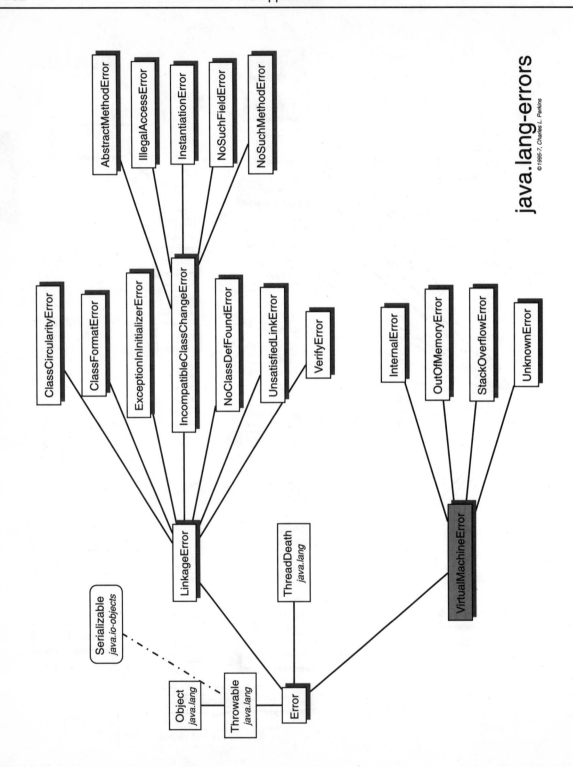

java.lang-errors

© 1995-7, Charles L. Perkins

java.lang-exceptions

© 1995-7, Charles L. Perkins

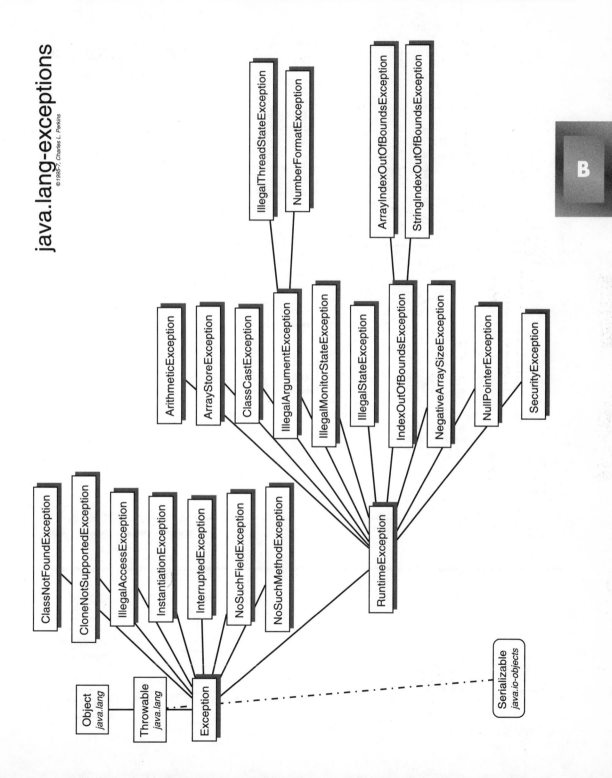

java.lang.reflect

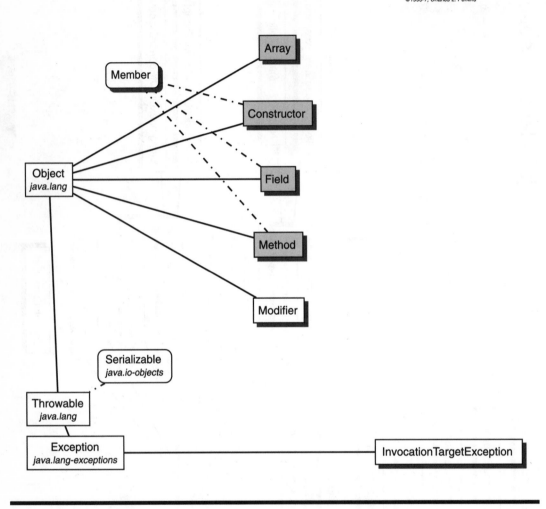

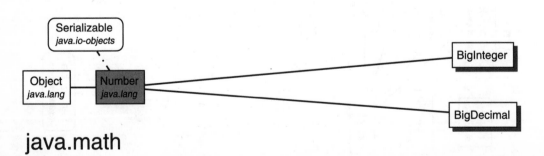

java.math

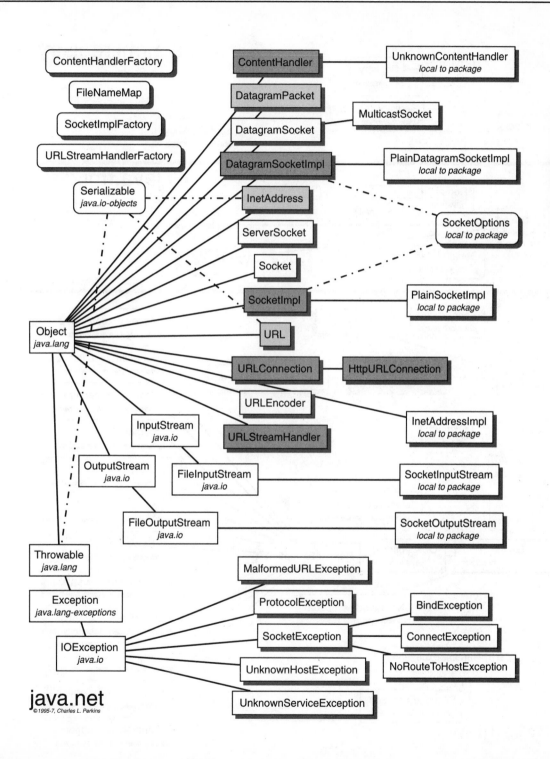

ContentHandlerFactory

FileNameMap

SocketImplFactory

URLStreamHandlerFactory

Serializable
java.io-objects

Object
java.lang

ContentHandler — UnknownContentHandler
local to package

DatagramPacket

DatagramSocket — MulticastSocket

DatagramSocketImpl — PlainDatagramSocketImpl
local to package

InetAddress

ServerSocket

SocketOptions
local to package

Socket

SocketImpl — PlainSocketImpl
local to package

URL

URLConnection — HttpURLConnection

URLEncoder

InetAddressImpl
local to package

URLStreamHandler

InputStream
java.io

OutputStream
java.io

FileInputStream
java.io

SocketInputStream
local to package

FileOutputStream
java.io

SocketOutputStream
local to package

Throwable
java.lang

Exception
java.lang-exceptions

IOException
java.io

MalformedURLException

ProtocolException

SocketException

BindException

ConnectException

UnknownHostException

NoRouteToHostException

UnknownServiceException

java.net
©1995-7, Charles L. Perkins

B

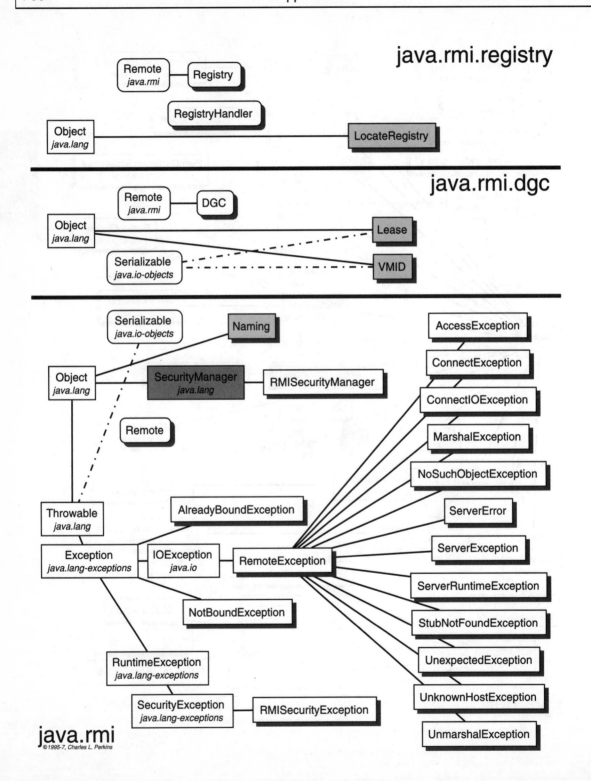

java.rmi.registry

java.rmi.dgc

java.rmi
©1995-7, Charles L. Perkins

java.rmi.server
©1995-7, Charles L. Perkins

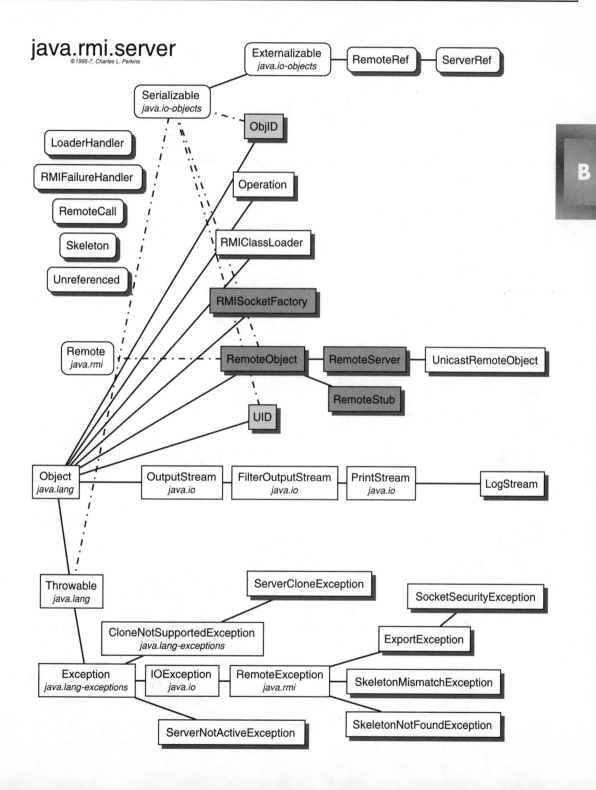

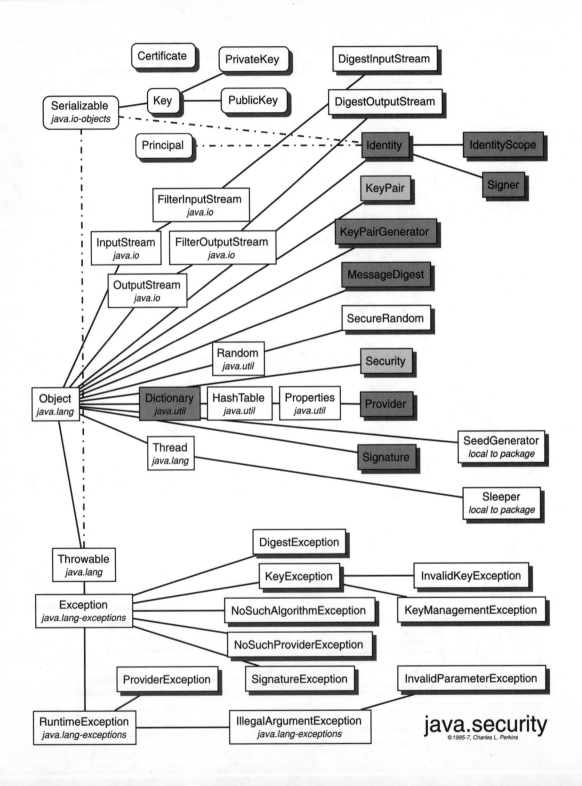

java.security
©1995-7, Charles L. Perkins

java.security.interfaces

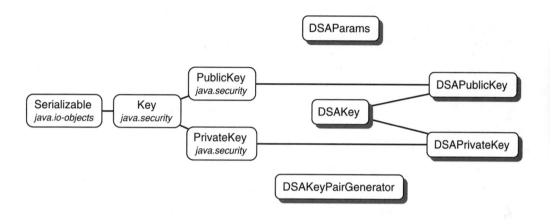

B

java.security.acl

©1995-7, Charles L. Perkins

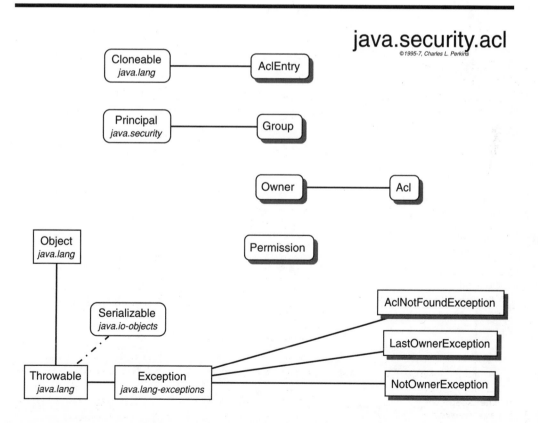

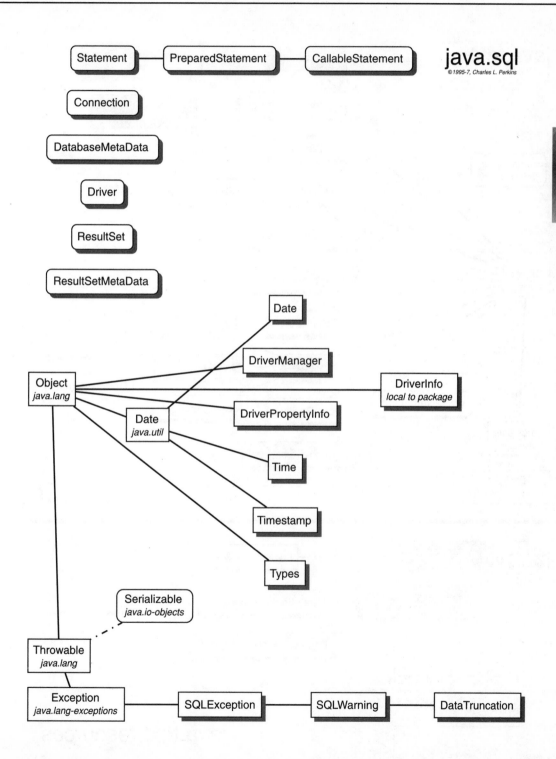

java.sql
©1995-7, Charles L. Perkins

java.text
©1995-7, Charles L. Perkins

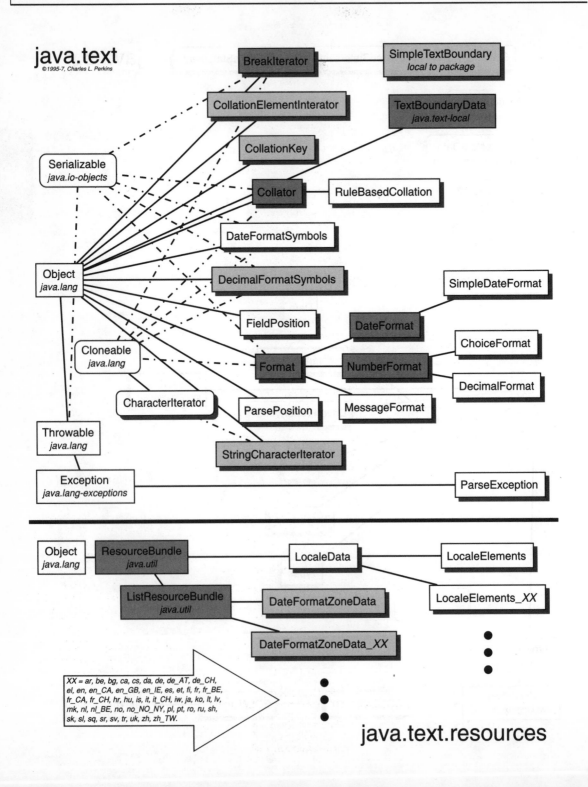

java.text.resources

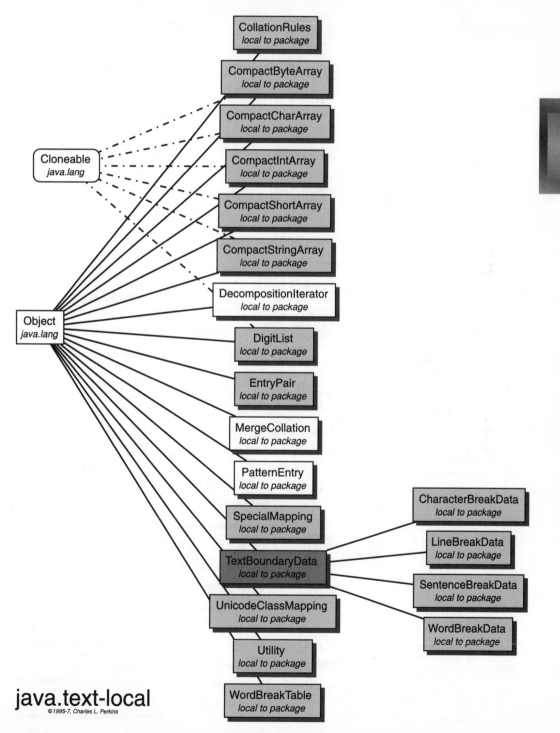

java.text-local
©1995-7, Charles L. Perkins

java.util
©1995-7, Charles L. Perkins

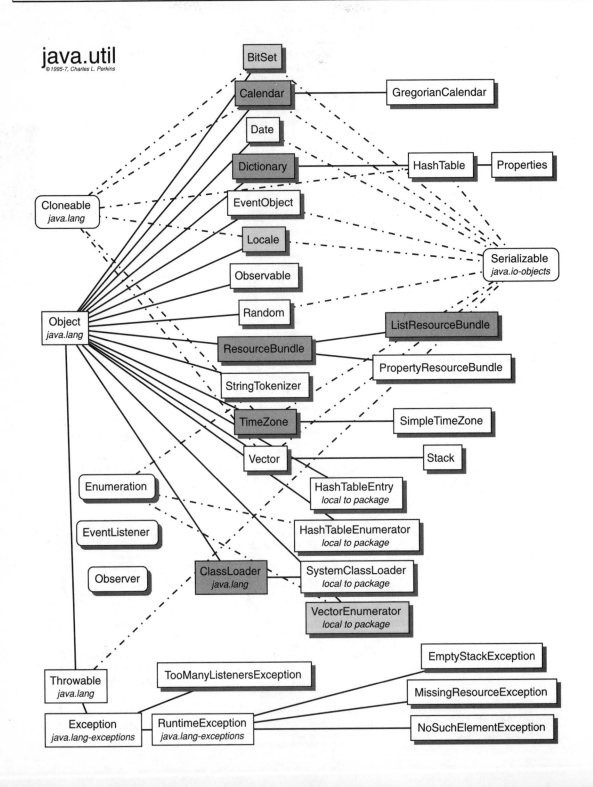

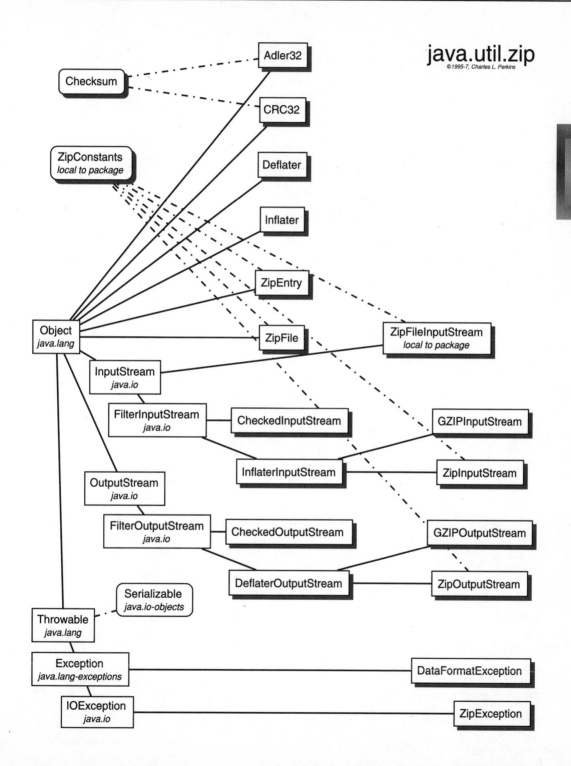

java.util.zip
©1995-7, Charles L. Perkins

APPENDIX C

The Java Class Library

by Laura Lemay

- [ ] `java.lang`
- [ ] `java.util`
- [ ] `java.io`
- [ ] `java.net`
- [ ] `java.awt`
- [ ] `java.awt.image`
- [ ] `java.awt.peer`
- [ ] `java.applet`

This appendix provides a general overview of the classes available in the standard Java packages (that is, the classes that are guaranteed to be available in any Java implementation). This appendix is intended for general reference; for more specific information about each variable (its inheritance, variables, and methods), as well as the various exceptions for each package, see the API documentation from Sun at `http://java.sun.com`. A copy of the 1.1 API documentation is on the CD-ROM included with this book.

java.lang

The `java.lang` package contains the classes and interfaces that are the core of the Java language.

Interfaces

Cloneable	Interface indicating that an object may be copied or cloned
Runnable	Methods for classes that want to run as threads
Serializable	Interface for tagging an object to be serializable (Java 1.1)

Classes

Boolean	Object wrapper for `boolean` values
Byte	Object wrapper for `byte` values (Java 1.1)
Character	Object wrapper for `char` values
Class	Runtime representations of classes
ClassLoader	Abstract behavior for handling loading of classes
Compiler	System class that gives access to the Java compiler
Double	Object wrapper for `double` values
Float	Object wrapper for `float` values
Integer	Object wrapper for `int` values
Long	Object wrapper for `long` values
Math	Utility class for math operations
Number	Abstract superclass of all number classes (`Integer`, `Float`, and
Object	so on) Generic `Object` class, at top of inheritance hierarchy
Process	Abstract behavior for processes such as those spawned using methods in the `System` class

Runtime	Access to the Java runtime
SecurityManager	Abstract behavior for implementing security policies
Short	Object wrapper for short values (Java 1.1)
String	Character strings
StringBuffer	Mutable strings
System	Access to Java's system-level behavior, provided in a platform-independent way.
Thread	Methods for managing threads and classes that run in threads
ThreadDeath	Class of object thrown when a thread is asynchronously terminated
ThreadGroup	A group of threads
Throwable	Generic exception class; all objects thrown must be a Throwable
Void	Object wrapper for void types (Java 1.1)

`java.lang.reflect` (Java 1.1)

The `java.lang.reflect` package is used to find out information about loaded classes such as what methods and fields they have.

Interfaces

Member	Methods to find out information about a member

Classes

Array	Methods to dynamically create and access arrays
Constructor	Methods to find out about and access constructors
Field	Methods to find out about and access variables
Method	Methods to find out about and access methods
Modifier	Decoder for static class and member access modifiers

java.math (Java 1.1)

The java.math package contains two classes that can hold numbers of arbitrary size.

Classes

BigDecimal	A very big floating point number
BigInteger	A very big integer number

java.util

The java.util package contains various utility classes and interfaces, including random numbers, system properties, and other useful classes.

Interfaces

Enumeration	Methods for enumerating sets of values
EventListener	Methods for listening to events (Java 1.1)
Observer	Methods for enabling classes to be Observable objects

Classes

BitSet	A set of bits
Calendar	A generic calendar (Java 1.1)
Date	The current system date as well as methods for generating and parsing dates
Dictionary	An abstract class that maps between keys and values (superclass of HashTable)
EventObject	A event object associated with another object (Java 1.1)
GregorianCalendar	A Gregorian Calendar, which is the type you probably use (Java 1.1)
Hashtable	A hash table
ListResourceBundle	A resource supplier for a Locale (Java 1.1)
Locale	A description of a geographic location (Java 1.1)
Observable	An abstract class for observable objects

Properties	A hash table that contains behavior for setting and retrieving persistent properties of the system or a class
PropertyResourceBundle	A resource supplier which uses properties from a file (Java 1.1)
Random	Utilities for generating random numbers
ResourceBundle	A set of objects related to a Locale (Java 1.1)
SimpleTimeZone	A simplified time zone (Java 1.1)
Stack	A stack (a last-in-first-out queue)
StringTokenizer	Utilities for splitting strings into individual "tokens"
TimeZone	A generic time zone (Java 1.1)
Vector	A growable array of Objects

java.util.zip (Java 1.1)

The java.util.zip package provides classes for dealing with zip and gzip files.

Interfaces

Checksum	Methods for calculating a checksum

Classes

Adler32	Calculates an Adler 32 checksum
CRC32	Calculates a CRC 32 checksum
CheckedInputStream	Input stream with an associated checksum
CheckedOutputStream	Output stream with an associated checksum
Deflator	Compressor for uncompressed files
DeflatorOutputStream	Output stream that compresses
GZIPInputSteam	Input stream from a GZIP file
GZIPOutputStream	Output stream to a GZIP file
Inflater	Decompressor for compressed files
InflaterInputStream	Input stream that decompresses
ZipEntry	A file entry inside a ZIP file
ZipFile	A whole ZIP file

`ZipInputStream`	Input stream from a ZIP file
`ZipOutputStream`	Output stream to a ZIP file

java.io

The java.io package provides input and output classes and interfaces for streams and files.

Interfaces

`DataInput`	Methods for reading machine-independent typed input streams
`DataOutput`	Methods for writing machine-independent typed output streams
`Externalizable`	Methods to write/read an object's contents with a stream (Java 1.1)
`FilenameFilter`	Methods for filtering filenames
`ObjectInput`	Methods for reading objects (Java 1.1)
`ObjectInputValidation`	Methods to validate an object (Java 1.1)
`ObjectOutput`	Methods for writing objects (Java 1.1)
`Serializable`	Tag to say that this class can be serialized (Java 1.1)

Classes

`BufferedInputStream`	A buffered input stream
`BufferedOutputStream`	A buffered output stream
`BufferedReader`	A buffered reader (Java 1.1)
`BufferedWriter`	A buffered writer (Java 1.1)
`ByteArrayInputStream`	An input stream from a byte array
`ByteArrayOutputStream`	An output stream to a byte array
`CharArrayReader`	A reader from an array of characters (Java 1.1)
`CharArrayWriter`	A writer to an array of characters (Java 1.1)
`DataInputStream`	Enables you to read primitive Java types (`ints`, `chars`, `booleans`, and so on) from a stream in a machine-independent way

`DataOutputStream`	Enables you to write primitive Java data types (`ints`, `chars`, `booleans`, and so on) to a stream in a machine-independent way
`File`	Represents a file on the host's file system
`FileDescriptor`	Holds onto the UNIX-like file descriptor of a file or socket
`FileInputStream`	An input stream from a file, constructed using a filename or descriptor
`FileOutputStream`	An output stream to a file, constructed using a filename or descriptor
`FileReader`	A reader from a file, constructed using a filename or descriptor (Java 1.1)
`FileWriter`	A writer to a file, constructed using a filename or descriptor (Java 1.1)
`FilterInputStream`	Abstract class that provides a filter for input streams (and for adding stream functionality such as buffering)
`FilterOutputStream`	Abstract class that provides a filter for output streams (and for adding stream functionality such as buffering)
`FilterReader`	A class that provides a filter for readers (and for adding functionality such as buffering) (Java 1.1)
`FilterWriter`	A class that provides a filter for writers (and for adding functionality such as buffering) (Java 1.1)
`InputStream`	An abstract class representing an input stream of bytes; the parent of all input streams in this package
`LineNumberInputStream`	An input stream that keeps track of line numbers
`ObjectInputStream`	A class that deserializes data and objects (Java 1.1)
`ObjectOutputStream`	A class that serializes data and objects (Java 1.1)
`ObjectStreamClass`	A descriptor for classes that can be serialized (Java 1.1)
`OutputStream`	An abstract class representing an output stream of bytes; the parent of all output streams in this package
`OutputStreamWriter`	A bridge between byte and character streams (Java 1.1)
`PipedInputStream`	A piped input stream, which should be connected to a `PipedOutputStream` to be useful
`PipedOutputStream`	A piped output stream, which should be connected to a `PipedInputStream` to be useful (together they provide safe communication between threads)

C

PipedReader	A piped reader, which should be connected to a PipedWriter to be useful (Java 1.1)
PipedWriter	A piped writer, which should be connected to a PipedReader to be useful (Java 1.1)
PrintStream	An output stream for printing (used by System.out. println(...))
PrintWriter	A writer for printing (Java 1.1)
PushbackInputStream	An input stream with a push back buffer
PushbackReader	A reader with a push back buffer (Java 1.1)
RandomAccessFile	Provides random access to a file, constructed from filenames, descriptors, or objects
Reader	An abstract class representing an input character stream; the parent of all readers in this package (Java 1.1)
SequenceInputStream	Converts a sequence of input streams into a single input stream
StreamTokenizer	Converts an input stream into a series of individual tokens
StringBufferInputStream	An input stream from a String object
StringReader	A reader from a String object (Java 1.1)
StringWriter	A writer to a String object (Java 1.1)
Writer	An abstract class representing an output character stream; the parent of all writers in this package (Java 1.1)

java.net

The java.net package contains classes and interfaces for performing network operations, such as sockets and URLs.

Interfaces

ContentHandlerFactory	Methods for creating ContentHandler objects
FileNameMap	Methods for mapping between filenames and MIME types (Java 1.1)
SocketImplFactory	Methods for creating socket implementations (instance of the SocketImpl class)
URLStreamHandlerFactory	Methods for creating URLStreamHandler objects

Classes

ContentHandler   Abstract behavior for reading data from a URL
                        connection and constructing the appropriate local
                        object, based on MIME types

DatagramPacket   A datagram packet (UDP)

DatagramSocket   A datagram socket

DatagramSocketImpl   Abstract base class for datagram and multicast
                        sockets   (Java 1.1)

HttpURLConnection   A connection can handle the HTTP protocol (Java 1.1)

InetAddress   An object representation of an Internet host (hostname, IP
                        address)

MulticastSocket   A server-side socket with support for transmitting data to
                        multiple client sockets (Java 1.1)

ServerSocket   A server-side socket

Socket   A socket

SocketImpl   An abstract class for specific socket implementations

URL   An object representation of a URL

URLConnection   Abstract behavior for a socket that can handle various Web-
                        based protocols (http, ftp, and so on)

URLEncoder   Turns strings into x-www-form-urlencoded format

URLStreamHandler   Abstract class for managing streams to object referenced by
                        URLs

java.awt

The java.awt package contains the classes and interfaces that make up the Abstract
Windowing Toolkit.

Interfaces

Adjustable   Methods for objects with adjustable numeric values (Java 1.1)

EventSource   Methods for objects that generate events (Java 1.1)

ItemSelectable   Methods for objects which contain a set of items which are
                        selectable (Java 1.1)

LayoutManager   Methods for laying out containers

LayoutManager2	Methods for laying out containers based on a constraints object (Java 1.1)
MenuContainer	Methods for menu-related containers
PrintGraphics	Methods for providing a print graphics context (Java 1.1)
Shape	Methods for geometric shapes (Java 1.1)

Classes

AWTEvent	The parent of all AWT events (Java 1.1)
AWTEventMulticaster	A multicast event dispatcher (Java 1.1)
BorderLayout	A layout manager for arranging items in border formation
Button	A UI pushbutton
Canvas	A canvas for drawing and performing other graphics operations
CardLayout	A layout manager for HyperCard-like metaphors
Checkbox	A check box
CheckboxGroup	A group of exclusive checkboxes (radio buttons)
CheckboxMenuItem	A toggle menu item
Choice	A pop-up menu of choices
Color	An abstract representation of a color
Component	The abstract generic class for all UI components
Container	Abstract behavior for a component that can hold other components or containers
Cursor	A screen cursor (Java 1.1)
Dialog	A window for brief interactions with users
Dimension	An object representing width and height
Event	An object representing events caused by the system or based on user input
EventQueue	A queue of events waiting to be processed (Java 1.1)
FileDialog	A dialog box for getting filenames from the local file system
FlowLayout	A layout manager that lays out objects from left to right in rows
Font	An abstract representation of a font
FontMetrics	Abstract class for holding information about a specific font's character shapes and height and width information

Frame	A top-level window with a title
Graphics	Abstract behavior for representing a graphics context and for drawing and painting shapes and objects
GridBagConstraints	Constraints for components laid out using GridBagLayout
GridBagLayout	A layout manager that aligns components horizontally and vertically based on their values from GridBagConstraints
GridLayout	A layout manager with rows and columns; elements are added to each cell in the grid
Image	An abstract representation of a bitmap image
Insets	Distances from the outer border of the window; used to lay out components
Label	A text label for UI components
List	A scrolling list
MediaTracker	A way to keep track of the status of media objects being loaded over the Net
Menu	A menu that can contain menu items and is a container on a menu bar
MenuBar	A menu bar (container for menus)
MenuComponent	The abstract superclass of all menu elements
MenuItem	An individual menu item
MenuShortcut	A keyboard shortcut for a menu item (Java 1.1)
Panel	A container that is displayed
Point	An object representing a point (x and y coordinates)
Polygon	An object representing a set of points
PopupMenu	A menu which pops up (Java 1.1)
PrintJob	A job to be printed (Java 1.1)
Rectangle	An object representing a rectangle (x and y coordinates for the top corner, plus width and height)
ScrollPane	A container with automatic scrolling (Java 1.1)
Scrollbar	A UI scroll bar object
SystemColor	A class containing the GUI colors for a system (Java 1.1)
TextArea	A multiline, scrollable, editable text field
TextComponent	The superclass of all editable text components
TextField	A fixed-size editable text field

C

| Toolkit | Abstract behavior for binding the abstract AWT classes to a platform-specific toolkit implementation |
| Window | A top-level window, and the superclass of the Frame and Dialog classes |

java.awt.datatransfer (Java 1.1)

The java.awt.datatransfer package is a subpackage of the AWT that provides interfaces and methods for talking to the clipboard.

Interfaces

| ClipboardOwner | Methods for classes providing data to a clipboard |
| Transferable | Methods for classes providing data to a transfer operation |

Classes

Clipboard	The clipboard itself
DataFlavor	The opaque concept of a data format
StringSelection	A transfer agent for a string

java.awt.event (Java 1.1)

The java.awt.event package is a subpackage of the AWT that implements the new event model for Java 1.1

Interfaces

ActionListener	Methods for listening to an action event
AdjustmentListener	Methods for listening to an adjustment event
ComponentListener	Methods for listening to a component event
FocusListener	Methods for listening to a focus event
ItemListener	Methods for listening to an item event
KeyListener	Methods for listening to a keyboard event
MouseListener	Methods for listening to a mouse event
MouseMotionListener	Methods for listening to a mouse motion event
TextListener	Methods for listening to a text event
WindowListener	Methods for listening to a window event

Classes

ActionEvent	An action event
AdjustmentEvent	An adjustment event generated from an adjustable object
ComponentAdapter	An adapter which listens to component events
ComponentEvent	An component event
ContainerAdapter	An adapter which listens to container events
ContainerEvent	A container event
FocusAdapter	An adapter which listens to focus events
FocusEvent	A focus event
InputEvent	An input event
ItemEvent	An item event generated from ItemSelectable object
KeyAdapter	An adapter which listens to keyboard events
KeyEvent	A keyboard event
MouseAdapter	An adapter which listens to mouse events
MouseEvent	A mouse event
MouseMotionAdapter	An adapter which listens to mouse motion events, such as drag
PaintEvent	A component-level paint event
TextEvent	A text event generated by a TextComponent
WindowAdapter	An adapter which listens to window events
WindowEvent	A windowing event

java.awt.image

The java.awt.image package is a subpackage of the AWT that provides interfaces and classes for managing bitmap images.

Interfaces

ImageConsumer	Methods for receiving image created by an ImageProducer
ImageObserver	Methods to track the loading and construction of an image
ImageProducer	Methods for producing image data received by an ImageConsumer

Classes

AverageScaleFilter	A filter that scales an image based on an average algorithm (Java 1.1)
ColorModel	An abstract class for managing color information for images
CropImageFilter	A filter for cropping images to a particular size
DirectColorModel	A specific color model for managing and translating pixel color values
FilteredImageSource	An ImageProducer that takes an image and an ImageFilter object and produces an image for an ImageConsumer
ImageFilter	A filter that takes image data from an ImageProducer, modifies it in some way, and hands it off to an ImageConsumer
IndexColorModel	A specific color model for managing and translating color values in a fixed-color map
MemoryImageSource	An image producer that gets its image from memory; used after constructing an image by hand
PixelGrabber	An ImageConsumer that retrieves a subset of the pixels in an image
ReplicateScaleFilter	A filter that scales an image (Java 1.1)
RGBImageFilter	Abstract behavior for a filter that modifies the RGB values of pixels in RGB images

java.awt.peer

The java.awt.peer package is a subpackage of AWT that provides the (hidden) platform-specific AWT classes (for example, Motif, Macintosh, Windows 95) with platform-independent interfaces to implement. Thus, callers using these interfaces need not know which platform's window system these hidden AWT classes are currently implementing.

Each class in the AWT that inherits from either Component or MenuComponent has a corresponding peer class. Each of those classes is the name of the Component with -Peer added (for example, ButtonPeer, DialogPeer, and WindowPeer). Because each one provides similar behavior, they are not enumerated here.

java.applet

The `java.applet` package provides applet-specific behavior.

Interfaces

AppletContext	Methods to refer to the applet's context
AppletStub	Methods for implementing applet viewers
AudioClip	Methods for playing audio files

Classes

Applet	The base applet class

java.beans

The `java.beans` package contains the classes and interfaces that make the JavaBeans technology possible.

Interfaces

BeanInfo	Methods that can be used to find out information explicitly provided by a bean
Customizer	Methods that define the overhead to provide a complete visual editor for a bean
PropertyChangeListener	Method that is called when a bound property is changed
PropertyEditor	Methods that provide support for GUI's that allow users to edit a property value a given type
VetoableChangeListener	Methods that get called when a constrained property is changed
Visibility	Methods used to determine whether a bean requires a graphical user interface and whether a graphical user interface is available for the bean to use

Classes

BeanDescriptor	Provides global information about a bean
Beans	Provides some general purpose beans control methods
EventSetDescriptor	Represents a set of events that a bean is capable of generating
FeatureDescriptor	Serves as a common base class for the EventSetDescriptor, MethodDescriptor, and PropertyDescriptor classes
IndexedPropertyDescriptor	Provides methods for accessing the type of an indexed property along with its accessor methods
Introspector	Provides the overhead necessary to analyze a bean and determine its public properties, methods, and events
MethodDescriptor	Provides methods for accessing information such as a method's parameters
ParameterDescriptor	Allows bean implementors to provide additional information on each of their parameters
PropertyChangeEvent	Stores information relating to a change in a bound or constrained property
PropertyChangeSupport	A helper class for managing listeners of bound and constrained properties
PropertyDescriptor	Provides methods for accessing the type of a property along with its accessor methods and describes whether it is bound or constrained
PropertyEditorManager	Provides a means of registering property types so that their editors can be easily found
PropertyEditorSupport	A helper class implementing the PropertyEditor interfaces that is used to make the construction of custom property editors a little easier
SimpleBeanInfo	A support class designed to make it easier for bean developers to provide explicit information about a bean
VetoableChangeSupport	A helper class for managing listeners of bound and constrained properties

java.rmi

The java.rmi package contains the classes and interfaces that enable the programmer to create distributed Java-to-Java applications, in which the methods of remote Java objects can be invoked from other Java virtual machines, possibly on different hosts.

Interfaces

Remote   Methods for identifying all remote objects

Classes

Naming   Methods for obtaining references to remote objects based
                         on Uniform Resource Locator (URL) syntax
RMISecurityManager   Methods defining the RMI Stub security policy for
                         applications (not applets)

java.rmi.dgc

Interfaces

DGC   Methods for cleaning connections for unused clients

Classes

Lease   Contains a unique VM identifier and a lease duration
VMID   Methods for maintaining unique VMID across all Java virtual machines

java.rmi.registry

Interfaces

Registry   A class used to obtain the Registry for different hosts
RegistryManager   Methods used to interface to the private implementation

Classes

LocateRegistry	Used to obtain the bootstrap Registry on a particular host

java.rmi.server

Interfaces

LoaderHandler	
RMIFailureHandler	Methods for handling when the RMI runtime is unable to create a Socket or ServerSocket
RemoteCall	Methods for implementing calls to a remote object
RemoteRef	Represents a handle for a remote object
ServerRef	Represents the server-side handle for a remote object implementation
Skeleton	Represents the server-side entity that dispatches calls to the actual remote object implementation
Unreferenced	Methods to receive notification when there are no more remote references to it

Classes

LogStream	Provides a mechanism for logging errors that are of possible interest to those monitoring the system
ObjID	Used to identify remote objects uniquely in a VM
Operation	Holds a description of a Java method
RMIClassLoader	Provides static methods for loading classes over the net work
RMISocketFactory	Used by the RMI runtime in order to obtain client and server sockets for RMI calls
RemoteObject	Provides the remote semantics of Object by implementing methods for hashCode, equals, and toString
RemoteServer	A superclass to all server implementations that provides the framework to support a wide range of remote reference semantics

RemoteStub	Stub objects are surrogates that support exactly the same set of remote interfaces defined by the actual implementation of the remote object
UID	Abstraction for creating identifiers that are unique with respect to the the host on which it is generated
UnicastRemoteObject	Defines a non-replicated remote object whose references are valid only while the server process is alive

java.security

The java.security package contains the classes and interfaces that enable the programmer to implement certificates and digital signatures in Java components.

Interfaces

Certificate	Methods for managing a certificate, including encoding and decoding
KeyParams	An interface to alogrithm-specific key parameter interfaces such as DSAParms
Principal	Represents the principal component of a certificate

Classes

DigestInputStream	Represents an input stream that has a message digest associated with it
DigestOutputStream	Represents an output stream that has a message digest associated with it
Identity	Methods for managing identities, which can be objects such as, people, companies or organizations that can be authenticated using a public key
IdentityScope	Methods for defining the scope for an identity including the name of the identity, its key, and associated certificates
Key	An abstract class representing a cryptographic key
KeyPair	A simple holder for a key pair (a public key and a private key)
MessageDigest	Methods that provide the functionality of a message digest algorithm

PrivateKey	A subclass of Key representing a private key
Provider	Represents a Security Package Provider (SPP) for the JavaSecurity API
PublicKey	A subclass of Key representing a public key
SecureRandom	Generates a random number
Security	Metohods for managing Security Packgage Providers(SPP)
Signature	Provides the algorithm for digital signatures
Signer	Represents an identity that can also sign

java.security.acl

The java.security.acl package provides the interface to a data structure that guards access to resources.

Interfaces

Acl	An interface representing an Access Control List (ACL) which is a data structure used to guard access to resources
AclEntry	Methods that allow programmers to add, remove, or set permissions for the Principals of each ACLEntry in the ACL
Group	Methods that allow programmers to add or remove a member from the group of Principals
Owner	Represents the owner of an ACL
Permission	This interface represents the type of access granted to a resource such as a Principal in the ACL

java.security.interfaces

Interfaces

DSAKey	Methods used to authenticate components including Java applets and ActiveX controls distributed via the Web
DSAParams	Methods allowing programmers to get the base, prime, and subprime
DSAPublicKey	An interface to a DSA public key

`java.sql`

The `java.sql` package includes classes, interfaces and methods that you can use to connect your Java applications to back-end databases.

Interfaces

`CallableStatement`	Methods used to execute stored procedures and handle multiple result sets
`Connection`	Represents a session with the database
`DatabaseMetaData`	An interface allowing programmers to get high-level information about the database
`Driver`	Methods used to connect to a database
`PreparedStatement`	Methods for running precompiled SQL statements
`ResultSet`	Methods for retrieving values from and executed SQL statement
`ResultSetMetaData`	Methods that provide information about the types and properties of the columns in a `ResultSet`
`Statement`	Used for static SQL statements

Classes

`Date`	Provides methods for formatting and referencing date values
`DriverManager`	Allows for the managing of a set of JDBC drivers
`DriverPropertyInfo`	Provides methods for obtaining different properties of a driver
`Time`	Provides methods for formatting and referencing time values
`Timestamp`	A wrapper that holds the SQL `TIMESTAMP` value
`Types`	Defines constants that are used to identify SQL types

`java.text`

The `java.text` package includes classes and methods used to format objects such as numbers, dates, times, datetime, and so on to a string, or parse a given string to an object such as number, date, time, and so on.

Interfaces

CharacterIterator	Methods to traverse a string and return various information about it

Classes

ChoiceFormat	Methods that allow the attaching of formats to numbers
CollatedString	Provides a way to use international strings in a hashtable or sorted collection
Collation	Allows the comparing of Unicode text
CollationElementIterator	Provides a way to iterate over an international string
DateFormat	An abstract class that includes several date-time formatting subclasses
DateFormatData	Methods to set the date-time formatting data
DecimalFormat	Methods to format numbers
Format	A base class for all formats
FormatStatus	Used to align formatted objects
MessageFormat	Methods to create concatenated messages
NumberFormat	An abstract class for all number formats, includes subclasses; you can use their methods to format and parse numbers
NumberFormatData	Encapsulates localizable number format data
ParseStatus	Gets the status of parsing when you parse through a string with different formats
SimpleDateFormat	Methods to format a date or time into a string
SortKey	Methods to do bitwise comparison of strings
StringCharacterIterator	Methods for bidirectional iteration over a string
TableCollation	Implements Collation using data driven tables
TextBoundary	Used to locate boundaries in given text

APPENDIX

D

How Java Differs
from C & C++

This appendix contains a description of most of the major differences between C, C++ , and the Java language. If you are a programmer familiar with either C or C++, you may want to review this appendix to catch some of the common mistakes and assumptions programmers make when using Java.

Pointers

Java does not have an explicit pointer type. Instead of pointers, all references to objects—including variable assignments, arguments passed into methods, and array elements—are accomplished by using implicit references. References and pointers are essentially the same thing except that you can't do pointer arithmetic on references (nor do you need to).

References also allow structures such as linked lists to be created easily in Java without explicit pointers; simply create a linked list node with variables that point to the next and the previous node. Then, to insert items in the list, assign those variables to other node objects.

Arrays

Arrays in Java are first class objects, and references to arrays and their contents are accomplished through implicit references rather than via point arithmetic. Array boundaries are strictly enforced; attempting to read past the end of an array is a compile or run-time error. As with other objects, passing an array to a method passes a reference to the original array, so changing the contents of that array reference changes the original array object.

Arrays of objects are arrays of references that are not automatically initialized to contain actual objects. Using the following Java code produces an array of type MyObject with ten elements, but that array initially contains only nulls:

```
MyObject arrayofobjs[] = new MyObject[10];
```

You must now add actual MyObject objects to that array:

```
for (int i=0; i < arrayofobjs.length; i++) {
    arrayofobjs[i] = new MyObject();
```

Java does not support multidimensional arrays as in C and C++. In Java, you must create arrays that contain other arrays.

Strings

Strings in C and C++ are arrays of characters, terminated by a null character ('\0'). To operate on and manage strings, you treat them as you would any other array, with all the inherent difficulties of keeping track of pointer arithmetic and being careful not to stray off the end of the array.

Strings in Java are objects, and all methods that operate on strings can treat the string as a complete entity. Strings are not terminated by a null, nor can you accidentally overstep the end of a string (like arrays, string boundaries are strictly enforced).

Memory Management

All memory management in Java is automatic; memory is allocated automatically when an object is created, and a run-time garbage collector (the "gc") frees that memory when the object is no longer in use. C's `malloc()` and `free()` functions do not exist in Java.

To "force" an object to be freed, remove all references to that object (assign all variables and array elements holding it to null). The next time the Java gc runs, that object is reclaimed.

Data Types

As mentioned in the early part of this book, all Java primitive data types (`char`, `int`, `long`, and so on) have consistent sizes and behavior across platforms and operating systems. There are no unsigned data types as in C and C++ (except for `char`, which is a 16-bit unsigned integer).

The `boolean` primitive data type can have two values: `true` or `false`. boolean is not an integer, nor can it be treated as one, although you can cast `0` or `1` (integers) to boolean types in Java.

Composite data types are accomplished in Java exclusively through the use of class definitions. The `struct`, `union`, and `typedef` keywords have been removed in favor of classes.

Casting between data types is much more controlled in Java; automatic casting occurs only when there will be no loss of information. All other casts must be explicit. The primitive data types (`int`, `float`, `long`, `char`, `boolean`, and so on) cannot be cast to objects or vice versa; there are methods and special "wrapper" classes to convert values between objects and primitive types.

Operators

Operator precedence and association behaves as it does in C. Note, however, that the `new` keyword (for creating a new object) binds tighter than dot notation (.), which is different behavior from C++. In particular, note the following expression:

```
new foo().bar;
```

This expression operates as if written like this:

```
(new foo()).bar;
```

D

Operator overloading, as in C++, cannot be accomplished in Java. The , operator of C has been deleted.

The >>> operator produces an unsigned logical right shift (remember, there are no unsigned integer data types).

The + operator can be used to concatenate strings.

Control Flow

Although the if, while, for, and do statements in Java are syntactically the same as they are in C and C++, there is one significant difference: The test expression for each control flow construct must return an actual boolean value (true or false). In C and C++, the expression can return an integer.

Arguments

Java does not support mechanisms for variable-length argument lists to functions as in C and C++. All method definitions must have a specific number of arguments.

Command-line arguments in Java behave differently from those in C and C++. The first element in the argument vector (argv[0]) in C and C++ is the name of the program itself; in Java, that first argument is the first of the additional arguments. In other words, in Java, argv[0] is argv[1] in C and C++; there is no way to get hold of the actual name of the Java program.

Other Differences

The following other minor differences from C and C++ exist in Java:

☐ Java does not have a preprocessor, and as such, does not have #defines or macros. Constants can be created by using the final modifier when declaring class and instance variables.

☐ Java does not have template classes as in C++.

☐ Java does not include C's const keyword or the ability to pass by const reference explicitly.

☐ Java classes are singly inherited, with some multiple-inheritance features provided through interfaces.

☐ All functions must be methods. There are no functions not tied to classes.

☐ The goto keyword does not exist in Java (it's a reserved word, but currently unimplemented). You can, however, use labeled breaks and continues to break out of and continue executing complex switch or loop constructs.

What's on the CD-ROM

On the *Teach Yourself Java 1.1 in 21 Days* CD-ROM you will find all the sample files that are presented in this book, as well as a wealth of other applications and utilities.

NOTE
Please refer to the readme.wri file on the CD-ROM (Windows) or the Guide to the CD-ROM (Macintosh) for the latest listing of software.

Windows Software

Java

- [ ] Sun's Java Development Kit for Windows 95/NT, version 1.1 (Solaris versions included)
- [ ] Sun's Beans Development Kit for Windows 95/NT (Solaris versions included)
- [ ] Sample Java applets
- [ ] Sample JavaScripts
- [ ] JFactory
- [ ] Trial version of Jamba for Windows 95/NT
- [ ] JPad
- [ ] JPad Pro demo
- [ ] Kawa demo
- [ ] Studio J++ demo
- [ ] Javelin demo
- [ ] JDesigner Pro database wizard for Java

HTML Tools

- [ ] Hot Dog 32-bit HTML editor
- [ ] HoTMeTaL HTML editor
- [ ] HTMLed HTML editor
- [ ] WebEdit Pro HTML editor
- [ ] Spider 1.2 demo
- [ ] Web Analyzer demo

Graphics, Video, and Sound Applications

- ☐ Goldwave sound editor, player, and recorder
- ☐ MapThis imagemap utility
- ☐ Paint Shop Pro
- ☐ SnagIt screen capture utility
- ☐ ThumbsPlus image viewer and browser
- ☐ Image Library from The Rocket Shop

Utilities

- ☐ Adobe Acrobat viewer
- ☐ WinZip for Windows NT/95
- ☐ WinZip Self-Extractor

Macintosh Software

Java

- ☐ Sun's Java Development Kit for Macintosh v1.0.2
- ☐ Sample applets
- ☐ Sample JavaScripts

HTML Tools

- ☐ BBEdit 3.5.1 freeware
- ☐ BBEdit 4.0 demo
- ☐ HTML edit
- ☐ HTML Editor
- ☐ HTML Web Weaver
- ☐ HTML Markup
- ☐ WebMap
- ☐ Web Painter

E

Graphics

☐ Graphic Converter

☐ GIFConverter

☐ Image Library from The Rocket Shop

Utilities

☐ Adobe Acrobat reader

☐ SnagIt Pro

☐ SoundApp

☐ Sparkle

☐ ZipIt 1.3.5 for Macintosh

About Shareware

Shareware is not free. Please read all documentation associated with a third-party product (usually contained with files named `readme.txt` or `license.txt`) and follow all guidelines.

INDEX

A VIACOM SERVICE

The Information SuperLibrary™

Bookstore

Search

What's New

Reference

Software

Newsletter

Company Overviews

Yellow Pages

Internet Starter Kit

HTML Workshop

Win a Free T-Shirt!

Macmillan Computer Publishing

Site Map

Talk to Us

You'll find thousands of shareware files and over 1600 computer books designed for both technowizards and technophobes. You can browse through 700 sample chapters, get the latest news on the Net, and find just about anything using our

We're open 24-hours a day, 365 days a year.

You don't need a card.

We don't charge fines.

And you can be as **LOUD** as you want.

MACMILLAN COMPUTER PUBLISHING USA

A VIACOM COMPANY

Technical ---- Support:

If you need assistance with the information in this book or with a CD/Disk accompanying the book, please access the Knowledge Base on our Web site at **http://www.superlibrary.com/general/support**. Our most Frequently Asked Questions are answered there. If you do not find the answer to your questions on our Web site, you may contact Macmillan Technical Support **(317) 581-3833** or e-mail us at **support@mcp.com**.

Web Programming with Java

— Harris & Jones

This book gets readers on the road to developing robust, real-world Java applications. Various cutting-edge applications are presented, allowing the reader to quickly learn all aspects of programming Java for the Internet.. CD-ROM contains source code and powerful utilities. Readers will be able to create live, interactive Web pages. Covers Java.

Price: $39.99 USA/$56.95 CDN
ISBN: 1-57521-113-0

User Level: Accomplished - Expert
500 pages

Java Unleashed, Second Edition

— Michael Morrison, et al.

Java Unleashed, Second Edition, is an expanded and updated version of the largest, most comprehensive Java book on the market. Covers Java, Java APIs, JavaOS, just-in-time compilers, and more. CD-ROM includes sample code, examples from the book, and bonus electronic books. Covers Java.

Price: $49.99 USA/$70.95 CDN
ISBN: 1-57521-197-1

User Level: Intermediate
1,224 pages

Java Developer's Reference

— Mike Cohn, et al.

This is the information, resource-packed development package for professional developers. It explains the components of the Java Development Kit (JDK) and the Java programming language. Everything needed to program Java is included within this comprehensive reference, making it the tool developers will turn to over and over again for timely, accurate information on Java and the JDK. CD-ROM contains source code from the book and powerful utilities. Includes tips and tricks for getting the most from Java and your Java programs. Contains complete descriptions of all the package classes and their individual methods. Covers Java.

Price: $59.99 USA/$84.95 CDN
ISBN: 1-57521-129-7

User Level: Accomplished - Expert
1,296 pages

Laura Lemay's Web Workshop: Netscape Navigator Gold 3, Deluxe Edition

— Laura Lemay & Ned Snell

Netscape Gold and JavaScript are two powerful tools to help users create and design effective Web pages. This book details not only design elements, but also how to use the Netscape Gold WYSIWYG editor. The accompanying CD-ROM contains a fully licensed edition of Netscape Navigator Gold 3! Teaches how to program within Navigator Gold's rich Netscape development environment. Explores elementary design principles for effective Web page creation. Covers Web Publishing.

Price: $49.99 USA/$56.95 CDN
ISBN: 1-57521-292-7

User Level: Casual - Accomplished
400 pages

Laura Lemay's Web Workshop: Microsoft FrontPage 97

— Laura Lemay & Denise Tyler

The latest release of Microsoft's FrontPage not only integrates completely with the Microsoft Office suite of products, but also allows a Web author to develop and manage an entire Web site. This allows Excel spreadsheets and Word documents to be added easily to a Web page or site. The previous version allowed only single-page development and did not work with Office. This book shows readers how to exploit those new features on their Web or intranet site and teaches basic design principles, link creation, and HTML editing. CD-ROM contains the entire book in HTML format, templates, graphics, borders, scripts, and some of the best Web publishing tools available.

Price: $39.99 USA/ $56.95 CDN   User Level: Casual - Accomplished
ISBN: 1-57521-223-4   650 pages

Laura Lemay's Guide to Sizzling Web Site Design

— Laura Lemay & Molly Holzschlag

This book is more than just a guide to the hottest Web sites; it's a behind-the-scenes look at how those sites were created. Web surfers and publishers alike will find this book to be an insightful guide to some of the most detailed pages. The latest Web technologies are discussed in detail, showing readers how they have been applied, and how they can implement those features on their own Web pages. CD-ROM includes source code from the book, images, scripts, and more. Covers Web Site Design.

Price: $45.00 USA/$63.95 CDN   User Level:Casual - Accomplished
ISBN: 1-57521-221-8   400 pages

Official Marimba Guide to Castanet

— Laura Lemay

Castanet is Marimba's technology for distributing and receiving Java applications across the Internet or an intranet. Written by best-selling author Laura Lemay, this clear, hands-on guide explains what this new technology is, why it's important, how to effectively use it, and how to develop content for it. CD-ROM includes special versions of the Castanet components from Marimba, plus author's examples from the book and additional tools and utilities.

Price: $39.99 USA/$56.95 CDN   User Level: Casual - Accomplished
ISBN: 1-57521-255-2   500 pages

Official Marimba Guide to Bongo

— Danny Goodman

Designed for programmers and non-programmers alike, Bongo is Marimba's visual tool for designing and implementing graphical user interfaces for Java applications and Castanet content. Written by best-selling author Danny Goodman, this hands-on guide teaches users how to create sophisticated, well-designed applications with this powerful tool. CD-ROM contains special versions of Bongo, the Castanet Tuner and Transmitter, all from Marimba, as well as examples from the author and additional tools and utilities.

Price: $39.99 USA/$56.95 CDN   User Level: Casual - Accomplished
ISBN: 1-57521-254-4   500 pages

Add to Your Sams.net Library Today
with the Best Books for Internet Technologies

ISBN	Quantity	Description of Item	Unit Cost	Total Cost
1-57521-113-0		Web Programming with Java (Book/CD-ROM)	$39.99	
1-57521-197-1		Java Unleashed, Second Edition (Book/CD-ROM)	$49.99	
1-57521-129-7		Java Developer's Reference (Book/CD-ROM)	$59.99	
1-57521-292-7		Laura Lemay's Web Workshop: Netscape Navigator Gold 3, Deluxe Edition (Book/CD-ROM)	$49.99	
1-57521-223-4		Laura Lemay's Web Workshop: Microsoft FrontPage 97 (Book/CD-ROM)	$39.99	
1-57521-221-8		Laura Lemay's Guide to Sizzling Web Site Design (Book/CD-ROM)	$45.00	
1-57521-255-2		Official Marimba Guide to Castanet (Book/CD-ROM)	$39.99	
1-57521-254-4		Official Marimba Guide to Bongo (Book/CD-ROM)	$39.99	
		Shipping and Handling: See information below.		
		TOTAL		

Shipping and Handling: $4.00 for the first book, and $1.75 for each additional book. If you need to have it NOW, we can ship product to you in 24 hours for an additional charge of approximately $18.00, and you will receive your item overnight or in two days. Overseas shipping and handling adds $2.00. Prices subject to change. Call between 9:00 a.m. and 5:00 p.m. EST for availability and pricing information on latest editions.

201 W. 103rd Street, Indianapolis, Indiana 46290

1-800-428-5331 — Orders   1-800-835-3202 — FAX   1-800-858-7674 — Customer Service

Book ISBN 1-57521-142-4

Installing the CD-ROM

The companion CD-ROM contains all the source code and project files developed by the authors, plus an assortment of evaluation versions of third-party products. To install, please follow these steps.

Windows 95 / NT 4 Installation Instructions

1. Insert the CD-ROM into your CD-ROM drive.
2. From the Windows 95 desktop, double-click on the My Computer icon.
3. Double-click on the icon representing your CD-ROM drive.
4. To run the CD-ROM installation program, double-click on the icon titled `setup.exe`.

Windows NT 3.51 Installation Instructions

1. Insert the CD-ROM into your CD-ROM drive.
2. From File Manager or Program Manager, choose Run from the File menu.
3. Type `<drive>\setup` and press Enter, where `<drive>` corresponds to the drive letter of your CD-ROM. For example, if your CD-ROM is drive D:, type `D:\SETUP` and press Enter.
4. Follow the onscreen instructions.

NOTE

Windows NT 3.51 users will be able to access the source code, listings, and applets from the book in one of two ways. You may run the source code installation program (`SOURCE.EXE`) located in the root directory, or choose to unzip each element separately. These zipped files are located in the `\WINNT351\BOOK\` directory.

Windows NT 3.51 users will be unable to access the `\WIN95NT4` directory because it was left in its original long filename state with a combination of upper- and lowercase characters. This lettering enables Windows 95 and Windows NT 4 users direct access to those files on the CD. All other directories were translated in compliance with the Windows NT 3.51 operating system, and you will be able to access them without any trouble. Attempting to access the `\WIN95NT4` directory will cause no harm; you simply won't be able to read the contents.

Macintosh Installation Instructions

1. Insert the CD-ROM into your CD-ROM drive.
2. When an icon for the CD appears on your desktop, open the disc by double-clicking its icon.
3. Double-click the icon named `Guide to the CD-ROM`, and follow the directions that appear onscreen.

5. Disclaimer of Warranty. Software is provided "AS IS," without a warranty of any kind. ALL EXPRESS OR IMPLIED REPRESENTATIONS AND WARRANTIES, INCLUDING ANY IMPLIED WARRANTY OF MERCHANTABILITY, FITNESS FOR A PARTICULAR PURPOSE OR NON-INFRINGEMENT, ARE HEREBY EXCLUDED.

6. Limitation of Liability. SUN AND ITS LICENSORS SHALL NOT BE LIABLE FOR ANY DAMAGES SUFFERED BY LICENSEE OR ANY THIRD PARTY AS A RESULT OF USING OR DISTRIBUTING SOFTWARE. IN NO EVENT WILL SUN OR ITS LICENSORS BE LIABLE FOR ANY LOST REVENUE, PROFIT OR DATA, OR FOR DIRECT, INDIRECT, SPECIAL, CONSEQUENTIAL, INCIDENTAL OR PUNITIVE DAMAGES, HOWEVER CAUSED AND REGARDLESS OF THE THEORY OF LIABILITY, ARISING OUT OF THE USE OF OR INABILITY TO USE SOFTWARE, EVEN IF SUN HAS BEEN ADVISED OF THE POSSIBILITY OF SUCH DAMAGES.

7. Termination. Licensee may terminate this License at any time by destroying all copies of Software. This License will terminate immediately without notice from Sun if Licensee fails to comply with any provision of this License. Upon such termination, Licensee must destroy all copies of Software.

8. Export Regulations. Software, including technical data, is subject to U.S. export control laws, including the U.S. Export Administration Act and its associated regulations, and may be subject to export or import regulations in other countries. Licensee agrees to comply strictly with all such regulations and acknowledges that it has the responsibility to obtain licenses to export, re-export, or import Software. Software may not be downloaded, or otherwise exported or re-exported (i) into, or to a national or resident of, Cuba, Iraq, Iran, North Korea, Libya, Sudan, Syria or any country to which the U.S. has embargoed goods; or (ii) to anyone on the U.S. Treasury Department's list of Specially Designated Nations or the U.S. Commerce Department's Table of Denial Orders.

9. Restricted Rights. Use, duplication or disclosure by the United States government is subject to the restrictions as set forth in the Rights in Technical Data and Computer Software Clauses in DFARS 252.227-7013(c) (1) (ii) and FAR 52.227-19(c) (2) as applicable.

10. Governing Law. Any action related to this License will be governed by California law and controlling U.S. federal law. No choice of law rules of any jurisdiction will apply.

11. Severability. If any of the above provisions are held to be in violation of applicable law, void, or unenforceable in any jurisdiction, then such provisions are herewith waived to the extent necessary for the License to be otherwise enforceable in such jurisdiction. However, if in Sun's opinion deletion of any provisions of the License by operation of this paragraph unreasonably compromises the rights or increase the liabilities of Sun or its licensors, Sun reserves the right to terminate the License and refund the fee paid by Licensee, if any, as Licensee's sole and exclusive remedy.

Java™ Development Kit
Version 1.1
Binary Code License

This binary code license ("License") contains rights and restrictions associated with use of the accompanying software and documentation ("Software"). Read the License carefully before installing the Software.

By installing the Software, you agree to the terms and conditions of this License.

1. Limited License Grant. Sun grants to you ("Licensee") a non-exclusive, non-transferable limited license to use the Software without fee for evaluation of the Software and for development of Java(tm) compatible applets and applications. Licensee may make one archival copy of the Software and may re-distribute complete, unmodified copies of the Software to software developers within Licensee's organization to avoid unnecessary download time, provided that this License conspicuously appear with all copies of the Software. Except for the foregoing, Licensee may not re-distribute the Software in whole or in part, either separately or included with a product. Refer to the Java Runtime Environment Version 1.1 binary code license (`http://java.sun.com/products/JDK/1.1/index.html`) for the availability of runtime code which may be distributed with Java compatible applets and applications.

2. Java Platform Interface. Licensee may not modify the Java Platform Interface ("JPI", identified as classes contained within the "java" package or any subpackages of the "java" package), by creating additional classes within the JPI or otherwise causing the addition to or modification of the classes in the JPI. In the event that Licensee creates any Java-related API and distributes such API to others for applet or application development, Licensee must promptly publish an accurate specification for such API for free use by all developers of Java-based software.

3. Restrictions. Software is confidential copyrighted information of Sun and title to all copies is retained by Sun and/or its licensors. Licensee shall not modify, decompile, disassemble, decrypt, extract, or otherwise reverse engineer Software. Software may not be leased, assigned, or sublicensed, in whole or in part. Software is not designed or intended for use in on-line control of aircraft, air traffic, aircraft navigation or aircraft communications; or in the design, construction, operation or maintenance of any nuclear facility. Licensee warrants that it will not use or redistribute the Software for such purposes.

4. Trademarks and Logos. This License does not authorize Licensee to use any Sun name, trademark or logo. Licensee acknowledges that Sun owns the Java trademark and all Java-related trademarks, logos and icons including the Coffee Cup and Duke ("Java Marks") and agrees to: (i) to comply with the Java Trademark Guidelines at `http://java.sun.com/trademarks.html`; (ii) not do anything harmful to or inconsistent with Sun's rights in the Java Marks; and (iii) assist Sun in protecting those rights, including assigning to Sun any rights acquired by Licensee in any Java Mark.

Appendixes   **677**

Overview

Copyright © 1997 by Sams.net Publishing

SECOND EDITION

International Standard Book Number: 1-57521-142-4

Library of Congress Catalog Card Number: 96-68602

00   99   98   97   4   3   2

Interpretation of the printing code: The rightmost double-digit number is the year of the book's printing; the rightmost single-digit, the number of the book's printing. For example, a printing code of 97-1 shows that the first printing of the book occurred in 1997.

Composed in AGaramond and MCPdigital by Macmillan Computer Publishing

Printed in the United States of America

President, Sams Publishing   Richard K. Swadley
Publishing Manager   Mark Taber
Acquisitions Manager   Beverly M. Eppink
Managing Editor   Cindy Morrow
Director of Marketing   Kelli S. Spencer
Assistant Marketing Managers   Kristina Perry, Rachel Wolfe

Acquisitions Editors
Mark Taber
David Mayhew
Beverly M. Eppink
Lorraine Schaffer

Development Editors
Scott Meyers
Fran Hatton

Software Development Specialist
Bob Correll

Editors
Mitzi Gianakos
Charles Hutchinson

Indexer
Tom Dinse

Technical Reviewers
Jeff Shockley

Editorial Coordinator
Deborah Frisby

Technical Edit Coordinator
Lorraine Schaffer

Editorial Assistants
Carol Ackerman
Andi Richter
Rhonda Tinch-Mize

Cover Designer
Tim Amrhein

Book Designer
Gary Adair

Copy Writer
David Reichwein

Production Team Supervisors
Brad Chinn
Charlotte Clapp

Production
Rick Bond
Georgiana Briggs
Carl Pierce
Mark Walchle

Teach Yourself JAVA™ 1.1
in 21 Days
Second Edition

Laura Lemay
Charles L. Perkins

201 West 103rd Street
Indianapolis, Indiana 46290

Teach Yourself JAVA™ 1.1

in 21 Days
Second Edition

Conventions

 NOTE

A note box presents interesting pieces of information related to the surrounding discussion.

 TECHNICAL NOTE

A technical note presents specific technical information related to the surrounding discussion.

 TIP

A tip box offers advice or teaches an easier way to do something.

 WARNING

A warning box advises you of potential problems and helps you steer clear of disaster.

 NEW TERM New terms are introduced in new term boxes, with the new term in italics.

 TYPE A type icon identifies some new Java code that you can type in yourself. You can also get the code from the CD that accompanies this book.

 OUTPUT An output icon shows the output from a Java program.

 ANALYSIS An analysis icon alerts you to the author's line-by-line analysis.

About This Book

This book teaches you all about the Java language and how to use it to create applets for the World Wide Web as well as for standalone applications. By the time you finish *Teach Yourself Java 1.1 in 21 Days*, you'll know enough about Java and the Java class libraries to do just about anything—inside an applet or out.

Who Should Read This Book

This book is intended for people with at least some basic programming background, which includes people with years of programming experience or people with only a small amount of experience. If you understand what variables, loops, and functions are, you'll be just fine for this book. The sorts of people who might want to read this book include you, if

- ☐ You're a real whiz at HTML, understand CGI programming (in Perl, AppleScript, Visual Basic, or some other popular CGI language) pretty well, and want to move on to the next level in Web page design.
- ☐ You had some BASIC or Pascal in school; you have a grasp of what programming is; and you've heard Java is easy to learn, really powerful, and very cool.
- ☐ You've programmed C and C++ for many years, you've heard this Java thing is becoming really popular, and you're wondering what all the fuss is about.
- ☐ You've heard that Java is really good for Web-based applets, and you're curious about how good it is for creating more general applications.

What if you know programming, but you don't know object-oriented programming? Fear not. This book assumes no background in object-oriented design. If you know object-oriented programming, in fact, the first couple days will be easy for you.

What if you're a rank beginner? This book might move a little fast for you. Java is a good language to start with, though, and if you take it slow and work through all the examples, you may still be able to pick up Java and start creating your own applets.

How This Book Is Structured

This book is intended to be read and absorbed over the course of three weeks. During each week, you'll read seven chapters that present concepts related to the Java language and the creation of applets and applications.